W9-AUU-460

SOCIOLOGY

SOCIOLOGY

David B. Brinkerhoff
Lynn K. White
University of Nebraska—Lincoln

West Publishing Company
St. Paul   New York   Los Angeles   San Francisco

Copyright © 1985 by West Publishing Company
50 West Kellogg Boulevard
P.O. Box 64526
St. Paul, MN 55164-0526

All rights reserved
Printed in the United States of America

Library of Congress Cataloging in Publication Data

Brinkerhoff, David B.
  Sociology.

  Bibliography: p.
  Includes index.
  1. Sociology. I. White, Lynn K. II. Title.
HM51.B8535 1985   301   84-27009
ISBN 0-314-85220-4
2nd Reprint—1985

COPY EDITOR: Jo-Anne Naples
ILLUSTRATIONS: House of Graphics
COMPOSITOR: Parkwood Composition, Inc.
COVER: Grace Hartigan *City Life*. National Trust for Historic Preservation, Nelson A. Rockefeller Collection. Photo by Lee Boltin.

Acknowledgments

Quotation on page 56 is reprinted with the permission of librettist Joseph Stein from the musical "Fiddler on the Roof". Copyright © 1964 by Joseph Stein. Used by permission only—all rights reserved. Published by Crown Publishers.

Quotations on pages 95, 96, and 97 are from Ruth Horowitz, *Honor and the American Dream*. Copyright © 1983 by Rutgers, The State University of New Jersey.

Quotations on pages 130, 217–220, 311 are from WORLDS OF PAIN by Lillian Breslow Rubin. Reprinted by permission of Basic Books, Inc., Publishers.

Table 11.2. Robinson, I. E., and Jedlicka, D., "Change in Sexual Attitudes and Behavior of College Students from 1956 to 1980: A Research Note", JMF Feb. 1982. Copyrighted © 1982 by the National Council on Family Relations, 1219 University Avenue Southeast, Minneapolis, Minnesota 55414. Reprinted by permission.

Table 11.3. Spanier, G. B., "Married and unmarried cohabitation in the United States: 1980", JMF May 1983. Copyrighted © 1983 by the National Council on Family Relations, 1219 University Avenue Southeast, Minneapolis, Minnesota 55414. Reprinted by permission.

Table 11.4 and quotations on pages 309 and 310. Greenblat, C. S., "The Salience of Sexuality in the Early Years of Marriage", JMF May 1983. Copyrighted © 1983 by the National Council on Family Relations, 1219 University Avenue Southeast, Minneapolis, Minnesota 55414. Reprinted by permission.

Figure 14.3. Graph adapted from Graham T. T. Molitor. 1981. The Futurist. With permission from Public Policy Forecasting, 9208 Wooden Bridge Road, Potomac, Md. 20854.

Figures 18.3, 18.4, and 18.5. Reprinted from "The nature of cities" by Chauncy D. Harris and Edward L. Ullman in volume no. 242 of The Annals of the American Association of Political and Social Science. Copyright © 1945. All rights reserved. Permission also granted from C. D. Harris.

Photo Credits

xx Rogers, Monkmeyer Press Photo Service; **1** Tom Sobolik, Black Star; **2** Lukas, Photo Researchers; **4** Brown Brothers; Peter Menzel, Stock, Boston; **7** Brown Brothers; **8** Brown Brothers; **9** (Top) Brown Brothers; **9** (Bottom) Brown Brothers; **12** The Bettmann Archive; **13** Brown Brothers; **14** Ethan Hoffman, Archive Pictures; **16** Rogers, Monkmeyer Press Photo Service; **18** James Nachtwey, Black Star; **20** Chris Steele, Perkins/Magnum; **21** Charles Gatewood, Stock, Boston; **27** Bruce Roberts, Photo Researchers; **34** Cartoon copyright Peter Mueller; **36** Ellis Herwig, Stock, Boston; **37** Richard Stack, Black Star; **43** Sepp Seitz, Woodfin Camp & Associates; **45** Victor Friedman, Photo Researchers; **48** AP/Wide World Photos; **50** AP/Wide World Photos; **55** J. M. Labat, Peter Arnold, Inc.; **57** (Left) Martha Cooper, Peter Arnold, Inc.; **57** (right) Robert Ginn, EKM-Nepenthe; **61** Cary Wolinsky, Stock, Boston; **66** Olivier Rebbot, Stock, Boston; **67** Homer Sykes, Woodfin Camp & Associates; **68** UPI; **69** Victor Encliffert, Black Star; **71** The Gorilla Foundation; **74** H. L. Mathis, Peter Arnold, Inc.; **75** Michael S. Yamashita, Woodfin Camp & Associates; **77** John Messenger; **80** Wendy Watriss, Woodfin Camp & Associates; **83** Stock, Boston; **86** (top) David R. Frazier, Photo Researchers; **86** (bottom) Tex Fuller, Woodfin Camp & Associates; **86** (left) Phyllis Graber Jensen, Stock, Boston; **90** Elizabeth Hamlin, Stock, Boston; **93** Shirley Zeiberg, Taurus Photos; **95** Frank Siteman, Stock, Boston; **98** Mimi Forsyth, Monkmeyer Press Photo Service; **101** Brown Brothers; **103** George Gerster, Photo Researchers; **104** Alpha; **105** John Running, Black Star; **112** Ethan Hoffman, Archive Pictures, Inc.; **113** Jean-Marie Simon, Taurus Photos; **114** Burt Glinn, Magnum Photos, Inc; **115** James H. Karales, Peter Arnold, Inc.; **117** From *The Battered Child*, Roy E. Helfer and C. Henry Kempe, Reproduced with permission of The University of Chicago Press; **118** University of Wisconsin Primate Laboratory; **120** Marilyn Sanders, Peter Arnold, Inc.; **122** Larry

(Continued Following Index)

Contents in Brief

Contents

UNIT TWO

Conformity and Nonconformity   113

CHAPTER 5—SOCIALIZATION   114

CHAPTER 10—GENDER AND AGE DIFFERENTIATION   259

UNIT FOUR
▄▄▄

Social Institutions 291

UNIT FIVE

Change 467

CHAPTER 17—POPULATION 468

CHAPTER 18—URBAN LIFE 496

Preface

Sociology is a balanced, research-based overview of an exciting discipline; it includes the most recent developments in the professional literature as well as in the world around us. Our goal has been to strike a balance between the tremendous intellectual enjoyment that can come from considering new ideas and points of view with a down-to-earth consideration of empirical data about our society.

The design of *Sociology* reflects the authors' active involvement in sociological research and their deep commitment to high quality undergraduate instruction. Over the past 15 years, the authors have taught introductory sociology to close to 10,000 students at the Universities of Nebraska, Notre Dame, and Washington. Our text reflects a knowledge of what has worked for us to make introductory sociology a success—for students and teachers. In our experience, this means that the text needs to use data and events that are up-to-the-minute and that it must appeal to student interest. *Sociology* does this. In addition, a stimulating course involves students in the process of doing sociology: it introduces the research process as a voyage of discovery. Finally, an effective text must be designed so that today's students can read it and come away feeling that it can be understood and mastered. When this is done successfully (and we think *Sociology* does), it goes without saying that the text will be easier to teach from.

The 20 chapters of *Sociology* cover all the standard areas, plus they provide additional material on increasingly important subareas: age and gender stratification are covered in Chapter 10 and sport, science, and medicine in Chapter 16. Two other areas, political and economic institutions (Chapters 13 and 14) receive fuller coverage than in many other books. All of the basics in the field are covered, plus many new and exciting theories and topics—from the segmented labor force to Reagan's proposals at the 1984 World Population Conference. This full coverage provides an opportunity for instructors to branch out in any direction, secure in the knowledge that the text provides the basic background of the field.

Plan of the Book

━━

Sociology is designed to give a comprehensive, contemporary view of the discipline in a format that students would enjoy reading and be able to master. The following features are designed to meet these goals.

Prologues Each chapter begins with a short prologue which makes a direct appeal to the student's personal experience. All prologues are in a "Have You Ever..." format which encourages students to consider how material covered in the chapter applies to their own experiences.

Application to Social Issues The last section of each chapter, Issues in Social Policy, brings the student full circle to a concern with another application, this time on the societal level. In Chapter 17, for example, the issue is policy regarding illegal aliens. Often these sections end with questions instead of firm conclusions; they are issues yet to be decided upon, issues on which the student's views may have an impact.

Focus Ons One boxed insert is used in each chapter to introduce provocative and interesting issues. Because we believe that the practice of social research can be provocative and interesting, some of these cover measurement issues. Others add historical and cross-cultural breadth by covering such issues as the Black Death (Chapter 17), the relocation of Japanese Americans in World War II (Chapter 9), or sexual repression in Inis Beag (Chapter 4).

Tables *Sociology* is a research-based introduction to the discipline, designed to give students an awareness of the methods and materials that sociologists use in studying human societies. In keeping with this goal, we have included a wealth of tables and figures in every chapter. Chapter 2 introduces the student to the art of table reading and the following chapters allow the student to develop an appreciation of sociology as an empirical discipline.

Chapter Summaries A short point-by-point summary lists the chief points made in each chapter. This will aid the introductory student in studying the text and discriminating the important from the supporting points.

Vocabulary Learning new concepts is vital to developing a new perspective on the world and this learning is facilitated in three ways. When new concepts first appear in the text, they are bold-faced and complete definitions are set out clearly in the margin. Whenever a group of related concepts are introduced (for example, power, coercion, and authority), a concept summary is included in a text table to summarize the definitions, give examples, and clarify differences. Finally, a glossary appears at the end of the book for handy reference.

Supplementary Materials

Three kinds of supplementary materials have been developed to ease the tasks of teaching and learning from *Sociology:* a large testbank, a unique instructor's manual, and a student study guide.

Test Bank The authors have constructed 100 multiple choice and 10 essay questions for each chapter. The test bank is available in hard copy, as MicroTest II on microcomputer diskettes, and as WesTest II on tape for mainframe access.

Instructor's Resource Manual The authors have developed a unique instructor's manual that provides innovative and exciting classroom activities—for the instructor with 350 students as well as the instructor with 35. In addition to chapter outlines, suggested films, and essay topics, each chapter provides at least one fully developed exercise and several major discussion topics. A unique feature of the resource manual is the inclusion of a questionnaire that may be used to collect sociological data from students. Many of the questions on this instrument are identical to those discussed in the text. We have found the comparison of class data to national data an invaluable aid for engaging student interest and for teaching about the merits and pitfalls of survey research. Suggested uses for the questionnaire are presented in the Instructor's Resource Manual on a chapter-by-chapter basis.

Student Study Guide The student study guide, written by Charles O'-Connor (Bemidji State University) and Charles M. Mulford (Iowa State University), will be invaluable in helping students master the material. The study guide contains an outline of each chapter, practice questions in matching, multiple-choice, and essay form.

Software A computerized study guide developed by Danny Hoyt (Iowa State University) is available for Apple personal computers. A student has the option to select different formats for review including self scoring multiple choice tests, a race and a quiz game. (The program is imaginatively done and students who have access to personal computers will enjoy it.)

Acknowledgments

In a project of this magnitude, we have had to rely on the goodnatured and generous advice of many of our colleagues at the University of Nebraska-Lincoln. Special thanks go to Nicholas Babchuk, Hugh Whitt, Helen Moore, Suzanne Ortega, Alan Booth, Jerry Cloyd, and Miquel Carranza. They were always willing to share their expert knowledge and to comment and advise on our own forays into their substantive areas. We thank all of them for their encouragement and support.

Special thanks go to the people at West Publishing. Our editor, Clyde Perlee, was generous with encouragement and advice and we benefited greatly from his knowledge of what makes a college textbook usable. His staff, especially Carole Grumney, orchestrated all of the exchanges between reviewers and authors as the manuscript advanced from one stage to the next. Our copyeditor, Jo-Anne Naples, was invaluable in saving us from technical gaffes and inconsistencies; the text is much improved as a result of her efforts. Bill Stryker's imaginative design layout and expertise in production and Cynthia Albrecht's assistance in photo selection proved invaluable in turning our manuscript into a finished product. The visual appeal of the book is a result of their substantial contribution. At all levels, the people at West have been delightful to work with—ready to help us make our book the best possible, but always leaving the substance and direction of the book in our hands.

During the course of writing this book, we have benefited from the conscientious reviews of dozens of sociologists across the country. Special thanks go to Charles O'Connor of Bemidji State University and to Charles M. Mulford of Iowa State University for their thoughtful reviews, constructive criticisms, and persistence: both have been with the project from the beginning. Other reviewers who provided helpful commentary include:

Paul J. Baker
Illinois State University

Carolie Coffey
Cabrillo College, California

Paul Colomy
University of Akron, Ohio

David A. Edwards
San Antonio College, Texas

William Egelman
Iona College, New York

Constance Elsberg
Northern Virginia Community College

Daniel E. Ferritor
University of Arkansas

Charles E. Garrison
East Carolina University, North Carolina

James R. George
Kutztown State College, Pennsylvania

Rose Hall
Diablo Valley College, California

Michael G. Horton
Pensacola Junior College, Florida

Sidney J. Kaplan
University of Toledo, Ohio

James A. Kithens
North Texas State University

Mary N. Legg
Valencia Community College, Florida

Joseph J. Leon
California State Polytechnic University, Pomona

J. Robert Lilly
Northern Kentucky University

Richard L. Loper
Seminole Community College, Florida

Carol May
Illinois Central College

Rodney C. Metzger
Lane Community College, Oregon

Vera L. Milam
Northeastern Illinois University

James S. Munro
Macomb College, Michigan

Lynn D. Nelson
Virginia Commonwealth University

J. Christopher O'Brien
Northern Virginia Community College

Robert L. Petty
San Diego Mesa College, California

Will Rushton
Del Mar College, Texas

Rita P. Sakitt
Suffolk Community College, New York

Barbara Stenross
University of North Carolina

Ida Harper Simpson
Duke University, North Carolina

James B. Skellenger
Kent State University, Ohio

James Steele
James Madison University, Virginia

Steven L. Vassar
Mankato State University, Minnesota

Jane B. Wedemeyer
Santa Fe Community College, Florida

Thomas J. Yacovone
Los Angeles Valley College, California

David L. Zierath
University of Wisconsin

This project consumed our weekends and evenings for two years—years during which family and friends made allowances for our absences and preoccupation. We are particularly grateful for the support of Doug, Laura, Leslie, and Steve, our children, and most of all to our spouses—each other.

SOCIOLOGY

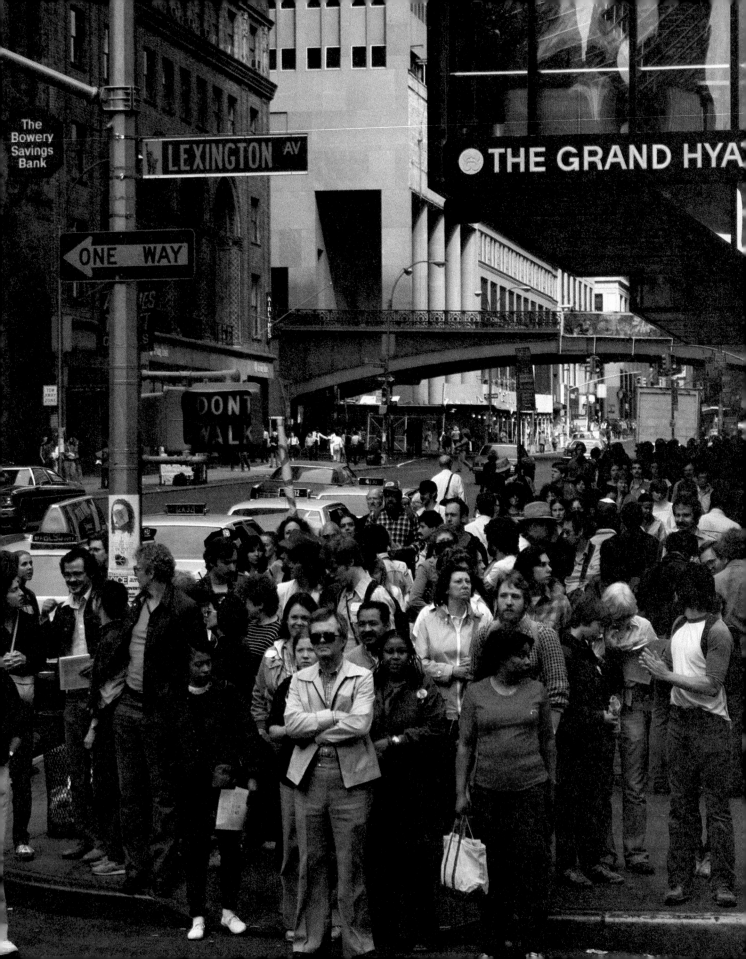

UNIT ONE

Introduction

CHAPTER 1

THE STUDY OF SOCIETY

PROLOGUE

Have You Ever . . . wondered why people act the way they do? When you see a man and a woman having lunch together for several days in a row, do you try to figure out what is going on? Do you think to yourself, "Are they lovers? What do they see in each other?" Do you look for clues (wedding rings, briefcases, how close the people sit to each other) that will help you explain the nature of their relationship and why they're having lunch together?

If you are a people watcher, you have the makings of a good sociologist. Sociologists are interested in people—why they do the things they do. They want to know why people get married, why they get divorced, why some join cults and others go jogging, why some are rich and others are poor.

You probably have developed some opinions of your own on these issues. You say to yourself, "Of course, I know why people get married!" But can you explain why nearly one out of five women who had babies last year failed to get married beforehand? You may know why you intend to marry, but can you explain why others don't marry?

All of us are limited in the amount of the world we can see for ourselves. We are bounded by our race, class, sex, age, nationality, and place in history. Thus we may understand why we do the things we do, but we may not understand why others do the things they do. Why do punkers dye their hair orange and stick safety pins through their ears? For that matter, why do many women pierce holes in their ears and put paint on their faces? Why do teenage boys continually ask people to feel their biceps? Why do parents seem to believe that the world would be a better place if everyone turned down stereos? From your own vantage point on the world, you cannot have insight into all the others who come from different worlds. The study of sociology will help you gain that insight.

Sociology should be one of your most interesting courses. You'll be looking at the behavior of women and men; adolescents and the elderly;

whites, blacks, and browns; religious cult members and homosexual activists; Kenyans, Chinese, and Russians. After studying sociology, you should become a better people watcher with a better grasp of why we do the things we do.

What is Sociology

Each of us starts the study of society with the study of individuals. We wonder why Theresa keeps getting involved with men who treat her badly, why Mike never learns to quit drinking before he gets sick, why our aunt puts up with our uncle, and why anybody likes Barry Manilow or, perhaps, Boy George. We wonder why people we've known for years seem to change drastically when they get married or change jobs.

If Theresa were the only person who ever got into this predicament and if Mike were the only person who ever drank too much, then we might try to understand their behavior by peering into their personalities. We know, however, that there are thousands, maybe millions, of men and women who have disappointing romances and who drink too much. To understand Mike and Theresa, then, we must place them in a larger context and examine the forces that compel so many people to behave in a similar way.

Sociologists tend to view these common human situations as if they were plays. They might, for example, title a common human drama "Boy Meets Girl." Just as Hamlet has been performed all around the world for 400 years with different actors and different interpretations, "Boy Meets Girl" has also been performed countless times. Of course, the drama occurs a little bit differently each time, depending on the scenery, the people in the lead roles, and the century—but the essentials are the same. Thus we can read 19th or even 16th century love stories and understand even now why those people did what they did. They were playing roles in a play that is still performed daily.

More formal definitions will be introduced later, but the metaphor of the theater can be used now to introduce two of the most basic concepts in sociology: role and social structure. By *role* we mean the expected performance of someone who occupies a specific position. Mothers have roles, teachers have roles, students have roles, and lovers have roles. Each position has an established script that suggests appropriate lines, gestures, and relationships with others. Thus each generation of mothers seems to have learned the line, "Just wait until you have kids of your own; then you'll know what I've gone through!" Each generation of students seems to have picked up the line, "Although I should study my economics tonight, I'll really learn it a lot better if I put it off until tomorrow, when I'm fresh." Discovering what each society offers as a stock set of roles is one of the major themes in sociology. Sociologists try to find the common roles that appear in any society and to determine why some people get one role rather than another.

The other major sociological concept is *social structure*, which is concerned with the larger structure of the play in which the roles appear. What is the whole set of roles that appears in this play, and how are the roles interrelated? Thus the role of mother is understood in the context of the social structure we call the family. The role of student is understood in the context of the social structure we call education. Through these two major ideas, role and social structure, sociologists try to understand the human drama.

The Sociological Imagination

The ability to see the intimate realities of our own lives in the context of common social structures has been called the **sociological imagination** (Mills, 1959:15). Sociologist C. Wright Mills suggests that the sociological imagination is developed when we can place such personal troubles as poverty, divorce, or loss of faith into a larger social context, when we can see them as common public issues. He suggests that many of the things we experience as individuals, such as divorce and loss of faith, are really beyond our control. They have to do with society as a whole, its historical development, and the way it is organized. Mills gives us some examples of the differences between a personal trouble and a public issue:

> When, in a city of 100,000, only one man is unemployed, that is his personal trouble, and for its relief we properly look to the character of the man, his skills, and his immediate opportunities. But when in a nation of 50 million employees, 15 million men are unemployed, that is an issue, and we may not hope to find its solution within the range of opportunities open to any one individual. The very structure of opportunities has collapsed. Both the correct statement of the problem and the range of possible solutions require us to consider the economic and political institutions of the society, and not merely the personal situation and character of a scatter of individuals....
>
> Consider marriage. Inside a marriage a man and a woman may experience personal troubles, but when the divorce rate during the first four years of marriage is 250 out of every 1000 attempts, this is an indication of a structural issue having to do with the institutions of marriage and the family and other institutions that bear on them. [Mills, 1959:9]

In everyday life, we do not define personal experiences in these terms. We frequently do not consider the impact of history and social structures on our own experiences. If a child becomes a drug addict, parents tend to blame themselves; if spouses divorce, their friends tend to focus on their personality problems; if you flunk out of school, everyone will tend to blame you personally. To develop the sociological imagination is to understand how outcomes such as these are, in part, a product of society and not fully within the control of the individual. Many people flunk out of school, for example, not because they are stupid or lazy but because they are confused about which play they are appearing in. The "this is the best time of your life" play calls for very different roles than the "education is the key to success" play. Some actors manage to appear with success in both plays simultaneously, but many find that a starring role in one interferes with success in the other. To the extent that society presents alternative and contradictory social expectations, we can expect some people to fail.

Sociological imagination, the ability to see our own lives and those of others as part of a larger human drama, is central to sociology. Once we

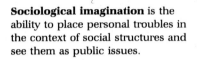

Sociological imagination is the ability to place personal troubles in the context of social structures and see them as public issues.

Figure 1.1
C. Wright Mills, 1916–1962

Figure 1.2

In mid-1983, the unemployment rate in the United States was 9.8 percent, nearly two times greater than it was a decade earlier. This photograph of people lined up outside of a hiring hall in the hope of getting work suggests that unemployment is no longer the personal trouble of a small percent who are unemployable or unwilling to work. Rather, the condition of unemployment has become a public issue, a structural problem of our economy. The **sociological imagination** *involves understanding the connections between our personal experiences and the larger social forces that structure our behavior.*

develop this imagination, we will be less likely to explain others' behavior through their personality and will increasingly look to the roles and social structures that determine behavior. We will also recognize that the solutions to many social problems lie not in changing individuals but in changing the social structures and roles in which they appear. Although poverty, divorce, illegitimacy, and racism are experienced as intensely personal tragedies, they are unlikely to be reduced effectively through massive personal therapy. To solve these and many other social problems, we need to change social structures; we need to rewrite the play. Sociological imagination offers a new way to look at—and a new way to search for solutions to—the common troubles and dilemmas that face individuals.

Sociology as a Social Science

Sociology is concerned with people and with the rules of behavior that structure the ways in which people interact. As one of the social sciences, sociology has much in common with political science, economics, psychology, and anthropology. All these fields share an interest in human social behavior and, to some extent, an interest in society. In addition, they all share an emphasis on the scientific method as the best approach to knowledge. The scientific method is based on the assumption that biological, physical, and social phenomena occur in an orderly fashion and that, by using systematic methods of observation, one can uncover the general laws underlying this order. Several methods of observation are used by social scientists; those employed by sociologists are discussed in chapter 2.

The subject of social science inquiry is **patterned social regularities**, phenomena that occur over and over in a similar way. A search for these regularities shows that most human behavior, from big and momentous

Patterned social regularities are social phenomena that occur over and over in the same way.

acts to small and insignificant ones, is patterned. For example, in our society, casual observation of hands would lead to the conclusion that women's fingernails are generally longer than men's and that many women, but few men, polish their nails. This is a patterned social regularity (it certainly is not biological). What does it mean? One interpretation is that long fingernails are a symbol of what sociologist Thorstein Veblen called conspicuous leisure. They are an advertisement of the fact that this woman does not have to work with her hands, that she doesn't have to work in the fields or in a factory. The interpretation that long fingernails are used as a symbol of leisure is supported by evidence from 19th century China, where fingernails of an inch or more in length were a characteristic status symbol for upper-class men.

All of the social sciences are interested in patterned regularities in human social behavior. The distinctions among the social sciences are chiefly in the kinds of regularities of interest. Economics focuses on patterns in the production, distribution, and consumption of goods and services; the distribution of world resources; and business and consumer behavior. Political science investigates the ways people govern themselves or are governed; the primary concern is with patterns in the distribution of power and participation in formal organizations, especially public bureaucracies. Sociologists also analyze the distribution of power, but in more diverse areas of social interaction—for example, between wives and husbands, friends, delinquent gangs, and complex organizations.

Psychology occupies itself principally with patterns of learning, motivations, and mental disorders. Because mental behavior also has a biological base, psychology is related to the natural sciences as well as the social. Anthropology has traditionally limited its inquiry to small, preliterate societies and has tended to focus on culture and cultural systems. The focus on such societies provides anthropologists with field laboratories in which they study many of the same concerns of the other social sciences: personality, economics, government, and structured social interaction. To the extent that anthropologists turn their attention to modern societies, there is little difference in the subject matter of anthropology and sociology; in many colleges and universities, they are in the same department. The chief differences continue to be in methodology and level of analysis.

Summary.   Analysis of human relationships shows that a wide variety of behavior is socially structured. That is, society provides a pattern for our goals and activities. Our family life, education, economic participation, and daily interactions are all structured by patterns that come ready-made for each new generation. From number of spouses and typical age at marriage to fingernail length, our behavior follows well-used scripts. The goal of sociology is to find out what these scripts are and how roles are allocated and learned.

In summary, although sociology is similar to the other social sciences in many respects, there are some important differences. The unique province of **sociology** is the systematic study of human social interaction. The emphasis is on patterned social regularities that govern people's interactions with one another—how they develop, how they are maintained, and how they change.

Sociology is the systematic study of human social interaction.

Figure 1.3
In most societies children work from an early age, typically alongside their parents in the fields, forests, or tending flocks. When agriculture was replaced by industry, however, child labor became separated from the family and large numbers of children, particularly among the poor, were put to work in mines, stoking furnaces, transporting garmets, and tending machinery. The work was menial, arduous, and poorly paid. As a result, early industrialization is noted for its exploitation of child labor. These conditions, along with massive immigration and urbanization, resulted in social problems that gave birth to the discipline of sociology.

The Emergence of Sociology

The emergence of sociology as a field of study resulted from a combination of circumstances in western Europe during the 18th and 19th centuries. Of particular importance was the industrial revolution, which began in Great Britain in the 1700s and spread to western Europe and the northeastern United States in the next century. The revolution was a major turning point in history: from domestic or cottage industry to power-driven machinery in factories, from agriculture and rural living to large cities and urbanization, from powerful monarchs and rich landowners to capitalists and voting blocs. In its wake, the social, economic, and political conditions of society were revolutionized.

The industrial revolution produced radical changes in the basic structures of society. These changes created stress by producing situations for which there were no preset patterns. It was as if society had changed the play without bothering to provide the actors with new scripts; people were making up the scripts as they went along. The immediate results of industrialization were thus disruption and disorder. As large numbers of people migrated to the cities to work in the factories, housing shortages became acute, serious sanitation problems developed, and most workers lived and worked under harsh conditions. The average worker spent 12 to 14 hours a day, 6 days a week, on a job that was more specialized and consequently more monotonous than before. There were few schools, so children who were not working drifted into the streets, where they created additional problems. Most of those who moved to the cities were strangers to urban life and to their new neighbors. Like immigrants to a foreign country, they were adrift in a sea of strangers and strange ways.

The picture of urban life during the early years of industrialization—in London, Chicago, or Hamburg—was one of disorganization, poverty, and dynamic and exciting change. This urban vitality was the inspiration for much of the intellectual effort of the 19th century. Charles Dickens wrote great novels about it; some people, among them Jane Addams of Hull House, tried to reform it; others turned to the scientific study of society. These were the years in which science was a new enterprise and nothing seemed too much to hope for. After electricity, the telegraph, and the x-ray, who was to say that science could not discover how to turn stones into gold or how to eliminate poverty or war? Thus, many hoped that the tools of science could help in understanding and controlling a rapidly changing society.

The Founders

The men who provided the foundation for sociology were not themselves sociologists. They were philosophers, economists, and preachers whose ideas provided the basis for the new discipline. Sociology has been influenced by dozens of major social theorists—Hobbs, Rousseau, de Tocqueville, Machiavelli, and many more. Two, however, deserve special mention for their early influence on the field: August Comte and Herbert Spencer.

August Comte (1798–1857).   The first major figure to be concerned with the science of society was the French philosopher August Comte. He coined the term *sociology* in 1839 and is generally considered the founder of this science.

Comte was among the first to suggest that the scientific method could be turned to social events (Konig, 1968). He developed the philosophy of **positivism**, arguing that social behavior and events could be observed and measured scientifically. Once the laws of social behavior were learned, he believed, scientists could accurately predict and even control events. Although thoughtful people wonder whether we will ever be able to predict human behavior with the same kind of accuracy that we can predict the behavior of molecules, the scientific method remains central to sociology.

Another of Comte's lasting contributions was his recognition that an understanding of society requires a concern for both the sources of order and continuity and the sources of change. Comte called these divisions the theory of statics and the theory of dynamics. Although sociologists no longer use his terms, Comte's basic divisions of sociology continue under the labels social structure (statics) and social process (dynamics).

Herbert Spencer (1820–1903).   Another pioneer in sociology was the British philosopher-scientist Herbert Spencer, who advanced the thesis that social, as well as natural, life has arisen by progressive evolution (Carneiro, 1968). In two books that were widely read by the U.S. upper classes in the late 19th century, Spencer applied the principle of survival of the fittest to social classes. He believed that class structure was the result of a process of natural selection: Those best adapted to society occupied the top ranks; the poor were those who were less fit. Thus he argued that the rich had nothing to feel guilty about and that the state should do nothing to relieve the conditions of the poor. He reasoned that if the less fit were protected, this would interfere with the evolution of society to higher forms. Spencer's philosophy thus gave "scientific" approval to inequality and to capitalism, an economic form based on competition.

Positivism is the belief that the scientific method can be applied directly to the study of social behavior.

Figure 1.4
Auguste Comte, 1789–1857

Spencer viewed society as being similar to a giant organism: Just as the heart and lungs work together to produce the life of the organism, the parts of society work together to maintain society. In his analogy to the process of evolution in animals, Spencer argued that social patterns contributing to the maintenance (survival) of society would be repeated in future generations, but patterns having negative consequences for society's survival would be dropped by the next generation. This evolutionary view had a strong impact on one branch of sociological theory—structural functionalism.

The Founders of Modern Theory: Durkheim, Marx, and Weber

Toward the end of the 19th century, a few scholars explicitly considered themselves to be sociologists rather than philosophers or economists. Among them, two giants who made lasting contributions to the discipline in a wide variety of areas stand out. The names Durkheim and Weber appear in half a dozen later chapters in this book, and their work continues to be influential. In addition, economist Karl Marx must be included as a 19th century scholar whose work continues to influence research and theory in sociology.

Karl Marx (1818–1883). A philosopher, economist, and social activist, Karl Marx was born in Germany of middle-class Jewish parents. His father, a lawyer, grieved over his son's ''demonic genius'' and early intellectual interests, factors that eventually alienated Marx from his family. Marx received his doctorate in philosophy at the age of 23, but because of his radical views he was unable to obtain a university appointment and spent most of his adult life in exile and poverty (Rubel, 1968).

Marx was repulsed by the poverty and inequality that characterized the 19th century. Unlike Spencer, he was unwilling to see them as natural products of the evolution of society, viewing them instead as social products. Specifically, he regarded private property and capitalism as the causes of poverty and alienation. As a result, he bent his intellectual efforts to understanding—and eliminating—capitalism. Many of Marx's ideas are of more interest to political scientists and economists than to sociologists, but Marx left two enduring legacies to sociology: economic determinism and the dialectic.

ECONOMIC DETERMINISM. Marx began his analysis of society by assuming that the most basic task of any human society was providing food and shelter to sustain itself. Marx argued that the ways in which society did this—its modes of production—would provide the foundations on which all other social and political arrangements would be built. Thus he believed that family structure, law, and religion all develop after and adapt to the economic structure; in short, they are determined by the form of economic relations. He called this idea **economic determinism**.

As an example, the traditional family style of children being obedient to their parents in all things, even allowing their parents to choose their spouses and their occupations, exists because parents control economic assets. This style occurs most often in agricultural societies, where the

Figure 1.5
Herbert Spencer, 1820–1903

Figure 1.6
Karl Marx, 1818–1883

Economic determinism suggests that economic relationships are the basis for all other social relationships.

quantity of land is fixed and young people have no other ways to support themselves. In industrial societies, however, family members have independent access to economic assets; father works for one company, mother for another, and young people for McDonald's or Safeway. Because they are economically independent, neither young people nor women need to be as obedient as they once were. Some people might see these changes as the result of a spirit of independence and equality. Marx would argue that the ideals of equality came after the fact and that the real determinant of a shift in family styles is the changing mode of production. Because Marx saw all human relationships as stemming ultimately from the economic system, he suggested that the major goal of a social scientist was to understand economic relationships: Who owns what, and why?

Dialectic philosophy views change as a product of conflict and contradictions among the parts of society.

THE DIALECTIC.   Marx's other major contribution was the **dialectic**, the philosophy that views change as a product of contradictions and conflicts between parts of society. This view of change was directly counter to the then-prevailing view that change came about through evolution. Marx's thinking on conflict was influenced by the German philosopher Georg Hegel, who suggested that for every idea, a counter-idea develops in conflict with it. Over time the two ideas blend to produce a new idea, or synthesis. Ideological change occurs as this pattern continually repeats itself (see Figure 1.7).

Marx's contribution was to apply this model of ideological change to change in economic and material systems. Marx suggested that the haves (the ruling class) are the thesis and the have-nots (the working class) are the antithesis. He predicted that the conflicts between them would lead to a new economic system, a new synthesis that would be communism. Indeed, in his role as a social activist, Marx hoped to encourage conflict and ignite the revolution that would bring about the desired change. With a stirring cry, he proclaimed that the workers "have nothing to lose but their chains. . . . Working men of all countries, unite!" (Marx & Engels, 1848/1965).

These ideas, discussed in more detail in chapter 8, were at once controversial and influential—and still are. Some scholars reject Marx's ideas about society, and others embrace them; nobody ignores them. Although relatively few sociologists are revolutionaries, Marx's emphasis on conflict and economic relationships provides an important perspective on human society.

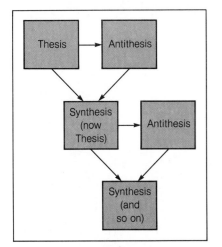

Figure 1.7 The Dialectic
The dialectic model of change suggests that change occurs through conflict and resolution rather than through evolution.

Emile Durkheim (1859–1917).   Like Marx, Durkheim was born into a middle-class Jewish family. Although Durkheim renounced his parents' faith—and, indeed, all religious faith—he never rejected society, as Marx did. He remained a conventional middle-class Frenchman. While Marx was starving as an exile in England, Durkheim spent most of his career occupying a prestigious professorship at the Sorbonne. Far from rejecting society, Durkheim embraced it, and much of his outstanding scholarly energy was devoted to understanding the stability of society and the importance of social participation for individual happiness. Thus, whereas the lasting legacy of Marx is a conflict theory that looks for the coercive and changing aspects of social practices, the lasting legacy of Durkheim

FOCUS ON YESTERDAY

Durkheim's Division of Labor

Durkheim was strongly influenced by the 19th century's preoccupation with biology and evolution (Turner, 1982:25). His basic assumptions about society were thus drawn from biological analogies. For example, he assumed that just as the parts of the body had to work together to produce a healthy organism, so the parts of society had to work together to produce a healthy society.

One of the most insightful of Durkheim's applications of this perspective was his work on the *division of labor*. A division of labor occurs when group members take on specialized tasks and then exchange the products of their labors for those of other specialists. For example, in a modern two-person household, one person might agree to specialize in cooking dinners in exchange for the other's doing all the cleaning. Of course, each person could agree instead to vacuum half the living room, make half the bed, and cook dinner for one. A lot of people who live the latter way eat macaroni and cheese for dinner. If someone specializes in cooking, however, both people might get lasagna and apple pie. A division of labor usually produces a higher-quality product with greater efficiency than does independent labor.

Durkheim acknowledged the efficiency of the division of labor, but he went on to note a more subtle contribution. He argued that the economic benefits of a division of labor are "picayune compared to the moral effect it produces, and its true function is to create in two or more persons a feeling of solidarity" (1893/1964:56). Thus Durkheim pointed out that human

associations from friendship groups to marriages to society are held together by the mutual dependence created by a division of labor.

In an analysis that is still compelling, Durkheim noted that this process of exchange is essential not only to the solidarity of society but also to the integration and satisfaction of the individual. What happens to the individual who is not part of the division of labor— who doesn't have a job, who is dependent on no one, and on whom nobody else depends? Pretty soon this individual becomes a loner, a drifter, someone outside society, someone who lacks a reason to get out of bed in the morning and, finally, a reason to go on living. Some people might call the condition of having no obligations "freedom"; Durkheim called it *anomie* (an-oh-mee) and argued that it is one of the primary causes of suicide and mental illness.

Durkheim's work on the division of labor continues to provide insight into the human condition. Yet, just as our vision of society is limited because we are male or female, black, white, or Hispanic, young or middle-aged Americans in the 20th century, Durkheim's vision of society was limited because he was a 19th century French male. Although he managed to rise above some of the limitations, his writings are affected by the limited knowledge and biases of his day. For example, his views on women appear to the modern reader to be insulting in the extreme. In common with the rest of Europe's intellectual community, he believed that, because women's heads are smaller than men's, they must contain fewer brains and thus

women must be less intelligent than men (Durkheim, 1893/1964:56–61). Durkheim thought this was a good thing. Why? Because the inequality in intelligence helps encourage mutual dependence, a division of labor, between men and women. Because they have different biological potentials, they become specialized in their functions and have to exchange things with each other. Men rely on women for their ability to bear children and their talent for affection and nurturance; women rely on men for their strength and intelligence (1893/1964:60). Durkheim argued that this mutual dependence was the cornerstone of marriage and the family.

From our historical vantage point, Durkheim seems like a sexist. Yet, although his evidence on intelligence was wrong, his analysis was probably right. Marriages were less likely to end in divorce when men's and women's roles were very different—when women couldn't support themselves and when men couldn't get their dinners at McDonald's and their shirts at Penney's.

Questions to Consider

Try to imagine what a family would be like if nobody was dependent on anybody—say that all family members could drive and had their own cars and all had independent incomes that would allow them to pay all the bills themselves. How many families do you know that would break apart tomorrow? How many teenagers, mothers, or fathers do you know who would leave tomorrow if they did not depend on one another economically?

is a theory that examines the positive contributions of social patterns. Together they allow us to see both order and change.

In four books still considered essential reading in sociological training, Durkheim laid the foundations for scientific methodology, the definition of sociological inquiry, and for structural-functional theory. One of Durkheim's major contributions was to define patterned social regularities as the appropriate subject matter of sociology. He called them social facts. In a study of suicide, for example, Durkheim pointed out that the concern of sociology is not with the unique, personal factors that may lie behind a particular suicide; rather, sociology is concerned with patterns of suicide. Thus, on the one hand, if Joe Moravic commits suicide in Oregon, this is a personal trouble and not a suitable subject of sociological inquiry. On the other hand, the fact that Oregon's suicide rate is two times higher than that of New York or that men are four times more likely to commit suicide than women are social facts. These are patterned social regularities, and we can inquire into the factors that create and maintain these patterns.

Durkheim took from Comte an emphasis on positivism, using empirical methods to investigate social phenomena. In his *Rules of Sociological Method,* he identified some of the major issues involved in investigating social facts. These rules include the need for objectivity and advance clarification of the social facts to be analyzed and measured and the importance of looking for cause-and-effect relationships. These issues persist in sociological research today and are discussed more thoroughly in chapter 2.

Max Weber (1864–1920). A German economist, historian, and philosopher, Max Weber (Veh-ber) was also born into a Jewish family with an intellectual tradition. Weber's parents had renounced Judaism in order to raise their social position, and it is possible that the fact of being a religious outsider—neither one thing nor another—was critical to Weber's ability to offer a clear-sighted analysis of world religions. Because of a nervous breakdown and persistent poor health, Weber never held a permanent academic position (Bendix, 1968). Yet his work provides the theoretical base for half a dozen areas of sociological inquiry. He wrote on religion, on bureaucracy, on methodology, and on politics. In all these areas, his work is still valuable and insightful; it will be covered in detail in later chapters. Three of Weber's most general contributions, however, were an emphasis on the subjective meanings of social actions, a stress on social as opposed to material causes, and a warning that sociologists must be objective in studying social issues.

Weber believed that in order to understand the behavior of an individual, it is necessary to understand the meanings the individual attributes to that behavior. Weber's work provided the foundation for **verstehen sociology** (from the German word meaning "understanding"), which emphasizes the subjective meanings of human actions. Advocates of this approach question whether the scientific method can be applied directly to human behavior (Martindale, 1968). Although a hydrogen atom in India is the same as a hydrogen atom in Chicago, the same is not true for social

Figure 1.8
Emile Durkheim, 1858–1917

Verstehen sociology emphasizes the subjective meanings of human actions.

events. A premarital pregnancy, for example, may mean very different things, depending on the historical and cultural context. Weber was more interested in analyzing the meaning of a social pattern within its own historical and cultural context than in looking for universal laws of human behavior. This criticism of positivism remains an important issue in social science.

Weber had been trained as an economist, and much of his work concerned the interplay between things material and things social. He rejected Marx's idea that economic factors were the determinants of all other social relationships. In a classic study, *The Protestant Ethic and the Spirit of Capitalism*, Weber tried to show how social and religious values may be the foundation of economic systems. This argument is developed more fully in chapter 15, but its major thesis is that the religious values of early Protestantism (self-discipline, thrift, and individualism) provided the foundation for capitalism.

One of Weber's most difficult principles to follow is his declaration that sociology must be **value-free**. Weber argued that sociology should be concerned only with establishing what is and should avoid making conclusions about what ought to be: "It is one thing to state facts, to determine mathematical or logical relations or the internal structure of cultural values, while it is another to answer the question of the *value* of culture . . . of how one should act in the cultural community and in political associations" [Weber, 1918/1970d:146].

If sociology is a science, then Weber is undoubtedly right: It should be concerned with uncovering the patterns that exist, not with making recommendations about how society ought to be. On the other hand, most people who enter the field of sociology—both in Weber's day and our own—are concerned about social problems. It is difficult for them to take a neutral, value-free attitude toward poverty or racial inequality. Though nearly everyone agrees with Weber in principle, it takes constant vigilance to keep from slipping into a judgmental posture.

Figure 1.9
Max Weber, 1864–1920

Value-free sociology concerns itself with establishing what is, not what ought to be.

The Development of Sociology in the United States

Sociology in the United States developed somewhat differently than in Europe. Although U.S. sociology has the same intellectual roots as European sociology, it has some distinctive characteristics. Three features that have characterized U.S. sociology from its beginning are a concern with social problems, a reforming rather than a radical approach to social problems, and an emphasis on the scientific method. The following section introduces some of the people who played a major role in the founding of U.S. sociology.

The Pioneers. Sociology dates back about a hundred years in U.S. experience. The first sociology course in the United States was taught at Yale University in 1876 by William Graham Sumner (1840–1910). Sumner was a follower of Spencer and an outspoken advocate of Social Darwinism, the application of evolutionary theory to human social life (Leyburn, 1968). Although Social Darwinism is no longer important in sociology, Sumner

Figure 1.10
Baptism is a common religious ritual in most Christian faiths. Verstehen sociology stresses that this common experience, however, may not be similar in that it depends on the symbolic meaning participants attach to it. The typical Presbyterian baptism in which an infant's head is sprinkled with a few drops of water during Sunday services is quite different in meaning from this older woman's baptism by immersion. Verstehen sociology asks, "What does this mean to the people involved?"

made a lasting contribution to the field through his study of *folkways*, a term he coined to describe the rules that govern everyday behavior.

Fifteen years after Sumner's first course, formal instruction in sociology was offered at 18 colleges and universities in the United States. In 1892, the first department of sociology was established at the University of Chicago under Albion Small. Perhaps more than any other early U.S. sociologist, Small contributed to the recognition of sociology as an academic discipline. He authored the first textbook in sociology in 1894 and in the following year founded the *American Journal of Sociology*, which he edited until his death. Under his direction, the Chicago school of sociology developed as the leading sociology department in the country.

By 1910, most colleges and universities in the United States offered sociology courses, although separate departments were slower to develop. Most of the courses were offered in joint departments, most often with economics but frequently with history, political science, philosophy, or general social science departments.

The Chicago School.   In the first 40 years of this century, the University of Chicago dominated U.S. sociology. During these years, the Chicago school was noted for two major contributions: a strong and enduring interest in social problems and the development of a sociology that stressed the subjective meanings of social action.

Many of the people who worked and taught at Chicago in those years were social activists who wanted not just to understand the world but to reform it. Robert Park (1864–1944), for example, worked as a secretary to Booker T. Washington and was active in the Congo Reform Association, an anticolonial group (Hughes, 1968). Other Chicago sociologists were concerned with eliminating the poverty and disorganization that made the city of Chicago a living laboratory of social problems.

W. I. Thomas (1863–1947) was one of the first PhD graduates of the University of Chicago sociology program (Volkart, 1968). He stood out from others of his period in his insistence on the social causes of social behavior and his disdain of Sumner's and Spencer's evolutionary perspective. In addition, he made a unique contribution by developing a research methodology for verstehen sociology, a methodology that provided systematic ways of uncovering the subjective meanings of human behavior. This research style is called participant observation, and, true to its name, it involves observation of and participation in social action. For Thomas it was not enough in a study of fertility to ask people how many children they wanted or to count the children they actually had; rather, one had to find out what having children meant to people individually—how children affected their hopes and dreams, their definitions of themselves, and their values. To reach this understanding required in-depth interviewing, during which the respondents talked about what was on their minds; it also meant reading people's letters and diaries and observing the day-to-day behaviors that often speak louder than words. This research tradition, which Thomas most successfully applied to a study of Polish immigrants, is one of his greatest legacies and still a rich tradition at the University of Chicago.

Thomas's other major contribution was the admonition that "if men define situations as real, they are real in their consequences" (Thomas & Thomas, 1928:572). Called the **definition of the situation**, this concept reminds us that the subjective meanings that individuals attach to situations have important consequences, consequences that may be as important as the objective conditions themselves. Thus, if John assumes that Sarah will not go out with him, he will never ask her. In this situation, it does not matter whether Sarah would or would not go out with John. His definition of the situation becomes reality: They will never go out together. In this way, Thomas emphasized again the importance of going beyond people's behavior to a study of the subjective meanings of that behavior.

Two other early scholars were instrumental in extending this perspective: Charles Horton Cooley and George Herbert Mead. Cooley (1864–1929) at the University of Michigan and Mead (1863–1931) at Chicago were contemporaries of Thomas who made major contributions to the development of social psychology and a theoretical perspective called symbolic interactionism. Their contributions are still required reading, and their work will be discussed in detail in chapter 5.

The University of Chicago is still an important force in sociology, but beginning in about 1940 it lost its dominant position as other universities and other perspectives became influential. Table 1.1 provides a list of the universities whose sociology departments are among the current leaders in the field.

The Growth of U.S. Sociology. In 1905, about 100 sociologists met in Baltimore to discuss their dissatisfaction with the American Historical, American Economic, and American Political Science associations. In the following year, the American Sociological Society (now called the American Sociological Association, largely because ASA looks better than ASS) was founded. By 1930, the ASA had 4,000 members, and the count now shows more than 12,000.

By 1960, almost all colleges and universities had departments of sociology, and approximately 70 offered doctorate programs. The popularity

Definition of the situation suggests that "if men define situations as real, they are real in their consequences."

Table 1.1 The Top 10 Sociology Departments in 1974
As with the best-dressed list, there is always some controversy over the designation of a top 10. This list is based on the fact that sociologists from these schools are most likely to have had their work cited by others. Other ways of ranking schools would move such schools as Wisconsin, North Carolina and UCLA into the top 10.

RANK	UNIVERSITY
1	Harvard
2	Columbia
3	Chicago
4	Berkeley
5	Yale
6	Pennsylvania
7	Michigan
8	Cornell
9	Northwestern
10	Washington (Seattle)

SOURCE: Roche and Smith. Reprinted with permission of the University of Texas press from Sociological Inquiry 48, 1, 1978:52.

of higher-degree sociology programs is greater in the United States than in any other country in the world. This is partly because sociology in the United States has always been oriented toward the practical as well as the theoretical. The focus has consistently been on finding solutions to social issues and problems, with the result that U.S. sociologists not only teach sociology but also work in government and industry.

Current Perspectives in Sociology

As the brief review of the history of sociological thought has demonstrated, there are many ways of approaching the study of human social interaction. The ideas of Marx, Weber, Durkheim, and others have given rise to dozens of major and minor theories about human behavior. In this section, we bring together and summarize the ideas that form the foundation of the three dominant theoretical perspectives in sociology today: structural functionalism, conflict theory, and symbolic interactionism.

Structural-Functional Theory

Structural functionalism addresses the question of social organization and how it is maintained.

Structural functionalism is the legacy of Durkheim and Spencer. It has its roots in natural science and the analogy between society and an organism. In the analysis of a living organism, the scientist's chief task is to identify the various parts (structures) and determine how they work (function). In the study of society, this perspective directs attention to identifying the structures of society and how they function; hence the name **structural functionalism.**

The Assumptions behind Structural Functionalism.   In the sense that any study of society must begin with an identification of the parts of society and how they work, structural functionalism is basic to all perspectives. Scholars who use this perspective, however, are distinguished from other social analysts by their reliance on three major assumptions:

1. *Stability*—The chief evaluative criterion for any social pattern is whether it contributes to the maintenance of society.
2. *Harmony*—As the parts of an organism work together for the good of the whole, so the parts of society are also characterized by harmony.
3. *Evolution*—Change occurs through evolution—the adaptation of social tructures to new needs and demands and the elimination of unnecessary or outmoded structures.

Because it emphasizes harmony and adaptation (see Figure 1.12), structural functionalism is sometimes called consensus theory.

Structural-Functional Analysis.   Earlier in this chapter, *social structure* was defined as a set of interacting roles guided by a preset script; examples included the family and the school. Structural-functional analysis is concerned with identifying such social structures and the roles and rules that make them up. The structural-functional analysis of a college, for example,

Figure 1.11
On a busy streetcorner, the comings and goings of pedestrians and vehicles are socially structured to maintain traffic and pedestrian flow. Without such a structure, it is easy to imagine the chaos that would result. The structural-functional approach to the analysis of human social behavior examines how the social structures of family, religion, government, and other major institutions contribute to the organization and stability of society.

might begin by noting all the roles that are performed there and the expectations (scripts) that guide their performance. It would probably begin by looking for patterned regularities, for behaviors that occur again and again in the same way. It would include a description of the formal rules and regulations as well as the informal rules that make behavior predictable. Professors regularly meet with their classes, and students, with somewhat less regularity, attend classes. In patterns repeated for generations, students spend too much time drinking coffee at the union and start to write term papers three days before they are due. These are some of the recurring social regularities that pattern life at a college.

The second aspect of structural-functional analysis involves determining the consequences of these social structures for society. Do the structures work in harmony with other social structures? Do they contribute to the maintenance of society? This analysis usually follows the pattern of looking for positive consequences, called **functions**, and for negative consequences, called **dysfunctions**. In addition, a distinction is drawn between those consequences that are manifest and those that are latent. **Manifest functions** are consequences that are intended and recognized by participants in the system; **latent functions** are consequences that are neither intended nor recognized by participants.

How do we tell whether a consequence is positive (functional) or negative (dysfunctional)? This is a difficult question to answer from a neutral point of view, and it is here that the assumptions behind structural-functional theory guide its analysis. Following the assumption that the major criterion for judging a social structure is whether it contributes to the maintenance of society, functional analysis has tended to call structures that preserve the status quo "functions" and those that challenge the status quo "dysfunctions." For example, one analyst has pointed out that one of the functions of poverty is that it scares the rest of us into working (Gans, 1973). As this example suggests, there is an important distinction between whether a social pattern is considered functional for society and whether it is regarded as desirable by the members of society.

Evaluation of Structural Functionalism.   Structural-functional theory tends to produce a static and conservative analysis of social systems (Turner, 1982). This tendency is not a requirement for functional analysis, but it is commonplace. For example, an enumeration of the ways in which poverty contributes to the maintenance of society (an argument outlined in chapter 8) is not the same thing as saying that poverty is good. The distinction is a fine one, however, and in general structural functionalism tends to be a more attractive perspective to those who want to preserve the status quo than to those who want to challenge it.

Conflict Theory

If structural-functional theory sees the world in terms of consensus and stability, then it can be said that **conflict theory** sees the world in terms of conflict and change. Conflict theorists contend that a full understanding of society requires a critical examination of the competition and conflict in society, especially of the processes by which some people are winners and others losers.

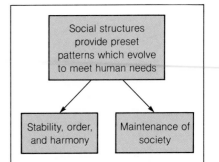

Figure 1.12   The Structural-Functional Model
The structural-functional model tries to identify the social structures that exist in society and to examine how these structures relate to the rest of society. Do they work in harmony together? Do they contribute to the maintenance of society?

Functions are consequences of social structures that have positive effects on the stability of society.

Dysfunctions are consequences of social structures that have negative effects on the stability of society.

Manifest functions are consequences of social structures that are intended and recognized.

Latent functions are consequences of social structures that are neither intended nor recognized.

Conflict theory addresses the points of stress and conflict in social structures and the ways they contribute to social change.

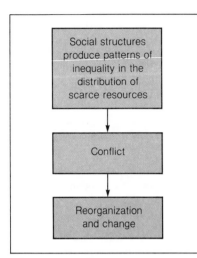

Figure 1.13 The Conflict Model
The conflict model is concerned with the stresses and conflicts that emerge in society because of competition over scarce resources. It focuses on the inequalities that are built into social structures rather than on those that emerge because of personal characteristics.

Assumptions Underlying Conflict Theory.   Although earlier thinkers commented on the importance of competition and conflict in human interaction, conflict theory looks back to Marx for its three guiding assumptions:

1. *The dialectic*—that change occurs through conflict rather than through evolution.
2. *Economic determinism*—that economic competition is at the root of all social relationships.
3. *Social activism*—that the first task of social analysis is social criticism.

Analyzing Conflict.   Like structural functionalists, conflict theorists are interested in social structures (see Figure 1.13). The questions they ask, however, are different. Basically, conflict theorists ask two questions: How is unequal access to scarce resources built into the social structure? How do tensions arising from this inequality affect change and stability?

Some conflict over scarce resources is inevitable. Not only are there limited supplies of goods and services, but there are also limited opportunities for such things as education, jobs, decision making, and leisure. Conflict theory is concerned with identifying the way social structures give people unequal access to these scarce resources. It is also concerned with the processes through which those with advantages manage to protect them. For example, when conflict theorists look at the family, they ask: Who has the power? How did that person get it? How does the person manage to keep it?

The second stage of conflict analysis is to examine the consequences of inequality and competition, to look at the tensions they create and the pressures for change. Conflict theorists see these stresses as inevitable. For every idea, there is a counter-idea; for every winner, there is a loser. The result is that there will be antagonisms and stresses that lead to conflict and change. The antagonisms need not always be between the upper and lower classes; they may also occur among competing factions within the same class. Wherever they occur, however, they are likely to lead to change. The change may be a revolution, or it may be only an adaptation, but conflict is seen as the ultimate source of change.

Within this perspective, neither conflict nor change is seen as necessarily detrimental or destructive. Rather, conflict can be a positive force for change. The conflicts related to the civil rights movement in the United States three decades ago served just such a purpose.

An Evaluation of Conflict Theory.   Conflict theory is a necessary balance to structural functionalism. To focus just on consensus ignores important conditions related to the process of conflict and the dynamic character of society. To focus just on conflict, however, ignores important issues related to stability, order, and predictability in society.

Conflict theory tends to produce a critical picture of society. Whereas structural functionalists evaluate social patterns by whether they promote or reduce stability, conflict theorists tend to evaluate social patterns by whether they are good or bad. Of course, this is not value-free sociology, and social criticism poses a difficult dilemma. Many conflict theorists are careful to distinguish analysis from value judgments; but when one reads that the elite is manipulating the working class, the message of social criticism is clear. Thus conflict theory tends to attract scholars who are more liberal and who would like to change society.

The Symbolic-Interaction Perspective

Conflict and consensus perspectives are based on the assumption that human social behavior and society can be understood by examination of the social structures that guide behavior. Symbolic interaction, by contrast, directs attention to analysis of the interaction of persons in face-to-face communications. **Symbolic interactionism** addresses the subjective meanings of human acts and the processes through which people come to develop and communicate shared meanings. Consequently, this perspective focuses on the everyday aspects of social life. Social psychologists who have a primary interest in small groups, interpersonal relationships, and the development of the self-concept are most inclined to use this approach.

Symbolic interactionism addresses the subjective meanings of human acts and the processes through which people come to develop and communicate shared meanings.

Guiding Assumptions. The major premise behind symbolic interactionism is that interaction is made possible by the development of shared symbolic meanings. At the most elementary level, this means that we learn the language of our culture and are able to understand such simple messages as "the dog is brown." Social interaction, however, also requires coming to share more subtle symbolic meanings. For example, we learn that "Hi, how are you?" is not usually a sincere request to hear about our health and that a pounding heart and shortness of breath may sometimes be attributed to love rather than illness.

A major concern of symbolic interactionists is the process through which people learn the symbolic frameworks of their cultures. How do Navajo children in the U.S. learn to value sharing and cooperation, whereas the vast majority of U.S. children learn to be competitive and achievement-oriented? How do some children learn to accept delinquent behaviors and others do not? Symbolic-interaction theory directs our attention to two major mechanisms that explain how learning takes place. First, we learn to believe what our family and friends believe. Second, we learn by playing the roles that society sets out for us. These theoretical assumptions guide symbolic-interaction analysis to focus on the groups we belong to and the roles we play.

Role Theory and the Dramaturgical Perspective. The emphasis on role playing is the foundation for the *dramaturgical perspective*. This approach, developed extensively by Erving Goffman (1922–1982), analyzes social situations in terms of the roles people are cast into, the scripts that have been written, and the opportunities for improvisation. Whereas structural-functional and conflict theorists are concerned with what might be called established dramas (the patterns of interaction that have become standard parts of our culture), dramaturgy is interested in the minor dramas of everyday life.

Figure 1.14
This march on Washington in August, 1983 is a cogent reminder that the social structure of our society benefits some more than others. These inequalities are the focus of conflict theory. Based on the theories of Karl Marx, the conflict perspective focuses on how those with economic power ensure that the system works to their benefit. It also focuses on the protests and demands for change, which—like the one pictured here—are an inevitable outcome of inequality.

Figure 1.15
By selecting our clothes and life-styles, we manage impressions about ourselves and symbolically communicate our statuses and the roles we have chosen to play. The symbolic interaction perspective focuses on the meanings of these symbols and how they affect our interaction with others in the common ordinary interaction of everyday life.

Goffman uses a variety of analogies to the theater to provide insight into social interaction. For example, he distinguishes between front-stage performances (those meant to be observed and interpreted) and back-stage performances (those we hope the audience will not see). Presenting a neat and tidy appearance in class while your bedroom floor is covered with dirty clothes is one example of the difference between front- and back-stage performance. In this case, it suggests that your fellow students rather than your roommates or family are the relevant audience. Goffman also notes that numerous props, including clothing, mannerisms, and possessions, may be used to foster or manage a particular type of impression. People going on a first date or to a job interview are particularly sensitive to managing impressions. An important dimension of the dramaturgical perspective is that personal identity shifts along with the roles we play, both in the course of a day and in the course of a lifetime.

An Evaluation.   The value of symbolic-interaction perspectives is that they focus attention on small group relationships, which are so much a part of everyday life. They also help us explain how the roles provided by social structures come to be such an inseparable part of ourselves that we regard them as natural. The fact that this perspective ignores the larger societal relationships analyzed through conflict or structural-functional theory is its major weakness.

Interchangeable Lenses

A variety of theoretical perspectives are used in the field of sociology. They can be regarded as interchangeable lenses through which to view society. Just as a telephoto lens is not always superior to a wide-angle lens, one sociological theory will not always be superior to another.

Occasionally, the same subject can be viewed through any of these perspectives. For example, one can examine prostitution through the theoretical lens of structural functionalism, conflict theory, or symbolic interactionism. Following are three snapshots of prostitution using these perspectives.

The Functions of Prostitution.   The functional analysis of prostitution begins by examining its social structure. It identifies the network of expectations that tie together the positions of pimps, prostitutes, and customers. Then it examines the consequences or functions of this social structure. In 1961, Kingsley Davis listed the following latent functions of prostitution:

— It provides a sexual outlet for men who cannot compete on the marriage market—the physically or mentally handicapped, the very poor.
— It provides a sexual outlet for men who are away from home a lot—salesmen and sailors.
— It provides a sexual outlet for the kinky.

Davis called these consequences "functions" because they help protect the institution of marriage from malcontents who, for one reason or another, do not receive adequate sexual service through the institution of

Figure 1.16

Prostitution can be viewed from several sociological perspectives. Symbolic interactionists would emphasize the social setting where hookers do business, the kind of clothing worn to signal intent to passersby, and the facial expressions and mannerisms of the participants. The conflict perspective, by contrast, would focus on prostitution as an economic relationship in which women without much education or job skill are reduced to trading sexual favors to gain access to scarce resources in society. A structural functional perspective would emphasize that prostitution is a voluntary exchange that helps meet unmet needs of both women and men thereby contributing to the stability of society.

marriage. He speculated that prostitution may also help reduce the incidence of rape.

Prostitution: A Scarce Resource.   Conflict theorists analyze prostitution as part of the larger problem of unequal allocation of scarce resources. Women, they argue, have not had equal access to economic opportunity. In some societies, they are forbidden to own property; in others, they suffer substantial discrimination in opportunities to work and earn. Because of this inability to support themselves, women have had to rely on economic support from men. They get this support by exchanging the one scarce resource they have to offer: sexual availability. To a Marxist, it makes little difference whether a woman barters her sexual availability by the job (prostitution) or by contract (marriage); the underlying cause is the same.

This perspective helps explain why many respectable women have been opposed to prostitution and promiscuity. To the extent that someone else is selling sex cheaper or giving it away, the respectable woman's bargaining power is reduced. Sexual availability is no longer a scarce resource. This perspective may also help explain why nonmarital sex is less condemned than it used to be. As women have gained increasingly independent access to economic resources, they no longer need to use sex as a bargaining tool and are freer to use it noneconomically.

Prostitution: Learning the Trade. Symbolic interactionists who examine prostitution will take an entirely different perspective. They will want to know how women learn the trade and how they manage their self-concept so that they continue to think positively of themselves in spite of engaging in a socially disapproved profession. One such study was done by Barbara Heyl, who intensively interviewed a middle-aged woman who had spent her career first as a prostitute and then as a madam and trainer of prostitutes. Heyl found that much of the training in the prostitute's role consists of business training, not sex. Women learn how to hustle—how to get the maximum amount of money for the minimum amount of work. In speaking of what her training produces, the madam says she is turning out professional hustlers, not whores. She is proud of her work. She says, "They find that I am teaching them how to make money, to dress tastefully, to converse and be poised with men, to be knowledgeable about good hygiene, to have good working habits, such as punctuality, which will help them whether they stay in the rackets or not, and to have self-respect" (Heyl, 1979:105).

Summary. As these examples illustrate, many topics can be fruitfully studied with any of these three theoretical perspectives. Just as a photographer with only one lens can shoot almost any subject, the sociologist with only one perspective will not be unduly limited in what to examine. One will generally get better pictures, however, by selecting the theoretical perspective that is best suited to the particular subject. In general, structural functionalism and conflict theory are well suited to the study of social structures, or **macrosociology**. Symbolic interactionism is well suited to the study of interactions among individuals, or **microsociology.**

Macrosociology studies human social behavior by identifying the basic patterns of society and their interrelationships.

Microsociology analyzes interactions among individuals.

CONCEPT SUMMARY

Major Theoretical Perspectives in Sociology

	STRUCTURAL FUNCTIONALISM	CONFLICT THEORY	SYMBOLIC INTERACTIONISM
Nature of society	Interrelated social structures that fit together to form an integrated whole	Competing interest groups, with each group seeking to secure its own ends	Interacting individuals, social networks, and groups
Basis of interaction	Consensus and shared values	Constraint, power, and conflict	Shared meaning regarding symbols
Focus of inquiry	Social order and maintenance of society	Social change and conflict	Development of self and adaptation of individual to society
Level of analysis	Social structure	Social structure	Interpersonal interaction

ISSUES IN PUBLIC POLICY

Sociologists at Work

A concern with social problems has been a continuing focus of U.S. sociology. This is evident both in the kinds of courses that sociology departments offer (social problems, race and ethnic relations, crime and delinquency, for example) and in the kinds of research sociologists do.

The majority of U.S. sociologists are employed in colleges and universities, where they teach and do research. Much of this research is *basic, or pure, sociology*, which has no immediate practical application and is motivated simply by a desire to understand some aspect of human social behavior more fully. Even pure research, however, often has implications for social policy. For example, an understanding of the ways people learn can be used in schools, prisons, and the military—all institutions concerned with teaching people new behaviors and values.

In addition to the pure research motivated by scholarly curiosity, an increasing proportion of sociologists are engaged in *applied sociology*, seeking to provide immediate practical answers to problems of government, industry, or individuals. The proportion of sociologists who are engaged in applied work has doubled (from 9 to 18 percent) in the brief period between 1976 and 1981. As Table 1.2 indicates, this increase is evident in government, business, and nonprofit organizations.

WORKING IN GOVERNMENT

A long tradition of sociological work in government has to do with measuring and forecasting population trends. This work is vital for decisions about where to put roads and schools and when to stop building schools and start building nursing homes. In addition, sociologists have been employed to design and evaluate public policies in a wide variety of areas. In World War II, sociologists designed policies to increase the morale and fighting efficiency of the armed forces. During the war on poverty, sociologists helped plan and evaluate programs to reduce the inheritance of poverty.

Sociologists work in nearly every branch of government. Sociologist William Darrow, for example, is employed by the Center for Disease Control. His assignment: to examine aspects of homosexual life-style that might be related to AIDS (Acquired Immune Deficiency Syndrome). While the physicians and biologists at CDC examine the medical aspects of AIDS, Darrow works at understanding the social aspects. Among his activities is an

Table 1.2 Where Sociologists Work

Although the majority of sociologists teach and do research in colleges and universities, a growing proportion do applied work.

	1976	1981	PERCENT CHANGE
Educational institutions	84%	74%	− 10%
Government	5	8	+ 3
Business/industry	1	5	+ 4
Nonprofit organizations	3	6	+ 3
Not employed	6	6	0
Total percent	99%	99%	
Total number	7,102	10,612	

SOURCE: Bettina Huber. Reprinted with the permission of the American Sociological Association from *Footnotes*, May, 1983 (Volume 11, pp. 1, 6–7).

application of W. I. Thomas's research strategies; Darrow hangs out in bathhouses and does long hours of in-depth interviewing in an attempt to understand the structure of the gay community. In speaking of his choice of work, Darrow says:

> John F. Kennedy had just become president and I thought I heard him asking me what I could do for my country. Rather than accepting a decent job as a management trainee for Bauer and Black, I chose to work with the Sharks and the Jets on the West Side of Manhattan for $4,490 a year. *West Side Story* is ancient history, but I am still trying to figure out how diseases spread in communities, and how chains of disease transmission can be broken. (Cited in Howery, 1983)

WORKING IN BUSINESS

Sociologists are employed by General Motors and Pillsbury, as well as by advertisers and management consultants. Part of their work concerns internal affairs (bureaucratic structures and labor relations), but much of it has to do with market research. Business and industry employ sociologists so that they can use their knowledge of society to predict which way consumer demand is likely to jump. For example, the recent sharp increase in single-person households has important implications for life insurance companies, for food packagers, and for the construction industry. To stay profitable, companies need to be able to predict and plan for these kinds of changes. Another area of extensive involvement for sociologists is the preparation of environmental impact statements, in which they try to assess the likely impact of, say, a coal slurry operation on the social and economic fabric of a proposed site.

WORKING IN NONPROFIT ORGANIZATIONS

Nonprofit organizations range from hospitals and clinics to social-activist organizations and private think tanks; sociologists are employed in all of them. Sociologists at Planned Parenthood, for example, are concerned with determining the causes and consequences of teenage fertility, with evaluating communication strategies that can be used to prevent teenage pregnancy, and with devising effective strategies to pursue some of that organization's more controversial goals, such as the preservation of legal access to abortion on demand.

The training that sociologists receive has a strong research orientation and is very different from the therapy-oriented training received by social workers. Neverthe-less, a thorough understanding of the ways that social structures impinge on individuals can be useful in helping individuals cope with personal troubles. Consequently, some sociologists also do marriage counseling, family counseling, and rehabilitation counseling.

WHAT CAN YOU DO WITH A DEGREE IN SOCIOLOGY? HOW ABOUT A NOBEL PRIZE?

Swedish sociologist Alva Myrdal used her sociological background for service to her country and the world. In 1982, she was the joint recipient of the Nobel Peace Prize for the 11 years she spent as Sweden's representative at the Geneva arms negotiations and for her unflagging efforts to increase awareness of the dangers of nuclear armament.

Myrdal's early sociological work was in the area of the family and women's roles. In 1940, this work became the basis for Sweden's first family policy. Between 1950 and 1955, Myrdal served as director of social services at UNESCO; later, she became Sweden's ambassador to India (Howery, 1983). Myrdal's long record of distinguished public service shows how thoroughly practical an understanding of society can be.

SUMMARY

1. Sociology is the systematic study of human social behavior. It is concerned with patterned social regularities rather than with unique personal experiences. Sociologists use the concepts role and social structure to analyze common human dramas.

2. Sociology is based on the premise that personal troubles and experiences are best understood in the context of social structure, as public issues rather than unique personal experiences. This way of looking at human social behavior is called the sociological imagination.

3. The scientific method is based on the assumption that phenomena occur in an orderly fashion and that, by using systematic methods of observation, the general laws underlying this order can be discovered. The belief that this method can be applied directly to social as well as biological and physical phenomena is called positivism. Those who advocate caution in this regard adhere to a branch of sociology called verstehen, which suggests that human behavior cannot be fully understood without attention to the subjective meanings people attach to their behavior.

4. The rapid social change that followed the industrial revolution was an important inspiration for the development of sociology. Problems caused by disorganization and rapid change made people demand accurate information about social processes. This social-problems orientation remains an important thread in sociology.

5. There are three major theoretical perspectives in sociology: structural-functional theory, conflict theory, and symbolic-interaction theory. The three can be seen as alternate lenses through which to view society, each having value as a tool for understanding society.

6. Structural functionalism has its roots in evolutionary theory. It is concerned with describing the interrelationships of social structures and analyzing their consequences for social stability. Major figures in its development include Spencer and Durkheim.

7. Conflict theory developed from Karl Marx's ideas about the importance of conflict and competition in structuring human behavior. It analyzes points of stress and conflict in society and their impact on social change.

8. Symbolic-interaction theory is concerned with the subjective meanings of human interaction and the processes through which people come to develop and communicate shared symbolic meanings. This perspective is based on the work of Thomas, Cooley, Mead, and Goffman.

9. Most sociologists teach and do research in academic settings. A growing minority are employed in government and business, where they do applied research. Regardless of the setting, sociological theory and research has implications for social policy.

SUGGESTED READINGS

Bart, Pauline, & Frankel, Linda. (1981). The Student Sociologist's Handbook (3rd ed.). Glenview, Ill.: Scott, Foresman. Information on sociological perspectives, research materials, and sociological writing for the beginning student.

Berger, Peter L. (1963). Invitation to Sociology: A Humanistic Perspective. Garden City, N.Y.: Doubleday Anchor. A delightful, well-written introduction to what sociology is and how it differs from other social sciences. Blends a serious exploration of basic sociological understandings with scenes from everyday life— encounters that are easy to relate to and that make sociology both interesting and relevant.

Huber, Bettina J. (1982). Embarking upon a Career with an Undergraduate Sociology Major. Washington, D.C.: American Sociological Association. A pamphlet containing useful information for students wanting to know how the study of sociology relates to various careers and how sociological skills acquired in college can be used in finding a job.

Mills, C. Wright. (1959). The Sociological Imagination. New York: Oxford University Press. A penetrating account of how the study of sociology expands understanding of common experiences.

Riis, Jacob A. (1971). How the Other Half Lives. New York: Dover Publishers. A photo essay and narrative of conditions in New York City in the second half of the 19th century. Riis, a police reporter turned social reformer, documents through pictures and statistics the deplorable conditions in New York that accompanied industrialization and that eventually spawned the development of modern sociology.

Truzzi, Marcello (Ed.). (1968). Sociology and Everyday Life. Englewood Cliffs, N.J.: Prentice-Hall. A collection of readings that draw on the common experiences of everyday life, illustrating how sociology pertains to ordinary and real experiences.

Willson, Everett K., & Selvin, Hanan C. (1980). Why Study Sociology? A Note to Undergraduates. Belmont, Calif.: Wadsworth. An introduction to sociological perspectives and methods, written especially to provide undergraduates with practical information about the discipline.

CHAPTER 2

DOING SOCIOLOGY

PROLOGUE

*Have You Ever . . . heard about the medical study designed to mea-
sure the extent to which the side effects of birth control pills are psychological rather than physical? The physicians involved in the study reasoned that if the effects were psychological, they would occur among
women who thought they were taking the Pill, whether they were or not.
To test this hypothesis, they recruited a group of women who were interested in contraception and gave half of them real birth control pills and
half of them sugar pills. All of the women thought they were taking the
real Pill. The results showed that the side effects were more pronounced
among the group taking the real Pill, thus substantiating a physical cause;
of course, one particular side effect—pregnancy—was much more pronounced among the women taking the sugar pill.*

*The physicians involved in this study were unconcerned about the ef-
fect an unwanted pregnancy might have on their subjects; their only concern was learning about the side effects. When asked why they didn't explain the experiment to the subjects, the physician in charge said, "If you
think you could explain [this experiment] to these women, you haven't
met Mrs. Gomez from the West Side" (cited in Seaman, 1972).*

*A similar lack of concern is evident in a study sponsored by the U.S.
Public Health Service between 1932 and 1972. In the so-called Tuskegee
Study, more than 400 black men who had syphilis were misled about the
nature of their illness and deliberately left untreated so the doctors
could observe the course of the disease (Jones, 1981). It is probably no
accident that in both of these experiments the subjects were members of
minority groups.*

*Both studies were unethical and irresponsible. Although the research-
ers began with legitimate questions, they ignored the rights of the individuals who participated in their studies. The pursuit of truth must not
be achieved at the expense of research subjects; it is unethical to experiment with human beings if such experiments may damage their health or
happiness. This is true not only in medical research but also in many*

areas of social research. Experiments concerning the effects of child abuse, poverty, or racism, for example, would be as unethical as these medical experiments.

Because of such ethical issues, social scientists have generally forsaken the efficiency of the experimental method for the humanism of less efficient methods. This chapter describes the compromises through which social science ethically produces accurate data on human social interaction.

The Application of Science to Sociology

The things that sociologists study—for example, deviance, marital happiness, and poverty—have probably interested you for a long time. You may have developed your own opinions about why some people have good marriages and some have bad marriages, why some people break the law and others do not. Sociology is an academic discipline that uses the procedures of science to critically examine commonsense explanations of human social behavior. Science is not divorced from common sense but is an extension of it.

Defining Science

The ultimate aim of science is to better understand the world. Science directs us to find this understanding by observing and measuring what actually happens. This is not the only means of acquiring knowledge. Some people get their perceptions from the Bible or the Koran or the Book of Mormon. Others get their answers from their mothers or their husbands or their girlfriends. When you ask such people "But how do you know that that is true?" their answer is simple. They say "My mother told me" or "I read it in *Reader's Digest.*"

Science is a way of knowing based on systematic, critical, and empirical investigation.

Science differs from these other ways of knowing in that it requires empirical evidence as a basis for knowledge; that is, it requires evidence that can be confirmed by the normal human senses. We must be able to see, hear, smell, or feel it. Before we would agree, for example, that marijuana use is a cause of low grades, we would have to have evidence showing that at least one student got worse grades after starting to smoke marijuana. Without this observed evidence, we would reject the proposition that marijuana use is a cause of low grades—no matter how many times our father told us it was true.

The Relationships between Observation and Theory

Science has two major goals: an accurate description of reality and an accurate explanation of it. In sociology, we are concerned with describing patterns of human interaction (how many people marry, how many people abuse their children, how many people flunk out of school). After we do this, we hope to be able to explain these patterns, to develop a theory. We hope to be able to say why people marry, abuse their children, or flunk out of school. Theory and observation work hand-in-hand to advance knowledge and understanding.

Induction. The strategy of gathering observations that can be used to develop theories is called **induction.** Scientists who use this strategy begin with observations of reality, find recurring patterns, and then develop explanations of observed patterns. A hypothetical example shows how this process works.

Induction is the process of moving from observations to theory.

OBSERVATIONS. Let us assume that after years of reading in the newspaper about the negative effects of marijuana use, your professor decides to critically examine the idea that marijuana use leads to underachievement in school. After finding out all she can about previous research in this area, she will begin by gathering systematic evidence about students' grades and their use of marijuana.

GENERALIZATIONS. After collecting and analyzing the data, your professor should be in a better position to make judgments about this commonsense idea put forth in the media. If support is found, then the generalization that students who use marijuana are the same students who get low grades is justified. This is a statement of **correlation.** It says that the two factors, marijuana use and low grades, tend to occur together. It is not a statement of explanation, however; it does not say why the relationship exists.

Correlation is a statistical association between two variables showing that they have a patterned relationship.

THEORY. Observing a correlation is a step toward forming an explanation. The difficulty is that there are often many different explanations for a particular correlation. In this case, for example, poor achievement could lead to drug use or drug use could lead to poor achievement. Your professor's theory may run something like this:

> Students who use illegal drugs have to develop a rationalization for their illegal behavior. This rationalization often includes a rejection of authority and the right of others to direct their activities. When this attitude becomes generalized to other social situations, users come to resent taking instructions from others in anything, including history and biology. Thus poor school performance among drug users is a result of reduced respect for authority.

Notice that this explanation goes beyond the facts at hand. The only empirical evidence so far is that low grades and marijuana use are correlated. The mechanism by which one causes the other has not been empirically supported. It is a **theory**—a set of interrelated assumptions that provide an explanation of why an observed pattern exists.

A **theory** is an interrelated set of assumptions that provides an explanation of why correlations exist.

Deduction. Arriving at theories that are supported by the evidence is not the end of the scientific process. The critical attitude taken toward evidence is also applied to theory. Thus we have to critically evaluate our explanations to see if they are supported by the evidence or if they need to be qualified or revised. This way of approaching science is called **deduction.** It begins with established theory, forms hpotheses, and tests them.

Deduction is the process of moving from theory to observations by devising tests of hypotheses drawn from existing theory.

HYPOTHESES. In order to evaluate our theories, we deduce **hypotheses**—statements about relationships we expect to find if our theory is correct. From the marijuana theory, for example, we could deduce two hypotheses, that marijuana users are more likely than nonusers to reject authority and

Hypotheses are statements about the expected relationships between two or more variables.

that people who reject authority get lower grades than people who accept others' authority.

OBSERVATIONS.   These hypotheses could be tested by gathering data from students on marijuana use, grades, and extent to which they reject authority. If either of those hypotheses is not empirically supported then we must revise our theory to take this new information into account.

The Research Process

Science is a never-ending circle of inquiry in which the investigator moves continually between observations and theory (see Figure 2.1). There is no beginning point or ending point on this circle. You can start your investigations by observing the world around you (induction) or by testing an already developed theory (deduction). Regardless of which strategy you pursue, however, there is a common pattern to research projects (see Figure 2.2).

Reviewing the Literature.
Most researchers begin their work with a vaguely defined interest in a topic. Perhaps something you read or observe or something someone says will spark your curiosity. The first step in turning this curiosity into a research project is to begin a review of the literature. In order to prevent yourself from rediscovering the wheel, it is essential that you find out what is already known.

Defining the Problem.
After you discover what is already known, you are in a position to design your own research project. It may be inductive or deductive, depending on the knowledge in the area, but either strategy requires that you spell out the research questions to be addressed. In deductive research, this means formulating specific hypotheses to test; in inductive research, it means stating in advance the specific information you are looking for.

Choosing a Research Design.
The questions you specify will determine the research design you use. At this point, you need to consider

Figure 2.1 The Wheel of Science
Science is a process of moving between theory and observation according to shared guidelines.
SOURCE: Adapted from Walter Wallace, Sociological Theory, Chicago: Aldine, 1969.

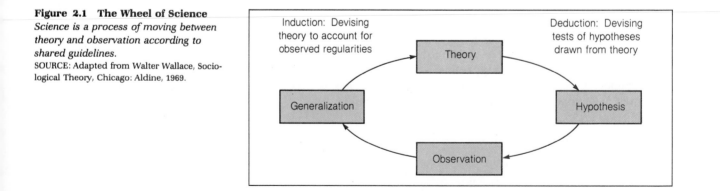

issues of measurement, sampling, and collection of observations. Some of these design considerations are addressed in the next sections.

Gathering Data.   In most research projects, data gathering is the most expensive and time-consuming step. Depending on the research design you have specified, it may involve setting up a lab, recruiting subjects, choosing locations for observation, or making up questionnaires and choosing a sample. After the data are gathered, they must be processed. Survey data must be entered on terminals for computer analysis; interview and observation data must be written up and coded.

Analyzing the Data.   Once the data are processed, you must begin making sense of them. What generalizations are supported? What hypotheses are supported? Analysis is a complex task, often requiring advanced statistical training and computer programming skills.

Drawing Conclusions.   The final step of the research process is drawing conclusions and presenting your findings to others. Typically, sociologists report their research in professional sociology journals, where the entire research process is described in detail. Their reports enable other sociologists to critically assess the research design and compare the results to those of similar studies. Research reports bring us full circle by providing literature for others to review prior to doing their own projects.

General Principles of Research

At each stage of the research process, certain conventional procedures are used to make sure that your findings will be accepted as scientific knowledge by others. These procedures are covered in classes on research methodology, statistics, and theory construction. At this point, we introduce four principles that underlie almost all research: variables, operational definitions, sampling, and notions of causality.

Variables

A medical specialist who studies cancer may have dozens and dozens of tissue samples to examine. Each sample comes from a unique human being, who might have other ailments and problems as well. The cancer specialist, however, is interested only in the tumors. In a similar fashion, sociological researchers are seldom interested in all aspects of individuals; instead they are interested in **variables**—measured characteristics of individuals that vary from one person to the next (Babbie, 1983).

In the fictitious study described earlier, we were concerned with two variables: marijuana use and grades. Someone could probably write a book about each of the students in this study, but for the purposes of our research we are interested in only the two pieces of information. These variables, then, rather than the individuals themselves, are the topic of our research. When we hypothesize a cause-and-effect relationship between two variables, the cause is called the **independent variable** and

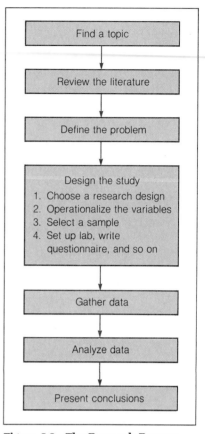

Figure 2.2 The Research Process
Whether they use an inductive or a deductive model, research projects go through a process in which general topics of inquiry become formulated into specific research questions.

Variables are measured characteristics that vary from one individual or group to the next.

The **independent variable** is the variable that does the causing in cause-and-effect relationships.

The **dependent variable** is the effect in cause-and-effect relationships. It is dependent on the actions of the independent variable.

the effect is called the **dependent variable.** In our example, marijuana use is the independent variable and grades are the dependent variables; that is, grades are dependent on marijuana use.

Operational Definitions

A vital step in providing empirical evidence about a phenomenon is to define what we are studying. Before we can test the theory that marijuana users get worse grades than nonusers, we need to be able to sort people systematically into two categories: users and nonusers. The exact rules that we use to measure a variable are called **operational definitions.** Reaching general agreement about them often poses a problem. For example, following are two possible operational definitions of *marijuana user:*

Operational definitions describe the exact procedures by which a variable is to be measured.

1. A marijuana user is any person who answers yes to the question: Have you ever smoked marijuana?
2. A marijuana user is any person who answers yes to the question: Do you generally smoke marijuana more than three times a week?

If one researcher uses the first definition and another uses the second, there will be substantial differences in the way they classify people. People who tried marijuana once, former users, and current users will all be classified as users by the first definition; only current, regular users will be called users by the second. As research consumers, we should always keep in mind that the data reported in sociological research, or any research, are based on operationally defined variables rather than on the full breadth of reality. These definitions may be only partial reflections of reality.

Sampling

In science, it is seldom possible to look at all instances of any phenomenon, whether hydrogen atoms or marriages. Thus science usually proceeds by looking at a **sample**—a systematic selection of representative cases from the larger population. There is considerably more variation among marriages than there is among hydrogen atoms, however, and the method of sample selection is often more important in social research than it is in the natural or physical sciences. Three general criteria operate in selecting and evaluating a sample:

A **sample** is a systematic selection of a group of individuals from a larger pool using random procedures.

1. From what population was the sample chosen?
2. How was the sample chosen?
3. What is the size of the sample?

The first principle concerns the list from which the sample was drawn. This list is the only population that the results can be said to describe. For example, if we draw a sample of telephone numbers from the directory, the sample can represent only households that are listed in the directory. Similarly, a sample drawn from students enrolled in the introductory sociology course at Midwestern State University can be generalized only to other students enrolled in introductory sociology at Midwestern State.

If Midwestern State is a public institution and introductory sociology is taken by students from a broad array of majors, we may be able to stretch the generalization to apply to midwestern college students. The findings from a study are generally limited to the population from which the sample was drawn and similar populations.

The second principle in evaluating a sample concerns the procedures used to draw the sample. A sample is representative of the population from which it is drawn only if the sample is drawn randomly. If we put the names of all introductory sociology students in a hat and blindly draw 50 out, we comply with this requirement and have a random sample of these students. If, however, we ask for volunteers or take only students with good grades, we do not have a random sample of students, and our results cannot be generalized to the entire group of students.

The third principle in selecting and evaluating a sample is size. When the sample is small, the random inclusion of one individual rather than the next (say the selection of John rather than Juan) can have a large effect on the results. Because of this, findings based on small samples may not adequately represent the population. In general, the larger the sample, the more the results can be depended on.

Notions of Causality

Sociologists assume that all events have causes, which is the same as saying that they assume that behavior is not random. For example, there are reasons why you have enrolled in introductory sociology. Perhaps your adviser recommended it; perhaps it was the only class that fit your schedule; perhaps you are interested in the social sciences. The causes may be many and complex, and they may differ among students, but they do exist. Something caused you to take introductory sociology.

In looking for the causes of human behavior, sociology relies on a probabilistic notion of causality. That is, if the presence of the independent variable increases the probability of the dependent variable occurring, then we are willing to consider it a cause. We do not require that the effect always occur; but only that it becomes more probable. For example, many students who do not smoke marijuana get low grades anyway, and some students who smoke marijuana get excellent grades. If smoking marijuana increases the likelihood that students will get low grades, however, then we are willing to say that marijuana is a cause of poor grades.

Generally, sociology adopts a model of multiple causation. Instead of looking for the only cause of an event, we anticipate that there will be many causes. Marijuana may or may not be a cause of low grades, but certainly there are many other causes; intelligence, work load, ambition, and health are other factors related to school achievement. The complexity of human behavior leads to complex explanations.

Three Strategies for Gathering Data

The theories and findings reported in this book have been produced using a variety of research strategies. Three of the most general strategies are outlined here: experiments, survey research, and field studies. First, each method is reviewed, with mention of its advantages and disadvantages. Then, research projects that demonstrate the three methodologies are discussed.

The Experiment

An **experiment** is a method in which independent variables are manipulated in order to test theories of cause and effect.

The **experiment** is a research method in which the researcher deliberately manipulates the independent variable in order to observe cause-and-effect relationships. Sometimes experiments are conducted in carefully controlled conditions in laboratories, but often they are field experiments that take place in normal classrooms and work enviroments. In the classic controlled experiment, a group of subjects is divided randomly into two groups—the control group which does not receive the experimental stimulus and the experimental group which does. The crucial aspect of an experiment is that the researcher controls the extent to which the subjects experience the independent variable.

In our study of marijuana use, a field experiment might begin by observing student grades for several weeks until students' normal performance level had been established. Then the class would be randomly divided into two groups. If the initial pool is large enough, we can assume that the two groups are probably equal on nearly everything. For example, we can assume that both groups probably contain an equal mix of good and poor students, of lazy and ambitious students. The control group might be requested to abstain from marijuana use for five weeks and the experimental group might be requested to smoke marijuana three times a week during the same period. At the end of the five weeks, we would compare the grades of the two groups. Both groups might have experienced a drop in grades because of normal factors such as fatigue, burnout, and overwork. The existence of the control group, however, allows us to determine whether marijuana use causes a reduction in grades over and above that which normally occurs.

Experiments are excellent devices for testing hypotheses about cause and effect. They have 3 drawbacks, however. First, experiments are often unethical because they expose subjects to the possibility of harm. The

CONTROL GROUP   OUT OF CONTROL GROUP.

study on marijuana use, for example, might damage student grades, introduce them to bad habits, or otherwise harm them. A more extreme example is the question of whether people who were abused as children are more likely to abuse their own children. We could not set up an experiment in which one of two randomly assigned groups of children was beaten and the other not. Because of such ethical issues, many areas of sociological interest cannot be studied with the experimental method.

A second drawback to experiments is that subjects often behave differently when they are under scientific observation than they would in their normal enviroment. For example, although marijuana use might normally have the effect of lowering student grades, the participants in our study might find the research so interesting that their grades actually improved. In this case, the subjects' response to the independent variable is different under experimental conditions than it would be under normal conditions. This response is called the **guinea-pig effect** and has been documented in many studies (Webb, et al., 1966). It reduces the likelihood that experimental results will apply to real life situations.

> The **guinea-pig effect** occurs when participants in an experiment act differently than they would outside the laboratory because of their knowledge that they are participating in an experiment.

A final drawback to the experiment is especially relevant to laboratory experiments such as that described later in this chapter. When researchers try to set up social situations in laboratories, they often must omit many of the same factors that would influence the same behavior in a real-life situation. The result is often a highly artificial social situation. Like the guinea-pig effect, this artificiality has the effect of reducing our confidence that the same results that appear in the experiment can be generalized to the more complex conditions of the real world.

Because of these disadvantages and because of ethical limitations, relatively little sociological research uses the controlled experiment. The areas in which it has been most useful are the study of small-group interaction and the simulation of situations that seldom occur in real life.

The Survey

Survey research involves asking a relatively large number of people the same set of standardized questions. These questions may be asked in a personal interview, over the telephone, or in a paper-and-pencil format. This technique is the one most commonly used to gather sociological data. Because it asks the same questions of a large number of people, it is an ideal methodology for providing evidence on incidence, trends, and differentials. Thus survey data on marijuana use may allow us to say such things as the following: 51 percent of the undergraduates at Midwestern State have smoked marijuana (**incidence**), the proportion using marijuana has gone up substantially in the last 10 years (**trend**), and the proportion using marijuana is higher for males than females (**differential**). Survey research is extremely versatile; it can be used to study attitudes, behavior, ideals, and values. If you can think of some way to ask a question about a subject, then you can study it with survey research.

> **Survey research** is a method that involves asking a relatively large number of people the same set of standardized questions.

> **Incidence** is the frequency with which an attitude or behavior occurs.

> **Trends** are changes in a variable over time.

> **Differentials** are differences in the incidence of a phenomenon across subcategories of the population.

Most surveys use what is called a **cross-sectional design;** they take a sample (or cross section) of the population at a single point in time and expect it to show some variability on the independent variable. Thus in our study of marijuana use we would take a sample of students, expecting

> The **Cross-sectional design** uses a sample (or cross section) of the population drawn from a single point in time.

Figure 2.3
The most common method of gathering data for sociological research is the survey, where relatively large numbers of people are asked the same question. The largest survey conducted in the United States is the Federal Census, taken every ten years.

Control variables are background factors whose effects must be eliminated in order to understand the relationship between the study variables.

The **longitudinal design** follows a sample over a period of time, during which some portion of the sample experiences the independent variable.

to find that some of them smoke marijuana and some do not. We could then compare these two groups to see which gets the best grades.

If we were to do this, we might find a correlation between marijuana use and grades. The difficulty with the cross-sectional design is that we cannot tell whether smoking marijuana causes bad grades or whether people who fail in school turn to marijuana. The independent variable is not randomly assigned to one of two equivalent groups; rather, some students choose to become smokers and some choose not to become smokers. It is entirely possible that the factors leading to this choice—for example, low attachment to parents or low ambition—are the real determinants of grades and that marijuana use is an accidental factor.

Under these circumstances, the researcher's strategy will be to introduce **control variables**—to specify the background variables that might be confusing the relationship of interest and to eliminate their effects. For example, we might control the possible effects of attachment to parents by dividing the sample into two or three groups according to strength of parental attachment. If marijuana use is found to be related to poor grades among those with strong parental attachment as well as among those with low parental attachment, then we may conclude that this particular background factor cannot explain the correlation between marijuana use and grades. This kind of design, however, can never get around the fact that subjects choose the independent variable; in this case, there is always the possibility that some other difference between smokers and nonsmokers causes the lower grades. Thus the cross-sectional technique will not give us the same assurance about causal explanations as will the controlled experiment.

Another kind of strategy used in survey research is the **longitudinal design.** To use this design for examining the effect of marijuana use on grades would require surveying a group of young people at several points in time, say from when they were 12 until they were 25. This design would not alter the fact that some people choose to smoke and others do not, but it would let us look at the same people before and after their decision. It would allow us to see whether students' grades actually fell after they started to smoke marijuana or whether they were always poor students. The major disadvantage of this design is that it is expensive and time-consuming. The study described here, for example, would take 13 years.

Both cross-sectional and longitudinal studies are less efficient than controlled experiments for demonstrating causal relationships. Nevertheless, they allow social scientists to build up a set of scientific observations and generalizations. If it is found that the relationship between marijuana use and bad grades holds for persons of varied backgrounds in both longitudinal and cross-sectional studies, then we begin to have some confidence that the relationship is a causal one.

Another important drawback of survey research is that respondents may misrepresent the truth. Prejudiced people may tell you that they are unprejudiced, and only a small fraction of those who abuse their children are likely to admit it. This misrepresentation is known as **social-desirability bias**—the tendency for people to color the truth so that they appear to be nicer, richer, and generally more desirable than they really are. The consequences of this bias vary in seriousness depending on the research aim and topic. Obviously, it is a greater problem for such sensitive topics as drug use and prejudice.

Survey research is designed to get standard answers to standard questions. It is therefore not the best strategy for studying deviant or undesirable behaviors or for getting at ideas and feelings that cannot easily be reduced to questionnaire form. For these areas we must turn to participant observation.

Social-desirability bias is the tendency of respondents to make themselves sound better and more desirable than they really are.

Participant observation is a method that uses interviewing, observation, and participation in order to examine the contexts of human interaction and their meanings for the individuals involved.

Participant Observation

Under the label **participant observation** we classify a variety of research strategies, all of which have in common a desire to see human behavior in context. Instead of sending forth an army of interviewers, participant observers go out into the field themselves in order to see firsthand what is going on. These strategies are an outgrowth of the verstehen school of sociology and W. I. Thomas's work at the University of Chicago. The concern is with discovering patterns of interaction and finding the meaning of the patterns for the individuals involved.

The three major elements of participant observation are interviewing, participating, and observing. A researcher goes to the scene of the action, where she may interview people informally in the normal course of conversation, participate in whatever they are doing, and observe the activities of other participants. Not every participant observation study involves all three dimensions equally. A participant observer studying drug use on campus, for example, would not need to get stoned every night. She would, however, probably do long, informal interviews with both users and non-users, attend student parties and activities, and attempt to get a feel for how marijuana use fits in with student life.

The data produced by participant observation are often based on small numbers of individuals who have not been selected according to random-

Figure 2.4

There are numerous areas of social behavior for which surveys and experiments are not suitable strategies for collecting data for research. Imagine the difficulties, for example, a middle-class interviewer would run into when using a standardized set of questions to collect data on homosexual life-styles. A better strategy for studying deviant behavior or uncooperative populations is participant observation.

sampling techniques. The data tend to be unsystematic and the samples not very representative; however, we do know a great deal about the few individuals involved. This detail is often useful for generating ideas that can then be examined more systematically with other techniques. In this regard, participant observation may be viewed as a form of initial exploration of a research topic.

In some situations, however, participant observation is the only reasonable way to approach a subject. This is especially likely when we are examining undesirable behavior, real behavior rather than attitudes, or uncooperative populations. In the first instance, social-desirability bias makes it difficult to get good information about undesirable behavior. Thus what we know about homosexual acts in restrooms (Humphreys, 1970), running a brothel (Heyl, 1979), or Satanism (Alfred, 1976) rests largely on the reports of participant observers. This style of research produces fewer distortions than would have occurred if a middle-class, middle-aged woman (the typical professional interviewer) had asked them about their activities.

In the second case, participant observation is well suited to studies of behavior—what people do rather than what they say they do. Behaviors are sometimes misrepresented in surveys simply because people are unaware of their actions or don't remember them very well. For example, individuals may believe that they are not prejudiced; yet observational research will demonstrate that these same people systematically choose not to sit next to persons of another race on the bus or in public places. Sometimes actions speak louder than words.

In the third case, we know that survey research works best with people who are predisposed to cooperate with authorities and who are relatively literate. Where either one or both of these conditions is not met, survey research may not be possible. For this reason there is little survey research on prison populations, juvenile gangs, preschoolers, or rioters. Participant observation is often the only means to gather data on these populations.

A major disadvantage of participant observation is that the observations and generalizations rely solely on the word of the investigator. The same events will never happen again in the same way, and there is no one else to confirm that the observer has correctly recorded and interpreted the event. Because researchers are not robots, it seems likely that one observer's conclusions would vary from another's. Thus the data that arise out of participant observation are often more suggestive than convincing.

Alternative Strategies

The bulk of sociological research uses these three strategies. There are, however, a dozen or more other imaginative and useful ways of doing research, many of them involving analysis of social artifacts rather than people. For example, a study of women's magazines of the 19th century has been used to show the changing attitudes toward spinsterhood (Hickok, 1981). A study of children's portraits over the centuries has shown how our ideas of childhood have changed (Aries, 1962). Studies of court records and government statistics have demonstrated incidence, trends, and differentials in many areas of sociological interest.

CONTROLLED EXPERIMENTS	
Procedure	Dividing subjects into two equivalent groups, applying the independent variable to one group only, and observing the differences between the two groups on the dependent variable.
Advantages	Excellent for analysis of cause-and-effect relationships; can simulate events and behaviors that do not occur outside the laboratory in any regular way
Disadvantages	Based on small, nonrepresentative samples examined under highly artificial circumstances; unclear that people would behave the same way outside the laboratory; unethical to experiment in many areas
SURVEY RESEARCH	
Procedure	Asking the same set of standard questions of a relatively large, systematically selected sample
Advantages	Very versatile—can study anything that we can ask about; can be done with large, random samples so that results represent many people; good for incidence, trends, and differentials
Disadvantages	Shallow—does not get at depth and shades of meaning; affected by social-desirability bias; better for studying people than situations
PARTICIPANT OBSERVATION	
Procedure	Observing people's behavior in its normal context; experiencing others' social settings as a participant; in-depth interviewing
Advantages	Seeing behavior in context; getting at meanings associated with behavior; seeing what people do rather than what they say they do
Disadvantages	Limited to small, nonrepresentative samples; dependent on interpretation of single investigator

CONCEPT SUMMARY

▬▬

Research Methods
There are three basic research strategies used in sociology, each with its own special uses, advantages, and disadvantages.

Examples of Sociological Research

▬▬

The Survey: The Sexual Revolution

Over 700 thousand teenage girls got pregnant in 1980. Two thirds of them ended the pregnancy with an abortion (U.S. Bureau of the Census, 1984:70, 71). Many of them will go on to have other unwanted pregnancies and other abortions. What lies behind these patterns? How can we account for the sharp increases in pregnancy and abortion among teenagers?

In a set of pioneering studies at Johns Hopkins University, John Kantner and Melvin Zelnik have begun to tackle these questions by studying teenage sexual activity. Their explicit purpose has been to "suspend efforts to account for the behavior until we had fully described it.... Thus, for example, we gave first priority to the question of ... how many young women have had intercourse and second priority to the factors that 'cause' premarital intercourse" (Zelnik et al., 1981:11). In short, they have not been trying to explain premarital sexual behavior but to describe its incidence, trends, and differentials.

As with most survey research, sampling is a vital concern. They want the results of their survey of young women to be representative of all females 15 to 19 years old. Where do you find these young women? School

FOCUS ON MEASUREMENT

Survey Research—Some Nuts and Bolts

The most common research methodology used in sociology today is survey research. Many of the findings reported in later chapters rely on survey data. Below are presented some guidelines for interpreting and evaluating these results.

The Problem

In 1984, to gather data for a class exercise, we conducted a survey on the relationship between marijuana use and grades among our introductory sociology students. The results of this survey are included here as an illustration of the mechanics of doing sociological research—the nuts and bolts of it.

In this student assignment, we wanted to examine the hypothesis that marijuana use was related to grades. We thought that closeness to parents might be an important control variable. That is, we hypothesized that marijuana use would be more likely to lead to bad grades among students who were more involved with their peers and less involved with their parents. This simple project therefore required information on three variables: marijuana use, time spent with parents, and grades.

Operationalizing Variables

Our first task was to decide how to measure each of these variables. The most important rule in survey research is to write clear, unambiguous questions. This means that the researcher should avoid questions that have complex or confusing words or several interpretations. The goal is to write questions that will mean the same thing to each respondent as they do to the researcher.

BAD:

> How much money do you make?
>
> $_____
>
> This is a bad question because it does not specify a period of time or what counts as income. One person might tell you the monthly salary and another the annual income after taxes.

Figure 2.5 A Sample Survey of College Students

To the student:

The results of this questionnaire are intended for instructional use only. Your participation is entirely voluntary, and you may decline to fill out the questionnaire. If, for any reason, you object to a particular question, leave that question out and go on. Because the questionnaire is to be entirely anonymous, we ask that you refrain from putting your name or student identification number on the questionnaire. Thank you for your cooperation.

1. How old were you on your last birthday? _____

2. What is your sex?
   ( ) Male
   ( ) Female

3. During your last year of high school, what was your grade-point average?
   ( ) A or A+
   ( ) B or B+
   ( ) C or C+
   ( ) D or lower

4. Which of the following statements best describes your use of marijuana during your senior year in high school?
   ( ) Never tried it
   ( ) Tried it once or twice
   ( ) Used it, but less than once a month
   ( ) Used it more than once a month

5. During your senior year in high school, how many hours each week did you spend with your family? This includes time spent with your whole family or alone with your mother or father.
   ( ) 5 hours or less each week
   ( ) More than 5 hours each week

GOOD: What was your total income last year before taxes, including wages, tips, bonuses, interest, and all other sources of income? Check one.
( ) Less than $10,000
( ) $10,000–$19,999
( ) $20,000–$29,999
( ) $30,000 or more

This question is much more precise and is likely to be interpreted in the same way by each respondent.

For our study we needed to measure marijuana use, grades, and time spent with parents. How could we measure these variables in such a way that the questions would be reasonably specific and mean the same thing to everybody? Because our sample consisted of college seniors as well as freshmen, we rejected the possibility of asking about current behavior. We reasoned that time spent with parents, grade-point averages, and marijuana use would all mean something different to seniors than to freshmen. To make the questions comparable for all subjects, we decided to ask about high school experiences. The actual questions and instructions are reproduced in Figure 2.5. Notice that the instructions encourage students to answer but give them the option of refusing. It would be unethical to require students to give personal information as part of a class assignment.

Analyzing and Reporting Data

The first step in the analysis of survey data is to put the data into a computer. In the past, this step often required access to a large mainframe computer, but increasingly researchers are putting their survey data onto disks and using microcomputers for their analysis. Computers are essential in helping researchers handle information on hundreds or thousands of individuals in a manageable way.

The Frequency, or Percentage, Table. The simplest way to present data is in a frequency, or percentage, table, which summarizes data about a single variable. (Frequencies are often converted to percentages so they will be easier to interpret.) Table 2.1

Table 2.1 Incidence of Marijuana Use, 1984*

"Which of the following statements best describes your use of marijuana during your senior year in high school?"

	NUMBER	PER-CENT
Never tried it	299	57%
Tried it once or twice	112	21
Used it, but less than once a month	59	11
Used it more than once a month	54	10
Total	524	99%

*Sample is 524 introductory sociology students at a midwestern state university.

is a percentage table for marijuana use. It shows that 299 students, or 57 percent of the total sample of 524, reported that they had never tried marijuana at the time they were seniors in high school; 54 students, or 10 percent, however, used it more than once a week.

Cross-Tabulations. In order to examine the general hypothesis that marijuana use results in lower grades, we need to compare the grades of users and nonusers. Table 2.2 presents this comparison. Because we are looking at two variables simultaneously, we refer to this table as a cross-tabulation. There are a few important guidelines to follow in reading such a table:

1. Read the headings carefully. A good table will tell you something about the origin and size of the sample as well as the operational definitions used in measuring the variables.

2. See how the percentages are calculated. The first number in this table is 46 percent. Before you can interpret the number, you must ascertain who the 46 percent are and what they are doing. In this case, 46 percent of those who never tried marijuana got As in high school.

Table 2.2 Cross-Tabulation of High School Grades by Marijuana Use in High School, 1984*

	MARIJUANA USE IN HIGH SCHOOL			
High School Grades	Never Tried It	Tried It Once or Twice	Used It Less than Once a Month	Used It More than Once a Month
A or A+	46%	27%	19%	7%
B or B+	42	54	56	65
C+ or below	12	20	25	28
Total	100%	101%	100%	100%
Number	299	112	59	54

*Sample is 524 introductory sociology students at a midwestern state university.

3. Compare percentages. In reading the top row of this table, note that 51 percent of those who never tried marijuana got As in high school, whereas only 7 percent of those who used it more than once a month got As. Comparing across the bottom row, note that 12 percent of the nonusers and 28 percent of the frequent users got Cs or below in high school.

4. Interpret the results. Before going on, study the table. Do marijuana users get lower grades?

Controls. Table 2.2 shows that there is a fairly strong relationship between marijuana use and high school grade-point average: The more frequent the marijuana use, the less likely students are to get As. This relationship could occur for a number of reasons, however, and the table does not really explain why.

To explore this question, Table 2.3 looks at the relationship between grades and marijuana use under a control for time spent with parents. This more complex table shows us that time spent with parents is a factor but that marijuana use is associated with lower grades even after family closeness is taken into account. The first row shows that among those who spent 5 hours a week or less with their parents, 30 percent of the nonusers and 7 percent of the regular users got As. The percentage getting As was higher among those who spent more than 5 hours a week with their parents but was still associated with marijuana use: 50 percent of the nonusers and 7 percent of the regular users got As. This table suggests that the negative effect of marijuana use is more pronounced among students who spend more time with their families.

Questions to Consider

Do you believe the results of this simple study? How would you design it differently so the results would be convincing? Do you think social desirability bias is affecting these results?

Table 2.3 Relationship between High School Grades and Marijuana Use, Controlling for Time Spent with Parents, 1984*

| | TIME SPENT WITH PARENTS | | | | | | | |
| | 5 Hours or Less a Week | | | | More than 5 Hours a Week | | | |
	Never Tried It	Tried It Once or Twice	Used Less than Once a Month	Used More than Once a Month	Never Tried It	Tried It Once or Twice	Used Less than Once a Month	Used More than Once a Month
A or A+	30%	23%	17%	8%	50%	28%	19%	7%
B or B+	40	54	50	46	42	53	57	71
C+ or below	30	23	33	46	8	19	23	22
Total	100%	100%	100%	100%	100%	100%	99%	100%
Number	53	26	12	13	246	86	47	41

*Sample is 524 introductory sociology students at a midwestern state university.

is an easy answer, but many of the older ones will not be in school, many of the disadvantaged ones will already have dropped out, and nearly all of the pregnant ones will be out of school. Kantner and Zelnik's solution was to select 5,000 young women randomly through a complex national sample of households. To draw their sample, they used census data to divide the entire United States into blocks. They randomly chose 216 blocks from across the country for inclusion in their sample. They then sent trained interviewers to each of the selected blocks. The interviewers were told to list the age and gender of each person who lived on these blocks. The final stage of the sampling was to select a fraction of the young women from these lists. In order to make the sample representative of all young women, not just those living in households, the same sampling strategy was repeated for college living units.

Sampling and interviewing of this sort are very expensive. Kantner and Zelnik estimate that it cost them an average of $100 for each interview in the 1976 survey, or a total of $0.5 million just for the sampling and interviewing. The expense is one of the drawbacks of good survey research.

Figure 2.6

Sharp increases in teenage pregnancy and abortion prompted John Kantner and Melvin Zelnik in 1971 to initiate a comprehensive study of premarital sexual behavior using survey research. Based on a random sample of 15–19 year old females, this study has provided important and useful information on the incidence, trends, and differentials related to premarital sexual activity in our society.

In designing a questionnaire Kantner and Zelnik were faced with some dilemmas. Would young women be willing to talk to strangers about intimate sexual matters? Was there a common and generally understood language that teenagers all over the country could and would use in talking about sexual matters? Would parents give their consent? Would it matter what age and race the interviewers were? What were the most important factors surrounding teenage sexual experience? All these questions had to be answered before the initial survey was undertaken.

To answer them, Kantner and Zelnik began by conducting 24 informal interview sessions at various locations across the country. In these sessions, the researchers chatted informally with groups of 5 to 10 young women, trying to get a feel for vocabulary, for sensitive versus matter-of-fact issues, and for issues important to the women themselves. (This is an example of the use of the less formal strategy of participant observation as a preliminary to survey research.) Following these sessions, they designed their first questionnaire and pretested it three successive times on a total of 406 young women. In the pretests, they experimented with alternative wordings for the questions. They also tested to see whether the age and race of the interviewer had much effect on the young women's willingness to participate. They found few age-race effects of interviewers on quality of data or response rate, so they settled for the middle-aged, middle-class white women who are the typical personal interviewers. The questions themselves were honed into a 1-hour interview that was unambiguous, inoffensive, and informative.

The study had a response rate of close to 80 percent; that is, 20 percent of the young women identified as part of the random sample were not interviewed. In some cases, the nonresponse was a direct refusal by the young woman or her parents; in many others, the young woman was never found at home in spite of repeated visits. If the 20 percent who were missed had the same sexual history as the 80 percent who were reached, there would be no problem. Unfortunately, nonrespondents are seldom a random sample of the initial sample. The lower a survey's response rate, the less likely it is that the results of the survey represent the desired population. An 80 percent response rate is a standard rate of response in a high-quality, relatively well financed survey research project. In many other projects the rate is not as high. Response rate is always something to take into consideration in evaluating survey results.

Kantner and Zelnik did their first survey in 1971; they repeated it in 1976 and 1979, thus covering a period when striking changes were taking place in the sexual behavior of young Americans. Evidence on these changes has given us a much clearer picture of what went on in the decade of the 1970s. Some of this information is presented in Table 2.4.

What was learned from this study? Kantner and Zelnik found that 23 percent of never-married white teenagers had had sexual intercourse in 1971; by 1979, this figure had nearly doubled. The increase in sexual activity is apparent at every age. The Kantner and Zelnik data also demonstrate the growing similarity of sexual experience for black and white teenagers. During the 8 years in which white teens experienced a sharp increase in the proportion having sexual experience (from 23 to 42 percent), black teens showed only a modest increase (from 52 to 65 percent). As a result, there is a growing convergence in the experience of the two racial groups.

Kantner and Zelnik's data show that sexual experience increased at every social-class level, at all levels of religious commitment, and at all ages. One of the most important findings is that among those who had had sexual intercourse, the most common answer to the question "How often have you had intercourse in the last month?" was 0. The documentation of the extremely sporadic and episodic nature of teenage sexuality, particularly of young teens, is important in understanding the dilemma of delivering contraceptive services to teenagers.

Participant Observation: Out on the Corner, Down in the Street

One of the best participant observation studies in recent decades is described in the book *Tally's Corner* (1967), a study of street-corner men in

Table 2.4   Sexual Experience among Never-Married Teenage Women: Percent 15 to 19 Ever Having Sexual Intercourse

Results from Kanter and Zelnik's survey of young women's sexual behavior show that increases in sexual activity took place in nearly every category between 1971 and 1979. The increases are particularly sharp for very young teens and for white teens.

	1971		1976		1979	
	White	Black	White	Black	White	Black
Total	23%	52%	34%	65%	42%	65%
By age:						
15	11	31	14	39	18	41
16	17	44	24	55	35	50
17	20	59	36	71	44	73
18	36	60	46	76	53	76
19	41	78	54	84	65	89

SOURCE: Zelnik and Kantner. Reprinted with permission from *Family Planning Perspectives*, 12, 5, 1980.

Figure 2.7
These men are shooting craps on a street in Brooklyn, New York. They are not working nor are they likely to have regular work. To study the meaning of work and family for men such as these, Elliot Liebow spent approximately one year hanging out on a street corner much like the one depicted here. He chose participant observation as the methodology best suited for studying the social structures of urban slums and its impact on the men who live there.

an urban slum. It provides a clear example of the strengths of this methodology; it also provides insight and understanding of a world with which few of us are familiar.

In spite of urban renewal, Head Start, and open-housing laws, urban slums in the United States have become poorer, blacker, and more despairing with every year. At one point in their development, they were just poor inner-city neighborhoods, but over the 40 years since World War II they have become the source of a hereditary class of the socially dispossessed. Little is known about the people who live in urban ghettos. Survey researchers are afraid to enter even the neighborhoods, much less the tenement buildings themselves. The U.S. Census, which spends billions of dollars trying to reach each citizen, misses 20 percent of the young men in central cities. Many do not have telephones or are so transient they are hard to reach. If someone from a survey research center does reach them to ask "How do you feel about your economic prospects: Would you say they're staying the same, getting better or getting worse?" a large proportion will decline to participate in such a personally meaningless and possibly threatening exercise.

What we know about the people who live in ghettos comes largely from the portion of the ghetto population that is in contact with authorities. Thus we know something about schoolchildren (their scores on standardized exams, their reading levels, their nutrition), about mothers on welfare, and about men who get picked up by the police. These people are not a representative sample of the people who live in ghettos. Overriding the question of sampling even is the question of whether information given involuntarily in welfare offices and police stations is truthful and open.

Obviously, people who live in central-city neighborhoods grow up, pair up, have children, support themselves, and belong to families and to networks of friends. They do not act randomly; their behavior is hedged around and directed by the social structures of their community. A major question for social science research is what these structures are and what they mean to the individuals involved.

Elliot Liebow, author of *Tally's Corner,* is an urban anthropologist (which is to say that he is virtually indistinguishable from a sociologist). For his doctoral dissertation he was assigned part of a larger research project that was designed to look at childrearing practices among lower-class families. For the reasons already given, survey research with question-naires and paper-and-pencil tests were out of the question. More impor-tantly, Liebow wanted to get an insider's view, a description of lower-class people and their lives in their terms and from their viewpoint. Because something was already known about lower-class women and children, Liebow chose to concentrate on the invisible character in the lower-class black family, the adult male.

With his only instruction being to go out there and make like an an-thropologist, Liebow chose a corner in Washington, D.C., and hung out there off and on for a year. He makes no pretense that this is a represen-tative corner or that the men he came to know were representative of the men in Washington's black slums. What he intends to do is offer a well-rounded picture of 15 to 20 men that enables us to see the social structure through their eyes. What does life look like in terms of their education, their economic opportunities, their environment?

Liebow is white and has an education far superior to that of the men he was studying. Nevertheless, he presented himself routinely at the cor-ner wearing T-shirts and khaki pants, prepared to use bad grammar and bad language. He came, as did the real participants, just to hang out, to see "what's happening." He did not carry a tape recorder, take notes, or ask questions. He just made small talk with the regulars. After each ob-servation period was finished, however, he returned to his office and made detailed notes of what he had observed. These field notes became his written record. When he came to write up his conclusions at the end of his year on the corner, the field notes enabled him to remember who had said what and what had actually happened.

The men on the corner knew that Liebow was there as part of his job, but since he took pains not to act, dress, or talk like an anthropologist, he felt he was soon accepted by them—although always aware of his separateness from them because of his color. He was eventually invited to their homes, went out drinking with them, and was asked to come to court with them on occasion to provide support or advice in cases of brushes with the law or the authorities. From this year's experience he came to see the differences between their public performance (the kinds of stories people tell about themselves to people they meet for the first time—and to survey researchers) and their real situations.

Some of Liebow's most insightful findings cover the relationship of these men to work. Although there are excuses of health and layoffs, Liebow concludes that it is undeniable that "getting a job, keeping a job and doing well at it is clearly of low priority" (p. 34). Does this make failure a matter of irresponsibility or a lower-class value that rejects conventional success? Liebow tells us the life stories of several men, all of whom are failures, who know they are failures—and who cannot see that taking and keeping a job will keep them from being failures. No matter how many years of school they may have had, they are largely illiterate and unskilled. The jobs they can get (janitor, dishwasher, day laborer at construction sites) are dead-end jobs with low wages. The only people who can hold such jobs and maintain their self-esteem are students who are taking the jobs only temporarily on their way to better things. A 35-year-old man who washes dishes is a failure, in his own eyes and those of society. In short, he can get from the job neither enough money to support himself and his family nor self-esteem and self-respect. How does this affect the rest of his life?

> He carries this failure home where his family life is undergoing a parallel deterioration. His wife's adult male models also failed as husbands and fathers and she expects no less from him. . . . (Nevertheless, she has hoped against hope that he would be a good provider and take on a role of "man of the house.") When he fails, it enlarges his failure in both of their eyes.
>
> Increasingly he turns to the streetcorner where a shadowy system of values constructed out of public fictions serves to accommodate just such men as he, permitting them to be men once again provided they do not look too closely at one another's credentials. [pp. 212–213]

These shadow values include the theory of manly flaws, an assertion that one is too much of a man to fulfill the expected man's role: that one's sexual urges are too strong for one to remain faithful, that one's independence is too strong for one to submit to authority on the job, and so on. In short, one has the characteristics accorded to manhood in our society in such great quantity that one is precluded from playing that social role successfully. The men did not blame the system—or they didn't in Washington, D.C., in 1962—and they were precluded from pointing out their own faults by a need for some sense of self-worth. They created an explanation for their failure that required neither social activism nor self-hate, a twilight world of values that paralleled their twilight place in the economic structure.

The 15 to 20 men who Liebow studied intensively may not be representative of all poor black men in Washington, D.C.; the street corner may not be representative of all black urban neighborhoods. It is sufficient, however, that these processes were at work among these people in this neighborhood. The study tells us much that is new in a way that makes human understanding possible and that gives us food for thought as we try to examine such patterned social interactions as marriage, working, and fathering. This rich and valuable information could have been provided only through participant observation.

The Experiment: Does Anybody Give a Damn?

In the spring of 1962, a young woman returned from her job as manager of a bar and parked her red Fiat in the parking lot 100 feet from the doorway of her apartment building in Queens, New York. It was 3 a.m., and the neighborhood was quiet. As she was locking her car, she became nervously aware of a man lurking nearby, and she headed for the police call box a short distance away. Before she could get there, the man attacked and stabbed her. The woman screamed, "Oh my God, he stabbed me! Please help me! Please help me!" One of her neighbors threw open a

Figure 2.8

At 3:29 A.M., Kitty Genovese drove into the parking lot at Kew Gardens railroads station and parked her car(1). Noticing a man in the lot, she became nervous and headed along Austin Street toward a police telephone box where the man caught and attacked her with a knife(2). She got away, but he attacked her again(3) and again(4). In all, 38 persons saw an assailant take 35 minutes to kill Kitty Genevese. None of them offered help or called the police to save her. Why?

window and hollered down, "Let that girl alone!" This caused the assailant to move off down the street. Nobody came to help, and the woman struggled to her feet. The lights went off again in the neighboring apartments, and the woman tried to get to the door of her apartment building. The assailant returned and stabbed her again. This time she shrieked, "I'm dying! I'm dying!" Windows were thrown up and lights turned on, but no one did anything. Apparently frightened off by the lights, the assailant got in his car and drove away. The woman managed to pull herself into the doorway of her apartment building but couldn't get up the steps. She lay there for perhaps 15 to 20 minutes before her assailant returned again and stabbed her a third time, this time fatally (Rosenthal, 1964).

Twenty minutes after Kitty Genovese died, the police received a call from one of her neighbors. He had waited until after the final attack and then called a friend to ask what he should do. Finally, he went to a neighboring apartment and got another tenant to make the call to the police. He didn't want to get involved. All in all, 38 of her neighbors watched the assailant take 35 minutes to kill Kitty Genovese on the street. None of them tried to rescue her; aside from the man who shouted from his window, no one tried to interfere; none of them even lifted the telephone to call the police to come and rescue her. Several of them went back to bed.

The incident stirred the entire nation. What are we coming to? was a prevailing question. Has our society become so callous that we care nothing about our fellow human beings? Many of the initial reactions focused personally on those 38 witnesses. What was wrong with them? More careful consideration suggested that the problem did not lie with those 38 individuals. One person's refusal to act could be interpreted as a personal problem—stupidity, indecisiveness, depravity, insensitivity. For 38 persons to behave in the same way suggests that there was something about the social structure that invited noninterference. After much soul-searching about apathy and insensitivity, a group of scholars finally started to investigate what is now called the bystander effect: Under what circumstances will people intervene to help a stranger?

The question is approached with experimental research rather than with participant observation or survey research. We forgo participant observation for the reason that such events, luckily, do not normally occur in any predictable way. Furthermore, a field researcher who stumbled on such a situation could not ethically stand by and examine the reactions of bystanders rather than offer help. We forgo survey research because few people would tell you that they would ignore a plea for help, that they wouldn't even make an anonymous telephone call to the police. Thus the study is done in the laboratory, where an emergency can be simulated and where the effects of circumstances surrounding the emergency can be carefully manipulated and the likelihood of offering assistance can be gauged.

The research reported here is done by sociologists Shalom Schwartz and Avi Gottlieb (1980). It is one of the more recent studies in the bystander tradition spawned by the Kitty Genovese murder. The previous research on the bystander effect led Schwartz and Gottlieb to hypothesize that two major factors worked to inhibit a helping response:

1. *Diffusion of responsibility among potential helpers.* Where bystanders are aware that there are other witnesses who also ought to do something, they are less likely to feel that they personally have a responsibility to help.

Hypothesis: Bystanders who know that there are other bystanders will be less likely to help than will those who believe that they're alone.

2. *Fear of what others will think.* Even among strangers, we want people to think well of us. Nobody wants to be seen as the kind of clod who would fail to help somebody in trouble.

Hypothesis: Bystanders who believe that their presence is unknown will be less likely to help than will bystanders who are known to be on the scene.

The subjects in the experiment were 127 undergraduates who were recruited to take part in an experiment allegedly on ESP (extrasensory perception). The experiments were carried on at night in an isolated wing of the social science building. As subjects arrived separately, they were conducted past an open doorway in which they could see a man sitting at a console. Each subject was then escorted into a separate cubicle, where a video monitor showed the front view of, apparently, the same man. The subjects were told that the man was going to exchange ESP messages with a third party and that their task was to intercept the messages if possible. The experimenter said that she herself was going to leave the area so that her presence would not interfere with the transmissions but that if any of the subjects wanted her, they could call on the telephone in the corner of the cubicle.

After the experimenter left, each subject watched the man for 7.5 minutes. The subject then saw on the screen a large, roughly dressed man entering the cubicle of the transmitter's room, grabbing a calculator from the desk, and throwing the other man against the wall, hitting him in the stomach, and, after he had fallen to the ground, kicking him several times. The stranger left 35 seconds after having grabbed the calculator. The research question: What will each subject do?

The experiment used two manipulations to test the hypotheses. To test the hypothesis about the importance of other bystanders, the experimenters created two conditions. In the other-bystanders-absent condition, the subject believed that the third party had not arrived yet and that he or she was the only person in the building besides the man at the console. In the other-bystanders-present condition, the subject believed that the ESP experiment was in process and that the third party was also watching.

To test the hypothesis about the importance of being a known bystander, two additional conditions were created. In the first condition, the subject was told that neither the man at the console nor the third party knew of the subject's presence; in other words, the subject believed that she or he was an unknown bystander. In the second condition, the subject believed that both the attacked man and the third party knew that she or he was watching. In this situation, the subject was a known bystander.

Figure 2.9
In December, 1983, the Soul Clinic Mission in downtown Los Angeles handed out nearly 2000 Christmas trees. In the process of receiving help themselves, these passersby are nearly oblivious to the street person along the curbside. Studies of bystanders generally suggest that when other bystanders are present responsibility for helping becomes more diffuse and a person is less likely to be helped.

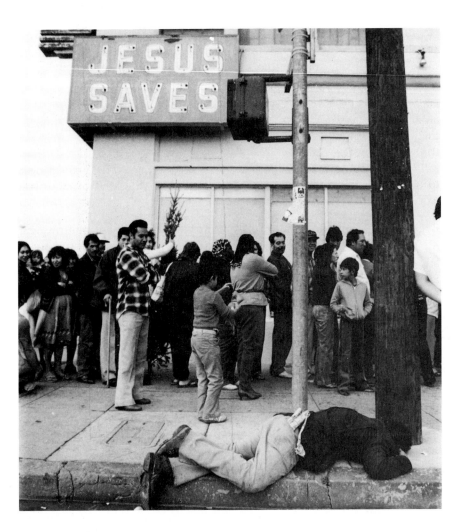

Thus four conditions were created in order to examine the circumstances in which people help:

1. *No one else is present; the subject's presence is known to the victim.* This condition should produce the maximum response. The subject knows that he or she is the only one who can help and that he or she is known to be on the scene.

2. *A third party is present; neither he nor the victim know of the subject's presence.* This condition should produce the minimum response. Not only are there others who can shoulder the burden but the victim will not know that the subject could have helped.

3. *A third party is present; both he and the victim know the subject is present.* This is an intermediate condition. Being a known bystander should encourage helpfulness, but the diffusion of responsibility among others may reduce helping.

4. *No one else is present; the subject's presence is unknown to the victim.* This is another intermediate condition. Although being an unknown by-

stander may reduce pressure to help, the absence of other bystanders should increase the subject's sense of responsibility.

The 127 students were assigned randomly and in equal numbers to these four conditions. This random assignment means that other relevant factors—such as kindness, courage, and intelligence—should be equal among all four groups. The results were measured by whether the subjects took any action to help (either called on the telephone or tried to go to the rescue), how long it took them to take action, and the kind of action.

The results showed that 89 percent of the subjects made some attempt to provide help within the first 5 minutes. This was true regardless of experimental conditions. The speed with which they tried to help, however, was significantly related to experimental conditions (see Table 2.5). If you are the only bystander, you are quite likely to give help regardless of whether your presence is known or unknown (75 percent of the known subjects and 70 percent of the unknown helped in the first minute); there is hardly any way to shirk your responsibility to help without damaging your self-esteem. However, if there are others present and the responsibility to help is not as clearly yours, whether or not you help is strongly affected by whether or not you think you can get away unrecognized. When others were present, only 40 percent of those whose presence was unknown helped, whereas 80 percent of the known bystanders helped within the first minute.

The results from the Schwartz and Gottlieb experiment help us understand why 38 of Kitty Genovese's neighbors watched her die without making any effort to help her. Her situation matched the condition of lowest response in this experiment: Other bystanders were present, and the presence of each individual bystander was unknown to the victim or other observers. It is worth noting that the man who eventually had the police called had been caught looking out his window by another neighbor; in short, he was a known bystander. This experiment provides an excellent example of how the laboratory can simulate situations that seldom occur in real life and that suffer from bias and unreliability in personal reporting.

Summary

This chapter has described three strategies for understanding structured social interaction as well as the general philosophy that underlies social science research. Sociological research requires courses in sampling, statistics, observation and interviewing, questionnaire design, and data anaysis. The material in this chapter, however, covers the major issues in sociology as a scientific enterprise.

Table 2.5 Percent Helping within 60 Seconds

Schwartz and Gottleib's experiment on the bystander effect shows that bystanders are more apt to help if there is no one else around and if their presence is recognized.

NO OTHER BYSTANDERS:	
Victim knows student is there	75%
Victim doesn't know student is there	70
THIRD PARTY PRESENT:	
Others know student is there	80
Nobody knows student is there	40

SOURCE: Adapted from Schwartz, Shalom and Avi Gottlieb. 1980. "Bystander anonymity and reaction to emergencies." Journal of Personality and Social Psychology 39(3):418–440.

Can Sociology be Harmful to Your Health?

Sociologists are interested in what people do and why. Often they are more interested in knowing about their subjects and respondents than the latter are in being known about. Sometimes the subjects are doing things they would like to keep quiet; more often they have developed their own interpretations of their behavior, and these interpretations give them comfort and reassurance. In any case, they would just as soon not be subjected to the hard light of scientific scrutiny. Do we have the right to disturb them? Do people have a right to privacy from social researchers?

The answer is: Sometimes.

In the early 1970s, several scandalous cases of unethical medical and biological experiments (such as the experiments described in the introduction to this chapter) raised everybody's consciousness about the ethics of scientific work. The federal government decreed that all federally funded studies that used human subjects, in any discipline, had to be approved by an institutional review board. Not wanting to seem insensitive to ethical issues, many universities, colleges, and even departments set up their own human-subjects committees to cover nonfunded and even student research. In each case, the researchers had to demonstrate that their subjects would not come to any physical or psychological harm through participation in a study. Careful measures were taken to ensure that subjects had the right to refuse to participate and that their consent to participate was given with full knowledge of the possible consequences.

The latest government guidelines, however, explicitly exclude most social science research from such reviews ("Final research regulation," 1981). After 10 years of review, it appears that there is little likelihood that people will be damaged by participation in sociological research, assuming that the investigators follow some general guidelines. These guidelines have recently been issued by the American Sociological Association as a revised Code of Ethics.

ETHICAL ISSUES IN PARTICIPANT OBSERVATION

Some of the most serious ethical issues in sociological research concern participant observation, which is often a disguised form of research. In order to avoid social-desirability bias or the guinea-pig effect, researchers often try to hide their presence so that people will act naturally. This means, of course, that they do not ask the subjects if they are willing to be studied.

This issue has raised serious ethical questions. A classic example of the problem is Laud Humphrey's (1970) study of homosexual encounters in public bathrooms. In this study, Humphreys presented himself in the bathrooms as a "watch queen," a person who likes to watch others' sexual encounters but doesn't want to take part. It provided a handy cover for his real role of sociological observer. This procedure may raise some eyebrows, but the real fuss is associated with the fact that Humphreys took down license plate numbers and used them to track these men to their homes. One year after his bathroom observations, Humphreys disguised his appearance and did a general interview with the men on mental health and related issues under the fiction that they were part of a random sample. Humphreys was extremely careful in ensuring that no one would see his list of names; likewise he was careful not to mention the bathroom incidents or in any way threaten his subjects with his knowledge of their sexual behavior. The question: Did he violate the right to privacy of his research subjects or expose them to the risk of substantial harm?

The answers are unclear. The consensus is that people do not have a right to privacy regarding their actions in public places. People who choose to have sexual encounters in public bathrooms have given up their right to privacy. They are, however, entitled to biographical immunity ("Revised code of ethics," 1982); that is, their names and any biographical details that would give their identity away must be protected. Also, when "the subject's responses, if known, would place them at risk of criminal or civil liability or . . . when the research deals with sensitive aspects of a subject's own behavior, such as illegal behavior, drug use, sexual behavior or use of alcohol," assurance of the researcher's ability and willingness to protect confidentiality must be given to a human-subjects review committee ("Revised code of ethics," 1981:10). In short, what you do in public can be studied whether you like it or not, but the researcher must not publicize your identity.

ETHICAL ISSUES IN SOCIOLOGICAL EXPERIMENTS

In spite of the fact that experimental work in other fields was the cause of the ethical furor, ethics is only a minor issue in sociological experiments. The major issue that arises in experimental research is that deception is almost always involved. Although the subjects do agree to take part, they are seldom told what the purpose is; to do so would reduce the validity of their response. Whether they were trying to help or confound the experimenter, they would be responding to something other than the experimental stimulus.

Experimenters are usually careful to debrief their subjects after the experiment, explaining the real purpose and answering any questions, and the deception is not usually important or challenging. Special criticism, however, has been directed at experiments such as the Schwartz and Gottieb one reported in this chapter. Such experiments expose the subjects to a stressful situation and, for those who don't help, to a painful self-knowledge. This is not what the subjects bargained for when they volunteered for an experiment on ESP.

ETHICAL ISSUES IN SURVEY RESEARCH

Survey research raises the fewest ethical questions. If I call you on the telephone, all you have to do is decline to be interviewed. I cannot interview you without your consent. Also, any time you object to a question, you can either refuse to answer it or hang up on me. At one point, there was some concern that survey research might expose people to the risk of substantial harm by putting ideas into their heads. For example, my asking you whether you have been thinking about divorce might cause you to think about it for the first time. There is no evidence that respondents are as suggestible as this, however, and most people enjoy talking about themselves as part of survey research.

SUMMARY

All in all, it does not seem likely that sociological research is likely to be harmful to those participating in it—willingly or not. The American Sociological Association guidelines enjoin researchers to provide confidentiality for all subjects, even those engaged in public acts in public places. And as a matter of public policy, the federal government has concluded that sociological research is not likely to be harmful to your health.

SUMMARY

1. Science is not a specific set of methods but rather a process of moving between data and theory that requires the utmost respect for the accuracy of observations and the utmost in skepticism toward theories and generalizations that go beyond the data.

2. In the wheel of science, we move from observations to generalizations to theory (induction); then we move from theory to hypotheses to observations (deductions). The circle is never-ending; one can begin at any point.

3. Scientific research focuses on measured attributes, or variables, rather than on whole individuals. When these variables are hypothesed to have a cause-and-effect relationship, the cause is called the independent variable and the effect is called the dependent variable.

4. Operational definitions specify how research concepts are to be measured. They are often an incomplete representation of the entire concept and must be carefully evaluated.

5. Sampling is critical to social research because there is so much variability between one research subject and the next. Systematic procedures must be used to ensure that a sample is drawn from a comprehensive list

of the members of a population, chosen by random procedures, and of adequate size to provide reliable data.

6. Sociologists assume a probabilistic notion of causality. We say that one thing causes another if its occurrence increases the likelihood of the effect occurring. We assume that everything has a cause and that most events have multiple causes.

7. The experiment is a methodology designed to test cause-and-effect hypotheses deduced from theory. Although it is the best method for this purpose, it has the disadvantage of using unrepresentative samples in highly artificial conditions. It is most often used for small-group research and for simulation of situations not often found in real life.

8. Survey research is a methodology that asks a large number of people a set of standard questions. It is good at describing incidence, trends, and differentials for random samples, but it is not as good at describing the contexts of human behavior.

9. Participant observation is a method in which a small number of individuals who are not randomly chosen are observed or interviewed in depth. The strength of this method is the detail about the contexts of human behavior and its subjective meanings; its weaknesses are lack of generalization and verification by independent observers.

10. Sociological research is unlikely to cause substantial harm to subjects or respondents. Nevertheless, the ethics code of sociology requires that subject identities be carefully guarded.

SUGGESTED READINGS

Babbie, Earl R. (1983). The Practice of Social Research (3rd ed.). Belmont, Calif.: Wadsworth. A textbook for undergraduates that covers the major research techniques used in sociology. Coverage is up-to-date, thorough, and readable.

Golden, M. Patricia. (1976). The Research Experience. Itasca, Ill.: Peacock Publishers. An excellent collection of research articles that discuss a variety of strategies. The unique part of this collection is the inclusion of a special report by each author on the problems and considerations that led to the particular research design.

Jones, James H. (1981). Bad Blood: The Tuskegee Syphilis Experiment. New York: Free Press. Covers the long history of the Tuskegee experiment noted in the introduction to this chapter, including lessons about ethics, experimentation, and race relations in the United States.

Liebow, Elliot. (1967). Tally's Corner. Boston: Little, Brown. A classic study that provides an excellent introduction to the richness of participant observation studies.

Lofland, John, & Lofland, Lyn. (1984). Analyzing Social Settings (2d ed.). Belmont, Calif.: Wadsworth. In case you think participant observation is a matter of just hanging around, the Loflands' text on doing field work will set you straight and give you direction.

CHAPTER 3
CULTURE

PROLOGUE

Have You Ever . . . *had a serious discussion with friends or parents about whether society's definitions of right and wrong are justified? For example, why is liquor generally considered socially acceptable whereas marijuana is a killer weed? Why is teenage sex often considered immoral whereas sex among older or married people is believed to be fulfilling and desirable?*

The answers to these questions rest on value judgments, not empirical evidence. A scientist can demonstrate that early sexual activity increases the risk of cervical cancer in women, but this fact is not what upsets parents when they find out that their 15-year-old daughter is sexually active. Nor is pregnancy their sole concern. Many will be just as upset, perhaps even more, if they find out that their daughter is on the Pill. They are upset because they define sexual activity as inappropriate for 15-year-old girls; they think it is wrong.

Whether a society or an individual considers sexual activity right or wrong, appropriate or inappropriate, for 15-year-olds is a value judgment. Just as all the nutritional evidence in the world would not encourage most of us to eat worms, so empirical evidence tends to be irrelevant to our values. Social science simply cannot say whether values are right or wrong. What it can do is document a culture's values and determine how they relate to the social structures of a society—how they fit in with the family system, religion, and the central ideas of society.

Introduction to Culture

Regardless of whether people live in tropical forests or in the crowded cities of New York, London, or Tokyo, they confront some common problems. They all must eat, they all need shelter from the elements (and often from each other), and they all need to raise children to take their place and continue their way of life. Although these problems are universal, the solutions are highly varied. For example, responsibility for childrearing may be assigned to the mother's brother, as is done in the Trobriand Islands; to the natural mother and father, as is done in the United States; or to communal nurseries, as is done in the Israeli Kibbutz.

Throughout the world, humans have devised very different methods for adapting to their environments and solving their basic problems. Over time, these methods become patterned and shared within the population. The patterned responses become a way of life, passed from one generation to the next as a design for living. Each succeeding generation may modify and add to the design, but the basic patterns show remarkable stability.

Culture is the total way of life shared by members of a society. It includes material products as well as patterned, repetitive ways of thinking, feeling, and acting.

The total way of life shared by members of a society is what sociologists refer to as **culture**—which includes tools and technologies, laws and customs, ideas and goals. All of these elements are part of the way people address common problems of everyday life. Consider how American culture provides patterned responses to eating: We share a common set of tools and technologies in the form of refrigerators, ovens, broilers, toasters, microwaves, and coffee pots. We share more-or-less common tastes for potato chips, hamburgers, and apple pie; but we gag at the thought of horsemeat or blood pudding. Both the equipment and technology of eating and our ideas about what is tasty and nutritious are part of our culture.

Culture can be roughly divided into two categories: material and nonmaterial. *Nonmaterial culture* consists of the beliefs, knowledge, values, and norms shared by the members of society. *Material culture* is the physical objects produced—tools, streets, homes, and toys, to name a few. These tangible objects are at once the result of culture and determinants of it. For example, the automobile has had dramatic effects on courtship practices and residence patterns.

The Carriers of Culture: Values and Norms

In the Broadway musical *Fiddler on the Roof*, the lives of the Jewish peasants of an impoverished village in Tsarist Russia are portrayed as being precariously balanced—as is the fiddler on the roof:

> And how do we keep our balance? That, I can tell you in one word. TRADITION! . . . We have our traditions for everything!
>
> . . . Because of our traditions everyone knows who he is and what God expects him to do!
>
> Tradition! Tradition! Without our traditions, our lives would be as shaky as . . . as a fiddler on the roof!*

So it is with Tevye, the father of five daughters, all of marriageable age. The age-old laws of tradition require the village matchmaker, Yente, to make a match for each of the daughters. When the daughters fall in love with young men of their own choosing, however, Tevye succumbs to the new ways and develops an elaborate scheme, also based on tradition, to help his daughters marry persons other than those chosen by the match-maker.

*Copyright © 1964 by Joseph Stein. Used by permission only—all rights reserved. Published by Crown Publishers.

One way of thinking of culture is as a composite of traditions and customs. Sociologists are particularly interested in two such aspects of culture: values and norms.

Values

Shared standards of desirability are **values**; they are the goals a culture suggests are worth pursuing. Values are typically couched in terms of whether a thing is good or bad, desirable or undesirable (Williams, 1970:27). For example, many Americans believe that a happy marriage is an important goal. In this case and many others, values may be very general. They do not, for example, specify what a happy marriage consists of.

Some cultures value tenderness, others toughness; some value cooperation, others competition. Nevertheless, because all human populations face common dilemmas, certain values tend to be universal. For example, nearly every culture values stability and security, a strong family, and good health. There are, however, dramatic differences in the guidelines that cultures offer for pursuing these goals. In societies like ours, an individual may try to ensure security by putting money in the bank or investing in an education. In many traditional societies, security is maximized by having a large number of relatives. In societies, such as that of the Kwakiutl of the Pacific Northwest, security is achieved not by saving your wealth but by giving it away. The reasoning is that all of the people who accept your goods are now under an obligation to you. If you should ever need help, you would feel free to call on them and they would feel obliged to help. Thus, although many cultures place a value on establishing security against uncertainty and old age, the specific guidelines for reaching this goal vary. The guidelines are called norms.

Norms

Shared rules of conduct are **norms**. They usually occur in the form of things that people ought to or ought not to do. The list of things we ought

Values are shared standards of desirability.
Norms are shared expectations of how people are supposed to behave.

Figure 3.1
The central values of any culture are generally accepted and shared by most members of society. A major characteristic of values, however, is that they cannot be proven right or wrong; they are merely shared statements of what is considered good. As the signs of these opposing groups suggest, sometimes conflicts between values are unanswerable. Is God a man of war? Are nuclear weapons good or bad? Value conflicts like these cannot be resolved by scientific evidence.

to do sometimes seem endless. We begin the day with an "I'm awfully tired, but I ought to get up", and many of us end the day with "This is an awfully good show, but I ought to go to bed." In between, we ought to brush our teeth, eat our vegetables, work hard, love our neighbors, and on and on. The list is so extensive that we seldom have to think for ourselves. Of course, some things are optional and require us to make decisions, but the whole idea of culture is that it provides a blueprint for living, a pattern to follow.

Norms and values are intricately connected. Norms specify the means for achieving socially valued ends. Consider some contemporary American norms about marriage:

1. Choose a spouse similar to yourself in background.
2. Wait to marry until you are able to support yourselves so that you don't have to live with or depend on your parents.
3. Don't start marriage with a baby on the way.
4. Have children, preferably just two—one boy and one girl.
5. Share the decision making around the house.
6. Have sex three times a week until you're 40, after which twice a week is okay.

As we can see, the norms that guide our behavior in family life range from very general to very specific. These norms represent the conventional wisdom in our society about the means necessary to achieve the socially desired goal of a happy marriage.

As the list demonstrates, some norms specify what we are supposed to do and some specify what we are not supposed to do. Some norms are enacted into law, but many are not. Whether enacted into law or not, however, norms are an important form of social control, directing and regulating the behavior of society's members.

Universal norms are norms that are binding on all members of society. **Specialty norms** pertain to only certain groups or subgroups.

Not all norms apply equally to each member of society. Some, such as thou shalt not kill, are **universal norms**, binding on all members of society. Others are **specialty norms**, applying only to some groups or subgroups of society: to men only, to women only, to the upper classes, to the young. Premarital chastity, for example, has often been a specialty norm—a standard applied largely, though not entirely, to women. Specialty norms help distinguish the major roles in society. Thus the norms that govern professors differ somewhat from those that govern students; there are different norms for mothers than for fathers.

Norms vary enormously in their importance both to individuals and to society. Some, such as fashions, are powerful while they last but are not central to society's values. Others, such as those supporting monogamy and democracy, are central to our culture. Generally, we distinguish between two kinds of norms: folkways and mores.

Folkways are norms that are the customary, normal, habitual ways in which a group does things.

Folkways.   In the 19th century, **folkways** was coined by William Graham Sumner to describe norms that are simply the customary, normal, habitual ways a group does things. Folkways is a broad concept that covers relatively permanent traditions (such as Christmas trees, white wedding dresses, and thank-you notes) as well as short-lived fads and fashions (such as checkered tennis shoes or sweatshirts with torn necklines).

A key feature of all folkways is that there is no strong feeling of right or wrong attached to them. They are simply the way people usually do things. For example, if you choose to have hamburgers for breakfast and oatmeal for dinner, you will be violating American folkways. If you sleep on the floor or become a vegetarian, you will also be deviating from the usual pattern. If you violate folkways, you may be regarded as eccentric, weird, or crazy, but you will not be regarded as immoral or criminal.

Mores. Some norms are associated with strong feelings of right and wrong. These norms are called **mores** (more-ays). Whereas eating oatmeal for dinner may only cause you to be considered crazy (or lazy), there are some things you can do that will really offend your neighbors. If you eat your dog, spend your last dollar on liquor rather than your child's shoes, or beat your children, you will be violating mores. At this point, your friends and neighbors may decide that they have to do something about you. They may turn you in to the police or to a child protection association; they may cut off all interaction with you or even chase you out of the neighborhood. Not all violations of mores result in legal punishment, but all result in such informal reprisals as ostracism, shunning, or reprimand. These punishments, formal and informal, reduce the likelihood that people will violate mores.

Mores are norms for which fairly strong ideas of right or wrong have developed; they carry a moral connotation.

Laws. Norms that are officially enforced and sanctioned, generally by the authority of government, are **laws.** Very often the important mores of society become laws and are enforced by regulatory agencies of the government. If the laws cease to be supported by norms and values, they are either stricken from the record or become dead-letter laws, no longer considered important enough to enforce. Not all laws, of course, are supported by public sentiment; in fact, many have come into existence as the result of lobbying by powerful interest groups. Laws regulating marijuana use in the United States, for example, owe their origins to the vested-interest politics of the 1930s (see chapter 7). Similarly, laws requiring the wearing of seatbelts are not a response to social norms. In these cases, laws are trying to create norms rather than responding to them.

Laws are norms that are officially enforced and sanctioned, generally by the authority of government.

Social Control

From our earliest childhood we are taught to observe norms, first within our families and later within peer groups, at school, and in the larger society. After a period of time, the norms we have been taught come to be so habitual that we can hardly imagine living any other way. Following these rules becomes so much a part of our lives that we may not even be aware of them as constraints. We do not think, "I ought to brush my teeth or else my friends and family will shun me"; instead we think, "It would be disgusting not to brush my teeth, and I'll hate myself if I don't brush them." For thousands of generations, no human considered it disgusting to go around with unbrushed teeth. Even today, in Inis Beag (described in the Focus section of this chapter), it is considered uppity to brush your teeth. For most Americans, however, brushing their teeth is so much a part of their feeling about themselves, about who they are and the kind of person they are, that they would disgust themselves by not observing the norm.

Through indoctrination, learning, and experience, a norm may become so habitual that we observe it automatically, without thought or reflection; it becomes natural to us. When this happens, it is more difficult to violate the norm than to conform to it. For example, we are so used to being quiet in libraries and respectful in church that it would take a great deal of courage for most of us to act differently. To shout in church would offend our own sense of what is right as much as it would offend the others in church. (The process of learning social norms is covered in detail in chapter 5.)

Because rules are broken, sociologists have found it useful to distinguish between ideal norms (statements of how we ought to behave) and real norms (what we actually do). In our own society, the ideal norm of marital fidelity is embodied in law and encouraged by religious, educational, and family organizations. Research in the 1970s, however, has shown that nearly half of all married men and women in our society have committed adultery (Thompson, 1983). In this instance, the ideal culture expresses expectations that differ significantly from actual behavior. The discrepancies between what people do and the ideal norms of society are the subject of one of the major areas of sociological research and inquiry: deviance (see chapter 7).

Sanctions are rewards for conformity and punishments for nonconformity.

Conformity to norms is encouraged by **sanctions**—rewards for conformity and punishments for nonconformity. Some sanctions are formal, in the sense that the legal codes identify specific penalties, fines, and punishments that are to be meted out to individuals found guilty of violating formal laws. Formal sanctions are also built into most large organizations to control absenteeism and productivity. Some of the most effective sanctions, however, are informal. Such positive sanctions as affection, approval, and inclusion encourage normative behavior, whereas such negative sanctions as a cold shoulder, disapproval, and exclusion discourage norm violations.

The use and threat of sanctions are important mechanisms of social control in every society. When sanctions are minimal or unenforced, norms are often violated. If the highway patrol is largely indifferent to people driving 60 to 65 mph on the interstate highways instead of observing the 55 mph federal speed limit, it is likely that a significant proportion of drivers will deviate from the law.

Subcultures and Countercultures

Subcultures are groups that share in the overall culture of society but that have their own distinctive values, norms, and life-styles.

Sharing a culture does not mean that all individuals will behave alike. This is especially true in societies that are large and complex. The United States, for example, is diverse in its ethnic, religious, racial, and economic composition. Many of these distinctive dimensions form the basis of **subcultures**, which share in the overall culture of society but also maintain a distinctive set of values, norms, and life-styles. Examples of subcultures are religious, ethnic, occupational, and youth groups whose styles of dress, language, and values are uniquely different from those of the larger culture. Although they share many of the same norms and values men and women, young and old, farmers and central-city residents may be regarded as distinct subcultures.

Figure 3.2
These upper-class English ladies and gentlemen attending Epsons Derby represent a distinct subculture. Top hats and bonnets distinguish their status and life-style from the working and middle-class. Attendance at the derby is itself a subcultural difference in recreation based on social class distinctions.

The existence of subcultures sometimes contributes to an appearance of nonconformity when, in fact, people may simply be conforming to the norms of different subcultures. For example, having—or even wanting—eight children is deviant by the norms of our society. However, certain subgroups within our society—Catholics and Mormons, to name two—encourage and reward large families.

Countercultures are groups that have acquired a set of unique values, interests, beliefs, and life-styles that are in conflict with the dominant characteristics of the larger culture. This theme of conflict can be observed for groups as varied as hippies, punkers, delinquent gangs, revolutionary Marxists, and such religious sects as the Moonies, the Hare Krishnas, and even the early Christians. These groups are not just different from the dominant culture, they are against it.

Countercultures are groups that have acquired a set of unique values, interests, beliefs, and life-styles that are in conflict with the dominant characteristics of the larger culture.

Society

Culture is a way of life. In some places, it cuts across national boundaries and takes in people who live in two, three, or four nations. In other places two distinct cultures (English and French in Canada) may coexist within a single national boundary. For this reason, we distinguish between cultures and societies. **Societies** are units of territorial organization where members are economically and politically interdependent. Often the members share a common culture, but not always. A society is thus any group of people who have lived and worked together long enough to become organized or to think of themselves as a social unit with well-defined territorial limits (Linton, 1936:91).

Societies are groups of interacting individuals who share the same territory and are bound together by economic and political ties.

Summary

Each of us is born into a culture that strongly influences the ways in which we live, behave, think, and feel. We learn from our culture what is appropriate and inappropriate, what is required and not required, and what is expected from others who share our culture. Culture provides us with ready-made solutions to problems, solutions that have evolved over a long time and that need not be reinvented with each new generation. In this sense, our culture provides us with an established design for living. It is only when we compare ourselves with people from other cultures that we become aware of how our own culture profoundly influences us in ways quite different from those of other cultures.

Culture is an all-inclusive term; it covers knowledge and technology, art and ideas, tools and houses, values and norms. In a sense, then, all academic disciplines are the study of culture. Within this broad arena, the field of sociology concentrates on the normative aspects of culture. Norms and values constitute the basic script for the roles we play in society. They are basic aspects of social structure (See chapter 4) and a major focus of sociological inquiry.

American Culture

American culture is a unique blend of complex elements. It is a product of its environment, its immigrants, its technology, and its place in history. It closely resembles the cultures of two close cousins, Australia and Canada, with which it shares vital characteristics. All three are new countries settled by diverse groups of immigrants yet dominated by English culture, all three have uncrowded spaces and a sense of frontier, and all three offer high levels of industrialization and wealth. Yet American culture is distinguishable from the cultures of these first cousins as well as from those of more distant relatives in Europe, with which the United States shares a general Western culture.

American Values

Values tend to be so general that it is hard to put a finger on them. Nevertheless, there have been many attempts to pin down the central values of Americans—the goals on which there is consensus that these things are worth pursuing; these are the things that a good American believes in.

Two general strategies are used for identifying central values. The simple strategy is just to ask people, "How important is this value to you?" The results of such a survey in 1983 are presented in Figure 3.3. They show that having a good family life is ranked number 1; closely following are good health, a good self-image, personal happiness, and freedom of choice. Having a nice home or car and having a high income appear far down the list. Does this mean that Americans don't value money and material goods? Hardly. What it means is that they don't value income and possessions by themselves; rather, they wish to have a reasonable amount of money and goods as a side benefit of doing "what one wants" (no. 5), "living up to one's potential" (no. 6), "having an interesting job" (no. 7), and "having a sense of accomplishment" (no. 8). A central component of many of these values is a concern with what is good for the individual rather than a concern for family or others.

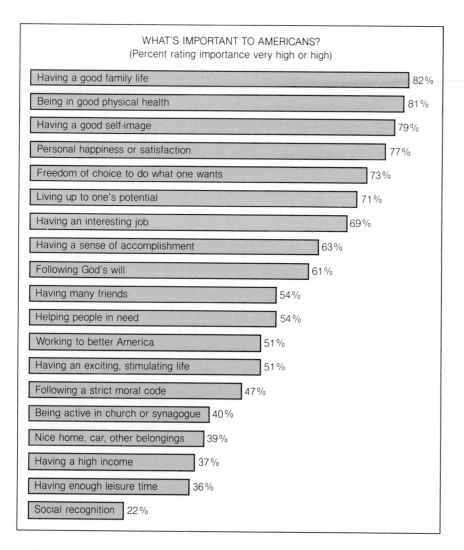

WHAT'S IMPORTANT TO AMERICANS?
(Percent rating importance very high or high)

Having a good family life	82%
Being in good physical health	81%
Having a good self-image	79%
Personal happiness or satisfaction	77%
Freedom of choice to do what one wants	73%
Living up to one's potential	71%
Having an interesting job	69%
Having a sense of accomplishment	63%
Following God's will	61%
Having many friends	54%
Helping people in need	54%
Working to better America	51%
Having an exciting, stimulating life	51%
Following a strict moral code	47%
Being active in church or synagogue	40%
Nice home, car, other belongings	39%
Having a high income	37%
Having enough leisure time	36%
Social recognition	22%

Figure 3.3 American Values in 1982
A majority of Americans endorse values that emphasize self-fulfillment and personal satisfactions. Values related to the general welfare of society or to others are not as widely shared.

SOURCE: The Gallup Report, March, 1982, Report No. 198.

The values that top this list are major American values. All important subgroups of Americans rank having a good family life, good health, and freedom of choice in the top 5. Blacks and whites, old and young, women and men, Easterners and Southerners—all put these values at the head of their lists.

A different approach to analyzing American values is to look at what Americans do. What do people make speeches about, make sacrifices for, and work toward? As with best-dressed lists, all observers have their own favorites; there is general consensus, however, that the following values are of central significance in understanding American culture (Williams, 1970):

1. *The importance of work and activity.* Americans have a positive attitude about work, often investing it with an aura of virtue. In the United States, one works not because one has to but because work is a good thing. According to this value, you should work even if you do not need the money. Granted many Americans have jobs that are dull and disgusting,

but this is regarded as a misfortune. Work is supposed to be good for you!

2. *The importance of practicality and efficiency.* Americans pride themselves on their engineering and technology, on their willingness to sacrifice tradition for rational solutions. One of the worst things you can call an American is old-fashioned or backward. As a result, Americans often regard change as equivalent to progress.

3. *The importance of achievement and success.* For many Americans, the mark against which they measure themselves is not their absolute standard of living but their achievements relative to others'. To be content with what you have is considered fatalistic; to aspire to better things, to be discontented with your present lot, is considered virtuous. In this sense, Abe Lincoln is the classic American hero: studying by firelight to rise from rural poverty to the presidency of the country.

4. *The importance of being moral.* For all their emphasis on practicality and efficiency, Americans tend to place a high value on morality. We talk of justice, equality, and charity, and we wish to be thought a just, egalitarian, and liberal nation. Thus, for example, we could not bear to justify a war as a desire to protect our economic interests; this would shock our vision of ourselves. Instead all of our wars have been justified as battles against tyranny and as self-sacrificing efforts to protect the little guy. It is important to Americans to be seen as a kindly, moral, generous people.

Changing American values: The Importance of No. 1.   A recent review of American values concluded that the major American value in the 1980s is self-fulfillment. Daniel Yankelovich, a psychologist, has conducted several national studies aimed at identifying changing values. For the new generation of Americans, Yankelovich argues, it is not enough to achieve wealth, security, or a sense of a job well done. People are insisting that they reach their full potential. Yankelovich quotes a man now reaching retirement: "Sure it was a rotten job. But what the hell. I made a good living, I took care of my wife and kids. What more do you expect?" (1981:9). This man was satisfied with both himself and his life. Increasingly, however, men like him are feeling trapped, seeking psychological counseling, and searching for meaning. The evidence for this new value is evident in survey data such as those reported in Figure 3.3, where freedom and potential rank so highly. It is also evident in such best sellers as *Number One* and *I'm OK, You're OK.*

Recent decades have seen a sharp change in many of the norms guiding American life. Premarital sex, childless marriages, working women, interracial marriages—many of the things that were considered plainly wrong two decades ago are increasingly being accepted by the American public (see Table 3.1). It would be incorrect, however, to assume a massive change in values. American norms now allow a wider variation in the means people use to achieve the value of a happy family life, but the value itself hasn't changed at all. Some people may court success by selling dope, others by becoming stockbrokers; some may seek self-fulfillment through drugs, others through prayer. Across America, however, there remains broad consensus that a good family life, work, success, and self-fulfillment are good things.

Table 3.1   Change and Stability in American Norms

The most rapidly changing norms in the United States have to do with sexuality and sex roles. In many other areas of life—such as family, religion, and work—there is still a great deal of continuity in norms and values.

SOME SIGNS OF CHANGE

1.	Disapprove of a married woman earning money if she has a husband capable of supporting her.	1938	75%
		1978	26%
2.	Believe that for a woman to remain unmarried she must be sick, neurotic, or immoral.	1957	80%
		1978	24%
3.	Would vote for a qualified woman nominee for president.	1937	31%
		1980	76%
4.	Condemn premarital sex as morally wrong.	1967	85%
		1979	37%

SOME SIGNS OF CONTINUITY

5.	Men: Would go on working for pay even if they didn't have to.	1957	82%
		1976	81%
6.	Would welcome more respect for authority.	1978	94%
		1981	94%
7.	Find religion very important in personal life.	1978	53%
		1982	57%
8.	Believe that most important characteristic of a good father is spending time with his children, reading, playing, etc.	1924	63%
		1977	69%

SOURCES: Items 1, 3, 6, and 7 are from The Gallup Reports; Items 2 and 5 are from the Institute for Social Research; Item 4 is from Yankelovich, Skelly, and White (1979); Item 8 is from Caplow, et al. (1982).

American Subcultures

In spite of general agreement on dominant cultural values, a great deal of cultural diversity exists in the United States. This diversity is particularly noticeable in language, life-style, and folkways. The most prominent subcultures are those based on region, ethnicity, race, and class. Thus, for example, blacks and whites, lower class and middle class share the values of success, health, and a good family life. The norms by which they structure their success, their health, and their family life, however, differ in important respects.

Consider the stereotypes you hold about what it would be like to live in the South. Some of these stereotypes reflect actual regional differences in subculture. Surveys demonstrate that people in the South do differ somewhat in norms and values and life-style from the rest of the nation. They are more likely to be born-again Christians, to go to church, and to be conservative on social issues. They are less likely to approve of gun control, unions, or divorce. Although people who live in the South—and the West and New England—share in the common American culture, they also have distinctive life-styles and norms.

Distinct subcultures also develop within most large organizations. In high schools all over the country, for example, you can usually distinguish at least three subcultures. Although the names change from region to region, there are (1) the socials/preppies, who get at least reasonable grades, wear fashionable clothing, and actually like high school for the social life;

Figure 3.4
Among the most distinctive subcultures in American society are those based on race and ethnicity. In most large cities distinct ethnic subcultures are segregated in neighborhoods where language, customs, and life-styles continue as expressions of particular immigrant groups. This parade through New York City's Chinatown is symbolic of numerous ethnic parades held annually across the United States by Puerto Ricans, Czechs, Greeks, and Irish.

(2) the intellectuals/eggheads/dexters, who carry multiple-function calculators everywhere they go, study on Saturday nights, and are generally well liked by teachers; and (3) the freaks/hippies, who are constantly in trouble, whom the teachers hate and sometimes fear, and whose only purpose for being in school is to find good parties. In addition, there may be jocks and punkers and other distinct subcultures, each of which possesses a set of folkways to which its members conform. These folkways help strengthen ties among group members and create barriers to interaction across subcultures (preppies do not date freaks).

American Countercultures

Groups whose needs are not being met by the dominant cultural values of society develop alternative cultures, or countercultures, that help them adapt to their unique problems. Among the major American countercultures are the gays, the hippies and beats, and the punkers.

For 30 years, the counterculture of the beats and the hippies has challenged the major values of society. It has challenged the meaningfulness of success and achievement, of possessions and middle-class morality. Marxist analysts see in countercultures the operation of the dialectic: The counterculture challenges the dominant culture and often a synthesis emerges. The hippie slogan "if it feels good, do it" can be seen to be the advance movement of the new middle-class emphasis on self-fulfillment.

Youth Culture and Punkers. For about as long as people have been able to leave written records, middle-aged people have been complaining about teenagers:

> The young people of today love luxury. They have bad manners, they scoff at authority and lack respect for their elders. Children nowadays are real tyrants,

they no longer stand up when their elders come into the room where they are sitting, they contradict their parents, chat together in the presence of adults, eat gluttonously and tyrannise their teachers. [Cited in Brake, 1980:1]

This complaint, by Socrates, was written more than 2,400 years ago. Youths have often occupied a sort of no-man's land between childhood and adulthood, facing the special problem of living up to dominant values with relatively few resources. The problem is particularly intense for lower-class youths, who have to cope with the difficult awareness that the goals may be forever beyond their reach.

One response to blocked goals is to create a counterculture—a language, style of dress, and music that are uniquely associated with youth. Sometimes youth cultures are simply subcultures, acceptable variations on a dominant theme. At other times they can become countercultures. Delinquent subcultures, whose folkways are characterized by leather jackets, nazi emblems, and a violent exploration of masculinity, are a counterculture. A more recent form of counterculture is punk, a deliberate attempt to outrage the establishment by language, appearance, and behavior. "What it manages to do successfully is to upset everyone, left, right, centre, avantgarde, and reactionary. The punk followers create an appearance of outrage which appeals to those who feel there is no future, no work and bleak prospects" (Brake, 1980:81). Thus punk is particularly attractive to working-class youths.

Middle-class youths, who have a shot at success but choose to reject it (at least temporarily), more often turn to the hippie or beat culture. Unlike punk culture, which is anti everything and for nothing, the hippie culture has an alternate set of values to propose. As befits a generally well-educated middle-class group, hippies tend to create free universities, magazines, and newspapers to espouse their creed. They are against the establishment, but they are not fatalists or anarchists.

Figure 3.5
One of the most recent countercultures of youth is Punk, a deliberate attempt to outrage the establishment through dress, adornment, and behavior. Punk counterculture originated in London among working-class youth and has subsequently spread to other industrialized countries where its strongest appeal is to youth who are working class.

High Culture/Popular Culture

Social scientists always make a point of saying that culture has to do with the norms and values of society as a whole and that they are not referring to culture with a capital C—high culture, as in art, opera, and symphony. Yet culture is influenced by social class, and, like everything else, the norms and values of the upper classes tend to be perceived as superior to the norms and values of the lower classes. If we prefer Doritos to crepes, Johnny Cash to Leonard Bernstein, we know we are supposed to be embarassed about it.

Generally, popular culture is what we do; high culture is what we think we ought to do. The distinction helps explain why Nielsen ratings give such television shows as *The A-Team* extremely high ratings but *nobody admits to watching them*. Even if you like such programs, you are smart enough to know that you should not. You know that they have no redeeming social value, that they explore no new ideas, that they do not expand your mind or the minds of their creators.

Popular culture is what people like and what people do. As Mick Jagger said, "I know it's only rock and roll, but I like it." The same can be said

Figure 3.6
Culture includes not only ballet and the symphony, it also includes Michael Jackson, break dancing, and stock car racing. All are equally important aspects of nonmaterial culture, reflecting society's changing norms and values. Popular culture may originate at any class level, but more often than high culture, it is a product of the lower and middle classes.

of popular culture. The analysis of popular culture focuses on the realities of everyday life, life as we really live it as opposed to the idealized norms and values we would like to project. Studies of American popular culture include studies of sports, rock and roll, and television.

Determinants of Human Behavior

This book was begun with the general intent of studying why we do the things we do. One response to that question is that we do them because of tradition, because they are what our culture says we should do. Others might suggest, however, that much of our behavior is just "human nature." In this section, we will explore the nature of humans and the nature of culture.

Biology and Cultural Universals

The common biology of human beings probably explains much that is common to various cultures—the universal faces of mirth and grief and the universal existence of the family, religion, aggression, and warfare. The unanswered question is whether these aspects of human societies are common adaptations to similar problems or whether they are encoded into our genetic makeup. In short, are these behaviors cultural or instinctual?

Biological explanations are most likely to be offered for behavioral patterns that are **cultural universals**. When the same pattern is found in cultures as diverse as those of Victorian England and Timbuktu, it begins to seem possible that common biology explains the pattern. One such pattern is dominance, which is a cultural universal. In even the simplest and poorest societies, men dominate women and adults dominate children. Dominance patterns also exist for many animal species. For chickens, we call it a pecking order. The dominant hen may peck all those beneath her, the second may peck all but the leader, and so on down to the lowliest hen, who may peck no one but may be pecked by all. Dominance patterns do not exist for all animal species, not even for all primate species. They are characteristic, though, of all primate species that live on the ground instead of in trees—a category that includes humans, of course. All known human societies display patterns of dominance by age and sex—which raises the question of whether such patterns are natural. Could they have been built into our blood and bones and chromosomes through thousands of years of genetic evolution?

Sociobiology and Evolution.   Most sociologists accept an evolutionary view of the human species, believing that our physiological and anatomical characteristics are the result of a long evolutionary process. Over tens of thousands of years, our species developed larger brains, more upright posture, and more complex vocal cords. What else did we develop?

The past decade has witnessed increased interest in the role of evolution in human behavior. A relatively new field, **sociobiology**, focuses on the biological and evolutionary bases of social behavior. Sociobiologists as-

Cultural universals are behavioral patterns and institutions that are found in all human cultures; among them are inequality, marriage, body adornment, and religious ritual.

Sociobiology focuses on the biological and evolutionary bases of social behavior.

Figure 3.7

In trying to uncover what may be the common nature of our species, social scientists have emphasized the search for cultural universals. They have reasoned that if the same cultural pattern is evident in all societies, it may have a biological or genetic basis. Dominance is one such universal pattern; another is mothering. In all societies, bearing children and caring for them is an important role for women.

sume that some human social behavior has evolved as genetic adaptation (van den Berghe, 1978; E. O. Wilson, 1975, 1978). They argue, for example, that since the children of better mothers are most apt to survive and reproduce themselves, a gene favoring mothering (a maternal instinct) has come to be bred into the human species. Likewise, they argue that dominance and territoriality are behavioral characteristics of our species that are genetically based.

The majority of social scientists remain skeptical about the extent of biological determinism, and some even consider the concept dangerous. Critics are concerned that sociobiology may provide new fuel for racism. After all, distinct races have developed because of generations of inbreeding, and it is possible that they have evolved a little differently. Different is not the same as better or worse, but many worry that it is too short a step from this kind of reasoning to Hitler's rhetoric of the superiority of the Aryan race. Similarly, sociobiology offers an explanation for women's "natural" subordination to men that challenges many people's values. Because sociobiology can be viewed as justifying the oppression of one group by another on the basis of biological inferiority, critics regard it as a dangerous idea (Rogan, 1978).

People are animals. They have biologically determined needs for food, sleep, and sex. These factors undoubtedly influence the cultural adaptations that they make. The basic sociological position is that although there may be some genetic factors that influence human behavior, most human behavior and most group differences are the result of cultural factors.

The Importance of Language

Probably the most important biological characteristic of the human species, the one that most clearly sets humans apart from other animals, is

THE FAR SIDE   By GARY LARSON

"And now, Randy, by use of song, the male sparrow will stake out his territory . . . an instinct common in the lower animals."

the capacity to use language. Language is the ability to communicate with symbols—orally first and later in writing.

What does *communicate with symbols* mean? It means that when you see the combinations of circles and lines that appear on your textbook page as the word *orally,* you are able to understand that it means "speaking aloud." Almost all communication is done through symbols. Without symbolic communication we would be back on the level of the apes. Visualize for a moment what it would be like if none of the people in your classroom shared a common language. Like chimpanzees, you would have to gesture at each other—grimacing, pointing, smiling, tugging at each other to get attention.

Language is the foundation of culture. It allows the accumulation and transmission of experience. Because humans possess both superior intelligence and well-developed capacities for symbolic communication, culture is uniquely human. Humans are the only species that can adapt to the environment through culture as well as biology.

Culture as Uniquely Human.   Social scientists have studied the capacities for symbolic communication among primates for many years. Early studies attempting to teach oral language to chimpanzees were not successful, leading to the general conclusion that the vocal apparatus enabling humans to talk differs substantially from that of our closest relatives (Kellogg & Kellogg, 1933). Since the 1960s, research efforts have shifted to trying to ascertain the symbolic abilities of primates. Research on chimpanzees and gorillas has shown that apes can learn to use, though not speak, true language. The first experiment in this area focused on teaching Washoe, a 1-year-old female chimpanzee, American Sign Language. Washoe gradually learned to distinguish and sign more than 200 gestures and to combine these gestures into rudimentary sentences having meaning (Gardner & Gardner, 1969). Similar results for other chimpanzees (Premack & Premack, 1972; Rumbaugh et al., 1973) and for gorillas (Patterson, 1978) have revolutionized our understanding of the language-learning abilities of apes. Clearly, the potential for abstract reasoning and communication in higher-order primates exists.

A critical point in distinguishing humans from other animals is not just the ability to learn but the ability to *teach*, to transfer what we have learned to others. Although animals are capable of learning, humans alone seem able, in any marked degree, to pass on acquired knowledge and habits to their offspring. This, of course, is not to say that other primates do not adapt to changes in their environment, learn, or transmit these adaptations to the next generation. They do. But the absence of language severely restricts their adaptations and their capacity to transmit learning.

In 1952, scientists at the Japan Monkey Center observed macaques adapting to new food resources they introduced to the island. The artificial feeding consisted of throwing sweet potatoes onto the beach. Over a period of time, the macaques shifted their foraging areas from the trees and mountains to the sandy beaches of the island. One year after the feeding started, a 2-year-old female was observed carrying a sweet potato to a nearby brook to wash the sand from it. In the following years, the technique of washing potatoes spread throughout the troup, with females and ad-

Figure 3.8
This photo shows Koko, a 7 year old female gorilla, communicating in sign language with developmental psychologist Penny Patterson. After being told the story of the "Three Little Kittens," Koko signs that the mother cat is "mad."

Koko's total working vocabulary is about 375 signs. Her abilities at linguistic abstraction, reasoning, and a sense of the past and future are important breakthroughs in research, suggesting far more symbolic capabilities and potentials for primates than previously realized.

olescents being the first to adapt. Eventually, the technique shifted from the brook to the sea, and potato washing became an established tradition, with infants of both sexes learning the behavior from their mothers as a natural adjunct to eating.

This change paved the way for other changes. The macaques no longer foraged in the mountains, as tree dwellers, but adapted to the sea. Infants clinging to their mothers as they washed potatoes acquired an association with the water, and new generations were observed bathing, playing, diving for seaweed, and swimming (Kummer, 1971:124). As Kummer notes, "This is the closest primate parallel of human culture studied in detail to date, although it is a tradition of behavior forms only, not of symbols" (p. 125). It is a precultural adaptation in which imitation is the principal form of behavior modification.

Human beings' capacity for language provides a distinct advantage in the accumulation of knowledge and experience from one generation to the next. Only after language is invented can pieces of practical knowledge (such as "don't use electricity in the bathtub") or ideas (such as "God exists") be transmitted from one generation to the next. Inventions, discoveries, and forms of social organization are socially bestowed and intentionally passed on so that each new generation potentially elaborates on and modifies the accumulated knowledge of the previous generations. In short, culture is cumulative only because of language.

Because of language, human beings are not limited to the slow process of genetic evolution in adapting to their circumstances. **Cultural evolution** is a uniquely human way for a species to adapt to its environment.

Cultural evolution is the use of specific social arrangements and technology as a mechanism for adapting to environmental and social change.

Whereas biological evolution may require literally hundreds of generations to fully adapt the organism to new circumstances, cultural evolution allows the changes to be made within a short period of time. In this sense, cultural evolution is an extension of biological evolution, one that speeds up the processes of change and adjustment to new circumstances in the environment (van den Berghe, 1978).

The Hidden Culture. Although language is a wonderful tool for vastly increasing our abilities to accumulate knowledge and work together, it has certain hazards. One hazard is that language often tells us much more about culture than about reality. For example, when we say that the controversial 1983 Miss America, Vanessa Williams, is black, this tells the listener more about race relations in the United States than it does about the color of Williams's skin.

Language is a set of culturally agreed-upon symbols that we use to describe reality. These symbols shape and confine what we experience as reality. For example, you may tell me that you're feeling angry. In trying to understand this symbolic communication, I can look in my thesaurus to find that you may mean that you're frustrated, furious, vexed, or hurt. You may agree that hurt best fits your mood. Fitting real feelings and experiences into available symbols is often frustrating and inaccurate.

For the most part, we can communicate only with the symbols offered by our culture, and these symbols impose a structure on reality. They direct our attention to things we expect to see (things for which we have symbols) and away from things we do not expect to see (things for which we have no symbols). Perhaps the clearest example of this is our notion of time. Time is an extremely abstract concept. We cannot see it, feel it, or hear it. As with the wind, we can tell it has been here only by the changes it makes.

In societies where there are few changes to mark the passage of time, time itself is hardly noticed. Even today, in many parts of the world, people have no notion of their age or when were born. Increasingly, however, we devise symbols to measure the passage of time. First, we devised calendars, then clocks, finally watches. Now we all wear watches with second hands so that we can measure time by fractions of a minute. These symbols for time have made time real to us. It is a commodity like coins. We can waste it, spend it, lose it, and make it up (Hall, 1976:16). Because we have symbols for it, time is real to us and we're very conscious of it. We think about time and how fast it is ticking away (symbols again) while we're eating, sleeping, and even loving. Because many other cultures do not have symbols for time, however, they do not have the same sensation. If herdsmen in rural Sudan are held up for hours because of a convoy on the road, they do not get tense and worry about wasting time. Our experience is molded by our symbolic world.

The Cultural Basis of Behavior

The importance of culture in explaining the behavior of our species cannot be overemphasized. Biological factors help explain what is common to humankind across societies, but culture explains why people and societies differ from one another.

Culture is not instinctive; nor is it transmitted through genes. Rather, it is composed of learned ways of responding to the environment. Eating, for example, is not cultural. Humans eat because they must; what, when, and how they eat, however, is learned and varies from one culture to the next. Eating beef is almost as American as eating apple pie; yet in India the cow is sacred, and Hindu religious law forbids the slaughter of cows for food. Societies of the Middle East—Israel and Egypt, for example—are strongly opposed to eating ham, a frequent holiday dish in our society. These attitudes toward food are learned responses, acquired by individuals through experiences after birth.

Each culture provides a set of guidelines for solving the recurrent problems that human beings face. Needs for food, shelter, and survival are among these problems; so are needs for self-fulfillment, identification, and belongingness. Culture is a design for living that details ways of dealing with such varied things as birth, marriage, death, strangers, and food production. The particular solutions to problems vary from culture to culture, but all cultures must provide them.

Cultural Relativity and Ethnocentrism. The solutions that each culture devises may be startlingly different. Among the Wodaabe of Niger, for example, mothers are not allowed to speak directly to their first- or second-born children and, except for nursing, are not even allowed to touch them. The babies' grandmothers and aunts, however, lavish affection and attention on them (Beckwith, 1983). The effect of this pattern of childrearing is

CULTURE IS	IMPLICATION
Learned	Culture is not transmitted through biological inheritance but is learned from interaction with other people.
Taught	Culture is uniquely human and is transmitted symbolically through language. Each generation passes its accumulated knowledge and experience on to its children.
Normative	Culture tells us how we ought to act and believe.
Problem solving	Culture helps us adapt to the problems presented to us by our biological imperatives, our physical and social environments.
Relative	Cultural practices must be evaluated on how well they help a particular society adapt. They cannot be evaluated with universal criteria but must be evaluated in context.
Integrative	By providing group members with a common set of expectations and solutions, culture encourages the integration of a society.

CONCEPT SUMMARY

Culture

to emphasize loyalties and affections throughout the entire kin group rather than just to one's own children or spouse. The norm provides solidarity and helps ensure that each new entrant will be loyal to the group as a whole. Is it a good norm or a bad norm? That is a question we can answer only with regard to how it fits in with the rest of the Wodaabe culture. Does the norm help the people meet recurrent problems and maintain a stable society? If so, then it works; it is functional. This way of evaluating norms and values is called **cultural relativity**; each cultural trait must be evaluated in the context of its own culture. A corollary of cultural relativity is that no practice is universally good or universally bad; goodness and badness are relative, not absolute.

This type of evaluation is sometimes a difficult intellectual feat. For example, no matter how objective we try to be, most of us believe that infanticide, human sacrifice, and cannibalism are absolutely and universally wrong. This attitude, called **ethnocentrism**, refers to the tendency to use the norms and values of our own culture as standards against which to judge the practices of others.

Ethnocentrism usually means that we see our way as the right way and everybody else's way as the wrong way. When American missionaries came to the South Sea Islands, they found that many things were done differently in Polynesian culture. The missionaries, however, were unable to view Polynesian folkways as simply different. If they were un-American, then they must be wrong and probably wicked. As a result, the missionaries taught the islanders that the only acceptable way (the American way) to have sexual intercourse was in a face-to-face position with the man on top, the now famous missionary position. They taught them that women must cover their breasts, that they should have clocks and come on time to appointments, and a variety of other Americanisms that the missionaries accepted as morally right behavior.

Ethnocentrism is often a barrier to interaction between people from different cultures, leading to much confusion and misinterpretation. It is not, however, altogether bad. In the sense that it is pride in our own culture and confidence in our own way of life, ethnocentrism is essential for social control. We learn to follow the norms of our culture because we believe that they are the right norms. If we did not share that belief, then there would be little conformity in society. Ethnocentrism, then, is a natural and even desirable product of growing up in a culture. The consequence, however, is that we simultaneously discredit or diminish the value of other ways of thinking and feeling.

Cultural Variation and Change

Culture provides solutions to common and not-so-common problems. The solutions devised by societies are immensely variable. Part of this variation can be explained by unique environmental conditions. Other conditions that produce diversity include isolation, technology, and dominant cultural themes. Each of these conditions affects the elaboration of culture and the development of society.

Cultural Relativity refers to evaluating the traits of a culture on the basis of how a trait fits into the overall cultural patterns.
Ethnocentrism is the tendency to view the norms and values of one's culture as absolute and to use them as a standard against which to judge the practices of other cultures.

Figure 3.9
In the "land of giraffe women," 20 pounds of brass loops measuring 12 inches in height have been twisted around this Padaung tribeswoman's neck. Draped with silver chains and coins, the loops are a symbol of elegance, wealth, and social status. An additional 30 pounds of brass worn in rings on a woman's arms and legs may further burden her mobility. In addition to signifying social status, tribal law decrees removal of the coils for adultery, an act which is usually followed by suffocation and death.

Environment

Why are the French different from the Australian aborigines, the Finns different from the Navajo? Although it is just possible that there are differences in genetic backgrounds, a far more obvious difference is their physical environments. Hot or cold climates, fertile or sandy soils, dense or sparse vegetation, the presence of animals, rainfall, and fuels—all are environmental conditions to which people must adapt.

The physical and natural environment of an area sets the stage for the cultural adaptations of a society. For example, the great southwest monsoons that annually cross India, Pakistan, Burma, and Indo-China bring seasonal rainfalls from June through August that are vital to the agricultural economy of these countries. Over the years, these societies have evolved cultures that reflect the importance of the monsoons to their survival. Traditionally, one of the most important of these adaptations is religion. In India, for instance, the chief of the Vedic gods is Indra, the god of rain. As the people wait for the monsoons to arrive, they do so with considerable anxiety and religious ceremony. Modern adaptations to the same phenomenon include government planning agencies, disaster relief organizations, and agricultural extension agents.

American society has been shaped by its environment in innumerable ways. The mobility, independence, and thirst for change that characterize the United States may justly be traced to the existence of an open frontier. Transplanting English culture to a rich and largely empty environment caused changes in that culture. More recently, the declining abundance of fossil fuels has influenced the way we live. People drive smaller cars, and they heat their houses less in the winter and cool them less in the summer. Resource shortages have affected national defense efforts, altered the ways homes are built, changed the industrial economy, and forced the average citizen to adopt a different (and frequently less comfortable)

Figure 3.10
The hot, dry land of Somalia is inhabited largely by nomadic tribes who raise camels, cattle, goats, and sheep. One of the few remaining pastoral societies, the nomads live in small, collapsible, beehive-shaped huts that are covered with skins and grass mats. Limited water and pasture makes for a relatively hard life requiring that huts, people, and herds move periodically in search of new grazing land.

life-style. Such changes reflect the impact of decreasing natural resources throughout the world and are a reminder of the extent to which human social behavior is influenced by the natural physical environment.

Isolation

When cultural patterns evolve as adaptations to the physical environment of an area, the absence of contact with other societies tends to perpetuate the patterns. Many of the geographically isolated societies located along the headwaters of the Amazon, in the back country of Australia, in the interior of Africa, and in the dense forests of Malaysia have been cut off from the rest of the world until just recently. The cultural patterns of these societies have evolved over centuries as distinct adaptations to conditions unique to their environment. In modern Western societies, specific groups wishing to escape the influences of the dominant culture have intentionally isolated themselves. The Hutterites, Amish, 19th century Mormons, and, more recently, Jonesville cultists are examples of religious sects that have used geographical isolation as a means to preserve the stability of their subcultures.

Isolation can be socially as well as geographically imposed. An important factor that increases isolation is ethnocentrism. Because we believe that our ways are the right ways, we may erect a symbolic wall between our culture and others'. Our negative judgments become a barrier to contact and to borrowing or adapting cultural characteristics from others. In this case, ethnocentrism is the cultural equivalent of geographic isolation, cutting one society off from the influence of others.

Technology

Cultural variation also results from the technological position of a society. The accumulation of cultural artifacts and designs for living that have previously evolved sets some limits as to what will be developed in the future or how readily alternatives will be adapted into an existing culture. This particular cause of cultural variation is stressed by Marxists. Marx argued that the mode of economic production—the technology and resources used in production—determined all of the other social structures in society. Thus Marxists emphasize that differences in level of technology and in physical resources may be among the most important causes of diversity. They may also be among the most potent causes of change.

Consider, for example, the development of the cotton gin. Prior to the invention of the cotton gin, cotton—and slavery—was confined to a narrow belt along the East Coast. The state of Georgia experimented with a new kind of cotton and found that it grew well inland, but it could not be processed with existing equipment. Thus, although large amounts of cotton were grown, only a small percentage was ever processed and brought to market. Lured by a commission from the state of Georgia, Eli Whitney in 1793 invented the cotton gin, a machine designed to mill the new cotton. As a result, cotton—and slavery—spread throughout the Deep South. King Cotton and the spread and profitability of slavery owed much to the technological advances of the industrial revolution (Wright, 1978).

FOCUS ON ANOTHER CULTURE

Hard Times in Inis Beag

Inis Beag, a remote 2-square-mile island settled during the 17th century by a group of Irish emigrants escaping political conflict, provides a unique example of how factors such as isolation, physical environment, dominant cultural themes, and unique historical events affect the evolution of culture. Isolation in particular has severely restricted contact with outsiders, enabling the islanders to retain their culture relatively unchanged for the last 300 years.

Inis Beag is an island of rock located off the coast of Ireland. Because of the absence of any deep-water ports, the islanders are virtually cut off from shipping and trade with outsiders. Any exchange requires shipping vessels to anchor off the coast, where canoes are used to transport both limited trade goods and visitors to and from the island.

Much of the island's farmland is found on the northeastern side, where stone fences mark off hundreds of plots used for simple subsistence agriculture. Over the years, the soil of these plots has been deepened and enriched by the addition of seaweed, sand, and human wastes. A relatively simple subsistence technology consisting of digging sticks, spades, and scythes has persisted for centuries. The island lacks electricity and running water, and its only vehicles are donkey-drawn carts. As with most peasant communities, the standard of living is low, the family is of central importance, and the birthrate is high (the average couple has seven children). Unlike other folk societies, however, Inis Beag has a low deathrate and a low illiteracy rate.

Today, there are approximately 350 residents, making up 59 families located in four villages on the island. The people's lives are strongly determined by the very small physical size of their island and by the difficulty of supporting themselves. They share this dilemma with much of the rest of Ireland, but with greater urgency; their small island places clear boundaries on growth. The plots are already so small (an average of 12 acres per family) that any further subdivision would make them too small to support a family. The Irish solution, one shared by Inis Beag, is to pass all of the family's land to one son. This solution has its costs. In the first place, only the chosen son will be able to support a family of his own—and he cannot do this until his parents pass their land on to him. Because life expectancy has increased, this often does not occur until the son has reached middle-age. His sisters and brothers face an even less desirable situation. They usually have a choice of staying home and working as free labor for their parents or their brother or emigrating to the Irish mainland or the United States. Of course, some of the girls manage to snag a middle-aged bachelor as he comes into his inheritance.

Figure 3.11

The islanders of Inis Beag survive on a subsistence economy based primarily on hoe agriculture. Conditions on the island are severe and a growing population has sharply restricted the availability of small garden plots to support the more than 350 families who reside on the island. Isolated from the rest of Irish culture, Inis Beag has maintained a culture relatively unchanged for the past three centuries. One of their most distinct cultural characteristics is a significant amount of sexual repression.

As a result of this situation, the average person who remains on Inis Beag marries many years after reaching sexual maturity; many never marry at all. The average age at marriage is 36 for men and 25 for women. Unlike the contemporary United States, being single on Inis Beag means total abstinence from sexual activity. In order to squash sexual desires thoroughly, the entire cultural apparatus is geared to depress sexual thoughts and opportunities. This culture has been branded the most sexually repressed in history.

Almost from infancy, girls and boys are raised separately. They do not play together or pray together; they are separated at home, church, and school. Courtship is practically nonexistent; most marriages are arranged, primarily on the basis of economic considerations.

These normative practices are reinforced by a strong sense of modesty. Anything to do with the body is regarded as shameful; such things as pregnancy, urination, and defecation cannot be spoken of in public. (In fact, although human wastes are an essential element of their agricultural technique, islanders will not admit that they use them.) Both men and women on Inis Beag abhor nudity, and the body is always fully covered. As a result, the people never bathe, contenting themselves with washing only their hands, face, and feet. Even sexual intercourse takes place with the couple as fully clothed as possible. Intercourse is viewed as physically unhealthy, to be engaged in only for the purpose of procreation. Although sexual relations are regarded as a woman's duty (as opposed to pleasure) in many societies, Inis Beag may be the only culture in the world where sex has also been defined as a man's duty. As a result, intercourse is an infrequent, speedy, and secretive act.

Sexual repression on Inis Beag stems from a combination of circumstances—a harsh environment, a limited land supply, and a religion that stresses the overwhelming fear of damnation. This particular form of Catholicism was at one time common to much of Ireland. Although it has been supplanted on the mainland, the isolation of Inis Beag has allowed it to persist as a dominant cultural theme.

Note: Inis Beag is not the real name of this island. The name has been changed in order to provide biographical immunity for the community and the people who live there.

Questions to Consider

1. How can the late age at marriage and the sexual repression of Inis Beag be seen as problem solving for the inhabitants?
2. Consider the possibility that a harsh climate and a hard life make a harsh religion and an unforgiving God seem more natural.

SOURCE: John Messenger (1969). *Inis Beag: Isle of Ireland.* New York: Holt, Rinehart, and Winston.

Dominant Cultural Themes

Cultural patterns generally contain dominant cultural themes that further contribute to variations between cultures. These themes give a distinct character and direction to a culture; they also create, in part, a closed system. New ideas, values, and inventions are usually accepted only when they fit into the existing culture or represent changes that can be absorbed without too greatly distorting existing patterns. The Native American hunter, for example, was pleased to adopt the rifle as an aid to the established tradition of hunting. Western types of housing and legal customs regarding land ownership, however, were rejected because they were alien to a nomadic and communal way of life.

Weber was one of the first sociologists to stress the importance of cultural themes as a determinant of cultural variability. He suggested that cultures tend to select and reinterpret the new ideas that are meaningful to them. If they can find no point of correspondence between the new ideas and their usual ones, then the new ideas are abandoned (Gerth and Mills, 1946/1970:63).

Diffusion

As noted earlier, the processes of cultural evolution are much more rapid than are the processes of biological evolution. In part this is because learning is accelerated by **diffusion**, the spread of cultural traits when one culture comes into contact with another. Where the conditions of isolation preclude contact, as on Inis Beag, a culture continues on its own course, unaltered and uncontaminated by others. Inis Beag, however, is unusual in this regard. Since the middle of the 18th century, industrialization and colonialism have extended Western culture to many previously isolated societies, producing rapid cultural change through contact and diffusion.

American society itself is an amalgamation of native populations and immigrant groups from around the world. This form of contact has produced a culture that is the accumulation of traits from many cultures. The "100 percent American," for example:

> awakens in a bed built on a pattern which originated in the Near East but which was modified in Northern Europe before it was transmitted to America. He throws back covers made from cotton domesticated in India, or linen, domesticated in the Near East, or silk, the use of which was discovered in China. All of these materials have been spun and woven by processes invented in the Near East. He slips into his moccasins, invented by the Indians of the Eastern woodlands, and goes to the bathroom, whose fixtures are a mixture of European and American inventions, both of recent date. He takes off his pajamas, a garment invented in India, and washes with soap invented by the ancient Gauls. He then shaves, a masochistic rite which seems to have been derived from either Sumer or ancient Egypt. [Linton, 1936:326]

After describing these rituals, Linton follows our solid American citizen through the rest of the morning as he dresses, has breakfast, smokes, and settles down to read the news. While he reads about problems in Beirut, Nicaragua, and Ireland, our man is likely to thank a Hebrew deity in an Indo-European language that he is 100 percent American (Pinney, 1968:5).

Since World War II, the diffusion of Western culture around the world has occurred at an accelerated rate, prompting anthropologist Margaret Mead (1970) to describe contemporary societies as being part of a world community. People born since 1940, in vastly different cultural traditions, are entering the present world community at approximately the same point in time. All people are equally immigrants in this new era, one based on the world. In the final chapter of this book, we will examine the processes of social and cultural change, particularly theories of modernization and world systems.

Diffusion is a process by which an aspect of material or nonmaterial culture is spread from one culture to another.

Transplanting Food Production

Food production and technology are cultural patterns that vary enormously around the world. In the developed countries, agricultural technology has revolutionized food production. In the United States, less than 3 percent of the total population lives on farms, where 12 percent of the world's meat, 46 percent of the world's corn, and 68 percent of the world's soybeans are produced. In the mid 1970s, only the United States, Canada, Argentina, Australia, and New Zealand produced enough excess grain to export it to other countries.

In the aggregate, the total production of food throughout the world is sufficient to meet the dietary needs of the world's population (almost 5 billion). Yet half of the world's population is inadequately fed, and more than 500 million people suffer extreme malnutrition and starvation (Murphy, 1984). World hunger, malnutrition, and starvation are in part problems of distribution. If the excess food produced by rich countries could be redistributed to the poor countries, the basic nutritional and dietary needs of the world's current population could be met.

Figure 3.12

The distribution of drought relief in Niger over the past several years is both humane and essential. Much of the world's current hunger and malnutrition could also be alleviated by redistributing the food surpluses of rich countries. Unfortunately, any redistribution program may disrupt existing indigenous food markets. In addition it obligates the receiving country and tends to create dependency.

Food redistribution as a form of foreign aid raises a number of political and moral issues. Any form of aid, regardless of motivation, increases the dependence of the recipient country and broadens the international power and influence of the benefactor. Viewed in this context, the poor countries of the world are potential pawns of the rich. Aid may also have unforeseen effects on the receiving economy.

In February 1976, for example, the earthquakes that hit Guatemala left approximately 24,000 people dead and another 1.2 million homeless. The rural farm Indians living north of Guatemala City were especially hard hit by the disaster. Their disaster was not the earthquake but United States aid. The farmers had just harvested a record grain crop, most of which was undamaged by the earthquake. Unfortunately for them, the U.S. disaster aid consisted of thousands of tons of grain given to rural villages for free distribution. This aid, though based on good intentions, created an oversupply in the economy. Native farmers could not sell their crops; many faced bankruptcy and were swallowed up by larger landholders.

One alternative to direct food assistance is aid aimed at making poor countries more self-sufficient. This is precisely what has been done in many parts of the world, where disease-resistant hybrid rice and wheat have been introduced to subsistence farmers. Referred to as the Green Revolution, these programs are based on Western methods of farming, which require expensive machinery, fertilizers, pesticides, systematic irrigation, and the production of one main cash crop. The end results are higher yields and greater economic self-sufficiency.

To be effective, however, the Green Revolution also means the ultimate disruption of a population's existing cultural patterns. It requires not just a change in the plants grown but major changes in the social organization of rural areas. It means relying on the agricultural extension agent rather than God, relying on booklearning rather than tradition, relying on machines and technology rather than one's family. All these changes favor the young over the old and further upset traditional family relations and traditional authority patterns. In addition, the traditional subsistence farmer, accustomed to growing a variety of crops, must now rely on one major crop, a major risk in the event of crop failure. The economic costs of participating in Western high-yield agriculture are also generally prohibitive to the subsistence peasant farmer. It is only the small proportion of well-to-do landowners who are able to benefit from such programs in underdeveloped countries.

Economic development programs such as these succeed or fail to the extent to which the traditional social, political, and economic characteristics of the recipient are taken into account. Diffusion of cultural traits from another culture is successful only when the new traits are easily incorporated into the existing culture. Ignoring this basic social science observation and imposing development programs on underdeveloped countries has produced many failures. Merely introducing new technology, regardless of its promise, may not help and may, in fact, hurt underdeveloped countries.

The technological progress of the West has resulted in the diffusion of Western culture throughout much of the world. In part, this has resulted from early colonialization, when colonial powers imposed Western cultural ways on non-Western societies. In more recent years, economic development programs have extended the influence of Western culture. As Third World countries attempt to become self-sufficient, adopt Western technology, and compete in international markets, many of their social problems are intensified. These cultural disruptions produce political instability, soaring population growth, unemployed and dislocated peasant farm families, rapid urban growth, continued malnutrition, and larger gaps between the rich and poor. (These topics are discussed in more detail in chapter 20.)

SUMMARY

1. Culture is a design for living that provides ready-made solutions to the basic problems of a society. It includes both material and nonmaterial traits that help people adapt to their circumstances.
2. Nonmaterial culture is embedded in norms and values, which determine the goals that the culture finds worth pursuing and specify the appropriate means to reach them.
3. The cultures of large and complex societies are not homogeneous. Subcultures and countercultures with distinct life-styles and folkways develop to meet unique regional, class, and ethnic needs.
4. In the United States, dominant values center on the family, achievement, activity, morality, and efficiency. Within the last decades there has been a growing emphasis on the value of self-fulfillment.
5. People are animals, and some of their social behavior represents adaptations to the demands that biology places on them. Although it is possible that some specific behavioral patterns, especially cultural universals, are embedded in our genes, social scientists assume that most human behavior and most group differences are the products of culture.
6. Culture is made possible by language, the ability to communicate in symbols. Without this symbolic communication, humans could not accumulate knowledge and pass it on to new generations. Because only humans have the biological capacity to use language, they are the only animals with culture.
7. Culture is learned, taught, normative, problem solving, relative, and integrated.
8. The most important factors accounting for cultural variation are the physical and natural environment, isolation from other cultures, ethno-

centrism, level of technological development, cultural themes that are elaborated over time, and diffusion.

9. Because cultural practices are highly integrated, it is sometimes disruptive to try to introduce new technology or values into a culture. What is intended to help may instead create problems. Both new and old cultural practices must be judged on whether they help a society adapt to its circumstances.

SUGGESTED READINGS

Kephart, William M. (1983). Extraordinary Groups: The Sociology of Unconventional Life-Styles (2d ed.). New York: St. Martin's Press. A fascinating tour of some of the most interesting subcultures and countercultures in the United States—both past and present: the Amish, gypsies, Shakers, and Hutterites. Painless sociology—the application of basic concepts and theory to truly extraordinary groups.

Mead, Margaret (1935). Sex and Temperament in Three Primitive Societies. New York: Morrow. First published a half century ago, this classic work compares the impact of culture on shaping sex-role behavior in three New Guinea societies. A major theme is the extent to which sex roles are biological versus social in origin.

Mead, Margaret (1970). Culture and Commitment: A Study of the Generation Gap. New York: Doubleday. A brief and concise treatment of how cultural changes around the world have created major differences between pre– and post–World War II generations. The implications for the diffusion of culture throughout the world are explored in terms of a movement toward a world culture.

Messenger, John C. (1969). Inis Beag: Isle of Ireland. New York: Holt, Rinehart and Winston. A report of Messenger's fieldwork over a period of years among the Inis Beag islanders. Illuminates the joys and perils of fieldwork as well as the culture and life-styles of the people of Inis Beag.

Ruesch, Hans. (1950). Top of the World. New York: Harper & Bros. A brilliant novel, based on authentic anthropological evidence, describing the difficulties encountered when different cultures come into contact. Particularly useful in understanding cultural relativity.

Slater, Philip. (1976). The Pursuit of Loneliness (rev. ed.). Boston: Beacon Press. A penetrating and critical account of American culture, emphasizing the extent to which major social forces are pulling America apart.

Williams, Robin W., Jr. (1970). American society (3rd ed.). New York: Knopf. Perhaps the most extensive and best analysis of American culture, society, and institutions, especially the dominant values operating in society today.

Wilson, Edward O. (1978). On Human Nature. Cambridge, Mass.: Harvard University Press. A critical examination of the influence of our biological heritage on culture by a leading sociobiologist. Essential reading for anyone interested in the interplay between culture and biology in explaining human behavior.

Yinger, Milton J. (1982). Countercultures: The Promise and the Peril of a World Turned Upside Down. New York: Free Press. An examination of various social groups characterized by values and norms that are contradictory to the dominant values and norms of society.

CHAPTER 4

SOCIAL PROCESS AND SOCIAL STRUCTURE

PROLOGUE

Have You Ever . . . tried to play a simple game and instead spent all your time haggling over the rules? If you have watched children playing or can remember when you were a child, you can probably cite instances where a simple game, such as baseball, degenerated into arguments about the rules. For example, does it count if someone throws the ball and you're not ready? Do you lose your place in line if you have to go in to eat? Who gets to go first? Is it fair if the bigger kids get to play? Do you have to let boys/girls play?

Luckily, many of the social structures we encounter as we get older are already well established. The players are all identified and the rules all spelled out. For example, most of us understand that in the marriage game the rules limit us to one spouse at a time, no sexual contacts outside the marriage, and a financial and emotional obligation to the other spouse. Similarly, the rules of the education game describe who can play and how the players should behave. At work, in bridge groups, even in bars, shared norms evolve, and newcomers must learn them if they are to fit into the group.

An important part of understanding human social behavior is identifying the rules of the games we play. This chapter introduces the rules— social process and social structure.

The subject matter of sociology is structured social interaction: how people get along together, fight together, work together. The study of structured interaction has two aspects: process and structure. Process is concerned with the dynamics of a relationship; structure is concerned with the normative constraints that guide the interaction.

For example, suppose that you want to understand the social interaction of husbands and wives. To understand what goes on in a marriage, you need to understand how the spouses respond to each other, how they cooperate, compete, exchange, and fight. You must also put their interaction in the context of the script that society has written for marriage. Few spouses create unique norms and values to structure their interaction. Instead, they improvise from a socially established script that describes what they are supposed to do. Thus, in order to understand the marriage, you need to understand both the original script and the dynamics between the actors. This is what Comte meant in the 18th century when he said that sociology is the study of statics and dynamics. Contemporary sociology refers to it as the study of structure and process. Both structure and process are essential to understanding social interaction.

Social Processes

The social interaction that occurs between people is critical to the stability of any group. Some kinds of interaction help maintain the group; others undermine its social structure, causing change. All interaction can be included in the concept **social processes**—the forms of action and reaction through which people and organizations relate to one another. Social processes are directly concerned with the dynamic aspect of society—not just what the script is but how actors develop and live their roles.

> **Social processes** are mechanisms of interaction. They are concerned with change, development, and the dynamic aspects of social relationships.

The ways in which people act and react are many. This section looks closely at four processes that regularly occur in the patterned social relationships between individuals as well as groups: exchange, cooperation, competition, and conflict.

Exchange

When individuals voluntarily interact together in the expectation of receiving some reward, **exchange** occurs. A wide variety of social relationships include elements of exchange. Friendships, love affairs, and business deals all involve situations where people enter into relationships with the anticipation that they will benefit from them. In friendships and marriages, exchanges usually involve such intangibles as companionship, moral support, and a willingness to listen to the other's problems. In business or politics, an exchange may be more direct; politicians, for example, openly acknowledge exchanging votes on legislative bills—I'll vote for yours if you'll vote for mine.

> **Exchange** is the mutual giving and receiving of material or nonmaterial benefits.

Exchange relationships are based on the expectation that if you do something for somebody, then you've created a debt that the other must pay. This expectation is called the **norm of reciprocity** (Gouldner, 1960). If you help your sister-in-law move, then she is obligated to you. Somehow she must pay you back. If she fails to do so, then the social relationship is likely to end, probably with bad feelings. A corollary of the norm of reciprocity is that you avoid accepting favors from people with whom you do not wish to enter into a relationship. For example, if someone you do not know very well volunteers to type your term paper, you will probably

> The **Norm of reciprocity** specifies that people should return favors and should seek to maintain a balance of obligation in their social relationships.

be suspicious of the person's motives. Your first thought is likely to be, "What is this guy trying to prove? What does he want from me?" If you do not want to owe this person a favor, you will say that you prefer to type your own paper. Nonsociologists might sum up the norm of reciprocity by concluding that there's no free lunch.

Exchange is one of the most basic processes of social interaction. Almost all voluntary relationships are entered into as situations of exchange. In traditional American families, these exchanges were clearly spelled out. He supported the family, which obligated her to keep house and look after the children; or, conversely, she bore the children and kept house, which obligated him to support her.

In exchange processes, each party to the interaction gets something out of it; the parties may, however, receive unequal benefits. The basis of unequal power is usually unequal dependence (Emerson, 1962). When one person depends on the relationship more than the other does, that person loses power. Consider the dating relationship in which John loves Mary desperately and has eyes for no one else; Mary, however, only likes John and is dating several other men too. Because John is more dependent than Mary on the relationship, he has less power than Mary in it; she can stand him up, demand favors, or be generally unkind, and he will stay with her. This unpleasant situation remains a form of exchange; they stay together because each is getting something out of the relationship: She gets power; he gets her—at least some of the time.

Cooperation

Exchange is a voluntary trade-off. When each person has something the other wants, the two make a deal. **Cooperation** occurs when both parties work together for something that neither could achieve alone. Such endeavors help us meet individual and collective goals, often at a much lower cost than if we tried to reach them individually. Consider, for example, a four-way stop. Although it may entail some waiting in line, in the long run we will all get through quicker and more safely if we cooperate and take turns. Most continuing relationships involve some element of cooperation. Spouses cooperate in raising their children; children cooperate in tricking their substitute teachers.

Cooperation is when people work together to achieve shared goals.

Competition

It is not always possible for people to reach their goals by exchange or cooperation. If your goal and my goal are mutually exclusive (for example, I want to sleep and you want to play your stereo), we cannot both achieve our goals. Similarly, in situations of scarcity, there may not be enough of a desired good to go around. In these situations, social processes are likely to take the form of either competition or conflict.

Competition is a form of interaction that involves a struggle over scarce resources (Friedsam, 1965). The struggle is regulated by norms and values that do not allow the use of violence or force. The rules usually specify the conditions under which winning will be considered fair and losing will be considered tolerable. When the norms are violated, competition may erupt into conflict.

Competition is a struggle for scarce resources that is regulated by shared rules.

Competition is a common characteristic of interaction in American society. Jobs, grades, athletic honors, sexual attention, marriage partners, and parental affection are only a few of the scarce resources for which individuals or groups compete. In fact, it is difficult to identify many social situations that do not entail competition. One positive consequence of competition is that it stimulates achievement and heightens people's aspirations. It also, however, often results in personal stress, reduced cooperation, and social inequalities (elaborated on in chapters 7 to 10).

Competition takes place within social structures and scripts that define appropriate strategies. If you are competing for grades, for example, the rules pretty much confine you to two strategies: studying harder and trying to impress the teacher. Cheating or deliberately sabotaging others' performance is illegitimate. In spite of this social structure, the process of competition is often a force for change. As groups and individuals look

Figure 4.1

Cooperation, competition and conflict are basic social processes found in all societies. These photographs depict the people of Idaho Falls cooperating to protect their community from flooding during the 1978 Teton Dam collapse, children competing in a sack race, and a looter facing the police in a direct conflict over scarce resources. These basic social processes are the dynamic aspects of social structure.

for ways in which they can get an edge, they innovate, they redefine, they jockey for position. Just as competition between business firms is often the spur for technological innovation, so competition between individuals and groups often leads to changes in their social structures.

Because competition often results in change, groups that seek to maximize stability often devise elaborate rules to avoid the appearance of competition. Competition is particularly problematic in such informal groups as friendships and marriages. Thus friends who want to stay friends will not compete for valued objects; they might compete over bowling scores, but they won't compete for the same promotion. Similarly, couples who value their marriage will not compete for their children's affection or loyalty. To do so would be to destroy the marriage.

Conflict

When individuals or groups competing for a scarce resource not only try to block others from reaching it but also attempt to neutralize, injure, or eliminate their rivals, **conflict** occurs (Coser, 1956:8). Where conflict is intense, these attempts to block others may result in overt hostility, injury, defeat, or even annihilation. Conflict between the superpowers, for example, carries the threat of nuclear disaster and the potential destruction of society.

A certain amount of conflict is always present in society. It may even have positive consequences. When a group experiences conflict with outsiders, group members often draw closer together and achieve a greater sense of solidarity (Coser, 1956; Simmel, 1955). For example, although Britain's dispute with Argentina over the Falkland Islands cost billions of dollars and hundreds of lives, it also became a rallying point of the Thatcher administration in its effort to demonstrate Britain's strength and military superiority and to restore the pride of the nation.

When conflict takes place within groups, however, the effect is seldom positive. The result is usually destruction of the group or significant alteration in its members' relationships. If, for example, in a competition over their children's loyalties, parents openly criticize each other to the children, competition will have burst into conflict. The parents will have passed the normal boundaries of competition and have begun to try to injure and eliminate their rival. Regardless of who wins, the marriage will be changed—and probably broken. After this episode, one of the parents will define themselves as a loser, the other as a winner. Win, lose, or draw, conflict changes the relationship. Within groups, it is a process of change, not stability.

Conflict is a deliberate attempt to destroy or neutralize one's rivals in order to attain valued ends.

Summary

People interact on the basis of shared norms and values. Sometimes these norms and values take on a structured form, offering a clear script to follow in our interactions. When you interact with your parents, for example, you are all following a script that has been used by others like yourselves for generations. This script provides a structure that defines how your family will cooperate and make exchanges. If it works well, it will regulate the competition between you and your parents and will eliminate conflict. It will constrain your interactions and guide them into well-worn paths. No script fully constrains people, however, and the daily interactions of real and unique human beings—their continual exchanges, cooperations, conflicts, and competitions—can profoundly influence their experiences even in well-defined social structures.

Social Structures

Interaction with others is the substance of social life. When this interaction occurs over and over in a similar way, it is called a social structure. Chapter 1 defined *social structures* informally as the scripts of common human dramas. At this point, the term can be defined more technically: A **social structure** is a network of interconnected statuses and corresponding roles that structure interaction.

Whenever people interact over a period of time, social structures emerge. They develop in families, in neighborhoods, and in dormitories. Some of them endure for many generations; others last only for a school year or less. Regardless of their length, however, social structures give definition and direction to social relationships. The analysis of these structures is one of the central tasks of sociology (Blau, 1964:12.)

Basic Elements of Social Structure

Whether we're talking about baseball games, families, or friendships, social structures can be divided into three components: roles, status networks, and sanctions.

Roles. Although many of the norms in society are universal, others are specialties—they apply to some people and not to others. The norms pertaining to teachers are different from those applying to students. If a teacher skips class, the meaning is entirely different than if a student skips class. The specialty norms are usually organized around **roles,** which specify the rights and obligations of persons performing special functions for a group. The role of student, for example, includes the *right* to expect free inquiry in classes; to have their work evaluated without regard to age, sex, race, or religion; and to have a fair hearing on charges of academic dishonesty. Students also have an *obligation* to attend classes, be honest in their work, respect the right of others to learn, and not disrupt campus activities. Similarly, the role of teacher includes the *right* to expect a decent salary from the school board and respect from students; it includes the *obligation* to provide conscientious instruction.

Being a student or teacher or parent involves many roles. Parents, for example, are supposed to provide financial support, teaching, and care-taking. The collection of roles performed by an individual occupying a specialized position in a particular group is called a **status.** The status of a high school teacher, for example, might have attached to it the roles shown in Figure 4.2.

Status Networks. A status and its roles do not exist independent of other statuses and roles. If we have rights and duties, then these must be

---

A **social structure** is a network of interconnected statuses and corresponding roles that structure interaction.

Roles are the rights and obligations of persons performing special functions for a group.

Status is the collection of roles associated with a specialized position in the group.

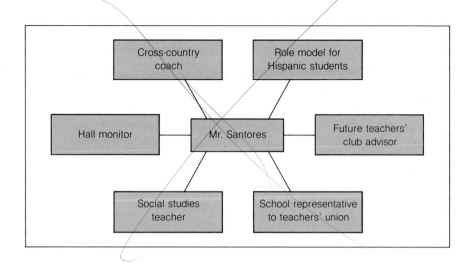

Figure 4.2 The Set of Roles Attached to the Status of High School Teacher
The person holding a particular status is expected to play many roles. Each role includes specific rights and obligations to others.

to someone. In fact, statuses always occur in pairs: teacher/student, parent/child, employer/employee. The interacting statuses within a group, organization, or social system are called a **status network.** The status network of a high school, for example, might look like the one in Figure 4.3. Teachers, administrators, service workers, and students all occupy statuses whose interaction is structured by shared norms and values. They each have duties to one another and rights from one another.

Individuals occupy statuses, but they *play* roles. This vocabulary from the theater is useful in reminding us that some people perform their roles better than others: Some people meet their role expectations and others do not. Have you ever had a teacher who came to class every day and talked about last night's ball game or who took 2 months to grade a major paper and then returned it unread with an "OK" on the last page? The individual who occupies the status of teacher will not necessarily fulfill the duties and obligations normatively associated with it. Thus careful analysis of social structures requires that we distinguish between expected and actual role behavior.

Status network is the total set of interacting statuses within a group, organization, or social system.

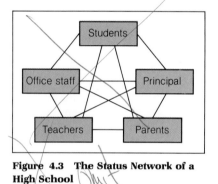

Figure 4.3 The Status Network of a High School

Sanctions. Failure to meet role expectations can have serious results. If just one person in a status network fails to meet obligations, then others are likely to relax their role performance too. If teachers don't discriminate between lazy and hardworking students, then fewer students will work hard. If the system is to work, people must be motivated to meet their role expectations. This motivation is accomplished through **sanctions**— rewards for conformity or penalties for nonconformity. Positive sanctions reinforce conforming role behavior; negative sanctions discourage nonconforming role behavior.

The existence of sanctions increases the probability that we will do as expected. The sanctions can be either symbolic or tangible. For example, individuals who conform may be given a pat on the back, a bonus at work, or a merit badge. Nonconformists may be subjected to embarrassment, rejection, fines, imprisonment, or even death. Positive sanctions increase an individual's integration and prestige within the group; negative sanctions are a form of group withdrawal. Teachers who want raises and praise instead of rude students and hostile colleagues will be motivated to meet

Sanctions are rewards for conformity or penalties for nonconformity.

Figure 4.4
Most social behavior occurs in groups that are socially structured. In the above picture, there are two statuses, teacher and student. Each status has roles that specify what is expected of the occupant. For example, sitting at attention, wearing similar clothing, and following the teachers instructions are socially structured expectations of these students.

Role strain results whenever there are tensions or contradictions built into the role expectations of a particular status.

their obligations; students who want good grades and enthusiastic support instead of failing grades and a cold shoulder will be motivated to meet their obligations.

A System of Action.

Ideally, a social structure is a well-integrated set of statuses; the individuals occupying each status behave according to a shared set of norms and values. When this occurs, the social structure can be visualized as being like a machine: All the cogs, cams, and belts perform their own part in an integrated pattern that produces some outcome. Schools produce educated young people, families produce new generations, and friendship groups produce security and support.

Sometimes, however, the cogs, cams, and belts do not behave as they are supposed to. Husbands beat their wives, schools turn out students who are illiterate, and friends fail to support one another. What accounts for these failures? Are the expectations too high? Are the sanctions inadequate? Is it the fault of individual personality defects? The factors that lead to deviation from normative expectations are reviewed in detail in chapter 7; one that is appropriate to consider here, though, is conflicting expectations caused by multiple roles. Whether these roles are built into the same status (role strain) or into different statuses (role conflict), they may create problems. They can lead to poor role performance and to a sense of personal failure that damages self-esteem and mental health.

Role Strain. Sometimes people fail to fulfill role requirements despite their best intentions. This failure is particularly likely under conditions of **role strain,** where contradictory expectations are built into the same status. Some of the clearest examples of contradictory expectations occur in the family. For example, the wife/mother status includes obligations to both husband and children. Sometimes, a woman is unable to meet both sets of obligations satisfactorily. A 35-year-old woman who takes care of

CONCEPT SUMMARY

Social Structure

CONCEPT	DEFINITION	EDUCATION EXAMPLE
Role	The rights, duties, and obligations associated with a particular group function	Teacher instructs; student studies
Status	A constellation of roles associated with a specialized position in a specific group	Teacher instructs and counsels students and supervises lunchroom activities.
Status network	The total collection of statuses that interact in a particular group	Teachers, students, administrators and staff members
Sanctions	Rewards for conformity and penalties for nonconformity to ensure adequate role performance	Good grades or being kicked out of class; promotions or demotions

a husband, six children, and an aging, sick father speaks of the many role obligations associated with the wife/mother status:

> It feels like somebody's always wanting something from me. Either one of the kids is hanging on to me or pulling at me, or my father needs something. And if it's not them, Tom's always coming after me with that gleam in his eye. Then it's not enough if I just let him have it, because if I don't have a climax, he's not happy. I get so tired of everybody wanting something from me. [Cited in Rubin, 1976:151]

Teachers often experience role strain when they are torn between their obligation to help students learn and their obligation to evaluate student performance. Often teachers spend the most time with the students they will eventually have to fail: Although the student has worked hard and perhaps made substantial progress, performance is still below average. The result may be merely a feeling of discomfort and guilt or it may be that the instructor's concern with helping students gets in the way of a fair assessment of performance.

Role Conflict. A second circumstance in which people are unable to meet all their role requirements occurs under conditons of **role conflict,** where the expectations of two or more statuses are incompatible or inconsistent. College students who try to combine school with work or marriage, or both, often discover that the role demands of one status interfere with the expectations of another. Not surprisingly, a spouse may expect a little attention in the evening, whereas the student role obliges one to stay at the library or lock oneself up in the bedroom to read. An employer is likely to demand overtime at Christmas, which is when a student needs time off to prepare for final exams. In circumstances such as these, it becomes almost inevitable that a person will fail to meet some role obligations. Even with the best will in the world, the person is likely to be regarded as a disappointment by teachers, employers, or spouse.

Role conflict occurs when the role expectations of two or more statuses held by an individual are incompatible or inconsistent.

Mechanisms for Resolving Role Strain and Role Conflict. In complex societies, where people are involved in many social structures and organizations, role strain and role conflict are inevitable. As a result, people may end up disappointing others and themselves. On the individual level, strain and conflict can be the basis for such personality disorders as guilt, anxiety, and aggression; they can also contribute to instability and disorder in society. Yet, in spite of the many potential causes of role strain and conflict, most people remain reasonably sane and most social structures continue to operate. Mechanisms that help people balance multiple roles and participate in diverse groups include role segmentation, establishment of dominant role and withdrawal (Merton, 1957).

ROLE SEGMENTATION. A means of resolving conflicting norms by relegating each set of norms to specific circumstances is **role segmentation** (Merton, 1957:116). Basically, this is a case of "when in Rome, do as the Romans do." The idea of role segmentation draws heavily on the analogy of life as a stage: As we move from scene to scene, we change costumes, get a new script, and come out as a different character. Thus a young man may play

Role segmentation occurs when roles are compartmentalized and used in some situations but not others.

the role of dutiful son at home, heavy-duty partier at the dorm, and serious scholar in the classroom. None of these images is necessarily false; but because the roles are difficult to carry on simultaneously, the young man does not try to do so. Most of us engage in role segmentation without even thinking about it. We adjust our vocabularies, topics of conversation, and apparent values and concerns automatically as we talk to our parents, our friends, and our co-workers. In this sense, we are like the elephant described by the six blind men; somebody trying to find out what we are really like might have a hard time reconciling the different views that we present.

ESTABLISHMENT OF DOMINANT ROLES.   Effective role segmentation requires that we play one role at a time and ignore the obligations associated with other roles. This is not always easy or even possible. In fact, competing demands often develop within the same situation, forcing us to choose between different sets of expectations. If our parents and peers appear in the same scene, which part should we act? One mechanism for making such choices centers on establishing **dominant roles**—assigning priorities to conflicting roles and choosing the most important one. In the movie *Kramer versus Kramer*, Mr. Kramer came to view being a parent as his dominant role; in situations of role conflict, he chose the role demands of fatherhood over those of advertising executive. The establishment of dominant roles helps one avoid conflict and stress by assigning less importance to the potentially threatening roles.

Dominant roles are established when individuals assign priorities to their roles and choose to act in terms of the normative demands of the most important role.

WITHDRAWAL.   Another mechanism sometimes used to resolve role conflict is **withdrawal**. Here individuals choose not to meet the expectations of either role by escaping from the field of conflict. For example, a woman whose union has endorsed the Democratic nominee and whose church has urged her to vote Republican may resolve the conflict by not voting at all; caught in the cross-pressure, she may lose interest in the political campaign. Similarly, college students may be torn between their parents' demand that they come home for Thanksgiving and their professors' equally urgent demand that they finish two term papers before December 1. A not infrequent response in this situation is to do neither. The student may stay at the dorm and spend all the time watching television and being depressed or may go home and spend all the time being surly to the parents.

Withdrawal is a mechanism for resolving role conflict in which individuals choose not to meet the expectations of either role.

Social Structures and Social Groups

Any group of people who interact together for a long period of time will develop a social structure. In informal groups, the structure will be informal, but it will exist. Thus in bridge groups, neighborhoods, and friendships, shared patterns of norms and values emerge in the course of interaction. Here we will see how group interactions are shaped by emerging social structures.

Figure 4.5

In on-going groups, our behavior is socially structured. The rules of the card game structure some of these men's interactions. In addition, these men probably share norms about whether it is permissible to bet, how long they play, where they meet each day and so on.

Social Structure in Groups

The concepts group and social structure almost overlap. A **group** is a set of people whose interactions are guided by a social structure, who have developed patterned ways of interacting on the basis of shared norms and values.

In informal groups, such as those that emerge on dormitory floors, the social structure may be simple. The norms may specify such things as who should be included in the group, who can borrow from whom, how loud stereos can be played, and how much effort you can put into your school work without being considered a drudge. A set of sanctions also exists. People who try to worm their way into a group where they are not wanted, who try to borrow more than is considered acceptable (not only your book and your notes but your whole term paper), or who play their stereos at 6 a.m. will be negatively sanctioned. People who are easy to get along with and who are cooperative and generous will be rewarded with invitations, confidence, and social support. In such a social structure, there will be few well-defined roles, perhaps not many beyond those of follower and leader, insider and outsider. The established social structure, however, will provide some guidelines for interaction. It will set the ground rules for exchange, regulate competition, and try to reduce conflict.

A fundamental observation of sociology is that people who are thrown together for a prolonged period of time will tend to develop a shared social structure to guide their interactions; a group will emerge from the collection of people. Put strangers together on dorm floors, in work groups,

A **group** is a collection of people who interact together on the basis of a shared social structure.

or on desert islands and they will develop a social structure. Following is a brief description of the social structure that has developed among adolescents in an urban Chicano neighborhood.

Dudes and Chicks: Structure and Process on 32nd Street

In the mid 1970s, sociologist Ruth Horowitz (1983) did a participant observation study of Chicano youth in Chicago. She calls their neighborhood 32nd Street, although that is not its real name. It is an older neighborhood, now running to seed, close to Chicago's business district. Its schools are so old and deteriorated that the school board considers them beyond repair. Fifty years ago the neighborhood was inhabited by Italians and Poles and other ethnic groups; by 1960 it began to assume its prominent Hispanic character.

The people who live on 32nd Street are poor by contemporary American standards, but few are on welfare. Instead, they rely on an extensive system of family obligations. Families are large and close. Often, all of a woman's married children will live within six blocks of her. Somebody who is out of work will visit each relative in turn for dinner until work starts again. Of course, the person must reciprocate when other relatives need help.

The values of 32nd Street are in part the values of America. The people want to get ahead, to drive big cars, to dress well, and to be successful. They also subscribe to a set of values from their Mexican heritage that stresses the importance of the family, male dominance, female sexual purity, and honor. Honor is a value that has almost disappeared from the larger American culture. In the Hispanic culture it means receiving proper respect in face-to-face relationships.

The young men and women of 32nd Street form a community. They all know one another and one another's families. Because apartments and homes are small and crowded, they live almost all their social lives outdoors, hanging out in the four city parks that exist within the Chicano community. Through continual interaction, they have evolved norms, roles, and sanctions that structure their lives.

The Dudes: Gangs, Guns, and Honor. The image of manhood in this subculture requires that each man be in control at all times. This means that the man must be free to make his own decisions—free especially of pressure from women but also of pressure from other men. By the time boys are 13 or 14, they are independent of their parents' control. Were a mother to tell her son that he ought to come in on time, quit drinking, or attend school, she would be regarded as robbing him of his manhood and offering him a grievous insult. However, as a man of honor, the boy knows that he must not insult his parents or his sisters and must offer them politeness and respect. This means that although he drinks, he should not insult his mother by coming in drunk. A young heroin addict relates the following incident that led him to admit his problem and enter a treatment program: "I used to steal all the time from my brothers and sisters and went through my old man's pockets many times . . . even stole his watch once and pawned it, but you know when I took some bread (money) from my old lady, then I knew I had to do something. Taking from your old lady's real bad" [Horowitz, 1983:71].

On 32nd Street, maintaining the honor of one's mother, one's sister, one's friends, and oneself is a major activity for young men. For many, this is their dominant role. In case of conflicting roles, for example, whether one should go to school or get in a fight to defend one's honor, the fight will usually win. Horowitz distinguishes three major roles for men, depending on whether they choose honor or achievement as their dominant value.

REALLY BAD DUDES.   The young men who are governed by the code of honor rather than by achievement norms are considered really bad dudes. They spend much of their time fighting. They fight to defend their honor from slights or imagined slights, and they fight to build up their reputations and the amount of respect they can claim from others. This means that not only must they meet every challenge, every insult to their honor, they must also actively challenge others. They have to find others who are reputed to be tougher than they are and insult *their* honor.

Because of the intense amount of fighting going on, the young men form gangs in order to protect one another. The gangs are largely defensive organizations that can be counted on to stand behind their members if the members are challenged. They also defend their part of the neighborhood against intrusions by outside gangs. For the gang to be preserved, no direct competition occurs within it; it is one group in which a man can relax and be free of the constant pressure to challenge and be challenged.

Within each gang there is a status hierarchy based on reputation. This reputation is acquired through fights with outsiders and through the way one handles women. When a younger boy is accepted into the gang, he engages in a fight with two or three of the older boys. Since he is younger, he is expected to lose, and there is no insult to his honor. (One young boy, however, came so close to winning the fight that the older boys had to break his arm in order to protect their honor.)

Being a bad dude is a hard role to drop, and many young men remain part of the street scene long into their 20s. One young man who decided to leave the street life and go to junior college explained why it was so hard to leave: "It's difficult when dudes are chasing you with a gun to turn around and say, 'Hey, wait a minute, I'm not into that shit any more, would you lay off please?' You tell the dudes to cool it, but they ain't going to believe you just like that." [Horowitz, 1983:183]. Since refusing to answer a man's challenge is an insult to his honor and makes him madder yet, it is very difficult for young men to drop out of the street scene without conflict.

REPUTATION DEFENDERS.   Significantly down the status hierarchy on 32nd Street are reputation defenders. These young men care about their reputations and will defend them if challenged; however, they tend to avoid situations where challenges might be made—they do not look for trouble. As a result, they get significantly less respect than the tougher boys. Their

Figure 4.6
In the Chicano neighborhood Horowitz studied, young people value "styling out." Because housing is crowded, young people hang out on street corners and in parks where personal appearance is important to maintaining an image of self-respect. These young people, although poor by contemporary American standards, live in an Hispanic subculture that values Honor as well as the broader values of American culture.

gangs are also less cohesive because they do not form mutual defense units but are more like ordinary friendship groups.

REPUTATION AVOIDERS.   Finally, some boys adopt the role of reputation avoidance. These boys play down the whole issue of honor. If someone insults them, they define it as poor taste or bad manners rather than a direct insult; however, they will fight to defend the honor of their mother or their sisters. For the most part, the reputation avoiders are boys whose major interests lie in the world of conventional achievement: school and work. They are interested in making a place for themselves in the prestige hierarchy of the larger society, not the prestige hierarchy of 32nd Street. Although they are held in low regard on 32nd Street, they do not care. They may live there, but 32nd street is not their world.

The Chicks: Virginity, Submission, and Motherhood.   Within the sub-culture of 32nd Street, girls face a conflicting set of norms: Virginity is highly prized, but so is submission to men. This means that a girl must walk a careful line, maintaining, at least in public, the image of virginity and sexual purity but giving in to her boyfriend's demands.

The image of virginity is carefully guarded by the girl's brothers and other relatives. One 16-year-old girl who was at a dance she probably should not have attended, said to Horowitz:

> Please tell me if you see my brother because I can't drink with him around, he'll beat me. Me and my sisters are not supposed to drink, he doesn't like that. You know when we go to dances on the north side, we got to sneak 'cause if he ever found out he would follow us around and we'd never get to go anywhere. [Horowitz, 1983:67]

Because the girls nevertheless manage to spend a considerable amount of time away from their brothers and their parents, few remain virgins for long. Under certain circumstances, however, they are allowed to maintain a public role as respectable women. (If they are unable to negotiate a respectable identity, then they take on the role of loose women.)

RESPECTABLE WOMEN. Girls can negotiate a role of sexual respectability while still being sexually active, even with a premarital pregnancy. To do so, however, requires that they explain their sexual behavior in terms of passion and submission. To maintain this appearance, they must never wear suggestive clothing or appear to be actively pursuing or inviting male attention, they must not be promiscuous, and they must not take birth control pills. To do any of these things would make it appear that their sexual relations were calculated rather than acts of passion and submis-sion. A pregnancy or even a birth before marriage is not a critical blow to a woman's image of sexual purity. Motherhood is an honorable role on 32nd Street, and an unmarried woman who performs it well may retain her good reputation.

For example, Laura, who had an illegitimate child at 17, would occa-sionally bring her baby to the park after she finished work. Because the baby was always clean and well cared for and because Laura talked to the girls and not the boys, she was referred to by everyone as a good mother. Her reputation remained unsoiled. Importantly, her chances for marriage were not damaged because she was seen as still having the reserve and submissiveness that a woman ought to have. Elena, however, was not saved by motherhood. When she brought her baby to the park, the baby was frequently grubby and in wet diapers. Moreover, Elena would leave the child with the girls while she went over to flirt with the boys. In this case, both the girls and the boys had little respect for her, and it was considered unlikely that anyone would ever marry her.

LOOSE WOMEN.   Like Elena, certain other girls and women on 32nd Street do not maintain a public image of sexual purity. These girls may be unfaithful, may openly chase and flirt with men, may use birth control, or may wear suggestive clothing. They still have a place in the social structure—they still fill a role—but it is a place with few rights and little respect. A gang member remarks about Alicia: "She's OK, she helps us carry the heats [guns], sneaks them into dances, and she'll take them off you if the cops are coming. Remember the time she had that .45 in her kid's carriage with him asleep?" [Horowitz, 1983:127]. None of the fellows on 32nd Street was interested in marrying Alicia, however, and no one would feel compelled to offer her respect or defend her honor.

LIBERATED WOMEN.   There is no role available on 32nd Street for a liberated woman. Women may work, but only for the extras and only if they do not use their income as a lever with which to increase their power in their relationships with men. Husbands or boyfriends, fathers or brothers must always be the bosses. There are a few independent young women on 32nd Street, but they are outcasts. Says a young man: "I can't understand them and where we (men) fit in. They are always going places and doing things without us. They don't seem to *need* us at all. I get confused about how to act with them." [Horowitz, 1983:175].

Summary.   The young people on 32nd Street are engaged in frequent and, for many, lifelong interactions. These interactions have become patterned. Several definite roles are open for boys and girls, each governed by a set of norms that define what is appropriate and inappropriate for people occupying the roles. The patterns that have developed on 32nd Street help the young people cooperate and make exchanges with one another, help regulate competition so it doesn't harm ongoing groups, and help direct conflict in ways that support rather than challenge the values of the community. The social structure helps the people adapt to life in their community.

Institutions as Social Structures

Social structures provide routine ways of interacting that help people adapt to their circumstances; they are problem solvers. Some of the circumstances to which people must adapt are constant and predictable. Every society, for example, must deal with the problems of producing new generations, of caring for infants and other dependents, of providing food

Figure 4.7
Each society provides a set of ready-made social structures to guide common interactions. The family is one of these. People who grow up in our society know that a family like the one shown here is the socially approved goal toward which they should aim. Knowing this—and achieving it—provides a sense of belongingness and stability. If this is not the kind of family you want, however, you may find society's expectations oppressive.

Institutions are relatively stable clusters of interconnected statuses and roles centered around the basic needs of society.

and shelter, and of maintaining social order. As a society evolves, the solutions to these problems become embedded in its culture as **institutions**—enduring social structures that provide ready-made answers to basic human problems.

Basic Institutions

Modern society has five basic institutions: family, economy, government, education, and religion. The family provides a solution to the universal problem of caring for dependents and rearing children. The economy provides a solution to the universal problem of producing and distributing goods. The government provides for social order and the control of conflict. Education ensures that the new generation is trained to step into the statuses of the old. Religion provides answers to the apparently universal question: Why?

The social structures that have evolved to deal with these universal problems are many and varied. In simple societies, the solutions are contained within one major social institution—the family or kinship group (Adams, 1971:90). In these societies all the basic needs (production, reproduction, education, and defense) are organized and met through social relationships based on kinship obligations. The family institution is also a political, economic, educational, and religious institution.

As societies grow larger and more complex, the kinship structure is less able to provide solutions to all the recurrent problems. As a result, some activities gradually are transferred to more specialized social structures outside the family. Thus the economy, education, religion, and government become fully developed institutionalized structures that exist separately from the family. (The institutions of the contemporary United States are the subjects of chapters 11 to 15.)

As the social and physical environment of a society changes and the technology for dealing with that environment expands, the problems that individuals have to face increase. Thus institutional structures are not static; new structures emerge to cope with new problems.

Among the more recent social structures to be institutionalized in Western society are medicine, science, sport, the military, law, and the criminal justice system. Each of these areas can be viewed as an enduring social structure, complete with interrelated statuses and a unique set of norms and values. (Chapter 16 reviews the social structures of medicine, science, and sport as secondary institutions that have grown up to meet new problems.)

Institutional Interdependence

Each institution of society can be analyzed as an independent structure, but none really stands alone. Instead, institutions are interdependent; each affects the others. This occurs on both a structural and an individual level. As individuals, we occupy statuses in many institutions simultaneously. Our status in one institution is likely to affect our status and behavior in another. On the macro level, the actions of one institution are likely to affect the actions of others.

In a stable society, the values underlying one institution will usually be compatible with those underlying other institutions. Thus a society that stresses male dominance and the rule of the elderly in the family will also stress the same values in its religion, its economy, and its political system. What happens, however, when expert knowledge rather than landholding becomes the basis of the economy, when achievement rather than hereditary position becomes the chief criterion for economic reward? Can this alternative set of values be contained within the economic institution, or is it likely to spill over and contaminate other institutions? The sociological answer is that of course other institutions will change too. In the case of Western culture, the break-up of traditional rule in the economy has had the effect of breaking up the traditional political structure (monarchy) and, increasingly, the traditional family structure. In short, the notion of institutional interdependence means that you can never change only one thing. A change in one institution almost always leads to changes in other institutions.

Institutions: Agents of Stability or Oppression?

Sociologists use two major theoretical frameworks to approach the study of social structures: structural functionalism and conflict theory. The first looks at the way institutions meet universal needs; the second looks at the constraints imposed by institutions.

A Structural-Functionalist View of Institutions. Institutions develop in response to both the individual and the collective needs of society's members. One of the most important aspects of institutions is that they regulate human behavior and provide the basis for social order. They pattern conduct and compel people to follow grooves established by earlier generations (Berger, 1963:87). By providing such standard patterns, they are an important agent for producing conformity, stability, and predictability in social interaction.

As people participate in society, acquiring institutional statuses and roles, they learn what is approved of and acceptable as well as what is disapproved of and forbidden. Membership in such institutional groups as family, church, and school links people to status networks that encourage conformity to role expectations.

A Conflict View of Institutions.   By the very fact that they regulate human behavior and direct choices, institutions also constrain behavior. By producing predictability, they reduce innovation; by giving security, they reduce freedom.

Granted that there are universal human problems for which society must provide institutionalized answers; still, any particular institutionalized pattern will favor one group over another. The grooves into which institutions force people are likely to be those that serve the status quo, that help keep the rich rich and the poor poor. The antisocial behavior that institutions help eliminate is often merely behavior that challenges the current distribution of power and wealth.

A conflict theorist interprets the normative structures of institutions as mechanisms for disguising inequality. For example, the normative structure of the traditional family directs the wife to be subordinate to her husband. Women who fulfill this role may never even consider the issue of how the inequality is created or maintained; they fulfill the role without question because they have learned that women should be subordinate to their husbands. When subordinates accept the norms that subjugate them, then we say that inequality is institutionalized. Institutionalized norms in our culture also assign greater value to pleasant white-collar jobs than to physically demanding blue-collar jobs; these norms help maintain the income and prestige of the educated. The cloak of tradition obscures the way inequality is created and maintained in society and helps to reduce opposition to it.

Institutions stifle social change by giving normative support to the status quo. The family, capitalism, and religion become not merely one way of fulfilling a particular need but the only acceptable way.

Summary.   Institutions create order and stability; in doing so, they suppress change. In creating order, they preserve the status quo. In regulating, they constrain. In this sense, both conflict and structural-functional theories are right; they simply place a different value judgment on stability and order. The two theoretical perspectives prompt us to ask somewhat different questions about social structures. Structural functionalism prompts us to ask how an institution contributes to order, to stability, and to meeting the needs of society and the individual. Conflict theory prompts us to ask about which groups are benefiting the most from the system and how they are seeking to maintain their advantage. Both are worthwhile questions, and both will be addressed when social structures ranging from deviance to science are looked at (in chapters 7 to 16).

The Mormon Challenge

In the early part of the 19th century, several religious groups in the United States attempted to establish social structures that were radically different from the existing institutional structures. Among the more successful of these groups were the Mormons, a religious group that began in New York in 1830 and migrated to the Utah Territory in the decade before the Civil War. The almost complete absence of any other settlers in the Utah Territory plus the large and growing number of Mormons (150,000 by 1880) allowed for the full flowering of Mormon institutions.

The Mormons challenged three traditional American institutions: the family, the economy, and the separation of church and state. First, the Mormons endorsed the practice of polygyny, a form of plural marriage in which men are allowed to have more than 1 wife. It is estimated that approximately 10 percent of Mormon men had more than 1 wife. Of these, most had 2 or 3 wives, although one church leader, Brigham Young, had 27 (Young, 1954). Second, the Mormons practiced a collective form of economic organization called the United Order. Under church sponsorship, cooperative economic enterprises were established throughout Mormon communities: retail stores, various factories and mills, banking and finance. Patronizing Mormon businesses was considered a sign of religious loyalty. The communal economic system challenged the value of free enterprise and made it virtually impossible for outsiders to compete. Third, the religious and economic integration of church members was supplemented by political integration through the People's Party, a political party directed by church leaders. Thus the Mormons formed an integrated unit in Utah; religious leaders were also political and economic leaders.

Throughout the second half of the 19th century the economic and political power of the Mormon church grew rapidly. The church came to dominate the Utah Territory, and non-Mormons were not welcome there. As the church grew, so did its opposition. Much of the opposition was directed at plural marriage, but in retrospect it seems clear that economic and political areas were also important.

Shortly after the Civil War a series of federal laws prohibiting some of the Mormon practices were passed. The Edmunds Act of 1882 provided heavy penalties for plural marriages, including the loss of voting rights and of the right to hold office. Although officially aimed at preventing plural marriages, the law had the effect of removing Mormon leaders from political office and destroying the political power of the Mormon leadership in the Utah Territory. In 1886, the Edmunds-Tucker Act reinforced the penalties for polygyny and prohibited the Mormon church from holding property.

Initially, Mormons evaded the consequences of these laws. Plural marriages were performed by the church, not in the civil courts, and the corporate holdings of the church were transferred to individual church leaders. Continued pressure from federal and territorial officials, however, eventually drove many church leaders into hiding or jail. During this period, considerable church property was confiscated,

Figure 4.8
The practice of polygyny in the 19th century allowed some well-to-do Mormon men to have several wives. This patriarch, Joseph F. Smith, appears to have had at least four wives and dozens of children. The practice of polygyny flourished for approximately 40 years but was finally abandoned by the church in 1890.

undermining the communal economic organization of Mormon communities.

By 1890, the Mormon church surrendered. The president of the church issued a manifesto that officially ended the practice of plural marriages (and the church's challenge to the institution of monogamous marriage). The People's Party was dissolved, and the collective economic efforts of the church were substantially reduced. In exchange, convicted polygynists were granted amnesty and some church property was returned. In 1896, the Utah Territory was granted statehood, bringing to a close one of the most radical challenges to the basic institutions of 19th century American society.

In the 1980s, the Mormon church remains a central institution in the state of Utah. Over 75 percent of the population of Utah belongs to the Mormon church, and the church continues to dominate the political and economic life of the state. The entire congressional delegation from Utah (two senators and two representatives) is Mormon, as are the governor and much of the state legislature (Barone & Ujifusa, 1981). The Mormon church holds extensive property in Utah and elsewhere and is believed to be the richest church in the United States on the basis of holdings per member (Kephart, 1983). And although the Mormon church officially opposes polygyny, splinter groups have broken away from the church in order to maintain the practice. Because it is illegal, there is no official count of how many people practice polygyny in Utah today. One plural wife, however, suggests that there are more practicing polygynists in Utah today than there were a century ago (Kephart, 1983:271).

Questions to Consider

1. How does this example illustrate institutional interdependence? Could American society have accepted plural marriage without changing some of its other institutions?
2. How would a structural-functionalist interpret the outcome of this challenge? How would a conflict theorist's interpretation differ?

Types of Societies

In chapter 3, *society* was defined as a territorially organized group of people who are bound together by political and economic dependence. This definition is one way of saying that society is a territorially defined group that shares common institutions. Its members live under the same government and the same economic system and share similar religions and educational and family systems.

Across human history there have been many different kinds of societies, each characterized by a different arrangement of basic institutions. In some societies, the military has been dominant; in others, it has been the church or the economy. Whatever the circumstance, scholars have found that understanding the basic institutions of society and the relationships between them is the first step toward understanding society itself.

The history of human societies is the story of ever-growing institutional complexity. In simple societies, there was only the family; in modern societies, there may be a dozen institutions. What causes this explosion of institutions? The triggering event appears to come from changes in the economic institution. The knowledge and technology of food production and the relative abundance or scarcity of food have enormous implications for institutional patterns.

In this section we will briefly review three revolutions in food production knowledge and technology. We will also see how changes in this one institution have had profound effects on society.

Figure 4.9
These people in Upper Volta are digging in a dry river bed for the potato-like roots of water lilies. Their economy provides a bare subsistence and continuous dedication to finding enough to eat prevents the development of elaborate institutions beyond the family.

Hunting, Fishing, and Gathering Societies

The chief characteristic of hunting, fishing, and gathering societies is that they have subsistence economies. This means that in a good year they produce barely enough to get by on; that is, they produce no surplus. There are, of course, years when game and fruit are plentiful, but there are also many years when starvation is a constant companion. The techniques used to produce food are primitive and inefficient; as a result, members of the society must often spend hours each day in the search for necessities.

The basic units of social organization are the household and the local clan, both of which are based primarily on family bonds and kinship ties. Most of the activities of hunting and gathering are organized around these units. A clan rarely exceeds 50 people in size and tends to be nomadic or seminomadic. Because of their lack of leisure to produce luxury goods and because of their frequent wanderings, members of these societies accumulate few personal possessions.

The division of labor is simple, based solely on age and sex. The common pattern is for men to participate in hunting and deep-sea fishing and for women to participate in gathering, shore fishing, and preserving. Although women often contribute half of all the food, they occupy a status inferior to that of men (Lenski, 1966). Aside from inequalities of status by age and sex, there are few structured inequalities in subsistence economies. Members possess little wealth; there are few, if any, hereditary privileges; and the societies are almost always too small to develop class distinctions. In fact, a major characteristic of subsistence societies is that individuals are homogeneous or alike. Apart from differences by age and sex, members generally have the same everyday experiences.

Horticultural Societies

The first major breakthrough from subsistence economy to economic surplus was the development of agriculture. When humans changed from harvesting whatever nature provided to planting and cultivating crops, stable horticultural societies developed. The technology was often primitive—a digging stick, occasionally a rudimentary hoe—but it produced a surplus.

The regular production of more than the bare necessities revolutionized society. It meant that some people could take time off from basic production and turn to other pursuits: art, religion, writing, and frequently warfare. Of course, the people who participate in these alternate activities are not picked at random; there develops instead a class hierarchy between the peasants, who must devote their full time to food production, and those who live off them.

Because of relative abundance and a settled way of life, horticultural societies tend to develop complex and stable institutions outside the family. Some economic activity is carried on outside the family, a religious structure with full-time priests may develop, and a stable system of government—complete with bureaucrats, tax officers, and a hereditary ruler—often develops. Such societies are sometimes very large. The Inca empire, for example, covered an estimated population of over 4 million.

Agricultural Societies

Approximately 5,000 to 6,000 years ago there was a second revolution, in agriculture, and the efficiency of food production was doubled and redoubled through better technology. The advances included the harnessing

Figure 4.10

Agricultural societies typically produce more surplus than simple hunting and gathering societies, but relatively primitive technology keeps surplus small. Only by ruthlessly taking the excess from workers like these can the society support a small elite class of bureaucrats, scholars, and artisans.

of animals, the development of metal tools, the use of the wheel, and improved knowledge of irrigation and fertilization. These changes in material culture dramatically altered social institutions.

The major advances in technology meant that even more people could be freed from direct production. The many people not tied directly to the land congregated together, and large urban centers became possible. In these centers, there developed a complex division of labor. Technology, trade, reading and writing, science, and art grew rapidly as larger and larger numbers of people were able to devote full time to these pursuits. Along with greater specialization and occupational diversity came greater inequality. In the place of the rather simple class structure of horticultural societies grew a complex class system of merchants, soldiers, scholars, officials, and kings—and, of course, the poor peasants on whose labor they all ultimately depended. This last group still contained the vast bulk of the society, probably at least 90 percent of the population (Sjoberg, 1960).

One of the common uses to which societies put their new leisure and their new technology was warfare. With the domestication of the horse (cavalry) and the invention of the wheel (chariot warfare), military technology became more advanced and efficient. Military might was used as a means to gain even greater surplus through conquering other peoples. The Romans were so successful at this that they managed to turn the peoples of the entire Mediterranean basin into a peasant class that supported a ruling elite in Italy.

Industrial Societies

The third major revolution in knowledge and technology appeared only 200 years ago in Western Europe with the onset of industrialization: the substitution of mechanical, electrical, and gasoline energy for human and animal labor. Prior to the industrial revolution, most of the energy used for production was based on muscle power, either of humans or of domestic animals. In the United States, in 1850, muscle power accounted for 65 percent of the energy used for work; water, wind, and wood accounted for another 28 percent. A century later, the combined energy of these sources supplied only 1.6 percent of the energy used for work (Lenski, 1966). The new energy resources of hydroelectric power and fossil fuels (coal, petroleum, and natural gas) became the drivers of industry.

Launched by the development of science and technology, the knowledge base of industrial societies exploded, transforming predominantly agricultural societies into societies based on the mechanized production of goods. In the space of a few decades, the work activities of vast numbers of people shifted from rural farm labor to urban factory production. The enormous increases in available energy, in technology, and in knowledge meant that less than 5 percent of the population had to be involved in direct production, freeing the rest of the population for other activities. In more recent decades, this revolution has continued, freeing the bulk of the work force not only from agricultural production but also from industrial production. The overall effect on society was to transform its political, social, and economic character.

Figure 4.11

With industrial technology, it is possible for a small proportion of the population to produce rich surpluses of food. This frees the large majority of the population for less-essential tasks such as research, health care, and industrial production. The large surpluses also make it possible to reduce the amount of inequality that exists in society.

Industrialization stimulated urbanization, mass education, and ever-greater technological development and specialization. Life expectancies doubled and tripled, and the standard of living for the average citizen increased tremendously. For the first time in the history of humankind, there was a reversal in the evolutionary trend toward increasing inequality. As people became more literate and more involved in politics and community affairs, there was a corresponding shift toward the common person in legislation and politics. Various programs, ranging from FDR's New Deal to Johnson's Great Society reflect policy and legislation designed to ensure a greater measure of equality for all of society's members.

CONCEPT SUMMARY

Types of Societies

HUNTING, FISHING, AND GATHERING

Technology:	Very simple—arrows, fire, baskets
Economy:	Bare subsistence, no surplus
Settlements:	None—very small (bands of under 50 people)
Inequality:	Very little—differentiation by age and sex only
Social organization:	All resting within family
Examples:	Plains Indians, Eskimos

HORTICULTURAL SOCIETIES

Technology:	Digging sticks, occasionally blade tools
Economy:	Simple crop cultivation, some surplus and exchange
Settlements:	Semipermanent—some cities, occasionally kingdoms
Inequality:	Substantial inequality between food producers and rulers
Social organization:	Military, government, religion becoming distinct social units
Examples:	Mayans, Incas, Egyptians under the pharaohs

AGRICULTURAL SOCIETIES

Technology:	Irrigation, fertilization, metallurgy, animal power used to increase agricultural productivity
Economy:	Largely agricultural, but much surplus; increased market exchange and substantial trade
Settlements:	Permanent—urbanization becoming important, empires covering continents
Inequality:	Great inequality
Social organization:	Educational, military, religious, and political institutions are well developed
Examples:	Roman empire, feudal Europe, Chinese empire

INDUSTRIAL SOCIETIES

Technology:	New energy sources (coal, gas, electricity) leading to mechanization of production
Economy:	Industrial—few engaged in agriculture or direct production; much surplus; fully developed market economy
Settlements:	Permanent—urban living predominating, nation-states
Inequality:	Vast abundance leading to reduction in inequality in comparison with agricultural societies
Social organization:	Complex set of interdependent institutions
Examples:	Contemporary United States, Europe, Japan

Theoretical Overview

After examining this description of the evolution of societies—from simple subsistence economies whose only well-developed institution is the family to industrial economies with complex institutional structures—it is reasonable for us to consider what such a tale says about the nature of society. It is immediately apparent that this evolutionary picture of human societies shows the economy as the driving force. The level of technology and the organization of food production are the major causes of change and the major determinants of social organization. This description appears to be straight Marxist economic determinism. It is. It is also, however, compatible with structural-functional theory, in which institutions arise in order to meet the basic needs of society—the first of which, of course, is to produce enough food to sustain the population. Thus structural-functional theory also assumes that the way societies solve this basic problem will have a vital influence on how other institutions develop.

Whether Marxist or conservative, whether conflict theorists or structural functionalists, sociologists who study institutions and societies give great importance to economic institutions and relationships. Future chapters, on deviance (7), stratification (8), racial and ethnic relationships (9), and urbanization (18), will be directly concerned with economic relationships and inequalities.

The Mental Illness of Women

Learning to recognize the importance of social structure in determining individual behavior is a crucial turning point in many areas of social policy. Why do people abuse their children, have illegitimate children, or go crazy? Is it because they have unique personality disorders? Or is their deviance in some way socially structured? In the first explanation the blame is placed on the individual, and correction of the deviance requires individual treatment or therapy; it is a personal trouble. In the second explanation the blame rests on the social structure, and correction of the deviance requires structural change—a public issue.

One of the differences between social work and sociology is the emphasis each places on individual versus structural causes of deviance. In the case of a failed marriage, a social worker is likely to look for an explanation in terms of the individuals' inability to communicate or to compromise. The sociologist is more likely to look for role strain and role conflict—the larger structural forces that make marriage difficult to sustain.

As one example, consider the insanity of women. Study after study has shown that women are more likely than men to say they are unhappy, to report symptoms of neurosis, and to be admitted to mental institutions. Why? Is it because women are biologically more predisposed to mental illness? Because the sex roles of women make it less threatening for them to admit to mental illness? Or is it because the particular roles women play in society drive them crazy?

Gove (1972) considered each of these explanations and concluded that the greater amount of mental illness in women is due to the social structure of marriage and the roles that married women play. If either the first or the second explanation were correct, women would show mental illness rates greater than men's in almost all comparisons. Instead, Gove found that unmarried women (whether never married, widowed, or divorced) are less likely than unmarried men to be mentally ill. In fact, the greater rate of mental illness in women occurs only for the married.

Gove suggested that the contemporary social role of wife is more stressful than that of husband. Several reasons exist for this interpretation. First, a married man can get gratification and a feeling of self-esteem from both his work roles and his family roles, whereas a married woman is often confined to family roles. Second, the social role of housewife has relatively low prestige and allows little opportunity to demonstrate intellectual or technical competence. Third, even if a married woman works, she is less likely than her husband to have a job commensurate with her education. Points 2 and 3 are potentially more stressful as women's educational levels increase.

Finally, Gove suggested that the rapid change in women's roles has created a great deal of role conflict. If a wife/mother works, she may feel guilty about not preparing gourmet meals each night and about being too tired for her family; if she decides not to work, she may be resentful of her lack of income or feel guilty about her free time. And no matter which role she chooses, there will be somebody to suggest that her choice was the wrong one.

Is the mental Illness of women an individual or a structural problem? Although structural analysis does not point directly to social policy solutions to this problem, it takes the first step by helping us define the nature of the problem.

SUMMARY

1. Sociology is about how people structure their social interactions. This means that we need to look at both the dynamics of their interactions (social processes) and at the established patterns that guide the interactions (social structures).

2. There are four basic social processes: exchange, cooperation, competition, and conflict. Exchange and cooperation are generally mechanisms for maintaining social structures; competition and conflict are more likely to be sources of change.

3. Whenever people interact over a period of time, social structures develop. Each structure can be divided into three components: roles, status networks, and sanctions. When the parts are properly integrated, they produce a system of action.

4. Roles are the active part of a status. We occupy a status, but we play a role. Sanctions work to encourage good performance or punish bad performance.

5. Each of us occupies multiple roles—roles that may not complement one another. Role failure may result from conflicting roles within a single status (role strain) or from conflicting roles in two or more statuses (role conflict). Role segmentation, dominant role establishment, and withdrawal are means of dealing with role conflict and role strain.

6. Because societies share common human needs, they also share common institutions. The common institutions are family, economy, government, education, and religion. Each society has some enduring social structure to perform these functions for the group.

7. Institutions serve to regulate behavior and to maintain stability of interaction over the generations. They promote stability rather than change and, by regulating behavior, constrain it into the patterns established by previous generations.

8. Institutions are interdependent; none stands alone, and a change in one results in changes in others. On the individual level, status in one institution affects status and role performance in another.

9. An important determinant of institutional development and inequality is the ability of a society to produce a surplus. Each major improvement in food-producing efficiency has led to revolutionary changes in the institutional patterns of societies.

10. Sociologists differ from social workers in that they usually look for socially structured rather than individual causes of personal problems. Instead of viewing deviance as a personal trouble, they are likely to look for role conflict and role strain. As a result, sociologists may see the solution to deviance as being a change in institutional arrangements rather than rehabilitation of the individual.

SUGGESTED READINGS

Erikson, Kai T. (1976). Everything in Its Path: Destruction of Community in the Buffalo Creek Flood. New York: Simon & Schuster. A sociologist's look at the devastating effects of a natural disaster on a community's social structure.

Horowitz, Ruth. (1983). Honor and the American Dream: Culture and Identity in a Chicano Community. New Brunswick, N.J.: Rutgers University Press. An ethnographic community study that focuses on the social structure of a Chicano community, especially the differences in role expectations for young adult men and women.

Lenski, Gerhard. (1966). Power and Privilege: A Theory of Social Stratification. New York: McGraw-Hill. A major work distinguishing the fundamental characteristics of different types of societies, particularly in terms of socially structured inequality.

Merton, Robert K. (1968). Social Theory and Social Structure (enl. ed.). New York: Free Press. Uses structural-functional theory to draw out the basic concepts and relationships used in the analysis of social structures. Bureaucracies, deviance, religion, and politics are only a few of the illustrations used to show the application of these concepts.

O'Dea, Thomas F. (1957). The Mormons. Chicago: University of Chicago Press. An interesting and readable sociological account of the unique development and growth of Mormonism. The religious organization as a social structure embedded in the society of an isolated people gives uniqueness to the history and development of the Mormon church.

Rubin, Lillian. (1978). Worlds of Pain. New York: Basic Books. A detailed study of working-class families based on in-depth interviews. This penetrating description illustrates how the social processes and social structure of American society affect the working class.

Spiro, Melford E. (1963). Kibbutz: Venture in Utopia. New York: Schocken Books. An anthropologist analyzes the basic aspects of social structure that have been designed by young Jewish adults in their attempts to create a utopia. Both successes and failures are examined.

UNIT TWO

Conformity and Nonconformity

CHAPTER 5

Socialization

PROLOGUE

Have You Ever . . . wondered why some kids are so awful? They swear at their mothers, steal from their friends, and are not even kind to dumb animals. These same kids may have brothers and sisters who get along with their folks, and seem to be decent human beings. How do people come to be so different?

You have probably been tempted to think that they must have been born that way. It is just possible that biological factors may have something to do with it. More importantly, however, people have different experiences in life. They get different amounts of attention, have different friends, and develop different styles of interaction. In this chapter, we will examine the processes by which we learn to be the people we are—how we come to act like other Americans and yet like no other American.

In chapter 3 we examined how differences in culture affect our behavior—how we learn to become Americans or Koreans or Germans. In this chapter we examine the learning process more closely. How is it that individuals come to accept the norms and values of their culture? What accounts for individual differences within the same culture, community, and family? How do we come to be the people we are?

Learning to Be Human: The Beginning Steps

What is human nature? Are we born with a tendency to be cooperative and sharing or with a tendency to be selfish and aggressive? The question of the basic nature of humankind has been a staple of philosophical debate for thousands of years. It continues to be a topic of debate because it is so difficult (some would say impossible) to separate the part of human behavior that arises from our genetic heritage from the part that is developed after birth. The one thing we are sure of is that nature is never enough.

The Necessity of Nurture

Each of us begins life with a set of human potentials: the potential to talk, to walk, to love, and to learn. By themselves, however, these natural capacities are not enough to enable us to join the human family. Nature is never enough. Without nurture—without love and attention and hugging—the human infant is unlikely to survive, much less prosper. The effects of neglect are sometimes fatal and, depending on severity and length, almost always result in retarded intellectual and social development.

How can we determine the importance of nurture? There are a few case studies of tragically neglected children, but luckily the instances are rare. Some of the first clinical evidence on the effects of limited social interaction on human development was provided by René Spitz's (1945) study of an orphanage where each nurse was in charge of a dozen or more infants. Although the children's physical needs were met, there was little time for nurses to give individual attention to each child.

Children who spend the first years of their lives in this type of institutional environment are devastated by the experience. Because of limited personal attention, such children withdraw from the social world; they seldom cry and are indifferent to everything around them. The absence of handling, touching, and movement is the major cause of this retarded development. In time, the children become increasingly retarded intellectually and more susceptible to disease and death. Of the 88 children Spitz studied, 23 died before reaching the age of 2½. Even if they live, Spitz found, socially deprived children are likely to become socially crippled adults.

A number of studies confirm the effects of institutionalized care described by Spitz (see, for example, Bowlby, 1969: Rutter, 1974). Provence and Lipton (1962) compared 75 physically healthy institutionalized infants with a control group of infants raised at home. The institutionalized infants received excellent food and physical care but limited social stimulation. During the first few weeks of life, there was little difference between the two groups. At about 3 months, however, the institutionalized infants showed increasing signs of retardation. They seldom cried or babbled, lost interest in their surroundings, and by the age of 1 were noticeably retarded in their language development. Because the infants were healthy to begin with, physical and genetic abnormalities cannot have caused their disabilities. Provence and Lipton concluded that the differences between the control group and the institutionalized infants clearly indicate the devastating effects of deprivation. In recent years, the medical profession has described this condition of neglect, isolation, and absence of mothering as an **environmental deprivation syndrome.**

Deprivation can also occur in homes where parents fail to provide adequate social and emotional stimulation. Children who have their physical needs met but are otherwise ignored by their parents have been found

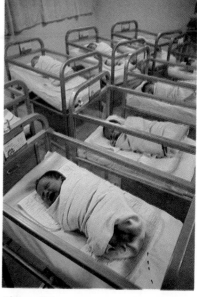

Figure 5.1

Social scientists generally assume that, at birth, the human infant does not possess a self concept or sense of individual identity. Rather, there exists a potential for development which is influenced by the infant's environment. As this picture of newborns illustrates, infant male and female children are handled and treated quite differently. As they are nurtured, acquire motor and language skills, and experience society, a self concept and sense of individual identity emerges consistent with their different experiences.

Environmental deprivation syndrome is a condition of neglect, isolation, and absence of mothering.

Anna and Isabelle

Two of the more thoroughly documented case studies of socially isolated children are Anna and Isabelle (Davis, 1940, 1947). These girls, discovered in the 1930s, had been kept in seclusion for several years because they were illegitimate.

Anna. On February 6, 1938, the *New York Times* carried a story of a child, age 5, who had been confined to the attic room of a farmhouse in Pennsylvania for nearly her entire life. She was the second of two illegitimate children of a young woman who shared the farmhouse with her parents. Because of the shame associated with illegitimacy, the maternal grandfather hid the child in an upper room, where she was fed almost nothing but milk. She was not bathed or trained in personal hygiene. She received virtually no personal attention and spent most of her time in a crib or in a half-reclining, half-sitting position in a chair tilted against a coal bucket. When she was finally discovered, she could not walk, talk, or do anything that showed normal intelligence. She had skeletal legs and a bloated abdomen.

After her discovery, Anna was placed first in the county home, then with foster parents, and later in a special school for defectives. At first she stayed in a supine position, immobile and apathetic. By all appearances, she was deaf and dumb. With a sound diet and physical therapy, her posture and motor coordination improved rapidly. Two years later, at the age of 7, she could walk, chew food, control bowel and bladder elimination, follow simple commands, and remember people. Her mental ability was that of a 19-month-old, and her score on a social maturity scale was 23 months. Anna never recovered from the effects of her isolation and died 3 years later at the age of 10.

Isabelle. In November 1938, a 6-year-old girl named Isabelle was discovered in Ohio living with her mother in a secluded dark room. Her mother was a deaf-mute, and Isabelle was illegitimate. Isabelle's grandfather locked both mother and daughter away in order to reduce the embarrassment their presence caused. When Isabelle was found, her legs had been deformed by rickets (probably from improper diet and lack of sunshine), she walked with a skittering gait, and she could not speak, although she made certain croaking sounds and simple gestures. Her reaction toward strangers, especially men, was almost like that of a wild animal; she exhibited much fear and hostility. At first it was thought that, like her mother, Isabelle was deaf. When it was discovered that she could hear, she was given various intelligence tests and pronounced feeble-minded. It was the general impression that she could not be educated and that any attempts to teach her to speak after so long a period of silence would end in failure.

Despite poor initial performance, Isabelle's caretakers started her on a systematic program of training using pantomime and dramatization. Within a few weeks, she was trying to talk. Her ability to learn accelerated, and within 2 years she had acquired knowledge and skills that ordinarily take 6 years to develop. Starting from an educational level somewhere between 1 and 3 years, she reached a normal level by the age of 8½. At the age of 14 she was in the 6th grade and doing well in both her schoolwork and her social-emotional adjustment to her classmates.

The extreme experiences of Anna and Isabelle give important insight into human development in the absence of interaction. To become fully human—to talk, to laugh, to love, even to walk—requires being with humans.

Questions to Consider

What differences do you note between the situations of Anna and Isabelle that might explain why Anna died and Isabelle eventually recovered?

to exhibit many of the same symptoms as institutionalized infants. In some cases, lack of stimulation can result in deprivation dwarfism, a glandular disturbance that slows normal growth (Gardner, 1972). Once children with this type of dwarfism are placed in nurturant homes, they quickly recover and grow rather rapidly.

Studies of the effects of isolation and deprivation on children suggest that children need intensive interaction with others in order to survive

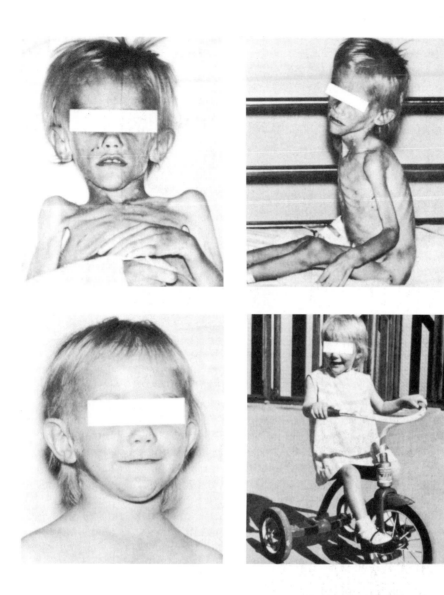

Figure 5.2
This child was admitted to the University of Colorado Medical Center for treatment of environmental deprivation syndrome, a condition produced by neglect, an absence of mothering, and in this case abuse. Five weeks after treatment, Jody's physical condition has improved dramatically. Recovery in terms of social, emotional, and intellectual development is typically slower.

and develop normally. Much of the evidence for this conclusion, however, is derived from atypical situations in which unfortunate children have been subjected to extreme and unusual circumstances. In order to assess the limits of these findings and to examine the reversibility of deprivation effects, researchers have turned to experiments with monkeys.

Monkeying with Isolation and Deprivation

For more than 20 years, researchers have been experimenting with mother deprivation and isolation of infant monkeys. In a classic series of experiments, Harry Harlow and his associates raised infant monkeys in total isolation. The infants lived in individual cages with a mechanical mother figure, which provided milk. Although the infant monkeys' nutritional needs were met, their social needs were not. As a result, both their physical

Figure 5.3

Social scientists assume that normal development requires both tactile stimulation and nurturance. Harry Harlow's studies of infant monkeys raised under different conditions show the importance of close bodily contact. This infant clings to a terry cloth surrogate for psychological comfort when threatened by strange objects placed in the cage even though the wire mesh surrogate is the source of food. Infant monkeys left alone with just the wire mesh surrogate typically show fear and anxiety towards a strange object, reject the surrogate, and cower in the corner of the cage until the object is removed.

and social growth suffered. They exhibited such bizarre behavior as biting themselves and hiding in corners. As adults, these monkeys refused to mate; if artificially impregnated, the females would not nurse or care for their babies (Harlow & Harlow, 1966). These experiments provide dramatic evidence about the importance of being with others; even apparently innate behaviors such as sexuality and maternal behavior must be developed through interaction. On the bright side, the monkey experiments affirm that some of the ill effects of isolation and deprivation are reversible. As with the children suffering from deprivation dwarfism, young monkeys experienced almost total recovery when placed in a supportive social environment (Suomi, et al., 1972).

Summary.   Although it is dangerous to generalize from monkeys to humans, the evidence from the monkey experiments confirms the observations about human infants: Physical and social development depends on interaction with others. Even being a monkey does not come naturally. To walk, to talk, to love, and to laugh all depend on sustained and intimate interaction with others. Clearly, our identities, even our lives, are socially bestowed and socially sustained (Berger, 1963:98).

Socialization Theory

From the moment of birth, we are continuously learning. We learn about ourselves and about society, about what we want for ourselves and what society wants for us. Research on learning takes place in two rather different contexts. Within the field of psychology, emphasis is placed on the development of **personality**—the unique attributes and abilities of the individual. Sociology is concerned primarily with socialization—the process of learning the roles, statuses, and values necessary for participation in social institutions. Psychology concentrates more on the unique, sociology more on the shared.

Bridging both psychology and sociology is a concern for **self-concept**—our assessment of how our personality characteristics and our role performance compare to others'. It is a composite of our feelings about our personality (do you hate yourself because you never know what to say?) and our perception of our social roles. We are students, daughters or sons, perhaps short-order cooks, parents, or bus drivers. Are our roles valuable or degrading? Do we play them well or poorly? The self-concept reflects all of these things. It is an image of self that we develop by comparing ourselves to others.

Within the field of sociology, theories about socialization and the development of the self-concept are dominated by symbolic interactionism. In addition, sociological perspectives on learning have been influenced by two perspectives from psychology: behaviorism and developmental theory. After reviewing the contributions of symbolic interactionism, we will look briefly at the two perspectives.

Symbolic Interactionism

The theory of **symbolic interactionism** emphasizes interaction, negotiation and role-taking as mechanisms for learning social roles and self-concept. Three premises are contained in this definition:

1. People interact on the basis of symbols (gestures, words), which are subjectively interpreted (Turner, 1978).
2. Roles and self-concept are created and re-created through a process of negotiation (Gecas, 1981).
3. We learn social norms and acquire our self-concept by playing roles.

The Self.   In common with other theories of human development, symbolic interactionism divides the human personality into two parts. One part responds to our individual desires and wants; the other responds to social demands for appropriate behavior. Together the parts form the **self**, a complex blend of individual motivations and socially desirable responses. George Herbert Mead (1934) called the two parts of the self the *I* and the *me*. In English grammar, *me* is used when we speak of ourselves as the object of others' actions; *I* is used when we are the actor. Sociological use follows this convention. *Me* is the self as social object, the part of the self that responds to others; *I*, by contrast, is the spontaneous, impulsive part of the self; it may lead us to act on impulse without consulting the me.

As this description of the self implies, the two parts may pull us in different directions. For example, many people face a daily conflict between their I and their me when the alarm clock goes off in the morning—the I wants to roll over and go back to sleep, but the me knows it is supposed to get up and go to class. Some of these conflicts are resolved in favor of the me and some in favor of the I.

Personality is the unique attributes and abilities of the individual.

Socialization is the process of learning the roles, statuses, and values necessary for participation in social institutions.

Self-concept is the individual's evaluation of his or her personality and social roles in comparison to others'.

Symbolic interactionism addresses the subjective meanings of human acts and the processes through which people come to develop and communicate shared meanings. It emphasizes interaction, negotiation, and role-taking as mechanisms for learning social roles and self-identity.

The **self** consists of two parts, one (the I) responding to individual needs and the other (the me) responding to social demands.

This distinction between the I and the me is similar to the Freudian distinction between the id (basic impulsive nature) and the superego (conscience, or learned morality). Unlike Freudian theory, however, symbolic interactionism does not assume that the I represents unlearned or instinctual motivations. Rather, it assumes that the I represents learned personality characteristics as well as innate impulses. Thus both aspects of self may be learned. How is this learning accomplished?

Looking-Glass Self.   Charles Horton Cooley (1902) provided a classic description of how we develop our self-concept. He proposed that we learn to view ourselves as others view us. He called this the **looking-glass self.** According to Cooley, there are three steps in the formation of the looking-glass self:

1. We imagine how we appear to others.
2. We imagine how others judge our appearance.
3. We develop feelings about and responses to these judgments.

The **looking-glass self** is Cooley's term for a self-concept that is based on how we think we appear to others.

For example, an instructor whose students openly talk to each other or doze during class and who frequently finds himself talking to a half-empty room is likely to gather that his students think he is a bad teacher. He need not, however, accept this view of himself. The third stage in the formation of the looking-glass self suggests that the instructor may either accept the students' judgment and conclude that he is a bad teacher or reject their judgment and conclude that the students are simply not smart enough to appreciate his profound remarks. Thus our self-concept is not merely a mechanical reflection of those around us; rather it rests on our interpretations of and reactions to those judgments. We are actively engaged in defining our self-concept, using past experiences as one aid in interpreting others' responses. Thus a person who considers herself witty will assume that others are laughing with her, not at her; someone used to making clumsy errors, however, will derive the opposite interpretation from the laughter.

We also actively define our self-concept by choosing among potential looking-glasses. That is, we try to choose roles and associates supportive of our self-concept (Gecas & Schwalbe, 1983). The looking-glass is thus a way of both forming and maintaining self-concept.

As Cooley's theory indicates, symbolic interactionism considers subjective interpretations to be extremely important determinants of the self-concept. It is not only others' judgments of us that matter; our subjective interpretation of those judgments is equally important. This premise of symbolic interactionism is apparent in W. I. Thomas's classic statement: If people "define situations as real, they are real in their consequences" (Thomas & Thomas, 1928:572). People interact through the medium of symbols (words, gestures) that must be subjectively interpreted. The interpretations have real consequences—even if they are *mis*-interpretations.

Figure 5.4
Each of us negotiates a self concept. Based on the reflections we receive from others and the ways we interpret our interaction with others, we develop a sense of who we are. If our personality and the roles we play are well received, we may, like this young woman, think we're terrific. If we play socially devalued roles or play valuable roles poorly, however, we may develop a poor self concept.

Role Theory.   The most influential contributor to symbolic-interaction theory during this century is George Herbert Mead. Mead argued that we learn who we are during the process of learning roles. Eventually, the roles we play become the me; they shape and direct the conforming part of our self.

According to Mead, role-learning begins in childhood, when we learn the rights and obligations associated with being a child in our particular family. In order to understand what is expected of us as children, we must also learn our mother's and father's roles. We must learn to see ourselves from our parents' perspective and to evaluate our behavior from their point of view. Only when we have learned their roles as well as our own will we really understand what our own obligations are.

Mead maintained that children develop their role knowledge by playing games. When children play house, they develop their ideas of how husbands, wives, and children relate to one another. As the little boy comes in saying "I've had a hard day; I hope it's not my turn to cook dinner," or as the little girl warns her dolls not to play in the street and to wash their hands before eating, they are testing their knowledge of family role expectations. By doing so, they clarify what is expected of them in their role and the norms that govern family life.

In the very early years, role-playing and role-learning are responsive to the expectations of **significant others**—those who occupy roles that deal intimately with us. Parents, siblings, and teachers, for example, are decisive in forming a child's self-concept. As children mature and participate beyond this close and familiar network, the process of role-learning helps them understand what society in general expects of them. They learn what the bus driver, their friends, and their employers expect. Eventually, they come to be able to judge their behavior not only from the perspective of significant others but also from what Mead calls the **generalized other**—the composite expectations of all the other role-players with whom they interact. Being aware of the expectations of the generalized other is equivalent to having learned the norms and values of the culture. One has learned how to act like an American or a Pole or a Nigerian.

If we learn through interaction, a crucial question is: Who will we interact with? The answer is determined largely by the social roles we occupy (Stryker, 1981:23). Professors, for example, interact largely with other professors and with students. Thus, if 40-year-old professors seem to be different from 40-year-old lawyers, a major factor is that the professor role determines that the person playing it will spend a major portion of each day interacting with 18- to 22-year-old students.

Role theory suggests that the social roles we acquire shape both our behavior and personality. If your first job after college is in a counseling office, you may believe that your role requirements include a pair of sandals; you will have to develop a style of interaction that is open, accepting, and relaxed. If you get a job in a law office, you may believe that you have to acquire a briefcase, a three-piece suit, and a style of interaction that demonstrates your analytic steel-trap mind.

Role theory views the self as a performance, a product of specific social roles. If you change your roles, you will also change your self. In this sense, social roles can be viewed as the bridge between social structure and self-concept (see Figure 5.5). The roles we play and the quality of our performance are the basis for our self and our self-concept.

Because each of us has multiple statuses and roles, we also have multiple **role identities** (Burke, 1980:18). For example, a woman who is a professor, a wife, and an aerobics student will have a different role identity in each setting. Her self-concept will be a composite of these multiple identities

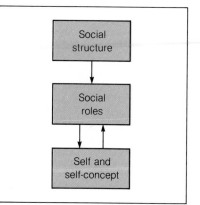

Figure 5.5 Social Roles as the Bridge between Social Structure and Self-Concept
Participation in social structures such as the family determines many of the social roles we play. These roles in turn shape our self and our self-concept. To some extent, however, we may choose social roles on the basis of their compatibility with our previously developed self-concept.

Significant others are those occupying roles that deal intimately with us.

The **generalized other** is Mead's term for our awareness of social norms; it is the composite expectations of all the other role-players with whom we interact.

Role theory suggests that the social roles we acquire shape both our behavior and personality.

Role identity is our evaluation of our performance in a specific social role.

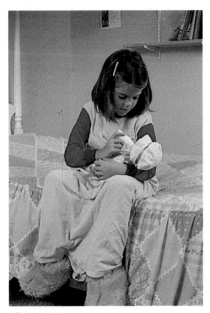

Figure 5.6

By assuming the role of mother, this child behaves toward her doll in much the same way her own mother behaves toward her. Mead suggests that throughout our lives we learn about ourselves by playing roles, first in the context of our families and later in larger and less intimate social structures. This process involves learning what others expect of role occupants and learning to evaluate ourselves in terms of these generalized expectations.

The **mutable self** is a self-concept based more on personality characteristics than on institutional statuses and roles; it is highly flexible and adaptable.

(Stryker, 1981). Some role identities are more important than others. Those that are most important tend to be merged into our self-definition. Thus the norms and values we hold as a result of our dominant roles tend to become part of our personality and definition of self.

Research suggests that in choosing dominant roles, we give preference to roles that provide us with the most positive self-image. Thus the high school student who does poorly in class but is an excellent athlete is likely to choose athlete as a dominant role and to base the self-concept on the requirements of this role. Coaches and teammates become the most important looking-glass. Students who cannot throw balls or run, swim, or do flips are likely to base their self-concept on their performance in the classroom, on the dance floor, or wherever it is that they excel.

The Mutable Self.   If the self is a product of the roles we play, then it follows that our self-concept changes when we change roles. As we take on new roles—become parents or managers or spouses—our identities change. A corollary of this is that a stable self-concept depends on a relatively stable set of roles. If our roles are in flux, our self-concept will be too.

A number of scholars have suggested that the rapid pace of change in modern society makes it difficult for many of us to maintain stable role identities. Many will experience career changes; 50 percent are likely to change spouses. Because of the temporary nature of many modern roles, it has been suggested that the basic source of self-concept has shifted away from institutionalized social roles toward personality (Berger et al., 1972; Sennett, 1978; Turner, 1976; Zurcher, 1977). The shift in the determinants of self has been described as the development of a **mutable self.** This new self-concept is highly adaptable and flexible (Zurcher, 1977), but it also provides less stability.

Over the years, the Twenty Questions Test has been the primary research instrument for measuring self-concept. In this test, the respondent simply completes 20 statements that begin "I am ...." The statements are then coded into those that reflect institutionalized roles and statuses (for example, I am a student, I am a female, I am middle class) and those that reflect personality (for example, I am selfish, I am competitive).

Twenty-five years ago, this technique showed that most college students tended to think of themselves in terms of institutional statuses and identities. Today's students are more apt to think of themselves in terms of their personality characteristics. They tend to view their institutional statuses as instrumental: temporary roles they have assumed in order to earn a living or reach some goal. They do not see these roles as becoming an integral part of their self-concept (Zurcher, 1977; Snow & Phillips, 1982). A late 1970s study of 1,125 college students showed that fully two-thirds of their statements reflected noninstitutional identity concepts and only 16 percent reflected institutionalized roles (Snow & Phillips, 1982). These findings do not suggest that role theory is wrong. They do, however, emphasize the fact that the longer you play a role, the more likely it will be to affect your self-concept. Roles that you play for only a short time are unlikely to become important determinants of your self-concept.

Negotiated Identity.   Implicit in the discussion of role theory and Cooley's looking-glass self is the notion of an active individual creating a personal identity. In fact, the central idea of symbolic interactionism is that we negotiate our identity by choosing to accept or reject others' judgments and by choosing which roles will be dominant. Of course, we do not have complete freedom of choice. Most importantly, we cannot choose our parents. Whether they are rich or poor, zany or humorless, black or white, rural or urban, they form our first looking-glass. Their roles help determine the roles we will play. Yet our self is not something directly imposed upon us; rather it is something that emerges during the process of interaction.

A striking example of the negotiation of self-concept is the consistent research finding that black adolescents have greater feelings of self-esteem than do white adolescents. Given the conditions of our society, one might have predicted the opposite. The high self-esteem of black youths reflects the process of identity negotiation. Through selective perception of others' judgments, through judicious selection of dominant roles, and through emphasis on the importance of noninstitutionalized characteristics, black youths develop a largely positive reflection of themselves (Hoelter, 1982).

According to symbolic interactionists, then, social roles and self-concept emerge from a process of negotiation between the self and others. This view of interaction as negotiated scripts for role-playing is explicit in the dramaturgical perspective.

Dramaturgy.   Role theory's emphasis on the importance of social roles as a basis of learning provides the foundation for a relatively new perspective in sociology, **dramaturgy.** Using the theater as a metaphor for social life, this perspective analyzes the ways in which our behavior is guided by social roles. In the words of Shakespeare:

> All the world's a stage
> And all the men and women merely players:
> They have their exits and their entrances;
> And one man in his time plays many parts. [*As You Like It*, Act II, Scene 7]

The dramaturgical view of social interaction is concerned primarily with the sociology of everyday life. It analyzes the rituals that we use to structure such common encounters as those with strangers on elevators, people passed on sidewalks, and greetings of acquaintances. For example, when we meet an acquaintance on the street, we engage in the ritual greeting: "Hi, how are you?" "Fine, fine. And how about you?" So far the encounter has followed the common script for this everyday scene. If your friend deviates from the script and starts to tell you about his health problems, however, you may be taken aback. A situation has come up that is not covered in the script, and you are going to have to improvise. Dramaturgy is concerned with understanding the norms that govern such everyday situations and the ways individuals negotiate their roles.

The chief architect of the dramaturgical perspective is Erving Goffman (1959, 1963). To Goffman, all the world is a stage. There is both a front region, where the performance is given, and a back region, where rehearsals take place and behavior inappropriate for the stage may appear. For example, in the dining room of an expensive restaurant, a waiter is

Dramaturgy is a version of role theory that views social situations as scenes, complete with stages, actors, scripts, props, and audiences.

acutely aware of being on stage and he acts in a dignified and formal manner. However, once in the kitchen, his behavior and bearing may be dramatically transformed. He may swear at the chef because the soup isn't ready, scratch himself, or just slouch down to have a smoke.

The ultimate back region for most of us, the place where we can be our real selves, is at home. Even here, however, front-region behavior is called for when company comes. ("Oh yes, we always keep our house this clean.") On such occasions, the spouses function as a team in a performance designed to manage their guests' impressions. People who were screaming at each other before the doorbell rang suddenly start calling each other dear and honey. The guests are the audience, and they too play a role. By seeming to believe the team's act (Goffman calls this giving deference), they contribute to a successful evening.

One of the central concepts of the dramaturgical perspective is the **art of impression management.** The actor or team tries to control the conduct of others by influencing the way the audience views the situation and the actor. By selecting among appropriate roles, costumes, and props, people can manipulate and manage performances to convey the desired impression.

Summary. Symbolic interactionism is a broad theoretical perspective that includes role theory and dramaturgy as well as other interpretations. It helps us understand how infants born in the United States learn to become recognizably American and yet still retain enough individuality so that none is exactly like any other. A brief review of two other learning theories—behaviorism and developmental theory—illuminates some of the constraints within which symbolic interaction takes place.

Behaviorism

In the first half of this century, behaviorist theory became an important influence on the development of psychology. **Behaviorism** assumes that we are motivated by the desire to avoid pain and receive pleasure. It argues that we learn to repeat behaviors that produce rewards and avoid behaviors that give us pain. A child, for example, learns that keeping his room clean makes his mother cooperative and generous. The first time he cleaned his room may have been because he was bored. Now that he has found out that it brings rewards, however, he may continue to do it (especially if he wants something). He will also learn that following norms is generally rewarding and that breaking them often leads to hassles and unpleasantness.

This model of learning is often called a stimulus-response model. It argues that every act produces consequences. These consequences become stimuli (feedback) that affect the likelihood that we will repeat the act. If the behavior is rewarded, we will repeat it. If it is punished or, worse, ignored by those around us, then we will eventually cease to engage in it. Behaviorism is not concerned with the motivations, desires, or impulses that led us to engage in the behavior in the first place. It attempts only to explain the processes by which we learn that such behaviors should or should not be repeated in the future.

The **art of impression management** is the attempt to control others' conduct and influence their definition of the situation and their impression of the actor.

Behaviorism assumes that individual acts are conditioned by events external to the individual. We learn to repeat behavior that brings rewards and avoid behaviors that give us pain.

Behaviorism had its foundations in a series of classic experiments performed by Pavlov. Pavlov rang a bell every time he fed his dog, and the dog soon learned to associate bell-ringing with eating. Within a short period, Pavlov could make the dog salivate simply by ringing the bell. Behaviorism argues that this same process of learning can be used to shape, or condition, human behavior. John Watson, an American who is generally considered to be the founder of modern behaviorism, demonstrated this point by training a baby to fear the furry animals he previously had loved. Watson wrote:

> Give me a dozen healthy infants, well formed, and my own special world to bring them up in and I'll guarantee to take anyone at random and train him to become any type of specialist I might select—doctor, lawyer, artist, merchant chief, and yes, even beggar and thief, regardless of his talents, penchants, tendencies, abilities, vocations and race of his ancestors. [1958:104]

The most radical version of behaviorism is contained in the works of contemporary psychologist B. F. Skinner (1948, 1971). Skinner argues that behaviorist techniques could be used to produce a truly good society. All we would have to do is decide what behaviors we wanted to encourage and see that they were rewarded; we would also have to define the behaviors that we wanted to eliminate and see that they were punished or at least unrewarded. In his book *Walden II*, Skinner describes such an ideal society.

Nobody has yet applied Skinner's techniques on a societal level, but they have been extensively applied in treatment settings. Skinner's theory (known as behavior modification, or B-mod) is used with nursery school children, with the mentally ill, in drug and alcohol treatment centers, and even in marriage counseling. In one application, prison psychologists tried to teach child molesters that assaulting children was unrewarding. The offenders were shown pictures of children and, when they showed signs

Figure 5.7
Behaviorists, such as B. F. Skinner, assume that behavior is a response to rewards and punishments from our environment. Through closely controlling all aspects of a person's environment, desirable behavior can be reinforced and undesirable behavior extinguished. The extreme version of this assumption is the "Skinner Box" where the rewards and punishments of an infant's environment are continuously monitored.

of sexual arousal, received an unpleasant shock (Kennedy, 1976). The analogy to Pavlov's dog is direct: When the offender saw a small child, he would think pain.

Such tactics are extremely controversial—and now illegal to use on involuntary subjects (Kazdin, 1978). Moreover, there is little evidence that B-mod can be used to bring about long-lasting behavioral changes (Schwitzgebel & Kolb, 1974:83). Since it does not seek to change attitudes and values, people often revert to their old patterns of behavior once they are away from the experimental environment.

Despite some practical successes in modifying behavior, at least in the short run, there is much criticism of behaviorism as a theory of human learning. One criticism concerns the ethics of modifying people's behavior, and another concerns the lack of attention to individual motives and processes.

The ethical criticism of behaviorism takes aim at the appropriateness of deliberately manipulating human behavior. Skinner's talk of building a perfect society by extinguishing all undesirable behavior scares many people. What is undesirable—long hair, belief or disbelief in God, being childless or having four children? What right did Watson have to deliberately frighten a child? This ethical concern is not a matter of whether behaviorism works but whether it should be used.

The second major criticism is that behaviorism may be able to change behavior, but it cannot explain it. Behaviorism ignores the subjective interpretations that are the heart of symbolic interactionism. Instead, it argues that regardless of the individual's values, self-concept, and personality, a judicious blend of reinforcers will change behavior. For many people, this is an unsatisfactory explanation; it treats individuals as merely passive objects rather than as actors who are actively engaged in determining their own fate.

Developmental Theory

Cognitive Development.   All of us recognize that the development of bones, teeth, and secondary sexual characteristics is related to physical maturation. These changes occur in an age-graded sequence that is predictable under normal conditions. What is less recognized is that thought processes also take time to develop and that the readiness for developing specific abilities is predicated on age. **Developmental theory,** pioneered by Jean Piaget, assumes that there are a series of stages in cognitive development that correspond to physiological maturation. Just as we must learn to walk before we can run, Piaget suggested, we must learn how to master early ways of knowing before we can advance to higher levels of reasoning. Piaget (1929, 1932) identified four stages in cognitive development:

Developmental theory assumes that there are a series of stages of cognitive and moral development that correspond to physiological maturation.

1. *Sensorimotor stage (0 to 2 years).* For approximately the first 2 years of life, the child's cognitive structure is limited primarily to organizing sensory experience. Thumb-sucking, grasping, smiling, and crying are sensory experiences related to the rewards and punishments of the immediate environment. In the beginning, the infant's actions are largely reflexive,

Figure 5.8
These ten year old boys have reached what child psychologist, Jean Piaget, calls the concrete operations stage of development. They can reason about the logical relationship between the chain and the gear sprocket—and, they can attempt to fix it. In order to reach this level of analytical ability, Piaget believes children must first pass through two prior stages of cognitive development. Because logical thinking depends upon these earlier stages of development, Piaget suggests that younger children are unable to master the mechanical relationships of a bicycle.

but gradually they become organized and integrated into a higher level of complexity. By the age of 2, children are able to begin solving problems in their environment symbolically.

2. *Preoperational stage (2 to 7 years).* This stage is marked by the acquisition of language, which greatly increases the capacity for representational thought and symbolic play. For example, children can now pretend that small sticks are cars, soldiers, or tanks. They also understand that objects have permanence and continue to exist even when out of sight. During this stage, however, children are extremely egocentric and are unable to take the point of view of others.

3. *Concrete operations stage (7 to 11 years).* The ability to think logically about concrete objects develops rapidly at this stage. Children are able to recognize that certain properties of an object remain constant even though the object's appearance may change (for example, pouring liquid from a glass into a differently shaped glass). They are able to reason about the whole and parts of the whole simultaneously, arrange objects into classes, think numerically, and construct mental images of complex actions.

4. *Formal operations stage (12 + years).* At this stage, the capacity for abstract reasoning and logic is developed. Children are able to deal with assertions, propositions, and quasideductive reasoning. This form of reasoning is considered to be quite advanced; not all adults reach this level.

Moral Development. Piaget's theory is concerned primarily with the development of cognitive structures. Harvard education specialist Lawrence Kohlberg (1980) suggests that children's ability to make moral decisions about right and wrong parallels the development of cognitive structures. At first, children judge their actions in terms of obedience and the physical consequences of misbehaving. If a behavior leads to punishment, then it should not be done. In time, children learn that certain acts bring rewards and that it is in their best interest to act in ways that bring these rewards. Kohlberg calls this self-centered period *hedonistic morality.*

As children grow older, they acquire conventional morality. Attending to rules and social conventions and receiving the approval of others become more important than immediate gratification. This good-boy/nice-girl orientation is closely associated with children's ability to conceptualize their actions in the light of what others are doing.

Eventually, Kohlberg believes, individuals acquire a law-and-order orientation to morality. At this stage of moral development, the established rules and laws of society require respect for authority and observation of the law because it is the law. With increased experience, individuals may reach a more advanced level of morality, where they think about how to improve the rules of conduct (legalistic orientation) within society. In the highest stage of moral development, behavior is guided by moral principles—principles that are followed even if they contradict the law or established social rules.

Kohlberg's stages of moral development are summarized as follows:

Preconventional Level
1. Punishment and obedience orientation.
2. Hedonistic orientation.

Conventional Level
3. Good-boy/nice-girl orientation.
4. Law-and-order orientation.

Postconventional Level
5. Social contract or legalistic orientation.
6. Orientation of universal ethical principles.

Research on children supports Kohlberg's argument that moral development, like physical and cognitive development, is a process of maturation (Kuhn et al., 1977). Because advanced stages of moral reasoning require the manipulation of complex symbolic structures, the progress of moral reasoning tends to parallel the acquisition of language skills and the ability to think abstractly. These characteristics are rarely found in 3-year-olds or even 10-year-olds.

Socialization Theory: A Review and Integration

The three major theories of socialization that have been discussed differ substantially. Symbolic interactionism stresses the role of the actor in learning and negotiating roles during the process of interaction. Behaviorism stresses the extent to which learning is determined by the reinforcers provided by the environment. Developmental theory stresses the stagelike unfolding of human cognitive and moral processes that corresponds to physiological maturation.

In spite of their differences, the three theories of behavior are not incompatible. Neither a developmentalist nor a symbolic interactionist would deny that we learn to repeat behavior that is rewarding to us. Both, however, would stress the importance of individual evaluation of rewards. For example, we read daily about people who are arrested, jailed, and harassed for demonstrating against nuclear power and nuclear armament. These people are being punished, yet they persist in their behavior. Does their persistence contradict behaviorist principles? No. At higher levels of moral development, people receive more gratification from following their principles than they do from conventional rewards.

Similarly, symbolic interactionists would not disagree that learning is affected by rewards and punishments. They would simply argue that rewards and punishments are symbolically communicated and received, filtered through the social roles and personality of the individual.

The core of learning theory in sociology is that we learn our social roles and our self-concept by interacting with others. What we learn depends on our social environment and our previous learnings and experiences.

Socialization over the Life Course

Socialization is a lifelong process. Our self-concept and initial social roles are learned in childhood, but we continue to learn new roles and to renegotiate our self-concept throughout our lives. Each time we join a new group or assume a new role, we learn new norms and redefine our identity. Both the form and content of socialization, however, vary over the life course. The three major kinds of socialization are primary socialization, anticipatory socialization, and resocialization.

Primary Socialization

Early childhood socialization is called **primary socialization.** It is primary in the sense that it occurs first and is vital for later development. During this period, children develop personality and self-concept, acquire motor abilities, reasoning, and language skills, become aware of significant others, and are exposed to a social world consisting of roles, values, and norms.

During the period of primary socialization, children are expected to learn and embrace the norms and values of the society. They learn that conforming to the rules is an important key to gaining acceptance and

Primary socialization is personality development and role learning that occurs during early childhood.

Figure 5.9

Anticipatory socialization prepares us for the roles we will occupy at a later stage in the life course. These boys are being shown how to use a hand saw and miter box. In other contexts, they will also learn attitudes, values, and social skills centered on what will be expected of them as fathers, husbands, and neighbors. As this photograph suggests, much of the anticipatory socialization that goes on in the United States reflects traditional sex role expectations.

love, first from significant others and then from a larger network. Because they care about others, they learn to become conforming members of society—people to whom following the rules comes naturally. If this learning does not take place in childhood, then conformity is exceptionally difficult to develop in later life.

Continuing Socialization

As we progress from infancy to old age, we must continually shed old roles and adopt new ones in the process of **role transition.** Many of our role transitions are relatively easy because of **anticipatory socialization**—role-learning that prepares us for roles we are likely to assume in the future. Because of this socialization, most of us are more-or-less prepared for the responsibilities we will face as spouses, parents, and workers. Goals have been established, skills acquired, and attitudes developed that prepare us to accept and even embrace adult roles.

With disconcerting frequency, however, individuals find that their anticipatory socializaton has taught them the ideal norms about their new statuses rather than the real norms. Thus people who marry at 18 to escape the hassles of living with their parents may not be fully aware of the different kinds of hassles that come with maintaining a home, a spouse, and a child. The statement of a 33-year-old automobile painter, the father of three, married 13 years, illustrates the point:

> I had to work from the time I was thirteen and turn over most of my pay to my mother to help pay the bills. By the time I was nineteen, I had been working for all those years and I didn't have anything—*not a thing.* I used to think a lot about how when I got married, I would finally get to keep my money for myself. I guess that sounds a little crazy when I think about it now because I have to support the wife and kids. I don't know *what* I was thinking about, but I never thought about that then. [Rubin, 1976:56–57]

This man was naive, but he did know what was expected of him. He knew he was supposed to spend his money on his family first and himself later; he just didn't understand how little was likely to be left over. As this quotation suggests, it is seldom possible to prepare fully for a new role. No matter how many books we read or how many others we observe, we still find that a new job, a new spouse, or a new child requires some on-the-job training.

Resocialization

The most extreme example of role transition comes about when we exchange our established self-concept for an entirely different one. **Resocialization** occurs when we abandon our self-concept and way of life for a radically different one. Changing the social behavior, values, and self-concept acquired over a lifetime of experience is difficult, and few people undertake the change voluntarily.

A tragic example of resocialization occurs when people become permanently disabled. Those who become paralyzed experience intense resocialization to adjust to their handicap. All of a sudden, their social roles and capacities are changed. Their old self-concept no longer covers the

---

Role transition is the process of shedding old roles and adopting new roles over the life course.

Anticipatory socialization is role-learning designed to prepare the individual for future roles.

Resocialization occurs when we abandon our self-concept and way of life for one that is radically different.

Figure 5.10
People with spinal cord injuries which impair normal motor abilities and body functions are almost always confronted with extremely difficult adjustments. Not only must they adjust to more limited physical ability, but their whole sense of self must be redefined. Resocializing mature individuals typically requires a radical redefinition of self-worth. New role expectations and attitudes supporting a radically different life-style and view of self are required in order to participate in society and avoid being labeled or treated as a shut in.

situation. They may have lost bladder and bowel control, they are severely limited in their ability to get around, and they may be incapable of full sexual functioning. If they are single, they must face the fact that they are unlikely ever to marry and become parents; if they are older, they have to reevaluate their adequacy as spouses or parents. These changes require a radical redefinition of self. If the self-concept is to remain positive, priorities will have to be rearranged and new, less active roles given prominence.

Resocialization may also be deliberately imposed by society. When an individual's behavior leads to social problems—as is the case with habitual criminals, problem alcoholics, and the mentally disturbed—society may decree that the individual must abandon the old identity and accept a more conventional one.

Total Institutions.   Most of those attempting to resocialize people assume that a radical change in self-concept requires a radical change in environment. Drug counseling one night a week is not likely to drastically alter the self-concept of a teenager who spends the rest of the week among kids who are constantly stoned. Thus the first step in the resocialization process is to isolate the individual from the past environment.

Monasteries, prisons, and mental hospitals are designed for this purpose. They are **total institutions,** controlling all aspects of inmates' lives (Goffman, 1961). Within them, past statuses are wiped away. The old social roles and relationships that formed the basis of self-concept are systematically eliminated. New statuses are symbolized by regulation clothing, rigidly scheduled activity, and new relationships. Inmates are encouraged to engage in self-analysis and self-criticism, a process intended to reveal the inferiority of past perspectives, attachments, and statuses.

Total institutions are facilities in which all aspects of life are strictly controlled for the purpose of radical resocialization.

A Case Study: Moonie Socialization and Resocialization.   People who join the Unification Church (Moonies) must radically alter their life-styles,

Figure 5.11
Our learning and the development of a self-concept is influenced by many factors. In the early formative years, parents are particularly important sources of socialization. The environments they provide as well as their values and beliefs determine in large part our own personality and self concept. Through indoctrination and training, these youngsters are developing the attitudes, values and practices of relatively small minority group in the United States.

values, and beliefs. They must reject their old identity and often their old relationships. How does the church attract volunteers for such a radical program?

The recruitment strategy of the Unification Church does not emphasize the higher truth of church doctrine. Instead, it offers the promise of fellowship and love. The Moonies refer to this process as love bombing—overwhelming the individual with the embrace and welcome of the group. Like other resocialization programs, this one stresses

1. Segregating or isolating new recruits from competing social environments.
2. Controlling the interaction of new recruits.
3. Placing novices in groups where they have identifiable roles to play.
4. Giving novices an activity to perform (for example, street-hawking or working in one of the church's economic enterprises).

New members are kept very busy each day giving religious testimony on the street, giving and listening to lectures, attending church functions, and so on (Robbins et al., 1975:115). In addition, both eating and sleeping rhythms are altered to throw novices off balance and to keep them too tired or too busy for independent action or thought.

Taken together, these efforts have proven to be successful strategies of recruitment, particularly among young adults. They have not, however, contributed to long-term commitments; the average recruit remains only 2 years (Long & Hadden, 1983). One reason for the high rate of defection is the unresolved disparity between American cultural norms and the norms of the church. The organizational structure of the church provides few opportunities for upward mobility, something that most young Americans have learned to value. Moonie doctrine also places a 3-year ban on marriage and sexual relationships, a difficult requirement for young people who are at the peak marrying age. The combined effects of weak doctrinal commitment, limited opportunities for upward mobility, and a 3-year period of celibacy prove to be too much for many converts. People socialized from infancy to value achievement, marriage, and family living cannot easily give it all up.

The church's recruitment strategies, especially segregation and isolation, have caused a great deal of tension in families. Irate parents have hired deprogrammers to kidnap their children and rescue them from the clutches of the church. When this happens, the convert must once again be resocialized, this time abandoning the church identity and resuming the old identity.

Agents of Socialization

Socialization is a continual process of learning. Each time we encounter new experiences, we are challenged to make new interpretations of who we are and where we fit into society. This challenge is most evident when we make major role transitions—when we leave home for the first time, join the military, change careers, or get divorced, for example. Each of these shifts requires us to expand our skills, adjust our attitudes, and accommodate ourselves to new social roles. Child psychologists have noted that these periods of transition tend to herald both intellectual and moral growth. They constitute a crisis that challenges our old assumptions about ourselves and prompt a fundamental reappraisal of who we are.

Learning takes place in many contexts. We learn at home, in school and church, on the job, from our friends, and from television. These agents of socialization have a profound effect on the development of personality, self-concept, and the social roles we assume.

Family

The most important agent of socialization is the family. As the tragic cases of child neglect and the monkey experiments so clearly demonstrate, the initial warmth and nurturance we receive at home is essential to normal emotional and physical development. In addition, our parents are our first teachers. From them we learn to tie our shoes and hold a pencil, and from them we also learn the goals and aspirations that will stay with us for the rest of our lives.

The activities required to meet the physical needs of a newborn provide the initial basis for social interaction. Feeding and diaper-changing provide opportunities for cuddling and for smiling at and singing and talking to the baby. These nurturant activities are all vital to the infant's social and physical development. This is one reason, of course, why breast-feeding is often recommended over bottle-feeding; the mother cannot leave the child in a crib with a bottle but must stay with the child, giving it warmth, eye contact, and baby talk. Whether these interactions take place at breast or bottle, they are essential; without them, the child's social, emotional, and physical growth will be stunted (Gardner, 1972; Lynch, 1979; Provence & Lipton, 1962; Spitz, 1945).

In addition to these basic developmental tasks, the child has a staggering amount of learning to do before becoming a full member of society. Much of this early learning occurs in the family as a result of daily interactions: The child learns to talk and communicate, to play house, and to get along with others. As the child becomes older, teaching is more direct and parents attempt to produce conformity and obedience, impart basic skills, and prepare the child for events outside the family.

One reason the family is the most important agent of socialization is that the self-concept formed during childhood has lasting consequences. In later stages of development, we pursue experiences and activities that integrate and build upon the foundations established in the primary years. Although the personality and self-concept are not rigidly fixed in childhood, we are strongly conditioned by childhood experiences (Mortimer & Simmons, 1978).

What children learn is affected by the circumstances of the family. One of these circumstances is family composition. Children from small families have an advantage over children from large families in cognitive development and achievement motivation (Gecas, 1981). The reason is that children from small families have more one-to-one interaction with adults. Not surprisingly, a 2-year-old learns more from interacting with adults than from interacting with a 4-year-old. For the same reason, the first-born child in the family typically shows greater achievement motivation and more conscientious behavior than do later-born children (Blake, 1981). This does not mean that first-borns or those from small families are better human beings; it means only that, on the average, they achieve more.

The family is also an important agent of socialization in that children inherit many characteristics from their parents. Most importantly, the parents' religion, social class, and ethnicity influence social roles and self-concept. They influence the expectations that others have for the child, and they determine the groups with which the child will interact outside the family. Thus the family's race, class, and religion shape the child's experiences in the neighborhood, at school, and at work.

Schools

In Western societies, schooling has become institutionalized as the natural habitat for children. The central function of schools in industrialized societies is to impart specific skills and abilities necessary for functioning in a highly technological society.

Figure 5.12
In the United States, adolescents generally spend much of their time with each other, segregated both from younger and older people. In adolescent peer groups, young people are able to test their self concepts on an audience less biased than their families. They may also explore values and beliefs different than those of their parents and perhaps begin to experiment with behaviors that their parents have chosen not to teach them.

Schools do much more than teach basic skills and technical knowledge, however; they also transmit society's central cultural values and ideologies through their hidden curriculum of rules, rights, and responsibilities. Unlike the family, in which children are treated as special persons with unique needs and problems, schools expose children to situations in which the same rules, regulations, and authority patterns apply to everyone. In schools, children first learn that levels of achievement affect status in groups (Parsons, 1964:133). In this sense, schools are training grounds for roles in the workplace, the military, and other bureaucracies in which relationships are based on uniform criteria.

Peers

Compulsory education and the late age at which most youths become full-time workers have contributed to the emergence of a youth subculture in modern societies. In recent years, this development has been accelerated by the tendency for both parents to work outside the home, creating a vacuum that may be filled with peer interaction.

Peer-group membership places the child in a social context where much of the learning that takes place is nondeliberate and nonauthoritative. The peer group represents a choice in companions, relationships, and activities based on the interests of individual members. It is the first agent of socialization that the child actively chooses. Because the peer group is chosen, it is usually a reflection of prior learning as well as a source of new knowledge.

Peer-group socialization has a vital influence on three major areas of child development (Gecas, 1981). First, it has an important effect on the development and validation of the self-concept. Unlike one's family or teachers, one's peers provide a looking-glass unclouded by love or duty. Second, the peer group provides an important arena for learning the effective presentation of self through role-taking and impression management. Finally, the peer group is often a mechanism for learning social roles and values that adults don't want to teach. For example, much sexual knowledge and social deviance is learned in the peer group. (Few people learn to roll a joint at their mother's knee.)

Mass Media

Throughout our lives we are bombarded with impersonal messages from radios, magazines, films, and billboards. The most important mass medium for socialization, however, is undoubtedly television. Nearly every home has one, and the average American spends many hours a week watching it.

The effect of television viewing on learning is vigorously debated, and the evidence is somewhat contradictory. The most universally accepted conclusion is that the mass media can be an important means of supporting and validating what we already know. Through a process of selective perception, we tend to give special notice to material that supports our own opinions and to ignore material that contradicts our beliefs. Thus a confirmed bigot will note only those incidents where blacks are portrayed as foolish and irresponsible and will overlook the instances in which blacks are shown as responsible, heroic, or intelligent.

Figure 5.13

The average American child is estimated to watch 5 hours of television each day. As a result, television has become a significant agent of socialization in our society. Some groups and authorities are concerned that television programs (cartoons included) may develop very distorted images of the real world, contributing to problems of adjustment in later years.

To the extent that selective perception governs our response to the mass media, the media have a relatively minor effect—at least on adults, whose self-concept is already firmly established. The more vital question, therefore, has been: How much does television affect children?

Judging from the content of the broadcasts, children could learn a lot by watching television. They could learn how medical units work in the army (*M*A*S*H*), how police departments work (*Hill Street Blues*), or how to be a nice guy (*Mr. Rogers' Neighborhood*). They could also, however, learn 50 ways to commit murder. The extent to which television watching contributes to violent behavior is addressed in the Issues in Social Policy section at the end of this chapter.

The extent to which the content of television influences children's attitudes and behaviors independent of their other socialization is still being debated. What is clear, however, is that children spend a tremendous amount of time passively sitting in front of a television. Bronfenbrenner (1970) argues that this passivity is far more damaging than the content of the programs. If it is through interaction that the child develops and negotiates the self-concept and a sense of competence, then reduced interaction may impede successful development.

Religion

In every society religion is important in regulating behavior in ways consistent with the society's moral codes. In addition to teaching the doctrines of a particular faith, religion also provides a set of general values that guide behavior and shape the self-concept. Many religious teachings reinforce values learned elsewhere. For example, honesty and caring for others are often stressed at home and at school as well as in church and synagogue. In addition, specific church doctrines may affect nonreligious roles. For example, because Catholic and Mormon doctrines emphasize the importance of large families, young people raised in these faiths typically desire larger families than do people raised in other faiths.

Workplace

Almost all of us will spend a significant portion of our adult lives working outside the home for wages or salaries. The environments in which we can expect to work, however, are very different. Some of us will work with machines, others with ideas; some will work with people, others on people. Work is found in cities, factories, offices, and fields. Much of it is impersonal, monotonous, and regulated by time clocks; but some is highly personal, challenging, and flexible.

Long-term research by Kohn and his associates indicates that the nature of our work affects our self-concept and behavior. The amount of autonomy, the degree of supervision and routinization, and the amount of cognitive complexity demanded by the job have important consequences. If your work demands flexibility and self-discipline, you will probably come to value these traits—at home, in government, and in religion. If your work instead requires subordination, discipline, and routine, you will come to find these traits natural and desirable (Kohn & Schooler, 1978). This is a clear example of how roles affect personality and self-concept.

Status is another aspect of work that has an important impact on self-concept and behavior. People with little power and few opportunities for upward mobility tend to reject their occupation as a dominant status. Instead they base their self-concept on such nonwork roles as runner or mother, volunteer or motorcyclist. Frequently, however, people are unable to brush aside low achievement in their work roles. As a result, those who have little opportunity or power at work may be bossier, more authoritarian, and more alienated than those whose work provides a validation of their self-worth (Kanter, 1977).

Others

In addition to the just-described agencies of socialization, we all experience a multitude of associations and networks throughout the life course that continually contribute to our adjustment and learning. The clubs and organizations we join, our children, and our neighbors influence our behavior and the attitudes we hold.

Television—Socialization to Aggression?

The average American child spends 5 hours a day in front of a television set. During these hours, the child is exposed to an overwhelming amount of violence and aggression. There are brawls, shootings, shoving matches, hijackings, and verbal threats. It has been estimated that children see as many as 20,000 murders by the time they reach 16.

What do children learn from watching violence on television? In 1969, the National Commission on the Causes and Prevention of Violence concluded that "violence on television encourages violent forms of behavior, and fos-

Figure 5.14
An important element of television drama is violence. Cartoons, soap operas, and sports show people hitting each other, yelling at each other, and wishing each other dead. The most violent form of televised violence, however, is heavyweight boxing. These are real men, drawing real blood, as they deliberately attempt to injure one another. Some social science research suggests that watching this kind of violence can desensitize viewers to others' pain, teach techniques of violence, and appear to make violence a socially-approved strategy of social interaction.

ters moral and social values about violence in daily life which are unacceptable in a civilized society" (Eisenhower, 1969:5). Since 1969, there have been hundreds of additional studies. Almost without exception, they support the contention that watching televised violence encourages violent behavior.

In one of the most extensive studies of the effect of televised violence on children, Eron interviewed all third-graders in a semirural New York county in 1960. Measures of aggressive behavior came from interviews with parents and teachers as well as fellow students. Each child interviewed was asked to name classmates "who were always starting fights for nothing" or "who were always saying mean things." In 1970, Eron reinterviewed the same children and their classmates, parents, and teachers. He concluded that "the single best predictor of how aggressive a young man would be when he was 19 years old was the violence of the television programs he preferred when he was 8 years old" (Eron, 1980:246).

Interestingly, Eron found no association between the watching of televised violence and aggressive behavior among girls. He suggests that this may be because almost all aggressive role models on television are men; few violent women are portrayed. Also, girls are less likely to find the shows believable. Boys, especially the aggressive ones, see the violent shows as realistic, whereas girls are more likely to think that they are just stories. Finally, girls are not reinforced for their own aggressive acts. They are neither punished nor rewarded for such acts; therefore, as behaviorist theory suggests, the behavior tends to disappear.

This study provides an excellent example of why the link between aggression and televised violence is still a matter of debate. Did watching violence on television at age 8 cause boys to become aggressive, or did these boys choose to watch violent shows because they were already aggressive at age 8? It may be that watching violence simply reinforces aggressive behavior among children who already have aggressive tendencies.

A review of the many studies of television and aggression suggests that violence is most likely to result in aggressive responses under the following conditions (Comstock, 1977): when the violence in the story is (1) rewarded, (2) exciting, (3) real, and (4) justified; and when the perpetrator of the violent act (5) is not criticized for his behavior, and (6) intends to injure his victim.

Much of the violence on television meets these criteria. Often the good guys are as violent as the bad guys, and their behavior is usually portrayed as intentional, justifiable, and rewarded. Most of the violence on television, however, is not real. A major exception to this is contact sports, and the most deliberate example of pure intended violence is professional boxing. Unlike in football or basketball, the object is to hit or injure the other person.

In a clever study, Phillips (1983) examined homicide rates in the United States on the days before and after highly publicized heavyweight fights. He found that homicide rates do indeed increase in the days immediately after a fight. Furthermore, the increase is directly proportional to the amount of publicity a fight receives. After one of the most publicized fights of the decade, the so-called "Thrilla in Manilla" between Ali and Frazier, the homicide rate was 24 percent higher than would have been expected without the fight.

How does television watching encourage violence? There appear to be three mechanisms of encouragement: desensitization, role-modeling, and apparent approval. The first path through which television may encourage violence is desensitization. Watching innumerable murders, rapes, and other hostile acts hardens a viewer to others' suffering. People who watch a lot of televised violence are simply not as upset by such events—on the screen or in real life—as people who are less frequent watchers. The second learning mechanism is role-modeling. Regardless of whether there is any innate tendency to aggress, the specific techniques of aggression must be learned. People have to learn the swear words, weapons, and styles of violence of their culture. Television offers a comprehensive, free education in the techniques of violence. Finally, televised violence suggests that aggression is a frequent and acceptable means of interaction: "A youngster who is continually bombarded with violence on television may well come to think that aggressive behavior is typical and therefore an appropriate way to solve life's problems" (Eron, 1980:247).

This consistent evidence concerning the relationship between televised violence and aggressive behavior poses a difficult dilemma for social policy. Would we like to have a society in which people were less aggressive and in which there were fewer acts of violence? Most of us would answer yes. Several organized groups, including the American Medical Association and Americans for Children's Television, would like to eliminate violence from television shows that children are likely to watch. Others oppose any sort of censorship and suggest that it is the parents' responsibility to keep their children from watching violence. To these groups, censorship of television programs is an unwarranted intrusion on individuals' freedom to watch what they choose to and perhaps a violation of the networks' right to free speech.

The ultimate question is how much control the public should exert over its own and others' behavior. We have speeding laws, laws about how you can dispose of your sewage, and laws about how loud your dog can bark. Some of these laws are to protect you from yourself, and others are designed to protect you from your neighbors (and vice versa). Would a law banning televised violence in order to reduce the aggressiveness of individuals and the violence in society be much different from these other laws? The final social policy decision rests with Congress and the federal judiciary, both of which are still grappling with the problem of when the public interest outweighs the vested interests of the networks.

What do you think? Did all those years of watching *Starsky and Hutch, Monday Night Football,* and *Hill Street Blues* increase your own aggressiveness? Would society be better off—would you be better off—if there had been less violence on television when you were growing up?

SUMMARY

1. Our self-identity is socially bestowed and socially sustained. Through sustained interaction, we learn to be human—to walk, to love, to talk. None of our innate capacities can develop without social interaction.

2. Symbolic interactionism is the dominant theoretical framework in sociological studies of human development. It emphasizes that learning takes place through subjectively interpreted interaction, role-playing and role-taking, and negotiated scripts and roles.

3. Individuals are not merely passive products of their environments. Rather they negotiate their identity and, through their own subjective interpretation of cues and scripts, achieve a unique self-concept.

4. The individual's self-concept is strongly affected by the roles and statuses occupied. Because each of us has many roles and statuses, our identities are complex and multifaceted. They change to reflect role transitions.

5. Behaviorism attempts to explain and predict *behavior*; it is concerned not with individual mental processes but with outcomes. It is criticized because it advocates the manipulation of human behavior and because it treats humans as passive objects of the environment.

6. Developmental theory suggests that cognitive and moral development unfold in a stagelike progression parallel to physical maturity. This development poses a set of constraints against which symbolic interaction takes place.

7. The foundation of the self-concept is laid during early childhood socialization and is subsequently difficult to change. This is why resocialization is much resisted and difficult to accomplish.

8. The family is the major agent of socialization. It is responsible for the early nurturance that helps the infant develop into a human being, and it is central in laying the foundation of the self-concept. In addition, the family provides a background (social class, religion, and so on) that determines much of the child's other interactions.

9. Consistent evidence shows that a steady diet of televised violence encourages aggressive behavior. It desensitizes viewers, teaches techniques of aggression, and appears to suggest that aggression is an appropriate solution to life's problems.

SUGGESTED READINGS

Benedict, Ruth. (1961). Patterns of Culture. Boston, Mass.: Houghton Mifflin. Originally published in 1934.) A classic that draws on several different cultures to illustrate how behavior and personality are consistent with the culture in which a person is reared. The emphasis is on the continuity of socialization.

Brake, Mike. (1980). The Sociology of Youth Culture and Youth Subcultures. London: Routledge and Kegan Paul. An examination of adolescent subcultures and the socialization of youth by peers.

Erikson, Erik H. (1963). Childhood and Society (rev. ed.). New York: Norton. A developmental framework based on the idea that at different stages of maturation each individual confronts crises that, when resolved, advance the person to the next stage. Eight stages in the life cycle are presented, as are historical and cross-cultural illustrations focusing on the importance of nurture and the social environment for development.

Goffman, Erving. (1959). Presentation of Self in Everyday Life. Garden City, N.Y.: Anchor/Doubleday. An insightful discussion of the dramaturgical perspective and how the social self emerges through the experiences a person encounters in everyday living.

Goffman, Erving. (1961). Asylums. Garden City, N.Y.: Anchor/Doubleday. A penetrating account of total institutions and the significance of social structure in producing conforming behavior. Primarily an analysis of mental hospitals and mental patients, although the analysis is applicable to other total institutions.

Rose, Peter I. (ed.). (1979). Socialization and the Life Cycle. New York: St. Martin's Press. A collection of articles examining the socialization process at various ages and in different groups.

Spiro, Melford. (1975). Children of the Kibbutz. Cambridge, Mass.: Harvard University Press. A study specifically concerned with the collective childrearing practices and socialization of children in kibbutzim—agricultural communes in Israel.

Zurcher, Louis A. (1977). The Mutable Self: A Self-Concept for Change. Beverly Hills, Calif.: Sage Publications. An examination of the multiple identities of individuals and the increasing reliance on personality as opposed to institutionalized roles in adapting to the ever-changing world.

CHAPTER 6

GROUPS, ASSOCIATIONS, AND ORGANIZATIONS

OUTLINE

PROLOGUE

Have You Ever . . . met friends after a long absence and been startled by the changes in them? Perhaps they have been off to college, in the army, or just married and moved away, but you may have found that they'd changed so much you hardly knew them. It was not just their appearance but their values and concerns that were altered—and so were yours.

One of the most basic reasons that we change is that we start to associate with new groups of people. Sometimes this happens by accident: We change jobs or neighborhoods. When we take a new job, we are often unknowingly making a commitment to a whole life-style and outlook. You will become a very different person if your first job after college is with IBM rather than the Sierra Club. Organizations mold us into their sort of people. In this chapter, we will look at the different kinds of groups we belong to and how they influence the shapes of our lives. No one is an island. We are linked to others by complex ties of duty, obligation, and need. These ties have profound impacts on us. They determine what time we get up in the morning, the people we interact with all day, and the kinds of demands that are made on us. If we want to understand why people do what they do, one of our first tasks must be to identify who they do it with—their groups, associations, and organizations.

Groups

What is a group? A **group** is not just any collection of people; rather, it possesses two distinct features that set it apart from other collections of people. Its members are dependent on each other for shared activities, and their interactions are guided by a set of shared expectations.

A **group** is a collection of people who interact together on the basis of a shared social structure.

The distinctive characteristics of a group stand out when we compare the group to two collections of people that do not have these characteristics. An **aggregate** is people who are temporarily clustered together in the same location (for example, all the people on a city bus, those attending a movie, or shoppers in a mall). Although these people may share some norms (such as walking on the right when passing others), they are not mutually dependent. In fact, most of their shared norms have to do with procedures to maintain their independence despite their close physical proximity. The other nongroup is a **category**—a collection of people who share a common characteristic. Dorm residents, Greeks, bald-headed men, and Samoans are categories of people. Most of the people who share category membership will never meet, much less interact.

The distinguishing characteristics of groups hint at the rewards of group life. Groups are the people we take into account and the people who take us into account. They are the people with whom we share norms and values. Thus groups are a major source of solidarity and cohesion, reinforcing and strengthening our integration into society. The benefits of group life range all the way from sharing basic survival and problem-solving techniques to satisfying personal and emotional needs.

How Groups Affect Individuals

When a man opens a door for a woman, do you see traditional courtesy or intolerable condescension? When you listen to Led Zeppelin or Black Sabbath, do you hear good music or mindless noise? Like taste in music, many of the things we deal with and believe in are not true or correct in any absolute sense; they are simply what our groups have agreed to accept as right.

The tremendous impact of group definitions on our own attitudes and perceptions has been cleverly documented in a classic experiment by Asch (1955). In this experiment, the group consists of nine college students, all apparently unknown to each other. The experimenter explains that the task at hand is an experiment in visual judgment. The subjects are shown two cards similar to those in Figure 6.1 and are asked to judge which line on Card B is most similar to the line on Card A. This is not a difficult task; unless you have a bad squint or have forgotten your glasses, you can tell that Line 2 most closely matches the line on the first card.

The experimental part of this research consists of changing the conditions of group consensus under which the subjects make their judgments. Each group must make 15 decisions and, in the first few trials, all of the students agree. In subsequent trials, however, the first eight students all give an obviously wrong answer. They are not subjects at all but paid stooges of the experimenter. The real test comes in seeing what the last student—the real subject of the experiment—will do. Will he go along with everybody else, or will he publicly set himself apart? Photographs of the experiment show that the real subjects wrinkled their brows, squirmed in their seats, and gaped at their neighbors; in 37 percent of the trials the naive subject publicly agreed with the wrong answer, and 75 percent gave the wrong answer on at least one trial.

In the case of this experiment, it is clear what the right answer should

An **aggregate** is people who are temporarily clustered together in the same location (e.g., busloads of people, those attending a movie, and shoppers in a mall).

A **category** is a collection of people who share a common characteristic (for example, the elderly, females, managers, and students).

Figure 6.1 The Cards Used in Asch's Experiment
In Asch's experiment, subjects were instructed to select the line on Card B that was equal in length to the line on Card A. The results showed that many people will give an obviously wrong answer in order to conform to the group.
SOURCE: From "Opinions and Social Pressure," by Solomon E. Asch. Copyright © November, 1955 by Scientific American, Inc. All rights reserved.

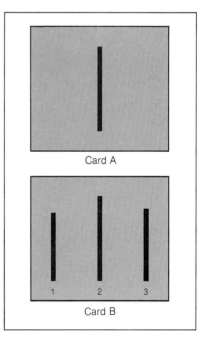

Card A

Card B

Figure 6.2

In this sequence of pictures from the Asch experiment, the subject shows the strain and consternation that come from disagreeing with the judgments of the six other members of the group. This particular subject disagreed with the majority on all 12 trials of the experiment. He is unusual, however, as seventy-five percent of the experimental subjects agree with the majority on at least one trial. In fact, subjects who initially yield to the majority find it increasingly difficult to make independent judgments as the experiment progresses.

be. Many of the students who agreed with the wrong answer probably were not persuaded by group opinion that their own judgment was wrong, but they decided not to make waves. When the object being judged is less objective, however—for example, whether Willie Nelson is better than Boy George—then the group is likely to influence not only public responses but also private views. Whether we go along because we are really convinced or because we're avoiding the hassles of being different, we all have a strong tendency to conform to the norms and expectations of our groups. Thus our group memberships are vital in determining our behavior, perceptions, and values.

Interaction in Small Groups

We spend much of our lives in groups. We have work groups, family groups, and peer groups. In class we have discussion groups, and everywhere we have committees. This section reviews some of the more important factors that affect the kind of interaction we experience in small groups.

Size.   The smallest possible group is two people. As the group grows to three, four, and more, its characteristics change. With each increase in size, each member has fewer opportunities to share opinions and contribute to decision making or problem solving. In many instances, the larger group will be better equipped for solving problems and finding answers, but this practical utility may be gained at the expense of individual satisfaction. Although there will be more ideas to consider, the likelihood that our own ideas will be influential diminishes. As the group gets larger, interaction becomes more impersonal, more structured, and less personally satisfying.

Proximity.   Dozens of laboratory studies demonstrate that interaction is more likely to occur among group members who are physically close to one another. This effect is not limited to the laboratory.

In a classic demonstration of the role of proximity in group formation and interaction, Festinger and his associates (1950) studied a married-student housing project. All of the residents had been strangers to one another before being arbitrarily assigned to the housing unit. The researchers wanted to know what factors influenced friendship choices within the project. The answer: physical proximity. Festinger found that people were twice as likely to choose their next-door neighbors as friends than they were to choose people who lived only two units away. In general, the greater the physical distance, the less likely friendships were to be formed. An interesting exception to this generalization is that people who lived next to the garbage cans were disproportionately likely to be chosen as friends. Why? Because many of their neighbors passed by their units daily and therefore had many chances to interact and form friendships.

Communication Patterns.   Interaction of group members can be either facilitated or retarded by patterns of communication. Figure 6.3 shows some common communication patterns for five-person groups. The communication structure allowing the greatest equality of participation is the *all-channel network.* In this pattern, each person can interact with every other person with approximately the same ease. Each participant has equal access to the others and an equal ability to become the focus of attention.

The other three common communication patterns allow for less interaction. In the *circle pattern,* people can speak only to their neighbors on either side. This pattern reduces interaction, but it does not give one person more power than others. In the *chain pattern* and *wheel pattern,* on the other hand, not only is interaction reduced but a single, pivotal individual gains greater power in the group. The wheel pattern is characteristic of the traditional classroom. Students do not interact with each other; instead they interact directly only with the teacher, thereby giving that person the power to direct the flow of interaction. In a chain pattern, the only way Persons A and B can communicate with D and E is through C. At the least, this pattern reduces the amount and intimacy of interaction. To the extent that C edits communications before passing them on, it may also distort the content of the interactions. This pattern tends to give C a great deal of power. The others are dependent on C's good offices for the passing of messages, and C can manipulate communications in order to achieve personal goals.

Communication structures are often created, either accidentally or purposefully, by the physical distribution of group members. The seating of committee members at a round table tends to facilitate either an all-channel or a circle pattern, depending on the size of the table. A rectangular table, however, gives people at the ends and in the middle of the long sides an advantage. They find it easier to attract attention and are apt to be more active in interactions and more influential in group discussions. Consider the way communication is structured in the classes and groups you participate in. How do seating structures encourage or discourage communication?

Social Cohesion.   An important characteristic of small groups is their **cohesion**, the forces that attract members to the group. Cohesion has to do with how much people care whether the group is continued. Research

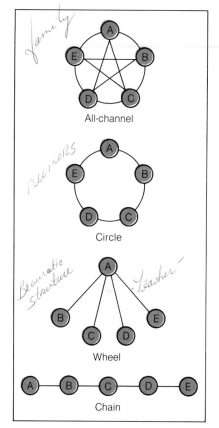

Figure 6.3   Patterns of Communication

Patterns of communication can affect individual participation and influence. In each figure the circles represent individuals and the lines are flows of communication. The circle and all channel networks provide the greatest opportunity for participation and are more often found in groups where status differences are not present or minimal. The chain and wheel, by contrast, are one way flows of communication and are typically associated with important status differences within the group.

Cohesion refers to the forces that attract members to the group.

Figure 6.4
Frequent and intense interaction, such as occurs among members of the same basketball team, tends to produce high levels of group cohesion. Cohesive groups experience a strong we-feeling; they tend to be more productive and more satisfying for the individual participants. Groups that experience high levels of turnover and relatively infrequent interaction, however, are less likely to persist or to be important to the members.

shows that cohesive groups are more productive and provide greater individual satisfaction than do noncohesive groups (Palazzolo, 1981).

Although a number of factors contribute to group cohesion, the amount of interaction and the absence of turnover are especially important. Study after study documents that extensive interaction tends to produce positive feelings. No matter how strange people seem when you first meet them, if you work with them year in and year out, you come to have a certain affection for them, to understand their problems and their quirks. Because these positive feelings may lead to even greater interaction—going to lunch together, playing cards in the evening—this mutual dependence between interaction and sentiments is a powerful force in binding group members together (Homans, 1950).

The more extensive the interaction among group members and the longer it persists, the more cohesive the group becomes. This is perhaps most obvious in marriage. Although persons married 25 to 30 years are often less enthusiastic about their marriages than are younger people, they are extremely unlikely to get divorced. The marriage has become increasingly important to them as a source of identity, and they want to maintain it.

Social Control.   Small groups rarely have access to legal or formal sanctions, yet they exercise profound control over individuals. As Asch's experiments demonstrate, groups can control their members by influencing both perceptions and behavior. The most effective control technique is the threat to exclude nonconformists from the group. This threat is more real in cohesive groups, but exclusion is always unpleasant. From "you can't sit at our lunch table any more" to "you're fired," exclusion is the ultimate sanction.

Exclusion occurs informally in all human groups—from marriages, to play groups, to work groups. When we are cross with others or wish them to know that they are acting in ways we disapprove of, a common strategy is to give them the silent treatment. Sanctions such as ridicule, humiliation, and contempt are also effective at bringing people into line.

Decision Making.   A common outcome of group processes is decision making. Whether planning what to have for dinner or planning foreign policy, groups make decisions. Their decision-making processes have been the focus of a large body of experimental work.

Generally, groups strive to reach consensus; they would like all their decisions to be agreeable to every member. As the size of the group grows, consensus requires lengthy and time-consuming interaction so everybody's objections can be clearly understood and incorporated. Thus, as groups grow in size, they often adopt the more expedient policy of majority rule. This policy results in quicker decisions, but often at the expense of individual satisfaction. It therefore reduces the cohesiveness of the group.

THE RISKY SHIFT AND THE TAME SHIFT.   One of the most consistent findings of research is that it is seldom necessary to resort to majority rule in most small groups. Both in the laboratory and in the real world, there is a strong tendency for opinions to converge. One of the classic experiments on

Figure 6.5
The type of interaction that takes place within groups depends on the similarity and proximity of the actors; it also depends on physical arrangements. A rectangular table, such as the one in this picture, tends to focus interaction on people sitting at the ends. As a result, people at the ends of the table tend to dominate the interaction. In on-going groups, from family dinners to board meetings, the dominant member of the group tends to select this position. Even when dominance has not previously been established in a group, however, seating position can determine which actors have the most influence.

convergence was done 50 years ago by Sherif (1936). In this experiment, strangers were put into a totally dark room. A dot of light was flashed onto the wall, and each participant was asked to estimate how far the light moved during the experimental period. After the first session, the participants recorded their own answers and then shared them with the other participants. There was quite a bit of variation in the estimates. Then they did the experiment again. This time there was less difference. After four trials, all participants agreed on an estimate that was close to the average of the initial estimates. (The dot of light was, in fact, stationary.)

The convergence effect has been demonstrated in dozens of studies since. Convergence, however, is not always to a middle position. Sometimes, the group reaches consensus on an extreme position. This is called the **risky shift** when they converge on an adventurous option and the **tame shift** when their choice is extremely conservative.

Initial research on the risky shift seemed to suggest that diffusion of responsibility allowed groups to take risks that individuals would find unacceptable (Wallach et al., 1964). Diffusion of responsibility, however, cannot explain the tame shift. Why would groups be more conservative than individuals? More recent research suggests that both the risky shift and the tame shift occur when group discussion uncovers a shared but secret tendency (Brown, 1974). For example, suppose a group of people are sitting around planning the annual employee picnic. They may be going through the usual, "Well, of course, we'll have horseshoes for the men and a penny hunt for the kids" routine, when one of planners says, "You know, I hate these stupid picnics." If this is what all the group members had been secretly thinking but had been afraid to admit, the committee may experience a risky shift. It may decide to cancel the picnic altogether or to do something radically different.

Risky shift is a process of decision making during which group members converge on a decision that is more adventurous than their initial individual choices.

Tame shift is a process of decision making during which group members converge on a decision that is more conservative than their initial individual choices.

Groupthink is a process of decision making in which we-feeling and unanimity rate higher than critical evaluation and rationality.

Primary groups are groups characterized by intimate, face-to-face association and cooperation.

Secondary groups are groups that are formal, large in size, and impersonal.

Figure 6.6
Although we all belong to dozens of groups, those that are most important to us are the few primary groups in which there is a high level of intense and personal interaction. Our family and our childhood friendship group are two of the most important of these primary groups. Thirty years from now these boys will remember each other's nicknames, the funny way the other held a baseball bat, and so on. This total familiarity produces a strong sense of we-feeling and acceptance in the group. Such a feeling of belongingness is a vital instrument of social control; we conform in order to maintain our membership in the group.

GROUPTHINK.   A decision-making process that is in many ways the direct opposite of the risky or tame shift is **groupthink**, in which an apparent convergence occurs because people do not share their true feelings. They stifle their criticisms so that there is an appearance of consensus. Sometimes groupthink results in nothing more awful than another dull company picnic. In other situations, however, the results can be devastating.

A classic example of groupthink is offered by President Kennedy's 1962 decision to allow the CIA to attempt an invasion of Cuba. The Bay of Pigs invasion was an embarrassing fiasco, not only a failure in fact but also badly flawed in theory. Later studies showed that many members of the Kennedy cabinet had serious reservations about the decision but did not voice them. They were trying so hard to maintain a we-feeling in the midst of crisis that they did not speak of their doubts. They thought it was more important to be supportive than to be right (Janis, 1971).

Summary.   Whether the small group arises spontaneously among neighbors or schoolchildren or whether it is a committee appointed to solve a community problem, the operation of the group depends on the quality of interaction among the members. Research suggests that interaction will be facilitated by small size, open communication networks, and physical proximity. This high level of interaction will promote conformity, productivity, and morale. Although the cohesiveness of a group is vital to productivity and individual satisfaction, it can be dangerous when it places we-feeling above critical thinking.

Types of Groups

Some groups are more important than others in their impact on our lives. All of you, for example, probably belong to a family group as well as to the student body of your college or university. Except for an occasional student activist, membership in the family is far more important than membership in the student body and will have a more lasting effect. Sociologists call small, intimate, and lasting groups **primary groups**; they call large, impersonal groups **secondary groups.**

Primary Groups.   Groups that are primary are characterized by intimate, face-to-face association and cooperation (Cooley, 1909/1967). These groups represent our most complete experiences in group life. The closest approximation to an ideal primary group is probably the family, followed by adolescent peer groups and adult friendships. The relationships formed in these groups are relatively permanent and constitute a basic source of identity and attachment.

The ideal primary group tends to have the following characteristics: (1) personal and intimate relationships, (2) face-to-face communication, (3) permanence, (4) a strong sense of loyalty or we-feeling, (5) small size—often fewer than 20 or 30 people, (6) informality, and (7) traditional or nonrational decision making (Rogers, 1960). In addition to the family, other examples of primary groups include friendship networks, coworkers, and gangs (such as those described in chapter 4). Groups such as these are major sources of companionship, intimacy, and belongingness, conditions that strengthen our sense of social integration into society.

Brainwashing Prisoners of War

At the conclusion of the Korean War, in September 1953, the United Nations Command and the communists completed the exchange of more than 88,000 prisoners of war (POWs). The U.S. soldiers taken captive were men who had fought bravely in combat and had surrendered only under hopeless conditions. Unlike previous POWs, however, some of these men had cooperated with the enemy during their captivity. Although only 21 Americans defected to communism rather than return home, the majority were passive prisoners. It is estimated, for example, that approximately 1 out of 3 were informants and 1 out of 10 gave reliable and regular information to the enemy. There were also no organized attempts at escape, something for which previous U.S. POWs had been well known. As a result, the Chinese were able to use just 1 armed guard for every 100 prisoners. Most astonishing was the deathrate; nearly 38 percent of the POWs died in captivity. Many of these men died of what has been called give-up-itus, the lack of a will to live.

When these facts came to light after the war, the military was both alarmed and embarrassed. What had brought about the passivity? the collaboration with the enemy? the overall demoralized condition of these men? Although conditions in the POW camps were terrible, they were not that much worse than what U.S. POWs had experienced in earlier wars, and torture was not widespread enough to account for the general passivity.

What was effective was a new pattern of brainwashing used by the Chinese: a systematic attack on group cohesion. Several techniques were used to bring about this effect. First, potential leaders (officers, the highly educated, the religiously devout) were separated from followers. The Chinese assumed that the rank-and-file soldiers, the draftees, would be less knowledgeable about the reasons for the war and less committed to U.S. positions and to military discipline. Second, prisoners were moved about frequently so that stable groups could not be formed. Individuals were moved from camp to camp and from solitary confinement to group quarters and back again. These techniques effectively prevented groups from forming. Each man remained isolated. Censorship of mail served to cut off ties from previous groups. The only mail allowed to reach prisoners consisted of bad news, bills, and "Dear John" letters, the kind of information that effectively cut off feelings and ties with intimate groups back home.

To create internal divisiveness and mistrust, each prisoner was required to be an informer. This was accomplished in part by requiring prisoners to engage in self-criticism in the presence of fellow prisoners. The Chinese weren't particularly concerned about what was said. What they wanted was confession, self-criticism, and the promise not to repeat the wrongdoing. This process left prisoners vulnerable. If they talked too much, an atmosphere of mistrust was created among them. If they talked too little, they and other members of their group were denied food and sleep. Thus, it was in each individual's immediate best interest to talk and to coerce others into talking. The end result was internal mistrust and divisiveness.

Through a systematic attack on group loyalties, both to fellow prisoners and to intimate attachments from home, the Chinese effectively demoralized the U.S. soldiers. Although these techniques did not lead the POWs to convert to communism, they were extremely effective in neutralizing them during captivity. The intention was to destroy group cohesiveness and individual identification. And, by all accounts, it worked.

It is under conditions such as these that we are reminded of the powerful impact of group memberships on our lives. When these ties are weakened or cut off, we are vulnerable, even sometimes to the point of losing the will to live.

Questions to Consider

1. Compare the situation in Korean POW camps with that of television's *Hogan's Heroes*. What group characteristics distinguish the successful fictional resistance fighters from the U.S. POWs in Korea?
2. Are there any parallels between the circumstances that cause demoralization in POWs and the circumstances giving rise to suicide or mental illness? Explain.

Secondary Groups.   By contrast, secondary groups are formal, large, and impersonal. Whereas the major purpose of many primary groups is simply to provide companionship, secondary groups usually form in order to accomplish some specific task. An ideal secondary group is entirely rational and contractual in nature; the participants interact solely to accomplish some purpose (earn credit hours, buy a pair of shoes, get a paycheck). Their interest in each other does not extend past this contract. If you have ever been in a lecture class of 300 students, you have firsthand experience of a classic secondary group. The interaction is temporary, anonymous, and formal. Rewards are based on universal criteria, not on such particularistic grounds as your effort or need. The Concept Summary shows the important differences between primary and secondary groups.

CONCEPT SUMMARY

Differences between Primary and Secondary Groups

	PRIMARY GROUPS	SECONDARY GROUPS
Size	Small	Large
Relationships	Personal, intimate	Impersonal, aloof
Communication	Face-to-face	Indirect—memos, telephone, etc.
Duration	Permanent	Temporary
Cohesion	Strong sense of loyalty, we-feeling	Weak, based on self-interest
Decisions	Based on tradition and personal feelings	Based on rationality and efficiency
Social structure	Informal	Formal—titles, officers, charters, regular meeting times, etc.

Expressive describes activities or roles that provide integration and emotional support to group members.

Comparing Primary and Secondary Groups.   Primary and secondary groups serve very different functions for individuals and societies. From the individual's point of view, the major purpose of primary groups is **expressive** activity, providing social integration and emotional support for individuals. Your family, for example, provides an informal support group that is bound to help you, come rain or shine. You should be able to call on your family and friends to bring you some soup when you're down with the flu, to pick you up in the dead of night when your car breaks down, and to listen to your troubles when you are blue. All of us need this kind of group support. Because we need primary groups so much, they have tremendous power to bring us into line. From the society's point of view, this is the major function of primary groups: they are the major agents of social control. The reason most of us don't shoplift is because we would be mortified if our parents, friends, or coworkers found out. The reason most soldiers go into combat is because their buddies are going. We tend to dress, act, vote, and believe in ways that will keep the support of our primary groups. In short, we conform. The law would be relatively helpless in keeping all the millions of us in line if we weren't already restrained by the desire to stay in the good graces of our primary groups. One corollary of this, however, which chapter 7 will address, is that if our primary groups accept shoplifting or streetfighting as suitable behaviors, then our primary-group associations may lead us into deviance rather than conformity.

The major functions of secondary groups are **instrumental** activities, the accomplishment of specific tasks. If you want to build an airplane, raise money for a community project, or teach introductory sociology to 2,000 students a year, then secondary groups are your best bet. They are responsible for building our houses, growing and shipping our vegetables, educating our children, and curing our ills. In short, we could not do without them.

Instrumental describes activities or roles within a group that are task oriented.

The Shift to Secondary Groups. In preindustrial society, there were few secondary groups. Vegetables and houses were produced at home by families, not by Georgia Pacific or Del Monte. Parents taught their own children, and neighbors nursed one another's ills. Under these conditions, primary groups served both expressive and instrumental functions. As society has become more industrialized, more and more of our instrumental needs are the obligation of some secondary group rather than of a primary group.

In addition to losing their instrumental functions to secondary groups, primary groups have suffered other threats in industrialized societies. In the United States, for example, approximately 21 percent of all households move each year (nearly 30 percent in the western states). This fact alone means that our primary ties to friends, neighborhoods, and coworkers are seldom really permanent. People change jobs, spouses, and neighborhoods. One consequence of this breakdown of traditional primary groups is that many people rely on secondary contacts even for expressive needs; they may hire a counselor rather than call their neighbor.

Many scholars have suggested that these inroads on the primary group represent a weakening of social control; that is, the weaker ties to neighbors and kin mean that people feel less pressure to conform. They don't have to worry about what the neighbors will say because they haven't met them; they don't have to worry about what mother will say, because she lives 2,000 miles away and what she doesn't know won't hurt her.

There is apparently some truth in this suggestion, and it may be one of the reasons that small towns with stable populations are more conventional and have lower crime rates than do big cities with more fluid populations—an issue addressed more fully in chapter 18. The rest of this chapter describes the social organizations of modern society and looks at how they serve both society and individuals.

Social Networks

Our society is frequently described as a nation of joiners. From informal card games and sports to formal participation in unions, churches, clubs, and special-interest groups, we involve ourselves in relationships with others.

A **social network** is the total set of linkages a person has with others through participation in social groups.

Primary ties are people for whom we have feelings of love, loyalty, and caring.

Weak ties are people known personally but not intimately.

Secondary ties are people known in the context of specific instrumental relationships.

Through cooperation and interdependence, each of us develops a **social network**, which consists of all the people to whom we are linked by ties of affection, association, or business. Many of us have social networks that include a large number of other people (see Figure 6.7). Among them are our family, our insurance agent, the store clerks with whom we regularly interact, our classmates and coworkers, and the people who belong to our clubs. Through these group memberships, we are linked to hundreds of people in our communities and perhaps across the country.

Although our insurance agent and our mother are both part of our personal network, there is a qualitative difference between them. We can divide our social networks into three general categories of intimacy: primary ties, weak ties, and secondary ties. **Primary ties** include members of our primary groups, those toward whom we have feelings of love, loyalty, and caring. They are the people for whom we would make sacrifices and who we expect to make sacrifices for us. **Weak ties** are people whom we know personally but not intimately—the ones we work with and the ones who go to our school and belong to our clubs and organizations. We know their first names and maybe even their children's and spouses' names, but we would not confide our deepest secrets to them and we probably would not loan them money. At the other end of the continuum are **secondary ties,** people known only in a secondary context. Physicans

Figure 6.7 Example of a Social Network

A social network includes all of the people we interact with. It includes close friends and family (primary ties), the people we know personally but not intimately (weak ties), and the people we know only in more formal and impersonal relationships (secondary ties). These ties to others integrate us into our communities and provide sources of stability and satisfaction.

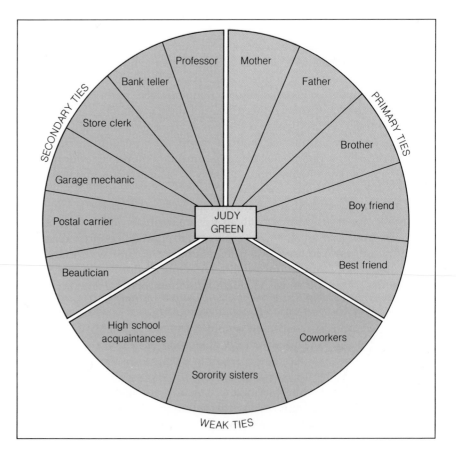

and insurance agents probably fall into this category. We know these people, but only in the context of specific instrumental relationships.

Primary Ties.   Research on primary groups suggests that primary ties are vital for integration into society, encouraging conformity and building a firm sense of self-identity. Because of their importance for the individual and society, documenting the trends in primary ties has been a major focus of research.

In a study of 1,050 residents living in 50 northern California communities, Fischer (1982) examined how modern industrial life has affected primary ties. Contrary to the expectations of theorists who had expected primary ties to be edged out by geographic mobility, urbanization, and large secondary groups, Fischer found that primary ties continue to be important. The average person in his sample named 15 to 19 primary ties.

The most important factor affecting the number of a person's primary ties is education. People with higher levels of education are more socially active, have larger personal networks, express more companionship and intimacy in their relationships, and are more likely to be tied to others outside their own community.

Fischer also found that the number of primary ties varies by residence, age, and sex. Urban residents have more primary ties than rural residents, perhaps in part because they have a greater variety from which to choose. Older respondents, especially men, are among the least active, whereas middle-aged women are the most active. Women's ties are more apt than men's to be from within the kin group, and women's ties tend to be more intimate than men's. As might be expected, marriage expands social ties, but the presence of children restricts them, particularly for mothers.

Most primary ties are formed voluntarily out of mutual interest. Over time, we decide which ties to cultivate and which to drop. Even our

Figure 6.8
This cheerful group of friends, neighbors, and kin illustrates the positive consequences of primary ties. Ties of family and friendship bind us to the larger community and give us a stable sense of self identity. Without such ties, we tend to become alienated and divorced from society.

participation in kin networks eventually becomes a matter of individual choice; some people can and do elect to sever ties with relatives. Not all people would include their mother among their primary ties.

Voluntary Associations

Voluntary associations are nonprofit organizations designed to allow individuals an opportunity to pursue their shared interests collectively.

In addition to our primary ties, most of us voluntarily choose to join other groups and associations. We may join the PTA, a bowling team, the Elks, or the Chamber of Commerce. These groups, called **voluntary associations**, are nonprofit organizations designed to allow individuals an opportunity to pursue their shared interests collectively. They vary considerably in size and formality. Some—for example, the Elks and the PTA—are very large and have national headquarters, elected officers, formal titles, charters, membership dues, regular meeting times, and national conventions. Others—for example, bowling teams and sewing circles—are small, informal groups that draw their membership from a local community or neighborhood.

Voluntary associations perform an important function for individuals. Studies document that people who participate in them generally report greater satisfaction and personal happiness, greater self-esteem, more political effectiveness, and a greater sense of community (Hanks, 1981; Knoke, 1981; Litwak, 1961; Pollock, 1982). The correlation between high participation and greater satisfaction does not necessarily mean that joining a voluntary association is the road to happiness. At least part of the rela-

Figure 6.9
Most Americans are members of at least one voluntary association. These are typically nonprofit organizations which allow individuals the opportunity to experience some of the intimacy and informality typical of primary groups. Cub Scouts of America, a national voluntary association, sponsors local packs where small groups of boys participate in numerous outings, activities, and special interests intended to give them experiences they otherwise might not have.

tionship is undoubtedly due to the fact that it is precisely those happy persons who feel politically effective and attached to their communities who seek out voluntary associations. It also appears to be true, however, that greater participation can provide an avenue for achievement and lead to feelings of integration and satisfaction.

The Mediation Hypothesis. An important characteristic of voluntary associations is that they combine some of the features of primary and secondary groups—for example, the companionship of a small group and the rational efficiency of a secondary group. Some scholars have therefore suggested that voluntary associations mediate (provide a bridge) between primary and secondary groups. They allow us to pursue instrumental goals without completely sacrificing the satisfactions that come from participation in a primary group. Through participation in voluntary associations, we meet some of our needs for intimacy and association while we achieve greater control over our immediate environment. Take, for example, the hunter who wishes to protect both wildlife and the right to have guns. This individual can write letters to his member of Congress, but he will believe, rightly, that as an individual he is unlikely to have much clout. If this same individual joins with others in, say, the National Wildlife Federation or the National Rifle Association, he will have the enjoyment of associating with other like-minded individuals and the satisfaction of knowing that a paid lobbyist is representing his opinions in Washington. It is in this sense that voluntary associations provide a bridge between the individual and large secondary associations.

Correlates of Membership Participation. Most Americans belong to at least one voluntary association, and approximately one-fourth participate in three or more. Among those who report membership, a large proportion are passive participants—they belong in name only. They buy a membership in the PTA when pressured to do so, but they don't go to meetings. Similarly, anyone who subscribes to *Audubon* magazine is automatically enrolled in the local Audubon Club, but few subscribers become active members. Because so many of our memberships are superficial, they are also temporary. Most Americans, however, maintain continuous membership in at least one association.

Several characteristics are related to membership participation. Among them are residence, social class, age, gender, and religion (Tomeh, 1973).

1. *Urban-rural residence.* Urban residents are more frequently involved in voluntary associations than are rural residents. One reason may be that urban areas offer a greater variety of associations to choose from and less competition from traditional primary groups.
2. *Social class.* Most studies show that people from higher social classes are more involved in voluntary associations than are people from lower classes. Furthermore, the types of organizations joined vary by social class. Upper-class persons are more involved in historical societies and country clubs, middle-class persons in civic groups (Rotary, Chamber of Commerce), and working-class persons in fraternal and veteran's associations.
3. *Age.* Membership in voluntary associations tends to increase contin-

Figure 6.10

This Shriner is in many ways typical of the people who join voluntary associations; he is male, probably middle to upper-middle class, middle-aged, and urban. His is probably also active in several other voluntary associations, including a church and civic organizations. Membership in such voluntary associations is generally associated with a greater feeling of integration into one's community and greater personal satisfaction.

uously through adulthood but begins to decline near retirement age. During early adulthood, the presence of young children has a depressing effect on the involvement of parents, particularly mothers. Age also affects the types of organizations joined. Young people's organizations tend to be almost exclusively expressive in nature; parents are active in youth-oriented groups such as the scouts and the PTA; middle-aged people are more active in civic groups.

4. *Gender.* In general, men participate more than women. In addition, the associations they belong to tend to be larger, more formal, and more instrumental than the associations women join.

5. *Religion.* Church membership and participation is the most widespread and intensive voluntary association in our society. People who are religious belong not only to a church but also to church boards, study groups, sewing circles, and fund-raising committees.

Primary ties and voluntary associations abound in modern society and, as noted, serve important functions for both individuals and society. Of course, they constitute only a limited aspect of the total social network. In addition to these groups and associations, individuals are also involved in larger and more complex organizations.

Complex Organizations

——

Few people in our society escape involvement in large-scale organizations. Unless we are willing to retreat from society altogether, a major part of our lives is organization-bound. Even in birth and death, large, complex organizations (such as hospitals and vital-statistics bureaus) make demands on us. Throughout the in-between years, we are constantly adjusting to organizational demands (Kanter, 1981).

Complex organizations are large in size and characterized by complex interrelationships among their parts.

Sociologists use the term **complex organizations** to refer to these highly structured organizations. They are complex not merely because they are large in size but because they are complicated. They have numerous divisions and branches; dozens, hundreds, or thousands of separate roles; and complex ties of authority and subordination (Brinkerhoff & Kunz, 1972). Examples include universities, government agencies, business organizations, and some voluntary associations, such as the Masons and the Catholic church.

These complex organizations have many merits and make a major contribution to the overall quality of life within society. Increased organization, however, has meant that individuals become constrained by the organizations they serve. Individual sentiments are subordinated to efficiency, and creativity and imagination frequently are stifled. Much of the feeling of alienation that people in industrialized societies develop can be attributed to organizations that deal with people in highly impersonal ways (Roszak, 1969). This impersonality is particularly characteristic of bureaucracies.

Bureaucracy is a complex organization characterized by the rational operation of a hierarchical authority structure and explicit procedures and rules.

Bureaucracy

A special type of complex organization, **bureaucracy** means literally "rule by the office"—or bureau. It is a complex "organization characterized by the rational operation of a hierarchical authority structure and explicit procedural rules" (Dushkin, 1974:30). In popular usage, *bureaucracy* often has a negative connotation: red tape, silly rules, and unyielding rigidity. In social science, however, it is simply an organization in which the roles of each actor have been carefully planned in order to maximize efficiency.

The sociological framework for understanding bureaucratic organizations was first developed by Max Weber nearly 100 years ago (Weber, 1910/1970a). Weber focused on organizations deliberately established for the attainment of specific goals through principles of efficiency, rationality, and expertise. In such a system, all details are planned so that individual members will act in ways consistent with the accomplishment of organizational objectives.

Most large, complex organizations are also bureaucratic: IBM, General Motors, U.S. Steel, the Catholic church, colleges, and hospitals. All share the following major characteristics:

1. *Division of labor and specialization.* Bureaucratic organizations employ specialists in each position and make them responsible for specific duties. Job titles and job descriptions specify who is to do what and who is responsible for each activity. Such specialization is akin to assembly-line methods of mass production, where the specific contributions of several people are necessary to produce a final product. In bureaucracies, however, much of the production involves paper-processing and documentation (the files) as opposed to material goods.

2. *Hierarchy of authority.* Positions are arranged in a hierarchy so that each position is under the control and supervision of a higher position. Frequently referred to as chains of command, these lines of authority and responsibility are easily drawn on an organization chart, often in the shape of a pyramid. They link together the organization's positions and functions for the purpose of identifying task responsibility and authority throughout the organization.

Figure 6.11
For many people, bureaucracy means standing in line, filling out forms, and being treated as a number. This view of bureaucracy is epitomized in the picture of an unemployment office. The procedures of the office have been designed to process the maximum number of applicants quickly and impersonally. All of the clerks use the same rules and no personal exceptions are made. Although bureaucracies are very efficient, their impersonality raises dilemmas for both employees and clients.

3. *System of rules and regulations.* All activities and operations of a bureaucracy are governed by abstract rules or procedures. These rules are designed to cover almost every possible situation that might arise: hiring, firing, and the everyday operations of the office. The object is to standardize all activities.

4. *Impersonality in social relationships.* Bureaucracies share many of the secondary-group characteristics discussed earlier. Relationships, both with clients and among personnel, are impersonal. Communications are frequently in the form of memos, telephone calls, and documents rather than face-to-face. The elimination of emotions, loyalties, and personal considerations is intended to make the bureaucracy more efficient.

5. *Careers, tenure, and technical qualifications.* Candidates for bureaucratic positions are almost always selected on the basis of technical qualifications such as high scores on civil service examinations, education, or experience. Once selected for a position, persons advance in the hierarchy by means of achievement and seniority. After a period of probation, employees are evaluated and granted tenure (a form of job security) if their work has been satisfactory throughout the probationary period. Within limits, tenure guarantees employees a career within the bureaucracy until they choose to retire or resign.

6. *Efficiency.* Bureaucratic organizations are one of the clearest examples of structured social interaction: Norms, roles, and sanctions are deliberately developed to coordinate the activities of a large number of people in the pursuit of organizational goals. All have been designed to maximize efficiency. From the practice of hiring on the basis of credentials rather than personal contacts to the rigid specification of duties and authority, the whole system is designed to keep individuality, whim, and particularism out of the operation of the organization.

Strains in Bureaucracies. Bureaucracies are not always totally efficient, reliable, or precise. The very characteristics that are intended to produce efficiency sometimes contribute to inefficiency and may even prove dysfunctional (Merton, 1957). For example, the specialized training and skills of the expert may produce rigid thinking. These trained incapacities may impede flexibility and innovation. Similarly, rigid adherence to rules may lead to the situation where a rule is followed regardless of whether it helps accomplish the purpose for which it was designed. The rule becomes an end in itself rather than a means to an end. Insistence on conformity may stifle initiative and prevent the development of more efficient procedures (Blau & Meyer, 1971).

As secondary-group structures, bureaucracies face two additional problems. First, the enforced impersonality of bureaucratic routine frequently annoys clients—the people the organization is supposedly set up to serve. Students who have waited in line for 2 hours to register for a course only to find that they're missing some essential piece of paper that can be obtained only by standing in yet another line (but that office closes at noon) will know the feeling. Students, taxpayers, and hospital patients all share the feelings of powerlessness and resentment at being pushed around by bureaucrats.

Second, the stress on impersonal routine can create resentment and alienation within an organization, particularly when exceptions are made.

Accusations of apple-polishing, nepotism, and favoritism result when personal considerations are given some people but not others. Yet the avoidance of personal considerations often creates stress for the actors. A teacher, for example, might like to nudge a B + to an A for a student who is obviously able and sincere but whose performance on the midterm was spoiled by personal problems. In a bureaucracy, which is what schools are, this kind of personal consideration is forbidden. The rules say that all students must be judged on the same (written) criteria. So the student gets a B +, the instructor feels like a heel, and the student feels that the university is a cold, uncaring place. Such problems are likely to reduce morale, motivation, and, ultimately, the effectiveness of the organization (Merton, 1957).

The Growth of Bureaucracies and Complex Organizations

The number of organizations modeled on the principles of bureaucracy has grown tremendously, and recent trends indicate that bureaucracies will continue to grow in size, scope, and complexity (Lincoln et al., 1978; Meyer, 1979; Useem, 1979). National firms become multinational conglomerates, government bureaucracies increase their scope of operations, and ordinary organizations become even more bureaucratic.

For many of us, our paychecks and prosperity depend on these large-scale bureaucratic organizations. Government alone employs more than 16 million people, and the vast majority of the remaining 94 million in the labor force in 1982 were employed by large, complex organizations. Employment, however, is only one of the areas in which people experience bureaucratic organization. Education, health care, and religion are all delivered through large-scale bureaucratic structures.

Not only are more organizations adopting a bureaucratic style of management, but bureaucratic organizations are becoming more bureaucratic (Meyer, 1979). Within the past decade there have been sharp increases in the number of rules and regulations that govern organizational operations. The Department of Energy, for example, now mandates the types of fuel that can be used in industries and the settings for government thermostats. One directive during the Carter administration stipulated a $10,000 fine for employees who set their office thermostat above 68 degrees in the winter. Often the regulations have desirable objectives (such as saving energy, protecting privacy, or ensuring fair hiring), but the consequence is that more and more aspects of life are subjected to bureaucratic regulation. (In the employee bulletin of one local restaurant, rule III. A.[2] requires that "all employees shall wear appropriate undergarments.")

Work in Organizations

Weber's description of an ideal bureaucracy makes it sound like a deadly place—a place in which all interaction would be formal, anonymous, and routine and all human interaction would take place through memos in triplicate, duly routed through all appropriate channels. No one would ever exercise any ingenuity or creativity, smile (unless it is part of the job description), or make an exception because "Stan's worried about his wife." In short, it sounds dull, impersonal, and a terrible place to spend your working days.

Figure 6.12
A common feature of most large organizations is the development of informal social networks among coworkers. These mill workers, for example, spend time together informally during shift changes, coffee breaks, and lunch hours. These exchanges provide the basis for primary ties within large organizations. Such ties generally contribute to the productivity of the organization and the satisfaction of individual employees.

Luckily, bureaucracies turn out to have a human side too. Because people who interact together frequently tend to develop a liking for one another (Homans, 1950), primary ties do develop at work, even in the stuffiest of bureaucracies. Sometimes these ties help support the aims of the bureaucracy. Many people, for example, show up regularly for work so they won't miss the lunch bridge game or so they can tell the news about their latest adventure. Others show up so their coworkers won't be overburdened by having to do all the work themselves. And as people develop a sense of caring about what their coworkers think of them, their caring becomes a strong source of social control. People who wouldn't worry much about whether General Motors could afford to miss a calculator would not like their coworkers to think they were dishonest.

The development of primary ties at the office may also work against bureaucratic efficiency, however. Many studies show that workers respond to the demands of management only when these demands are consistent with the demands of their primary group within the work setting. Informal agreements within a primary group may stand in the way of implementing the most rational method. For example, individual incentive plans that pit members of a work group against one another so that one member's gain becomes others' loss have generally been unsuccessful. As a result, group incentive plans that take these informal ties into account have generally replaced individual incentive plans in industry. These issues will be taken up in more detail in chapter 13.

Beyond Bureaucracy

The antiauthority movements of the 1960s spawned several organizations intentionally designed to avoid bureaucratization. These alternative organizations, or collectives as they are sometimes called, are attempts to avoid the impersonality and authority that tend to dominate bureaucratic structures. The Japanese model of organization provides yet another alternative to the standard Western bureaucracy.

Alternative Organizations

Alternative organizations have been designed to meet the social and economic needs of their members without bureaucratic regulation and authority. They provide a wide variety of services—for example, legal aid, free schools, and food and health cooperatives. They also include grassroots business cooperatives requiring relatively small amounts of capital outlay: bookstores, clothing shops, newspapers, auto repair shops, and alternative energy installations. In 1973, it was estimated that there were more than 800 free schools operating in the United States, and a conservative estimate in 1976 indicated well over 5,000 alternative organizations nationwide (Rothschild-Witt, 1979).

Alternative organizations have been deliberately designed to be the polar opposite of bureaucratic organizations. They differ in the following ways (Rothschild-Witt, 1979):

1. *Authority*. Collective organizations emphasize democracy and consensus. All members participate in decision making, and the goal is to reach decisions supported by the entire group: "All major policy issues, such as hiring, firing, salaries, the division of labor, the distribution of surplus, and the shape of the final product or service, are decided by the collective as a whole" (p. 512).

2. *Rules*. There is a marked attempt to minimize the use of the rules to run collectives. Instead, decisions are made on an individual basis, taking into account the particular circumstances of each situation. Here, again, decisions are arrived at through membership consensus and collective participation.

3. *Social control*. Because collectives do not rely on standardized rules or central authority to maintain control, they must rely on personal and moral appeals. Because this type of influence is possible only in homogeneous groups, recruitment emphasizes the selection of individuals who share the basic views and values of the collective.

4. *Social relations*. Alternative organizations strive to maintain primary-group relationships. They often speak of themselves as communities rather than organizations, and they endeavor to create relationships that are holistic, personal, and of value in and of themselves.

5. *Recruitment and advancement*. Instead of expertise, training, and lifelong careers, emphasis is placed on individual personality characteristics, friendship networks, and self-direction. Although collectives attempt to recruit skilled and competent persons, hiring and staffing is based more on such criteria as friendship and shared social and political values. There is no hierarchy of positions and thus no concept of individual advancement.

6. *Incentive structure*. Material incentives or rewards take a back seat to moral incentives. Work is construed as a labor of love. At a free medical clinic, one of the members describes motivation this way: "Our volunteers are do-gooders. . . . They get satisfaction from giving direct and immediate help to people in need. This is why they work here" (cited on p. 515).

7. *Status distinctions*. The absence of status distinctions is a central feature of collective organizations. Wage differences occur, but they are largely

Figure 6.13
Alternative organizations, such as this food cooperative in Portland, Oregon, are designed to eliminate the stiffling and negative characteristics often associated with bureaucracies. They are attempts to create a work environment based on primary group characteristics, where workers collectively make decisions, minimize the use of rules, and appeal to group interests over individual interests. Over the past two decades, the number of alternative organizations in the United States has grown rapidly.

the result of special circumstances (number of dependents, for example) rather than worth of the individual to the organization: "Through dress, informal relations, task sharing, job rotation, the physical structure of the workplace, equal pay, and the collective decision-making process itself—collectives convey an equality of status" (p. 517).

8. *Specialization.* Little emphasis is placed on specialization and technical expertise. Through job rotation, teamwork, and task-sharing, administrative and performance tasks are combined and the division between intellectual and manual work is reduced. Everyone manages and everyone works.

Although laudable in many ways, collectives are not without constraints and social costs. Arriving at consensus and maintaining a high level of communication require the devotion of large amounts of time to staff meetings and discussion. The demand for consensus and full participation means some sacrifice of efficiency. The practice of job rotation and a lack of clear authority further hamper quick and efficient action. Individual costs may be high because of high levels of emotional exchange, the intimacy of face-to-face communication, and the potentials for conflict. It takes a lot of emotional energy to reach and maintain agreement with even half a dozen other individuals.

The spread of alternative organizations is an active rejection of the impersonal efficiency valued by bureaucratic organizations. Although some researchers have argued that the trend toward alternatives indicates a movement away from bureaucracy, the overall growth of bureaucratic organizations does not appear to be diminishing (Bennis, 1979; Meyer, 1979; Shariff, 1979). Instead, there is now greater diversity of organizational structures and increased bureaucratization coexists with alternative organizations (Bennis, 1979). Somewhere between these two extremes is the Japanese model of organization, which, with the growth of Japanese multinationals, has recently been imported to the United States (Lincoln et al., 1978).

The Japanese Model of Organization

Since World War II, Japan has dramatically improved its industrial capabilities, and currently it dominates a variety of world markets: compact cars and motorcycles, cameras and optics, electrical components (television, radio, stereos, video recorders), musical instruments, shipbuilding, textiles, and numerous related areas. Japan's rapid expansion has led some to conclude that Japan is the foremost industrial nation in the world today (Vogel, 1979).

Japan's rise to economic prominence in world trade is due to a unique combination of Japanese culture and the adoption of Western management practices in industrial organization. Shortly after World War II, the Japanese government spearheaded a move to revamp several basic institutions, especially commerce and industry. The result was the development of what is referred to as the paternalistic lifetime commitment model of organization (Dore, 1973; Marsh & Mannari, 1976; Masatsugu, 1982). This model, which is fashioned after the bureaucratic forms of organization in the West, contains several distinct characteristics of Japanese culture and tradition. Among them are a system of permanent employment, a seniority-based system of promotion, bottom-up management, an emphasis on small-group responsibility, and a long-term perspective (Masatsugu, 1982; Vogel, 1979).

Permanent Employment. The feudalistic tradition of Japan emphasizes the lifetime of loyal service of the samurai warriors to their feudal lords. This tradition was extended into industry in the early 1900s (1912–1926), at a time when relatively high levels of turnover among blue-collar workers in factories prompted several companies to offer lifetime employment. After World War II, lifetime employment became a standard, though not universal, practice in large firms.

The relationship between an employee and the firm is one of lifetime commitment. Upon completing school, an employee enters a firm and remains there until retirement. The company assumes a paternalistic attitude, agreeing to provide for both the economic and noneconomic needs of employees, including housing, health care, recreation, and continued education.

A Seniority-Based System of Promotion. Japanese organizations have hierarchical structures much like those of bureaucracies in the West. A person's base pay, benefits, and promotions, however, depend more on age and length of service than on job performance. New employees start out together and receive the same pay for their work. Although some differences begin to occur over time, the emphasis on equal pay by seniority level tends to reduce competition and strengthen camaraderie among work groups.

The hierarchical structure of Japanese companies is largely age-graded; thus higher-status officials are almost always older than those in lesser statuses. The major exception to the seniority system is educational level. The starting positions of high school graduates are lower than those of university graduates, and students graduating from first-rate universities earn more than those from mediocre schools. Because education determines entry-level status, there is substantial emphasis on educational attainment in Japan.

Bottom-Up Management. Frequently referred to as the ringi system of management, bottom-up management is a procedure for decision making in which decisions flow from the bottom of the organization to the top. The underlying assumption is that company decisions should be made on the basis of broad consensus within the organization rather than imposed by corporate or executive rule. It is also based on the belief that workers will feel a personal responsibility for their particular assignment and will show initiative in improving work procedures (Vogel, 1979).

Probably over 90 percent of all large companies and many smaller ones currently use the bottom-up system of management (Masatsugu, 1982:171). Proposals related to section activities originate within the section and circulate upward through the organization to other concerned sections and departments. Along the way, each person who receives the proposal has the opportunity to study it and make suggestions or revisions before passing it along. By the time a proposal has circulated upward through the organization, it has obtained general consensus. This process leads to good internal communication between sections and divisions and serves as a reporting device to others in the company. When company officials finally approve a proposal, it is relatively easy to implement it and no longer feasible to oppose it. Everyone knows about it, has cooperated in its development and is committed to assisting in its implementation.

Small-Group Responsibility.   The philosophy of Japanese management entails a strong emphasis on developing group identification and company loyalty. Many of its features are designed to make work groups one of the most cohesive groups that employees experience.

The process of developing group identification begins in the spring of each year, when most companies do the majority of their hiring. New graduates from high schools and universities enter the company at the same time and will be advanced together through the seniority system in much the same way that they advanced together in school. There are other parallels with the school system. Special ceremonies are held to induct new employees into the company and to foster their sense of identity with one another. Group identification is further reinforced through the use of company uniforms, badges, mottos, and songs. Many companies also provide special-interest activities (clubs, courses, lectures, exhibitions) as well as gymnasiums, recreational facilities, team sports, and company housing. The result is that individual workers are integrated into the company at several levels: a particular factory or store, a department, a section, an immediate work group, and an age group that advances at the same time.

Long-Term Perspective.   Japanese firms are more interested in building for the future than in realizing short-term profits. Permanent employment, seniority-based promotion, and bottom-up management reflect this attitude. The firms invest heavily in technology, modernizing their plants and sponsoring training programs to upgrade the skills of employees. This long-term perspective is not simply a matter of philosophy, however; it is also due to the willingness of the Japanese government to provide long-term financing.

The Future of Paternalism.   The paternalistic lifetime commitment model is unique to Japan, but it may no longer be characteristic of Japan. In a study of three large Japanese factories (electric, shipbuilding, and sake), Marsh and Mannari (1976:338) conclude that this model exaggerates the uniformity, uniqueness, and traditionalism of Japanese firms. They find considerable diversity in the extent to which the predominant features of the model are present. More importantly, they find that those organizational variables distinct to the model (paternalism, company housing, participation in company activities, company identification, and so on) have less impact on worker performance than do such organizational variables as employee status in the company, gender, job satisfaction, and knowledge of organizational procedures. On the basis of their research, Marsh and Mannari predict that the organizational structure of Japanese firms will become increasingly like that in the West. Referring to this change as a convergence theory of modernization, they argue that the technological and structural forces of modernization and production require similar forms of organization within industrial countries.

ISSUES IN SOCIAL POLICY

Career-Seeking and the Use of Weak Ties

Presumably, readers of this text were motivated to attend college in part to improve their chances of obtaining satisfying jobs. This is a reasonable expectation and a college education will increase your job prospects dramatically. A growing body of research, however, indicates that the size of your social network is also important.

Regardless of the occupational field you choose to enter, finding a job and advancing in your career can be strongly influenced by your social networks. This does not mean that you need to cultivate a lot of close friends or have a big family; it just means that you have to know a lot of people. It is through these weak ties rather than through the close ties of friendship or kinship that information passes and people first hear about jobs they later obtain (Granovetter, 1973, 1974; Lin et al., 1981; McPherson & Smith-Lovin, 1982). Similarly, information leading to career mobility in professional, technical, or managerial jobs is more likely to come from someone

Figure 6.14

Parties may not only be enjoyable, they may also be good business. While these people are sharing a drink and a joke, they are also establishing a relationship that may be the basis for informal information about jobs and business deals. Research demonstrates that weak ties, such as those established between members of voluntary organizations or among conventioning business people, may have a direct pay off.

you barely know (a weak tie) who is highly placed in an organization than it is from a close friend.

These findings provide yet another set of evidence supporting the rewards of belonging to voluntary associations. Participation in these associations can greatly enhance your interpersonal contacts, and it frequently provides information outside your immediate environment. Of particular importance is the size of the voluntary association; large organizations have large networks. Although the ties between members are weaker, this element turns out to be less important than the increased number of contacts. The larger the number of people you know, the more likely you are to know somebody who has a friend who . . .

All of this, of course, is a long way of saying that what is often called the old-boys' network really works. There is a certain amount of irony in this network. The old-boys' network does turn out to be largely of and for men. This occurs because women belong to fewer voluntary associations than men and, more importantly, because the voluntary associations they belong to are smaller. Since men's organizations are, on the average, three to four times larger than women's, men have many more weak ties (McPherson & Smith-Lovin, 1982).

These differences by gender are important in terms of job information and resources. Because men's social networks tend to be larger than women's, men have many more potential contacts and resources related to jobs. This difference appears to give them a substantial advantage in looking for work as well as in career advancement.

The practical implications of these findings have been obvious to insurance salespeople for years. Those who make their living from sales are the biggest joiners in any community, calculating that more contacts mean more sales. The lesson may also apply to you. Even if your major is much in demand, a broad social network may significantly increase the likelihood that you will be successful in finding the job you want.

SUMMARY

1. Groups are distinguished from aggregates and categories in that members interact and take each other into account and their interaction is shaped by shared expectations.

2. Group interaction is affected by group size and the proximity and communication patterns of group members. The amount of interaction in turn affects group cohesion, the amount of social control the group can exercise over members, and the quality of group decisions.

3. A fundamental distinction between groups is the extent to which they are primary or secondary. Primary groups are essential to individual satisfaction and integration; they are also the primary agents of social control in society. Secondary groups are generally task-oriented and perform instrumental functions for societies and individuals.

4. Each person has a social network that consists of primary, weak, and secondary ties. The number of these ties is generally associated with satisfaction and community integration as well as career advancement.

5. Voluntary associations may mediate between the primary and secondary group, providing a bridge that links the individual to larger groups. Voluntary associations combine some of the expressive functions of primary groups with the instrumental functions of secondary groups.

6. Bureaucracies are rationally designed organizations whose goal is to maximize efficiency. The chief characteristics of a bureaucracy are division of labor and specialization, a hierarchy of authority, a system of rules and regulations, impersonality in social relations, and emphasis on careers, tenure, and technical qualifications.

7. We all participate in bureaucracies. Most Americans work for them, and the rest are clients of bureaucratically run schools, hospitals, and governments.

8. As a result of the alienation and impersonalization encountered in bureaucratic organizations, antibureaucratic organizations have emerged in recent years. Based on principles of democracy and cooperation, these organizations minimize the use of rules and authority, status distinctions, and specialization.

9. The paternalistic lifetime commitment model found in Japanese organizations is an adaptation of Western bureaucratic organization and Japanese culture. This organizational style emphasizes permanent employment, promotion based on seniority, bottom-up management, and small-group cohesion.

SUGGESTED READINGS

Barker, Larry L., et al. (1979). Groups in Process: An Introduction to Small Group Communication. Englewood Cliffs: N.J.: Prentice-Hall. An easy-to-read description of interaction in small groups that expands on the basic ideas at the beginning of this chapter regarding the social structure and group processes that make up the dynamics of small groups.

and violations of the criminal code; the latter focuses more on minor offenses. Together they give us a picture of how conformity, nonconformity, and deviance operate in society.

The Traditional Approach

The traditional approach to deviance concerns itself with the incidence and causes of rule violation. It sidesteps the question of the origin of rules by focusing on such law-breaking behavior as murder and armed robbery, for which there is disapproval across almost all subcultures and age groups.

The sections that follow will review briefly three major theories that offer explanations of rule violation: anomie theory, cultural-transmission theory, and social-control theory. Each has contributed to our understanding the causes of deviance.

Social Structure, Anomie, and Deviance. One of the most important sociological explanations for the cause of deviance is anomie theory, initially formulated by Durkheim in his classic study of suicide (1897/1966). Durkheim was trying to explain why people in industrialized societies are more likely to commit suicide than are people in other societies. He suggested that in traditional societies the rules tend to be well known and widely supported. As a society grows larger, becomes more heterogeneous, and experiences rapid social change, the norms of society may be unclear or no longer applicable to current conditions. Durkheim called this situation **anomie;** he believed that it was a major cause of suicide in industrializing nations.

The anomie thesis was first applied to the study of deviance by Robert Merton (1957), who suggested that individuals who find society's rules irrelevant to their own situation have an increased potential for deviance. The potential for **anomic deviance** in the United States is greatest in the case of our strong cultural emphasis on economic success and achievement. This goal is widely shared, and people of all classes, social backgrounds, and races are expected to aspire to high educational and economic achievement. The means for achieving success, however, are not always readily or equally available. People from the lower social classes in particular have less opportunity to become successful. The discrepancy between their goals and means, Merton believes, encourages them to use illegitimate means to achieve success.

Of course, not everyone who is blocked in attempts to achieve socially defined goals will turn to a life of crime. Merton identifies four ways in which people adapt to situations of anomie (see Table 7.1): innovation, ritualism, retreatism, and rebellion. The mode of adaptation depends on whether an individual accepts or rejects the society's cultural goals and accepts or rejects appropriate ways of achieving them.

People who accept both society's goals and society's suggestions about how to reach them are conformists. Most of us conform most of the time. When people cannot successfully reach society's goals using society's rules, however, deviance is a likely result. One form deviance may take is innovation; people accept society's goals but develop alternative means of reaching them. Innovators, for example, may pursue academic achieve-

Anomie is a situation in which the norms of society are unclear or no longer applicable to current conditions; the individual has few guides as to what is expected.

Anomic deviance occurs among individuals who accept society's goals but are blocked from achieving them through the usual means.

Table 7.1 Merton's Types of Anomic Deviance

Merton's anomie theory of deviance suggests that deviance results whenever there is a disparity between institutionalized goals and the means available to reach them. Individuals caught in this dilemma may reject the goals or the means or both. In doing so, they become deviants.

MODES OF ADAPTATION	CULTURAL GOALS	INSTITUTIONAL MEANS
CONFORMITY	Accepted	Accepted
DEVIANCE		
Innovation	Accepted	Rejected
Ritualism	Rejected	Accepted
Retreatism	Rejected	Rejected
Rebellion	Rejected/replaced	Rejected/replaced

SOURCE: Adapted from Robert K. Merton, 1957:140.

Figure 7.2

Anomie theory suggests that one of the major causes of deviance and crime is blocked opportunities. Merton argued that people trapped in crowded slums and urban ghettos may find themselves blocked from conventional achievement in education and the labor force. Consequently, people who live in these environments are more likely to use illegitimate means (deviance and crime) in order to achieve success.

ment through cheating, athletic achievement through steroids, or economic success through joining the Mafia. In these instances, deviance rests on using illegitmate means to accomplish socially desirable goals.

Other people who are blocked from achieving socially desired goals respond by rejecting the goals themselves. Ritualists slavishly go through the motions prescribed by society, but their goal is security not success. Their major hope is that they will not be noticed. Thus they do their work carefully, even compulsively. Although ritualists may appear to be overconformers, Merton says they are deviant because they have rejected our society's values on achievement and upward mobility. They have turned their back on normative goals but are clinging desperately to procedure. Retreatists, by contrast, adapt by rejecting both procedures and goals. They are society's dropouts: the vagabonds, drifters, and street people. The final mode of adaptation—rebellion—involves the rejection of society's goals and means and the adoption of alternatives that challenge society's usual patterns. Rebels are the people who start communes or revolutions to create an alternative society. Unlike retreatists, they are committed to working toward a different society.

The basic idea of Merton's theory is that, in the normal operation of complex societies, there are dislocations between ends and means that encourage individuals to commit acts that are socially defined as deviant (Douglas & Waksler, 1982). This theory explicitly defines deviance as a social problem rather than a personal trouble; it is a property of the social structure, not of the individual. As a consequence, the solution to deviance lies not in reforming the individual deviant but in changing the structure that produces deviant behavior.

There are two basic criticisms of the anomie theory of deviance. First, conflict theorists object to its structural-functional roots. Anomie theory suggests that deviance results from a lack of integration among the parts of a social structure (norms, goals, and resources); it is viewed as an abnormal state produced by extraordinary circumstances. Conflict theorists, however, see deviance as a natural and inevitable product of competition in a society in which groups have different access to scarce resources. They suggest that the ongoing processes of competition should be the real focus of deviance studies (Lemert, 1981).

Second, critics question Merton's assertion that anomic deviance is more characteristic of lower-class people. There is evidence that most lower-class people are able to adjust their goals downward sufficiently that they can be reached by respectable means (Thio, 1983). In addition, there is evidence that many highly successful individuals adjust their goals so far upward that they still cannot reach them by legitimate means. President Nixon resorted to illegitimate means to secure his high position; already wealthy brokers turn to stock manipulations when their aspirations are beyond the usual means. Thus it is not at all clear that the means-goals discrepancy is particularly acute among members of the lower class.

In spite of these criticisms, sociologists continue to find anomie theory both interesting and useful as an explanation of deviance. It underscores the sociological view that society, not the individual, is an important cause of deviant behavior.

Cultural-Transmission Theory. At about the same time that Merton was proposing anomie theory as a cause of deviance, Edwin Sutherland introduced the theory of differential association to explain the cultural transmission of deviance. His observations of delinquency patterns in Chicago showed that there were high-crime-rate areas where deviance appeared to be learned through personal and group contacts (for example, play groups and gangs). The standards and values of delinquent neighborhoods differed from those of nondelinquent neighborhoods, he found. Thus he assumed that deviance is learned or transmitted as a cultural characteristic of one's neighborhood.

Sutherland believed that differential association might explain patterns of deviance on both the neighborhood and the individual level. The transmission of deviance through group membership would explain why some neighborhoods and groups had consistently high levels of deviance and others consistently low ones. Similarly, an individual's group memberships and contacts could be used to explain why some individuals become deviant and others do not. In short, Sutherland's **differential-association theory** assumes that deviance is learned through the same mechanisms as conformity. It is basically symbolic-interaction theory applied to deviance. We learn deviant norms and values by interacting with others and coming to share their symbolic framework.

Sutherland's theory of differential association has been the springboard for much of the research and theory in deviance in the last 40 years. One of the more recent extensions of his work has been made by behaviorists, who argue that criminal behavior is learned through differential reinforcement (Burgess & Akers, 1966). They suggest that people will continue to engage in criminal behavior if they have been rewarded for such behavior. Individuals choose a life of crime over one of convention if they find criminality more rewarding than conformity.

Social-Control Theory. One of more important theoretical contributions to the study of crime and delinquency in recent years is **social-control theory** (Hirschi, 1969; Nye, 1958; Reckless, 1973). This perspective assumes that deviance is a natural condition and that its absence, not its

Figure 7.3
The cultural transmission theory of deviance is based on the assumption that deviance, like other behaviors, is learned. Neighborhood gangs like the Ghetto Brothers and Savage Skulls are microcosms of their communities and neighborhoods where there is an excess of definitions that favor violating the law. It is difficult to imagine, in fact, how a young person growing up in such an environment could avoid the pressure to conform to the subcultural standards that are characteristic of the neighborhood.

Differential-association theory assumes that deviance is learned through the same mechanisms as conformity—essentially through interaction with intimates.

Social control theory assumes that deviance is a natural condition which may be controlled by strong bonds that tie the individual to society.

presence, needs to be explained. Hirschi (1969) suggests that deviance is absent when people have strong social bonds to society; in this situation, informal social control is powerful. When individuals lack strong bonds to society, however, informal social control is weak or absent.

Hirschi identifies four ways in which people are bonded to society: attachment to other people, belief in the morality of social rules, commitment to conventional things, and involvement in conventional activities. Where individuals have strong bonds of attachment, belief, commitment, and involvement they are likely to conform. Where they do not, there is nothing to prevent their nonconformity. Social-control theory is similar to differential-association theory in that it traces deviance and conformity to an individual's group memberships. Whereas Sutherland's theory directs our attention to conforming versus nonconforming groups, however, Hirschi's theory directs our attention to the individual's attachment and integration to others.

Empirical support for Hirschi's social-control theory has been provided by many researchers (Hirschi, 1969; Krohn & Massey, 1980; Wiatrowski et al., 1981). It appears, however, that the theory explains mild forms of deviance better than it does serious offenses (Krohn & Massey, 1980).

Modernist Theories of Deviance

The modernist perspective on deviance is concerned with how acts and persons become defined as deviant. This perspective finds its voice in labeling and conflict theories.

As symbolic interactionists remind us, the meaning of any act depends on the symbolic meanings people attach to it. Thus a concern for the definition of deviance leads to a concern with subjective meanings. It also leads to a concern for the process by which one group's subjective meanings become preferred over another's. Within this perspective, labeling theory concentrates on how some acts come to be defined as deviant and conflict theory concentrates on the role of power and in equality in defining deviance.

Labeling Theory.   The processes by which some groups are able to attach the label *deviant* to the behavior of other groups or individuals is the concern of **labeling theory.** This theory is concerned not with why some people go bad but with why some people's acts are thought to be bad. It is also interested in how the *deviant* label comes to be shared by both the deviant and the conformist—the labeled and the labeler—and what consequences the labeling has for their future interactions. An important assumption behind this theory is that deviance is relative. As the chief proponent of labeling theory puts it, "Deviant behavior is behavior that people so label" (Becker, 1963:9). Thus the interpretation (label) that people attach to an act is more important than the act itself.

According to this theory, labelers generally consist of control agents: teachers, police, probation officers, mental-hospital attendants, psychiatrists, and so on. The labeled, of course, are the deviants: troublemakers, criminals, the insane. Labeling theory points out that those who do the labeling are usually more powerful than those they label.

The **Labeling theory of deviance** is concerned with the processes by which some groups are able to attach the label *deviant* to the behavior of other groups or individuals.

The process through which a person becomes labeled as deviant depends on the reactions of others toward nonconforming behavior. The first time a child acts up in class, it may be the result of a prank or a bad mood. This is an example of **primary deviance.** What happens in the future depends on how others interpret the act. If teachers, counselors, and other children label the child a troublemaker *and* if she accepts this definition of herself, then she may take on the role of troublemaker. This continued and deliberate deviance is called **secondary deviance.**

Researchers have found that labeling helps explain why some youths become increasingly delinquent as they get older whereas others eventually accept conformity and conventionality. Of the many youths who steal cars, smoke marijuana, or shoplift, only a portion are caught and only a portion of those caught end up with police records. Labeling theory suggests that those who are caught and publicly labeled are more likely to go on to deviant careers than are those who are able to escape the label. For example, a youth who is sent to jail for selling a small amount of marijuana comes out of prison an ex-con. This label may prevent him from getting a job, joining the army, or even getting into school; it may also cut him off from friends and family. Because some respectable alternatives are closed to him, a deviant career becomes more attractive. The many other youths who sell or trade small amounts of marijuana but do not get caught may go on to be respectable pillars of their community. It is society's differential treatment that produces secondary deviance. As this explanation suggests, labeling theorists are interested mainly in secondary deviance and the process by which labels are assigned.

FROM SIN TO SICKNESS.   Labeling theory's emphasis on subjective meanings gives us a framework for understanding the changing definitions of deviance. In recent years there has been an increasing tendency for acts to be labeled as sickness rather than deviance. Prominent examples include alcoholism, drug use, and even incest. Individuals who acquire *sick* rather than *bad* labels are entitled to treatment rather than punishment and are allowed to absolve themselves from blame for their behavior (Conrad & Schneider, 1980). Even with the general shift toward the medicalization of deviance (see chapter 16), there is still a great deal of subjectivity in the application of labels. For example, the upper-class woman who shoplifts is likely to be labeled neurotic, whereas the lower-class woman who steals the same items is likely to be labeled shoplifter. The middle-class boy who acts out in school may be defined as hyperactive, the lower-class boy as a troublemaker.

POWER AND LABELING.   Marxists suggest that the definitions of deviance are the result of a competition between vested interest groups (Troyer & Markle, 1982). Those with greater access to scarce resources get to decide what is called deviant. In a classic study, Becker (1963) describes how this competition between interest groups caused marijuana users in the United States to be labeled deviant. Prior to 1937, marijuana use was not illegal in the United States. In 1937, however, a powerful vested-interest group, the Federal Bureau of Narcotics, campaigned to have it declared illegal. (Since Prohibition had ended, the bureau had to either find a new enemy

Primary deviance is an individual's first instance of a nonconforming act. If the act is labeled deviant and the person accepts the label, then the person may become a real or secondary deviant.

Secondary deviance occurs when a person accepts the label of deviant and elects to play that role in society by repeatedly engaging in deviant acts.

Figure 7.4
Posters such as this one were distributed in the early 1930's when vested interest groups such as the Federal Bureau of Narcotics and the Consolidated Brewers Association of America joined together to make marijuana illegal. The zealous campaign of these moral entrepreneurs was successful and in 1937 marijuana use was declared a crime.

Moral entrepreneurs are people who are in a position to create and enforce new definitions of morality.

or go out of business.) The FBN launched a major media campaign to stigmatize marijuana use by associating marijuana with violence and other criminal behaviors. As a result of its successful campaign, it created a new group of deviants. Becker refers to those who are in a position to create and enforce new definitions of morality as **moral entrepreneurs.**

EVALUATION.   Labeling theory has become extremely popular in sociology in the last 20 years and has been applied in diverse situations (see chapter 12 for a discussion of labeling in the schools, for example). It does, however, have some important limitations. First, the assumption that deviance is relative tends to limit this perspective to explanations of minor or victimless crimes. There are few who would like to argue that the only thing wrong with murder is that some powerful group has arbitrarily chosen to define it as deviant. Second, labeling theory tends to ignore the causes of primary deviance in favor of a focus on the reactions of others to deviance. Finally, labeling theory has not been useful in explaining the deviance of the powerful; this is because the primary deviance of business and government (for example, price-fixing or the dumping of toxic wastes) is not seriously stigmatized or labeled in the United States. Nor do those who commit such acts experience the same consequences for their deviance as do the less powerful.

Conflict Theory.   The conflict theory of deviance is concerned with how competition and inequality within society create deviance. In a classic conflict analysis, Marx argued that low wages and unemployment pressured the working class into acts of crime in order to maintain a decent living. Conflict theorists argue that nearly all crimes among the working class are a means to survival: "Crime under capitalism has become a response to the conditions of life" (Quinney, 1980).

Capitalism is alleged to encourage not only property crimes but also acts of violence such as murder, rape, and assault. It is suggested that economic marginality leads to a lack of self-esteem and a sense of powerlessness and alienation, which leads some people to vent their frustration in violence (Balkan et al., 1980). Others become self-destructive, turning to suicide, alcoholism, or mental illness.

Conflict theorists point out that the class differentials in crime rates are also caused by discrimination against the poor in law enforcement. Formal controls have been aimed more heavily at lower-class kinds of crime than at upper-class kinds of crime. For example, we spend more money deterring muggers than embezzlers. In addition, even when people from the upper and lower classes commit similar crimes, those from the lower class are more likely to be arrested, prosecuted, and sentenced (Williams & Drake, 1980).

Summary

Within the field of sociology there are two general perspectives on deviance: traditional and modernist. Both are sociological, not psychological, theories; they place the reasons for deviance within the social structure rather than within the individual. The two perspectives differ in part in the kinds of deviance they seek to explain (see Concept Summary). Traditional theory seeks to explain acts that are widely regarded as deviant, whereas modernist theory seeks to explain acts that are only sometimes regarded as deviant. Thus traditionalists tend to deal with rape, murder, and arson and modernists with the deviance of everyday life—cheating, troublemaking, and marijuana smoking.

Crime as Deviance

Much of the behavior that is regarded as deviant or nonconforming is subject only to informal social controls. Acts that are subject to legal or civil penalties are called **crimes.** Many of the acts that we call crimes have been so labeled because they represent serious threats to the well-being of individuals and society and must be controlled. Such individual threats as murder and assault and such societal threats as treason are examples of acts that are called crimes because they violate important norms and values. Some acts, however, are called crimes because one

Crimes are deviant acts that are subject to criminal or civil penalties.

CONCEPT SUMMARY

Theories of Deviance

	MAJOR QUESTION	MAJOR ASSUMPTION	CAUSE OF DEVIANCE	MOST USEFUL FOR EX-PLAINING DEVIANCE OF
TRADITIONAL THEORY				
a. Anomie Theory	Why do people break rules?	Deviance is an abnormal characteristic of the social structure	A dislocation between the goals of society and the means to achieve them.	The working and lower classes who cannot achieve desired goals by means at hand.
b. Cultural Transmission Theory	Why is deviance more characteristic of some groups than others?	Deviance is learned like other social behavior	Subcultural values differ in complex societies; some subcultures hold values that favor deviance. These are learned through socialization.	Delinquent gangs and those integrated into deviant subcultures and neighborhoods.
c. Social Control Theory	What keeps people from breaking the rules?	Deviance is normal and it is conformity which must be explained.	Absence of strong ties to others and to society's values and activities.	Individuals who are poorly integrated into families, neighborhoods, and communities (particularly youth from broken homes).
MODERNIST THEORY				
d. Labelling Theory	How do acts and people become labelled deviant?	Deviance is relative and depends on how others label acts and actors.	People whose acts are labelled deviant and who accept that label become career deviants.	The powerless who are labelled deviant by more powerful individuals.
e. Conflict Theory	How does unequal access to scarce resources lead to deviance?	Deviance is a normal response to competition and conflict over scarce resources.	Inequality and competition.	All classes. Lower class driven to deviance to meet basic needs and to act out frustration; upper class use deviant means to maintain their privilege.

Victimless crimes are illegal acts for which there is no complainant.

segment of society successfully imposes its definitions on other segments. So-called **victimless crimes**—illegal acts for which there is no complainant, such as homosexuality, prostitution, and vagrancy—are examples. In this section, we will examine the incidence and characteristics of crime in the United States and the responses of society to crime. The examination will include major crimes of violence and property as well as white-collar and victimless crimes.

Measuring Crime Rates

Crime statistics for the United States are based primarily on two sources of information: the *Uniform Crime Report* and the *National Crime Survey.* The *Uniform Crime Report (UCR)* has been issued annually by the FBI since 1927. It summarizes crimes known to the police in seven major categories of criminal offense: murder and nonnegligent manslaughter, forcible rape, robbery, aggravated assault, burglary, larceny-theft, and motor vehicle theft; in 1979, an eighth crime, arson, was added. These statistics are widely used to monitor levels of crime.

The official statistics are criticized on two major grounds. First, it is argued that the statistics may not be comparable from year to year or from jurisdiction to jurisdiction. Levels of crime reported to the Federal Bureau of Investigation (FBI) depend on (1) differences from jurisdiction to jurisdiction in the definition of the crime, (2) changing rates at which the public reports crime to the police, and (3) variations in the way police officers handle crime reports. Whether police officers find or officially report a crime may depend on the victim's social characteristics, the relationship between the victim and the accused, and organizational pressures on the police. Prior to a political campaign, for example, there may be pressure to make the crime rate look low; at budget time, the need to justify expenses and ward off budget cuts may cause pressure to make the crime rate look high. All these factors lead to bias and error in official reports.

Second, because not all crimes are reported, especially the less violent crimes, the UCR underestimates the crime rate. For example, it is estimated that only 26 percent of the instances of personal larceny and only 50 percent of rape incidents are reported to police (O'Brien et al., 1980). Thus victimization surveys are used to supplement official statistics. Twice each year, the Department of Justice asks a random sample of 65,000 householders about any crimes they or any members of their household have experienced during the last 6 months. These *National Crime Surveys* provide information on crimes known to victims and allow changes in crime reporting to be monitored. The following discussion relies heavily on official statistics (*UCR*) in reporting the incidence of crime by major categories and uses findings from both sources in its discussion of the correlates of crime.

Crimes of Violence

Crimes involving the use of force or the threat of force are known as crimes of violence. The *UCR* taps four such crimes: murder and nonnegligent manslaughter, rape, assault, and armed robbery.

Murder.   The most violent criminal acts are murder and nonnegligent manslaughter. Murder is a relatively rare form of crime, constituting about 2 percent of all violent crimes committed in the United States. In 1982, there were 9 murders for every 100,000 persons, with southern states and urban areas reporting the highest murder rates. The murder rate over all has remained almost unchanged over the last 10 years, although it showed a noticeable decline between 1980 and 1982. In 1981, the chance of being a murder victim over one's lifetime was estimated to be 1 out of 153. The odds were highest for nonwhite males (1 out of 28) and lowest for white females (1 out of 450). As these figures suggest, the chances of being a murder victim are unevenly distributed; in 1982, 52 percent of all murder victims were black and 76 percent were male. Although the social class of victims is hard to identify, it is estimated that as many as 90 percent of murder victims are lower class (Mulvihill et al., 1969; Swigert & Farrell, 1976; Wolfgang, 1958). Many murders involve situations in which the victim and the offender know each other. In 1982, 46 percent of the murders were committed either by relatives or by persons acquainted with the victim; 17 percent of all murders were within families, and one-half of these involved a spouse killing a spouse.

Rape.   Forcible rape accounts for approximately 6 percent of the violent crimes in the United States (U.S. Department of Justice, 1983). In 1982, there were 77,763 rape offenses reported, a rate of 34 per 100,000 population. Studies of rape victimization suggest that in nearly half of the cases the victim and the assailant were previously acquainted (Amir, 1971). Although reported rapes declined somewhat in 1981 and 1982 (see Figure 7.5), current rates of rape are much higher than they were a decade ago. Some of this increase may be due to a change in reporting patterns. Revised police procedures may have made it less embarrassing for women to report rapes and rape attempts.

Robbery.   Taking or attempting to take anything of value from another person by force, threat of force, violence, or putting the victim in fear is

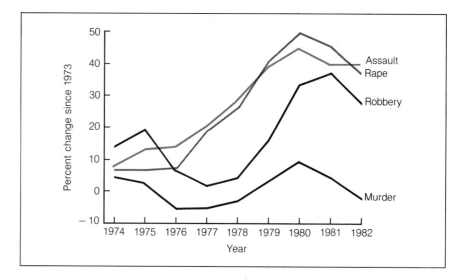

Figure 7.5   Changes in Violent Crime Rates, 1973–1982
Since 1973, rape, robbery, and assault have become more frequent. Nevertheless, the last two years have witnessed a decline in nearly all forms of violent crime.
SOURCE: U.S. Department of Justice, 1983, table 1.

known as robbery. Unlike simple theft or larceny, robbery involves a personal confrontation between the victim and the robber and is thus a crime of violence.

In 1982, more than half a million robberies were officially reported in the United States. Although all types of robbery have increased in the last decade, armed robbery has increased at a faster rate than unarmed robbery, which indicates a greater tendency toward violence during the act of robbery.

Assault.   Aggravated assault is an unlawful attack for the purposes of inflicting severe bodily injury. Kicking and hitting are included in assault, but increasingly assault involves a gun, knife, or other weapon. Nearly half of all violent crimes are aggravated assault.

Since 1973, the aggravated-assault rate has increased 40 percent in the United States. It is the only crime in the *UCR* that did not decline between 1981 and 1982. Like homicide, aggravated assault is most often a crime of passion, with the offender and the victim knowing each other personally.

Property Crimes

The other major offenses officially reported in the *UCR* are the property offenses of burglary, larceny-theft, motor vehicle theft, and arson (see Figure 7.7). These are by far the most frequent crimes committed in the United States, occurring 9 times more often than crimes of violence. Property losses from these crimes are estimated to have exceeded $9 billion in 1981. Burglary and motor vehicle theft each accounted for approximately $3.5 billion. These estimates of total loss are undoubtedly conservative, however, as many larceny-thefts (shoplifting, purse-snatching, and thefts from office buildings, for example) go undetected or unreported.

Figure 7.6
Assaults, such as this attack on a woman in Boston's high crime area, the so-called combat zone, are among the most feared crimes in America today. Nearly half of all crimes of violence reported in the U.S. are aggravated assaults. For the past two years, the assault rate has been increasing while other major crimes of violence have decreased. As a result, more people express fear in their homes and neighborhoods.

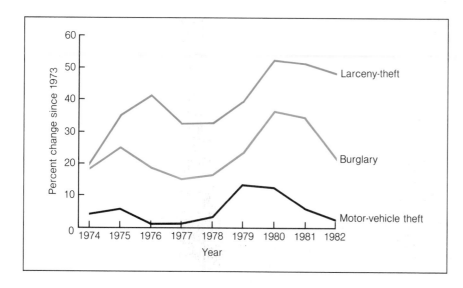

Figure 7.7 Changes in Property Crimes, 1973–1982
Property crimes, especially larceny-theft, have increased over the last decade. In all categories, however, crime is down from the 1980–1981 rates.
SOURCE: U.S. Department of Justice, 1983, table 1.

Summary of Crime Trends

Crime rates are higher now than they were a decade ago. One major crime was committed every 2 seconds in the United States during 1982. Nevertheless, in all major crime categories except aggravated assault, there has been a general downward trend since 1980 and 1981. This trend is attributed largely to the aging of the baby-boom generation. Because young people account for a high proportion of all crime, a decrease in the proportion of the population that is 15 to 24 years old generally results in a decrease in the crime rate.

Correlates of Crime: Age, Gender, Race, and Class

In 1981, only 20 percent of the crimes reported in the *UCR* were cleared by an arrest. This means that the people arrested for criminal acts represent approximately a 1 in 5 sample of those who commit reported crimes; they are undoubtedly not a random sample. The low level of arrests coupled with the low levels of crime reporting warn us to be cautious in applying generalizations about arrestees to the larger population of criminals. With this caution in mind, we note that the persons arrested for criminal acts are overwhelmingly male and disproportionately young and from minority groups. The highest incidence of violent crime is for black male 18-to-20-year-olds; the rate for this group is 22 times greater than that for white male 18-to-20-year-olds and 300 times greater than that for the least offensive group, white female adults (Hindelang, 1981). The incidence of household crimes (burglary, household larceny, and vehicle theft) is also much higher for this group.

An important question for sociologists studying deviance is: What causes these differences? Some of the answers come from the traditional perspective and some from the modern.

Gender Differences. The gender differential in crime can be attributed to both physical and social causes. Women's smaller size and lesser strength

Figure 7.8

Property crimes, such as this woman shoplifting cosmetics, are among the most frequent and costly crimes committed in the United States. Because much property crime either goes undetected or unreported, it is difficult to estimate the real dollar value of all property crimes.

make them less effective than men in situations of personal confrontation and threat. Although guns are appropriately known as equalizers, women have not made much use of them. This may be because the traditional female role stresses nonaggression. It may also be because most deviant groups lack affirmative-action officers—women have generally not had the same opportunity as men to join deviant networks (Steffenmeier, 1980). Moreover, the criminal-justice system, from the police on their beats to the court system, is generally more lenient toward women, letting them off in situations where men would be held (Frazier et al., 1983).

These sex-role explanations raise questions about whether changing roles for women will affect women's participation in crime. Will increased equality in education, labor-force participation, smoking, and drinking also show up in greater equality of criminal behavior? The evidence shows little tendency for this to happen (Hartnagel, 1982; Steffenmeier & Cobb, 1981). It is true that the crime rate for women has increased faster than the crime rate for men in a few areas (vagrancy, disorderly conduct, property crimes), but there has been no increase in women's participation in violent crime.

Differences by Social Class.   The effect of social class on crime rates is more complex. Although sociologists have historically held that social class is an important explanation of criminality (Braithwaite, 1981; Elliott & Ageton, 1980; Thornberry & Farnworth, 1982), some recent studies have found that the relationship is not very strong and in some cases is nonexistent (Hirschi, 1969; Johnson, 1980; Krohn et al., 1980; Tittle et al., 1978). Much of the inconsistency appears to center on difficulties in measuring both social class and crime.

Braithwaite's (1981) review of more than 100 studies leads to the conclusion that lower-class people commit more of the direct interpersonal types of crimes normally handled by the police than do people from the middle class. These are the types of crimes officially reported in the *UCR*. Middle-class people commit more of the crimes that involve the use of power, particularly in the context of their occupational roles: fraud, embezzlement, price-fixing, and other forms of white-collar crime. There is also evidence that the social-class differential may be greater for adult crime than for juvenile delinquency (Thornberry & Farnworth, 1982).

Both traditional and modernist theories offer explanations for these social-class differences. Traditionalists suggest that the lower-class is more likely to engage in crime because of blocked avenues to achievement, poor social integration, and growing up in neighborhoods containing exposure to deviant subcultures. Modernists point out that primary deviance in the lower class is likely to receive a negative label and thus lead to secondary deviance. Furthermore, social-control agencies concentrate more heavily on lower-class forms of deviance and are less lenient with lower-class offenders (Williams & Drake, 1980). Finally, frustration over inequality is likely to lead to increases in property crimes and crimes of violence.

Differences by Race. Although blacks are only 12 percent of the population, they are 50 percent of those arrested for murder and rape, 61 percent of those arrested for robbery, and 39 percent of those arrested for assault. Hispanics, who compose about 6 percent of the total population, are between 10 and 15 percent of those arrested for violent crimes. These strong differences in arrest rates are explained in part by social-class differences between minority and Anglo populations. Even after this effect is taken into account, however, blacks and Hispanics are still much more likely to be arrested for committing crimes.

Because many crimes, especially crimes of violence, occur among friends and acquaintances, minority-group members are also much more likely to be the victims of violence. The explanation is complex. Part of it lies in the difficulties that minority-group members face in standard achievement. Like the men on Tally's Corner, they have fathers who are failures, and the signs of failure are all around them. The likelihood that they can pull themselves out of poverty appears low. Thus, it is argued, lower-class minorities are more frustrated, angry, and despairing than are lower-class Anglos. As conflict theorists suggest, this may lead to crimes of aggression as well as crimes for economic gain. In addition, minority-group members often live in neighborhoods characterized by rapid turnover of renters, a situation that reduces the effectiveness of informal mechanisms of social control. There is also substantial evidence that whether we're talking about troublemaking in school, stealing cars, or petty theft, minority-group members are more likely than Anglos to be branded deviant and, if apprehended by the police, more apt to be cited, prosecuted, and convicted (Unnever et al., 1980). An additional factor, as noted in chapter 4's discussion of the gangs on 32nd Street, is that minority subcultures (like the southern white subculture) may place more emphasis on violence as part of life.

Victimless Crimes

The so-called victimless crimes—such as drug use, prostitution, homosexuality, gambling, and pornography—are voluntary exchanges between persons who desire goods or services from each other (Schur, 1979). Par-

FOCUS ON MEASUREMENT

How Deviant Are You?

Because the offenders who find their way into official statistics are such a biased sample of all offenders, many people argue that males, minorities, and lower-class people are getting too much blame for crime. One measurement technique that tries to get at the true differentials in deviance uses self-reports. The following self-report was designed by Hindelang, Hirschi, and Weis (1981:223–226) to measure deviance among high school youths. Try yourself out on it to see how deviant you were at 17.

Place a check next to things you had *ever* done by age 17:

— 1. Been questioned as a suspect by the police about some crime.

— 2. Been held by the police or court until you could be released into the custody of your parents or guardians.

— 3. Been placed on probation by a juvenile court judge.

— 4. Been caught shoplifting by the clerk or owner of a store.

— 5. Been sentenced to a reformatory, training school, or some other institution by a judge.

— 6. Sold something you had stolen yourself.

— 7. Broken into a house, store, school or other building and taken money, stereo equipment, guns or something else you wanted.

— 8. Broken into a locked car to get something from it.

— 9. Taken hubcaps, wheels, the battery, or some other expensive part of a car without the owner's permission.

—10. Taken gasoline from a car without the owner's permission.

—11. Taken things worth between $10 and $50 from a store without paying for them.

—12. Threatened to beat someone up if they didn't give you money or something else you wanted.

—13. Carried a razor, switchblade, or gun with the intention of using it in a fight.

—14. Pulled a knife, gun, or some other weapon on someone just to let them know you meant business.

—15. Beat someone up so badly they probably needed a doctor.

—16. Taken a car belonging to someone you didn't know for a ride without the owner's permission.

—17. Taken a tape deck or a CB radio from a car.

—18. Broken into a house, store, school or other building with the intention of breaking things up or causing other damage.

—19. Taken things of large value (worth more than $50) from a store without paying for them.

—20. Tried to get away from a police officer by fighting or struggling.

—21. Used physical force (like twisting an arm or choking) to get money from another person.

—22. Used a club, knife, or gun to get something from someone.

—23. Taken things from a wallet or purse (or the whole wallet or purse) while the owner wasn't around or wasn't looking.

—24. Hit a teacher or some other school official.

—25. Taken a bicycle belonging to someone you didn't know with no intention of returning it.

—26. Tried to pass a check by signing someone else's name.

—27. Intentionally started a building on fire.

—28. Grabbed a purse from someone and run with it.

—29. Forced another person to have sex relations with you when they did not want to.

—30. Taken little things (worth less than $2) from a store without paying for them.

—31. Broken the windows of an empty house or other unoccupied building.

—32. Let the air out of car or truck tires.

—33. Used a slug or fake money in a candy, coke, coin, or stamp machine.

—34. Fired a BB gun at some other person, at passing cars, or at windows of buildings.

—35. Taken things you weren't supposed to take from a desk or locker at school.

—36. Bought something you knew had been stolen.

—37. Broken the windows of a school building.

—38. Taken material or equipment from a construction site.

—39. Refused to tell the police or some other official what you knew about a crime.

—40. Purposely broken a car window.

—41. Picked a fight with someone you didn't know just for the hell of it.

—42. Helped break up chairs, tables, desks, or other furniture in a school, church, or other public building.

—43. Jumped or helped jump somebody and then beat them up.

—44. Slashed the seats in a bus, a

movie house or some other place.

—45. Punctured or slashed the tires of a car.

—46. Destroyed things at a construction site.

—47. Destroyed mailboxes.

—48. Kept money for yourself that you collected for a team, a charity (like the March of Dimes), or someone else's paper route.

—49. Driven away from the scene of an accident that you were involved in without identifying yourself.

—50. Taken mail from someone else's mailbox and opened it.

—51. Broken into a parking meter or the coin box of a pay phone.

—52. Drunk beer or wine.

—53. Drunk whiskey, gin, vodka or other "hard" liquor.

—54. Smoked marijuana (grass, pot).

—55. Gone to school when you were drunk or high on some drugs.

—56. Pretended to be older than you were to buy beer or cigarettes.

—57. Sold illegal drugs such as heroin, marijuana, LSD, or cocaine.

—58. Driven a car when you were drunk or high on some drugs.

—59. Taken barbiturates (downers) or methedrine (speed or other uppers) without a prescription.

—60. Used cocaine.

—61. Taken angel dust, LSD, or mescaline.

—62. Used heroin (smack).

—63. Been sent out of a classroom.

—64. Stayed away from school when your parents thought you were there.

—65. Gone out at night when your parents told you that you couldn't go.

—66. Been suspended or expelled from school.

—67. Cursed or threatened an adult in a loud and mean way just to let them know who was boss.

—68. Run away from home and stayed overnight.

—69. Hit one of your parents.

If you have never done any of these things, you are exceptional. You are probably also a white female. Like the official statistics, self-report measures show differentials by race and gender. Males report nearly twice as much deviance as females; the difference is least on the drug and alcohol items and greatest on the items involving violence. Black youths, especially girls, report somewhat more delinquent acts than whites of the same gender. This differential is particularly strong for items reflecting violent personal encounters. Self-report data, however, do eliminate the social-class differential. Middle-class youths report as much deviance as lower-class youths (Tittle et al., 1978; Hirschi, 1969). Does this mean that middle-class kids are as deviant

as lower-class kids but that they get away with it more? Some scholars believe that this is true; others believe that the lower-class kids really are more deviant than the middle-class kids but that they aren't about to admit it, even on an anonymous questionnaire. These scholars also raise questions about whether the truly deviant (a category that they presume overrepresents lower-class kids) are included in these samples (Kleck, 1982).

When this self-report was filled out by more than 14,000 youths in Seattle in 1975, it was found that the amount of self-reported deviance was highly related to police contact. Among males with no police record, the average number of items checked was 12; among those with a police (but not a court) record, the average was 22. Among females, the figures were 8 and 12. How did you stack up?

SOURCE: Hindelang, Michael J., Hirschi, Travis, & Weis, Joseph. "Appendix B, The Seattle Self-report Instrument," Pp. 223–226 in Measuring Delinquency. Copyright © 1981. Reprinted by permission of Sage Publications, Inc.

Questions to Consider

Do you think that this self-report is a comprehensive measure of deviance? Explain. Are there things that should be added to the list? How much of a problem do you suppose dishonesty is in such a questionnaire?

ticipants in the exchange typically do not see themselves as being victimized or as suffering from the transaction. Moreover, most offenders regard the laws regulating these illicit transactions as outmoded and discriminatory.

Because there are no complaining victims, these crimes are difficult to control. The drug user is generally not going to complain about the drug pusher, and the illegal gambler is unlikely to bring charges against a bookie. In the absence of a complaining victim, the police must find not only the criminal but also the crime. Efforts to do so are costly and divert attention from other criminal acts. As a result, victimless crimes are irregularly and inconsistently enforced, most often in the form of periodic crackdowns and routine harassment. In spite of these difficulties, though, approximately one-third of all arrests are for victimless crimes.

Many informed observers conclude that the laws regarding victimless crimes do more harm than good. Not only do they increase enforcement costs, but they burden an already overburdened court system, stimulate organized crime and criminal careers in the forbidden areas, and contribute to police corruption and public disrespect for the law (Schur, 1979). Despite these arguments, enforcement continues, largely because vocal community groups find such behavior morally repugnant and have pressured authorities to control it.

White-Collar Crime

A crime committed by respectable people of high social status in the course of their profession is **white-collar crime** (Sutherland, 1961). This type of crime includes offenses such as false advertising, price-fixing, embezzlement, auto and home improvement fraud, and tax evasion. In many ways, these types of crimes are more harmful than all of the street crimes combined. It has been estimated, for example, that in 1979 the property loss from white-collar crime ranged somewhere between $50 billion and $200 billion, far more than the loss from common crimes ("Crime in the Suites," 1979).

White-collar crime occurs at several levels. It is committed, for example, by employees against companies, by companies against employees, by companies against customers, and by companies against the public (the latter by dumping toxic wastes into the air, land, or water). In addition to the enormous economic costs of white-collar crime, there are social costs as well. Exposure to repeated tales of corruption tends to breed distrust and cynicism and, ultimately, to undermine the integration of social institutions. If you think that all members of Congress are crooks, then you quit voting. If you think that every police officer can be bought, then you cease to respect the law. Thus the costs of such crime go beyond the actual dollars involved.

The magnitude of white-collar crime in our society makes a mockery of the idea that crime is predominantly a lower-class phenomenon. Instead, it appears that people of different statuses simply have different opportunities to commit crime. Those in the lower statuses are hardly in the position to engage in price-fixing, stock manipulation, or tax evasion. They are in the position, however, to engage in high-risk, low-yield crimes

White-collar crime is crime committed by people of respectability and high social status in the course of their profession.

Figure 7.9
Laws against industrial waste, one form of white-collar crime, have proven difficult to enforce as well as costly. At this paper factory, waste containing high levels of mercury is dumped into the English-Wabigoon River where it is ingested by fish. The Ojibway Indians who rely on fishing eventually suffer the effects of mercury poisoning.

such as robbery and larceny. Since most white-collar crime goes undetected or unreported, higher-status individuals are in the position to engage in low-risk, high-yield crimes (Schur, 1979).

The Fear of Victimization

Victimization studies show that about one-quarter of all U.S. households were victims of crime in the last year. For most of these households, victimization was a minor annoyance (a broken window or the loss of a bicycle, for example) rather than a major trauma. Nevertheless, the relatively common experience of victimization, paired with sensational media coverage of gruesome cases of murder, torture, or rape, can cause widespread fear.

Although the likelihood of the average citizen experiencing violent crime is relatively remote and, in fact, declining, national surveys demonstrate increasing fear of victimization (see Table 7.2). One out of every two adults, for example, is afraid to walk alone at night in his or her neighborhood, and three out of every four women who live in urbanized areas express this fear (Gallup Report, 1983, no. 210). Moreover, 13 percent fear going out into their neighborhoods in broad daylight, and 16 percent do not feel secure even in their own homes at night. Those who are most fearful tend to be women, nonwhites, the elderly, low-income people, and city dwellers.

The fear of victimization is most acute among the elderly. In March 1981, both *Time* and *Newsweek* devoted cover stories to the fact that crime and the fear of crime are the major issues of concern to older Americans. To what extent are their fears real? How does fear affect neighborhood and community satisfaction? Are the elderly becoming prisoners of fear who dare not leave the security of their own homes?

Although the elderly tend to be the most fearful of victimization, they are actually among the least likely to be victimized. The fear of victimization, however, may have its own negative consequences. Those who are fearful are more dissatisfied with their neighborhoods, have lower morale, and feel slightly more isolated than they would prefer to be (Yin, 1982). Although these findings suggest that fear of victimization reduces the quality of life for older Americans, it must be remembered that these findings come from a cross-sectional survey. We cannot be certain, therefore, whether unhappiness and isolation lead to fear of crime or whether fear of crime leads to unhappiness and isolation.

Formal Social Control: Police, Courts, and Prisons

The formal mechanisms of social control discussed at the beginning of the chapter are administered through the criminal-justice system. In the United States, this system consists of a vast network of agencies set up to deal with persons who deviate from the law: police departments, probation and parole agencies, rehabilitation agencies, criminal courts, jails, and penitentiaries.

Because the U.S. Constitution reserves police powers to the states, law enforcement is largely a function of state and local agencies. Each has its

Table 7.2 Victimization and Fear of Victimization

Data from a 1983 Gallup Poll show that women, the elderly, and people in big cities are most likely to fear crime. However, they are generally no more likely than others to be the victims of crime. The elderly show a particularly large gap between their fear of crime and the likelihood that they will be victims.

	PERCENT AFRAID TO WALK ALONE AT NIGHT	PERCENT ACTUALLY VICTIMIZED
Total	45%	25%
Gender:		
Male	26	25
Female	62	25
Race:		
White	43	25
Black	58	24
Age:		
Under 30	45	31
30–49	39	29
50–65	47	18
65 and older	54	15
City size:		
Over 1,000,000	56	28
500,000– 999,999	49	32
50,000–499,999	54	27
2,500–49,999	40	21
Under 2,500 and rural	29	20

SOURCE: The Gallup Report, No. 210, March 1983:4–6.

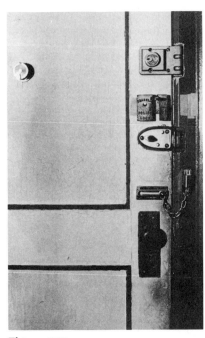

Figure 7.10
Many citizens report that they are afraid to walk outside in their neighborhood at night. As the locks on this door indicate, many also fear staying at home and take extra security measures to prevent burglary, assault, rape, and other major crimes. This fear of becoming a crime victim is most acute among the elderly, females, and persons in large cities.

Street-level justice is the decisions the police make in the initial stages of an investigation.

own criminal law, procedures of enforcement, and enforcement agencies. Although these systems of law enforcement resemble one another, there are often substantial differences in the treatment of similar offenses. Nevada, for example, is the only state where first-offense possession of the slightest amount of marijuana is a felony, punishable by up to 6 years' imprisonment. Ironically, until recently, Nevada was also the only state permitting casino gambling and prostitution (Galliher & Cross, 1982).

Law enforcement and the control of crime are the responsibility of three groups: those who investigate and arrest persons suspected of committing crimes, those who prosecute persons charged with crimes, and those who administer punishment or treatment to persons convicted of crimes.

The Police

Police officers occupy a unique and powerful position in the criminal-justice system because they are empowered to make arrests in a context of low visibility: Often there are no witnesses to police encounters with suspected offenders. Although they are supposed to enforce the law fully and uniformly, everyone realizes that this is neither practical nor even possible. In 1981, there were approximately 2 full-time law-enforcement officers for every 1,000 persons in the nation (U.S. Department of Justice, 1983). This means that the police ordinarily must give greater attention to the more serious crimes. Minor offenses and ambiguous situations are likely to be ignored.

Police officers have a considerable amount of discretionary power in determining the extent to which the policy of full enforcement is carried out. Should a drunk and disorderly person be charged or sent home? Should a juvenile offender be charged or reported to parents? Should a strong odor of marijuana among an otherwise orderly group be overlooked or investigated? The decisions the police make in the initial stages of an investigation are called **street-level justice.** Unlike the justice meted out in courts, street-level justice is relatively invisible and thus hard to evaluate.

In a recent study of 24 police departments in three large metropolitan areas, Smith and Visher (1981) report that street-level justice depends on how antagonistic the suspect is, whether there are bystanders present, and whether the victim and the suspect know each other. Suspects who are highly antagonistic and who directly challenge the authority of the investigating officer are likely to be arrested. Arrest rates are also higher when bystanders are present, probably because of the need for the police to appear to be in control. In situations where the victim and the suspect know each other, however, the police are less likely to make an arrest. This may be because they perceive that the victim is less likely to cooperate in getting a conviction (Smith & Visher, 1981). In addition, persons who are members of socially disadvantaged groups, such as blacks and youths, are more likely to be taken into custody, independent of the seriousness of the offense (Black, 1976; Galliher, 1971).

Although everyone realizes that police officers must exercise some discretion, there is concern that prejudice and bias may enter into their decision making. In short, there are many questions about the justice of street-level justice.

Figure 7.11
Police officers have considerable discretionary power in deciding when to make an arrest. Factors that contribute to arrest include the presence of bystanders, whether the assailant and victim know one another, and the hostility of a suspect. In this photograph a robbery victim (notice that his back pocket is still turned inside out) has pursued his assailants and angrily holds a gun on them while waiting for the police. Because of the victim's actions, the discretionary power of the police was minimized. The two suspects in the car were arrested and later convicted of armed robbery.

The Courts

The second stage of controlling crime involves the prosecution of people who have been arrested as suspects in the commission of a crime. This, of course, is a minority of all offenders. As Figure 17.12 shows, crimes of violence, especially murder and aggravated assault, are more likely to result in arrest and prosecution than are crimes of property.

Once arrested, an individual starts a complex trip through the judicial process. This trip can best be thought of as a series of decision stages through which some of those arrested will pass. Just as there is a high level of attrition in police work, there is also considerable attrition as defendants pass from arrest to prosecution to sentencing and punishment. Even in felony cases, it is not unusual to find that as many as 40 to 50 percent of those arrested will be rejected for prosecution after initial hearings because of problems with evidence or witnesses (Brossi, 1979). At the same time, approximately 90 percent of all convictions are the result of guilty pleas at this stage of prosecution (Blumberg, 1970). This means that only about 10 percent of criminal convictions are processed through public trials. Thus the pretrial phases of prosecution are often more crucial to arriving at judicial decisions of guilt or innocence than are court trials themselves. Like the police, prosecutors have considerable discretion in deciding whom to prosecute and on what charges.

Throughout the entire process, the prosecution, the defense, and the judges participate in negotiated plea bargaining. The accused is encouraged to plead guilty in the interest of getting a lighter sentence, a reduced charge, or, in the case of multiple offenses, the dropping of some charges. In return, the prosecution is saved the trouble of assembling evidence sufficient for a jury trial.

Figure 7.12 Proportion of Crimes in the United States Cleared by Arrest, 1982
The police are much more likely to identify and arrest an offender in cases of violent crime than in cases of nonviolent crime. Over all, only 1 out of every 5 crimes reported to officials results in an arrest.
SOURCE: U.S. Department of Justice, 1983.

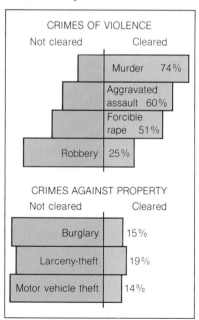

Sentencing, whether it results from trial proceedings, plea bargains, or guilty pleas, is officially decided by the judge. In reality, however, the prosecutor indirectly determines sentencing, since it is the prosecutor who decides what charges to file and what plea bargains to accept.

One of the critical problems throughout the judicial process is the disparity in sentencing that occurs across the country and even within the same jurisdiction. In general, judges have considerable leeway in determining a sentence, and there is little uniformity in decisions made. There is also considerable evidence that sentencing decisions are influenced by the social class and race of the criminal (Wolfgang & Cohen, 1970). Males, those from lower-class backgrounds, and blacks receive severer sentences; they are more likely than others to receive the death penalty, to receive longer sentences, and to be denied early parole (Frazier et al., 1983; Petersen & Friday, 1975; Thornberry, 1973). As a result of this disparity, several states have recently adopted determinate and mandatory sentencing as a solution; sentences and fines are regulated by statute rather than by the discretion of the judge. Determinate sentencing, however, may merely have the effect of shifting the discretionary power to prosecutors through plea bargaining or to prison officials who can recommend early release and probation (Clear et al., 1978).

Prisons and Punishment

Any assessment of prisons and punishment must come to grips with the issue: Why are we doing this? Before we can assess the adequacy of punishment, we need to be clear about its purpose. There seem to be five major rationalizations for punishment (Conrad, 1983):

1. *Retribution.* Society punishes offenders in order to revenge the victim and society as a whole; this is a form of revenge and retaliation.
2. *Reformation.* Offenders are not punished, but rather are corrected and reformed so that they will become upstanding members of the community.
3. *Specific Deterrence.* Punishment is intended to scare offenders so they will think twice about violating the law again.
4. *General Deterrence.* By making an example of offenders, society scares the rest of us into following the rules.
5. *Prevention.* By incapacitating offenders, society keeps them from committing further crimes against society.

Today, prisons in the United States represent an amalgamation of these different philosophies and practices. Currently, there are nearly 800 state prisons, with a total inmate population of approximately 330,000. An additional 160,000 people are confined in local jails. Approximately 40 percent of the inmates of local jails have not been convicted of a crime. They are in jail because they are awaiting trial and have been unable to post bail. Disproportionately, they are young men who are uneducated, unskilled, poor, and black. Urban jails are particularly overcrowded, mixing petty offenders and persons not yet convicted of crimes with hardened criminals. In many ways, jails are more punitive, dangerous, and degrading than are maximum-security prisons.

Figure 7.13
Prisons are total institutions where inmates are assigned numbers, wear identical uniforms, live in identical cells, and all follow the same routines. They are also environments full of anger, hatred, violence, and insecurity. In this totally negative environment, prisons become warehouses for the deviant and the violent. They are unlikely environments for rehabilitation.

In recent years, prisons have become increasingly overcrowded. Between 1970 and 1981, the proportion of the population in prisons jumped 58 percent—from 96.7 per 100,000 to 153.2 per 100,000. Even in facilities where there is only one inmate per cell, 58 percent provided less than 60 square feet per inmate—a space about the size of a bathroom (U.S. Bureau of the Census, 1984). These overcrowded conditions, many believe, have contributed to the violent outbreaks and revolts at penitentiaries in New York, New Mexico, and Missouri.

The effects of imprisonment are overwhelmingly negative. Prisoners are deprived of liberty, goods and services, heterosexual relationships, autonomy, and security (Sykes, 1974). The loss of liberty and autonomy is a deliberately imposed sanction; the loss of security is largely a latent dysfunction. The inmate is forced to associate with other criminals, many of whom have a long history of violent and aggressive behavior. The climate of violence and fear that pervades prisons and jails has no counterpart on the outside (Toch, 1977). As one prisoner commented, "It takes a pretty good man to be able to stand on an equal plane with a guy that's in for rape, with a guy that's in for murder, with a man who's well respected in the institution because he's a real tough cookie" (Sykes, 1974:78). Although imprisonment may prevent a man from abusing the rest of us, it does not prevent him from abusing fellow inmates. Many would argue that the fear and insecurity that accompany imprisonment are "cruel and unusual punishment" that cannot be justified by any of the rationales we use to justify punishment.

Is Capital Punishment Justified?

Consider the following situations:

During a quarrel, Rita picks up a nearby shotgun and kills her husband.
In the course of an armed robbery, Bill shoots and kills the owner of a liquor store.
Frank kidnaps a 4-year-old girl and tortures her for 2 days before he finally kills her.

Do you think the death penalty is justified in all of these cases? Just the last one? None of them?

In the last 10 years, nation after nation has abolished capital punishment, calling it barbaric and ineffective. In the United States, however, it seems to be making a comeback. Why does our society increasingly favor capital punishment?

We noted earlier that there are five major motivations for punishment: retribution, reform, specific deterrence, general deterrence, and prevention. Which motivation justifies capital punishment instead of life in prison? Capital punishment is not more effective than life in prison for prevention or specific deterrence; it is no better and no worse at reform. The chief advantages alleged for it are retribution and general deterrence.

The Deterrence Hypothesis

The idea behind the deterrence hypothesis is that raising the cost of crime will reduce people's likelihood of committing it. Since people value their life above all else, it is reasoned, they will be unlikely to do anything that will increase the risk of losing it. The death penalty is the ultimate threat in enforcing conformity.

Although the deterrence hypothesis may appeal to common sense, it is supported by neither logic nor empirical data. On the logical side, it can be expected to apply not to crimes of passion but only to such calculated crimes as burglary. This suggests that capital punishment would be a more effective deterrent to robbery or burglary than to murder.

Empirically, the hypothesis has fallen on hard times. For 30 years, researchers have rather consistently failed to find any empirical support for it (Conrad, 1983). Comparisons of states that have the death penalty with those that do not show no consistent differences in their mur-

der rates; nor did the murder rate increase during the decade of the 1970s, in which there were only three executions in the United States. Although there are many

Figure 7.14

Why do we kill people to punish them for killing people? Some believe in revenge and others hope it will be a grim warning to potential killers. In the last decade, Americans have become increasingly favorable toward the death penalty and, after a decade-long period of no executions, electric chairs and gas chambers are back in business in the United States. Because the death penalty tends to reflect public prejudices and revulsion, however, it is particularly prone to misuse.

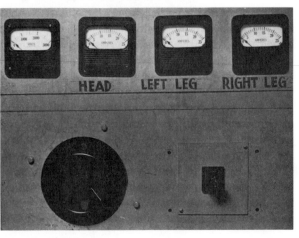

disputes about measurement, the over all conclusion is clear: "There is no empirical support for the deterrent effect of the death penalty as superior to that which is exerted by long incarceration" (Conrad, 1983:134).

The Brutalization Effect

Many, however, suggest that capital punishment may actually *increase* the amount of violence in society. First, media attention to the condemned person's crimes may desensitize the public and even inspire unstable people to commit similar crimes. Second, it is possible that publicly sanctioned murders may appear to condone violence. This so-called brutalization effect has found empirical support in a study by Bowers and Pierce (1983). Using data from New York State, they demonstrate that each public execution has been followed by an increase in homicides. The Bowers and Pierce data are suggestive rather than convincing, but there is sufficient evidence of copycat crimes to make their conclusion plausible.

RETRIBUTION

This leaves only retribution as a rationale for capital punishment. Although vengeance sounds like something we should rise above, it is a common human desire. In 1883, Victorian legal historian Sir James Stephen noted:

> In cases which outrage the moral feelings of the community to a great degree, the feeling of indignation and desire for revenge which is excited in the minds of decent people, is, I think, deserving a legitimate satisfaction. If a man commits a brutal murder . . . I think [he] should be destroyed, partly in order to gratify the indignation which such crimes produce . . . and partly in order to make the world wholesomer than it would otherwise be by ridding it of people as much misplaced in civilized society as wolves or tigers would be in a populous country. [Cited in Sellin, 1980:36]

This rationale was used a century later by Justice Stewart of the United States Supreme Court:

> The decision that capital punishment may be the appropriate sanction in extreme cases is an expression

of the community's belief that certain crimes are themselves so grievous an affront to humanity that the only adequate response may be the penalty of death. [Cited in Sellin 1980:37]

Unlike deterrence, no amount of empirical data can say whether retribution is justified. This is a moral question, not an empirical one. Whether the United States will or will not use capital punishment depends on public opinion. Right now, the public has swung in favor of it. In 1982, 72 percent of the public favored capital punishment for convicted murders; this is an abrupt increase from 54 percent in 1980 (Gallup Report, 1982, no. 206). It appears that public opinion is swayed by current events. In the face of particularly nasty murders, many people do want retribution.

THE PROBLEM WITH CAPITAL PUNISHMENT

For many people, both those who believe in retribution and those who do not, a serious problem with capital punishment is the possibility that bias and prejudice may enter into the decision to use it. A recent analysis of criminal sentencing between 1967 and 1978 showed that black homicide offenders are no more apt to be given the death penalty than are white offenders. However, homicides with black victims are less likely to result in a death sentence than are homicides with white victims (Kleck, 1981).

The issue of prejudice is a central problem with capital punishment. If capital punishment is justified because of public revulsion against the crime, then, by definition, punishment reflects public biases. If the public is more offended by white homicides, then retribution against those who kill whites will be more likely than retribution against those who kill blacks. As a motive for capital punishment, retribution leaves the door open for bias and discrimination.

This is an issue on which public policy rather closely reflects public opinion. In this sense, capital punishment is your decision. Is retribution a sufficient motive? What kinds of crimes justify the death penalty? Do you feel confident that society can use the death penalty justly?

SUMMARY

1. Most of us conform most of the time. We are constrained to conform through three types of social control: (1) self-restraint through the internalization of norms and values, (2) informal social controls, and (3) formal social controls.

2. Nonconformity occurs when people violate expected norms of behavior. Acts that go beyond eccentricity and that challenge important norms are called deviance. Crimes are a specific kind of deviance for which there are formal sanctions.

3. Deviance is relative. It depends on society's definitions, the circumstances surrounding an act, and the particular groups or subcultures one belongs to.

4. The traditional approach to the study of deviance concentrates on explaining who breaks rules and why. It focuses on major forms of deviance on which there is substantial public consensus. Anomie theory, cultural-transmission theory, and social-control theory fall within this tradition.

5. Modernists are concerned with how some behavior comes to be defined as deviant. Because they assume that deviance is relative, they tend to concentrate on the deviance of everyday life. Labeling theory and conflict theory fall within this approach.

6. Most crimes are property crimes rather than crimes of violence. Crime rates have decreased recently but are still considerably higher than they were a decade ago.

7. Males, blacks, lower-class people, and young people are disproportionately likely to be arrested for crimes. Some of this differential is due to their greater likelihood of committing a crime, but it is also explained partly by their differential treatment within the criminal-justice system.

8. One-third of all arrests are for victimless crimes—acts for which there is no complainant. Such crimes are the most difficult and costly to enforce.

9. The high incidence of white-collar crimes, those committed in the course of one's occupation, indicates that crime is not merely a lower-class behavior.

10. Although the crime rate has edged downward in the last 2 years, fear of becoming a crime victim has increased. Surveys show that women, nonwhites, the elderly, the poor, and the urban are the most fearful.

11. The criminal-justice system includes the police, the courts, and the prison system. Considerable discretion is available to authorities at each of these levels, and many individual circumstances influence the way an offender is treated.

12. Punishment is justified as retribution, reformation, specific or general deterrence, or prevention. There is little evidence that deterrence or reformation work. Rather, confinement and capital punishment prevent further criminal activity and provide retribution.

SUGGESTED READINGS

Becker, Howard S. (1963). Outsiders: Studies in the Sociology of Deviance. New York: Free Press. A labeling perspective used to describe and analyze outsiders, persons whose behavior has been socially defined as deviant. Analysis focuses on difficulties in defining deviance and the role of moral entrepreneurs in establishing deviant labels.

Clinard, Marshall B., & Yeager, Peter C. (1980). Corporate Crime. New York: Free Press. Research report examining the illegal practices of 500 large U.S. corporations. Includes important insights into the various dimensions of white-collar crime.

Conrad, Peter, & Schneider, Joseph W. (1980). Deviance and Medicalization: From Badness to Sickness. St. Louis, Mo.: C.V. Mosby. A fascinating examination of how our society has altered many of its definitions of deviance and how deviant behaviors are increasingly being treated as illnesses by the medical profession.

Erikson, Kai. (1966). Wayward Puritans: A Study in the Sociology of Deviance. Historical and sociological analysis of deviance during the 19th century in the Massachusetts Bay Colony.

Skipper, James K., Jr., et al. (Eds.). (1981). Deviance: Voices from the Margin. Belmont, Calif.: Wadsworth. A collection of readings covering a wide range of deviant practices described by the deviants themselves. Provides insights into the subjective meanings of deviance.

van den Haag, Ernest, & Conrad, John P. (Eds.). (1983). The Death Penalty: A Debate. New York: Plenum Press. A collection of articles critically examining the social issues raised in this chapter by describing our society's attitudes and values related to the death penalty. A detailed discussion of the facts, pros and cons, and opinions of the experts.

UNIT THREE

Differentiation and Inequality

CHAPTER 8
STRATIFICATION

198

PROLOGUE

*Have You Ever . . . considered where the kids you went to high
school with are now? Some may have gone to Harvard, some to major
state universities, some to community colleges, and some to vocational-
technical schools. Some may be working on assembly lines, and some
may be selling shoes; some may already have two children; some may be
on welfare.*

*What determines which path people will take? Are the people who go
to Harvard really that much smarter than those who are selling shoes?
Or are they harder working or maybe luckier? Or did their parents have
more money? Consider what the future holds for those who go to major
universities compared to those who are selling shoes or working on assembly lines. Their lives are bound to be very different; they already are
very different.*

*This chapter considers how occupations are assigned and what the
consequences are for individuals and societies. It also considers the issue of fairness and how Americans deal with the significant inequalities
that exist all around them. How did the kids who drove their parents' old
Ford station wagons cope with the knowledge that some kids got new Ca-
maros for their 16th birthday? As you read this chapter, you might consider how well it explains the origins and destinations of your high
school senior class and how its explanations compare with those that
you yourself have offered.*

Structures of Inequality

Inequality exists all around us. Maybe your mother loves your sister more
than you or your brother received a larger allowance than you did. So-

ciologists study a particular kind of inequality called **stratification,** in which social categories within a society are ranked according to the amount of scarce resources they receive.

If your parents give your brother more money because he is nicer than you are, then that is not stratification. Inequality becomes stratification when three conditions exist:

1. Two or more categories have unequal access to scarce but desirable resources.
2. The inequality is institutionalized—that is, backed up by long-standing norms about what *should* be.
3. The inequality is based on membership in a category (such as oldest son) rather than on individual characteristics.

Types of Stratification Structures

There are almost as many variations in structures of inequality as there are cultures. Nevertheless, we can distinguish two basic forms of stratification structures: caste and class. The major difference between the two is the balance between achieved and ascribed statuses. When a status important in allocating scarce resources is fixed by birth and inheritance, it is an **ascribed status.** When the status is optional, one that can be achieved in a lifetime, it is an **achieved status.** Being black or female, for example, is an ascribed status; being an ex-convict or a physician is an achieved status. Every society has some ascribed and some achieved statuses; the differences are in degree.

Caste. A society in which scarce resources are distributed on the basis of ascribed statuses is called a **caste society.** In this kind of society, whether you are rich or poor depends entirely on who your parents are.

Stratification is an institutionalized pattern of inequality in which social categories are ranked on the basis of their access to scarce resources.

class & caste

An **ascribed status** is one that is fixed by birth and inheritance and is unalterable in a person's lifetime.

An **achieved status** is one that is optional and that a person can obtain in a lifetime.

Caste systems use ascribed statuses as the basis for unequal resource distribution.

Figure 8.1
These plowmen in Bihar, India are working much as their parents and grandparents did before them—and for as little reward. People who live in societies where almost everybody is poor, have always been poor, and probably will always be poor are relatively accepting of poverty and inequality as a way of life. In societies such as the United States, however, poverty is not as inevitable. Consequently, the reasons why some are rich and others poor are of greater public concern.

Whether you are lazy and stupid or hardworking and clever makes little difference; what counts is your parents. Their social class and occupation fully determine your own.

This system of structured inequality reached its extreme form in 19th century India. The level of inequality in India was not a lot different from that in many European nations at the same time, but the system for assigning positions was markedly different. The Indian population was divided into castes that were roughly comparable to occupational groups. They were rigidly ranked from high to low on the basis of social honor. The distinctive feature of the caste society is that caste assignment is unalterable; it is destined to be a characteristic of one's children and one's children's children. The inheritance of position in India was ensured by rules specifying that everyone (1) follow the same occupation as their parents, (2) marry within their own caste, and (3) have no social relationships with members of other castes (Weber, 1916/1970b).

The current Indian government and the British colonial government before it tried to break down the caste system. The gradual collapse of the system, however, owes less to the efforts of various governments than it does to the impersonal forces of industrialization and urbanization. The system is suited only to a stable, preindustrial society; in fact, rigid adherence to the caste system precludes change. If each son follows his father's occupation, who is to program the computers? In periods of rapid social change, a class system provides more flexibility.

Class systems use achieved statuses as the basis of unequal resource distribution.

Class.   In a **class system,** achieved statuses are the major basis of unequal resource distribution. Occupation remains the major determinant of rewards, but it is not fixed at birth. Instead, you can achieve an occupation far better or far worse than that of your parents. The amount of rewards you receive is influenced by your own talent and ambition or their lack. Of course, ascribed characteristics also have an influence. Whether you are male or female, black or white, Jewish or Protestant is likely to influence which doors are thrown open and which barriers have to be surmounted. Nevertheless, these factors are much less important in a class than in a caste society. Because class systems predominate in the modern world, the rest of this chapter is devoted to them.

Classes—How Many?

A class system is an ordered set of categories. Which categories are included, and how many classes are there? Two theoretical answers to these questions are presented here.

The **bourgeoisie** is the class that owns the means of production.

The **proletariat** is the class that does not own the means of production and must sell its labor to the bourgeoisie in exchange for a wage.

Class refers to a person's relationship to the means of production.

Marx.   Karl Marx (1818–1883) believed that there were only two classes. We could call them the haves and the have-nots; Marx called them the bourgeoisie (boor-zhwah-zee) and the proletariat. The **bourgeoisie** are those who own the tools and materials necessary for their work; the **proletariat** do not. They must therefore support themselves by selling their labor to those who own the means of production. In Marx's view, **class** is determined entirely by one's relationship to the means of production.

Relationship to the means of production obviously has something to do with occupation, but it is not the same thing. According to Marx, your college instructor, the manager of the Sears store, and the janitor are all proletarians, because they work for someone else. Your garbage collector is probably also a proletarian who sells his labor to an employer; if he owns his own truck however, your garbage collector is a member of the bourgeoisie. The key factor is not income or occupation but whether individuals control their own tools and their own work.

Marx, of course, was not blind to the fact that in the eyes of the world managers of Sears stores are regarded as more successful than are truck-owning garbage collectors. Probably managers think of themselves as being superior to garbage collectors. In Marx's eyes, this is **false conscious-ness**—a lack of awareness of one's real position in the class structure. Marx, a social activist as well as a social theorist, hoped that managers and janitors could learn to see themselves as part of the same oppressed class. If they developed **class consciousness**—an awareness of their true class identity—he believed, a revolutionary movement to eliminate class differences would be likely to occur.

Weber: Class, Status, and Party. Several decades after Marx wrote, Max Weber developed a more complex system for analyzing classes. Instead of Marx's one-dimensional ranking system, which provided only two classes, Weber proposed three independent dimensions on which people are ranked in a stratification system (see Figure 8.2). One of them, as Marx suggested, is class. The second is **status**, or social honor, expressed in life-style. Unlike people united by a common class, people united by a common life-style form a community. They invite each other to dinner, marry each other, engage in the same kinds of recreation, and generally do the same things in the same places. The third dimension is **party**, which is roughly equivalent to political power; it is the ability to influence public action.

Weber argued that although status and party often follow economic position, they may also stand on their own and have an independent effect on social inequality. In particular, Weber noted that status often

False consciousness occurs when people are fooled by differences in income and prestige and fail to recognize their true class interests (that is, their relationship to the means of production).

Class consciousness occurs when people are aware of their relationship to the means of production and recognize their true class interests.

ability to create income

Status is social honor, expressed in life-style. *Prestige*

Party is a person's ability to influence communal action.

Power

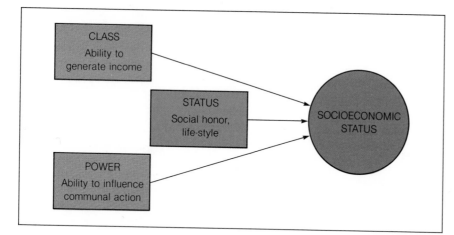

Figure 8.2 Weber's Model of Social Class
In Weber's work there are three independent dimensions of social class. This multidimensional concept is sometimes called socioeconomic status (SES).

FOCUS ON YESTERDAY

Sumptuary Laws

The necessity of clothing ourselves has almost universally been used as a way of declaring our social status. Across the centuries, people have adopted a startling variety of ways to demonstrate their superior status. In ancient China, women of the upper classes were systematically crippled by having their feet bound. This incapacitated them for work and symbolized that their families could afford to support merely decorative and reproductive objects. Corsets may have served a similar function in European history, emphasizing the fragility of upper-class women and rendering them incapable of work. In a witty analysis of the status games people play, sociologist Thorstein Veblen named this phenomenon conspicuous leisure.

In general, one's ability to maintain the outward appearances of status through dress is related to income. If you can afford it, you can look like you have high status. This has not always been the case, however. In Europe between 1300 and 1700 nearly every nation proclaimed sumptuary laws—laws relating to the consumption of goods. They covered the number of tassles your horse could wear, the number of guests you could invite to your wedding, and the quality of your clothing. Initially, they seemed to have been motivated by religious opposition to extravagance and unseemly display. They banned excessive expenditures for conspicuous consumption for all social classes and generally forbade new fashions that were considered indecent.

Beginning in 1500, however, another motive became apparent in the sumptuary laws: to preserve the distinctions of social class. As prosperity increased in Europe, it became possible for the lower classes to imitate their betters in terms of material consumption. The leading citizens of Nürnberg, Bavaria, wailed that "one can scarcely distinguish one class from the other any longer, so that foreigners riding through the city often confuse persons of high and low degree" (Greenfield, 1918:127). The express purpose of the sumptuary laws declared by Elizabeth I of England was to prevent the "disorder and confusion of the degrees of classes" (Baldwin, 1926:222). Elizabeth's sumptuary laws relating to women's apparel are printed here.

The laws specified that certain status-conferring fabrics were reserved for the nobility. Regardless of income, only countesses could wear purple silk. About halfway down the list, however, income began to compete with status as a criterion for wearing sumptuous clothing. If you had a net income of £200 per year, you could wear silk underwear even if you were a tradesman's wife. The same kinds of regulations existed for men and for horses—no gold pompoms for the horses of merchants, for example.

Questions to Consider

What kinds of clothing or objects do contemporary Americans use to demonstrate status? How do your classmates signal their status? How can you tell whether your fellow students come from wealthy or disadvantaged backgrounds?

Sumptuary Laws of Elizabeth I, 1597

NO WOMAN SHALL WEAR THE FOLLOWING	EXCEPT
Cloth of gold or silver, purple silk	Countesses and all above that rank
Silk or cloth mixed or embroidered with pearl, gold, or silver	Baronesses and all above that rank
Cloth of gold or silver in the linings of garments	Wives of barons' oldest sons and barons' daughters and all above that rank
Cloth of silver in gown	Knights' wives and all above that rank
Embroideries of gold or silver, lace of gold or silver or mixed with gold, silver, or silk; headdresses trimmed with pearls	Wives of barons' oldest sons and barons' daughters and all above that rank; wives of Knights of the Garter or of Privy Councillors; maids of honor, ladies, etc. of Privy Chamber; those with incomes of 500 marks per year for life
Velvet in upper garments; embroidery with silk; silk underwear	Knights' wives and all above that rank; those with net incomes of 200 pounds per year
Velvet in gowns or petticoats; satin in cloaks or other outer garments	Wives of knights' oldest sons and all above that rank; gentlewomen attendant upon countesses, etc.; those with net incomes of 100 pounds
Satin in robes; gowns of taffeta, damask, grosgrain	Gentlemen's wives and all above that rank

SOURCE: Frances E. Baldwin (1926). *Sumptuary Legislation and Personal Regulation in England.* Baltimore. Johns Hopkins University Press.

stands in opposition to mere economic power, depressing the pretensions of those who "just" have money. Thus, for example, a member of the Mafia may have a lot of money, may in fact own the means of production (a brothel, a heroin manufacturing plant, a casino)—but he will not have social honor. (The distinction between status and class is explored more fully in the Focus section of this chapter.)

Most sociologists use some version of Weber's framework to guide their examination of stratification systems. Rather than speaking of class, we more often refer to **socioeconomic status (SES),** which is a composite measure of a person's income, occupation, education, and other measures of status. This system allows for much more complex divisions of society than does Marx's class system. It allows us to distinguish between a salesperson who makes $12,000 a year and one who makes $100,000 or between a garbage collector and the manager of a Sears store. According to this system, there are many socioeconomic statuses, each reflecting various combinations of class, status, and party.

Explanations of Inequality

Within the field of sociology, explanations of inequality have been of keen interest. More than most subjects, inequality is hard to examine in an objective manner. Different social-class backgrounds and different political philosophies and experiences all shape individual moral judgments about inequality. Here we will review three major sociological explanations of inequality.

Structural-functional Theory

The structural-functional theory of stratification begins (as do all structural-functional theories) with the question: Does this social structure contribute to the maintenance of society? Functional theory is concerned not with whether the structure contributes to the happiness of individuals but with whether it contributes to the maintenance of society. A basic assumption of the theory is that since individual needs can be satisfied only within society, the good of society comes before the good of individuals.

This theoretical position is represented by the work of Davis and Moore (1945), who conclude that stratification is necessary and justifiable because it contributes to the maintenance of society. Their argument begins with the idea that each society has essential roles (functional prerequisites) that it must fill. Society encourages people to perform essential roles by offering high rewards. The amount of reward that must be offered depends on the scarcity of necessary talent and on the unpleasantness of the task. Some roles require only small rewards because they are fun and anybody can perform them. Other roles, however, require large rewards in order to motivate people to perform them. The occupation of physician, for example, requires quite a bit of skill, intelligence beyond that of the average person, and long years of training and commitment. Davis and Moore suggest that in order to encourage people who have this scarce talent and ability to undergo long years of expensive training, society must allow

Figure 8.3

An important element of stratification is status, social honor expressed as life style. A wedding is one such indicator of status. For example, this elaborate church wedding confers a very different level of status on its participants than does a marriage ceremony at the court-house. The expensive flowers and costumes signal the parents' status in the community; their choice of church and the formality of their invitations will also have telegraphed to guests the social honor attached to the occasion. Guests to this wedding did not come in jeans.

Socioeconomic status (SES) is a measure of social class that is based on indicators of income, occupation, and education.

Figure 8.4

How much should these men be paid for removing garbage? The Davis and Moore theory of stratification suggests that each task in society receives a reward which reflects the importance of the job to the community, the scarcity of the talent necessary to do the job, and the unpleasantness of the job. Removing garbage is both unpleasant and vital, but since almost anybody can do the task the pay can be quite low. Critics of this theory suggest that the generally low wages of garbage collectors has more to do with their lack of power than their lack of skill. When they increase their power through unionization, garbage collectors may make very good wages.

them to gain significant economic rewards. Society is likely to determine, however, that women do not need very much reward for being mothers. Although the function is vital, the potential to fill the position is widespread (about 50 percent of the adult population can do it) and the job has enough noncash attractions that people need not be paid to do it. In many ways, this is a supply-and-demand argument that views inequality as a rational response to a social problem. This theoretical position is sometimes called consensus theory because it suggests that inequality is the result of societal agreement about the importance of social positions and the necessity of paying to have them filled.

Criticisms.   This theory has been sharply attacked as an ideology that justifies inequality. One of the major criticisms is that the theory does not consider the ways in which the game may be rigged. No matter how many scarce talents and abilities they have, the children of sharecroppers do not have the same opportunities to get good jobs as do the children of physicians and lawyers. A second strand of criticism directly attacks the assumption that unequal financial rewards are necessary to motivate people to take high-status jobs. Most people would rather manage a store than pick up garbage. Do we really need to offer the manager a much higher salary than the garbage collector in order to motivate someone to fill the position of manager? Or do managers get higher salaries because they have the power to allocate profits?

The Conflict Perspective

A clear alternative to the Davis and Moore theory is given by scholars who adhere to Marxian theory. They explain inequality as exploitation. Those who own the means of production (land in an agrarian society, machines in early industrialization) seek to maximize their own profit by minimizing the amount of return they must give to the proletarians, who have no choice but to sell their labor to the highest bidder. In this view, inequality is an outcome of private property, where the goods of society are owned by some and not by others. In Marxian theory, stratification is neither necessary nor justifiable. Inequality does not benefit society; it benefits only the rich.

Although Marx did not see inequality as either necessary or justifiable, he did see that it might be nearly inevitable. The reason is that inequality is a direct outcome of the division of labor. Even if private property were eliminated, some people would still have power over others because of the division of labor. Individuals who coordinate the work of others have the power to pursue their own self-interest at the expense of others'—to hire their own children in preference to others', to give themselves more rewards than they give others, and generally to increase the gap between themselves and those they coordinate. Marx's patron and coauthor, Engels, explained it this way:

> It is therefore the law of the division of labor that lies at the basis of the division into classes. But this does not prevent the division into classes from being carried out by means of violence, and robbery, trickery and fraud. It does not prevent the ruling class, once having the upper hand, from consolidating its power at the expense of the working class, from turning its social leadership into an intensified exploitation of the masses. [Engels, 1880/1965:79]

Because Marxists place the origins of inequality in the division of labor (the forms of production), to some extent they see inequality as an inevitable outcome of a complex occupational structure. Socialist utopias therefore often emphasize the principle of job rotation in order to avoid inequality.

Criticisms. A major criticism of Marxist theory is that it entirely overlooks two issues:

1. People are unequal. Some people are harderworking, smarter, and more talented than others. Unless forcibly held back, these people will pull ahead of the others.
2. Inequality is a major motivation for human labor. In any society, an important reason for hard work is that people hope to get ahead or at least hope to keep from falling behind. In short, they are motivated by inequality.

Figure 8.5

A good education is not necessarily a guarantee of economic prosperity. Shifts in economic conditions or even in the age structure can throw groups of workers or even entire communities out of work. Persons like this unemployed school teacher, who depend on someone else for employment are relatively helpless against these kinds of economic shifts. By contrast, the smaller number of people who own their own capital are better able to control their own economic fate. This awareness was one of the important insights of Marx; those who work for others, school teachers and autoworkers alike, share a common economic condition.

Lenski's Evolutionary Theory

The evolutionary approach to inequality propounded by Lenski begins with the notion that inequality may be functional under some conditions. In relatively poor societies, such as early horticultural societies, high levels of inequality were required to sustain the nonproductive elites. Everything above the merest subsistence had to be taken from the producers in order to provide enough for the small ruling class of scholars and priests. Largely as a result of the technological innovations of those released from direct labor, however, productivity increased. This meant that more people could be freed from direct production, a wider variety of nonproductive positions could be supported, and there was less need to strip the peasants completely. In this view, the level of inequality in a society is directly related to the level of productivity. The more productive a society, the lower the level of inequality required to maintain specialization.

This theory suggests that inequality is necessary at low levels of productivity in order to provide the surpluses required for specialization (ultimately a prerequisite for further improvements in productivity); at high levels of productivity, however, inequality in consumption is not necessary. Lenski nevertheless expects it to continue because a division of labor gives some people more power than others and because it is human nature to maximize personal rewards and to seek to keep whatever advantages one has. If inequality declines, Lenski argues, it will be because government has restricted the ability of those with power to amass resources.

Synthesis

Structural-functional theory and conflict theory address important issues in the explanation of inequality; each also has a blind side. Structural-functional theory disregards the way the upper classes may rig the game for their own benefit; conflict theory generally ignores the positive functions of inequality. Lenski's evolutionary theory offers a partial synthesis of these two perspectives. It shows how inequality may be necessary under some conditions (low surplus), but it also recognizes that force and fraud may be used to extend inequality far beyond what is necessary or fair.

Inequality in the United States

Stratification exists in all societies. In Britain, India, and Russia there are social structures that ensure that some categories of society routinely get more rewards than do others. This section considers how the system works in the United States.

Measuring Social Class

If you had to rank all the people in your classroom by social class, how would you do it? There are many different strategies that you could use: their incomes, their parents' incomes, the sizes of their savings accounts,

BASIS OF COMPARISON	STRUCTURAL-FUNCTIONAL THEORY	CONFLICT THEORY	EVOLUTIONARY THEORY
1. Society can best be understood as . . .	Groups *cooperating* to meet common needs	Groups *competing* for scarce resources	Cooperation as well as conflict
2. Social structures can best be understood as patterns that . . .	Solve problems and help society adapt	Maintain current patterns of inequality	Help solve problems, but help some groups more than others
3. Causes of stratification are . . .	Importance of vital tasks; Unequal ability	Unequal control of means of production maintained by force, fraud, and trickery	Need for coordination giving some people power, which they use to amass privilege
4. Conclusion about stratification . . .	Necessary and desirable	Difficult to eliminate, but unnecessary and undesirable	Necessary under conditions of low surplus; currently much more inequality than is necessary or desirable
5. Strengths . . .	Consideration of unequal skills and talents and necessity of motivating people to work	Consideration of inheritance of privilege and ways in which the privileged manipulate the system to their advantage	Recognition that inequality may meet societal goals at the expense of some individuals and that costs and benefits vary by level of surplus
6. Weaknesses . . .	Ignores the inheritance of privilege and the role of ideology in rationalizing inequality	Ignores real inequalities in talent and the necessity to motivate people; glosses over the near-impossibility of eliminating greater power of coordinators	None; combines best of others in fairly complete general theory

or the ways they dress and the cars they drive. Some students would score highly no matter how you ranked them, but others' scores might be very sensitive to your measurement procedure. The same thing is true when we try to rank people in the United States; the picture of inequality we get depends on our measurement procedure. Here we will examine some of the most frequent measurement procedures.

Warner and the Upper-Uppers and the Lower-Lowers. One of the earliest attempts to describe the American class structure was that of W. Lloyd Warner. Warner used information on income source, occupation,

Table 8.1   Warner's Description of the American Class Structure

Warner used information about source of income, occupation, education, and homes to produce a description of the American class structure. Aside from the distinction between the upper-upper and the lower-upper, however, Warner's structure rests heavily on occupation.

SOCIAL CLASS	DESCRIPTION	OCCUPATION
Upper-upper	Old aristocracy	On boards of directors, bankers, owners of major businesses
Lower-upper	New rich	Bankers, owners or managers of businesses
Upper-middle	Good, respectable people	Professionals, merchants, midlevel managers of major businesses
Lower-middle	Good people, but nobody	Clerks and other white-collar workers, public school teachers, highly skilled blue-collar workers
Upper-lower	Poor but honest	Semiskilled and service workers, laborers
Lower-lower	Disreputable poor	Unemployed or irregularly employed

SOURCE: W. Lloyd Warner, Marcia Meeker, and Kenneth Eells, 1949.

Table 8.2   Prestige of Selected Occupations

Prestige scores are based on survey research asking about the social standing of men in these occupations. The same rankings have been found in the United States since 1927.

OCCUPATION	1963
Physician	93
College professor	90
Lawyer	89
Dentist	88
Public school teacher	82
Accountant for large business	81
Artist	78
Electrician	76
Trained machinist	74
Welfare worker	74
Police officer	72
Bookkeeper	70
Carpenter	68
Mail carrier	66
Plumber	63
Barber	63
Truck driver	59
Store clerk	56
Restaurant cook	55
Coal miner	50
Janitor	48
Garbage collector	39
Shoe shiner	34

SOURCE: Hodge, Siegel, and Rossi, 1964. "Occupational prestige in the United States, 1925–63." American Journal of Sociology, vol. 70(3), table 1. © 1964 by the University of Chicago.

neighborhood, and kind of house to rank all the men in several small communities. He concluded that there are six social classes in the United States: upper-upper, lower-upper, upper-middle, lower-middle, upper-lower, and lower-lower. A general description of the people in each category is presented in Table 8.1.

Warner's work has been influential, and his description of the American class structure is now part of the American language. Later scholars have pointed out, however, that except for his distinction between the upper-upper and lower-upper classes (which is based on whether one has old or new money), Warner's distinctions between social classes are based on only one variable: occupation. Today, many scholars use occupation alone as their indicator of social class.

Occupational Prestige.   Occupations are easy to identify but hard to rank. The device most often used to rank them is the Occupational Prestige Scale. The scale is based on survey research in which large random samples were asked: "What do you think is the general social standing of a man who is a . . . [plumber, doctor, shoe salesman]? Would you say it is excellent, good, fair or poor?" The prestige of an occupation is based on the proportion who say that the social standing of men in that occupation is excellent or good (Reiss et al., 1961). Repeated tests have demonstrated that this procedure yields consistent results; the same ordering of occupations has been demonstrated on American samples since 1927 as well as in other Westernized societies, from urban Nigeria to Great Britain (Hodge et al., 1964; Hodge et al., 1966). And in spite of the fact that the question is specifically about *men* who hold these occupations, occupations are ranked the same way for women too (Bose & Rossi, 1983). Thus we can be confident that the scale produces a reliable ordering of occupations (see Table 8.2 for a partial list of occupations).

Self-Identification.   A more direct way of measuring social class is simply to ask people what social class they think they belong to. One of the

Figure 8.6

Almost everything we do, say, or own gives off signals about our social class. From the moment we park in front of someone's house, we can begin to make guesses about their income and status. When we see their living room, their car, or hear about their vacations, our information becomes more precise. Did they visit all the great museums in New York or did they hit every bingo parlor between here and Duluth? Sociologists have found that education, income, and occupational prestige are good predictors of these variations in life-style.

disadvantages of this method is that people may place themselves incorrectly. Nevertheless, few respondents say, "What do you mean by *social class*?" The concept is meaningful to most Americans, and they have an opinion about where they fit in the hierarchy.

People's social-class identification is highly affected by the class labels used. If sociologists ask people whether they belong to the upper, middle, or lower class, the vast majority of Americans will say that they belong to the middle class. If they are asked whether they belong to the upper, middle, working, or lower class, nearly half of the middle class and some of the lower class will say they are working class. It appears that although many people recognize that they are below average in socioeconomic status, few are willing to call themselves lower class.

Economic Inequality

Within all contemporary class systems there are very high levels of inequality. This is true of capitalist and socialist systems, of democracies and dictatorships. In the United States income inequality has been substantial since the beginning of the republic. Despite wars on poverty, large-scale increases in educational attainment, and a fourfold increase in the number of two-earner households, inequality in the distribution of house-

Table 8.3 Income Inequality in the United States, 1950 and 1982

Distributions of income in the United States show little change in income inequality in the last 30 years. Forty-three percent of the total income in the United States goes to the richest twenty percent of the population where the poorest twenty percent of the population consistently receives only 4–5 percent.

	1950	1982
Poorest fifth	4%	5%
Second fifth	12	11
Third fifth	17	17
Fourth fifth	23	24
Richest fifth	43	43

SOURCE: U.S. Bureau of the Census, Statistical Abstract of the United States 1984, table 766 and Current Population Reports Series P-60, No. 132, 1982, table 18.

Figure 8.7 Percent of All Personal Wealth Held by the Wealthiest 1 Percent, 1810 to 1972.

There is much more inequality in the distribution of wealth than there is in the distribution of income. This inequality peaked in the early part of the century and has declined somewhat since 1939. SOURCE: For the years 1810 to 1900, Gallman, 1969; for years 1922 to 1972, U.S. Bureau of the Census, Statistical Abstract of the United States, 1984, table 794.

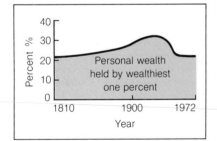

hold income has changed little in the last 35 years (see Table 8.3). The poorest 20 percent continue to receive only 4 to 5 percent of all personal income, whereas the richest 20 percent receive over 40 percent.

The significant and long-standing inequality documented by income distribution is actually an underestimate of inequality. If we measure material inequality by the distribution of *wealth*—not only what someone earned this year but also all that the person and the person's family have accumulated over the years (savings, investments, value of homes, land, cars, and other possessions), we find that the richest 20 percent of households held 76 percent of all wealth in 1962. A significant portion of Americans never accumulate any assets, and the richest 1 percent owned fully 21 percent of all assets in 1972. Historical research suggests that this unequal distribution of wealth is a long-standing pattern in the United States, dating back at least to 1810 (see Figure 8.7).

The Consequences of Social Class: Can Money Buy Happiness?

Do you prefer bowling to tennis? What is your preference in movies (films they call them in the upper class)? Would you rather drink beer or sherry? These choices and nearly all the others you make throughout your life are influenced by your social class. Consider the following:

— Women with lower-class backgrounds are seven times more likely to be overweight than are middle-class women (Goldblatt et al., 1965).
—Babies born in poor neighborhoods are 50 percent more likely to die before their first birthday than are babies born in better neighborhoods (Gortmaker, 1979).
—People who fail to graduate from high school are three times as likely to get divorced as are those who complete college (Glick & Norton, 1977).
—People with poor education and low incomes score lower on measures of mental health and physical health than do people with good educations and high incomes (Kessler, 1982).

The following chapters will point out the influence of social class in a number of areas—among them religious affiliation and participation, divorce, prejudice and discrimination, and work satisfaction. Here it suffices to say that almost every behavior and attitude we have (from sexual behavior to belief in democracy) is related to our social class. Knowledge of a person's social class will often tell us more about an individual than will any other single piece of information. This is why "What do you do for a living?" immediately follows "Glad to meet you."

Change and Continuity in the Consequences of Social Class

Levels of income inequality have changed little over the last 35 years, and differences in wealth have been remarkably constant over 170 years. Nevertheless, there have been some striking changes in the consequences of social class. Whether in infant mortality or recreational patterns, social class makes less difference now than it did only a few decades ago.

Perhaps the clearest evidence of this is from a study of Middletown (Muncie, Indiana) originally done in 1924–25. After the original investigation, the researchers concluded that social class

is the most significant single cultural factor tending to influence what one does all day long throughout one's life: whom one marries; when one gets up in the morning; whether one belongs to the Holy Roller or Presbyterian church; or drives a Ford or a Buick; whether or not one's daughter makes the desirable high school Violet Club; or one's wife meets with the Sew We Do Club or with the Art Students' League; whether one belongs to the Odd Fellows or to the Masonic Shrine; whether one sits about evenings with one's necktie off; and so on indefinitely throughout the daily comings and goings of a Middletown man, woman, or child. [Cited in Caplow & Chadwick, 1979]

In 1972 another team of investigators went back to see how Middletown had changed in the ensuing 50 years. The second study found a dramatic decline in class differences (see Table 8.4). The working class still gets up a little earlier and still places less stress on independence, but there is a marked convergence on all measures except the directly economic one— percent unemployed.

As the differentials reported on obesity, infant mortality, mental health, and divorce demonstrate, social class still does make a big difference. Nevertheless, the difference is less than it was 50 years ago. To some extent, this is a result of the major increases in real income that have been experienced in this country since 1924. The increases have been partic-

Table 8.4   Changes in Life-Styles by Social Class in Middletown between 1924 and 1972

Differences in social class declined sharply in Middletown between 1924 and 1972. With the exception of unemployment, the life-styles of working-class families and business-class families are more similar in 1972 than they were in 1924.

	1924	1972
Percent of families rising before 6 a.m. on workdays		
Business class	15%	31%
Working class	93	38
Percent of families where husband unemployed in last year		
Business class	1	4
Working class	28	25
Percent of families with a working wife		
Business class	3	42
Working class	44	48
Percent of mothers wanting their children to go to college		
Business class	93	90
Working class	23	83
Percent of parents stressing independence in children		
Business class	46	82
Working class	17	68

SOURCE: Caplow and Chadwick, 1979. "Inequality and life-styles in Middletown, 1920–1978." *Social Science Quarterly* 60(3). Reprinted with permission of The University of Texas Press and authors.

ularly important for those who were barely keeping their heads above water. Although the cars, televisions, and homes of the working class are not of the same quality as those of the middle class, the working class does have them. An additional factor in reducing some of the major differences in life chances is the extension of public services. Public schools, public health, the GI Bill, and veterans' benefits have helped reduce some of the severer consequences of lower social class.

Social Mobility in the United States

Social mobility is a change in occupation or social-class position between generations or over the career of an individual.

Intergenerational mobility is the change in social class from one generation to the next.

Intragenerational mobility is the change in social class within one person's career.

As shown earlier, the primary difference between caste and class systems is not the level of inequality but the opportunity for achievement. The distinctive characteristic of a class society is that it permits **social mobility.** This means that a person may have a different social class than the parents did. Technically, mobility between generations is **intergenerational mobility.** Change in occupation and social class during an individual's own career is **intragenerational mobility.** Both kinds of mobility may be downward as well as upward.

We can study social mobility at two distinct levels. On the macro level, we can examine the factors that lead a society to experience high or low levels of social mobility. On a micro level, we can ask about the individual characteristics that lead some people to move up, some to move down, and yet others to stay in the social class into which they were born.

Causes of Mobility: Macro Level

In a static society, where activities and occupations change little from generation to generation and where, in fact, there may be only a few occupations to choose from (the case with either a hunting-and-gathering or a simple agrarian society), there is little opportunity for social mobility. In a rapidly changing industrial society, however, there must be occupational mobility. The son of a harness maker cannot be a harness maker because horses are no longer used for work. Cross-cultural comparisons indicate that all countries undergoing industrialization experience high levels of occupational mobility regardless of their ideals about inequality.

Within the last 80 years, the occupational structure of the United States has changed rapidly. As Figure 8.8 shows, the number of positions at the top has expanded dramatically during this century, thus providing opportunities for upward mobility.

Changes in occupational structure determine the amount of social mobility in a society, but if we want to explain why some of your high school senior class went to prestigious universities, others went to vocational-technical schools, and still others began waiting on tables, we need to turn to individual factors. What determines who gets the advantages?

The Indirect Inheritance Model: Micro Level

If *Sports Illustrated* gave you the job of predicting the top 20 football teams in the country next year, you could go to the trouble of finding out the

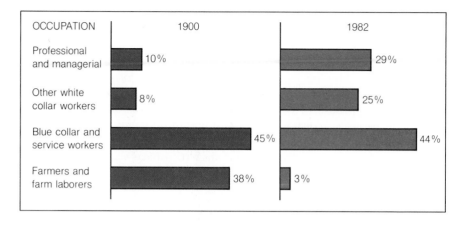

Figure 8.8 The Changing Occupation Structure, 1900–1982
Since the turn of the century the occupational structure of the United States has shifted away from farm labor. Today there are many more white collar, professional and managerial jobs.
SOURCES: U.S. Bureau of the Census, *Historical Statistics of the United States, Colonial Times to 1970*, Bicentennial Edition, Part 1. Washington, D.C. 1975, p. 139, and U.S Bureau of the Census, *Statistical Abstract of the United States 1984*, table 693.

average height, weight, and experience level of each team, the dollars allocated to the athletic department, the years of coaching experience, and the attendance at games. From this information you could devise some complex system of predicting the winners. You would probably do a better job for a lot less trouble, however, if you predicted that last year's winners will be this year's winners. The same thing is true in predicting occupational winners and losers. The simplest and most accurate guess is that of social continuity.

American culture values achievement rather than ascription, and occupations are not directly inherited. Yet people tend to have occupations of a status similar to that of their parents. How does this come about? The best way to describe the system is as an **indirect inheritance model.** The parents' occupations do not directly cause the children's occupations, but the family's status and income provide the children with surroundings and goals that ensure that they end up at the same place as the parents.

The **indirect inheritance model** argues that parents' status and income structure children's surroundings and aspirations so that the children end up at the same social class as their parents.

Education. The best predictor of eventual social class is education; education is a vital determinant not only of occupation but of success within that occupation. In a sense, though, this answer just moves us back a pace, and we must now ask what determines education? Some people achieve a good education through their own intelligence and determination. Study after study, however, demonstrates that the best predictor of education is parents' education (Duncan et al., 1972). The following section reviews the evidence of how education fosters indirect inheritance and how it may work to foster truly individual success or failure. (These issues will also be dealt with in greater detail in chapter 12.)

Inherited Characteristics: Help and Aspirations. How much education you get depends to a significant degree on how much you want. This amount, in turn, often depends on how much your parents have. If your parents graduated from college or have middle-class jobs, then you have probably always assumed that you too would go to college. You automatically signed up for algebra and chemistry in high school. If your parents didn't graduate from high school and tend to think that education is a necessary evil, then you probably bypassed algebra for a shop or sewing class.

Figure 8.9
Is there any doubt about this boy's eventual social class destination? Regardless of his intelligence or his aptitude for academic work, this boy undoubtedly plans to attend college and pursue a career that requires three-piece suits and a brief case—and incidentally which will provide him high income and occupational prestige. Because we model our aspirations on our parents, there is a great deal of inheritance of social class even within an achievement based class system like that found in the United States.

Achievement motivation is the continual drive to match oneself against standards of excellence.

The Middletown data reported in Figure 8.4 show that the majority of parents of all social classes now want their children to go to college. Parents' educations are still important, however, in determining whether this desire is a hope or an intention. Social class is also an important determinant of whether students finish their degree programs. Furthermore, parental background is important in determining where one goes to college. Regardless of whether they are bright or dull, working-class youths are likely to aspire to and attend community colleges and higher-status youths are likely to aspire to and attend prestigious universities (Thomas, 1979). This choice has been shown to have a major impact on occupational achievement 10 years later (Monk-Turner, 1983). Thus parents' social class has indirect influences on educational aspirations and achievement.

Parental education and social class can influence a child's attitude toward education in subtle ways too. Is the home crowded with books? Does the child have a desk in a quiet room for studying? Do parents encourage homework? Are they willing to help with math and English? To buy encyclopedias, dictionaries, and home computers? The atmosphere of the home and the parents' own support and encouragement may have important effects on the child's success. Bright and ambitious lower-class children may find it hard to do well in school if they have to study at a noisy kitchen table amidst a group of people who think that their studies are a waste of time; middle-class children with even modest ambitions and intelligence may find it hard to fail within their very supportive environment. Although there are some Abe Lincolns whose aspirations are not dampened by having to overcome difficulties, aspirations are highly correlated with social-class background.

The Wild Cards: Achievement Motivation and Intelligence. The social-class environment in which a child grows up is the major determinant of educational attainment. There are, however, two wild cards that keep education from being directly inherited: achievement motivation and intelligence. Neither of these factors is strongly related to parents' social class, and both offer filters that allow people to rise above or fall below their parents' social class (Duncan et al., 1972).

Achievement motivation is the continual drive to match oneself against standards of excellence. Students who have this motivation are always striving for As, are never satisfied with taking easy courses, and have a real need to compete. Not surprisingly, therefore, students with high achievement motivation do better than others in school. Because achievement motivation is not strongly related to parents' social class, it is one way for people to move out of their inherited position.

Intelligence is an important factor in determining educational and occupational success (Duncan et al., 1972). That is, it has an important effect on how much education is received and how well one does in an occupation. Because intelligent people are born into all social classes, however, intelligence is a factor that allows for both upward and downward mobility. (The issue of social class and intelligence will be pursued in greater detail in chapter 12.)

Summary. The indirect inheritance model explains the continuity of social class over generations (see Figure 8.10). The evidence, however, also indicates mechanisms through which people can achieve a social class different than their parents'. Achievement motivation and intelligence in particular are not closely related to parents' social class, and individuals may rise or fall in social status, depending on the degree to which they possess these attributes.

The American Dream: Ideology and Reality

A system of stratification is an organized way of ensuring that some categories of individuals get more social rewards than others. As we have seen, sometimes this means a great disparity not only in income but in health, honor, and happiness. Yet, in most highly stratified systems, there are no revolutionary movements, the rich aren't always fearing attack, and the poor don't sit around stoking the fires of resentment. For the most part, inequality is accepted as fair and natural, even as God-given.

This consensus about inequality indicates the role of the normative structure in reinforcing and justifying a system of stratification. Each system provides an **ideology**—a set of norms and values that rationalize the existing social structure (Mannheim, 1929). The ideology is built into the dominant cultural values of the society—often into its religious values. For example, the Hindu religion maintains that a low caste in this life is a punishment for poor performance in a previous life. If you live well in this life, however, you can expect to be promoted to a higher caste in the next life. Thus the Hindu religion provides the opportunity for mobility (extragenerational mobility, we might call it) and offers an incentive to accept one's lot in life. To attack the caste system would be equivalent to saying that the gods are unfair or this religion is stupid.

In the United States, the major ideology that justifies inequality is the **American Dream,** which suggests that the system is open to all people of talent and ambition and that one's position in the class structure is a fair reflection of what one deserves. That is, if you are worthy and if you work hard, you can succeed; since your success comes entirely from your

An **ideology** is a set of norms and values that rationalizes the existing social structure.

The **American Dream** is the ideology that Americans use to rationalize their class positions. It suggests that there is equality of opportunity in the United States, and everyone gets the class position they deserve.

Figure 8.10 Indirect Inheritance Model
Most people have the same social class as their parents. In the U.S. this occurs through an indirect inheritance process in which our parents' social class determines our educational aspirations and achievements. Neither achievement motivation nor intelligence, however, is closely related to our parents' social class and these two factors allow some people to move up and force some to move down.

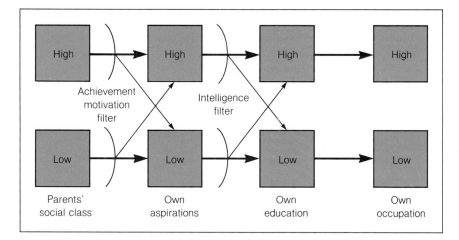

own efforts, no one but you can be blamed for your failures. The upper class is the most likely to believe that America is a land of opportunity and that everybody gets a fair shake, but the majority of the lower class believe this too. There are, to be sure, some grumblers, especially among minority respondents. One disenchanted person, for example, responded: "The rich stole, beat, and took. The poor didn't start stealing in time, and what they stole, it didn't value nothing, and they were caught with that!" (Huber & Form, 1973).

Although there are some grumblers about the operation of the system, they are not the majority; and most of them are less interested in changing the rules of the game than in being dealt into it. A recent survey of American adults found that equality was a dirty word: Fewer than 20 percent agreed that "it would be a good thing if the President decided to distribute all the money in the United States equally among all the population" (Bell & Robinson, 1978). Americans disapprove of eliminating inequality because they hope, in the future, to be on top themselves. A typical attitude toward the wealthy is represented by the comments of one unemployed laborer: "If a person keeps his mind to it, and works and works, and he's banking it, hey, good luck to him! That's good" (cited in Hochschild, 1981:116).

Variations on a Theme: The Rich, the Working Class, and the Poor

The United States is a middle-class nation. If given only three categories for self-identification, over two-thirds of the population considers itself middle class. American norms and values are the norms and values of the middle class. Everybody else becomes a subculture. This section will briefly review the special conditions of the non-middle class in America.

The Upper Class

The most outstanding characteristic of the upper class is that they have a lot of money. To a significant extent, they inherited it. Government estimates suggest that over one-third of the truly wealthy (those whose assets total $500,000 or more) inherited nearly all their wealth directly (Projector & Weiss, 1966).

There are approximately 570,000 millionaires in the United States, people whose assets total more than $1 million. At the top of the heap in 1980 were 4,112 families whose *incomes* totaled over $1 million in a single year. These people pursue a variety of occupations—most often business, less often the professions, and occasionally celebrity roles in sport or entertainment. In 1981, for example, the highest-paid businessman in the U.S. was William Agee, then Chairman of Bendix. His total compensation in 1981—$1,666,853.

An important thing about wealth is its cumulative nature. As Table 8.5 shows, the wealth of the wealthy is invested in income-producing assets: stocks and bonds, businesses, and other investments. This means that the assets of the wealthy are working to make more money for them. The wealth of those with smaller estates is invested largely in non-income-producing assets; 44 percent of the wealth of those with estates less than $50,000 is simply the equity in their homes. The moral of this is obvious. The rich get richer.

The Working-Class Family

The working class is the group of people that manages to hold onto a slot in the social hierarchy that is somewhat above the lower class but not really in the middle class. For the most part, the men work at jobs that require low skill and that therefore provide low wages and low prestige. The majority of women and men in younger working-class families have graduated from high school or at least completed a high school equivalency degree (GED), but an 11th grade education is more common than is college experience. Unemployment in the working class is high; in recent years, many working-class jobs have been permanently eliminated through automation (see chapter 14). Many of the people who have jobs have had to make wage concessions in order to help keep their employers afloat.

To find out what life is like for working-class families, Lillian Rubin conducted extensive interviews with 100 working-class couples in the San Francisco area. These families all had at least one child under the age of 12 still living at home. The husbands were employed in manual jobs, the wives were all under 40 years of age, and neither of the spouses had more than a high school education. Their personal stories help us see how social class affects our daily lives.

Table 8.5 The Rich and Their Assets
One of the differences between the rich and the middle class is the way they use their assets. The assets of the middle class are usually just their homes and cars. The wealthy, however, possess income-earning assets: stocks, businesses, and other investments. One consequence is that the rich get richer; they use their money to make money.

TOTAL VALUE OF ALL ASSETS	PROPORTION OF ASSETS THAT ARE INCOME PRODUCING
$1–999	8%
$1,000–4,999	10
$5,000–9,999	16
$10,000–24,999	23
$25,000–49,999	42
$50,000–99,999	62
$100,000–199,999	67
$200,000–499,999	84
$500,000 and over	89

SOURCE: Projector and Weiss, 1966. Survey of Financial Characteristics of Consumers. Washington, D.C.: Board of Governors of the Federal Reserve Board, table A32, p. 148.

Growing Up Working Class. Working-class children grow up in a world of overcrowded and run-down homes and tired parents. Television, magazines, and the movies, however, present the promise of a different future. Many working-class youths hope to have stable lives, happy marriages, clean and attractive homes, and well-behaved and successful children—just as the magazines at the checkout counters suggest.

For children reared in working-class families, the major route to independence and adulthood is marriage. One 30-year-old housewife, a mother of three who had been married 9 years when she was interviewed, comments on her desire to be independent:

> I was only seventeen when I got married the first time. I met him just after I graduated from high school, and we were married six weeks later. I guess that was kind of fast. I don't know, maybe it was rebound. I had been going with a boy in high school for a couple of years, and there was no other way if I wanted to get away from that house and to be a person in myself instead of just a kid in that family. All three of us girls married when were very young, and I guess we all did it for the same reason. All three of us got divorced, too, only for my sisters it didn't work out as lucky as for me. They've both had a lot of trouble. [Rubin, 1976:57]

"We all did it for the same reason"—the clearest possible expression of socially structured roles. For this woman and her sisters, marriage was the means of escape from the problems of the parents' working-class

Figure 8.11
This working class family lives in a trailer park in a West Virginia mining community. For these boys, growing up working class typically means early entry into the labor force, a life of menial or manual work, and lower levels of educational achievement. In search of escape, most working class youth marry young, jeopardizing their chances of escaping from the life-style conditions of the working class.

home. Occasionally, other ways of escape seem possible. Some people, women as well as men, hope to make it through education. More working-class people are making it than ever before, but many still find the way blocked:

> I was a good student, and somehow I could lose myself in school. And I used to love some of my teachers; they knew so much, and everybody treated them with respect. So I used to dream about wanting to be a teacher. . . .
>
> Then, when I was going into the twelfth grade, my father got sick and went to the hospital. My counselor told me then that she didn't think I would have the strength to go through with going to college all by myself. So she got me a scholarship. It wasn't much of a scholarship; it was to a beauty college instead of to a real college. (Sadly.) I don't know; I guess she was right. Anyway, she was sure she was, so I did what she told me. And then, not long after that —I was seventeen—I got married. [Rubin, 1976:44]

This young woman had worked as a live-in babysitter with a middle-class family from the age of 12. There she learned aspirations and ambitions that were "above her station." The institutional structure in which she was living, however, made these dreams unlikely to be realized. Her counselor didn't encourage her, and her family couldn't support her; probably most important is that she knew she was stepping out of the expected role for a woman of her class. When faced with obstacles, she chose the safety of the normatively prescribed path—marriage.

The problems of growing up working class are even more substantial when one or both parents are alcoholic, irregularly employed, or abusive. The social structure of such families may push the child into early work responsibilities to help support the family, into foster homes, or into the streets to escape abuse:

> Things were slim around the house; sometimes there wasn't enough food. By the time I was thirteen, I was working—doing all kinds of odd jobs. We needed the money. [Rubin, 1976:45]

> I ran away from home four or five times before I turned seventeen and finally stayed away. And they didn't come looking for me none of the time. The first time after I came back, my dad just walked in and beat me up. Another time when I ran away, the dude who was running the juvenile hall sent my family a telegram, and told them that I was there, and that they should come and get me. They sent back word that they should find me a job because they didn't have no more time for me. [34-year-old sheet-metal worker from a family of six, Rubin, 1976:24–25]

One way or another, these working-class children were usually out on their own, supporting themselves, at an early age. At an age when many young people worry about term papers, national championships, and what they want to do when they get out of school, these working-class kids are already stuck in a permanent rut. The girls are married at 17 and mothers at 18; the boys are stuck in dead-end jobs, often jobs they hate but can't give up because they have a wife, a baby, and bills to pay.

Marital Relations.　The fantasies and dreams of marriage typically remain unrealized for the children of the working class. Marriage brings new problems instead of independence and, like their parents, the children find economic problems intruding into their domestic life. Economic uncertainty and low incomes make it difficult for them to have happy marriages, attractive homes, or successful children. The larger economic setting in which the working-class family finds itself affects its interpersonal relationships:

> (I wanted) my own little family, in my own house, and everything pretty and shiny and new, like in magazine pictures.
>
> Life sure doesn't match the dreams, does it? Here I am living in this old, dumpy house and the furniture is a grubby mess. I still have those pictures of the storybook life in my head, but I have a lot more sense now than when I was young. Now I know we're lucky just to be able to keep up with the bills. [Rubin, 1976:72]

Another young woman, commenting on the effects of economic uncertainty on marital relations, says:

> When Chuck got laid off right after we were married, all I could think of was, "Here I go again." It was like I couldn't make myself believe that he wouldn't just go off and go on a drunken binge because that's what my father always did, and my mother used to tell us we should understand him and that he did it because his life was so hard. So now here was my husband, and *his* life was hard, so I figured that was what he would do too.
>
> God I was so scared. I didn't know what to do. I felt sorry for him and I felt angry at him. . . . Everytime he'd have a beer, everything would get worse because then I was *sure* he was just going to be another drunk. That's still a problem with us. I can't stand to see him take a drink because it scares me so much. [Rubin, 1976:76]

A young man caught in the dilemma of being unable to support his wife and kids the way he hoped to says:

> I couldn't figure out what the hell she wanted from me. I was trying and I didn't like how things were coming out any better than she did. (Did I) tell her? Who could tell her anything? She was too busy running off at the mouth—you know, nagging—to listen to anything. I just got mad and I'd take off—go out with the guys and have a few beers or something. When I'd get back, things would be even worse.
>
> Sometimes I'd feel like hitting her just to shut her up, I never could figure out why the hell she did that. Did she think I didn't care about not making enough money to take care of my family? [Rubin, 1976:77]

Some men turn to drink to escape their inability to fill a man's proper role; others become domestic tyrants, determined to fulfill at least part of a man's traditional role. Three men comment on the "naturalness" of this institutionalized inequality:

> That's just the way life is. It's her job to keep the house and children and my job to earn the money. My wife couldn't do my job and I couldn't be as good a cook and housekeeper as she is. So we just ought to do what we do best. [Rubin, 1976:100]

> I couldn't stand being home every day, taking care of the house, or sick kids, or stuff like that. But that's because I'm a man. Men aren't supposed to do things like that, but it's what women are supposed to be doing. It's natural for them, so they don't mind it. [Rubin, 1976:105]

Figure 8.12
The vast majority of working class jobs involve manual work requiring unskilled or semi-skilled labor. Construction workers, such as these men, are employed in jobs particularly sensitive to the vagaries of the economy. Work is often seasonal and in periods of economic decline or stagnation, they are among the first to become unemployed. The economic insecurity of such jobs poses a constant threat to family security and stability.

Figure 8.13
Working class neighborhoods in large cities are often older, crowded, and poorly kept up. In older cities in the U.S., these neighborhoods are often situated adjacent to factories or industrial plants. Since World War II, working class neighborhoods have also developed in the suburbs where single family homes continue to be modest and overly crowded.

(Speaking of his wife's desire to get a job) Dammit, no! A wife's got to learn to be number two. That's just the way it is, and that's what she better learn. She's not going to work. She's going to stay home and take care of the family like a wife's supposed to do. [Rubin, 1976:183]

The Consequences.   It is undoubtedly possible to be poor, to be economically insecure, and to still be happy—but it is hard. Thus poor people ask relatively little from their marriages—and usually get it.

I guess I can't complain. He's a steady worker; he doesn't drink; he doesn't hit me. That's a lot more than my mother had and she didn't sit around complaining and feeling sorry for herself, so I sure haven't got the right. [Rubin, 1976:93]

I really haven't got a right to gripe. I don't have a lot of the problems that a lot of women I know do. I feel very lucky. My husband doesn't drink; he never does anything mean to me; he's nice to anyone that comes over; he doesn't gamble. So I really can't complain too much. [Rubin, 1976:104]

The Present.   Rubin interviewed these working-class couples in 1974. Had they graduated from high school, they would have been part of the classes of 1960 through 1965. Are things any different for working-class families in 1985? Some things are different: Most students from working-class families are graduating from high school, many are going on to college, and fewer are getting married at 17. Yet the underlying factor, economic uncertainty, is still there. As the economic recession of 1981–83 showed, the working class is still economically vulnerable. Although its members may be able to accumulate snowmobiles and campers during the good years, the jobs are insecure. Few school teachers or accountants lost their jobs when unemployment hit 11 percent; the unemployed were auto workers, steel mill employees, and laborers—in fact, the working class.

The Poor in America

Each year, the U.S. government fixes a poverty level that is calculated to be the amount of money a family would need to meet the minimum requirements of a decent standard of living. The poverty level adjusts for family size and in 1982, the poverty level for a family of four was $9,862 (U.S. Bureau of the Census, 1984:447). Under this definition, 29.2 million people were classified as poor in 1981; by 1982 the figure was up to 34.4 million, the highest level of poverty since 1965.

Who Are the Poor?   Poverty cuts across several dimensions of society. It is found among whites as well as nonwhites, in rural areas as much as urban centers, in families as well as for single adults. As Table 8.6 indicates, a substantial number of the poor in 1982—at least 51 percent (the elderly, the children, and the disabled)—were unable to work. Of those who could work, a substantial proportion could not earn a wage that would lift them out of poverty. For example, one-third of American women working full time in 1980 earned an income that would place them below the poverty level for a family of four.

Table 8.6 The Population below the Poverty Level in 1982
Many of the people below the poverty level in 1982 were unable to work. Many of those who were able to work, could not have earned a wage that would put them above the poverty level.

	MILLIONS OF PEOPLE	PERCENT OF POVERTY POPULATION	PERCENT OF GROUP IN POVERTY
Total	34.4	100%	15%
Race			
White	23.5	68	12
Black and other	10.9	32	36
Residence			
Central cities	12.7	37	20
Other urban	8.6	25	9
Nonmetropolitan	13.2	38	18
Living in Families			
Male headed	15.6	45	9
Female headed	11.7	33	41
Living alone			
Male	2.3	7	19
Female	4.1	12	27
Children Under 15	11.6	34	23
People over 65	3.8	11	15
People 15–64 Disabled	2.2	6	11

SOURCE: U.S. Bureau of the Census, 1984. Current Population Reports, Series P-60, no. 144. Characteristics of the Population Below Poverty: 1982. Washington, D.C., tables A1, and 14.

A significant portion of the women and children who live in poverty do so simply because they have no husband or father in their house. Granted that having a man in the house is no guarantee of being out of poverty (15.6 million male-headed households are below the poverty level), it does significantly decrease the likelihood of being in poverty: 9 percent of all male-headed families are below the poverty level, whereas 41 percent of all female-headed families are below the level. Thus the poor are poor for a variety of reasons. This variety has to be taken into account if one is trying to design social policy to reduce poverty.

How Poor Are the Poor? An important issue that arises in discussing American poverty is how poor the poor actually are. Two concepts are particularly important here: absolute poverty and relative poverty. **Absolute poverty** means the inability to provide the requirements of life. **Relative poverty** means the inability to maintain what your society regards as a decent standard of living.

Few people in America are absolutely poor. They have running water, a roof over their heads, and enough food to survive on. Does this mean that poverty is not a concern? There are conflicting views on the subject. Some people argue that we have eliminated real poverty and that what we have left is statistical poverty. People are poor only in that they are below average (Lebergott, 1975). Others argue that it is nonsensical to compare the American poor to African tribesmen or medieval peasants: "The American poor are not poor in Hong Kong or in the sixteenth century;

Absolute poverty is the inability to provide the requirements of life.

Relative poverty is poverty relative to the average standard of living in a society.

they are poor here and now, in the United States. They are dispossessed in terms of what the rest of the nation enjoys" (Harrington, 1962:177).

Anybody who has driven through America's rural or urban slums knows that there are people in America who experience real poverty. About one-third of the people below the poverty level are living at less than half of that level. They are, for example, families of four trying to get by on less than $4,800 a year. Although these families may have water and a roof, most people in the United States would feel absolutely deprived at this level of income.

Blaming the Victim: The Culture of Poverty   The American Dream says that success and failure are in the individual's hands. Thus a substantial majority of Americans think that the poor are poor because of their own limitations (see Table 8.5). In a national survey, Feagin (1972) asked people to rank 11 reasons for poverty. The 5 reasons most often listed as very important were lack of thrift (58 percent), lack of effort (55 percent), lack of ability (52 percent), loose morals (46 percent), and sickness (46 percent). Not surprisingly, the rich are more likely than the poor to hold these views, but a substantial minority of the white poor do accept these views of themselves. The black poor, however, are more likely to believe that structural factors (lack of jobs, discrimination, low wages) are the causes of poverty (Nilsen, 1981; Rytina et al., 1970).

Anthropologist Oscar Lewis coined the term **culture of poverty** to explain why people stay poor. Lewis argued that in rich societies, people who are poor develop a set of values that protect their self-esteem and maximize their ability to extract enjoyment from dismal circumstances. These subcultural values initially develop as a result of poverty. Recognizing that success is not within their reach, that no matter how hard they work or how thrifty they are, they will not make it, the poor come to value living for the moment and put immediate gratification ahead of thrift, investment in the future, and hard work. Lewis argued that those living in the culture of poverty are aware of middle-class values but do not find them applicable to their own circumstances (Lewis, 1969). Thus they develop an alternate set of values—values that they can live by. The

The **culture of poverty** is a set of values that emphasize living for the moment rather than thrift, investment in the future, and hard work.

Figure 8.14
Despite a war on poverty and real increases in the average American's income and standard of living, some groups of people have been left behind. This Appalachia girl is from such a group. She is not starving, but her circumstances are bleak. Her chances of poor health, early childbearing, poor education, and early death are much greater than those of more affluent Americans.

Table 8.7   Why Are the Poor Poor?

The view from the poor:

The poor were poor from the beginning. Their foreparents were poor.

We're poor because we can't make much money.

It was handed down through the family like the rich. We lacked the opportunity.

The view from the rich:

The poor are lazy and shiftless as a class, although there are exceptions.

I don't think the average person on the lower economic scale wants to assume the responsibilities and obligations necessary to become rich. He doesn't want to be bothered.

The poor lack the ability to rise above their class situation. There is no lack of opportunity, but lack of ability.

SOURCE: Huber and Form, 1973, pp. 102–103.

shadow values of Tally's Corner (see chapter 2) serve just such a function. Thrift and hard work would not have allowed these men to achieve the American Dream, so they abandoned it for a dream that they could reach.

As we have seen, the impoverishment of a large portion of the poor can be explained without any recourse to personality defects or bad values. Critic Michael Harrington points out that

> the real explanation of why the poor are where they are is that they made the mistake of being born to the wrong parents, in the wrong section of the country, in the wrong industry, or in the wrong racial or ethnic group. Once that mistake has been made, they could have been paragons of will and morality, but most of them would never have had a chance to get out [of poverty]. [1962:21]

Until the poor have the opportunity to achieve and reject that opportunity because of their culture, we will never know whether it is the culture of poverty or simply poverty that holds them back (Gans, 1969).

The Creation of Poverty. The culture-of-poverty approach points to the categories of poor people who should be working; critics point to the lack of jobs. Gunnar Myrdal, a Swedish sociologist, coined the term **underclass** to refer to the group that is unemployed and unemployable, not an integrated part of the nation but a useless and miserable substratum (Myrdal, 1962). He is speaking of men such as those who hang out on Tally's Corner. Changes in America's economic structure have opened new opportunities for upward mobility for the well educated; at the same time the changes have shut the doors for others with finality. No matter how hard they are willing to work, there is no place for them. A youth unemployment rate of 25 percent and a high adult unemployment rate suggest that if the poor do look for work, they will not find it. If they do find it, it will not offer them a wage that will raise them over the poverty level.

The **underclass** is the group that is unemployed and unemployable, not an integrated part of the nation but a miserable and useless substratum.

Figure 8.15
The poor are poor for a variety of reasons. Some are unable to work; others are unable to find work. As a result, many of the poor exist as an underclass—persons unnecessary to our economic system. This man, for example, could probably qualify for welfare or medicaid, but like many other "unnecessary" citizens, his lack of work has eventually estranged him from society. Because he is not a part of society's division of labor, he has drifted almost completely outside of the usual conventions of society.

The Functions of Poverty.   If a survey researcher were to ask "Are you for or against poverty?" most people would say they were against it. Why, then, does it persist? An insightful answer has been offered by sociologist Herbert Gans (1973), who enumerates some of the functions of poverty. He suggests that poverty continues to exist because it contributes to the maintenance of society. Among its functions are

1. Each society has some jobs to be done that are nasty and dirty. Although we could bribe people to do these jobs by offering them high wages, a cheaper possibility has been to leave people no alternative. By excluding some people from jobs that are clean and dignified, society can force them to do the dirty work: picking up the garbage, digging the ditches, washing the dishes, cleaning other people's houses. Few people who had a choice would do these dirty and unpleasant jobs. Society ensures that the jobs get done by creating a class of people who have no choice but to do them. For example, in earlier times, many southern states eliminated welfare payments in the summer months. The purpose was to coerce people into taking ill-paid work harvesting cotton.

2. A second function of poverty is that it can be used to "justify the desirability of hard work, thrift, honesty, and monogamy" (p. 169). The threat of sinking into poverty is the goad that serves to encourage the rest of us to avoid idleness. In a sense, poverty serves the same function in society as hell does in traditional Christianity: If the lure of success does not spur you on, then perhaps fear of poverty will.

Conclusion.   One simple truth lies behind these very different approaches to the explanation of poverty: The poor are poor because they don't have good jobs. The elderly are poor largely because they never had good jobs. Even if the teenagers, the elderly, and the single mothers who are poor looked for work, many could not find any at all, much less work at a wage that would lift them out of poverty. Even if the women heading their own households got married, many would end up with a husband who was unemployed. The crux of poverty is a mismatch between jobs and the people available to fill them.

ISSUES IN SOCIAL POLICY

Inequality and Public Policy

IS IT FAIR?

Fairness is not a question to which science can provide an answer; it is a question of personal and social values. Nevertheless, we can review social values about fairness and the directions in which these values have led social policy.

As noted earlier, the majority of Americans are not keen on equality. They believe that as long as the greater reward is earned, it is fair that some people receive more money and status than others. In short, for Americans the issue of fairness has more to do with the process of distribution than with the outcome of it. This viewpoint is nicely summarized in the metaphor of a footrace. The goal of the race, of course, is to rank people by ability. The problem is to ensure that everyone starts out equally and has no unfair obstacles put in the way.

SOCIAL POLICIES

If the race is fair, inequality is acceptable to most Americans. The question is how to ensure that no one has an unfair advantage. Social policy has taken three different approaches to this: taxing inheritances, outlawing discrimination, and creating special education programs.

Estate Taxes

The policy regarding estate taxes is designed to reduce the direct inheritance of social position. There is substantial consensus even among conservatives that although it is acceptable for an ambitious, lucky, or clever man to amass a large fortune, it is not fair that his children should start their race with such a large advantage. Thus, since 1931, the United States has had a progressive estate tax. The maximum tax has varied over the years from 50 to 90 percent of the estate.

In fact, however, inheritance taxes have not significantly reduced unequal advantage. If a wealthy man dies at 70, his children are already middle aged. The $80,000 he spent to give them the best private education money could buy, the new homes he bought them when they married, the businesses he set them up in, the trusts he has set up for his grandchildren—none of these are part

Figure 8.16
Headstart programs and special education programs cannot reasonably be expected to yield equality of opportunity. If the children in these two pictures all went to the same school, their achievements would probably be very different. Equality of opportunity can only be achieved where there is already substantial equality in background. When children come to school from very unequal backgrounds, their achievements in school are likely to repeat the patterns of their parents.

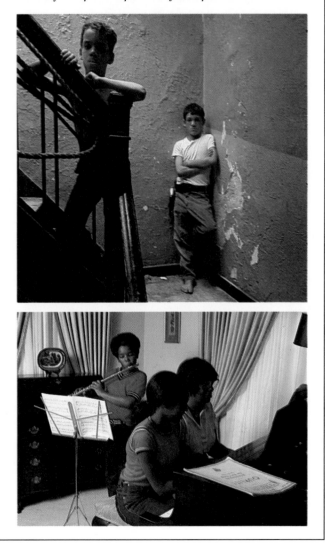

of his estate. By the time he dies, his children have already been established as rich themselves (Lebergott, 1975). Unless we ban private schools, transfers of money to one's children, and giving one's children good jobs, this inheritance is outside the scope of public policy.

Outlawing Discrimination

Antidiscrimination and affirmative-action laws are not aimed at reducing the inequalities that one starts the race with; rather they attempt to ensure that no unfair obstacles are thrown in the way during the race. Antidiscrimination laws have some effect. Able people have been and still are held back unfairly. If the race itself is not rigged, however, those who work very hard and are very able can overcome the handicaps they begin with. Because people start out with unequal backgrounds, however, they do not have an equal chance of success just by running the same course.

Education

Education is widely believed to be the key to reducing unfair disadvantages associated with poverty. Prekindergarten classes designed to provide intellectual stimulation for children from deprived backgrounds, special education courses for those who don't speak standard English, and loan and grant programs to enable the poor to go to school as long as their ability permits them to do so—all these are designed to increase the chances of students from lower-class backgrounds getting an education.

The programs have had some success. Certainly colleges and universities see many more students from disadvantaged backgrounds than they used to. Because students spend only 30 hours a week at school, however, and another 100 hours a week with their families and neighbors, the school cannot reasonably overcome the entire disability that exists for disadvantaged children. A recent study, entitled *Summer Learning,* documents the fact that disadvantaged children learn less quickly than advantaged children during the school year. Perhaps more importantly, they forget more during the summer. Their home environments do not include trips to the library and other activities that encourage them to use and remember their schoolwork. Consequently, for every step forward they take at school, they slide back half a step at home during the summer (Heyns, 1978).

SUMMARY

This review of programs designed to reduce unfair advantages or disadvantages leads to several conclusions. First, the family is at the root of the inheritance of both advantage and disadvantage. As long as some people are born in tenements or shacks, as long as their parents are uneducated and have bad grammar and small vocabularies, and as long as they have no encyclopedias or intellectual stimulation—while others are born to educated parents with standard speech patterns who flood them with intellectual stimulation and opportunity—there can never be true equality of opportunity. To some extent, the pursuit of equal opportunity will come at the expense of the family: Any attempt to reduce inheritance of status requires weakening the influence of parents on their children.

In any culture, individuals espouse values that conflict with one another and values that are so idealistic that few attempt to live by them. America's ambivalent feelings about inequality are no exception. Do we want equal opportunity badly enough to pay the costs, or will it remain, like premarital chastity or marital stability, an ideal but not a reality?

SUMMARY

—

1. Stratification is distinguished from simple inequality in that (1) two or more categories have unequal access to scarce resources, (2) it is based on social roles or membership in social categories rather than on personal characteristics, and (3) it is supported by norms and values that justify unequal rewards.

2. Marx believed that there was only one important dimension of stratification: class. Weber added two further dimensions. Most sociologists now rely on Weber's three-dimensional view of stratification, which embraces class, status, and power.

3. Following Davis and Moore, structural functionalists tend to see inequality as necessary and justifiable. Marxists see that some inequality may be inevitable because of the division of labor; nevertheless, they believe that inequality is maintained by force, fraud, and trickery.

4. The more complete view offered by evolutionary theory suggests that inequality may serve some functions for society, especially under conditions of low surplus, but that patterns of inequality do tend to be maintained for selfish reasons.

5. Inequality in income and wealth is substantial in the United States and has changed little over the generations. This inequality has widespread consequences and affects every aspect of our lives.

6. There is a great deal of continuity in social class over the generations. In the United States, this inheritance of social class is indirect and works largely through education. Achievement motivation and intelligence, however, are factors that allow for upward and downward mobility.

7. In spite of high levels of inequality, most people in any society accept the structure of inequality as natural or just. This shared ideology is essential for stability. In the United States, this ideology is the American Dream, which suggests that success or failure is the individual's choice.

8. Because of a variety of public programs, the negative consequences of being working class or lower class are less than they were 50 years ago. Nevertheless, substantial differences remain, and the lower class and working class continue to be disadvantaged in terms of health, happiness, and lifestyle.

9. Approximately 15 percent of the American population is below the poverty level. Many of the poor are children, the elderly, or the handicapped, who cannot work; many of the poor who can work cannot earn a wage that will lift them out of poverty. The essential problem is a mismatch between jobs and the people who need them.

10. Because families pass their social class on to their children, both indirectly and deliberately, any attempt to reduce inequality must take aim at the intergenerational bond between parents and children, reducing the ability of parents to pass on their wealth and values.

SUGGESTED READINGS

Hochshild, Jennifer. (1981). What's Fair? American Beliefs about Distributive Justice. Cambridge, Mass.: Harvard University Press. Addresses the issue of why there is so little support for redistribution among America's poor. The answer is found in loosely structured interviews with several dozen Americans, including both the poor and the rich. Their own words provide the body of this readable and provocative book.

Jencks, Christopher, et al. (1972). Who Gets Ahead? The Economic Determinants of Success in America. New York: Basic Books. A major work on inequality in the United States and the factors related to achieving success. Particular attention is given to family background, personality, and education.

Lenski, Gerhard. (1966). Power and Privilege: A Theory of Social Stratification. New York: McGraw-Hill. A major work distinguishing the fundamental characteristics found in different types of societies, particularly in terms of socially structured inequality.

Lundberg, Ferdinand. (1968). The Rich and the Super-Rich. New York: Lyle Stuart. What it is like to have money, power, and prestige in the ruling class of the United States.

Rossides, Daniel W. (1976). The American Class System. Boston: Houghton Mifflin. An analysis of stratification and social mobility in the United States.

Rubin, Lillian. (1978). Worlds of Pain. New York: Basic Books. A detailed study of working-class families based on in-depth interviews. This penetrating description illustrates how the social processes and social structure of American society affect being working class.

Terkel, Studs. (1975). Working. New York: Avon. An extensive account of how people feel about the occupations they have chosen, the work involved in their jobs, and the diversity of occupations in society. An enjoyable book, especially for those contemplating a profession and wanting to know how people in that profession feel about it.

CHAPTER 9

RACIAL AND ETHNIC INEQUALITIES

PROLOGUE

Have You Ever . . . seen signs that say "whites only," or "no Japanese?" Probably you haven't, for they are the product of an earlier generation. They have not been gone for long, however. Only 15 years ago, blacks were being shot for wanting to go to white colleges, and only 20 years ago they were being shot for registering to vote or for using white-only drinking fountains. Only 45 years ago, West Coast Japanese-Americans were rounded up and put in camps. The last major massacre of Native Americans occurred only 100 years ago.

When we see Bryant Gumbel doing the news or read about Daniel Inouye speaking in the Senate, it is easy to think we have put racism behind us. Certainly, we have come a long way since the bad old days, but we still have trouble. Every year, the Ku Klux Klan marches down the main streets of U.S. towns. Every year, swastikas are painted on synagogues. Black murderers are much more apt than white murderers to get the death penalty—but only if their victims are white. Blacks who kill other blacks get lighter sentences than in any other assailant-victim combination. Closer to home, the chances are that you have dated people only of your own race and that you would be hesitant to go out with those of another race. If you did go out with someone of another race, your parents and grandparents probably would be upset.

Race is still a major issue in U.S. society. As the Hispanic population continues to grow and as new immigrant groups are accepted from Vietnam, Laos, and Haiti, it will remain an important issue. The harshest forms of prejudice and discrimination may have gone, but racial and ethnic divisions are still deep and troublesome. Whether you are white, black, brown, or yellow, an understanding of your personal experiences requires an understanding of how race and ethnicity structure people's lives.

OUTLINE

229

Figure 9.1

Forty or even twenty years ago, signs such as this were commonplace in the United States. Although their disappearance does not mean an end to racism, there is much more racial tolerance and much less discrimination today than there used to be.

A **race** is a category of people who are socially defined as distinct because of genetically transmitted physical characteristics.

An **ethnic group** is a category of people who are distinct because of cultural characteristics handed down from generation to generation.

As we have seen, most of the theories concerned with inequality focus on inequality in achieved statuses. We also, however, need to consider differences in rewards and life chances that are associated with ascribed characteristics. In chapters 9 and 10, we will examine three such ascribed characteristics: race and ethnicity, age, and gender. In each case, we will deal with the differences in life chances that exist by virtue of ascribed characteristics and will consider whether these differences can be explained by the usual determinants of social class or whether there are some other processes at work. In short, we will ask whether the poverty of blacks, Hispanics, and Native Americans can be explained by the color-blind forces of educational and occupational attainment or whether it is in some way a direct product of being black, Hispanic, and Native American. To the extent that the latter is true, we will need to introduce some new ideas to explain how ascribed statuses work in a class system.

Race, Ethnicity, and Racism

Race and Ethnicity

A **race** is a category of people who are socially defined as distinct because of inherited physical characteristics. An **ethnic group** is a category of people who are distinct because of cultural characteristics handed down from generation to generation (language, religion, or national identification). Both race and ethnicity are handed down to us from our parents, but one is transmitted genetically and the other through socialization.

Although this distinction seems clear enough in theory, it is hard to apply in practice. When racial groups interact more among themselves than with other groups, they may develop distinct cultural practices. In these circumstances, racial groups may also be ethnic groups. In addition, ethnic groups often share physical as well as cultural characteristics. Generations of intermarriage create common physical characteristics; one can thus truthfully say that a person looks like a Slav or a Greek or a Swede. It is possible, however, for an ethnic group to have several races in it (for example, although most Hispanics are a combination of South American Indians and whites and are usually referred to as Caucasian, some are black).

The concept of race first developed in Western thought at the end of the 18th century. It was part of the scientific explosion in which, following Linnaeus, men classified, typed, and sorted plants, animals—and people. One of the first scholars in the area distinguished five divisions, or races: Caucasian, Mongolian, Ethiopian, American (Indian), and Malayan. He noted that each division was "connected with others by such an imperceptible transition that it is very clear that they are all related or only differ from one another by degrees" (Blumenbach, 1775/1975:24–25). This passion for dividing and classifying the human species peaked in the 19th century and has since fallen into scientific disrepute. Not only could no one decide which physical traits were essential but no one in the biological sciences or in anthropology could find that physical traits had anything to do with anything else.

Race lingers, however, as a social phenomenon. It is thus a category that is socially defined as different by virtue of inherited physical characteristics. Recognizing this socially imposed definition will keep you from wasting your time trying to find the logic by which a very dark Pakistani is caucasian and a light-skinned mulatto is black. Although there are physical differences among races, the differences that count are those with social not physical importance.

Racism

By itself, sorting people into racial groups is a harmless activity. Under some circumstances, however, racial awareness turns into **racism,** a belief that there are inherited differences in ability that justify unequal treatment.

Almost all groups are ethnocentric—believing that their group is superior to others—to some degree. Why does racism arise in some situations of intergroup contact and not in others? Specifically, why did racism develop and flower in 19th century Western thought? Two reasons appear likely (van den Berghe, 1967):

Racism is a belief that inherited physical characteristics determine the presence or absence of socially relevant abilities and characteristics and that such differences provide a legitimate basis for unequal treatment.

1. In most eras, the practice of slavery has been compatible with values and ideals and thus has not necessitated any special ideology. When the age of enlightenment popularized the ideals of liberty and democracy, however, society had to define exploited groups as subhuman or quit exploiting them. The choice is history. It should be clear that slavery did not by itself lead to racism; historically, slavery has been the fate of defeated nations regardless of their race or their conquerors' attitudes toward race. Slavery fostered the development of racism in the 19th century and not in the 1st century because modern slavery contradicted dominant cultural values whereas ancient slavery did not. Thus the 19th century needed to justify the practice of slavery by a belief in racial inferiority.

2. Racism was, however, compatible with popular ideas about social Darwinism that were in vogue in the 19th century. It was believed that the rankings of human groups, both within and between societies, were a reflection of genetic worth. Those who were on top had been naturally selected because of their better ability. Thus people who were having trouble squaring slavery or exploitation with their religious or political values were offered a safe out, with the apparent approval of science: Racial inequalities were the result of a natural process.

Racism as a Special Case of Stratification.   Chapter 8 defined stratification as structured social inequality by which entire categories of people are treated unequally on the basis of categorical membership. Race is clearly such a category in the United States and in much of the world. Not surprisingly, much of what has already been said about stratification also applies to inequalities among races. However, the existence of essentially castelike distinctions within a class society requires a careful look at the relationships between castes and the dimensions of class, status, and power.

Patterns of Intergroup Contact

Physical and cultural differences emerge because populations live and intermarry in isolation. Intergroup contact occurs when members of one group expand into the territory of another or, as in the class of slavery, are forcibly drawn into that territory. What happens when the two groups try to live in the same society? This chapter will later describe the circumstances and consequences of several such meetings in the United States. Here it introduces a vocabulary for describing these relationships.

Majority and Minority Groups

A **majority group** is a group that is culturally, economically, and politically dominant.

A **minority group** is a group that is culturally, economically, and politically subordinate.

Rather than speaking of white and black or Finn and Swede, sociological theories of intergroup relations usually refer to majority and minority groups. A **majority group** is a group that is culturally, economically, and politically dominant. A **minority group** is a group that is culturally, economically, and politically subordinate. Although minority groups are often smaller than majority groups, this is not always the case. In the Union of South Africa, for example, whites are the majority group, although they make up only 15 percent of the population, because they control all major political and social institutions. Relations between majority and minority groups may take one of four general forms: conflict, accommodation, acculturation, or assimilation.

Conflict is a deliberate attempt to destroy or neutralize one's rivals in order to attain valued ends.

Conflict.   Following the definition in chapter 4, **conflict** is a deliberate attempt to destroy or neutralize another group in order to attain valued ends. In European contact with the native populations of North America, the valued end was land and open conflict was the means used to achieve it. In other instances, racial conflict is less violently expressed through laws requiring segregation or forbidding social, political, or economic participation by the minority group. Conflict may also take the form of attacking another group's culture, such as forbidding group members to speak their native language or practice their religion.

Accommodation is a process of intergroup interaction in which two groups live side-by-side as parallel cultures.

Accommodation.   The two groups exist side-by-side in **accommodation.** They are essentially parallel cultures, each with its own institutions. Canada's French and English provinces and Switzerland's German, Italian, and French cantons are examples of this type of relationship. Although the two cultures are seldom equal, the relationship between them is not based on direct subordination. The idea of parallel cultures is sometimes referred to as pluralism.

Acculturation occurs when continuous contact causes the subordinate group to take on the material or nonmaterial culture of the dominant group.

Acculturation.   Another possible outcome of intergroup contact is for the minority group to adopt elements of the culture of the majority group. This process is called **acculturation.** It includes learning the language, history, and manners of the majority group; it may even include accepting its loyalties and values as one's own. As middle-class blacks in the United States have learned, however, full acculturation does not necessarily mean full acceptance.

Assimilation.   When full acceptance comes—when the minority group is fully integrated into the institutions of society and ceases to exist as a separate group—we speak of **assimilation.** It usually includes going to the same schools, living in the same neighborhoods, belonging to the same social groups, and being willing to marry one another. Under conditions of full assimilation, members of a minority group cease to be defined as a distinct group.

Assimilation is the integration of the minority group into the institutions of the majority group and the end of its identity as a distinct group.

Majority Group and Minority Group Patterns and Social Class

Social classes have been defined in terms of hierarchical ordering of class, status, and power. Majority and minority groups have been defined in the same terms. What are the relationships between these concepts? Many scholars of race relationships in the United States believe that we have a **semicaste structure,** which includes a ranking of social classes within castelike racial categories (see Figure 9.2). As in a caste system, race represents an unchangeable status associated with evaluations of worth; however, there are social-class groupings within both races. Still, the lowest spots in the social-class hierarchy are reserved for nonwhites and the highest spots for whites. Moreover, the nonwhite upper class is not as well off as the white upper class.

A **semicaste structure** is a hierarchical ordering of classes within castelike boundaries based on ascribed characteristics such as race or ethnicity.

There is evidence suggesting that such a model is an accurate description of U.S. race relations (see Table 9.1). Data from 1982 show that the stratification system operates within races as well as between them. Inequalities in personal income within each race are almost identical to the overall pattern noted in chapter 8. In both the white and black populations, the wealthiest 20 percent of families get nearly half of all income. The other implication of the semicaste model is also evident in this table; wealthy blacks have less money than wealthy whites, and poor blacks are poorer than poor whites.

Maintaining Group Boundaries

Acculturation, assimilation, conflict, and accommodation are different ways in which minority and majority group members interact. Given the evidence that interaction tends to lead to cohesion and attraction (see chapter 6), how is it that group differences remain? To answer this question,

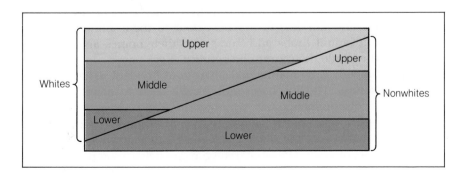

Figure 9.2 The Semicaste Model
Race and ethnicity are factors in the stratification system of the U.S. There is a social class hierarchy within each race, but there is also a caste-like barrier between them. Upper-class nonwhites are not as upper class as upper-class whites and the lowest positions in the social class hierarchy are reserved for nonwhites.

Table 9.1   Income Distributions among Families, by Race, 1982

Income data from the U.S. support the semi-caste model. The wealthiest 20 percent of black families receive 45 percent of all black family income, a figure very comparable to the 42 percent received by the wealthiest 20 percent of white families. Nevertheless, wealthy whites are more wealthy than wealthy blacks and poor blacks are poorer than poor whites.

	PERCENT OF FAMILY INCOME RECEIVED		UPPER LIMIT OF INCOME FIFTH	
	BLACK	WHITE	BLACK	WHITE
Poorest fifth	4%	5%	$ 5,596	$12,428
Second fifth	9	12	10,438	20,468
Third fifth	16	17	17,550	28,930
Fourth fifth	26	24	27,200	41,090
Richest fifth	45	42	42,510*	65,665*

SOURCE: U.S. Bureau of the Census, 1984:465.

*For this highest income category, the median of the top 5 percent rather than top income is reported.

it is necessary to look at the operation of social processes that maintain group boundaries. Roughly, they can be grouped into processes that ensure social distance and processes that ensure physical distance.

Social Distance

Social distance is the degree of intimacy in relationships between two groups.

The extent to which you are willing to admit people from another group into intimate social interaction with you is called **social distance.** It is often measured through the Bogardus Social Distance Scale, which asks: Would you accept members of this group...

1. As close kin by marriage?
2. As very good friends?
3. As neighbors?
4. As coworkers?
5. As speaking acquaintances only?
6. Only as visitors to the country?
7. Exclude from the country?

The higher the score, the higher the social distance. This scale, which has been filled in by college students for more than 50 years, produces similar rankings each time. A recent ranking of six ethnic groups is provided in Figure 9.3. It shows that, on the average, students would accept Canadians as good friends or as kin, but the closest the average student is willing to come to Arabs and Turks is to live next door to them. Although some students would admit Arabs and Turks into their homes and families, others would exclude them from the country.

Social distance can be maintained in spite of frequent association or physical closeness. The mechanisms typically used to maintain it are prejudice and discrimination.

Prejudice

The foundation of prejudice is stereotyping, a belief that people who belong to the same category share common characteristics—for example,

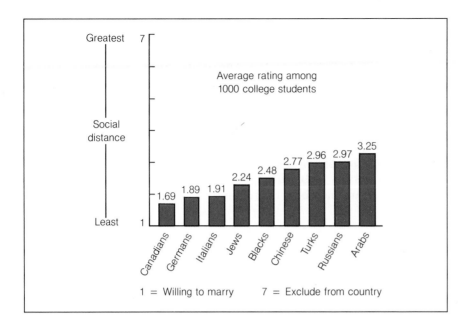

Figure 9.3   Social-Distance Ratings in 1975
For 50 years, college students have given very similar rankings of their social distance from various ethnic groups. The major change is the position of blacks; 20 or even 10 years ago, blacks ranked lower than Chinese, Turks, and Russians.
SOURCE: Sue R. Crull and Brent Bruton, 1979. "Bogardus social distance in the 1970s." Sociology and Social Research 63(July):775.

that athletes are dumb or that blacks are naturally good dancers. Stereotyping is not always bad. If your seatmate on a bus is an elderly woman, you might start a conversation about the high price of groceries; if your seatmate is a 30-year-old man, it might be about the prospects of next year's football team. These conversational topics are based on stereotyped notions of what these people are likely to be interested in. The woman might be able to give you details about middle guards and the man might be completely uninterested in sports, but stereotypes often prove useful at least as a starting point in secondary relationships.

Prejudice moves beyond stereotyping in that it is always a negative image and it is irrational. It exists in spite of the facts rather than because of them (Pettigrew, 1982). A person who believes that all Italian Americans are associated with the Mafia will ignore all instances of the law-abiding behavior of Italian Americans. If confronted with an exceptionally honest man of Italian descent, the bigot will rationalize him as the exception that proves the rule.

A startling example is the decision by the United States to intern its West Coast Japanese American citizens during World War II. The decision to go ahead with the internment in spite of a lack of evidence of treason is a fascinating study in the irrationality of prejudice. Said General John Dewitt (1943): "The very fact that no sabotage has taken place to date is a disturbing and confirming indication that such action will be taken."

Prejudice is a powerful barrier to the kinds of interaction that might reduce intergroup barriers. It ensures that when people from different groups interact with each other, they see not each other but only their conception of what the other is like. What causes prejudice? Basically, we learn to hate and fear through the same processes that we learn to love and admire. Prejudice is a shared meaning that we develop through our interactions with others. Learning negative attitudes is facilitated by both personal attributes and institutional factors.

Prejudice is irrationally based negative attitudes toward categories of people.

Figure 9.4
Prejudice is a negative and often irrational attitude toward others. Because it is based on feelings and values rather than facts or experiences, prejudice is often difficult to eliminate. This man almost certainly learned racial hatred before he learned his ABC's. Instead of trying to change people's beliefs, most public policy is designed to prevent acts of discrimination and to eliminate public demonstrations of racism such as cross burnings or swastikas on synagogues.

Personal Factors.   Some people are more prone to prejudice than are others. One predisposing factor is **authoritarianism**—a tendency to be submissive to those in authority coupled with an aggressive and negative attitude toward those lower in status (Pettigrew, 1982). Regardless of their own race or ethnic group, authoritarians in the United States tend to be strongly antiblack, anti-Semitic, and antiliberal.

Another personality characteristic associated with prejudice is frustration in attempting to reach one's goals. People who are blocked in their own goal attainment are likely to blame others for their failures. This practice, called **scapegoating,** has appeared time and again. From the anti-Chinese riots in 19th Century California to Nazi Germany, setbacks for majority group members often result in attacks against the minority group.

Institutional Patterns.   Personality factors alone cannot explain prejudice; nor can they explain the choice of target for authoritarian or frustrated individuals. An important reason for prejudice is simple ethnocentrism. When we learn to value the ways of our own culture, we simultaneously learn to devalue the ways of others. At bottom, then, prejudice (or prejudging) is a normal outcome of socialization.

When one group is politically and economically dominant in a heterogeneous society, prejudice becomes institutionalized and reinforced. Legal discrimination, for example, is a powerful source of prejudice. A child growing up in a legally segregated society is likely to develop prejudice. Social-class factors also intervene. People are likely to rate themselves and others in terms of their worth in the economic market. If no one pays highly for a group's labor, we are likely to conclude that the members of the group are not worth much. Through this learning process, members of the minority as well as the majority group learn to devalue the minority group (Stolte, 1983).

The Self-Fulfilling Prophecy

An important mechanism for maintaining prejudice is the **self-fulfilling prophecy**—a situation in which, by acting on the belief that something exists, it becomes real. A classic example is the situation of women in feudal Japan (or in more recent Western cultures). Because women were considered to be inferior and capable of only a narrow range of social roles, they were given limited education and barred from participation in the institutions of the larger society. The fact that they subsequently knew nothing of science, government, or economics was then taken as proof that they were indeed inferior and suited only for a role at home. And, in fact, they were unsuited for any other role. Having been treated as inferiors had made them ignorant and unworldly. The same process reinforces boundaries between racial and ethnic groups. If we assume that Jews are clannish, then we don't invite them to our homes. When we subsequently observe that they associate only with one another, we take this as confirmation of our belief that they are clannish.

Authoritarianism is the tendency to be submissive to those in authority coupled with an aggressive and negative attitude toward those lower in status.

Scapegoating is the practice of placing the blame for one's own frustrations on another group.

A **self-fulfilling prophecy** occurs when, by acting on a belief that a situation exists, it becomes real.

Discrimination

Treating people unequally because of the categories they belong to is **discrimination.** Prejudice is an attitude; discrimination is behavior. Often discrimination follows from prejudice, but it need not. Figure 9.5 shows the possible combinations of prejudice and discrimination. Most individuals fit into the two consistent cells: They are prejudiced, so they discriminate (bigots); or they aren't prejudiced, so they don't discriminate (friends). Some people, however, are inconsistent, usually because their own values are different from those of the dominant culture. Fair-weather friends do not personally believe in racial or ethnic stereotypes; nevertheless, they discriminate because of what their customers, neighbors, or parents would say. They do not wish to rock the boat by acting out values not shared by others. The fourth category, the timid bigots, have the opposite characteristics: Although they themselves are prejudiced, they hesitate to act on their feelings for fear of what others would think (Merton, 1949).

Public policy directed at racism is aimed almost entirely at reducing discrimination—allowing fair-weather friends to act on their fraternal impulses and putting some timidity into the bigot. As Martin Luther King remarked, "The law may not make a man love me, but it can restrain him from lynching me, and I think that's pretty important" (cited in Rose, 1981:90).

Segregation

The mechanisms of prejudice and discrimination may be carried out between groups in close, even intimate, contact; they create social distance between groups. Differences between groups are easier to maintain, how-

Discrimination is the unequal treatment of individuals on the basis of their membership in categories.

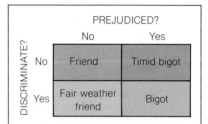

Figure 9.5 The Relationships between Prejudice and Discrimination

Prejudice is an attitude; discrimination is behavior. They do not always go hand-in-hand. Some people act on their attitudes, whereas others submerge their own attitudes to conform to community standards. Fair-weather friends are nonprejudiced people who will discriminate anyway; timid bigots are prejudiced people who are deterred from discrimination by community standards.

Figure 9.6

Segregated neighborhoods are a part of almost all diverse societies. The segregation is sometimes partially voluntary, a desire to preserve ethnic customs and reduce contact with other groups. In many situations, however, ghettos, barrios, and ethnic neighborhoods are involuntary reactions to prejudice and discrimination by the larger society. **De jure** *and* **de facto** *segregation are powerful means of preventing contact between groups and encouraging the persistence of prejudice.*

Segregation is the practice of physically separating minority and majority group members.

ever, if social distance is accompanied by physical distance, or **segregation.** Thus most societies with strong divisions between majority and minority groups have ghettos, barrios, Chinatowns, or Little Italies, where, by law or custom, members of the minority group live apart. This segregation protects majority group members from contact with the minority group and buttresses the boundaries between the groups by maintaining distinct cultures. Although segregation limits the minority group, it may also protect it. It allows the group to maintain its own community and culture and provides a haven from the hostility of the majority group.

Institutionalized Racism

Institutionalized racism is an indirect form of discrimination, one in which unjustifiable preconditions and prerequisites exclude a disproportionate number of minority group members.

Sometimes discrimination can occur without explicit reference to race or ethnicity; this pattern of discrimination is called **institutionalized racism.** The most common form is setting unjustifiable prerequisites that exclude a disproportionate number of minority group members. A clear example is the former practice of many southern counties of requiring payment of a fee (poll tax) to vote. This requirement effectively prohibited poor (that is, black) people from voting. Unnecessary educational requirements for jobs (high school education for garbage collectors, for example) are another instance. A political strategy that fits the label of institutionalized racism is the practice of electing local officials on a citywide basis. When city council or school board members, for example, are elected on a citywide basis, the political power of minority groups is diluted. If elections are held by district, however, residentially concentrated groups such as minorities are more apt to have political power and representation (Vedlitz & Johnson, 1982). The intent to discriminate may not be present in all such cases, but the effect is the same. The minority group is blocked from full participation. In a society where discrimination is illegal and overt racism is socially unacceptable, institutional patterns may still keep minority groups in subordinate positions.

Extraordinary Solutions

Prejudice, discrimination, and segregation are what might be called ordinary solutions that societies use to maintain boundaries between majority and minority groups (Daniels & Kitano, 1970). If they fail, however, or if the minority group is seen as particularly threatening, extraordinary solutions may be invoked: rigid segregation (such as that practiced in the Union of South Africa), concentration camps, expulsion, or extermination. All too often, the history of intergroup relations is the study of extraordinary solutions.

Race and Ethnic Relations in the United States

The United States, and indeed the entire Western hemisphere, is an ideal location for the study of racial and ethnic relations. For 400 years, floods of immigrants from diverse backgrounds have jostled against one another—assimilating, accommodating, and conflicting. Some have come to escape persecution, some have come to strike it rich, some were dragged here, and some were here in the first place. In this section, we will examine the histories of major racial and ethnic groups in the United States, tracing how the processes we have reviewed plus general ideas of stratification apply in each case.

White Immigrants

The earliest immigrants to North America were English, Dutch, French, and Spanish. By 1700, however, English culture was dominant on the entire Eastern Seaboard. The English became the majority group, and everybody who came after that time, regardless of degree or number, became a minority group in North America.

The Melting Pot. The dominant patterns of interaction between the majority group and the people who arrived prior to 1800 were acculturation and assimilation. Some idealistic observers of this scene believed that a new race would emerge in North America, where "individuals of all nations are melted into a great race of men" (Crèvecouer, 1782/1974). The final form of the melting-pot image was provided by an English Jew, Israel Zangwill, in his 1909 play *The Melting Pot:*

> There she lies, the great melting pot—listen! Can't you hear the roaring and bubbling? There gapes her mouth—the harbor where a thousand mammoth feeders come from the ends of the world to pour in their human freight. Ah, what a stirring and a seething—Celt, Slav, and Teuton, Greek and Syrian, black and yellow—. . . Jew and Gentile. [Cited in Rose, 1981:64]

The **melting pot** goes beyond assimilation to include a physical and cultural blending of groups. It envisions a blending of all groups to produce

The **melting pot** goes beyond assimilation to include a physical and cultural blending of groups.

Figure 9.7
Between 1880 and 1920, the United States accepted massive waves of immigrants from Europe. Many, such as these immigrants from Southern Italy, came with all their worldly possessions in a few parcels. These immigrants were accepted grudgingly and only under the condition that they abandon all the customs of their homelands and conform to Anglo-American culture.

a strong, new race and a stronger, more vibrant culture. Zangwill was exceptionally idealistic in assuming that Jew and Gentile (non-Jew) and black and yellow would all be equally welcome. In this regard, he was far ahead of his own generation, and we are still running to keep up with his vision of a society without prejudice.

Anglo-Conformity.   In fact, careful observers suggest that the melting pot never existed. Certainly, our language is peppered with words borrowed from other languages (frankfurter, ombudsman, hors d'oeuvre, chutzpah), and some of us are such mixtures of nationalities that we would be hard pressed to identify our national heritage. Instead of a blending of all cultures, however, what has occurred is a specific form of acculturation—**Anglo-conformity**, the adoption of English customs and English language. To gain admission into U.S. society, to be eligible for social mobility, one has to learn correct English, become restrained in public behavior, work on Saturday and worship on Sunday, and, in general, act like the American version of an Englishman.

Anglo-conformity is the process of acculturation in which new immigrant groups adopt English language and English customs.

The **triple melting pot** is the intermarriage and cultural blending of whites within the three major religions: Catholic, Protestant, and Jewish.

Some observers believe that a limited form of the melting pot, called the **triple melting pot,** has existed among white ethnic groups. This form of the melting pot allows intermarriage, but only within the three major religious groups: Catholic, Protestant, and Jewish. Thus a woman of Italian descent might marry an Irish Catholic, but not a Scot or a Swede. Likewise, a German Jew might marry a Russian Jew but not a German Catholic.

Summary.   To a significant extent, ethnicity has ceased to be a basis for stratification among white, Gentile, non-Hispanic Americans. Although ethnic differences do exist and assimilation is not complete for white ethnics, these differences are not related to structured inequality. Rather, feelings of group identity among Poles, Czechs, Germans, and Swedes often provide a basis for cohesion and solidarity, processes that produce a stronger, not a weaker, community.

The integration of 80 percent of the population from diverse sets of backgrounds and conditions is a remarkable achievement. Yet it leaves out a significant portion of Americans who are not white, Gentile, or non-Hispanic. Here we will consider the history of majority-minority relations for the other 20 percent: the nonwhites, the Hispanics, and the Jews.

Blacks

Black Americans are the largest racial minority in the United States, representing one-ninth (or 12 percent) of the entire population. Their importance goes beyond their numbers. Next to Native Americans, blacks have been the greatest challenge to the United States' view of itself as a moral and principled nation.

The history of blacks in the United States has two essential elements that distinguish it from the history of other ethnic groups. First, black migration was involuntary; blacks came as slaves, not as settlers. Second, black Americans are almost uniformly descendants of people who have been here since the founding of the nation, having roots in this country deeper than those of the Swedish, Norwegian, Italian, Irish, and German settlers who followed them.

At the beginning of the 19th century, over 90 percent of the blacks in the United States were slaves, mostly in the rural South. Occasionally, they knew a skilled trade; more often, they were laborers. The limited evidence available suggests that slave families were usually stable two-parent families and had health and life expectancies similar to those of lower-class whites (Sowell, 1981).

As the Civil War approached, southern society became more defensive about its "peculiar institution" and increasingly afraid of slave uprisings. For the first time, education of blacks was banned, and it appears that conditions affecting health and life expectancy deteriorated in this period (Eblen, 1974). The Civil War and the Emancipation did little to change these conditions. Rather, 4 million illiterate slaves were freed to go out and support themselves in a land ravaged by war. They began their career in freedom as a poor, rural, and southern people; they remained poor, rural, and southern until World War II.

In many ways, World War II was a benchmark for blacks in the United States. The move from the rural South to the industrial North and Midwest that had begun during World War I was vastly accelerated. The defense effort sharply increased the demand for labor and made possible some real gains in income for blacks relative to whites. In addition, the Nazi slaughter of 6 million Jews in the name of racial purity deeply shocked the Western world, causing a renewed soul-searching about racism in the United States. When World War II was in full swing, there were tens of thousands of black men in arms. They served in segregated units—good enough to die for their country but not good enough to eat with whites of their country.

Compared to the century before, the 40 years following World War II have seen rapid social change: segregation banned in the armed forces (1948), school segregation outlawed (1954), the Civil Rights Act passed (1964), affirmative-action laws passed (1968). For the first time, blacks appeared on television, on baseball diamonds, in ballet companies, and on the Supreme Court. In the following sections, we will review some evidence about the differences in life chances for blacks and whites. In many cases, comparisons over time show that these differences have been significantly reduced.

Political Change. Blacks in the United States have been entitled to vote and hold office since the passage of the Fourteenth Amendment immediately after the Civil War. For nearly 100 years, however, these rights existed on paper only. It took the Civil Rights Act of 1964, subsequent voter registration laws, and the civil rights activism of the late 1960s to make these political rights effective. The results have been dramatic. The proportion of southern blacks registered to vote surged from 29 to 63 percent in the decade after 1964. The number of black elected officials tripled between 1970 and 1982, and four of the six largest cities in the United States (Los Angeles, Philadelphia, Washington, D.C., and Chicago) elected black mayors. In addition to these impressive gains, blacks now have considerable optimism about their future political power. Despite Jesse Jackson's only slight chance at the 1984 presidency, an overwhelming three-quarters of blacks polled in 1983 thought that the chances of electing

Figure 9.8
Black Americans have had the right to vote since 1864 (a right, incidentally, not granted to Native Americans until 1924). Until the civil rights movement of the 1960s, however, many blacks were too intimidated to use their voting rights. Martin Luther King, a charismatic leader of the civil rights movement, was an important leader giving black and white Americans a vision of racial equality and a sense that justice could be achieved.

a black president in the next 20 years were good or excellent (ABC News Poll, 1983).

Education.   Blacks have made significant progress in education too. Data covering the period since World War II show a remarkable convergence among young people in attainment of a high school diploma (see Table 9.2). Even among the population 25 years of age and older, which includes many who went through the segregated school system of the 1940s and 1950s, the educational deficit of blacks is less than a single year. There still remain significant differences in the likelihood of graduating from college or getting advanced degrees, however. Blacks 25 to 29 years old in 1980 are only half as likely to be college graduates as is the total population of young adults.

Economic Attainment.   Black income continues to lag behind white income (see Table 9.3). In 1981, black families received only 62 percent of the income received by white families—only a slight improvement from 1960. Progress is most evident among black husband-wife families, who have significantly increased their economic position relative to whites. Even in this group, however, black family income remains only 76 percent of what white husband-wife families earn.

There are a variety of reasons that black family income is 62 percent of white family income. An increasingly important one is the greater likelihood that black families will be headed by a woman. This difference has grown over the past decade. Because rates of remarriage are much lower for black women than for white women, the consequences to children are striking. Fewer than 20 percent of all white children living in female-headed households will stay there for a significant portion of their childhood; for the vast majority, it is simply a brief stop before becoming part of another (more prosperous) husband-wife family. For black children, however, it is often a permanent condition of childhood; thus the income

Table 9.2 Gains in Black Educational Attainment, 1940–1982

Blacks have made tremendous gains in educational attainment in the last 40 years. The gap in education has been almost completely closed at the high school graduation level, but a large gap still remains in college graduation.

| | PERSONS AGED 25–29 | | | | MEDIAN YEARS OF SCHOOLING FOR ALL PERSONS AGED 25 + | |
| | Graduated from High School | | Graduated from College | | | |
	BLACK	*TOTAL*	*BLACK*	*TOTAL*	*BLACK*	*TOTAL*
1940	*	38%	2%	6%	5.7	8.8
1950	20%	50	3	8	6.8	9.7
1960	38	61	5	11	8.0	10.9
1970	56	75	7	16	9.9	12.2
1982	81	86	13	22	12.2	12.6

SOURCE: U.S. Bureau of the Census, 1984:144.

*Figure not available.

Table 9.3 Black-White Income Differences, 1982 and 1960

Over all, black family income has not improved relative to white family income in the last 20 years. Husband-wife families have made substantial improvements in income, but this is balanced by the deteriorating position of a growing segment of black families: female-headed households.

	1982 MEAN INCOME		RATIO OF BLACK TO WHITE INCOME	
	White	Black	1960	1981
All families	$26,934	$16,696	0.58	0.62
Husband-wife families	28,732	21,872	0.61	0.76
Female-headed families	18,226	11,096	0.70	0.61
Percent of all families with female heads	12%	41%	2.20	2.88

SOURCE: Bianchi, 1980, and U.S. Bureau of the Census, 1984, table 766.

difference between female- and male-headed households weighs much more heavily on black children than on white children (Bumpass & Rindfuss, 1979).

Other factors in explaining the black-white income difference are that blacks are less well educated than whites (this is especially true of older blacks) and that a relatively high proportion live in the South, where wages are low, *and* they are discriminated against. Repeatedly, studies show that blacks with college degrees are less apt than whites to achieve professional positions in the same occupation (Oliver & Glick, 1982); once in professional positions, blacks with college educations get paid less than others; blacks in any occupation (professional, sales, or skilled labor) are less apt than others to be in supervisory positions; and, if they are in supervisory positions, they get paid less than white supervisors with the same edu-

Figure 9.9

There have been real improvements for black Americans in the last 20 years; income, education, and political power have increased. Nevertheless, there is a substratum of black society that has not participated in these improvements, a group which experiences extraordinarily high rates of illegitimacy, female headship, and poverty. Thus, while some black Americans are able to use the educational system to pursue the American Dream, an important segment continues to be alienated from the economic benefits of American society.

cation and experience (Kluegel, 1978). Multiplied by all the various steps it takes to put together a career, these small discriminating acts end up producing a very different occupational distribution and a very different income picture for blacks and whites.

A recent study estimated that if discrimination were eliminated today—that is, if blacks had the same process of upward mobility as whites—the differences in earnings between black and white men would disappear within 50 years (Daymont, 1980). This is still two generations away at best. Because discrimination has not been eliminated, it will take much longer (Oliver & Glick, 1982).

In summary, the period since World War II has been one of steady improvement for blacks in the United States. They are still significantly behind the majority group in income and higher education, but the gap is narrowing. Some serious problems remain, though. An important one is the dramatic rise in the proportion of black births that are illegitimate and the proportion of families that are female-headed. These familial responses to poverty and lack of opportunity create a vicious circle that may perpetuate or even increase the economic disadvantages of blacks. Another important problem is the indignity, harassment, and anticipation of rejection that blacks continue to feel in contact with white society. Blacks still face significant disadvantages in the United States. One personal measure of these disadvantages comes from a 1984 Gallup survey: Only 58 percent of black adults, compared to 81 percent of white adults, reported being happy with the way things were going in their personal lives (Gallup Report, 1983).

Over all, it appears that there have been two opposing forces at work in the last decades: greater equality of education and job opportunity for working- and middle-class blacks, but greater poverty and family break-up for lower-class blacks. In 1978, fully 24 percent of nonwhites reported that the quality of life had gotten worse for blacks. We have presented evidence showing that, on the average, things have improved. Nevertheless, there is a sizable group at the very bottom of the social-class hierarchy that has not been included in this overall improvement; in fact, for it the situation may have deteriorated. This group, which has been called the black underclass, has been left behind by the more prosperous of all races (W. W. Wilson, 1978).

Hispanics

The general term *Hispanic* includes immigrants and their descendants from Puerto Rico, Mexico, Cuba, and other Central American or South American countries. Hispanics constitute 6 percent of the U.S. population. The largest group of Hispanics is of Mexican origin (60 percent), with 15 percent from Puerto Rico and the remaining 25 percent from Cuba and elsewhere. The various Hispanic groups live in different parts of the country and have rather different cultural backgrounds and levels of social and economic integration.

Cubans.   The first wave of Cuban immigrants came to Florida after the Cuban Revolution of 1960; they were largely middle class or professionals.

Cuban immigrants who arrived in subsequent waves represent much lower economic and educational levels. As a result, the economic status of the Cuban population of the United States is worse now than it was a decade ago. Despite having educations almost equal to those of the average American and despite a high proportion of male-headed families, Cubans lag substantially behind other Americans in average income.

Puerto Ricans.   Of all the Puerto Ricans in the United States, 73 percent live in the greater New York area. Although Puerto Ricans who migrate to this country are better educated than the majority of the people in Puerto Rico, they are poorly educated in comparison to other Americans (only 42 percent were high school graduates in 1982). Because they also have a high incidence of female-headed households (45 percent), Puerto Ricans have the lowest average family incomes of any racial or ethnic group in the nation: 45 percent are below the poverty level, and median family income in 1982 was $11,200, compared to $16,402 for the Hispanic population as a whole (U.S. Bureau of the Census, 1984: table 46).

Chicanos.   The Mexican American, or Chicano, population of the United States is very diverse. Many Chicanos are not immigrants; their ancestors were here when the United States annexed the Southwest in 1848. Fol-

Figure 9.10
Hispanics are the fastest growing minority in the United States. Historically, this group has been a mainstay of American agriculture, providing a significant portion of the migratory labor force that harvests America's crops. For the most part, however, Hispanics are an urban people, living in major urban centers across the Southwest, Florida, and New York. The large urban density of this minority group increases the likelihood that the Spanish language and elements of Hispanic culture will be retained by this group.

lowing annexation, there have been three waves of immigrants. The first wave, between 1900 and 1930, was caused by civil unrest in Mexico and labor demand in the United States. The second wave, between 1942 and 1950, brought thousands to the United States under the bracero (contract labor) program to fill jobs opened by absent servicemen and the relocation of Japanese Americans. The third wave, from 1960 to the present, is due to the substantial wage differences between Mexico and the United States. Following the first two waves of immigration, there were massive deportations—1 million in 1951 alone. Despite the fact that the third, and current, wave of immigration is largely illegal, there has been little effective control of it. Deportation is relatively rare, and the U.S. border patrol has been helpless to stem the rising tide of job-seeking immigrants. (The whole issue of illegal immigration and its impact on the U.S. population is discussed in the Issues in Social Policy section of chapter 17.) In spite of the high levels of current immigration, however, 50 percent of all people in the United States of Mexican origin are estimated to be third-generation residents of this country (Sowell, 1981).

Because Hispanics are an urban people living in segregated neighborhoods, many have retained Spanish as their primary, sometimes their only, language. This language retention creates a significant handicap in the labor force and an almost insurmountable one in education. For decades, schools with large concentrations of Hispanic students (whether in Texas or New York) simply ignored the fact that many of their pupils could not speak English, thus producing some of the lowest achievement scores and highest dropout rates on record (Fitzpatrick, 1978). This situation is being slowly rectified, and 20 percent of Hispanic elementary school students now participate in bilingual education programs.

Hispanics in the United States suffer substantial prejudice and discrimination. They are a large enough group to be perceived as an economic threat, and they are culturally distinct enough to be seen as a threat to American culture. "If they don't want to be Americans and learn to speak English, they shouldn't come here" is the way many Anglos and blacks speak about Hispanics. The issue of Hispanic integration into American culture will become increasingly important in the future. Hispanics now constitute about 6 percent of the U.S. population. Even if all further immigration were blocked, the relative youthfulness and high birthrate of the Hispanic population will bring this figure to 10 percent in our lifetime. If immigration continues at current levels, it is estimated that Hispanics will constitute 18 percent of the U.S. population in 50 years (Davis, 1982).

Jews

Since they were driven out of Palestine in A.D. 70, Jews have been a minority group everywhere. Thus they brought a unique background with them to the United States—a background filled with prejudice, discrimination, and, all too frequently, extraordinary solutions. They had had nearly 2,000 years of practice in maintaining their own cultural world in an alien environment.

Jewish immigration to the United States consisted of two distinct groups at two time periods. The first wave of Jewish immigrants came in the early

19th century from Germany, where they had been fairly well integrated into economic and social life. These early immigrants achieved the same thing in the United States, spreading out across the country in a broad spectrum of urban professions. By 1880, many had come to feel they were Americans of Jewish religion rather than Jews in America. The second wave of Jewish immigration was sparked by outbreaks of violent anti-Semitism in Russia and Poland. Between 1880 and 1920, it is estimated that three-quarters of the Jewish population of Eastern Europe migrated to the United States. Jewish immigrants of the second wave were markedly different from those who preceded them; they were less literate, they were poorer (they were, in fact, the poorest of all immigrant groups to come to the United States in this period), and they were used to living in walled ghettos and not participating in the larger society. Thus they congregated together in the most crowded slums the world has ever seen on Manhattan's lower East Side. Here they established their own institutions and singlehandedly created the U.S. garment industry. The Singer who made sewing machines was an Isaac; the Strauss who made jeans was a Levi. By the turn of the century, 234 of the 241 garment factories in New York were owned and operated by Jews (Sowell, 1981).

First through hard work and then by zealous application to education, these Jewish immigrants pulled themselves out of the lower class. Despite the very real prejudice and discrimination they faced, their rate of upward mobility was twice as high as that of other immigrant groups (Peterson, 1978). By 1950, Jews far exceeded other Americans in education and income; in that year, 25 percent of all Jewish men had a college degree, compared to 10 percent of all men. More than one-quarter of all Nobel prizes won by Americans have been won by Jews, who constitute only 3 percent of the U.S. population (Sowell, 1981: 89). (Some of these Nobelists were not U.S.-educated, however, but were refugees from Nazi persecution).

Despite what seems the perfect example of the American success story, Jews have remained a minority group. Jewish separatism is partly by choice. The large population of Jews in several Eastern cities (for example, a Jewish population of 1 million in New York City) has made it possible for Jews to set up their own institutions—hospitals, nursing homes, cemeteries, and social clubs (Parenti, 1967). One of the reasons Jews have elected to set up separate institutions, however, is prejudice and discrimination. Until the last decade, Jews were commonly excluded from clubs and colleges across the country. This overt discrimination is now much reduced (though not completely eliminated), and assimilation appears to be nearing completion for Jews. An increased level of intermarriage (nearly one-third of all Jews now marry Gentiles) suggests that Jews may soon cease to be regarded as a minority group (Reiss, 1980:333).

Japanese and Other Asians

The Japanese, Chinese, Filipinos, and other Asians make up a little over 1 percent of the total U.S. population. Different groups of Asian Americans have followed different paths in the United States, but their immigration experiences are similar. The migrations were largely male, directed at the

West Coast between 1850 and 1900, and met by sharp and occasionally violent racism.

The last decades of the 19th century saw repeated and finally successful efforts to ban further Japanese or Chinese immigration to the United States. As a result of closing the door to immigration before many could bring their families, the predominantly male Asian American community declined in number over the next few generations. During this period, many struggled for an education only to find that the only place for college graduates of Japanese descent was back on their parents' farm. Nevertheless, substantial progress was made. In 1941, Japanese Americans owned more than half of all hotels in Seattle and 10 percent of all restaurants. At the height of the Depression, less than 1 percent of Los Angeles Japanese population was on the dole, compared to 12 percent of the white population (Gelernter, 1981).

In the ensuing years, each of the three Asian American groups has surpassed the educational achievements of the average American and Asian Americans now have the highest average incomes of any major racial or ethnic group in the United States (see Table 9.4). Despite the educational and economic success of Asian Americans, however, these groups are not fully assimilated into American society. Residential segregation is high, intermarriage rates are low, and Asian Americans get paid less than whites at comparable levels of education. Japanese men earn only 88 percent of the income that whites with the same education and occupation earn, a level of discrimination comparable to that against blacks (Woodrum, 1981).

Native Americans

By all accounts, Native Americans (American Indians) are the most disadvantaged minority group in the United States. They are one of the smallest minority groups (about 0.5 percent of the total population), and nearly half their members live in just four states: Oklahoma, Arizona, California, and New Mexico.

Almost from the beginning, whites used extraordinary solutions in their contacts with Native Americans. The current native population of 1.4 mil-

Table 9.4 A Comparison of the Major U.S. Ethnic and Racial Groups, 1980
Of the five major ethnic groups in this table, Hispanics have the lowest educational levels. Black families have lower incomes than Native American or Hispanic families because of a higher proportion of families that are female headed. Asian-American families have higher average education and income than white families.

	WHITE	BLACK	HISPANIC	ASIAN	NATIVE AMERICANS
Median family income	$20,835	$12,598	$14,712	$22,713	$13,724
Percent College Graduates	17%	8%	8%	33%	8%
Percent high school graduates	69	51	44	75	56
Percent families below poverty line	7	26	21	11	24
Percent families with female heads	14	41	22	13	26

SOURCE: U.S. Bureau of the Census, 1981, tables 121–139.

America's Concentration Camps

One of the darkest blots on the U.S. conscience is the relocation of 123,000 Japanese Americans during World War II. Although not as extreme as the enslavement of blacks or the extermination of Native Americans, the relocation startles and shames because it occurred only 40 years ago. It brings home the reality that racism in a virulent form was alive and well very recently; it is not something our nation left behind with the last century.

Anti-Japanese racism was strong on the West Coast almost from the beginning of Japanese settlement. The relative economic success of the Japanese immigrants only strengthened the resentment. Thus, when Japan bombed Pearl Harbor in December 1941, there were immediate demands to do something about the Japanese in the United States—two-thirds of whom were U.S. citizens. During this period, Japanese Americans huddled in front of their radios,

Figure 9.11

eager to hear the news but afraid to go out into the streets, to school, or to work. In fear, they burned or destroyed all their ties to Japan—books, letters, Bibles, and clothing (Sone, 1953).

There were relatively few hostile incidents, but the fears turned out to be justified. In February 1942, President Roosevelt signed Proclamation 9066, the document that gave the army the right to do what it thought necessary to protect national security. The army's solution was the relocation of the West Coast Japanese Americans.

The people were given less than 2 months to sell all their belongings or to find a trusted white to care for their property. Dealers in second-hand goods roamed like vultures through Japanese neighborhoods, trying to buy cheaply from people who had no time to look for a decent price. One woman remembers her mother breaking every piece of a treasured set of china rather than sell it for $15 (Houston & Houston, 1973). Long-term land leases were voided, and many lost their homes and businesses. Things left behind were vandalized or stolen.

The army had as little time to prepare as did the Japanese Americans, and initially the internees were confined on fairgrounds, housed in exhibition halls and barns. Within 6 months, however, large relocation camps had been thrown up in isolated regions of the Western United States—Tule Lake, Manzanar, Minedoka. The inmates themselves provided all the labor in the camps; they were cooks, nurses, and even internal security forces. The weather

was awful, and the conditions were Spartan at best.

Almost immediately, decent women and men began to try to undo the damage. Through the American Friend's Service Committee (a Quaker organization), Japanese college students were sent to the East Coast to resume their studies. Efforts were made to find jobs and relocate families in the Midwest and the East. As a result, the camps were entirely empty before the war itself ended. And although it did not come close to covering actual losses, the U.S. government paid out $37 million in property damages to the internees.

One of the tactics the government used to defuse anti-Japanese sentiment and to integrate the Japanese Americans into American society was to encourage their enlistment in the armed forces. It is hard to imagine the gall it took for a recruiter to enter an internment camp and urge young men to serve their country. Nevertheless, young men did volunteer and did serve with distinction in Europe and the Pacific, even in the army of occupation. For its size, the all-Nisei (American-born Japanese) 100th Battalion and 442nd Regimental Combat Team was the most decorated combat team in the war. Memorial services for dead soldiers were held in internment camps as well as at Arlington National Cemetery.

The deed of relocating Japanese Americans was shameful. Not a single act of sabotage or espionage was ever uncovered to justify the incarceration of a single individual, much less the entire West Coast Japanese American population

(Girdner & Loftis, 1969). Although wartime fear was a factor, so was racism; there was no move to imprison German Americans or Italian Americans. Racism plus fear resulted in the violation of the constitutional rights of more than 100,000 U.S. citizens. In evaluating our acts and our principles, it is useful to remember that we were not the only ones evacuating people of Japanese ancestry. Canada and Mexico also evacuated West Coast Japanese. In the case of Canada, it was done far less humanely than in the United States. For example, the Canadian government confiscated all the goods of Japanese Canadian citizens, sold them at sacrifice prices, and gave the people back the money minus a sales commission. It broke up families by putting the men into work crews and sending the women, children, and the elderly to fend for themselves in abandoned ghost towns (Kogamawa, 1981). Having company in a disgraceful act does not reduce the burden, but it does make it clear that racism is not a particularly American character fault.

P.S. The legislation making it possible to intern Americans without trial was repealed in 1969.

Questions to Consider

Could it happen again? Consider our reactions to Iranians at the time of the embassy crisis. What would happen if we got into a war with Cuba or Vietnam or Mexico?

lion represents a fraction of the number who lived here before white settlement (Dobyns, 1966). The native population of the Americas was decimated by disease and, to a lesser extent, warfare. The last major massacre is now a century behind us (Wounded Knee, 1890), and for the last 100 years ordinary solutions of prejudice, discrimination, and segregation have been employed in white relations to this minority group.

It is difficult to speak with authority about Native Americans as a group. They represent more than 200 tribal groupings, with different cultures and languages. Some have been successful: fish farmers in the Northwest, ranchers in Wyoming, bridge builders in Maine. In urban areas, Native Americans experience much less racial segregation than do other non-white groups (Bohland, 1982), and some have entered the professions and other occupations of modern industrial society. Many, however, have suffered the destruction of one culture without finding another to replace it.

More than any other minority, Native Americans have remained both unacculturated and unassimilated. In rural areas, reservations foster a sort of pluralism with segregation. In urban areas, Anglo-conformity is the rule. It is estimated that in the mid 1970s between 25 and 40 percent of Native American children were taken from their parents and reared in (white) foster homes because their own parents' homes didn't meet conventional (that is, Western industrial) standards of adequacy (Witt, 1980). Was this an impartial attempt to help children, or was it simple ethnocentrism, a preference for one way of life over another? These are difficult questions. Nevertheless, it is clear that Native American culture is not simply different from the dominant culture; in many ways it is a shattered culture. Those who cling to earlier values face a severe case of anomie, since the means to achieve the old goals are gone forever. In addition, prejudice and discrimination may stand in the way of achieving the new goals. The results are obvious in the following quote from John Kifner, a *New York Times* reporter covering the 1973 confrontation at Wounded Knee (Kifner, 1973:82):

Today the Pine Ridge Reservation is a bleak picture of some of the worst poverty in America. Abandoned, rusted cars cluster around tumbledown shacks and

Figure 9.12

Native Americans are one of the smallest and poorest racial groups in the United States. They are a people caught between two cultures, one which has been systematically destroyed and another which has hardly welcomed them. One result of this marginality is the despair and delapitation apparent on this Blackfoot reservation in Browning, Montana. An increasingly active Native American movement, however, is seeking to regain control over the economic and political destiny of reservations such as this one.

litter the prairie hills, the best acres of which are grazed by white men's cattle. The unemployment rate stands at 54 percent and goes up to 70 percent in the winter months. More than half of the families are on welfare, and every index of social disorder is higher than among the nation's black population. Hopeless drunk men lurch about the streets at mid morning.

The Newest Immigrants

If we went no further, it would appear that intergroup relations in the United States represent a continuing process of adjustment to the last generation's, even the last century's, immigrants. Yet the United States is still a haven for refugees—Haitians, Laotians, and Vietnamese today. For the most part, these recent immigrant groups have entered at the bottom of the economic and social ladder. As a result, prejudice and discrimination, as well as poverty, are common. As Figure 9.13 shows, many Americans are not pleased with the new immigrants—just as in 1920 they didn't want the Italians or the Jews. There is, however, a strong pattern in American ethnic relationships for social distance and segregation to decrease with improvements in economic position (Massey, 1981). Thus acceptance of the newest immigrants should increase as the immigrants and their children move up the socioeconomic ladder.

Intergroup Conflict

In their respective histories, each minority group has been implicitly compared to the Anglo majority group. It should also be noted, however, that there is substantial competition between minority groups. Aside from the Native Americans, blacks have the longest heritage in the United States. Like their white peers, they have thus occasionally objected to European, Asian, or Hispanic immigration. In part this was an economic judgment,

Figure 9.13 Americans Rating Group Contributions, 1982

Just as Americans were pretty unenthusiastic about Italians, Jews, and Poles earlier this century, surveys show that the newest immigrants are not warmly welcomed. As these groups improve their socioeconomic position, however, their ratings are likely to improve.

SOURCE: Edwin Harwood, "Alienation: American attitudes toward immigration" in Public Opinion, Vol. 6 (June/July, 1983), pp. 45–51.

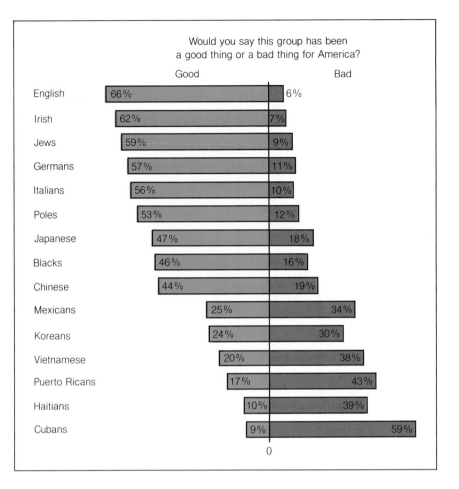

Would you say this group has been a good thing or a bad thing for America?

	Good	Bad
English	66%	6%
Irish	62%	7%
Jews	59%	9%
Germans	57%	11%
Italians	56%	10%
Poles	53%	12%
Japanese	47%	18%
Blacks	46%	16%
Chinese	44%	19%
Mexicans	25%	34%
Koreans	24%	30%
Vietnamese	20%	38%
Puerto Ricans	17%	43%
Haitians	10%	39%
Cubans	9%	59%

0

Figure 9.14

During the late 1970s and early 1980s, special legislation was passed by the U.S. Congress to allow Vietnamese boat people to immigrate to the United States. After a rocky start in American schools, Vietnamese children are now beginning to pursue the same upwardly mobile course of previous Asian ethnic groups.

the recognition that white unskilled labor would probably usurp the toehold that black labor was getting in industry. It also reflected simple ethnocentrism. Booker T. Washington, the famous black educator, is "reported to have considered Sicilian sulphur miners deserving of their fate as human beasts of toil—'they are superstitious Catholics who eat garlic.' Mr. Washington passed upon them the judgment of a middle-class American Protestant; quite naturally so, for that is what he was" (cited in Rose, 1981:198). In the 1940s, Hispanics argued before the Texas Supreme Court that their children should not be educated in segregated schools because the segregaton law referred only to "colored children" and they weren't colored (San Miguel, 1982). In short, the competitive disadvantage at which minority groups stand with regard to the dominant society has often led to competition between minority groups (Shankman, 1982). In fact, most ethnic and racial groups have more in common with the dominant Anglo culture than they do with each other.

Continuity and Change

Changing Attitudes

During the last 20 years, significant steps have been taken to secure the rights of minority groups in political life, in housing, and in the labor force. These changes have not eliminated discrimination by any means, though they have eliminated the most overt expressions of racism and have offered means of legal redress to victims of racial or ethnic exclusion.

Although, as Dr. King said, the law may not be able to make one person love another, there has been a substantial decrease in prejudicial attitudes. Both blacks and whites perceive more interracial tolerance and less dislike. Trend data on other indicators show that attitudes toward interracial marriage and integration have changed dramatically (see Table 9.5).

Table 9.5 Changes in Racial Attitudes

Over the last 15 years there have been substantial reductions in prejudice among both blacks and whites. A majority of Americans now say that they are unprejudiced.

Most whites dislike blacks:	1968	1978
Whites	77%	40%
Blacks	57	39
Most blacks dislike whites:		
Whites	75	57
Blacks	*	44
Approve of interracial marriage:	1968	1983
Total	20	43
Whites	*	38
Blacks	*	71
Would vote for a black for president:		
Total	38	77
Whites	*	76
Blacks		71

SOURCE: The Gallup Report, Nos. 168, 212, 213.

*Not asked.

People say that they are less prejudiced now. Is this just another level of timid bigotry, with people reluctant to admit prejudice, or is it real change? Probably some of both. Repeated studies show that although the majority are now favorable to integration, it is conditional; only 13 percent of whites would move if a black family moved in next door, but 51 percent would move if "blacks came to live in great numbers in your neighborhood" (Gallup Opinion Index, 1978). And although 86 percent think that black and white students should go to the same schools, 56 percent of whites would object to sending their child to a school where most of the children were black (Smith, 1981). Thus, although the decade has shown substantial progress in the reduction of racist attitudes, a significant majority of whites are still uncomfortable with blacks, and vice versa.

Prospects for the Future

There was a time not many years ago when many serious students of U.S. racial and ethnic problems believed that the issue would disappear. They thought that the Poles, Slavs, Italians, and Jews were already assimilated. They predicted that changes in law and in attitude would make it possible for blacks and whites to reach the same level of amicable integration as have whites and Japanese. In short, they saw a happy vision of Anglo-conformity.

This vision received a rude interruption. First came black awareness, accompanied by a rising pride in things distinctively black. In its footsteps came a rising ethnic awareness on the part of Hispanics and Native Americans. White ethnics soon followed. All this time, it turns out, the Italians, Poles, Greeks, and so on have not been assimilated at all but have been living in ethnic communities, that are easily mobilized into an assertion

Figure 9.15

In response to the increasingly vocal demands of black and brown racial and ethnic groups during the 1960s and 1970s, white ethnics became more assertive. Poles, Greeks, and Italians ceased to claim that they were just plain Americans who had put the old country behind them and began to take pride in their ethnic origins. This parade of New York's Greek community is just one manifestation of a renewed pride in ethnic heritage.

of distinct ethnic culture. Because it has often been motivated by competition with other organized groups that are making claims for special treatment, white ethnic assertiveness has been called **defensive pluralism.**

Can ethnic identity also be a positive force? Many people believe it can; they see it contributing to both the richness and integration of U.S. society. Cultural pluralism in a positive sense is far from being accomplished, however; throughout the Southwest and in the suburbs of northern industrial cities there is still powerful debate about the merits of Anglo-conformity versus pluralism. Will we as a nation insist on Anglo-conformity, or will we allow the development of pluralism, a federation of nations with more than one legitimate culture? This is a value issue; it is also a pragmatic policy issue. To provide education in Spanish is to accept cultural pluralism; to refuse it is to deny the legitimacy of cultural pluralism.

Defensive pluralism is an assertion of group identity motivated by competition with other organized groups that are making claims for special treatment.

Prejudice and Residential Segregation

Because prejudice is so difficult to eliminate, most policy programs have been directed at reducing discrimination. Nevertheless, a substantial body of research demonstrates that prejudice can be reduced. Prejudice is in part a response to the unknown. (As someone once remarked, it is being down on what you're not up on.) Sustained interaction with members of another group generally reduces this response.

The first empirical evidence came from studies of the armed forces during World War II. The army was taking tentative steps toward integration by experimenting with the introduction of black soldiers in white combat groups. The results gave evidence that familiarity led to acceptance. The acceptance of integration varied by degree of contact.

OF THOSE WITH:

— No blacks in the division, 38 percent accepted integration.

Figure 9.16
Racial integration in housing is a vital link in the effort to reduce prejudice and discrimination and produce racial equality and brotherhood in the United States. This birthday party in an integrated neighborhood includes anglo, black, and asian children. Although this integration will not make these children immune to the racism and prejudice in their society, it does make racial tolerance much more likely.

— Blacks in the division but not in the regiment, 76 percent accepted integration.
— Blacks in the regiment but not in the company, 80 percent accepted integration.
— Blacks in the company, 93 percent accepted integration.

More recent evidence confirms that whites who live closer to blacks and who work with them express significantly less social distance than do whites who have little contact with blacks (Robinson, 1980). This evidence suggests that an important mechanism for reducing prejudice and discrimination is an increase in the level of interracial interaction. The major barrier to interaction is residential segregation.

RESIDENTIAL SEGREGATION

In all major U.S. cities, there is a high and unchanging level of housing segregation. Before the current civil rights legislation, much of this *segregation* was de jure—established by law. Now *segregation* is de facto occurring because minorities often cannot afford to live in higher-class neighborhoods.

Sociologists measure segregation by the extent to which census tracts in a city depart from the total racial composition of the city. In a city with a population that is 80 percent Anglo and 20 percent Hispanic, perfect integration exists when each census tract is 80 percent anglo and 20 percent Hispanic. This measure, the segregation index, varies from 0 to 100 and can be interpreted as the proportion of the smaller group that would have to move to create total integration. Data from U.S. cities show that blacks are the most highly segregated ethnic group: 83 percent of the black population in U.S. cities would have to move to a different census tract in order to create integration with Anglos; 76 percent would have to move to achieve residential integration with the Hispanic population (Massey, 1979). The segregation between Hispanics and Anglos is much smaller (only 44 percent would have to move), but growing.

Repeated studies of racial and ethnic segregation demonstrate little change over time; a study of black-white segregation in 109 major cities showed that the index of segregation fell only slightly, from 85 to 82, between 1940 and 1970 (Sorenson et al., 1975). Moreover, the segregation differs little from North to South and from industrial centers to rural counties. Additional studies have demonstrated that segregation is not a simple result of socioeconomic differences. If we look only at professionals, we find that 83 percent of all black professionals would have had to move to another census tract in 1970 to achieve integration (Farley, 1977).

Only halfhearted efforts have been made to reduce segregation. In the late 1960s, open-housing laws (laws declaring it illegal to deny people the right to rent or buy housing because of their race) were passed in many communities, but their enforcement is weak. Redlining is illegal but difficult to prove. Black and Hispanic realtors are all too few, though some recent policy statements urge that increasing their number is essential to encouraging integration. One of the most potent forces encouraging continued segregation is, ironically, the federal government. With the intent of helping, it has erected low-cost housing in many U.S. cities—smack in the middle of black neighborhoods. Many people believe that if government housing policy had concentrated less on high-rise apartment buildings and more on small units spread throughout the city, it could have been a major force for integration (Bullock & Rodgers, 1976).

It should be apparent that school busing, one of the most controversial social programs of the decade, is an outgrowth of residential segregation. If neighborhoods were integrated, then neighborhood schools would be integrated and there would be no need for busing. We are left with an anomalous situation:

— 86 percent of the people prefer integrated schools
— 90 percent of the people prefer neighborhood schools to busing

The obvious solution to the dilemma is residential integration. Yet we still have no vigorous federal programs to encourage the end to de facto racial and ethnic segregation.

SUMMARY

1. Race and ethnicity are both passed on from parent to child, but race refers to the genetic transmission of physical characteristics and ethnicity refers to socialization into distinct cultural patterns.

2. Race and ethnicity interact with social class to determine an individual's position in the hierarchy of life chances. The history of racial and ethnic groups in the United States shows that prejudice, discrimination, and segregation tend to decrease as groups improve their educational and economic position.

3. Prejudice is attitudes; discrimination is behavior. They do not always go hand-in-hand, but one is likely to lead to the other. Prejudice is difficult to change because it is irrational; thus most social policy is aimed at reducing discrimination.

4. Four basic patterns of contact between majority and minority groups are conflict, assimilation, accommodation, and acculturation.

5. On almost all indicators, racial and ethnic minorities have improved their position in U.S. society. Nevertheless, prejudice and economic differentials still exist.

6. Native Americans are the least prosperous and least assimilated group in the United States; they are followed by Hispanics and blacks. Older Asian immigrant groups and Jews have made it—earning, on the average, more than whites, though not more than whites of comparable educations. Hispanics are the fastest growing minority group in the United States;

within 50 years, Hispanics are likely to replace blacks as the largest minority group.

7. One key to reducing prejudice is an increase in interaction. Interaction ultimately relies on housing integration. Unfortunately, studies of residential patterns show high levels of segregation for blacks and Hispanics. The levels have changed little since World War II.

SUGGESTED READINGS

Horowitz, Ruth. (1983). Honor and the American Dream: Culture and Identity in a Chicano Community. New Brunswick, N.J.: Rutgers University Press. An absorbing account of a Chicano community in Chicago, with special emphasis on how young people move back and forth between the demands of Chicano culture and the demands of the larger culture.

Liebow, Elliot. (1967). Tally's Corner. Boston: Little, Brown. Introduced in chapter 2, this classic study provides an insightful look at how poverty and lack of opportunity affect family and personal life in urban slums.

Rose, Peter I. (1981). They and We (3rd ed.). New York: Random House. An excellent short text that provides an overview of the major issues of pluralism, diversity, and democracy.

Sowell, Thomas. (1981). Ethnic America: A History. New York: Basic Books. Covering all of the major ethnic groups in the United States, this volume provides a fascinating account of divergent immigration experiences.

Steinberg, Stephen. (1981). The Ethnic Myth: Race, Ethnicity and Class in America. New York: Antheneum Publishers. Addresses the question of why minority groups are disadvantaged in American society and why some have made it and some have not.

Wilson, William J. (1978). The Declining Significance of Race. Chicago: University of Chicago Press. A controversial argument that class has replaced race as a determinant of socioeconomic position, suggesting that castelike features of race are not important any longer for the black working and middle classes.

CHAPTER 10

GENDER AND AGE DIFFERENTIATION

PROLOGUE

Have You Ever . . . thought about growing old? Have you perhaps peered closely at the mirror and discovered what might be the beginning of a wrinkle? Have you seen a few strands of grey? If you are male, are you already getting noticeably thinner on top? Do you find that you cannot touch your toes as easily as you used to?

Growing old is not something we start to do at 30 or 40; it is something that happens to us continuously. By the time we're 20, it already takes our bodies twice as long to heal as it did when we were 10 (Du-Noüy, 1936: 154, 155). In spite of these physiological changes, much of the way we age depends on our social roles. This is nowhere more evident than in the different concerns that men and women have with aging.

Probably 9 out of 10 students who admit to noticing their potential wrinkles are female. The physical signs of aging have far more significance for women than for men, in part because women's physical appearance has for many generations been a commodity—the chief bargaining tool in the marriage market. Sex and age still go together in many ways. After 40, men are three times more likely than women to marry. A woman who is single (or single again) past 40 tends to remain single forever. A man is still desirable; he may lose his hair but not his checkbook.

In all societies, gender and age are bases of differentiation. The social roles of women and men are different; children, adults, and the elderly each have their own rights and obligations. This chapter describes the differences in social roles by age and sex, looks at the causes of these differences, and considers whether the differences represent socially structured inequality.

259

Sexual Differentiation

Gender is biological sex, male or female.

Sex roles are the rights and obligations assigned to males and females in a particular culture.

Gender is biological sex—male or female. **Sex roles** are the rights and obligations assigned to each gender in a particular culture. Obligations include not only expected behaviors but also norms prescribing appropriate personality characteristics. Thus the norms that surround the traditional role for women may prescribe such duties as childbearing, childcare, and cooking and such personality characteristics as nurturance, passiveness, and emotionality.

Women and men are different. Biology differentiates them, and cultural norms in every society differentiate their roles. A question everybody is interested in is: How much is biological, and how much is cultural? Are sex roles really roles? Can we treat them as optional parts in the play of life? If we do not like the script provided by society, can we throw it away and rewrite our lines? Or are we bound by nature to play our parts a certain way? Psychologists, biologists, chemists, anthropologists, and sociologists are all working to discover the balance between cultural and biological forces. When the answer comes, it is bound to be complex and will undoubtedly say that both factors are important.

The chief point of concern for social scientists is that although biology provides two distinct and universal genders, cultures provide almost infinitely varied sex roles. Each man is pretty much like each other man in terms of gender—whether he's upper class or lower class, black or white, Chinese or Apache. Sex roles, however, are a different matter. The rights and duties of the male sex role are very different for a Chinese man than for an Apache man. Even within a given culture, men do not play the same sex roles. Some play an extreme form of the manly sex role; others may lean toward more womanly behaviors. Similarly, some women act more manly than some men do.

Social scientists are generally more interested in sex roles than in gender. They want to know about the variety of roles that have been assigned to women and men and, more particularly, about what accounts for the variation. Under what circumstances do women have more or less power, prestige, and income? What accounts for the changes that have occurred in our own sex roles?

Sex-Role Norms

Cross-Cultural Evidence

Most societies seem to have capitalized on obvious biological differences in devising a gender-based division of labor. That is, because women may be tied down by childbearing and nursing, they are given tasks that are close to home and easily interruptible (Brown, 1970). Cross-cultural evidence indicates that in the vast majority of cultures, men are the hunters, the herders, the fishers; women are the gatherers, the water carriers, the food preservers (Stephens, 1963:282). There are exceptions, but few societies have been in a position to overlook the physical differences between men and women.

Figure 10.1
Although the labor of women has been a mainstay of economic life in most societies, it is often a mark of prestige when a family can afford to do without her labor. This prestige is symbolically declared by these Afghan women whose attire incapacitates them for work and thus declares the ability of others to support them. In western culture, such devices as the corset and high heels serve much the same purpose.

Within these general constraints, however, there is wide variability in personality socialization and division of labor between women and men. Cross-cultural research shows that the behaviors we normally associate with being female and male are by no means universal. Among the New Guinea Arapesh, both genders are expected to be gentle and giving, subordinating their own needs to those of others. Their neighbors, the Mundugumors, are fierce, combative, and aggressive. Both genders exhibit what we would call compulsive masculinity. The Tchambuli, a third primitive society of New Guinea, adhere to sex roles opposite to what is expected in our society: Dominant women are considered normal; men are expected to be more passive, emotional, and dependent (Mead, 1935). In some societies, men rather than women wear makeup and spend hours preening themselves.

These societies demonstrate that it is possible to structure a society with sex roles different from our own. Human "nature" appears to be quite plastic, and culture molds us in many different ways. It is also important to note the universals, however: In all cultures women (though not necessarily the biological mothers) are responsible for childcare, and in all cultures women have less power than men.

Physically, women are different from men; in terms of social status, they are inferior. In spite of the fact that women do substantial amounts of work in all societies, often supplying large portions of food as well as taking care of stock, children, and households, women universally have less power and less value. A simple piece of evidence is parents' almost universal preference for male children. Table 10.1 includes data on gender preference for six nations. In these nations, parents who have a preference prefer a boy to a girl by a margin never lower than 10 to 1 and as high as

Table 10.1 Cross-Cultural Differences in Sex Preference

In most cultures there is a strong preference for the birth of a new child to be a boy. This preference is even stronger for first-born children.

"When a family has several children, both sons and daughters equally, and a new child is coming, is it preferable that the new child be a boy, either one, or a girl?"

	BOYS	GIRLS	EITHER	BOY/ GIRL RATIO
Argentina	33%	3%	63%	11/1
Chile	56	5	39	11/1
India	78	5	17	16/1
Bangladesh	91	2	8	46/1
Israel (non-Europeans)	44	4	52	11/1
Nigeria	67	2	31	34/1

SOURCE: Original data from the Harvard Project on the Socio-cultural Aspects of Development conducted by Inkeles and Smith. Presented in Williamson, Nancy. 1978. "Boys or girls: Parents' preferences and sex control." Population Bulletin 33(1), table 1, page 9.

46 to 1. This preference is less strong in modern industrial nations, but parents in the United States still prefer boys to girls and, by a 2 to 1 ratio, prefer their first child to be a boy (Pebley & Westoff, 1982).

Figure 10.2

Changing sex role norms have altered the expectations—and the opportunities—for both men and women in western culture. The roles which women and men play are still noticeably different, but there has been a marked convergence. Women are now more involved outside the household and men are more involved at home.

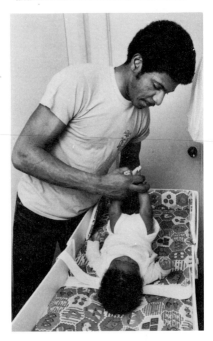

Changing American Sex Roles

The traditional sex role for men in the United States has been that of work outside the home, provision of the family income, and general responsibility for the moral and economic welfare of the family. Men have been expected to be physically strong and to have a great deal of emotional control. They have avoided expressing feelings and have not easily formed intimate relationships (Pleck, 1981). The traditional sex role for women has stressed home and family, attention to physical appearance, an emotional approach to people and issues, and a general ban on the expression of power or aggression (Schaffer, 1981).

These traditional roles have been supported by religious, legal, educational, and political norms. As a result, most men and women have agreed that it is right and proper that men should have more power and prestige than women. Because men have been considered less emotional and have had more contact with the outside world and more outside responsibility, most people have agreed that they should "wear the pants" and "have the final say." Within the past 15 years, however, there have been dramatic changes in sex-role norms. These changes are apparent in a longitudinal study of women in Detroit. In 1962, researchers studying family life selected a sample of 1,200 women in Detroit who had just had a child; 18 years later they interviewed the women again, this time including an interview with their grown children. The results (see Table 10.2) show that the women had become much less traditional in their norms about sex roles during the 18-year period. This is particularly noticeable in the area of power: By 1980, a majority (71 percent) did not agree that husbands ought to "have the final say."

The changes in sex-role norms reflected in these data have generally increased the power of women and the alternatives thought appropriate for them. They have simultaneously reduced the power of men and increased the competition that men have to face in many areas of life. Thus it is not surprising that the data in Table 10.2 show that boys in 1980 tended to be a bit more traditional than either their mothers or their sisters.

New Sex Roles.   Changing sex roles have brought stress to many people—to men who have had to give up rights and power and also to women. Women who grew up in an era when being a good mother and housewife was a sufficient goal are troubled to find that society no longer regards this as enough. Generally, the changes in sex roles mean that both women and men must add new roles, while retaining many of their traditional obligations. For women, the remodeled sex role appears in the superwoman complex. Each woman is expected to have a well-kept house, elegant meals, and cheerful and clean children; she must belong to the PTA, be a room mother, and have a successful career. There is a parallel in the postfeminist superman role: Each man is supposed to have a successful career as well as be a gourmet cook, a sensitive lover, and a dad who begins a life of total involvement with his children by going to Lamaze classes and staying in the delivery room (Gerzon, 1982).

In the short run, the increasing role demands on both men and women may create role strain, a feeling that too much is being demanded. In the long run, many expect that changed sex roles will produce more well-rounded human beings. The greater flexibility of sex roles will increase our freedom to discover the roles that we play well and that suit our interests.

Table 10.2   Changing Sex Roles, 1962 and 1980
A study of Detroit mothers found that their sex role attitudes have shifted towards a more equalitarian view over the last two decades. In 1980 there was little difference between the mother's sex role attitudes and those of their children, although boys tended to be slightly more traditional on two measures.

Normative Sex Roles in a Sample of Mothers Studied in 1962 and 1980 and Their 18-Year Old Children in 1980

| | MOTHERS | | CHILDREN, 1980 | |
	1962	1980	Boys	Girls
Most of the important decisions in the life of the family should be made by the man of the house.				
Percent disagree	32%	71%	44%	66%
It is perfectly all right for women to be very active in clubs, politics, and other outside activities before the children are grown up.				
Percent agree	44	68	73	72
There is some work that is men's and some that is women's, and they should not be doing each other's.				
Percent disagree	56	67	51	69
A wife should not expect her husband to help around the house after he comes home from a hard day's work.				
Percent disagree	47	69	76	72

SOURCE: Aarland Thornton, et al, "Causes and consequences of sex-role attitudes and attitude change." American Sociological Review 48 (April, 1983), Table 1, p. 214.

FOCUS ON MEASUREMENT:

What Kind of Man (or Woman) Are You, Anyway?

How well does the adjective *decisive* describe you?

Would you say . . .

1. Never or almost never true.
2. Usually not true.
3. Sometimes but infrequently true.
4. Occasionally true.
5. Often true.
6. Usually true.
7. Always or almost always true.

How about the adjective *warmhearted?*

Would you say . . .

1. Never or almost never true.
2. Usually not true.
3. Sometimes but infrequently true.
4. Occasionally true.
5. Often true.
6. Usually true.
7. Always or almost always true.

Docile?

Would you say . . .

1. Never or almost never true.
2. Usually not true.
3. Sometimes but infrequently true.
4. Occasionally true.
5. Often true.
6. Usually true.
7. Always or almost always true.

Resolute?

Would you say . . .

1. Never or almost never true.
2. Usually not true.
3. Sometimes but infrequently true.
4. Occasionally true.
5. Often true.
6. Usually true.
7. Always or almost always true.

If you scored yourself high on decisiveness and resoluteness but

low on docility and warmheartedness, you have a masculine sex-role identity. If you scored yourself high on docility and warmheartedness but low on decisiveness and resoluteness, you have a feminine sex-role identity. If you scored high on all the adjectives or even on three out of the four, then you may be *androgynous.* What if you're low on all of them? The sex-role literature labels you undifferentiated.

As we are growing up, we learn that there are some things that are girlish and some that are boyish. We learn that activities and feelings are *sex-typed*—more appropriate for one sex than another. In general, our culture has thought that the more instrumental activities (being physically active and concerned with getting the job done, for example) are masculine and that the more expressive activities (giving sympathy, help, and support, for example) are feminine.

These sex-role traits have been normative; that is, persons of the male gender *should be* masculine and persons of the female gender *should be* feminine. Moreover, traditional wisdom has suggested that the two characteristics are mutually exclusive. A masculine person could not and should not be feminine too. This view is increasingly being questioned, and many now believe that a person who combines both characteristics may be more well-rounded than others are.

Psychologist Sandra Bem devised the Bem Sex Role Inventory (BSRI) to determine empirically the degree of sex-typing in each individual's

personality. In the Bem inventory, respondents are asked to evaluate themselves on each of 60 adjectives. Of the 60 adjectives, a panel judged 20 to be desirable behaviors for men, 20 to be desirable for women, and 20 to be desirable but not sex-typed. The adjectives are sprinkled randomly throughout the questionnaire so that individuals who want to be thought manly, for example, cannot simply endorse a whole section without considering all of them.

Bem has explored some of the consequences of androgyny in laboratory studies. In one study, she gave subjects the choice of two tasks: one typed for the opposite gender and one for their own. (For example, women were given the choice of nailing boards together or ironing linen napkins.) The subjects were paid twice as much for doing the opposite-sexed task. Androgynous people were able to maximize their self-interest by pursuing the more profitable task regardless of its sex-typing; sex-typed individuals confined themselves to acting out their sex roles even when the roles were not in their best interest.

Summing up the results of dozens of different tests using many methodologies, Bem concluded that androgynous people "perform spectacularly. They shun no behavior simply because the culture happens to label it as male or female, and their competence crosses both the instrumental and expressive domains. They are firm in their opinions, cuddle kittens and bounce babies, and have a sympathetic ear for someone in distress" (Bem, 1976:58).

Bem and others argue that androgyny will produce individuals who are more adaptable and more mentally healthy than others. Some studies during the 1970s support this expectation. Less sex-typed individuals are reported to receive more awards during their school years, to date more, and to be sick less often than others (Spence et al., 1975). Other studies, however, have found that the advantages of androgyny are largely for women (Jones et al., 1978). In this case, it is not the combination of both sex-typed behaviors that brings advantages; instead it is that becoming more masculine brings more rewards for women. Being warmhearted may make a woman a nice lady, but she will get farther if she is also resolute and decisive.

Questions to Consider

1. Can you find anyone among your acquaintances who is a completely manly man or womanly woman? What are such people like to live and work with?
2. What is the likelihood that sympathy and understanding will someday be seen as deserving of status and prestige? If women want status and prestige, must they become more masculine?

Differences in Life Chances by Gender

In terms of race and social class, women and men start out equal. The nurseries of the rich as well as the poor contain about 50 percent girls. After birth, however, women and men experience very different life chances. This section examines some of the consequences of gender and sex roles for achievements and activities.

Differences in Life and Death

Childbearing.   Women still bear all the children, but they have far fewer than they used to, and active childbearing is a much smaller proportion of their lives than ever before. In 1790, the average American woman was having eight children; she was actively bearing children during much of the period between her 20th and 40th birthdays. In 1984, the average American woman was having fewer than two children, and their births generally were compressed into a 5-year period sometime in her 20s. As her life expectancy more than doubled in this period, the average American woman's social role has changed to the extent that she can now expect to live 35 years after her last child leaves home, 50 years after her last child enters school, and 55 years after her last child is born. As women spend fewer years of their adult lives being mothers, they have more time to be wives, thus changing the nature of marriage. In addition, most wives are spending a substantial portion of their newly freed time in the paid labor force.

Mortality.   Perhaps the most important difference in life chances is life itself. In 1982, men could expect to live 70.8 years and women 78.2 years. On the average, then, women live 7 years longer than men. Although some of men's greater mortality has to do with greater stress and more dangerous life-styles, perhaps half of it is biological (Hoover, 1983). The importance of inherited characteristics is evident in fetal mortality rates. Before the gender of the child is known and before cultural influence has

Figure 10.3
Throughout their entire lives men experience higher mortality than women. Although some of this is due to biological factors, a substantial portion is due to the different life-styles of men and women. Dangerous or rough occupations, smoking, drinking, and violence are important reasons that men have a life expectancy that is, on the average, 8 years lower than women's.

an effect, mortality is greater for males than females; miscarriage rates are higher for male fetuses, and neonatal mortality (mortality within the first week of life) is higher for male than female infants. This evidence strongly suggests that biology plays a part in giving women longer life-spans.

The social contribution to differential life expectancy, however, begins early. At high school and college ages, males are nearly three times more likely than females to die. Some of this difference is due to the greater likelihood, even at this age, of males dying of cancer and heart disease; to a significant extent, however, it has to do with the more dangerous life-style (particularly drinking and driving) associated with masculinity in our culture. As women become more competitive and intense about their work and as increasing proportions smoke cigarettes and drink alcohol, it is possible that the gender gap in mortality may be reduced.

Work—In the Labor Force and at Home

In 1900, only about 5 percent of married women worked outside the home. By 1940, the proportion had increased to just 15 percent. In every decade since, however, there have been dramatic increases in the percentage (see Figure 10.4). There are a variety of reasons for these increases: desire for a higher standard of living, for insurance against the possibility of divorce, for career continuity in a work life likely to last 30 to 40 years, and for a socially valued and respected role.

Of the women between the ages of 25 and 55, however, 40 percent are not working at outside jobs. Some are engaged in childbearing, but most

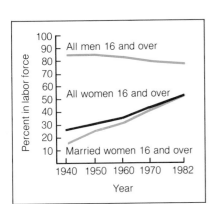

Figure 10.4 Changes in Labor-Force Participation
Since 1940 there have been dramatic increases in women's labor-force participation. These increases are most dramatic among married women. During the same period, men have slightly decreased their participation in the labor force.
SOURCE: U.S. Bureau of the Census, Statistical Abstract of the United States 1984, table 683.

Figure 10.5
World War II served as a benchmark in opening up paid employment for married women. During the war, government propaganda declared that it was women's duty to work in factories and offices to support the war effort. After the war, women were encouraged to leave the labor force and return to their kitchens, leaving jobs open for returning veterans. Although they did leave temporarily, women's employment has increased steadily since 1950 and work in the paid labor force is now a normal expectation for adult women, married and unmarried, mothers and nonmothers.

are engaged in the traditional social role of housewife and mother. They have forgone conventional achievement in business or industry and devoted themselves to raising children, keeping house, and, if middle or upper class, to community service. Although most young women expect to work most of their lives, for many women—working as well as nonworking—the role of wife and mother takes precedence over the role of worker. Except at the higher levels of occupational success, wife/mother continues to be the dominant role for many women, taking precedence over all other roles in case of conflict and determining which other roles will be held.

Household Work and Childcare.   Dozens of studies over the last decades demonstrate that childcare and housework are almost entirely women's province, whether they work outside the home or not. Normatively, most men and women say that the husband ought to help with the housework if the wife works (but it is still the woman's responsibility); in fact, however, husbands of working wives do little more than husbands whose wives are full-time homemakers (Hedges & Barnett, 1972), and the division of housework is a major source of strain in families with working wives (Hartman, 1981).

Conventional Achievement

In fields of conventional achievement, women have succeeded less well than men. Although they have almost closed the education gap, substantial differences remain in occupational prestige, earnings, and political power.

Education.   Women's educational attainment has increased faster than men's, with the result that men and women are now equally represented among high school graduates and among those receiving bachelor's and master's degrees. It is not until we reach the level of the PhD or advanced professional degrees (law and medicine) that women are disadvantaged in quantity of education. Probably more important than the differences in level of education are the differences in types of education. Although the gap has been closing, women are still overrepresented in the fields of education and the humanities and men are overrepresented in the fields of physical sciences, engineering, and law.

Occupations.   In part because of the differences in the focus of their educations, women are employed in different ways than are men (see Figure 10.6). Over one-third of female workers are in clerical occupations. These jobs are generally nonunion and poorly paid, with low benefits and a short career ladder (that is, there is no career ladder to climb). In contrast, approximately one-third of male workers are categorized as craft and kindred workers. These blue-collar workers also have short career ladders, but many are unionized and have high hourly wages and good benefit packages. The proportion of men and women in professional jobs is nearly equal. Generally, though, men are doctors and women nurses, men professors and women nursery school teachers.

Figure 10.6 Differences in Occupation by Gender, United States, 1982

Men and women continue to be employed in very different occupations in the United States. The most striking differences are in clerical and service work where women predominate and in various blue-collar jobs held primarily by men. Even within categories where men and women are equally represented, for example the professions and administration, men typically hold higher status positions relative to women.

SOURCE: U.S. Bureau of the Census, Statistical Abstract of the United States 1984, table 693.

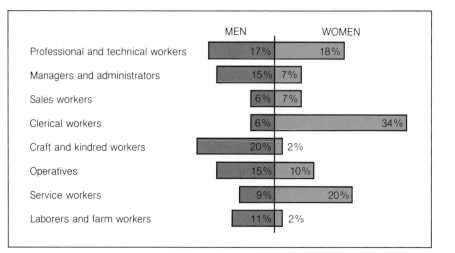

Earnings. In 1981, women who were full-time, full-year workers earned 59 percent as much as men. This percentage has not changed much since 1950. Some of the difference is due to the differences in educational preparation and occupation, but there is still a major gap between women's and men's earnings after these factors are taken into consideration (Duncan et al., 1972).

Political Power. Since the 19th Amendment gave women the vote, in 1919, women have not been legally barred from any level of political participation. Nevertheless, they have less political power than men do. The prejudice against female leaders has declined in recent years, and only a minority of people now say that they would not consider voting for a woman for president (Gallup Report, 1982). However, the higher the level of political power, the less is the participation of women. Whereas women represent 53 percent of the voting population, they comprise only 12 percent of all state legislatures and only 4 percent of the U.S. Congress.

Life Satisfaction: What Are the Costs?

Women are at a substantial disadvantage in most areas of conventional achievement. They pay for their lack of achievement in higher levels of mental illness (see chapter 4) and in a greater incidence of poverty (see chapter 8). Men too face some disadvantages from their traditional sex role. One of them, higher mortality, has already been covered. Additional costs include loss of intimacy and stress.

The deemphasis on nurturance and expressiveness in the male role appears to reduce men's ability to form close relationships with their children and with other kin and friends. Maintaining family relationships is usually viewed as women's work, and when men end up without women to do this work for them (never married, divorced, or widowed), they also frequently end up alone. Surveys demonstrate that children express much more affection toward their mothers than their fathers—a differential that extends to old age, when fathers see less of their children than do mothers

(Hoyt & Babchuck, 1983; Norman & Harris, 1981). It is not all a case of "poor dad," however, since men are socialized to depend less on interpersonal contacts (Chappell & Havens, 1980) and are not as negatively affected as women by the lack of close friends or kin. Nevertheless, it is obvious that in terms of intimacy and affiliation, men are significantly disadvantaged.

In addition, the emphasis of the male sex role on achievement and success can prove stressful. Even men who are successful by any reasonable standard may feel stressed by the constant striving, and those who fail often compensate by excessive agressiveness in other spheres. This constant emphasis on achievement, coupled with a normative demand to be confident and self-assured, may lead to the swaggering version of masculinity we call macho. Anybody who has watched a 15-year-old boy assume the swagger of confidence when it is obvious that he is quaking inside will recognize the strains posed by the masculine role. Assuming that the boy manages to perfect his acting of the role, the world of conventional achievement may be his oyster, but he will have sacrificed something on the way. This sacrifice will be reflected in a higher rate of hypertension, a suicide rate that is four times higher than women's, and an alcoholism rate that is five times higher (U.S. Bureau of the Census 1984).

Summary of Life Chances by Gender

An observer reviewing the evidence on differential life chances by gender comes to the inevitable conclusion that men have the advantages in terms of conventional achievement. Although there are individual exceptions, men as a group have more prestige, more income, and more power than women. They pay a price, however, in terms of forgone intimacy and higher stress and mortality. Many changes have occurred in the last decades, and most of them have reduced the disadvantages of women. In two areas, however—life expectancy and earnings—the gap between men and women is as large as or larger than it was 20 years ago.

The facts that women bear all the children and men are more likely to die as infants are due to physical differences between men and women. Most of the differences in life chances, however, are socially structured. We will now review three explanations for the existence of these differences.

Explanations of Gender Stratification

Traditionally, women have received fewer rewards than men. They have had fewer rights, fewer opportunities, and less status and income. What accounts for this? Biology almost certainly plays a role, but as sociologists we are more concerned with the influence of social factors. What accounts for the fact that most societies have thought it natural that women be accorded an inferior status? Perhaps as importantly, why is this assumption now being challenged?

Keeping Women Down: The Conflict Perspective

The conflict perspective uses a Marxist framework to explain differences between the status of men and women. Women are the proletarians in the gender division of labor, men the bourgeois (Engels, 1884/1972). This perspective suggests that men control the means of production and keep women in a dependent position by force, fraud, and trickery. The initial advantage fell to men because of their greater physical strength and women's frequent pregnancies, but the advantage has been maintained by institutionalized norms and values that keep women in an inferior position.

This Marxist framework has generally formed the ideological base of the 20th century feminist movement. This means not that individual men are supposed to be scheming to subordinate women through force, fraud, and trickery (though some are) but that our social institutions are set up to preserve power differentials between men and women. Thus decent and compassionate men may want to preserve the traditional woman's role because they have been taught to value it rather than because it helps restrict women's opportunities. Nevertheless, the feminist movement is an assault on the image of men as well-intentioned and democratic persons as well as on their privilege, and it is not surprising that many men have been resentful and angry (Skjei & Rabkin, 1981). As a result, conflict theory's view of change as battles between opposing forces is an accurate portrayal of some of the dynamics of sex-role change.

A conflict perspective of women's status can gain much from an analogy to race relations. Women can be viewed as a minority group and men as the majority (dominant) group. The same mechanisms that help maintain boundaries between racial groups also maintain boundaries between the genders: prejudice, discrimination, self-fulfilling prophecies, and segregation. The analogy extends to the use of labels to keep minority groups in their place. Just as black men were called boys to remind them of their inferior status, middle-aged women continue to be called girls. Is this just a friendly term that doesn't have any political meaning, or is it a subtle reminder that women are not full grown-ups with responsibilities equal to men's? Although people who use the term *girls* usually deny any negative intent, the fact that this usage is most common toward women in lower-status occupations (for example, typists and housewives) supports the suggestion that it is a mechanism for reinforcing status.

Prejudice and Discrimination.   One of the most important mechanisms for keeping women in their place is **sexism**—the belief that women and men have biologically different capacities and that these differences form a legitimate basis for the subordination of women. Recent studies show that women are significantly less likely than men to be promoted to positions of authority—that is, they are denied higher earnings and higher power. One study estimates that perhaps half of the exclusion of women from authority is based on simple discrimination (Wolf & Fligstein, 1979) and cannot be explained by women's lack of experience or education.

Conflict theorists explain this as part of the general strategy of stratification. Whenever any group has access to class, status, or power, its first step is to try to exclude others from it. To the extent that it can exclude

Sexism is a belief that women and men have biologically different capacities and that these differences form a legitimate basis for the subordination of women.

others categorically (that is, on the basis of gender or race), the need to compete individually is reduced. Sexism, then, is a means of restricting access to power.

Sexual Harassment. A special form of discrimination that is especially problematic for female workers and students is **sexual harassment**— unwelcome sexual advances, requests for sexual favors, and other unwanted verbal or physical conduct of a sexual nature. Harassment may be just an annoyance. It may, however, turn into real discrimination. The courts use the following guidelines to determine when flirting and sexual innuendo become harassment and constitute unlawful discrimination (Howard, 1980):

1. Submission to such conduct is either explicitly or implicitly a term or condition of an individual's employment or grade evaluation.
2. Submission to or rejection of such conduct is used as the basis for grading or employment decisions such as promotion.
3. Such conduct has the purpose or effect of unreasonably interfering with an individual's work performance or creating an intimidating, hostile, or offensive working environment.

Sexual harassment ranges from subtle hints about the rewards of being more friendly with the boss/teacher to outright rape. In the less severe instances (and sometimes even in the severe instances), the subordinate may be reluctant to make, literally, a federal case of it. New federal laws protecting male as well as female workers, however, have removed the legitimacy of this form of discrimination and may well help reduce it.

The Structural-Functional Perspective

The structural-functional explanation of sex-role differences begins with the unarguable fact that a division of labor is often the most efficient way

Sexual harassment consists of unwelcome sexual advances, requests for sexual favors, and other unwelcome verbal or physical conduct of a sexual nature.

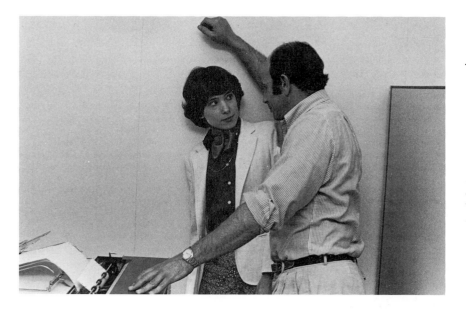

Figure 10.7
In the United States, full-time, full-year women employees earn about 58 cents for every dollar that a man earns. Even after experience, education, and years in the job are taken into consideration, women still earn much less than men. Part of this difference is due to discrimination. An important form of discrimination that strikes particularly hard at women workers is sexual harassment. Demands for sexual favors may be made a condition for promotion or unwelcome attentions may make it difficult for women workers (or students) to do their best.

to get things done. Because of biological differences, chiefly the size and strength of men and childbearing by women, gender has been a major criterion used to allocate the division of labor. He does the heavy work and work that requires being away from home; she does the light work and work that can be done while she is tied down at home, especially childcare. A classic functionalist statement argues:

> Some degree of specialization [on the basis of sex] is to be found in all economic systems, if for no other reason than the biological characteristics of the human species.... Biologically determined relevance is apparent in the usual associa- tion of women with tasks of the household and its environs, which is consistent with the primary female function of child-bearing and child-rearing. [Moore, 1967:293]

In our society, it is no longer generally accepted that women's primary function is childbearing and childrearing. Nevertheless, functional theo- rists still assume that a division of labor between the genders—that is, different roles for men and women—has positive consequences. They suggest that when men and women have different but complementary roles, there will be greater interdependence and solidarity in marriage and society. They believe that stable homes are easier to establish when there is mutual respect for different talents than when the same talents are expected of each (Parsons, 1942).

Functional theory explains why different roles exist for women and men, but it does not explain why women's roles are less highly rewarded than men's. Application of the Davis and Moore argument (see chapter 8) to gender stratification, however, suggests that men are more highly re- warded because their work is more important to the community or be- cause the skills and abilities necessary to do men's work are scarcer than those required to do women's work. These are pretty strong statements. What do you think? Is the work of women less important than the work of men? Is there greater scarcity of the talent it takes to do men's work?

Socialization

Observers from all theoretical perspectives agree that a primary mecha- nism for the perpetuation of different sex roles is socialization. From the time of birth, boys and girls are treated differently. Girls are hugged and caressed more, they are spoken to more (Goldberg & Lewis, 1969), and they are given different toys (Rheingold & Cook, 1975), dressed differently, and disciplined differently. It should hardly be surprising, then, that they turn out differently.

Socialization theorists explain women's lower achievement as a result of socialization practices that channel girls' aspirations differently than boys' and that generally undermine girls' sense of self-esteem and self- worth (Allen, 1980). Few girls or boys now see achievement itself as in- herently unfeminine; they no longer assume that a female engineer must be unattractive and unpopular. And an increasing number of girls are assuming that they can be successful at marriage, motherhood, and ca- reers. Nevertheless, an honest appraisal of the difficulties of managing these multiple roles causes many women with high potential to curtail their ambition, lower their expectations, and adjust their external roles to their home roles (Allen, 1980). For example, a 1976 survey of 50,000 high school students showed that only 17 percent of the girls compared to 31 percent of the boys aspired to be high-status professionals (Garrison, 1979).

Differential socialization continues to orient boys and girls toward different types of occupational participation in society. Current studies show that boys are much more apt than girls to be interested in and comfortable with computers. Analysis of enrollment figures in computer camps shows that, over all, boys outnumber girls by 3 to 1; in the advanced classes, the ratio is 20 to 1 (Hopper & Mandell, 1984). For girls, computers seem to fit into the traditional math-anxiety syndrome, so they shy away from using them. In addition, the computerized games that precede many children's experience with working computers are consistently oriented to boys' rather than girls' interests. In a society in which even typists use computers, this is likely to be a source of continuing disadvantage for women.

Implications

There are physical differences between women and men, and some of these differences do affect social roles. Because size and strength are no longer needed for most jobs in the American economy and because most women have severely curtailed their childbearing, the gross differences between women and men explain fewer and fewer of the differences in their social roles. Although there appears to be some biological predisposition toward nurturance in women and aggression in men, the wide variability in sex roles across cultures suggests that cultural roles explain a large share of the differences between women and men in society.

Although sex roles have a biological base, they are also cultural products closely related to the cultural heritage embodied in family, economic, religious, and political institutions. This means that as our institutions change, so will sex roles. Just as changing technology and changing social structures have given us new ways to adapt to the physical world around us, so they have given us new ways to adapt to the physical world inside us.

Age Differentiation

In all cultures, people have been assigned different roles according to age. At a minimum, all societies distinguish between the young, the adult, and the elderly. Some role differentiation by age is inevitable, especially at the two extremes. Infants and young children cannot perform as well as adults; the elderly experience declining strength and endurance as they age.

But what is young? What is elderly? There are many ways we can measure age. We can measure simple chronological age—whether a person has reached the 20th or 50th birthday. There is a certain merit to this measurement, since people of the same chronological age share many experiences. For example, everybody who is now 65 shares a remembrance of World War II and of a childhood without television. Nevertheless, it is important to recognize that just because people are the same age does not mean that they have reached the same place, have traveled a similar

Figure 10.8
Despite changing sex-role norms and changing roles for adult men and women, children are still socialized into traditional sex roles. Boys learn how to saw, mow lawns, and clean garages while girls learn how to sew, do laundry, and clean house. Although there is little difference in boys' and girls' educational attainments, traditional sex roles still guide boys and girls into very different fields of specialization.

way to get there, or are going in the same direction (Pearlin, 1982). In addition, chronological age may be a misleading indicator of physical condition and emotional and intellectual maturity. Some people are in better physical shape at 50 than others are at 20, and some are more mature at 20 than others will ever be.

Sociologically, we are interested in patterned regularities that occur in connection with age. In short, we want to know what is implied when we tell someone to "act your age." What norms govern age-graded behavior, and what roles are considered appropriate for particular age groups? Finally, we want to consider whether the rights and privileges associated with age roles represent a pattern of structured inequality. Is there a consistent pattern of unequal reward by age that is justified by age norms, and if so, to what extent is this inequality socially structured rather than biologically determined?

Age Roles in the United States

All of the other bases of differentiation that we have looked at (class, race, ethnicity, sex) tend to be mutually exclusive. That is, to be white means you will never be black; to be female means you will never be male; and to be middle class probably means that you will always be middle class. Age, however, presents a very different picture. We move through age roles sequentially, casting off one in favor of the next. We move from schooling, to marriage and childbearing, to career achievement, and to retirement. All these steps are age-graded; they are appropriate for some ages and not others. People who are not married by 25 or 30, who do not have a settled career by 40, or who have not retired by 65 are outside the usual expectations of society.

The **life course** is the structure of expectations and relationships through which one passes sequentially.

A key concept in examining age roles is that of the **life course**—the structure of expectations and relationships through which one passes sequentially (Clausen, 1972). The life-course perspective explicitly recognizes that we cannot understand where someone is now unless we understand the process by which the person got there. For example, the experience of the Great Depression has been shown to be very different for those who were young children in 1930 than for those who were older (Elder, 1974). For the youngest children, poverty and uncertainty were the conditions they were born into, and the post–World War II prosperity seemed to them to represent progress and security. Those who were older at the time of the Depression, however, saw a cyclical pattern in which prosperity was erased and then returned. Even 40 and 50 years later, these people are still saving their old socks in case hard times return. Thus these groups will experience old age differently because of the different paths they took to get there.

The following sections will briefly review general norms about age roles in the United States and their consequences for social inequality. The last part of the chapter will turn to the larger issue of how age interacts with gender, race, and social class.

The Role of Children

Historian Philippe Aries (1962) has argued that childhood was not a recognized social role until the 17th century; before then, children were regarded as miniature adults. From an early age, they were expected to be productive. Because of their lower capacities, however, they were generally accorded low status. For example, children were allowed to eat only after the adults had finished.

This attitude has changed substantially. Childhood is now seen as a special status. The helplessness of children is now seen not as a defect that lowers their ability to command respect but as a special vulnerability that demands adult protection and care. Children have a central importance in American families, and contemporary norms suggest that parents should sacrifice for their children rather than vice versa. In contemporary society, almost all obligations run from the parents to the children; few children do any work, and children have few responsibilities (Boocock, 1975). The obligations of the contemporary child are to accomplish certain developmental tasks, such as learning independence and self-control.

Rites of passage are formal rituals that mark the end of one status and the beginning of another.

Adolescence/Young Adulthood

Adolescence is a difficult period between childhood dependence and adult independence. In some societies, **rites of passage**—formal rituals that mark the end of one status and the beginning of another—indicate

Figure 10.9
Childhood is a special status in the United States, one with few obligations. Few children do any real work and most have only symbolic chores until they reach their teens. From infancy on, the major work of American children is to develop their emotional and intellectual capacities, to learn, and to explore. This attitude toward children is a luxury affordable only by a wealthy society that can afford to dispense with the labor of children. In less wealthy societies, children are expected to work from a very early age.

the end of childhood and the beginning of adulthood. They generally occur in societies with simple divisions of labor, where young people can be expected to fill adult roles relatively early in their lives. In our own society, the end of childhood is not clearly marked and depends a great deal on social class. Whereas some people, such as the working-class people described in chapter 8, take on full adult roles at 18, others may not assume such roles until they finish a protracted period of education at 22 or 25 or even 30.

Adolescence is often a period of irresponsibility. Because society has little need for youth, it contributes to a concern among young people for trivialities—concern over personal appearance and the latest music. Yet, because adolescence is a temporary state, the adolescent is under persistent pressure. Questions such as "What are you going to do when you finish school?" "Where are you going to college?" and "How serious are you about that girl?" have an urgent reality that creates strain amid the trivia of youth.

What are the rights and obligations of adolescence? Basically, there appear to be four (Campbell, 1969):

1. Adolescents are supposed to become independent of their parents. The change from family to peer group as a source of esteem is the first step in this process.

Figure 10.10

Adolescence is an awkward age in industrialized societies. The children in this picture are too young to work, to vote, or to go to R-rated movies. Yet they are still too old to fit comfortably into the role of dependent child. As a result, adolescence is often a time of conflict, one that both young people and their parents are glad to put behind them.

2. They are supposed to experiment with new roles and behaviors, to test the limits of their values and the worth of social roles. Throughout childhood they have taken their parents' word for what is valuable and normative. During adolescence they test these values and either make them their own or discard them.

3. They are supposed to acquire adult skills. These include social skills (how to work in committees and how to meet and impress new people, for example) and technical skills (how to make change, type and differentiate equations, for example).

4. Last, but not least, they are supposed to have fun. If they do not (if they stay home on Friday nights, if they are always serious and never silly), they will be violating a norm and will surely be sanctioned by their peers. Their parents will begin to worry about them, and they may find themselves seeing a psychologist.

Adolescence is one of the most stressful stages in the life course. Try taking an informal survey of adults, and you will find that most are emphatic about not wanting to be a teenager again. In fact, data from a national study show that twice as many adults picked their teens as the worst part of their lives as picked it as the best part of their lives (Harris et al., 1975). Thus, in spite of the fact that society does not appear to expect much of adolescents, they are under a great deal of role stress.

Adulthood

As defined in our society, adulthood begins somewhere between 18 and 25 and merges into old age somewhere after 65. Being an adult means settling down, raising a family, and achieving something in the world of work. The norms of our society suggest that it is appropriate that we all marry, somewhere between 20 and 25 for women and between 22 and 25 for men. Furthermore, we are all expected to have children—about two, although three is acceptable (Blake, 1979). One child is considered unsuitable, and to be childless implies that you are selfish. After the children reach their early 20s, it is expected that they will leave home and that their parents will live alone with each other. They will have grandchildren, of course, but will not be expected to provide much babysitting or economic help to their children. Aside from these very general norms about work, marriage, and parenthood, the norms that guide adult behavior are those of gender and class.

The busiest part of most adults' lives is between the ages of 20 and 45. There are children in the home and a marriage and career to be established. This period of life is frequently marked by role strain and role conflict—simply because there is so much going on at one time. The strain gradually eases, however, and studies show that both men and women tend to greet the empty nest with relief rather than regret (Glenn, 1975).

The norms of our society suggest that people should have achieved most of their life goals by the time they reach middle age. Thus middle age is a period of assessment (Neugarten, 1968). It is a time for evaluating one's own situation—family, career, standard of living, physical appear-

Figure 10.11
The parenting years are often the busiest years in an individual's lifetime. Demands of children compete with those of spouse, job, community, and household. As a result, it is often a time of role conflict and role strain for parents. Many parents experience relief when these demands begin to drop off after middle age and they have launched their children.

The **mid-life crisis** is an awareness that goals not yet reached are probably forever beyond one's reach.

ance—relative to the norms of society. For some people this evaluation results in what is called the **mid-life crisis**—an awareness that goals not yet reached are probably forever beyond their reach. More positively, people recognize that youthful norms are no longer as applicable as they used to be, and they reorganize life's priorities (Tamir, 1982). Good looks and a slim body are no longer such important priorities, and health and satisfaction become more important values.

Adults over 65

Older adults, those over 65, are extremely diverse, defying easy categorization. For the most part they are retired, although 20 percent of the men and 10 percent of the women are in the labor force. Social norms are more explicit about what they are not supposed to do than about what they are supposed to do. This has led some commentators to suggest that being elderly is a roleless role—an absence of both rights and duties. The socially appropriate role for the elderly is to be nonproductive, nonaggressive, and noncompetitive, but also independent and out of their children's hair— and homes, except when invited.

Figure 10.12
Old age has generally received a bad press in the United States. We hear of poverty, illness, and dependency. The most striking trend, however, is for an improvement in the status of the elderly. Their incomes are higher and their health is better than ever before. Most Americans look forward to retirement and an increasing proportion retire before they must. Declining vigor and dependency accompany aging, but many people find 10 or 15 enjoyable years after retirement in which they can, like this older couple, still get a kick out of life.

Many studies have demonstrated that the general public holds negative stereotypes about the aged. These stereotypes are generally shared by the elderly themselves (see Table 10.4). In fact, although the general public is willing to concede that the elderly, though not very bright or adaptable, are at least friendly and wise, the elderly generally describe other old people as not friendly or wise or adaptable or bright. There is a sharp difference, however, when the elderly person is asked for a self-description. Many devalued groups (women and minorities, for example) manage this same trick: to accept society's generally poor opinion of their group while holding themselves apart as an exception. In Marxist terminology, they are guilty of false consciousness.

Many observers suggest that the comparative rolelessness of the elderly reduces life satisfaction. Nevertheless, one of the most consistent findings in research on the aging is that retirement is generally a positive stage in the life course (Medley, 1976). Although some women and men may require a little adjustment (as one women said, "I'm getting twice as much husband for half as much money!"), almost all believe that their new leisure is legitimate (that is, normatively approved) and do not feel badly about not having more demanding social roles. As long as they stay healthy, older adults report high levels of life satisfaction. The best predictors of satisfaction among the elderly are the same factors that predict satisfaction at every other stage of the life course: good health, adequate income, and a satisfying family life (Larson, 1978; Medley, 1976).

Inequalities by Age

Society is controlled mainly by adults between the ages of 30 and 65. These adults control jobs, industry, education, and wealth. In the following sections, we will examine the extent to which youths and the elderly can be considered structurally disadvantaged relative to this middle-aged group.

Table 10.3 Views of the Elderly

A national study of how the public views persons over the age of 65 shows a number of stereotypes that are widely endorsed. Although the elderly share these views about others over the age of 65, elderly individuals are not as likely to see themselves in these ways.

	PERCENT SAYING THAT MOST PEOPLE 65 + ARE:		PERCENT OF THOSE 65 + SAYING *THEY* ARE:
	Public, Aged		
	18–24	65 +	
Very friendly and warm	82%	25%	72%
Very wise from experience	66	56	69
Very bright and alert	29	33	68
Very open-minded and adaptable	19	34	63
Very good at getting things done	35	38	55
Very physically active	41	43	48

SOURCE: Louis Harris and Associates, 1975. The Myth and Reality of Aging in America. Washington, D.C.: The National Council on Aging, p. 48 and p. 53.

Unequal Rights for Youths

In law, people under 18 are called infants (Sloan, 1981). They are not responsible for their contracts (thus they usually are not allowed to make any), and they are considered less responsible than adults for their bad deeds. Just as legal statutes once declared women and minority members incapable of self-government, the law still declares the young to be incapable. As you may be painfully aware from personal experience, young people have few legal rights. Their rights to drink, drive, work, own property, and marry are abridged. They have to pay adult prices, but cannot see adult movies. In church, school, and industry they find that there are age barriers they must pass before they are allowed full participation. Unlike the case of women and minorities, there is no movement to reduce inequality for teenagers. The voting age was reduced from 21 to 18 in 1970, but the drinking age appears to be on its way up again. Although this move springs from the praiseworthy objective of reducing deaths from drinking and driving, it is nevertheless a reminder that may people believe that the young cannot make responsible decisions themselves and need to be protected.

The unemployment rate for teenagers 16 to 19 is perennially four times higher than it is for the entire labor force; for black teenagers it is eight times higher. Youths are legally barred from some occupations by age and from others by age-related entrance requirements. Some of these requirements—for example, that of a high school diploma—can be regarded as institutionalized ageism, an artificial device that keeps young people out of the labor market.

Are the Elderly Rewarded Unequally?

It is conventional wisdom that modernization has led to a decline in the status and power of the elderly. This decline probably has been exaggerated. Recent examinations of cross-cultural data suggest that the elderly seldom have as much status as younger adults (Stearn, 1976) and that, in many societies, they have much lower status than they do in our own. Nevertheless, there is evidence that the status of the elderly has declined in Western society with modernization (Palmore, 1983). The leaders of many churches, for example, are called elders because historically they were the older members of the community. Studies of 18th century churches show that church seats were assigned in age-graded fashion, with the best seats in the house always going to the oldest. A century later, the seats were being sold to the highest bidder, and class replaced age as the means of deciding status in church (Fischer, 1979).

Although they may have less power than they used to, the elderly in our own society do not seem to be particularly disadvantaged—as long as they keep their health. The following sections review some of the basic findings about the elderly in the United States.

Income.   There is a great deal of emphasis in the media about the poverty of the aged. In fact, however, the proportion of the aged that is below the poverty level is no greater than the proportion of the entire population that is poor (U.S. Bureau of the Census, 1984:747). Furthermore, the elderly are overrepresented among the top wealth holders (U.S. Bureau of the Census, 1984:479). And the elderly may be the proportion of the population that is least likely to be living on fixed incomes; their social security checks are raised each year according to the cost-of-living index. Thus, in 1980, when many employees in public and private industry averaged 5 percent raises, social security checks were increased by 13 percent. Poverty among the aged is usually a continuation of poverty or near-poverty in middle age rather than a special condition of being old. However, the aged poor have no bootstraps to pull themselves up with—poverty past 65 means permanent poverty.

Discrimination. Mandatory retirement regulations have forced some people out of the productive labor force regardless of their physical ability, economic need, or desire to work. This problem is decreasing, however. In the first place, the age for mandatory retirement has been increased from 65 to 70 in many instances; more importantly, a large proportion of people retire before they are legally required to. This varies by income and by pension-related security, but for a majority of workers retirement is something to look forward to, not a restriciton of their freedom (Barfield & Morgan, 1979).

A far more important problem than mandatory retirement is age discrimination that begins during middle age, when women and men over 45 are considered too old to learn new skills or take new jobs. This discrimination goes hand in hand with the stereotypes reported earlier; many people, including the elderly, are prejudiced against older people. Only a minority believe that the elderly are bright and alert, adaptable, or good at getting things done. This **ageism** is particularly hard on people who need a new job after 45—especially women returning to work and men and women who have been laid off. Because of this, affirmative-action legislation against age discrimination uses age 45 as the definition of when age discrimination begins.

Political Power. Age and even infirmity in no way abridge one's legal rights. The elderly are more apt to vote than other age groups (see chapter 15) and, on issues where they form a voting bloc, most recently on threatened social security cutbacks, they have a great deal of political power. The fact that social security has gone up so much more than the average wage earner's income is clear evidence of the elderly's political power.

A Life Course Perspective on Today's Elderly. In speaking about the elderly, or any age group, it is important to distinguish between the consequences of age itself and the consequences of the age group's place in history. Today's elderly are different from the rest of the population not only because they are over 65 but also because they were born before the Great Depression. They grew up in a world vastly different from the one they currently live in. Many grew up on a different continent in a different culture: 54 percent of the white elderly in New York City are foreign-born (Cantor, 1976). They grew up in an era when an 8th grade education was considered sufficient for most people. Furthermore, they represent a group

Figure 10.13
Far from being a powerless group, older Americans wield an increasing amount of power. They are a growing proportion of the population—and they are organized to use that advantage. Maggie Kuhn, President of the Gray Panthers, is a leader of the senior movement. Among their goals are a protection of social security and other pension benefits. Because older people are the segment of the population most apt to vote, social security has become an almost untouchable political issue. Nobody wants to buck the older vote.

Ageism is the belief that chronological age determines the presence or absence of socially relevant criteria and that age therefore provides a legitimate reason for unequal treatment.

that experienced the lowest levels of childbearing in U.S. history (the group that passed their peak childbearing years during the Great Depression). As a result, fully 25 percent of today's elderly in the United States have no children to rely on for support and assistance. They are further disadvantaged in that they are a transition group between a pre-1935 dependence on self-support to a dependence on social security and pension plans. Compared to the group that will be 65 in 20 years, today's elderly are much less likely to be getting maximum social security benefits or dependable pensions.

To the extent that the problems of the elderly are a problem of their place in history rather than age itself, we can expect the situation to improve. The elderly in 2000 will be much less disadvantaged by history. They will have better retirement benefits, higher educations, and larger families. All this should improve the ability of the elderly to enjoy a full life.

Intergenerational Bonds

A crucial aspect of age differentiation is the nature of familial ties that bind one generation to the next through feelings of affection and obligation. Some people have worried that these ties might be weakened by geographical mobility and by the growing tendency to depend on the state rather than the family for help. In this respect, as in many others, the rumor of the death of the family has been much exaggerated. The majority of older people with children see at least one child regularly: Eight out of ten see a child once a week and two thirds see a child as often as every one or two days (Riley & Foner, 1968). Most children see their grandparents many times a year.

Similarly, the relationship between teens and their parents is not as bad as is often suggested. Although many families go through a prolonged period of conflict, with both parents and children being relieved when they get to live apart (Hopkins, 1983), they maintain a strong bond and many common values. As Mark Twain said, "When I was a boy of 14, my father was so ignorant I could hardly stand to have the old man around. But when I got to be 21, I was astonished at how much the old man had learned in seven years."

Explanations of Age Stratification

In everyday usage, most people rely on a physiological explanation of age stratification. The young and the old have less status because they are less competent and less productive. To some extent this explanation is correct. It does not, however, explain the cross-cultural or historical variations in the status of the aged. In all societies, the aged lose some of their productive skills when their physical powers decline, but they often retain important and status-giving roles as supervisors and traditional sources of wisdom. A full explanation of age stratification has to show why these variations exist as well as why the disadvantages associated with youth and old age are so loosely correlated with productive ability.

Figure 10.14
Despite high rates of geographic mobility, many families still stay closely in touch. As a result, there are close ties across generations. Like this great-grandfather, most older people see their children and grandchildren frequently. Such ties are one reason inequalities by age do not get out of hand. Older citizens are less likely to vote in support of schools and younger citizens are less likely to vote in support of social security, but close and intimate ties across generations gives both groups a vested interest in the welfare of the other.

The status of the aged is high when they are able to continue to perform valued and useful functions; this ability is directly contingent on both the capacities of the elderly and the values of society. The conflict and functionalist perspectives, as well as modernization theory, provide insightful explanations as to why age stratification exists and varies across societies.

Structural-Functionalist Perspective

The structural-functionalist perspective focuses on the ways in which age stratification helps fulfill societal functions. Briefly, the lower status of youth helps protect the family from strife in much the same way and for the same reasons as does the lower status of the wife. That is, the allocation of power on the basis of age rather than on the basis of competition reduces conflict (Parsons, 1942). As we saw when we considered the rights of children, not all conflict has been eliminated. The decision in favor of parents, however, is functional for society: the longer parents are responsible for their own offspring, the less burden is placed on government and other societal agencies. Furthermore, the relief from the obligation of supporting themselves and fulfilling other adult roles gives young people time to learn the complex skills necessary for operating in society. From the functionalist perspective, then, the lower status of young people ultimately benefits the individual as well as society.

At the other end of the age scale, the functionalist perspective becomes what the gerontology literature calls **disengagement theory**. The central argument of this perspective is that the aged voluntarily disengage themselves from active social participation, gradually dropping roles in production, family, church, and neighborhood even before actual disability connected with age requires it. This disengagement is functional for society because it makes possible an orderly transition from one generation to the next, avoiding the dislocation caused by people dropping dead in their traces or dragging down the entire organization by decreased performance. It is functional for the individual because it reduces the shame of declining ability and provides a rest for the weary. Disengagement theory is a perfect example of why functional theory is sometimes called consensus theory: The lack of participation of the aged is agreed upon by both the aged and others and is to the benefit of all (Hendricks & Hendricks, 1981).

Disengagement theory is the functionalist theory of aging that argues that the elderly voluntarily disengage themselves from active social participation.

Conflict Perspective

The conflict view of age stratification produces a picture of disengagement that is far less benign—one that is instead simple rejection and discrimination springing from competition over scarce resources. These resources are primarily jobs but also include power within the family. Conflict theorists suggest that barring youth and older people from the labor market is a means of categorically barring some groups from competition and improving the prospects of workers between 20 and 65.

There is empirical evidence to support this view. Early in American history, few people retired. Not only could they not afford to, but their labor was still needed. As immigration provided cheap and plentiful labor, however, the need for the elderly worker decreased. In addition, as unions established seniority as a criterion for higher wages, older workers became more expensive than younger ones. In response to these trends, management instituted compulsory retirement to get rid of older workers. The mandatory retirement rules occurred long before social security, in an era when few employees had regular pension plans. Thus compulsory retirement usually meant poverty for the older worker and was very much against the person's will (Atchley, 1982).

It was not until 1965 that social structures such as social security and private pensions began to make retirement a desirable personal alternative. Between 1967 and 1980, the proportion of the elderly who were poor declined dramatically, from 60 percent to 16 percent. At the present time, retirement suits both the aging worker and the economic system. As the growing elderly population becomes an increasing burden on a shrinking working-age population, however, there may once again be a conflict between generations over economic interests (an idea discussed more fully in the Issues in Social Policy section at the end of this chapter).

Modernization Theory

Modernization theory argues that modernization reduces the power of the elderly by reducing the value of their traditional resources: land, labor, and experience.

The elderly have low status in modern societies because the traditional bases of their power have been eroded, according to **modernization theory**. This is due to three simultaneous events: the decline in importance of land (disproportionately owned by the elderly) as a means of production, the increasing productivity of society, and a more rapid rate of social change (Cowgill, 1974).

Decline in Importance of Land.   When land is the most vital means of production, then those who own it have high status and power. In many traditional societies, land ownership is passed from father to son. This gives fathers a great deal of power even if they live to an age when they are physically much less able than their sons. This explanation, of course, applies only in a society where wealth resides in transferable property, either land or animals. In a hunting-and-gathering society—for example, Plains Indians of the 19th century—where there is little accumulated wealth, status comes from physical prowess, and consequently the elderly have much lower status.

Level of Productivity.   In societies with low levels of productivity, it is not feasible to exclude either the young or the elderly from productive activity. Everyone's labor is needed. In industrial societies, however, productivity is so high that we no longer need everybody's labor (Cohn, 1982). Mechanization and automation mean that many people can be freed from direct production. They can study, they can do research, they can write great novels, or they can do nothing at all. In short, a productive society can afford the luxury of omitting large groups of people from the labor force. A less positive way of putting the same thing is that the labor of youth and the elderly becomes expendable; society doesn't need it any more.

Speed of Change.   Technological knowledge has grown at an ever-accelerating pace. Since most of us learn the bulk of our technological skills when we are young, this rapid change produces an increasing disadvantage for older workers (Cohn, 1982). Their technical skills become outdated. In times of less rapid change, their greater steadiness and reliability was a virtue; now their mental skills are growing old faster than their physical skills. Thus rapid social change works to the disadvantage of the elderly.

Crosscutting Statuses—Age, Sex, Race, and Class

We began the section on stratification by examining inequalities in life chances. So far we have dealt with unequal life chances by social class, race and ethnicity, gender, and age. On each of these dimensions we have been able to demonstrate that there is a hierarchy of access to the good things in life and that some groups are substantially disadvantaged.

When a person has a lower status on more than one of these dimensions, we speak of **double or triple jeopardy.** This means simply that disadvantage snowballs. Thus black teenagers are twice as likely as white teenagers to be unemployed; old women are more likely than old men to be poor. People who are old and black and female are in even worse shape.

Being over 65 is a problem largely for the working or lower class. The greater income and education of the middle class give its members better access to services, better mobility, and more interest in and involvement with the community. Middle-class people are unlikely even to consider themselves old until age 75 and do not believe that the plight of the nation's elderly is relevant to them. The problem of today's elderly is to a large extent a problem of social class, only magnified.

It is also, to a significant extent, a problem of gender stratification. Many of the women who are old today earned no pensions themselves, and until recently many pension plans died with the earner. Thus the elderly widow must frequently rely solely on her survivor's benefit from social security; 40 percent of these older widows currently receive the minimum monthly payment: $112. The normative system that made these women financially dependent during their robust years has doubled their dependence during their old age. Instead of being dependent on their husbands, however, they are now dependent on the state.

Because women live longer than men, they are an increasingly larger proportion of the population as the population ages. Thus, in 1960, there were 83 men for every 100 women over age 65; by 1981, there were only 66 men. For people 85 and older, there are twice as many women as men. The change in the gender composition of the elderly has consequences for social roles. It means that heterosexual contacts, whether through marriage or just in bridge groups, are less important than before for structuring social life. It also means that fewer of the elderly are married and more of them live alone (Soldo, 1981). The feminization of old age contributes to the poverty of old age. Female-headed households are poorer than male-headed households at all ages, and the elderly are no exception. Thus the increasing proportion of the elderly that is female has the effect of increasing the poverty of the aged population.

Double or triple jeopardy means having low status on two or three different dimensions of stratification.

Figure 10.15
Stratification occurs when categories of people systematically and normatively receive fewer benefits than other categories. When an individual belongs to 2 or 3 devalued categories simultaneously, real poverty and disadvantage may result. In the U. S., being old is largely a problem for those who belonged to devalued categories as younger people—women, minorities, and the lower class.

ISSUES IN SOCIAL POLICY

Social Security—Will You Get Yours?

The social security system is our nation's most comprehensive program for dealing with the elderly. It is a system that is much misunderstood. It is only in part the insurance program it is advertised to be. One pays into it all one's working days and draws out from it after retirement on the basis of years and level of contribution. From the beginning, however, the system has been paying beneficiaries out of current earnings. In practice, it is a systematic program of intergenerational transfers in which the currently productive generation decides on the level at which it is willing to be taxed in order to provide a particular standard of living for the elderly.

In all cultures, adults of working age produce goods that are used for the benefit of themselves and their dependents. In traditional societies, the family is the distribution network, with the adults being responsible for their own children and their own parents. In modern industrial societies, this burden has been shifted in part to the state. The state collects taxes from the working population and redistributes them to dependents, thus depersonalizing the exchange process. Social security does what the family was expected to do in previous times. In some ways, it does it better. It regularly provides a guar-

anteed sum of money; it entails no feeling of obligation on the part of the aged and no feeling of direct resentment on the part of the working generation. That is, the workers may grumble about taxation and government inefficiency, but they don't resent their own parents. The changing age composition of the population, however, raises serious questions about whether the program can continue.

THE AGE STRUCTURE

The United States has historically been a society with a youthful population. Since the time of the first census, however, the average age of Americans has been increasing; the proportion over 65 has increased from 4 percent to 11 percent in the last 80 years. This means a tripling in the proportion of the population that must be supported by social security—and ultimately by those who are still working.

Ironically, the increased proportion of the elderly in our society is due not to decreased mortality but to decreased fertility. In a high-fertility population, the proportion of elderly is always small. If each couple has six

Figure 10.16 A Comparison of the Age Structure in 1980 and 2030

In the next 50 years, the percentage of the population over 65 is expected to nearly double, from 11 percent in 1980 to 18 percent in 2030. Unless fertility increases sharply in the future, there will be as many old people as there are children.

SOURCE: Bouvier, Leon. 1980. "America's Baby Boom Generation: The Fateful Bulge." Population Bulletin vol. 35, April, figure 4, page 19.

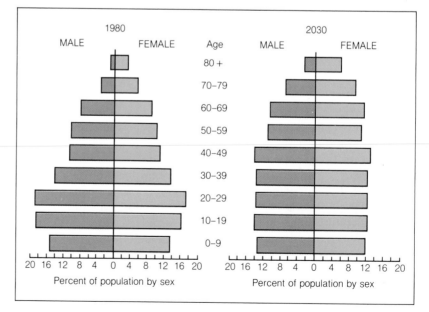

children and their children have six children, and so on, then there are many more young than old people. When fertility is relatively low, however, and each couple has only two or three children, then the elderly generation is about the same size as the children's and grandchildren's generation. The result is that an increasing proportion of the population is elderly and the ratio of the elderly to the working-age population is growing.

In the United States, the problem will be most severe around 2030. At this time, the huge baby-boom generation will be over 65 and the proportion 65 and older will climax at 18 percent of the total population (see Figure 10.16). If you were born between 1960 and 1965, you will be in that group (the biggest baby-boom cohort was born in 1962). There will be a lot of people your age wanting to retire and live off the taxes on the younger workers, but because of the low birthrates in the 1970s and 1980s, there won't be very many of these younger workers to support you (see Figure 10.17). There will be more people 65 to 75 than people 55 to 65. One solution, of course, is for all of you to have many children so that there will be many people to support you in your old age. (As you can see, our system isn't really much different from that of nonindustrialized countries, where having many children is the primary means by which couples protect themselves from want in old age.) Of course, this solution is not a very good long-term answer, as it would undoubtedly cause more problems than it would solve.

IMPLICATIONS FOR THE FUTURE

Because of changes in our age structure, some analysts believe that social security will have to be changed: "By 2020 there will simply be too many old and too few young to maintain the social structure, including retirement, as we know it in the 1980's" (Woodruff, 1983:141). But what are the alternatives?

In our society, there are a limited number of positions in the productive labor force. Largely by accident, we have increased the proportion of positions held by women and decreased the proportion held by the old. In this sense, working-age women have displaced older men. Thus the dependence burden has shifted from gender- to age-related criteria. This trade-off is important to recognize. Reduced dependence of the over-65 population cannot be achieved simply by removing institutional barriers to work or providing work incentives; there must also be jobs. If the number of jobs cannot be expanded, then a decision to encourage the old to work requires discouraging some other class of workers.

As a social policy decision, is it better to increase the number of households with at least one worker or to encourage two-earner families at mid-life and have intergenerational transfer payments? The clear implication of both policy alternatives is that families at mid-life will have to pay, one way or another, for the support of the elderly.

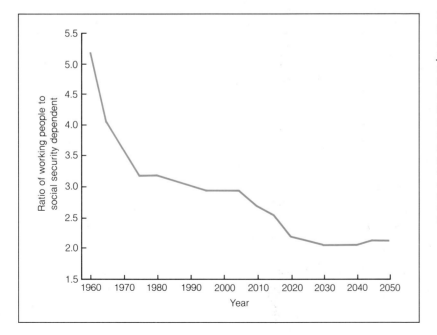

Figure 10.17 Ratio of Employees per Social Security Dependent, 1960–2050
In 1960, there were five people working for every person over 65 who was drawing a social security check. By the year 2030, there will be only two earners for every person over 65. If social security benefits are to remain at current levels, this suggests that payroll taxes will have to climb sharply. Will the workers be willing to pay?
SOURCE: U.S. House of Representatives, Select Committee on Population, Domestic Consequences of United States Population Change, 95th Cong., 2d sess., 1978, figure 13, p. 73. Cited in Bouvier, 1980, Population Reference Bureau.

SUMMARY

1. Although there is a universal biological basis for sex roles, there is a great deal of variability in the roles and personalities assigned to men and women across societies. Universally, however, women have been given less power than men.

2. Sex roles have changed substantially in the United States in the last 20 years. Although these changes have increased the options available for both sexes, the chief result has been to give women some of the opportunities previously open only to men.

3. In terms of conventional achievement, men have had the advantage over women. This gap is decreasing in education, in politics, and in employment, but remains unchanged in terms of earnings. There are costs, however; men have lower life expectancies, higher stress, and fewer affectional ties.

4. The feminist movement tends to use conflict theory to explain current inequalities by gender. It suggests that the same mechanisms used to keep other minority groups in their place (prejudice, discrimination, segregation, and self-fulfilling prophecies) are used to subordinate women.

5. Functional theory suggests that inequalities by gender are a tradition left over from the time when biological differences dictated a division of labor between women and men. It does not explain why women's labor was less highly valued.

6. Age roles are less highly structured than many others. Although there are accepted criteria for "acting your age," social class, sex, and race may have more effect on roles.

7. Childhood, adolescence, and old age are almost roleless roles in our society. We expect little from people in these age groups and specify few obligations for them. The ages from 20 to 65, however, are crowded with obligations, and role strain may result.

8. The young suffer many structured inequalities. They are legally barred from many rewarding activities but also are protected from many responsibilities.

9. The plight of the elderly is largely a problem of gender and class stratification. People over 65 are not disproportionately poor or powerless. Until they lose their health, the elderly are not a significantly disadvantaged group.

10. Modernization theory, functionalism, and conflict theory provide different perspectives on why the young and the elderly tend to have lower status in our society.

11. Because of changes in fertility, the burden of supporting a growing retired population will fall on a declining working-age population. Thus the social security system poses a potential problem of intergenerational conflict.

SUGGESTED READINGS

Atchley, Robert C. (1980). *The Social Forces in Later Life* (3rd ed.). Belmont, Calif.: Wadsworth. An overview of the field of social gerontology examining the major social forces that shape later life.

Gerzon, Mark. (1982). A Choice of Heroes: The Changing Faces of American Manhood. Boston: Houghton Mifflin. An examination of the changing sex roles for men and women in our society, emphasizing how current role expectations that are at odds with past ones contribute to individual stress.

Kanter, Rosabeth Moss. (1977). Men and Women of the Corporation. New York: Basic Books. An important work exploring the differences in opportunities for achievement, career patterns, and interaction between women and men working for corporations.

Karp, David A., & York, William C. (1982). Experiencing the Life Cycle: A Social Psychology of Aging. Springfield, Ill.: Charles C. Thomas. An overview of human development during the life course that dwells on adolescence as well as old age, combining social psychology theory with material from popular culture. An enjoyable and thorough introduction to the life course.

Maccoby, Eleanor Emmons, & Jacklin, Carol Nagy. (1974). The Psychology of Sex Differences. Stanford, Calif.: Stanford University Press. An examination of the biological, cultural, and psychological differences between the genders.

Stockard, Jean, & Johnson, Miriam M. (1980). Sex Roles: Sex Inequality and Sex Role Development. Englewood Cliffs, N.J.: Prentice-Hall. An analysis of sex-role socialization and sex-role inequality.

Weitzman, Lenore. (1979). Sex Role Socialization. Palo Alto, Calif. Mayfield. A concise analysis of sex roles and how they are learned in childhood as well as the limitations in educational and occupational achievement that result from women's early socialization.

UNIT FOUR

Social
Institutions

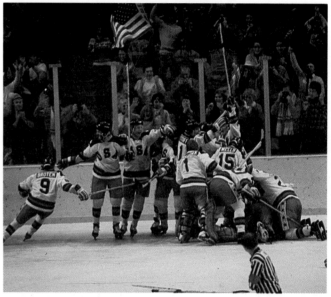

CHAPTER 11

THE FAMILY

292

PROLOGUE

Have You Ever . . . stopped to consider how many of the people in your family you would choose as friends? If you are like the average person, there are some people in your family whom you really like, people you would seek out whether you were obliged to or not. You might, however, be able to identify one or two family members whom you really don't like very well, people you would not choose as your friends. Probably ties of family loyalty bind you to these people so that you would come to their aid if they needed you, you would feel badly if they had troubles, or you would expect them to help you if you had problems. But you wouldn't shed any tears if you did not see them for the next 10 years.

The family is a remarkable arrangement for binding people together with ties of obligation. Your obligations to your parents, brothers, sisters, and children will bind you to them long after you have ceased to live together in the same household—and, to a significant extent, regardless of the affection between you. You may be able to divorce a spouse or end a friendship, but there is no such thing as an ex-child or an ex-brother. These relatives are with you forever.

If you have been out of high school even 3 or 4 years, you probably have found already that you no longer know many of the same people you did when you were 16. At 30 or 40 or 60, probably the only people you will know who can remember your first car, your first wedding, or your first child will be your family. Everybody else will have moved on. Thus your family is not only a safety net of obligations, it is a link to both your past and, most likely, your future. It is a major source of continuity over a lifetime, not only for society but also for the individual.

There have been many changes in American family life in recent decades. Birthrates have declined sharply, but adolescent pregnancy rates have doubled. Divorce rates have reached record levels, the proportion of single-parent families has increased, and, for the first time, women with small children have entered the labor force in large numbers. In addition to these statistical trends, major shifts in attitudes and values have occurred. Sexual activity outside marriage has become increasingly acceptable; unmarried couples living together and homosexuals have become more open. Related to many of these changes are the dramatic changes in the roles of women in our society.

These changes in family life have been felt, either directly or indirectly, by all of us. Is the family a dying institution, or is it simply a changing one? In this chapter, we will examine the question from the perspective of sociology. What has caused the changes? What do they mean for the future? We begin with a broad description of the family as a basic social institution.

Marriage, Family, and Kinship: Basic Institutions of Society

In order to place the changes in the American family into perspective, it is useful to look at the variety of family forms across the world. What is it that is really essential about the family, and what kinds of structures are possible to meet these needs? How is the structure of the family affected by surrounding institutions?

The Necessity of the Family—The Universals

In every culture, the family has been assigned major responsibilities, typically including (Murdock, 1949; Pitts, 1964):

to determine responsibility of off-spring.

1. Replacement through reproduction.
2. Regulation of sexual behavior.
3. Economic responsibilities for dependents—children, the elderly, the ill, and the handicapped.
4. Socialization of the young.
5. Ascription of status.
6. Provision of intimacy, belongingness, and emotional support.

Because these activities are important for individual development and the continuity of society, every society provides some institutional pattern for meeting them. No society leaves them to individual initiative. Although it is possible to imagine a society in which these responsibilities are handled by religious or educational institutions, most societies have found it convenient to assign them to the family.

The importance of these tasks varies across societies. Status ascription is an important responsibility in societies where social position is largely inherited; regulation of sexual behavior is important in cultures without contraception. In our own society, we have seen the priorities assigned to these family responsibilities change substantially over time. In colonial America, the family's primary responsibilities were care of dependent children and replacement through reproduction; the provision of emotional support was a secondary consideration. More recently, however, some of the responsibility for socializing the young has been transferred to schools and daycare centers; financial responsibility for the dependent

A **family** is a relatively permanent group of persons linked together in social roles by ties of blood, marriage, or adoption who live together and cooperate economically and in the rearing of children.

A **kin group** is a status network composed of people related by common ancestry.

Marriage is a socially recognized and institutionalized mating arrangement between males and females.

elderly has been shifted to the government. At the same time, intimacy has taken on increased importance as a dimension of marital relationships.

Unlike most social structures, the **family** is a biological as well as a social group—a relatively permanent group of persons linked together in social roles by ties of blood, marriage, or adoption who live together and cooperate economically and in the rearing of children. This definition is very broad; it would include a mother living alone with her child as well as a man living with several wives. The important criteria for families are that its members are bound together—if not by blood, then by some cultural ceremony such as marriage or adoption that ties them to each other relatively permanently—and that they assume responsibility for each other.

The family is usually embedded in a larger set of relatives—the **kin group**, which is the socially defined network of kin (not necessarily the same as all of one's blood relatives). In the Trobriand Islands, only kin descended on the mother's side are recognized; among the Zulu, kinship is organized around male siblings. In our society, the group we call kin covers both the male and female side of the family but seldom extends beyond first cousins. In addition to blood relatives, most Americans also include their in-laws as part of their kin group.

Marriage is a key concept in understanding the family as a social rather than a biological unit. By giving or withholding approval for marriage, society controls the formation of new family units, of kinship relationships, and of inheritance. This control is vital to ensuring the continuity of existing patterns of stratification, community integration, and support. Control of marriage is exerted through social norms defining who should marry and when and limiting the range of partners who can be considered. All societies bar the marriage of certain blood relatives, and many have explicit rules about which groups one must marry into and which groups one must not marry into.

Marriage is the approved social structure for sexual relationships and childbearing. Many cultures tolerate other kinds of sexual encounters—premarital, extramarital, or homosexual—but all cultures discourage childbearing outside marriage. In some cultures, the sanctions are severe and almost all sexual relationships are confined to marriage; in others, marriage is an ideal that can be bypassed with relatively little punishment.

Marriage is important for childrearing because it imposes socially sanctioned roles on parents and the kin group. When a child is born, parents, grandparents, and aunts and uncles are automatically assigned certain normative obligations to the child.

The network represents a ready-made social structure designed to organize and stabilize the responsibility for children. Children born outside marriage, by contrast, are more vulnerable. The number of people normatively responsible for their care is smaller, and, even in the case of the mother, the norms are less well enforced. One consequence is higher infant mortality for illegitimate children in almost all societies, including our own.

Marriage, family, and kinship are among the most basic and enduring patterns of social relationships. Although blood ties are important, the family is best understood as a social structure defined and enforced by cultural norms.

Cross-Cultural Variations and Patterns—The Differences

Families universally regulate sexual behavior, provide care for dependents, and offer emotional and financial security. That is where the universals end, however. Hundreds of different family forms can be used to fill these roles. Children can be raised by their grandmothers or their aunts; wives can have one husband or three; children can be cared for at home or sent to boarding school; the aged can be put out in the cold to die or put on social security. This section of the chapter reviews some of the most important variations in the ways cultures have fulfilled family functions. (The Focus at the end of this section describes in some detail the unique family system of a 19th century utopian community.)

Family Patterns.   The basic unit of the family is the wife-husband pair and their children. When the married pair and their children form an independent household living apart from other kin, we call them a **nuclear family**. When they live with other kin, such as parents or siblings, we refer to them as an **extended family**.

Extended families are found in all types of societies, although they are normatively defined as the ideal family form only in premodern, nonindustrialized societies. Where extended families occur in the United States, they are often the result of financial hardship. In most industrialized societies, the ideal family form is the nuclear family. It gives up the security that comes with a wider network of kin but provides greater mobility and independence. Thus the nuclear family is well adapted to contemporary society, where economic and geographic change are commonplace and where security comes from a good job rather than a large family.

Residence Patterns.   Whether a society favors nuclear or extended families has a great deal of influence on where a newly married couple will live. By definition, the nuclear family lives by itself; this is called **neolocal residence**. Extended families, however, may exhibit a wide variety of residence patterns. They may live with the wife's relatives (**matrilocal residence**), with the husband's relatives (**patrilocal residence**), or in some unique combination, such as with the wife's mother's sisters or the wife's relatives one year and the husband's the next. Like the extended family itself, complex residence patterns are gradually being displaced by the neolocal pattern of the nuclear family. There are still hundreds of small societies that prescribe complex residence patterns, but the vast majority of the world's population now lives in large societies practicing neolocal residence.

Courtship Patterns.   As for all recurring behaviors, society provides a set of standards for how and when to select a mate. It also specifies the extent to which parents and kin are involved (Goode, 1959). (See Figure 11.2.)

Whenever marriage has a strong impact on families or communities, it is unlikely that mate selection will be left up to individuals. When dowries or bride prices are exchanged, when the new spouse will move in with relatives, or when prestige is strongly related to family ties, then the activities leading to marriage are likely to be controlled by parents and kin.

Figure 11.1
The Wodaabe of Niger are a society where the extended family is extremely important. Wodaabe taboo prohibits a mother from speaking to her first and second born child and except for nursing, physical contact between mother and child is limited. Other relatives, such as this baby girl's grandmother, lavish care and affection on the children. As a result of this practice there is a wider network of kin who have responsibility toward one another.

A **nuclear family** consists of a husband, a wife, and their dependent children.

An **extended family** exists when the wife-husband pair and their children live with other kin and share economic and childrearing responsibilities with them.

Neolocal residence occurs when the rules of residence require that a newly married couple take up residence away from their relatives.

Matrilocal residence occurs when the rules of residence require newly married couples to take up residence with the wife's kin.

Patrilocal residence occurs when the rules of residence require a newly married couple to take up residence with the husband's kin.

Figure 11.2 Types of Courtship Systems and Their Determinants

Parental control over dating is more direct when the child's mate selection directly affects the parents.

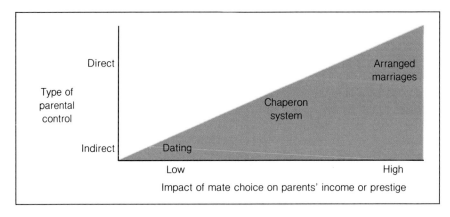

Under these circumstances, mate selection is based on the interests of the kin group rather than on any emotional bond between the young people. Love between a couple is regarded as a lucky accident and more likely follows than precedes marriage.

In the extreme case, this may mean that the family arranges a marriage between young people who have never met each other. In less extreme cases, chaperoning and careful supervision, especially of girls, gives some scope for individual choice while ensuring that young people will meet only those who are socially and economically acceptable to their parents. In extended family systems, family control of mate selection is important because marriage affects the economic interests of kin groups. Where the young people will live by themselves, however, and where the kin group's economic interests are not affected by the young people's choices, there is a corresponding decrease in the family's involvement in choosing children's mates (Lee & Stone, 1980).

In our own society, dating and courtship are relatively free of direct parental control. We have considerable freedom of choice and need not consider the wishes of others, including our parents, in choosing dating partners or spouses. Parental influence is still important, however, in both

Figure 11.3

Courtship practices are more likely to be restricted and supervised in cultures where marriage has an impact on the community or the economic welfare of families. Among the Old Order Amish, for example, this young couple observes church teachings by courting in an open buggy where their behavior is more open to supervision. After a couple is married they are entitled to the privacy afforded by a covered buggy.

indirect and direct ways. Where our parents live, where they send us to school, where they vacation, and what activities they engage in all serve to influence the types people we meet. Such arrangements increase the likelihood that the partner we choose will be acceptable to our parents in terms of race, religion, and social class.

Marriage Patterns. In the United States and much of the Western world, a marriage form called **monogamy** is practiced; each man may have only one wife (at a time), and each woman may have only one husband. Many cultures, however, practice some form of **polygamy**—marriage in which a person may have more than one spouse at a time. The most frequent pattern, that practiced by the 19th century Mormons, is to allow a man to have more than one wife at a time (**polygyny**). Less frequently, the form is **polyandry**, where a woman is allowed to have more than one husband at a time.

Viewed cross-culturally, polygyny has been the most popular marriage pattern. In a study of 250 cultures, Murdock (1949, 1957) found that 75 percent prefer polygyny as a marriage pattern, 24 percent prefer monogamy, and only 1 percent prefer polyandry. In the contemporary world, polygyny is most common in African societies. In the period 1960–1977, approximately 24 percent of married African men had more than one wife (Welch & Glick, 1981). The practice of polygyny is, of course, restricted by the nearly equal number of men and women in a society; if some men have more than one wife, other men will have to go without. Thus, even in societies where polygyny is the preferred marriage pattern, the majority of men have only one wife—and even though a clear majority of cultures favor polygyny, the vast majority of the population of the world practices monogamy.

Polygyny is by definition an extended family system. It tends to be best adapted to preindustrial societies in which both geographic and social mobility are limited. It is also characteristic of societies in which wealth depends on kinship ties. Polygyny enhances a man's wealth by bringing in more dowries, providing more women and children for labor, and producing more heirs (Reiss, 1980). Everywhere polygyny is practiced, it tends to become an important symbol of the prestige and status of the wealthy. Monogamy, on the other hand, tends to flourish when there are other means to demonstrate wealth and status and when the costs of supporting wives and children exceed their economic benefits.

Authority Patterns. Both in and out of the family, human societies have been characterized by **patriarchal authority**; the oldest male of the family typically controls economic resources, makes decisions, and has the final say in all matters related to the family. Although the influence or authority of wives varies from one society to another, there are no societies in which the cultural norms specify **matriarchal authority** and few in which the norms specify equality of authority. Increasingly, however, contemporary Western societies are coming to accept a new norm of **egalitarianism,** in which spouses jointly share in decision making, control of family resources, and childrearing. Even in the societies where equality is most highly developed, however, husbands continue to have more power than wives and are less involved in childrearing.

Monogamy is marriage in which there is only one wife and one husband.

Polygamy is any form of marriage in which a person may have more than one spouse at a time.

Polygyny is a form of marriage in which one man may be married to two or more women at a time.

Polyandry is a form of marriage in which one woman may be married to two or more men at a time.

Patriarchal authority is normatively approved male dominance.

Matriarchal authority is normatively approved female dominance.

Egalitarianism emphasizes spouses jointly sharing in decision making, control of family resources, and childrearing.

FOCUS ON YESTERDAY

Group Marriage in the 19th Century

The United States in the late 19th century was remarkably tolerant. The moral code of the dominant culture stressed premarital chastity and monogamy. Nevertheless, dozens of sectarian groups with very different ideas of sexual and familial morality emerged and briefly prospered. The Mormons are the only of them to have survived to the present day; and, as pointed out in chapter 4, one of the conditions of their survival was the adoption of the family structure of the dominant culture.

The Oneida community was one of the most successful and most daringly different of these 19th century groups. Oneida was founded in 1847 by a Yale-trained theologian named John Humprey Noyes. It began as a group of 20 to 30 in Oneida, New York, and grew to 300 children and adults before it disbanded, in 1879.

Noyes's community was based on the principles of Christian communism. (Acts 2:32–35 offers biblical support for Christian communism.) In the Oneida community, there was no private property, and monogamy, the exclusive ownership of a spouse, was not allowed. Although Noyes recognized that the early Christians applied the communistic principle only to material goods:

"Yet we affirm that there is no intrinsic difference between property in persons and property in things. . . . The new command is, that we love one another, and that, not by pairs, as in the world, but *en masse*. We are required to love one another fervently. The fashion of the world forbids a man and woman who are otherwise appropriated to love one another fervently. But if they obey Christ they must do this." [Noyes, 1869/1961:625–627]

In the Oneida community, the practice of complex marriage meant that all men were considered married to all women. Oneida, however, was hardly the place to go if one was looking for sex without commitment. Entrance into the community required signing over all of one's worldly goods to the community as well as embracing a life of considerable physical toil, and group marriage was not simply a matter of sleeping around. Rather, the selection of sleeping partners was done through a committee. At Oneida, all members lived together in a big mansionlike house. The women each had a private bedroom, whereas the men all slept together in a dormitory. When a man wished to sleep with a particular woman, he submitted a written request to the committee, which then referred it to the woman. The request could be denied by the woman on personal grounds or by the committee on the ground that too much particularism was developing in this relationship and that the brother did not show himself willing to love all his sisters. During the first 2 decades of the community's existence, the Oneidans avoided having children. They wished to establish both their economy and their family structure before adding the burden of children. During these 20 years they practiced a form of contraception

Figure 11.4

This photograph of the Oneida community depicts the women and men of the community on a free afternoon in front of the Mansion House. Note that the women wore pantaloons under their short skirts and bobbed their hair, styles which were unconventional for the time. Oneida was obviously economically successful as a community, a major factor that contributed to group marriage lasting as long as it did.

called *coitus reservatas*, in which the man does not ejaculate. Since this technique takes a great deal of willpower and some practice, it is reported that young men were required to sleep only with women past childbearing age until they had perfected the technique. (In a parallel practice, younger women were encouraged to sleep with older men. In this case, greater spiritual growth was given as the reason.) The teaching method must have worked reasonably well, as only 2 children were born during this period.

Between 1869 and 1879, the Oneidans produced 59 children. The women and men who became parents were "scientifically" matched by a committee. The selection process was designed to produce children with superior mental and physical abilities. The children were nurtured by their mothers for the first 12 months and then were raised in a communal nursery. As with spouses, there was to be no exclusive attachment;

adults were supposed to love all children equally. The children of Oneida apparently got exceptional care; their infant mortality rate was very low, and their educational training was excellent.

In 1879, the Oneida community disbanded. A major cause for the break-up was the erratic leadership provided by Noyes. Additional problems included the management of an increasingly large household and diversified economic enterprises. The problems were internal rather than external; the community never received a great deal of harassment from outsiders. It even advertised for visitors and sold Sunday lunches to day-trippers from New York who came up to satisfy their curiosity about these strange people. The community's hard work and economic success, as well as a strategic willingness to buy locally and help neighbors, meant that its members were generally well regarded in upstate New York in spite of their odd family system.

When the community disbanded, many members stayed on in Oneida, most of them legally marrying one of the other members. The financial enterprises of Oneida were incorporated and divided among the members. One of these enterprises, the Oneida Silver Manufacturing Company, is still a successful corporation providing tableware for millions.

Questions to Consider

1. Would men or women benefit more from a family system like the one developed by the Oneida community? What are the advantages and disadvantages to the individual of such a system?
2. Why do you suppose complex marriage was tolerated in the 19th century but Mormon polygyny was not (see chapter 4)?

SOURCES: Whitworth, John McKelvie. (1975). *God's Blueprints: A Sociological Study of Three Utopian Sects.* Boston: Routledge and K. Paul.

A Profile of the U.S. Family

The family in the United States has changed substantially in the generations since World War II. These changes are responses to changes in the economy, in education, and in values. In this section, we will examine the basic structure of the U.S. family, seeing how it has changed in the last 40 years. Then we will look at the normative structure of courtship and marriage institutions, especially how they work in practice.

Growing Up

American norms, like those of most other societies, specify that children should grow up in intact families, with both a mother and a father to see to their emotional and financial needs. Increasingly, however, U.S. families are not living up to this norm. As a result of divorce and illegitimacy, only three-quarters of U.S. children live with both of their natural parents. The other one-quarter live with a single parent, usually the mother (see table 11.1). Before they reach the age of 18, nearly half of all U.S. children will spend some time living with a single parent. Of those whose parents

Table 11.1 Living Arrangements of Children under 18 in the United States, 1970 and 1982

There has been a substantial increase in the number of children who do not live in two-parent families. At current rates of illegitimacy and divorce, it is estimated that half of U.S. children will spend some time in a one-parent family.

LIVING WITH:	1970	1982
Own mother and father	85%	75%
Mother only	11	20
Father only	2	1
Neither	3	3

SOURCE: U.S. Bureau of the Census, Current Population Reports, Series P-20, No. 380, 1983:51.

Figure 11.5
The nuclear family is considered to be the ideal family form by most Americans. Nevertheless, an increasing proportion, also divorce and remarry. Nearly one-half of all marriages are remarriages, and many families, now include stepparents and stepchildren.

divorce and remarry, nearly half will experience the break-up of the second marriage too (Bumpass, 1984). Children growing up in these circumstances may acquire a view of the family that is quite different from what it was just 2 decades ago. There is considerable speculation, though relatively little hard evidence, that children growing up in these circumstances may be more prone to illegitimacy and divorce themselves (Pope & Mueller, 1976).

Getting Married

Nearly all Americans marry. In fact, the United States is the "marryingest" of industrialized nations. By the time they reach the age of 30, nearly all Americans have been married at least once, and those who divorce tend to remarry quickly. The current generation of Americans, however, is marrying later than its parents did. In the past decade, the average age at marriage has increased nearly 2 years, and there has been a sharp increase in the percentage of young people who are still single in their early 20s. The percent of women married by the age of 21, for example, dropped from 56 to 37 percent between 1970 and 1982 (U.S. Bureau of the Census, 1983:2). Most observers believe that this increase in singleness, however, is merely a postponement of marriage rather than an increase in the proportion who will never marry.

Having Children

The majority of couples in the United States enter marriage with the expectation of becoming parents. Among the 90 percent who expect to have families, however, the size of family desired has declined dramatically. Young people starting marriage in the 1970s and 1980s expect to have an average of two children, a considerable decline from the fertility of their own parents. Among married couples, both Catholic and non-

Figure 11.6
Before children reach adolescence, their most important social contacts take place within the family—with their parents, brothers, and sisters. Although it appears that this boy may be clobbered by his big sister, their relationship will last 40 or 50 years into the future and be a source of stability and integration for both of them.

Catholic, contraceptive use is close to universal, and, increasingly, children born to married women are planned.

These decreases in family size have occurred during a period in which women have increased their participation in the labor force and their educational attainment. Although the average woman does not yet place career roles over family roles, she does desire more personal freedom and economic security, both of which are adversely affected by taking time out for childbearing (Wilkie, 1981). As women's commitment to the labor force grows, the fertility rate in the United States is expected to continue to decline (Ryder, 1979).

Early Childbearing.   Balanced against this pattern of planned decrease in family size is a sharp increase in illegitimacy. In 1982, nearly one out of six children was born to an unwed mother. Perhaps an additional 20 percent of all brides are pregnant at the time of marriage and will have a child within the first months of marriage. These pregnancies are generally unplanned and occur disproportionately to young women. Nearly half of all illegitimate births in 1979 were to teenage mothers. Thus, although some are postponing parenting, many are having children at relatively youthful ages.

Getting Divorced

In the United States, more than 2 million adults and approximately 1 million children are affected annually by divorce. And although remarriage is common, the increasing amount of divorce in recent years has resulted

Figure 11.7
The divorce rate in American society has increased dramatically over the past two decades. Many states have passed no-fault divorce legislation making it easier for a couple to terminate their marriage without contesting it in court. In some places around-the-clock divorce services are now available for those who wish to end a marriage immediately. This store front in Baja, California in fact, will apparently begin processing your divorce in the middle of the night if necessary.

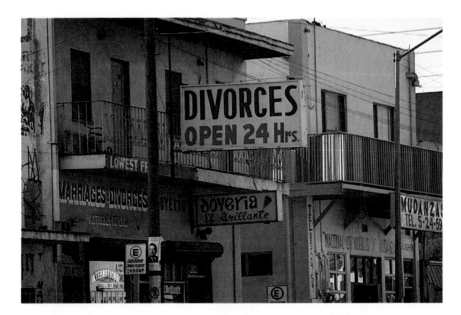

The **divorce rate** is calculated as the number of divorces each year per 1,000 married women.

Lifetime divorce probability is the probability that a marriage will ever end in divorce.

in a significant portion of the adult population currently divorced and a large portion of children living with a divorced parent.

The **divorce rate**, calculated as the number of divorces each year per 1,000 married women, has risen steadily in the post–World War II period and stood at 22 in 1982. That is, 22 out of 1,000, or 2.2 percent, of all married women in the United States became divorced in 1982. Another way of looking at divorce is to calculate the probability of its occurrence over the lifetime of a marriage—the **lifetime divorce probability**. Of marriages begun in 1890, for example, the proportion eventually ending in divorce was approximately 10 percent. For couples marrying in 1970, the proportion is estimated to be 48 percent (Cherlin, 1981). (See Figure 11.8.) This means that if current divorce rates persist, the chances that your marriage will end in divorce are about 50/50.

Remarrying

Although a large number of people end their first marriage with divorce, most remarry—often very quickly. Of those who divorce before they are 25, one-third remarry within the year. Remarriage is more common for young people, and aging is particularly hard on women's chances of remarriage; Three-quarters of the women who divorce before age 30 remarry, but this drops to half for those divorced in their 30s and one-quarter for those who divorce after age 40 (U.S. Bureau of the Census, 1977). Men, on the other hand, retain their eligibility and high remarriage rate well into their 60s.

Summary

Americans retain a high commitment to marriage. Almost all of them expect to marry and become parents. There have, however, been some

Figure 11.8 Changing Probability of Divorce, 1870–1970
There has been a dramatic increase in the likelihood that marriages will end in divorce. For those who first married after 1970, it is now expected that half will be divorced.
SOURCE: Cherlin, Andrew. 1981. Marriage, Divorce, Remarriage. Reprinted by permission, Harvard University Press.

important changes in how marriage and parenthood are carried out. The normative expectation that marriages are permanent and that children grow up with both parents is decreasingly a guide to what people experience. In the following sections, we will review the processes that go on in American family institutions—how people choose mates, how marriages work, and why some marriages succeed and others fail.

Courtship in the United States

Romantic Love and the Tendency to Marry

Ours is a marrying society. Fewer than 5 percent of Americans reach middle age without marrying. Some people marry for economic reasons, some to escape from their parents, and some to escape loneliness. In addition to these mundane reasons, most Americans marry because they are in love. No other society has believed that love in marriage is as important as contemporary America finds it.

What is love? First, we need to distinguish romantic love (the kind you fall into) from love for parents, children, dogs, or countries. The best definitions of **romantic love** probably are found in poetry and song, but a standard sociological definition is that it is a combination of such physical symptoms as breathlessness and a pounding heart with sexual desire and a disregard of practical or economic consequences. Romantic love is the learned association of uncomfortable physical sensations with positive emotional feelings. Certainly, the physical symptoms of breathlessness and a pounding heart could be interpreted very differently if they resulted, say, from meeting a mean dog in a dark alley (Schachter, 1964).

Romantic love has been around since at least the 12th and 13th centuries. At that time, however, it was considered a practical basis for choosing a lover, not a spouse. It has been considered a necessary precondition

Romantic love is a combination of such physical symptoms as breathlessness and a pounding heart with a sexual yearning for the other and a disregard of practical and economic consequences.

Figure 11.9
Beginning in the late 1960s, American youth became more open and permissive with respect to sexual behavior. For the first time, the premarital sexual behavior of girls was similar to that of boys: more permissiveness, less commitment, and a decline in the double standard. During this same period, teenage pregnancies and abortions have also risen dramatically.

A **double standard** exists when premarital or extramarital sexual activity is acceptable for men but not for women.

for marriage in very few societies, and probably in no society is it more important than in the United States. Romantic love can flower only when marriage is an arrangement between individuals rather than families. Thus it tends to be found only in societies where the nuclear family is strongly developed and kinship is relatively unimportant for other social roles.

The Dating Game

Even in societies where marriage choices are left pretty much to the individual, the decision to seek a partner is not left entirely to chance or to individual effort. Rather, many social structures encourage the development of love. In our society, the principal mechanism is dating. Generally, all young people are expected to date, and most youths begin dating in their early teens (14 is the most common age). Parents, peers, friends, and even churches and schools encourage heterosexual dating. Often, the expectations of these groups are so obvious that people without dates feel embarrassed about going alone to school or church events. Thus, although it may be fun, dating is also an obligatory form of social behavior—it is normative.

The Sexual Revolution.   Some of the more important norms surrounding dating behavior are concerned with the amount of acceptable sexual contact. These norms range from total abstinence (sexual contact is always wrong) to permissiveness with affection (sexual contact is okay if there is commitment to the relationship) to total permissiveness (sexual contact is okay with or without commitment).

In the United States, there have been two revolutions in premarital sexual norms and behavior. The first occurred in the 1920s, when there was a major increase in the proportion of both women and men who engaged in premarital sexual intercourse (Kinsey, 1948, 1953). The second began in the late 1960s and is continuing. Studies of adolescents and college students indicate that this second revolution has two components: an increase in permissiveness and a decline of the double standard.

All major surveys have found increases in permissiveness in recent years; more people engage in sex before marriage, and fewer see anything wrong with it (see Table 11.2). Increasingly, both men and women believe that a strong commitment is unnecessary for a sexual relationship to be acceptable. Moreover, these changes in the last decade have been more pronounced for women than for men, with the result that men and women are now much more alike in both attitudes and levels of experience. The **double standard** that allows premarital sexual activity for men but not for women appears to be gradually dying out. For example, a recent study of undergraduates asked students to rate the desirability of several hypothetical dating partners who varied on degree of sexual experience. If the double standard were operating, female students would prefer more experienced men and male students would prefer less experienced women. The study found that prior sexual experience was of little importance to either women or men (Istvan & Griffitt, 1980). The only exception was that the inexperienced of both sexes preferred a partner who was also inexperienced.

Studies of college students may underestimate the changes that have occurred in society's premarital sexual norms. One recent survey found

Table 11.2   Changing Attitudes toward Premarital Sex, 1965 to 1980

During the last 20 years, premarital sexual experience has become much more common among college women. As a result, the double standard has nearly disappeared. This change has been accompanied by a sharp decline in the percentage of students who believe that such behavior is immoral.

| | PERCENT OF COLLEGE STUDENTS WHO: | | | |
| | Have Had Premarital Intercourse | | Believe Premarital Intercourse Is Immoral | |
	Males	Females	Males	Females
1965	65%	29%	33%	70%
1970	65	37	14	34
1975	74	57	20	21
1980	77	64	17	25

SOURCE: Robinson and Jedlicka, 1982, table 3.

that both virginity and the double standard were more common among college students than among young people not in college: 28 percent of college men and 40 percent of college women had never had sexual intercourse, whereas 21 percent of young noncollege men and 21 percent of young noncollege women had never had intercourse (DeLamater & MacCorquodale, 1979).

Choosing a Marriage Partner

Given the fact that there are thousands of "pebbles on the beach," how is it that two individuals eventually discover that no other person will do quite as well? How do people arrive at loving one another? Why does John fall in love with Mary rather than with Sue or Carolyn? Several factors are important in moving a relationship from attraction to marriage.

Original Attraction.   Factors important in determining original attraction include propinquity, homogamy, and physical attractiveness. Obviously, you are unlikely to meet, much less marry, someone who lives in another community or another state. **Propinquity**, or spatial nearness, operates in more subtle ways, however, by increasing the opportunity for continual interaction. It is no accident that so many people end up marrying coworkers or fellow students. The more you interact with others, the more likely you are to develop positive attitudes toward them—attitudes that may ripen into love (Homans, 1950).

Propinquity is spatial nearness.

Spatial closeness is also often a sign of **homogamy**, or similarity. Research demonstrates that people tend to be drawn to others like themselves—people of the same class, race, religion, age, and interests. Of course, there are exceptions, but faced with a wide range of choices, most people tend to be attracted to others like themselves (Rawlings, 1978).

Homogamy is similarity in characteristics between individuals.

Advertisers have sought to convince people that physical attraction is the major determinant of whether one gains attention or love from the opposite sex. Although it isn't as important as the media suggest, research has found that physical attractiveness is important in gaining initial attention (Elder, 1969; Walster et al., 1966). When you first meet somebody, all you have to go on is the outside packaging; if that is attractive, it may prompt a closer look. Its importance in the courtship process, however, does not normally extend beyond the first meeting.

Figure 11.10

This Hindu wedding is an arranged marriage in the sense that approval by the parents of both the bride and groom was required before the marriage could be performed. This couple met in graduate school in Nebraska (propinquity) and their similarities in background (homogamy) increased their attraction to one another. Before they could marry, however, it was essential that their parents approve the marriage. One of the important conditions related to parental approval was the couple's similarity of caste background.

Dating is likely to progress toward a serious consideration of marriage if the couple discover similar interests, aspirations, anxieties, and values (Reiss, 1980). When dating starts to get serious, couples begin sharing information about marriage expectations. Do they both want children? How do they feel about traditional marriage roles for men and women? If he expects her to do all the housework and she thinks that idea went out with the hula hoop, then they'll probably back away from marriage.

This description of the courtship process is diagramed in Figure 11.11 as a set of filters that gradually narrows down the field of eligibles (Kerckhoff & Davis, 1962). At each stage in the courtship process the screens in the funnel become a little finer, and the pool of eligibles is finally reduced to the one best person. Is mate selection really all that sensible? Probably not. Some people do follow this sensible set of steps from top to bottom, but others jump to the final choice without passing through all the filters. Some get married in the fever of love at first sight, and some are caught by unwelcome pregnancies.

Dating can be viewed as a shopping trip in which each person is evaluating the available goods and searching for the best bargain. Each is trying to get the most in return for personal assets (looks, talent, money). If this sounds too crass, consider the times you've heard someone say "I know he can do better than that" or "she's throwing herself away on him." These are basically statements that the shopper has bought overpriced merchandise and should have done a little more shopping around. A commitment to marriage is likely to occur when the individual decides that a particular person is the best buy in the market (Adams, 1979).

Cohabitation

Cohabitation occurs when couples live together without legal marriage.

A major change in courtship is the significant rise in **cohabitation**—living together without legal marriage. In 1982, approximately 1.9 million couples in the United States were cohabiting. This number is a threefold increase since 1970 and a twofold increase just since 1977 (Spanier, 1983).

Some view the increase in cohabitation with alarm. Such an arrangement violates many people's religious views, and even those without strong religious principles wonder whether it is a rejection of the commitment required by marriage. Increasingly, however, cohabitation is viewed as an additional stage in the courtship process rather than as an alternative to marriage (Risman et al., 1981).

Changing rates of cohabitation are associated with a changing composition of the cohabiting population. In earlier decades, cohabitation was limited largely to those with low incomes and educations, many of whom already had had failed marriages and who lacked the economic and emotional resources to marry. Increasingly, however, cohabitation is a life-style embraced by middle-class youths as a prelude to marriage. The majority of cohabitors now are young never-married people (see Table 11.3). They too tend to have low incomes, but generally because they are still in school rather than because their economic prospects are poor (Spanier, 1983). Whether for the young or old, the never married or divorced, cohabitation is a big-city life-style. Few cohabitors reside in non-metropolitan areas (Glick & Spanier, 1980).

Roles and Relationships in Marriage

In fiction, the story ends with the wedding or even the engagement, and we are told that the couple lived happily ever after. In real life, though, the work has just begun. Marriage means the acquisition of a whole new set of duties and responsibilities, as well as a few rights. What are they? The following section considers work roles, sexual roles, and parenting roles.

The Division of Labor

The work roles of women and men in the United States, both at home and in the labor force, are changing in fundamental ways. This is due to many factors, among them improved technology that has altered domestic chores, rapid expansion of service work in the labor market, and changing attitudes and values about women's roles.

The Traditional View. In the traditional nuclear family, the roles of men and women were distinct. Men were responsible primarily for instrumental roles,—roles involved in economic production and task performance. Women were responsible primarily for expressive roles—roles involved in maintaining morale, reducing conflict, creating a pleasant environment, and seeing to emotional needs. In the traditional view, both husband and wife performed necessary functions for the family, and the complementarity of their roles gave strength and stability to the family (Parsons & Bales, 1955).

The instrumental/expressive view of men's and women's roles is a simplified picture designed to lay out the major features of role differences. It is doubtful that such a strict dichotomy existed in many families. Few

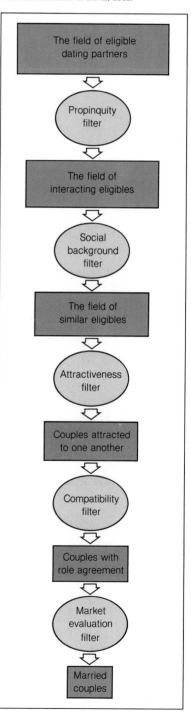

Figure 11.11 Process of Selecting a Mate

Mate selection can be viewed as a series of filters that help us narrow the field of eligibles to one or two people who share our interests and expectations—and who seem to be a good bargain.

SOURCE: Kerckoff & Davis, 1962.

Table 11.3 Number of Unmarried Couples Living Together in the United States, 1960–1981, by Presence of Children

As cohabitation has become common, it has changed character. It is no longer dominated by formerly married people who cannot afford marriage; now it is used more commonly by never-married young people as a prelude to marriage.

	PERCENT WITH CHILDREN	ABSOLUTE NUMBER OF COUPLES
1960	46%	425,000
1970	37	523,000
1980	27	1,589,000
1982	25	1,863,000

SOURCE: Glick and Spanier, 1980; Spanier, 1983.

husbands could afford a wife who was nonproductive, and few wives would tolerate a husband who was never expressive. Despite the many changes in marital roles in recent years, however, it is probably still true that the role of economic supporter falls more to the husband and the role of housekeeper and emotional supporter falls more to the wife.

Work Outside the Home. For married men, participation in the labor force is a role obligation, and most such men are employed full time if the economy permits. For women, the norms surrounding work are less clear: 10 or 20 years ago, women who chose to work had to defend their choice; today, women who choose not to work are on the defensive.

The participation of women in the labor force has increased continuously over the past several decades. In many instances, the wife's employment is an economic necessity; in others, it is an important contribution to raising the family's standard of living. In 1975, the median proportion of family income contributed by wives who worked full time (approximately 41 percent of all women) was 39 percent. In 12 percent of the families with working wives, over 50 percent of the total family income came from the wife's employment (Vanek, 1980).

One of the most dramatic changes in women's working has been the increased participation of mothers in the labor force, especially mothers of young children. In 1982, nearly two-thirds (63 percent) of the mothers with children between the ages of 6 and 17 worked outside the home and 49 percent of those with children under 6 did so (U.S. Bureau of the Census, 1984:414). The employment of mothers of young children is strongly related to the income of the husbands (Gordon & Kammeyer, 1980). Women married to men with lower incomes return to work more quickly after the birth of a child than do women married to men with higher earnings.

Household Labor. The dramatic increase in the role of wives as breadwinners has not been accompanied by an equal change in the domestic

Figure 11.12
Most people in our society marry. In recent years, however, there has been a notable tendency to postpone marriage. Consequently, many young people are still single until their mid-twenties.

division of labor. In recent years, studies consistently have found that household tasks continue to be defined as either women's work or men's work. Wives generally take responsibility for household and family care, meal preparation, cleaning up, laundry and mending, and childcare. Husband's tasks typically include yard work, home repair, some shopping and household errands, and a limited amount of childcare.

This sex-typed division of labor persists even when the wife works. It is still her kitchen and his garage. As a result, wives who work, and especially mothers who work, put in long hours. One study estimated that the average mother with a full-time job puts in a total of 80 hours of work a week, counting work at home and office, whereas the average father puts in a total of 62 hours (Vanek, 1980). Rather than increasing the husband's time spent in housework, the average family with a working wife adjusts by lowering its standards for cleanliness, meals, and other domestic services. They eat at McDonald's, let the iron gather dust, and vacuum once a week instead of every other day.

Sexual Roles in Marriage: A Changing Script

In few areas of our lives are we free to improvise. Instead, we learn social scripts that direct us toward appropriate behaviors and lines and away from inappropriate ones. Sex is no exception. Unfortunately, we know relatively little about the sexual script for marriage partners and about how it has changed. All the attention in the sexual revolution has gone to young people. Did the revolution pass married folks by, or have sexual roles changed within marriage as well as outside it?

Relatively few serious studies of this subject have been undertaken. Many of the popular surveys, such as those by *Redbook* (Levin & Levin, 1975) and *Playboy* (Hunt, 1974), are reports from biased samples. Neither the people who read these magazines nor the people who choose to send in information about their sex lives are random samples of the population. The few serious studies that have been done find that frequency of sexual activity seems to have changed very little among married people in the last 30 years (Gagnon, 1977; Gagnon et al., 1978). There have, however, been two notable trends. One is an increase in oral sex, a practice that was limited largely to unmarried sexual partners and the highly educated in earlier decades. The second is that women have reached parity with men in their probability of having an affair. The double standard has disappeared in adultery, and recent studies suggest that 50 percent of both men and women have had an extramarital sexual relationship (Thompson, 1983).

One of the most consistent findings about sexuality in marriage is that the frequency of intercourse declines steadily with the length of the marriage (see Table 11.4). The decline appears to be nearly universal and to occur regardless of the couple's age, education, or situation. After the first year, almost everything that happens—children, jobs, commuting, housework, finances—reduces the rate of marital intercourse (Greenblat, 1983).

> Oh, it's getting worse all the time. Maybe it's three or four times a month now instead of three or four times a week. But I guess it's natural—it's like "I'm tired, you're tired, let's forget it." [Cited in Greenblat, 1983:296]

Figure 11.13
Aside from rising divorce rates, the biggest change in American family life in the last 20 years is the entrance of mothers, especially mothers with preschoolers, into the labor force. The change may be sparked by women's better educational preparation, smaller families, and a desire to insure themselves against the possibility of divorce. Because working mothers continue to shoulder most of the burden of house and childcare, working may add role stress and role conflict. Studies indicate, however, that mothers' working has few negative effects on her children.

Table 11.4 Frequency of Sexual Intercourse per Month among Couples Married Five Years or Longer

The frequency with which married couples engage in sexual intercourse steadily declines after the first year of marriage for most couples. Couples attribute this decline to such things as work, childrearing, fatigue and familiarity.

YEAR OF MARRIAGE	AVERAGE	RANGE
First	14.8	4–45
Second	12.2	3–20
Third	11.9	2–18
Fourth	9.0	4–23
Fifth	9.7	5–18
Sixth	6.3	2–15

SOURCE: Cathy Stein Greenblat, "The salience of sexuality in the early years of marriage." Journal of Marriage and the Family 45 (May, 1983), table 3, page 292.

Sex has become less important now—in the beginning there was a feeling that newlyweds screw a lot; therefore, we ought to. It was great and I loved it, but now I think that other things have become more important as we found other things that are satisfying to do besides sex. [Cited in Greenblat, 1983:297]

The overall conclusion drawn from Greenblat's research is that, after the first year of marriage, sex is of decreasing importance to most people. Nevertheless, satisfaction with both the quantity and quality of one's sex life is essential to a good marriage (Blumstein & Schwartz, 1983).

Changing Sexual Scripts for Women. The lack of reliable survey data hampers descriptions of what people actually do. We can, however, get a pretty good idea of what people are supposed to do (that is, sexual norms) by looking at marriage manuals.

Marriage manuals of the 19th century generally expected sex to be a male right and a female duty. The sexual script for women is described as follows in an 1869 manual:

As a general rule, a modest woman seldom desires sexual gratification for herself. She submits to her husband, but only to please him; and but for the desire to maternity, would far rather be relieved from his attentions. [Cited in Weinberg et al., 1983:313]

An analysis of the content of sexual scripts contained in the best-selling sex manuals of the last few decades indicates that the sexual script for women has changed substantially in the last century (Weinberg et al., 1983). In the first period of change, covering roughly the years from 1950 to 1970, sex was viewed as positive for women as well as men, but as qualitatively different in meaning:

"Men can enjoy sex, in an animal sort of way, without love. Women can't," said Robert Hall in 1965. [Cited in Weinberg et al., 1983:315]

"Sex is a much more meaningful, deeper part of life for most women than for men," said Joyce Brothers in 1972. [Cited in Weinberg et al., 1983:315]

Furthermore, the double standard was still operative. Women were expected to be sexually naive and to be instructed by their more experienced mates.

"Ellen was lucky. She stumbled on . . . a patient and understanding man who was willing to teach her the basic facts of life," said Ruth Dickson in 1972. [Cited in Weinberg et al., 1983:315]

In the second revolution, beginning in the early 1970s, a more egalitarian model appeared in the sex manuals. Men and women were presented as having similar approaches to sex. Another major change was the de-emphasis on marriage and commitment; references to husband and wife were replaced with more generic terms, such as partner.

"Sex is no longer a male-oriented exercise," said Robert Hall in 1974. [Cited in Weinberg et al., 1983:317]

"Years ago . . . a 'good' and moral woman waited for her husband to entice and seduce her. Petting and sexual maneuvers were left entirely up to the male's prowess and imagination, or lack thereof. It was a solo act. Today the liberation of sexual ideas has made sex more of a duet. Both partners participate in more or less equal roles, providing themselves and each other similar experiences of

■ure 11.14
■st couples in the early years of mar-
■e want and have children. In America,
■norm is two: one of each sex. Chil-
■■ are expected to bring fulfillment, joy
■happiness, and to be symbolic of a
■ and woman's love for one another.
■■ite these expectations, couples with-
■hildren tend to have happier mar-
■s than couples with children.

Recent estimates suggest that it may cost as much as $150,000 to raise a middle-class child to adulthood. Parenthood, however, is one's of life's biggest adventures. Few other undertakings require such a large commitment of time and money on so uncertain a return. The list of disadvantages is long and certain: It costs a lot of money, takes an enormous amount of time, probably disrupts all the usual activities, and causes at least occasional stress and worry. And once you've started, there is no backing out; it is a lifetime commitment. What are the returns? You hope for love and a sense of family, but you know all around you are parents whose kids cause them heartache and grief. Parenthood is really the biggest gamble most people will ever make. In spite of this, or maybe because of it, most people want and have children.

Despite some major changes in parenting roles, there is still a great deal of gender differentiation in the roles generally assumed by mothers and fathers. Mothers are the ones most likely to drop out of the labor force to care for infants and young children; they are the ones most likely to take time off work to care for sick children or to go to school conferences.

A recent survey of parents found that mothers and fathers believed that they had equal responsibility for teaching the child norms and values, for developing the child's cognitive abilities, and for meeting the emotional needs of the child. However, both also believed that mothers had a greater responsibility for teaching the child social skills and helping the child develop physically and emotionally. There was nothing besides economic support for which these parents believed that fathers had more responsibility than mothers (Gilbert et al., 1981).

The substantial differences that exist between the roles of mothers and fathers have important consequences. In the short-run, the greater responsibility of mothers gives them a heavier burden of emotional and physical work. In the long-run, however, it may also give them a stronger relationship with the children. One recent study of 2,400 college students found that nearly twice as many felt close to their mothers as felt close to their fathers (White et al., 1985. The greater time mothers spend with their children and the tendency for mothers to be more nurturant probably account for this difference. The inequality in affection contributes to a lifelong disability for fathers. When they are old and widowed, men receive less support and help from their children than do women (Ortega, et al., 1983).

Stepparenting.   Over 10 percent of all children in the United States are being raised by a stepparent, most often by their natural mother and a stepfather. If parenting is difficult, stepparenting is more so. In addition to the problems all parents face, stepparents often face the continued presence of an ex-husband or an ex-wife, plus the trials of giving equal love and attention to his children, her children, and their children. As a result, both stepparents and stepchildren indicate more conflict and stress in stepfamilies than in original families (Duberman, 1975).

The Empty Nest: Crisis or Release?   In earlier centuries, when fertility was high and life expectancy was low, marriage and parenthood were

heightened pleasure," said Dominick Barbara in 1975. [Cited in Weinberg et al., 1983:317–318]

In addition, a third model appeared in feminist-oriented sex manuals, which urged women to take charge of their own sexual experience. Sexual independence was seen as part of the whole movement for women to gain greater control over their lives.

"There is an old saying that there are no frigid wives, just inept husbands. Although that sounds rather comforting from the female point of view, it was probably made up by some male who thought he could make any woman come. Nowadays most women like to think that they have something to do with their own orgasms and that they are not dependent on a man for sexual fulfillment," said Patricia Raley in 1976. [Cited in Weinberg et al., 1983:318]

"And once we become sexually independent and happy, we can apply what we've learned to other areas of our lives as well," said Carmen Kerr in 1977. [Cited in Weinberg et al., 1983:319]

In spite of the purported changes in sexual scripts, there is evidence that sex in marriage still tends to follow the old stereotypes about men's and women's roles. In Lillian Rubin's (1976) study of working-class families, for example, there was little evidence of the mutuality recommended by the manuals. Many of the working-class women reported that they responded to their husband's sexual demands rather than their own desires. This was particularly obvious in the case of husband's demands for oral sex. Some responded out of duty and some out of a sense of powerlessness; others used sexual response as a bargaining tool.

Duty

Even though I hate it, if he needs it, then I feel I ought to do it. After all, I'm his wife. [p. 139]

Powerlessness

I tell him I don't want to do it, but it doesn't do any good. If it's what he wants, that's what we do. [p. 140]

Bargaining Tool

He gets different treats at different times, depending on what he deserves. Sometimes I let him do that oral stuff you're talking about to me. Sometimes when he's *very* good, I do it to him. [p. 140]

The sexual role is an important part of marriage. Like any other marital role, however, it harbors the potential for role conflict and role stress. People who are overworked really do have headaches, and role strain reduces their ability to meet their role obligations. Others face role strain because they grew up with a sexual script different from the one now in use. And like most other marital roles, the sexual role remains substantially different for husbands and wives in spite of all the changes that have occurred.

The Parental Role: A Leap of Faith

The decision to become a parent is a momentous one. Children are extremely costly, both financially and in terms of emotional wear and tear.

largely overlapping. On the average, women still had children in the home at the time they lost their husband. In modern society, however, active parenthood takes up a much smaller portion of adult life. The average woman with two children is likely to have all of her children raised by the time she is 45 or 50. She can expect to live an additional 30 years, of which she will spend approximately 20 with her husband. Contrary to popular belief, this empty-nest stage of the family life cycle is a satisfying one for most couples. Reported marital satisfaction increases as the children leave home, and women especially report feelings of release and renewal (Glenn, 1975). Thus, although parenthood is a desired role for most people, it is also a tiring one, and parents are pleased to relinquish it when it is over.

Determinants of Marital Satisfaction and Marital Stability

Some marriages succeed and others fail; some are torn with conflict and others are extremely satisfying. The courtship processes described earlier work well for helping some people find satisfactory partners with whom to spend the next 50 years. For others, however, marriage leads to feelings of entrapment and disappointment, and eventually divorce. Important factors affecting marital satisfaction and stability are summarized here.

Homogamy

In the courtship process, couples that go beyond initial attraction to affection and marriage tend to have similar backgrounds. After marriage, this similarity will stand them in good stead. A large body of research shows that sharp differences in age, religion, social class, and race are associated with lower levels of marital satisfaction and higher levels of divorce (Lewis & Spanier, 1979). Although romantic love may develop across lines of class, race, and generation, it is rarer for marriages to thrive across these lines.

Age at Marriage

One of the strongest predictors of divorce is age at marriage. Marriages before age 20 are particularly vulnerable (Lee, 1977). Youthful marriages generally begin with several strikes against them. One is that youthful brides are often pregnant at the time of the marriage (U.S. National Center for Health Statistics, 1981). Premarital pregnancy at any age is stressful. It often causes a couple to enter marriage with resentment, to lack parental support, and to be quickly saddled with additional roles and financial demands. These conditions tend to promote marital conflict and divorce. Both premarital pregnancy and a youthful age at marriage have negative effects on marital quality; when they occur together, they are a serious obstacle to a happy or stable marriage.

Youthful marriages are also often characterized by a lack of maturity, few financial resources, inadequate role performance, and short engagements. In plain language, the partners do not know each other very well, they are uninterested in settling down, they are almost always broke, and they are not very good cooks, housekeepers, or earners. Given these obstacles, it is not surprising that the lifetime divorce probability of teenage marriages is close to 70 percent (Glick & Norton, 1977).

Income

Couples who have higher incomes consistently report happier marriages and lower divorce rates (Glick & Norton, 1977). In this instance, it appears that money can buy happiness. A higher income means greater material comfort, fewer arguments over spending, and more elbow room for daily living. In poor families, economic tensions are likely to spill over into marital tensions; these may be made worse by overwork, lack of vacations, and a feeling of failure.

Male Unemployment

The work role for married men is very clear; such men are supposed to be working full time. Men who fail to meet this expectation are usually defined as failures. This social definition tends to persist even when the individual himself can hardly be faulted for his unemployment, say when 20 percent of the men in his city are unemployed. Male unemployment causes both low income and a personal sense of failure. Not unexpectedly, then, male unemployment is related to marital dissatisfaction on the part of both husband and wife and a higher divorce rate (Ross & Sawhill, 1975).

Wives Working

When women first entered the paid labor force in large numbers, there was a great deal of concern about the effect this would have on marriages and children. Recent research, however, documents that a wife's employment has little effect on a couple's marital adjustment, degree of com-

Figure 11.15

Marital satisfaction and happiness depend on several factors. A consistent finding from research is that similarity of background makes for a more stable marriage. Persons who marry across lines of class, religion, or race are often confronted with additional obstacles to building a successful and happy marriage.

panionship, or sex-role attitudes (Gordon & Kammeyer, 1980; Locksley, 1980). It also does not substantially reduce the woman's effectiveness as a mother (Hoffman & Nye, 1974).

Although marital satisfaction is not related to the wife's work, divorce is. A wife who is not working and is economically dependent on her husband would have to be terribly unhappy before she would leave him; likewise, a man whose wife is totally dependent on him would have to be either a clod or terribly unhappy before he could leave her. The labor-force participation of wives gives both husbands and wives greater freedom to end their marriages. One consequence is that marriages may now be ending for less serious reasons than before. When divorce meant bankruptcy, it was usually limited to cases of abuse or adultery. As the financial cost of divorce has decreased, so has the level of unhappiness necessary to prompt it (Booth & White, 1980; Levinger & Moles, 1978). Thus, although women's labor-force participation does not reduce marital happiness, it does increase the likelihood of divorce (Booth et al., 1984).

Children

Couples with children in the home tend to be less happy than childless couples. Why is this? There appear to be two reasons. One is that children do, in fact, cause problems between the wife and husband. The birth of the first child doubles the spouses' role obligations. The marital dyad becomes a triad, with the newest member intruding on the marital relationship by disrupting sleep, interrupting schedules, and curtailing some of the joint activities the couple previously pursued (Feldman, 1971; Figley, 1973; Miller, 1976).

A second reason, however, may be just as important. Having children in the home reduces the likelihood that people in unhappy marriages will divorce. Preschoolers especially increase the emotional and financial costs of divorce (Cherlin, 1981). In households with preschoolers, the mother is somewhat less likely to be working, daycare expenses are enormous, and both spouses are likely to be at the bottom of their career ladders, with relatively low earnings. All of these factors mean that there are many barriers to breaking up the marriage even though it may be unsatisfactory. Because of this, a sample of families with preschoolers turns up more unhappy marriages than a sample of childless couples. In this case, the children don't cause the unhappiness; they just retard the divorce.

"Why, no...I thought he was from your previous marriage..."

Summary

In spite of high divorce rates—or perhaps because of them—the majority of married couples in the United States are relatively satisfied and happy. For example, approximately three out of four adults surveyed between 1973 and 1978 reported either a very great deal or a great deal of satisfaction with family life (National Opinion Research Center, 1978). Similarly, nearly 70 percent reported being very happy in their marriages, and most of the remaining 30 percent said they were pretty happy. Undoubtedly, these high levels of reported happiness owe something to the fact that the unhappy marriages had already ended in divorce.

Violence in the Family

Home is supposed to be the place where you can let your hair down and retreat from the tensions and problems of the workaday world. Instead, for millions, home is another place of tension and problems; for some it is a place of danger.

Estimates of the proportion of adults and children affected by family violence are unreliable. In the first place, most people are ashamed of violent acts within families and will not be truthful in surveys or on questionnaires. An even greater problem is definitional. What is family violence? Recent surveys of parents show that 80 to 90 percent spank their children at some stage in childhood development (Bybee, 1979). At what level does physical punishment become defined as abuse? And what about emotional abuse?

Abuse is a loaded term. It implies actions that are shameful, despicable, and intolerable. As with almost all social judgments, what constitutes abuse varies from time to time and place to place. A very general definition of *abuse* is deliberate action that is intended to harm another emotionally or physically and that is contrary to social norms. Generally, norms in our society specify that physical aggression and punishment are never justified against a spouse. Thus slapping one's wife is abuse. However, corporal punishment is generally approved of for children, and slapping or spanking one's child is not defined as abuse. A key to defining abuse, then, is not the nature of the act itself but society's reaction to it. Similarly, changing levels of abuse often reflect changing levels of tolerance rather than changing behavior.

WHAT ARE THE CIRCUMSTANCES OF ABUSE?

Using a rather broad definition of abuse, it is estimated that perhaps 1.5 to 2 million children in the United States are abused every year (Gelles, 1980). Largely on the basis of clinical data from families in treatment and survey data, several factors have been found to be associated with abuse.

One consistent conclusion is that persons who experience violence and abuse during childhood are more likely to be abusive and violent as adults than are those who do not have this experience in childhood. Domestic violence is also related to a number of structural char-

acteristics of families: income, employment status, gender, and family authority patterns (Dibble & Straus, 1980).

Research in the 1970s shows that family violence is not limited to any particular social class. Nevertheless, it is more prevalent among the lower socioeconomic classes. In part, this is because attitudes and values in the lower classes are more favorable to resolving problems through aggression. In addition, families living in poverty face many stresses: unemployment, part-time employment, and low job satisfaction of men, single parenting, financial problems, pregnancy, and wives working outside the home. These conditions are much more prevalent in low-income families and are likely to stimulate conflict that erupts into acts of violence. Families that experience violence are typically multiple-problem families (Bybee, 1979).

In addition to these major factors, severe violence against children or spouses is more likely when family members are socially isolated than when the family is integrated into the community, neighborhood, and larger kin group. A large family, alcohol problems, lack of attachment between spouses, and the absence of religious affiliation are additional conditions associated with violent family behavior. Mothers tend to abuse their children more often than fathers do, and sons are slightly more likely to be abused than are daughters. The greater abusiveness of mothers is explained, in part, by opportunity; mothers have greater involvement with their children in terms of discipline and control. The differential between sons and daughters, however, is probably the result of expected sex-role differences between males and females. Although adolescents are somewhat more likely to be targets of aggressive behavior from their parents, infants and young children are the ones most apt to be injured by their parents' aggression.

POLICY ALTERNATIVES FOR CHILD ABUSE

Historically, in Western culture, parents were seen as having absolute rights over their children—including the right to abuse them, maim them, sell them into slavery, or even kill them (Radbill, 1974). Children, like sofas, were private property to be used as parents saw fit. Increasingly, though, our culture defines children as having certain rights, one of which is the right to be free from abuse.

The rights of children, however, come directly into conflict with the rights of parents and the individual's right of privacy. If children are to have the right to be free of abuse, then some agency must have the authority to enforce that right and to observe and control what goes on within families. Even people who feel strongly about the need to protect children worry about the potential dangers of giving government the right to control what goes on within families. Big brother seems just around the corner.

The touchiness of the issue and the general wariness of officials in this area is well illustrated by the case of Mary Ellen, who, in 1871, was removed from her home because of severe physical abuse. In order to get official approval for removing her from her parents, the humane society (Society for the Prevention of Cruelty to Animals) had to demonstrate that Mary Ellen was an animal and hence subject to protection under the law that forbade cruelty to animals. There was no law preventing cruelty to children.

In the century since Mary Ellen was defended by the humane society, every state has passed laws intended to reduce child abuse. These laws are of two types. The first tries to increase the identification and reporting of abuse by making it mandatory for doctors, hospitals, and schools to report suspected instances of child abuse. The second tries to prevent such abuse.

Unfortunately, it is beyond the scope of public policy to resolve the situations in which child abuse develops: poverty, unsatisfactory jobs, and social isolation. Instead, social policy currently concentrates on devising temporary alternatives to help parents who find themselves in these situations. Included are a number of public programs: crisis lines for parents who need help handling their anger, crisis nurseries where parents at their wits' end can leave their children temporarily, counseling programs for families who have had previous problems and are at high risk for abuse, and foster grandparents' programs for parents who are temporarily unable to handle their children.

No one is in favor of child abuse. Reports of battered, maltreated, or murdered children cause anger in everybody. The crucial sociological insight into violence is the recognition that, like other recurrent behaviors, violence is socially structured. It is not a unique behavior that can be understood only through individual analysis. Rather, understanding and responding to family violence requires an understanding of the social patterns that support and encourage it.

SUMMARY

1. Marriage, family, and kinship are the most basic institutions found in society. In all societies, these institutions meet such universal needs as regulation of sexual behavior, replacement through reproduction, child-care, and socialization.

2. Cross-cultural comparisons demonstrate that the structure and function of the family vary considerably. Preindustrial economies tend to place greater emphasis on extended families, on family participation in mate selection, and on male dominance. In industrial societies, norms prescribe a nuclear family, individual choice in mate selection, and more egalitarian authority patterns.

3. Almost all Americans marry. Courtship practices encourage individual freedom in the selection of a marriage partner, although parental control occurs indirectly. Romantic love is stressed as a basis for selection.

4. In recent years, cohabitation has increased rapidly. For most people, living together is a prelude to marriage rather than an alternative to it.

5. Major changes in U.S. family patterns in recent decades include postponement of marriage, reduced fertility, increased illegitimacy, and increased probability of divorce.

6. The sexual revolution of the 1960s and 1970s has resulted in more people experiencing premarital sexual relationships and a decline in the double standard. The sexual scripts for marriage have changed, and spouses are expected to be more equal sexual partners.

7. The increasing participation of wives in the breadwinning role is a major change in family roles. This change has not been accompanied by significant increases in the husband's role at home.

8. The parenting role tends to rest more heavily on women than men. Although it is a role that most Americans are eager to embrace, it is stressful. Most people welcome the empty nest.

9. Approximately 50 percent of all marriages being contracted now are expected to end in divorce. Factors that affect the likelihood of divorce are homogamy, age at marriage, family income, employment (both husband's and wife's), and presence of children.

10. Family violence and abuse occur in all types of families. They are more common, however, in multiple-problem families—those facing unemployment, single parenting, or poverty.

SUGGESTED READINGS

Blumstein, Phillip, & Schwartz, Pepper. (1983). American Couples. New York: Morrow. An extensive study of marital relationships in the United States, based on thousands of questionnaires and hundreds of interviews. Primary emphasis is given to money, work, and sex as major dimensions around which couples choose to structure their most intimate relationships.

Cherlin, Andrew. (1981). Marriage, Divorce, Remarriage. Cambridge, Mass.: Harvard University Press. One of the best sources documenting the historical trends and patterns of marriage, divorce, and remarriage in the United States.

Finkelhor, David, Gelles, Richard J., Hotaling, Gerald T., & Straus, Murray A. (eds.). (1983). The Dark Side of Families: Current Family Violence Research. Beverly Hills, Calif.: Sage Publications. A collection of readings on family violence assembled by leading researchers in the field.

Kephart, William M. (1983). Extraordinary Groups: The Sociology of Unconventional Life-Styles (2d ed.). New York: St. Martin's Press. A fascinating tour of some of the most interesting variations in U.S. family practices within subcultures and countercultures, both past and present: the Oneidans, Mormons, Amish, gypsies, Shakers, and Hutterites. Painless and interesting sociology by a well-established family sociologist who has traced and analyzed the consequences of extraordinary family life-styles in the United States.

Masnick, George, & Bane, Mary Jo. (1980). The Nation's Families: 1960–1990. Cambridge, Mass.: Joint Center for Urban Studies of MIT and Harvard University. A report examining recent changes in the U.S. family and containing projections about the future.

Rubin, Lillian. (1976). Worlds of Pain. New York: Basic Books. One of the best descriptions of what it means to be working class in America. Based on in-depth interviews with husbands and wives, this book contains numerous quotes that illustrate growing up, getting married, parenting, and coping in families that are strained by low-paying jobs, unemployment, and economic difficulties. Essential reading.

Spiro, Melford. (1975). Children of the Kibbutz. Cambridge, Mass.: Harvard University Press. An exploration of the collective childrearing practices and socialization of children in agricultural communes in Israel.

Weitzman, Lenore. (1981). The Marriage Contract: Spouses, Lovers, and the Law. New York: Free Press. A comprehensive analysis of how laws related to marriage and family favor men and affect marital relationships. An excellent illustration of the interdependence of our legal institutions and the family. Also contains useful information on drawing up a marriage contract based on equalitarian relationships between partners.

CHAPTER 12

EDUCATION

PROLOGUE

Have You Ever . . . seriously considered not going to college? For many of you, going to college was as normal as starting first grade, and neither you nor your parents ever seriously considered whether it was a good thing. It was just assumed that you would go. (For this reason, you may now be a premajor, trying to make up your mind why you are here.) Others have had to break tradition to attend college. You may be the first in your family or your neighborhood to do so.

Regardless of which group you belong to, you have already been in school for at least 12 years. During those years, you hailed Christmas and summer vacations with a cheer and looked forward eagerly to high school graduation. Yet, here you are again, slogging away at the books, the homework, and the term papers. Why?

For those who have asked themselves this question, the answer probably rests on a realistic assessment of the job market. What kinds of jobs are available for a 17-year-old high school graduate, and what kind of future do such jobs hold? Clerking at Penney's or making hamburgers at McDonald's may be a good enough job at 17, but do you really want to be doing it when you're 40? Education is rightly seen as a way to a better future. This chapter describes the modern educational system and addresses some of the ways education affects our lives and life chances.

Education is one of our most enduring and familiar institutions. Most of us spend at least 12 years going to school, and some spend 16 or even 20 years as students. When we include the teachers, secretaries, janitors, and administrators who work in the schools, 65 million Americans are directly involved in education every day; 3 of every 10 Americans are either enrolled in school or employed within the educational system. Even those not actually in the system are involved as taxpayers, parents, or former students. However we choose to look at it, education is part of our lives.

The school system is designed to make us literate, teach us the values of our culture, and prepare us for adult statuses. The schools teach specialized skills for a changing labor force, promote the development of new knowledge, and integrate society's members through a common core of values (Parelius & Parelius, 1978).

These same educational institutions, however, have been criticized for promoting racism, sexism, and inequality. Critics charge that schools tend to exploit people by channeling them into programs of study and political attitudes that serve the interests of the powerful (Bowles & Gintis, 1976).

These contrasting views of education raise important sociological concerns about the characteristics of schools and the purposes they serve. What are all the people doing in schools? Why are vast amounts of money being spent on education? What purposes are being achieved? Who benefits? These are all critical questions that citizens, educators, and sociologists have raised.

Development of Mass Education

During the last 2 centuries, industrialization and urbanization have transformed the U.S. institutional landscape. Two major long-term trends in education during this period are a shift from elite to mass education and increasing bureaucratization (Katz, 1975; Parelius & Parelius, 1978).

The Shift from Elite to Mass Education

Prior to the 19th century, education was reserved primarily for the elite. General education for the masses began at the elementary school level in the 19th century, moved to the secondary school level in the first half of the 20th century, and spread to the college level only after World War II (Boocock, 1976).

The Preindustrial Era (1607–1812). In colonial America, education was a local responsibility, and communities varied in the extent to which formal schooling was available. Many early schools were church-sponsored, and their programs focused on reading, particularly the Scriptures. In 1647, the Massachusetts Bay Colony passed what is now affectionately referred to as "The Old Deluder Act." This law made education compulsory in the colony in order to foil that "old deluder Satan," who was thought to be intent on keeping people from knowledge of the Scriptures.

Formal schooling in the early colonies was instituted for moral and religious reasons. It was not designed to prepare children for work; nor was it a prerequisite for most jobs. In short, it was a luxury and, as such, was enjoyed more often by the wealthy than by the working class. Education for adult occupations took place outside the classroom; most children learned adult work roles by working beside their parents. Children of the poor often received their training through apprenticeship programs.

During this period, children from black families rarely received an education, and they were much less likely to be apprenticed than were the children of white families. In fact, prior to the Civil War, most southern states had "compulsory ignorance" laws—laws making it illegal to teach slaves to read or write. It was feared that education would heighten the aspirations of blacks and increase their ability to communicate and organize. In the northern states, schools were available for free blacks, but these schools were almost always segregated and poorly funded (Hare & Swift, 1976).

The Early Industrial Period (1812–1930). The early years of industrialization were turbulent in our society. Urban growth, technological development, changing labor demands, and massive numbers of immigrants at the turn of the century were among the many changes that led to a dramatic surge in educational opportunities.

THE LABOR MOVEMENT.   One outgrowth of the terrible working conditions of the early industrial period was the labor movement. In its concern for improving the conditions of the working class, labor organized in support of free public education. This support was based on the belief that education would help working-class children avoid poverty and exploitation. It was also based on a desire to keep young workers (cheap labor) out of the labor market, thereby preserving jobs for adults. By the 1850s, public schools had been established in all of the major cities where labor was organized. Although attendance was not compulsory, schooling was available.

IMMIGRATION.   Between 1850 and 1930, the United States experienced massive immigration. Many of the new immigrants, particularly those from Southern and Eastern Europe (Italians, Greeks, Russians), located in the

Figure 12.1

These adults are attending an Americanization class where their text is "English for Foreigners." These classes were intended to help immigrants prepare for their citizenship examinations and introduce them to American values, language, and customs. Some argued that the classes were necessary in order to help immigrants abandon their old ways and more rapidly adopt the ways of their new country. The teaching of English was also intended to increase the immigrants' skills and usefulness in the labor force.

large industrial cities. They brought with them the values, customs, and languages of their homelands, a diversity many viewed with alarm and concern. How could these diverse groups of people be assimilated into the American culture? The answer was found in the Americanization of immigrants through formal schooling.

The pressures of the labor movement and the need to absorb new immigrants were two of the forces behind the expansion of education. Others included the need to provide organized activity for urban children, a decreased need for child labor, and the demands of industry for literate workers. These combined forces led to a tremendous expansion in education at the end of the 19th century. Compulsory-attendance laws gradually spread throughout the country, and between 1870 and 1910 the number of high schools increased twentyfold, from 500 to 10,000 (Trow, 1973).

Although there was widespread consensus that compulsory education was in the best interests of society, debate existed over educational techniques and curriculums. Educators pushed for a liberal arts program to open children's minds and develop critical thinking. Industry favored a curriculum that emphasized the virtues of work and discipline. Union leaders and labor were committed to the idea that schools should be their children's road to upward mobility.

Throughout this early period, controversy raged over the shape of education. Wealthy Eastern elites operated free pauper schools, intended to reform the habits of the poor and the immigrants. By contrast, schools in the rural areas were usually financed and controlled by parents. There the local community controlled a curriculum that reflected local religious and moral values. A third alternative, private schools and military academies, also emerged. They were financed and controlled by wealthy parents and alumni.

Although private education and religious education still exist in the United States, by the end of the 19th century the basic framework of U.S. education had been established along the democratic lines of the earlier rural school districts. Education is locally financed and locally controlled, a public institution that reflects the public purse and the dominant cultural and social values of the community. This means, as one critical observer notes, that public education in the United States is "free, compulsory, bureaucratic, racist and class biased" (Katz, 1975:xviii).

The Mature Industrial Period (1930–present). Mass elementary school education was well established by the turn of the century. It was not until the 1930s, however, that high school graduation became common, and it was 1950 before half of America's 17-year-olds had graduated from high school. If your grandparents graduated from high school, they were part of a small minority.

The expansion in secondary and college education is largely a phenomenon of the post–World War II years. As Table 12.1 demonstrates, the vast majority of adult Americans in 1940 were not high school graduates, and only a small fraction attended college. These relatively low levels of education were even more pronounced in the nonwhite population. The

Table 12.1   Percent of Adults 25 and Older Who Have Graduated from High School and College, by Race and Gender, 1940–1982

There has been a sharp increase in high school and college graduation since 1940. Although all segments of the population have been included in this increase, nonwhites have increased their education faster than whites. The result is a narrowing gap between white and nonwhite education.

	WHITES		NONWHITES	
	Males	Females	Males	Females
Percent Graduated from High School				
1982	73%	72%	56%	54%
1980	71	70	51	51
1970	57	58	35	37
1960	42	45	20	23
1947	33	36	12	14
1940	24	28	7	8
Percent Graduated from College				
1982	23	14	9	9
1980	22	14	8	8
1970	15	9	7	6
1960	10	6	8	4
1947	9	5	2	3
1940	6	4	1	1

SOURCE: U.S. Bureau of the Census, 1975:380 and 1984:144.

South provided public elementary school education to black students in segregated facilities, but it offered them few secondary schools. Black parents who wanted their children to attend secondary school usually had to send them away from home to church-sponsored boarding schools. Although segregated schools have not been legal since the Supreme Court's 1954 decision against the Topeka, Kansas, Board of Education, many of today's black adults are products of this segregated and unequal school system. Thus, although the education gap is closing for the current generation, black adults over age 25 are still significantly disadvantaged relative to white adults.

From the 1940s on, changes in labor demand and a growing search for upward mobility meant that it would be only a matter of time before mass education extended itself into colleges and universities. Numerous social conditions contributed to this expansion. The GI Bill sent millions of veterans of World War II, the Korean War, and the Viet Nam War to college. During the 1960s, a desire to avoid being drafted encouraged many young men to stay in college. Later, the civil rights movement and expanding roles of women resulted in more minorities and women attending college. As a result of these forces, college enrollments rose dramatically. In the last decade, slightly over 25 percent of all 18-to-24-year-olds have been enrolled in institutions of higher education. There has also been a large increase in the number of persons over the age of 24 returning to college on a part-time basis.

Within this century, education has expanded enormously. Both the proportions and the numbers attending school at all levels have increased. One consequence of this growth is that education is becoming increasingly bureaucratic.

The Trend toward Increasing Bureaucratization

An institution that deals with 65 million people daily has got to be a complex organization. Thus it is no surprise to find that education in the United States is highly bureaucratic. This process began in the 19th century and still continues. Among the signs of bureaucratization are standardization, hierarchies of authority, and professionalization of staff.

Standardization. Rules and regulations within the school system are designed to promote standardization at a variety of levels. Course offerings, textbooks, lunch programs, length of the school year, and teacher certification standards are increasingly uniform. Although there are still local, state, and regional variations, these become smaller with every year.

Hierarchies of Authority. In place of the one-room schoolhouse, where the teacher was responsible only to parents, there has developed an increasingly complex hierarchy of authority. Beginning with the state of New York in 1812, local school boards have been consolidated into state boards of education, which are charged with coordinating and standardizing education across the state. An even higher level of supervision has been developing, although somewhat unevenly, at the federal level.

Specialization and Professionalization of Personnel. As education has become more bureaucratized, formal credentials have become more important in hiring, firing, and promotion. The teacher who covered all fields has been replaced by the specialist. The well-staffed school has a speech therapist, a media specialist, and a staff of counselors in addition to teachers who may teach only a narrow range of courses.

Local Control versus Standardization. Education is still financed largely by local taxes and controlled largely by state and local school boards, which means that there is a great deal of variety from state to state and even from county to county in textbook selection and curriculums. School boards can, as they recently did in Texas, require that creationism (the Genesis story) be taught in the public schools as an alternative to evolution. Local control and local financing also mean wide disparities in school financing: In 1981, the state of Alabama spent under $1,400 per pupil; in the same year, Oregon and Massachusetts spent over $3,000 per pupil. Differences in community prosperity and in willingness to fund public education create not just differences in education but also major inequalities in the quality of public education.

Increasingly, the federal government has intervened in order to create greater standardization among public schools. This intervention has been most apparent on issues of segregation and discrimination on the basis of race and gender. Federal funds may be withheld to force compliance,

Figure 12.2
After World War II, high school and then college education was opened to the masses. High school graduation has become the norm and college education is no longer restricted to the economic and intellectual elite. Large lecture classes such as this help colleges inexpensively process several hundred students. Those who have the talent or grit to continue their college education past the first year or two will undoubtedly be rewarded by smaller classes that are more personal.

Figure 12.3

Over the years, education has become more and more standardized. Students' scores on such standard examinations as the California or Iowa Achievement Tests show not only how a student fares compared to others, but also how their teachers, their school, and their school district compare. And, although the performance standards are shared, the resources to achieve them are still unequal and the quality of education is far from uniform across the United States.

and litigation may be sought to resolve cases of inequity. The vigor with which federal programs are pursued, however, has varied sharply from one administration to the next. Whereas the Carter administration pressed strongly for federal oversight of local programs, the Reagan administration has preferred local control. The long-term trend, however, has clearly been in the direction of reducing local control and increasing standardization.

Education in the United States: Three Models

The U.S. educational system, an extremely expensive system, was deliberately established to meet certain goals. What has the system accomplished, and for whom? In this section, we will examine three sociological perspectives of education: the structural-functional, conflict, and systems models. Each offers a different perspective on the major accomplishments of education.

Structural-Functional Model

A structural-functional analysis of education is concerned with the consequences of educational institutions for the maintenance of society. It points out both how education contributes to the maintenance of society and how educational systems can be forces for change and conflict.

The Functions of Education.   The educational system has been designed to meet multiple needs. Major manifest (intended) functions of education include cultural reproduction, social control, assimilation, training and development, selection and allocation, and promotion of change.

CULTURAL REPRODUCTION.   Schools transmit society's culture from one generation to the next by teaching the ideas, customs, and standards of the culture. We learn to read and write our language, we learn the pledge of allegiance, and we learn history. In this sense, education builds on the past and conserves traditions.

SOCIAL CONTROL.   Second only to the family, schools are responsible for socializing the young into patterns of conformity. By emphasizing a common culture and instilling habits of discipline and obedience, the schools are an important agent for encouraging conformity.

ASSIMILATION.   Schools function to assimilate persons from diverse backgrounds. By exposing students from all ethnic backgrounds, all regions of the country, and all social backgrounds to a common curriculum, they help create and maintain a common cultural base.

TRAINING AND DEVELOPMENT.   Schools teach specific skills—not only technical skills such as reading, writing, and arithmetic but also habits of cooperation, punctuality, and obedience.

SELECTION AND ALLOCATION.   Schools are like gardeners; they sift, weed, sort, and cultivate their products, determining which students will be allowed to go on and which will not. Standards of achievement are used as criteria to channel students into different programs on the basis of their measured abilities. Ideally, an important function of the school system is to ensure the best use of the best minds. The public school system is a vital element of our commitment to equal opportunity.

PROMOTION OF CHANGE.   Schools also act as change agents. Although we do not quit learning after we leave school, new knowledge and technology are usually aimed at schoolchildren rather than at the adult population. In addition, the schools promote change by encouraging critical and analytic skills and skepticism. Schools, particularly colleges and universities, are also expected to produce new knowledge.

Figure 12.4
Schools teach much more than the ABC's. After our family, they are probably the most important agent of socialization, introducing us to our culture and our history. We learn the Pledge of Allegiance and Star Spangled Banner, make pilgrim hats, and learn about Abraham Lincoln and George Washington. In this way, schools are an important conserver of tradition, helping to maintain continuity with the past.

Latent Functions and Dysfunctions.   In spite of its many positive outcomes, a system as large and all-encompassing as education is bound to have consequences that are either unintended or actually negative. They include generation gaps, custodial care, youth cultures, rationalization of inequality, and perpetuation of inequality.

GENERATION GAP.   As schools impart new knowledge, they may drive a wedge between generations. Courses in sociology, English, history, and even biology expose students to ideas different from those of their parents. What students learn in school about evolution, cultural relativity, or the merits of socialism may contradict values held by their parents or their religion.

CUSTODIAL CARE.   Compulsory education has transformed schools into settings where children are cooped up 7 to 8 hours a day, 5 days a week, for 9 months of the year (Bowles, 1972). Young people are kept off the streets, out of the labor force, and, presumably, out of trouble in small groups dispersed throughout communities in special buildings designed for close supervision. This setup enables their elders to command higher wages in the labor market and relieves their parents of the responsibility of supervising them.

YOUTH CULTURE.   By isolating young people from the larger society and confining them to the company of others their own age, educational institutions have contributed to the development of a unique youth culture. As one observer has noted, youth "constitute a small society, one that has most of its important interactions within itself, and maintains only a few threads of connection with the outside adult society" (Coleman, 1961:3).

RATIONALIZATION OF INEQUALITY.   One of the chief consequences of life in the schools is that young people learn to expect unequal rewards on the basis of differential achievement. Schools prepare young people for inequality. Some consider this preparation undesirable in that it leads young people to believe that all inequality is earned, that it is a fair response to unequal abilities.

PERPETUATION OF INEQUALITY.   The most significant criticism launched against education is that schooling benefits some groups more than others. Abundant evidence exists that ascriptive characteristics of students (race, gender, and social class) have an impact on how students are treated in school. The evidence supports the conclusion that schools perpetuate inequality, particularly for minorities and disadvantaged students, and function to maintain and reinforce the existing social-class hierarchy. This criticism is at the heart of the conflict theory of education.

Summary.   A structural-functional analysis begins with the premise that any ongoing institution of society must be contributing to the maintenance of society. The enumeration of the functions of education clarifies what some of these contributions are. Although there are unanticipated side effects, both positive and negative, functionalists tend to concentrate on how education benefits society and individuals.

Conflict Model

Conflict theory offers a critical perspective on the relationship between education and the social-class system. Conflict theorists argue that modern education serves the interests of the elite—in short, that education is a capitalist tool.

There is no question that the shift from elite to mass education paralleled the development of capitalism. This is history. Conflict theorists argue, however, that mass education developed in response to the economic interests of powerful capitalists. Capitalism required a steady supply of skilled workers who had acquired the values and behaviors conducive to industrial productivity. Educated workers were presumed to be more productive not only because they could read and write but also because their schools taught them obedience, punctuality, and loyalty to the economic and political system. Schools, it is argued, reinforce the idea that inequalities result from merit and achievement rather than coercion. These conditions have provided an ideal work force for capitalism by helping to legitimate inequality.

Credentialism.   In the modern world, the elite cannot directly ensure that their children stay members of the elite. Although status and social class are remarkably continuous over generations, the ability of parents to pass on their social-class attainments depends to a large extent on their ability to provide their children with appropriate educational credentials (Blau & Duncan, 1967).

This does not mean that discrimination on the basis of class background no longer occurs. Rather, according to conflict theorists, it means that a subtle shift has taken place. Instead of enquiring who your parents are, the prospective employer asks what kind of education you have and where you got it. Because these educational credentials are highly correlated with social-class background, they serve to keep undesirables out. Conflict theorists argue that educational credentials are mere window dressing; apparently based on merit and achievement, **credentialism** is really a surrogate for social-class background. As the level of education in society increases, educational requirements also must rise in order to maintain the status quo. This credential inflation can be seen in nursing, in public school teaching, and in government. Jobs that used to require a high school diploma now require a bachelor's degree; jobs that used to require a bachelor's degree now require a master's degree. Because the elite increases its pursuit of higher degrees as quickly as the lower class increases its pursuit of a high school diploma, no real change occurs. Credentialism, it is argued, is a way of manipulating the educational system for the benefit of the well-off (Collins, 1979).

Systems Model

The **systems model of education** (input/output model) focuses on how the output from schools depends on both the diversity of input (children) and life in the schools. Unlike the functional and conflict models, the systems model focuses on process; it is concerned with how the schools transform the raw material of 5- and 6-year-olds into finished products

Figure 12.5
American schools are based on competition not cooperation. "Me first, me first—call on me," is the guiding principle. We compete for teachers' attention, for grades, and for a spot on the team. In the process, we come to believe that the best, brightest, and hardest working are justified in getting the most reward. Conflict theorists suggest that fostering such attitudes in the schools helps children to rationalize and accept inequality in the economy.

Credentialism is the practice of using educational degrees as job requirements to ward off any encroachment of the lower class on upper-class jobs.

Systems model of education (input/output model) focuses on how the output from the schools depends on both the diversity of input (children) and life in the schools.

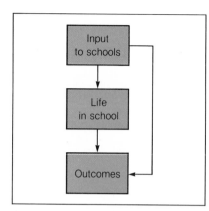

Figure 12.6   The Systems Model of Education

Does schooling make a difference? If people bypassed schools altogether, would they end up in roughly the same place in the social-class hierarchy of society? The systems model of education suggests that schools do not do a very good job of providing equal opportunity and that children leave the school system with the same inequalities they entered with.
SOURCE: Adapted from Boocock, 1976:1

12 or 16 years later (see Figure 12.6). Major questions posed by this perspective are: Does schooling make a difference? To what extent are differences in educational attainment a simple repetition of the inequalities in background with which students enter school? Or does schooling alter the effects of early background?

Although there are a few studies showing that teacher expectations and school climate can affect achievement (Brookover et al., 1979), most of the recent research concludes that schooling does not alter the effects of early background:

> Indeed, if there was a basic sociological finding of the 1960's, it was that it is difficult to document any enduring effects of school or school programs upon student learning—in most societies, including our own, a child's achievement and success in school are more related to the social status of his family and of the other students in his school than to any factors of school organization, curriculum, or teachers' training and techniques. . . . By the time children enter school, they have already been shaped by their background and environment, so that they each possess a set of qualities, experiences, and expectations through which the school experience must filter. [Boocock, 1976:1]

Of course, students learn. When they graduate from high school, many can type, write complete sentences, and maybe even differentiate equations. What research indicates is that what they learn depends significantly on the quality of the input. Students who enter kindergarten with the rank 1, 2, 3, or 4 on the basis of their parents' social class will tend to come out with the same rank on the basis of their own school achievements.

Input to Schools.   Children in the United States begin their formal education at the age of 6. Because of increasing proportions of working mothers, however, many children are starting their school experiences much earlier. In 1982, 49 percent of U.S. children between the ages of 3 and 5 were enrolled in preprimary schools; more than 99 percent of the population between the ages of 7 and 13 is enrolled in school (U.S. Bureau of the Census, 1984, table 219).

Children begin school with very different backgrounds in home environment, race, social class, and family composition. All these factors affect their experiences in the schools. Children reared in middle-class families, for example, are much more likely to have been socialized toward independence, self-direction, curiosity, initiative, and self-control. Parents from lower socioeconomic classes tend to emphasize qualities that make children acceptable to others: obedience, neatness and appearance, honesty, and docility (Kohn, 1969). Developed prior to school, these qualities represent differences that schools and teachers are somehow expected to minimize under the auspices of equal educational opportunities.

Parents' social class also determines the neighborhoods in which children are raised (inner city, suburb, farm), the types of schools in which they enroll, and the standard of living they have experienced thus far. Children from disadvantaged backgrounds are likely to experience economic hardships that work against them in all their daily experiences in school. They are likely to lack a set of encyclopedias and a home computer. Furthermore, it is likely that their parents will be too caught up in the struggles of day-to-day living to have the time or energy to help them with

Figure 12.7
These small boys will spend 12 or maybe 16 years in the school system. What will they be like when they emerge? The input-output model of education focuses on how the schools deal with their raw materials—how they track, sort, evaluate, and ultimately graduate students ranked from top to bottom on achievement. A central question is whether the processes that occur in the school favor children from more affluent and educated backgrounds.

their studies. Paying the bills may be more important than trying to improve their children's SAT scores.

Family size and birth order may also have an effect on school performance (see chapter 11). Research has shown that firstborns and children from smaller families perform better in school than do later-born children and those from larger families. Usually, this difference is attributable to greater adult stimulation in the early years, but it may also be due to fewer resources in larger families. Although this is a complex situation, available research indicates that large families reduce school achievement.

The systems perspective views these differences in social-class background and early socialization as important conditions affecting what children learn in school. The schools cannot eliminate these differences, and, in fact, they tend to reinforce them.

Life in School. The schools are highly bureaucratized organizations that are supposed to apply uniform curriculums to all students. A standard curriculum, however, may produce far from standard results when applied to students with very different backgrounds and preschool experiences. These differential results are also a product of four processes occurring in the schools: the hidden curriculum, the emphasis on evaluation and achievement, the tracking process, and the youth culture.

THE HIDDEN CURRICULUM. At home and in their own neighborhoods, U.S. children have few responsibilities, are relatively self-centered, and spend most of their days watching television and fooling around (Boocock, 1975,

The **hidden curriculum** is the unofficial program of studies in the schools, the three Rs of which are rules, regulations, and routines.

1976). One of the most wrenching aspects of starting school is trading this casual life-style for one that is regulated by clocks, bells, and seating charts. The three Rs of the **hidden curriculum**—rules, regulations, and routines—are the "things students and teachers must learn if they are to make their way with minimum pain in the social institution called the school" (Jackson, 1972:81). They must learn to be patient, to wait their turn, to obey rules, to be punctual, and to show respect. These behaviors are consistent with what is expected in the labor force, especially from the working class (Dale, 1977). A central role of schools, conflict theorists point out, is socialization for obedience and acceptance of inequality, values that enable youths to make the transition into adult economic roles fairly easily.

EVALUATION AND ACHIEVEMENT.   Life in the schools also means achievement through competition; schools reward or punish on the basis of structured competition. Children are supposed to want to raise their hands and say, "Call on me, call on me!" They are supposed to want to be first, to do best, to compete with their peers. From stars on the blackboard to senior class rankings, competitive rewards are the spur used to encourage learning. In this sense, life in the schools is a microcosm of the larger society, mirroring its values on achievement and competition.

TRACKING.   Schools constantly evaluate, sort, and select students on the basis of achievement and competition. Some students are directed into college preparatory tracks, others into vocational education, and still others into remedial classes.

Tracking occurs when evaluations relatively early in a child's career determine the educational programs the child will be encouraged to follow.

There is a great deal of controversy over this practice. Ideally, **tracking** is supposed to benefit the gifted and the slow learners. By having classes that are geared to their levels, both should learn faster and both should benefit from increased teacher attention. Instead, research suggests that bright students benefit substantially more than slow students (Alexander et al., 1978). The slow students no longer have the benefit of interaction with those whose achievements and ambitions are higher than their own. Furthermore, they are saddled with the formal label *remedial*. The labeling can result in a self-fulfilling prophecy. Because a child has been labeled a slow learner or even stupid, parents, teachers, and the child all lower their expectations; at the end of 12 years, it surprises no one that the child does not know very much.

The labeling and tracking process is of special concern because there is considerable evidence that evaluations by teachers often reflect the cultural stereotypes and prejudices of their communities. Gender, race, ethnicity, and social class often influence the extent to which a child is encouraged or discouraged. A middle-class child, for example, who blurts out answers in class may be considered bright but overeager, whereas a lower-class child who does the same may be viewed as disruptive. A boy who directs the activities of other children may be considered a leader when his female counterpart is judged aggressive or bossy.

The effect of the labeling and tracking process on both teacher expectations and children's performance was shown in an unusual experiment in an elementary school in San Francisco. At the beginning of the school year, 20 percent of the students in grades 1 through 6 were identified to their teachers as being potentially late bloomers. These children were in a school that had a relatively high rate of turnover and a high proportion of Mexican American children. Throughout the school year and into the next grade, additional IQ tests were administered. The improvement in IQ scores for this particular group during the school year confirmed that these students were indeed late bloomers. The children who showed the greatest gains were those from whom their teachers had previously expected the least (the Mexican American boys who looked most Mexican). What is of interest in this study is that the children identified as late bloomers were actually selected at random rather than on the basis of initial IQ scores. Since the researchers did not observe the classes or the teachers between the testing periods, it can be inferred that the teachers brought about the change in IQ by altering their expectations for these children and that the children themselves responded to a more positive label (Rosenthal & Jacobson, 1968).

THE YOUTH CULTURE.   A student's passage through the school system is affected not only by the formal and informal curriculum of the schools but also by the expectations of peers. In a 1961 study of high school values, Coleman found that a student's popularity and peer group status depended primarily on participation in extracurricular activities. Academic achievement was less important. The most important activity boys wished to be remembered for was being athletic, whereas girls wished to be remembered for being a leader in activities and being most popular. Having a good personality and reputation, being athletic, and having good looks, a car, and nice clothes were the most important ways to achieve success with your peers. In fact, high grades unaccompanied by achievement in other areas could detract from a student's popularity, especially for girls. The all-around boy, the one who was both an athlete and a scholar, was more popular than the boy who was an athlete only, however.

Figure 12.8
More than any other institution in society, schools are responsible for the creation of youth culture. Through enforced association, young people turn to one another for values and attitudes. Being popular, having a good time, the right clothes, or the right music become overriding concerns. Actual schoolwork is not forgotten, but it tends to be a minor focus of youth culture.

FOCUS ON MEASUREMENT

Measuring Mental Ability

● How many legs does a Kaffir have?

● Who wrote *Great Expectations?*

● Which word is out of place?
sanctuary—nave—altar—attic—apse

● If you throw the dice and 7 is showing on top, what is facing down?
7—snake eyes—boxcars—little joes—11

If you have answered 2, Dickens, attic, and 7, then you get the highest possible score on this test. What does that mean? Does it mean that you have genetically superior mental ability, that you read a lot, that you shoot craps? What could you safely conclude about a person who got only two questions right?

The standardized test is one of the most familiar aspects of life in the schools. Whether it is the California or the Iowa Achievement Test, the SAT or the ACT, students are constantly being evaluated. Most of these tests are truly achievement tests; they measure what has been learned and make no pretense of measuring the capacity to learn. IQ tests, however, are supposed to measure the innate capacity to learn—mental ability. People who rank highly on one kind of test tend to rank highly on the other, though, and both are effective predictors of grades and educational attainment (Jencks, et al., 1972). They are used for guiding students into various tracks and for college placement. In short, they are important; people

use them to make real decisions about real people. On these tests, black, Hispanic, and Native American students consistently score below Anglo students and working-class students score substantially below middle-class students. The differences in test scores help ensure that the stratification patterns of the next generation will look very much like those of this generation.

The obvious question is whether these tests are fair measures. Are black, Hispanic, Native American, and working-class youths lower in mental ability than middle-class or Anglo youths?

Before we can answer this question, we must first ask another: What is mental ability? Most scholars recognize that it is a combination of genetic potential and prior social experiences. It is an aspect of personality, "the capacity of the individual to act purposefully, to think rationally and to deal effectively with his environment" (Wechsler, 1958:7).

Do questions such as those that opened this section measure any of these things? No. We can all imagine people who act purposefully, think rationally, and deal effectively with the environment but do not know who wrote *Great Expectations* and are ignorant about dice or church architecture. These people may be foreigners, they may have lacked the opportunity to go to school, or they may have come from a subculture where dice, churches, or 19th century English literature are not important.

For this reason, good IQ tests try to measure reasoning ability as well

Figure 12.9

One of the first restrictions put on immigration to the United States was a ban on the "feeble minded." This picture shows officials administering an intelligence test to a potential immigrant at Ellis Island. The test appears to be an early attempt to create a culture free test for it does not require knowledge of English. The circumstances and tasks, however, may be so strange that difficulties with the test could occur regardless of actual intelligence.

Figure 12.10 Culture-Free Intelligence Tests?

What can we conclude about your intelligence from your score on this simple test? Does a high score mean that you are naturally intelligent or have some of your experiences in life and in school prepared you for these kinds of problems? Increasingly scholars believe that it is impossible to make an intelligence test that is free of cultural influences.
SOURCE: From *Frames of Mind: The Theory of Multiple Intelligences* by Howard Gardner © 1983 by Howard Gardner. Reprinted by permission of Basic Books, Inc., Publishers.

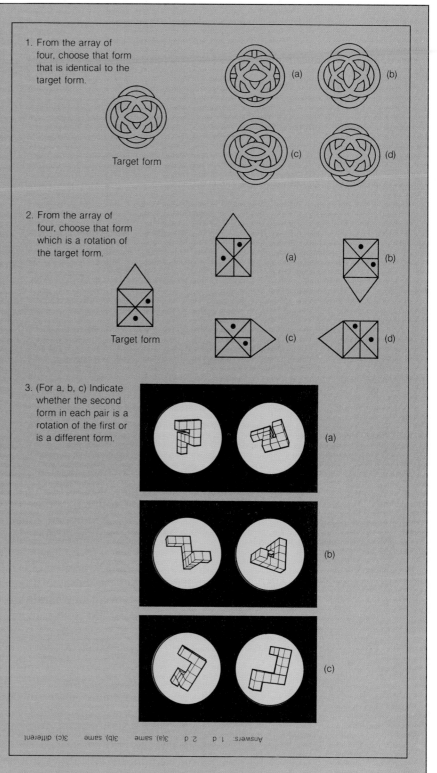

as knowledge. These nonverbal tests are supposed to measure the ability to think and reason without the assumption of formal educational opportunity. Examples of items from such a nonverbal test are reproduced in Figure 12.10. Do these nonverbal tests achieve their intention? Do they measure the ability to reason independent of years in school, subcultural background, or language difficulties? Again, the answer seems to be no.

There are two ways in which these tests are not culture-free. The first is that they reflect not only reasoning and knowledge but also competitiveness, familiarity with and acceptance of timed tests, rapport with the examiner, and achievement aspiration. Students who lack these characteristics may do poorly even though their ability to reason is well developed.

The more serious fault with such nonverbal tests is their underlying assumption. Reasoning ability is not independent of learning opportunities. How we reason, as well as what we know, depends on our prior experiences. The deprivation studies of infant monkeys and hospitalized orphans (see chapter 5) demonstrate that mental and social retardation occur as a result of sensory deprivation.

Just as the body does not develop fully without exercise, neither does the mind. Thus reasoning capacity is not culture-free; it is determined by the opportunities to develop it. For this reason, there will probably never be an IQ test that will not reflect the prior cultural experiences of the test-taker.

An IQ test score is a mixture of natural ability, exposure to appropriate stimuli, and drive to excel. A high score means that a person is likely to be a success in school, and a low score means that a person is likely to do poorly in school. Does the low score also mean that the person is stupid or lacks mental ability? No. It may mean that, but it may also mean that the student has lacked the opportunity or encouragement to learn. Since these elements cannot be untangled, many educators now recommend that IQ tests be used not as measures of natural ability but as measures of cultural deprivation. If this interpretation is generally accepted, then the test will begin doing what its originator intended nearly 100 years ago—identifying those who need help to live up to their potential.

Questions to Consider

Make two lists. In the first list, itemize the types of harm that could occur if a child's IQ score wrongly identified the child's mental ability. In the second list, itemize the advantages of correctly identifying a child's mental ability. Which list is more compelling? Explain.

Coleman's research showed that the extent to which a student is willing to work for high grades depends on how much status and popularity those grades will bring or, conversely, on how much will be lost by getting high grades. He concluded that "students with ability are led to achieve only when there are social rewards, primarily from their peers, for doing so" (Coleman, 1961).

There have been many changes in the 2 decades since Coleman investigated the presence of a youth subculture in schools. The use of drugs has increased, sexual attitudes and behavior have become more permissive, and girls participate more in athletics. In spite of these changes, though, the roles described by Coleman are still present. A 1975 replication of Coleman's study found that 56 percent of the boys wanted to be remembered as athletes, 24 percent as ladies' men, and only 19 percent as scholars (Eitzen, 1975). The names may vary, but in schools across the country students still can be divided into freaks, jocks, and socials (Varenne, 1982). These roles continue to be consequential; the crowd one runs with is both determined by and a determinant of academic achievement.

Output: The Final Product.   The outcomes of education could be measured in terms of reasoning skills, openness of mind, and other intellectual qualities. Most often, however, they are measured in terms of years of educational attainment.

TRENDS IN EDUCATIONAL ATTAINMENT.   By this criterion, two important trends have occurred. First, there has been a continual increase in educational attainment with each new generation. By 1982, 71 percent of those over the age of 25 had graduated from high school and 18 percent had completed college.

Second, race and gender differences in education are being reduced (see Table 12.1). In the case of women, it seems likely that the differential may even be reversed in the next generation. Since 1979, more women than men have entered college as new admissions, and the educational aspirations of current high school students indicate that larger proportions of women than men will pursue post-high school education in the near future (U.S. Education Department, 1982). A comparison of educational attainment by race and ethnicity reveals a more modest change. Over the last decade, the educational attainment of blacks and Hispanics has grown faster than that of whites, but the gap is still very large. The dilemma is particularly acute for Hispanics, who run an increasingly poor third in the education race. Although black and Hispanic educational achievements were virtually the same in 1970, Hispanics now lag considerably behind black as well as Anglo Americans.

DETERMINANTS OF EDUCATIONAL ATTAINMENT. In a follow-up study of 18,000 high school graduates, it was found that high school scores in mathematics and vocabulary were the best predictors of educational attainment 7 years later (U.S. Education Department, 1982). In addition, educational attainment is increased if one's friends plan to go to college (Jencks et al., 1983).

In the long run, however, the most important factor determining whether a student will go on to college is parents' socioeconomic status. The higher the education, income, and occupation of the parents, the higher the eventual educational attainment of the child (Sewell et al., 1969; Sewell & Hauser, 1975; U.S. Education Department, 1982). In part, socioeconomic background relates to whether parents can afford to send their children to college. In a less direct way, however, it affects students' attitudes and aspirations. (Conklin & Daley, 1981). Your vocabulary and math scores as well as your friends' aspirations are in many ways a product of the social class environment your parents have provided.

Consequences of a College Education

This chapter began by asking what you expected to get out of a college education. Among the most well documented benefits are that persons with higher educational levels obtain more prestigious jobs, earn more over their lifetimes, and experience lower rates of unemployment than do those with less education. These advantages are not as great as they used to be, however; nor are they equally available to all groups. Moreover, the type and level of post–high school education has a substantial impact on the quality of life and the socioeconomic status eventually attained.

Impact of Education on Earnings

For many people, a chief objective of college education is the enhancement of earnings. This objective has been and continues to be realistic. Nevertheless, a college education is worth less than it used to be. In 1968, the average male college graduate earned 42 percent more than the average male high school graduate; in 1980, he earned only 25 percent more (see Table 12.2). A 25 percent increase in income compounded over a 40-year working life is still a long way from peanuts, but a college education makes

Table 12.2 Economic Returns of Additional Education, 1968 and 1980

Although a college education continues to be a sound financial investment, the economic return from education has declined slightly since 1968. In 1980 college-educated men earned 25 percent more annually than did high school graduates and college-educated women earned 31 percent more than women who did not go beyond high school. A fifth year of college meant an additional 14 percent increase in income for men and an additional 20 percent increase for women.

	FEMALE		MALE	
	1968	1980	1968	1980
MEDIAN TOTAL MONEY INCOME FOR FULL-TIME, FULL-YEAR WORKERS 25 AND OVER WITH:				
4 years of high school	$4,835	$11,537	$ 8,302	$19,469
4 years of college	6,694	15,143	11,795	24,311
5+ years of college	8,257	18,143	12,803	27,803
PERCENT INCREASE IN INCOME FOR GOING FROM:				
4 years of high school to 4 years of college	38%	31%	42%	25%
4 years of college to 5+ years of college	23	20	8	14

SOURCE: U.S. Education Department, 1982.

less difference in income than formerly. Because the number of college graduates is expected to grow faster than the number of high-level entry jobs, the return on investment for a college education is expected to continue to deteriorate over the next several decades (Freeman, 1976).

Differences by Gender and Race. The average female college graduate who works full time earns less than a male high school graduate who works full time. She earned less in 1968, and she continued to earn less in 1980. Because women with only a high school diploma earn even less

Figure 12.11
College graduation is no longer rare, but it still makes you part of a minority: fewer than 20 percent of the adults in the United States have graduated from college. Those that do will get better jobs, earn more money, and probably have a different lifestyle. Increasingly, however, college graduation is no longer a guarantee of affluence or success. Instead, it is merely a required credential for lower-level professional jobs that used to be staffed by high school graduates.

than that, however, women continue to find that graduating from college substantially increases their earning power. In fact, in the changing labor market, women now experience a greater proportional boost to their income from graduating from college than men do (31 percent for women versus 25 percent for men).

Although white men have suffered a substantial deterioration in the financial return on their educational investment, the situation is reversed for black men. Studies from the 1970 census showed that the earning power of young college educated black men was 9 percent greater than it was for college educated white men (Freeman, 1976). A year of graduate school increased black men's income by 36 percent, compared to only 13 percent for white men. Black women with a college degree earned approximately the same as comparable white women, but black women who invested in schooling beyond college graduation could expect a slightly higher return than white women. At all levels of education below college graduation, however, blacks received substantially lower economic returns than whites (Parelius & Parelius, 1978:74).

Overeducation: Can You Have Too Much?

For decades, a college education has seemed like the best avenue to a secure and prestigious job. Relative to the past, however, incomes, jobs, and career paths are depressed, as highly educated young workers experience more trouble finding high-status jobs. Many of the people now in college will begin their careers in entry-level positions for which they are overqualified or that are outside their training areas.

This situation is what labor market analysts describe as **overeducation.** In 1958, about 1 out of every 10 workers had more education than their job required; recent estimates indicate that perhaps as many as 1 out of every 5 workers experiences this problem today. Being overeducated is more likely to be a problem for nonwhites, the middle class, and persons age 35 and under than it is for others. These are the people least likely to hold a job commensurate with their education.

There has been a great deal of debate about the consequences of overeducation. Should we expect people who have to take work below that for which they are qualified to be alienated, depressed, and dissatisfied? The evidence suggests that, with the exception of the very overeducated (people with doctorates who are driving cabs, for example), the effects of overeducation have been much exaggerated (Burris, 1983). Although overeducated workers tend to be somewhat more dissatisfied with their jobs, they are not hostile to the system or depressed about their own achievements. In fact, when they compare their current situation with the jobs they would have had with only a high school diploma, many still find the occupational rewards of a college education very substantial.

Responses to a Changing Job Market. The deterioration of job opportunity and lifetime earnings has been the greatest for white men. Not surprisingly, this group has responded by decreasing its investment in a college education (see Table 12.3). Although other factors have been at work (increased tuition charges, changes in draft laws, changes in the

Overeducation occurs when the level of education attained exceeds what is necessary for an occupation.

Table 12.3 Percent of High School Graduates Ages 18 to 24 Enrolled in College, by Race and Gender, 1970 and 1982

	1970	1982
WHITES:		
Females	26%	32%
Males	42	34
BLACKS:		
Females	24	28
Males	29	28

SOURCE: U.S. Bureau of the Census, 1984, table 256.

overall state of the economy), a major factor in this unprecedented drop has been the depressed job market (Freeman, 1976). This situation seems to have affected white men from all social strata, including those from more advantaged family backgrounds. Women, black men, and nontraditional students (those over the age of 30) have been exceptions to this downward trend in college enrollment. For both women and blacks, college enrollment has been virtually unchanged since the mid 1970s.

Where Is as Important as If

Going to college is no longer restricted to the white upper and middle class. Increasingly, minorities and working-class youths are attending college. The numbers for these groups, however, should not be interpreted to mean that access to high-status professional and managerial jobs is being equalized across the groups. Where you go to college turns out to have nearly as much effect on your future income and earnings as whether you go to college. A community college will simply not do the same things for you as will Harvard or even the local state university.

The community college movement was intended to provide a stepping stone for students whose test scores or finances would not allow immediate entrance into a 4-year school. They were conceived of as feeder schools that would allow disadvantaged groups to move gradually into college, and indeed the majority of community college entrants do say that they intend to transfer to a 4-year school. Fewer than 25 percent of them do so, however. Although a majority of students who enroll in 4-year schools graduate from college (60 to 70 percent), only a minority (21 percent) of community college entrants ever get even their 2-year (Associate of Arts) degree (Monk-Turner, 1983).

The lower likelihood of completing their education is not the only disadvantage of attending community colleges. When people with equal educations are compared (say people with exactly 4 years of college), those who began their college careers at community colleges achieve significantly less than those who began their careers at 4-year schools. Ten years after their initial college entrance, their earnings and their occupational prestige are lower (Monk-Turner, 1983).

Conflict theorists tend to put an entirely negative interpretation on these findings. They suggest that community colleges are yet another means of tracking students. The disadvantaged (working-class and minority) youths who are disproportionately attracted to community colleges find that the college education they get will not do for them what the same number of years at a state university would. Their credentials will declare their origins.

Community colleges can make a positive difference to students, however. They offer a chance to students who have lower grades, lower social-class origins, and fewer resources than the students who start in 4-year schools. For some students, this chance is a vital opportunity. Intelligence is a much greater predictor of success at the community college level than it is at the 4-year level. Although community colleges cannot make up for all the disadvantages with which their students begin, they do provide the opportunity for upward mobility.

What's the Bottom Line? What Will College Do for Me?

A major incentive for college attendance is the belief that it will prepare you for a career. Chances are that the career you want, whether in nursing, counseling, law, or management, requires a college education. Even if the return on your education isn't as great as it used to be, you would probably rather be a relatively poorly paid lawyer than a secretary or a construction worker; you would probably rather be a manager than a managee. In the sense that a degree is increasingly required for even middle-level jobs, your investment in a college education will still pay off.

It can pay off in other ways too. It is a value judgment to say that a college education will make you a better person, but it is a value judgment that the vast majority of college graduates are willing to make. Survey after survey demonstrates that people feel very positively about their college education, believing that it has made them better and more tolerant people (Bowen, 1977).

Whether it makes you a better person or not, a college education is likely to have a lasting effect on your knowledge and values. If you finish college, you will sit through 30 to 45 different courses. Even the least dedicated student is bound to learn something from these courses. In addition, students learn informally. Whether you go to college in your hometown or across the country, college will introduce you to a greater diversity of people than you're likely to have experienced before. This diversity will challenge your mind and broaden your horizons. As a result of formal and informal learning, college graduates are more knowledgeable about the world around them, more tolerant and less prejudiced, more active in public and community affairs, and more open to new ideas (Bowen, 1977).

Many of the changes that take place between a student's freshman and senior years would occur anyway as part of the normal process of mat-

Figure 12.12

A college education goes far beyond training for a specific career. It encourages creative and critical thinking and broadens one's view of the world. This happens not just in classes, but through interaction with other students outside of the classroom. Most college graduates agree that their college educations made them more tolerant and more open to new ideas; the college experience also encourages drinking, rejection of traditional religious values, and political liberalism.

uration. Nevertheless, research suggests that three changes can be attributed largely or entirely to the educational experience (Astin, 1977):

1. Conventional religious preference declines, and the proportion of students who say they have no religion increases substantially.
2. Partying (drinking, smoking, and staying up late) increases; this effect is most pronounced for women who join sororities.
3. Political liberalism increases.

Summary

The economic return on an investment in higher education is not what it used to be, and a college education is not a certain passport to a prestigious professional career. Nevertheless, higher education continues to be an excellent investment, one that would be justified on the basis of the monetary returns alone. When one also considers the nonmonetary rewards—the contributions to intellectual and social growth—there is "no doubt that American higher education is well worth what it costs" (Bowen, 1977:448)

Quality of U.S. Education

Modern education has expanded in dozens of directions in the last 30 years. It tries to provide a bootstrap for those desiring upward mobility, to meet the changing needs of industry, and to meet a variety of other social needs. It tries to babysit and to teach reading and writing, driving, contraception, responsible drinking, cooking, and carburetor cleaning. It does some of these things better than others.

Many observers believe that U.S. education is in a state of crisis. In 1983, an 18-member National Commission on Excellence in Education issued a report that was extremely critical of U.S. education. For example, the report indicated that 13 percent of all 17-year-olds and as much as 40 percent of minority youths are functionally illiterate. In a comparison of U.S. students with students from 21 other nations, Americans scored the worst on 7 of 19 achievement tests and never came in either first or second. The commission concluded that a "tide of mediocrity" had swept over U.S. education, and it blamed this tide on "weakness of purpose, confusion of vision, underuse of talent, and lack of leadership" (Gardner, 1983:13). The commission argued that the problem was caused not by factors beyond our control but simply by lack of insight and will. The solutions it recommended included longer school days, tougher educational requirements, and more basics.

The U.S. public agrees that U.S. schools are not good enough. As Table 12.4 demonstrates, a majority of the public thinks that students are not required to work hard enough. The parents who feel most strongly about this subject are college educated and nonwhite. Both groups see educational success as vital for their offsprings' success, and they want greater emphasis placed on educational achievement. There is less consensus, however, on the solutions to the problem. Only a minority of the public

Table 12.4 Public Perceptions of the Work Load of Public School Children, 1975 and 1983

There is growing consensus that public school students do not work hard enough in the U.S. Between 1975 and 1983 the percent believing that students should work harder increased to over 60 percent. Only a handful of adults believe that students work too hard.

In general, do you think students in the public (elementary/high) schools here are made to work too hard in school and on homework, or not hard enough?

	ELEMENTARY SCHOOL STUDENTS		HIGH SCHOOL STUDENTS	
	1975	1983	1975	1983
Too hard	5%	4%	3%	3%
Not hard enough	49	61	54	65
About right	28	19	22	12

SOURCE: The Gallup Report, 1983, No. 216:18–32.

favors longer school days or longer school years; the public does, however, favor more homework and stricter discipline at school.

In addition to lack of hard work, there seems to be general agreement among the public and educators that disorderly student behavior is a serious problem, particularly in secondary schools. Two interrelated factors contribute to the problem: the presence of a youth subculture and compulsory education requirements that force some students to stay in school even when neither they nor their teachers want them to be there.

How serious is the crisis in education? U.S. students routinely score less well on achievement tests than do students from other nations, and their SAT scores declined steadily in the 1970s. (Since 1980 they have remained about constant.) This situation may represent confusion of purpose and lack of will, but it may also be a measure of the success of the U.S. educational system—a system that is supposed to serve a democratic society by integrating and assimilating a diverse population as well as meeting other social needs.

To a substantial extent, the declines in SAT scores have occurred because of the school system's success in opening up secondary and college education to the nonelites. Rather than shunting a substantial proportion of students into vocational tracks after the 8th grade (as is done in the British and Russian systems), the U.S. educational system tries to maximize the opportunities for mobility by keeping all students in the academic track. As a larger and larger proportion of the high school senior class takes the SATs, the average score falls. This does not mean that the scores of the traditional college preparatory groups have fallen; it means only that more disadvantaged students are going to college. Would you want it to be otherwise?

If you only have one job to do, it is relatively easy to do it well; if you have a dozen jobs to do, it is less likely that you will excel at any of them. This is precisely the current situation in U.S. education. During this century, the public's expectations of the public schools have expanded dramatically. In addition to teaching reading, writing, and arithmetic, the schools are now expected to give alcohol and drug education and to teach young people how to cook, raise children, and drive (see Table 12.5). In fact, the public places more emphasis on teaching about drugs, drinking,

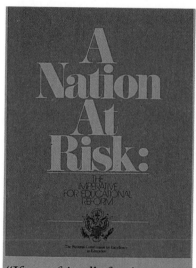

"If an unfriendly foreign power had attempted to impose on America the mediocre educational performance that exists today, we might well have viewed it as an act of war."

Figure 12.13

Table 12.5   What Subjects Should Be Required in High School? The Public's Response

The basics are increasingly in competition with non-academic courses for scarce school resources and hours. Although the basics are still emphasized, especially for college-bound students, the public seems to place equal weight on such courses as drug and alcohol abuse, parenting, and driver's education. As a result, there is less time and money to cover the basics.

	STUDENTS WHO WON'T BE GOING TO COLLEGE	STUDENTS WHO WILL BE GOING TO COLLEGE
Mathematics	87%	92%
English	83	88
Science	53	76
History/U.S. government	63	78
Foreign languages	19	50

	ALL STUDENTS
Drug abuse	81%
Alcohol abuse	76
Driver's education	72
Parenting	58

SOURCE: The Gallup Report, 1983, No. 216:24.

and driving than it does on teaching history or science. Is it any wonder that our schools do not produce people strong in the basics? Instead, the schools are giving the public what it wants. As long as the public will not support a longer school day or a longer school year, all these nonbasics mean that fewer minutes in the day will go to reading, writing, and arithmetic. When one adds in pep assemblies and all the other apparently necessary paraphernalia of the modern secondary school, it is no wonder that our students do not compete effectively with those from other nations.

U.S. schools do not do as good a job teaching the basics as do the schools of other nations. That does not mean that the schools are doing a bad job; it simply means that they are doing a different job. Only when there is consensus that the central task of our school system is teaching the basics will it be possible to conclude that the school system is in crisis. And only then will it be possible to seek solutions to the problems.

Equality of Educational Opportunity

A major issue in U.S. education is the provision of equal educational opportunity to young people of all races. An essential aspect of equal opportunity is school integration. In the 1954 Supreme Court decision that made it unconstitutional to maintain segregated school facilities, Chief Justice Earl Warren concluded that "to separate [black students] from others of similar age and qualifications solely because of their race generates feelings of inferiority as to their status in the community that may

Figure 12.14
Because education budgets depend largely on local property taxes, schools in affluent neighborhoods can afford much more luxurious facilities than schools in poor neighborhoods. The quality of the facilities is an important factor affecting the quality of education students receive. Just as important is the social class mix of the students. Students who attend schools where most of the children have high aspirations and middle-class values do better than those who must attend schools where the majority are from the lower class.

affect their hearts and minds in a way unlikely ever to be undone" (Warren, 1954).

The 1954 decision made it illegal to maintain segregated school facilities, and the chief lawyer for the plaintiff predicted that racial segregation in the schools would be eliminated within 5 years (Farley, 1982). This did not happen, and it now seems unlikely that schools in metropolitan areas will be racially integrated by the year 2000. Few in 1954 perceived the type of school segregation that would surface.

THE COLEMAN REPORT

In 1964, President Johnson and Congress commissioned a study to determine whether there was a "lack of availability of equal educational opportunities for individuals by reason of race, color, religion or national origin in public educational institutions" (Coleman et al., 1966). Directed by sociologist James Coleman, this study is the most comprehensive survey of U.S. schools ever undertaken. Information was collected from over 645,000 students as well as from school administrators and teachers. The study was designed to answer several important questions about the effects of segregation on educational achievement.

Are schools in the United States segregated? The Coleman study showed that the great majority of U.S. children attend schools that are largely segregated, a fact that is especially true for black children, although it holds for other minority children as well. Segregation also extends to teachers. Black teachers are concentrated in schools enrolling primarily black children, and white teachers generally teach white children.

Are there differences in academic achievement by racial groups? Coleman found that white children, on the average, outperform other children on achievement tests. Asian Americans who score as high or higher on these standardized tests are an exception. Coleman's study also found that the racial differences in achievement test scores increased the longer children remained in school. This finding is attributed to the fact that advantages and disadvantages associated with family background become increasingly crucial in later stages of education.

Do school characteristics differ? Although students attend segregated schools, Coleman found that the schools themselves do not differ on major characteristics. The

Figure 12.15
These first graders in Harlem are attending a school that is virtually all black. Families who can afford to live in the suburbs have migrated from the inner city, leaving behind schools that are predominantly poor and black, factors which retard minority achievement. Studies have shown that schools integrated on the basis of class and race contribute to achievement for disadvantaged children at little or no costs to the achievements of more advantaged children.

small differences he discovered, however, generally provide greater advantages for white students. These advantages include greater access to laboratories (physics, chemistry, and so on), more books per pupil in school libraries, a greater supply of textbooks, more access to college preparatory curriculums and accelerated programs, and positive differences in teaching staffs (higher salaries, more degrees, and higher test scores on achievement for white teachers).

One important difference in student characteristics, however, is the makeup of the student body. Schools that are segregated are segregated by both race and social class; all black schools are also predominantly lower class. As a result of this multidimensional pattern of segregation, the average disadvantaged child attends a school composed largely of other disadvantaged students, a con-

dition that reduces educational achievement. The relatively few disadvantaged and minority students enrolled in schools with more diverse racial and socioeconomic characteristics are more successful over all.

THE PROGRAM

Coleman's findings are important because they indicate that educational achievement can be improved by altering the composition of schools. Disadvantaged students may gain more from their education if they attend schools that are racially and socioeconomically mixed. When disadvantaged students associate with more advantaged and successful students, their work habits, motivation, and attitudes toward education should improve. And, in fact, the findings of hundreds of studies over the 20 years since Coleman's report indicate that mixed schools improve minority students' performance without reducing the performance of more advantaged students (Crain et al., 1982).

WHAT SHOULD BE THE OBJECTIVE OF SOCIAL POLICY?

One possibility for social policy is simply **racial balance,** the achievement of the same racial mixture in the schools as exists in the community at large. The difficulty with this objective is that some communities and many neighborhoods are segregated. A racially balanced school in downtown Los Angeles will be largely Hispanic; a racially balanced school in suburban Portland, Oregon, will be almost entirely white.

There is another dilemma with the goal of racial balance. Even in schools that represent several racial and ethnic groups, segregation may continue in classrooms, school activities, and student tracking. To be effective, desegregation must also result in **integration**—biracial interaction in which the minority group is accepted on a completely equal basis (Pettigrew, 1971).

How Can Integration Be Achieved?

A basic stumbling block to creating racially integrated schools is the pattern of residential segregation in U.S. cities. In recent years, almost all large cities have experienced a decline in the proportion of white residents. This decline has occurred for reasons unrelated to school integration; the housing is old, employment opportunities have declined or employers have moved to the suburbs, and the cities are perceived to be decaying and dangerous places to live in (Farley, 1982). Many whites and blacks who can afford to live elsewhere do—in the suburbs and outlying areas. The remaining urban pop-

Figure 12.16

In the late 1970s it became apparent that racism and racial violence were not confined to the South. Demonstrations and violence flared in northern industrial cities as court-ordered busing attempted to create integrated schools in racially segregated cities. Both black and white parents expressed reasonable concerns about having their children transported across town to potentially hostile environments. Busing, however, is considered by some to be a necessary opening wedge in the vicious circle between prejudice, segregation, and differential achievement.

ulation is disproportionately poor and black. If present trends persist, it is likely that three-fourths of the 50 largest cities in the United States will have majority black enrollments in the schools by the late 1980s (Farley, 1982).

Because of these trends, many believe that school integration can occur only if the concept of racial balance is expanded to include the entire metropolitan area, suburbs and all. That is, if an entire metropolitan area is 50 percent Anglo, 35 percent black, and 15 percent Hispanic, then racial balance will be achieved when each school has that same racial mixture. When many of the Anglos live in the suburbs and the minorities live in the central city, however, this mixture means busing. To a lesser extent, the same objectives can be achieved through redistricting, selective closing and opening of schools, and the creation of magnet or target schools that draw art or science students from the entire metropolitan area.

WHAT HAS BEEN ACCOMPLISHED?

It has been 20 years since Coleman's research. During those years there have been court cases, forced busings, and much self-recrimination. Where has it all led? Unless you count a great deal of research confirming Coleman's initial results, the answer has to be: Not far.

A very small proportion of all students in the United States are bused to achieve racial balance. Less than 9 percent of all high schools bus any students, and the proportion of students bused for the purpose of integration is much smaller than that (U.S. Education Department, 1982:72–73). As a result, segregation is increasing rather than decreasing in U.S. schools.

This pattern of increasing segregation has occurred not because anybody thought it was a good idea but because patterns of suburbanization continue to create white suburbs surrounding increasingly black central cities (see chapter 18). Busing is one attempt to reduce the impact of this pattern of housing segregation, but the ultimate challenge is to reduce the pattern of housing segregation. Residential integration will not only make racial balance easier to achieve in the schools, it will also increase the likelihood of real integration in schools and society. To the extent that this happens, it should also increase the educational achievement of minority students.

Do these goals seem to you to be worth pursuing? Are racial segregation and reduced minority achievement important enough social problems to merit government action? If so, what should that action be? Few people are enthusiastic about busing. What alternatives would you be willing to support—with your votes and tax dollars?

SUMMARY

1. There have been two major trends in U.S. education in the last 200 years: a shift from elite to mass education and a shift toward increasing bureaucratization.

2. The structural-functional model of education suggests that education has been a beneficial response to changing needs. Among the positive outcomes of education are cultural reproduction, social control, the teaching of specific skills, the selection of students for future adult roles, and the promotion of change. Education is also recognized as having latent functions and dysfunctions.

3. The conflict model suggests that the benefits of education go largely to the elite. Education, according to this model, produces a docile labor force instilled with the idea that differential rewards are a fair reflection of differential ability. Credentialism ensures that mass education is no threat to the elite.

4. The systems model looks at processes that occur in the school (hidden curriculum, testing and evaluating, youth culture, and tracking). Such processes do not change the relative social-class rankings of children.

5. IQ tests used to track students show that Anglos score higher than minorities and middle-class students score higher than working-class students. Such tests may be better measures of cultural deprivation than of innate ability.

6. Educational attainment has increased for all major groupings in our society. Educational differences between men and women have virtually disappeared, but the gap between white and minority educational attainment is decreasing more slowly.

7. The returns on a college education in terms of income and job prestige are smaller than they used to be. College remains a sound investment, however, and will increase lifetime earnings and job security and decrease unemployment. In recent years, the proportional increase in income from a college education is greater for blacks than whites and greater for women than men.

8. Many believe that there is a crisis in our public schools because U.S. students score lower on basic subjects than do students in other nations. An important reason for these lower scores is that our schools are burdened with many tasks besides teaching the basics—assimilation, integration, and the teaching of such nonbasics as driver's education and parenting.

9. Research demonstrates that minority students are not likely to have equal educational opportunity if their schools are racially segregated. In spite of a 20-year public commitment to integrated schools, little has been accomplished because neighborhoods have become more segregated.

SUGGESTED READINGS

Astin, Alexander W. (1977). Four Critical Years. San Francisco: Jossey-Bass. A longitudinal study examining the effects of college by comparing students who finish with those who don't, men with women, living on-campus with living off-campus, and so on in an effort to answer these types of questions: How does the experience of going to college change people? Do they become more open-minded, more liberal, less religious because of the experience?

Bowles, Samuel, & Gintis, Herbert. (1976). Schooling in Capitalist America: Educational Reform and the Contradictions of Economic Life. New York: Basic Books. An expanded treatment of the conflict perspective as applied to education in U.S. society.

Collins, Randall. (1979). The Credentialist Society: A Historical Sociology of Education and Stratification. New York: Academic Press. A well-written essay unraveling the historical relationships between education and the class structure. Using a conflict perspective, it critically examines the limited opportunities for upward social mobility that education has provided.

Eysenck, H. J., & Kamin, Leon. (1981). The Intelligence Controversy. New York: Wiley. A short but readable book in which two leading experts in the field of intelligence testing vigorously debate the issue of heredity versus environment in intelligence through attack and counterattack, addressing such topics as the validity of IQ tests, the relationship between race and intelligence, and how intelligence is formed throughout childhood.

Freeman, Richard B. (1976). The Overeducated American. New York: Academic Press. A critical examination of the changing value of a college education in terms of earnings, employment, underemployment, and so on. Discusses whether being a minority member, a woman, or a major in one of the humanities as opposed to computer science or engineering makes any difference in the job market.

Parelius, Ann Parker, & Parelius, Robert J. (1978). The Sociology of Education. Englewood Cliffs, N.J.: Prentice-Hall. One of the most readable, informative, and thorough texts in the area. Presents a solid overview of the historical development of education in the United States and examines some of the major issues confronting the educational system.

CHAPTER 13

POLITICAL INSTITUTIONS

PROLOGUE

Have You Ever . . . *considered the draft and what it might mean to you? If you're a young man, having to register for the draft is probably a sharp reminder of your obligations to the state. The draft is one of those issues that bring the mutual responsibilities between citizens and state close to home. What is the role of the state? If it is supposed to be ensuring the general welfare, why does it always seem to be pushing us around? One answer, of course, is that it is doing it for our own good. Usually this means that the demanded act is for the good of society as a whole or for the majority rather than for us as individuals.*

Taxation, the draft, and speed laws are instances where we give up some rights for the good of the whole. Nowhere is this process more obvious than in China's successful birth-control program (discussed more fully in chapter 17). The Chinese declare that the number of children you have is not a private decision. Because family size affects the welfare of your neighbors and the state, it is public business. Hence, records are kept of every woman's menstrual cycle. If her period is late, someone will shortly be visiting her to discuss abortion.

To talk about political institutions is to talk about power, to talk about how individual rights are given up, sometimes voluntarily and sometimes not. In our society, we have laws restricting dogs from barking, laws specifying how to dispose of sewage, laws restricting the circumstances under which we can marry, and laws restricting the speed at which we can drive. Will we soon have laws making it illegal to get pregnant? Why are some laws acceptable and others not? What is the process through which decisions are made and shared? In this chapter, we will focus on how decision making is institutionalized in societies.

Political institutions are institutions concerned with the social structure of power. In this chapter, we will examine the values and norms that structure how power is used in American society. In doing so, we will give special attention to the interdependence of the stratification structure, economic development, and democracy. We will begin with an introduction to the study of power, the nature of the state, and the formal and informal norms that structure America's political institutions.

Power

In any effective group, from a dyad to a nation, someone has to make decisions. Failure to make decisions ensures standing still or proceeding thoughtlessly in the same direction from inertia—as do people who cannot decide whether to go to the movies or out to dinner and so end up at home watching television again. Although decisions need not be made by a single individual, it would be tedious to negotiate every issue that comes up. Thus most ongoing organizations, from families to governments, develop procedures for determining who will make the decisions.

When you can make decisions that determine other people's behavior, then you have power over them. **Power** is the ability to get others to do something against their wishes, the ability to overcome resistance. Power operates in day-to-day encounters and in international relationships. Parents compel their children to eat their cauliflower; employers compel their employees to conform to a dress code; one nation compels another to rearm.

The primary characteristics of power are that there are competing or even conflicting viewpoints and that one group or person is able to exercise control. Some person or group has power over another. In cases where the parties have agreed to take turns or to hold periodic elections, it may be that power is rather evenly balanced over all. Nevertheless, the nature of power is that it involves inequality in the ability to get your own way. Thus the exercise of power is always a potential source of conflict.

Sociologists define two kinds of power: coercion and authority. These two kinds of power are described below along with a closely related phenomenon—influence.

Coercion

The exercise of power through force or the threat of force is **coercion**. Coercion is not limited to physical force; it can involve the use of any compulsory negative sanction. Thus, for example, you pay your taxes because of coercion. If you do not pay them, the government may fine you, confiscate your property, or even send you to prison. Another form of official coercion is the classic "stop or I'll shoot" police action.

Coercion exists in informal settings too, and threats of force or punishment are part of many relationships: between parents and children, between siblings, and sometimes between spouses. Power through coercion may or may not be legitimated by social norms and values. Normally, the activities of the tax collector are regarded as legitimate; the activities of the mugger who takes the same amount of money are not legitimate.

Political institutions are institutions concerned with the social structure of power.

Power is the ability to get others to do something against their wishes, the ability to overcome resistance.

Coercion is the exercise of power through force or the threat of force.

Figure 13.1
Power is an important part of all institutions and most social relationships. Coaches have power over their players, parents have power over their children, and teachers have power over their students. This power may be coercive (based on force or threat of force) or authoritative (based on norms attached to statuses). Power relationships are least problematic when they are based on authority, when the subordinates agree that the other has the right to make the decisions and they have a duty to obey.

Figure 13.2
Authority may rest on tradition, charisma, or on rational law. President Reagan's authority rests on rational law. Even those who disagree with his policies agree that he has the right to make them because he occupies the Presidency; his right has nothing to do with Ronald Reagan the man, but comes with the office of the Presidency. Because President Reagan also has a good deal of personal charm, he adds substantial influence to the authority granted to him by law. This increases the likelihood that he will get his way.

Authority is power supported by norms and values that legitimate its use.

Traditional authority occurs when an individual is given the right to make decisions for others because of the sanctity of time-honored routines.

Charismatic authority occurs when an individual is granted the right to make decisions for others because of perceived extraordinary personal characteristics.

Rational-legal authority occurs when an individual is granted the right to make decisions for others because of submission to a set of rationally established rules.

Similarly, it has been generally acceptable to spank your children (although this norm is changing) but not to use force or the threat of force in dealing with your spouse.

Authority

Power supported by norms and values that legitimate its use is **authority** (Wrong, 1979:35). Authority is explicitly concerned with legitimate power, where the subordinate agrees that, in this matter at least, the other has the right to make decisions. In his classic work, Weber distinguished three bases on which this agreement is likely to rest: tradition, extraordinary personal qualities (charisma), and legal rules.

Traditional Authority. Decision-making power that is based on the sanctity of time-honored routines is **traditional authority** (Weber, 1922/ 1970e:296). Monarchies and patriarchies are classic examples of this type of authority. For example, in our own society, many men and women have agreed that women should be subordinate to men. As the data reported in chapter 10 demonstrated, in 1962, only 31 percent of a sample of adult women disagreed with the statement that husbands should make all the major decisions for their families. These women gave their husbands the right to exercise authority in the family. As in this instance, traditional authority is often supported by religious or sacred attitudes toward past practices. A pattern of authority, such as male dominance, becomes time honored, and many people believe it is a sacrilege to try to change it. Traditional authority, according to Weber, is not based on reason, it is based on a reverence for the past.

Charismatic Authority. When individuals are given the right to make decisions because of perceived extraordinary personal characteristics, this is **charismatic authority** (Weber, 1922/1970e:295). These characteristics (often an assumed direct link to God) put the bearer of charisma on a different level than subordinates. Gandhi's authority was of this form. He held neither political office nor hereditary position, yet he was able to mold national policy in India. On a much smaller scale, one of John Humphrey Noyes's strongest assets in leading the Oneida community (see chapter 11) was his personal attractiveness to both women and men.

Charismatic authority may be very powerful, gaining followers' loyalty as well as obedience. By nature, however, it is an unstable form of power; it resides in an individual and is therefore mortal. If efforts are made to pass on charisma—if, for example, it is argued that charisma is a property of the son as well as the father—then charismatic authority evolves into traditional authority.

Rational-Legal Authority. Unequal authority based on rationally established rules is **rational-legal authority** (Weber, 1922/1970e:299). This form of authority is a chief characteristic of bureaucracy, but it is not limited to bureaucratic structures. It is involved whenever decision making is allocated on the basis of previously negotiated rules, such as taking turns or majority rule. An essential element of rational-legal authority is that it

Figure 13.3
Few people are able to direct others' activities on the basis of their personalities alone. Ghandi (shown here in 1947 with his two granddaughters) was such a person. Although he held no political office and occupied no position of traditional authority, Ghandi was able to guide a movement that crumbled the British Empire in India. His power was based on charisma, an unstable form of power that must usually be supplemented with or replaced by traditional or rational-legal authority.

is impersonal. You do not need to like or admire or even agree with the person in authority; you simply follow the rules.

In modern society, rational-legal authority has gradually supplanted traditional authority in church, government, home, and office. A chief advantage of rational-legal authority is that it is more flexible than traditional authority. The consensus behind it is based on a set of written rules and, more importantly, on the procedure for establishing them (for example, elections and legislative enactments). The distribution of power is recognized as a social product, something that can be changed by the same process by which it was established.

Analytically, we can make clear distinctions among these three types of authority. In practice, the successful exercise of authority usually combines two or more (Wrong, 1979). An elected official who adds charisma to the rational-legal authority stipulated by the law will have more power; the successful charismatic leader will soon establish a bureaucratic system of authority to help manage and direct followers.

All types of authority, however, rest on the agreement of subordinates that someone has the right to make a decision about them and that they have a duty to obey it. This does not mean that the decision will always be obeyed or even that each and every subordinate will agree that the distribution of power is legitimate. Rather, it means that society's norms and values legitimate the inequality in power. For example, if a parent tells her teenagers to be in at midnight, they may come in later. They may even argue that she has no right to run their lives. Nevertheless, most people, including children, would agree that the parent does have the right.

Because authority is supported by shared norms and values, it can usually be exercised without conflict. Ultimately, however, authority rests on the ability to back up commands with coercion. Parents may back up their authority over teenagers with threats to kick them out of the house or take the car away. Churches back up their authority by threats to excommunicate. Teachers back up their authority with threats to flunk, suspend, or expel students. Employers can fire or demote workers. Thus authority rests on a legitimation of coercion (Wrong, 1979).

Influence

A concept closely related to power, but separate from it, is **influence**. The wielder of influence has no right to make the decision and no formal or physical sanctions to apply; instead the person must rely on persuasion and personal appeals. Influence occurs when you try to persuade someone to change their opinion, party, or creed (or when you try to sell them a vacuum cleaner).

Influence is not institutionalized; it rests on individual appeals based on personal or ideological grounds rather than social structure. It is typically the strategy of groups that are structurally powerless. People without the right to order an action may be reduced to: "Won't you do it for little old me?" Even people who have a great deal of power must often use influence if they want to affect actions outside the scope of their authority. The president of the United States, for example, has no authority to compel congress to support his legislative proposals. To get congressional approval, he must try to exercise influence. He calls individual senators on the telephone, invites them to dinner, and generally courts their favor, using personal appeals and persuasive arguments to move them to his position.

As this example suggests, influence and power often exist side-by-side. For example, many parents first try to influence their children to do what they want and use authority and then coercion as last resorts. In bureaucracies, there are patterns of influence as well as authority. Thus the old-boys' network and who eats lunch with whom may be more important in determining decision making than are the formal rules of authority.

CONCEPT SUMMARY

Power

CONCEPT	DEFINITION	EXAMPLE FROM FAMILY
Power	Ability to get others to act as one wishes in spite of their resistance; includes coercion and authority	"I know you don't want to mow the lawn, but you have to do it anyway"
Coercion	Exercise of power through force or threat of force	"Do it or else"
Authority	Power supported by norms and values	"It is your duty to mow the lawn"
Traditional authority	Authority based on sanctity of time-honored routines	"I'm your father, and I told you to mow the lawn"
Charismatic authority	Authority based on extraordinary personal characteristics of leader	"I know you've been wondering how you might serve me, . . ." (unlikely)
Rational-legal authority	Authority based on submission to a set of rationally established rules	"It is your turn to mow the lawn; I did it last week"
Influence	Not power but ability to persuade others to change their decisions	"I don't feel very well today; would you help me mow the lawn?"

Political Institutions

Power is not exercised randomly in relationships. To a significant extent it is socially structured. That is, the roles associated with such statuses as student/teacher, parent/child, or officer/soldier specify unequal power relationships as the normal and appropriate standard. To the extent that power relationships are attached to norms, roles, and statuses, we say that power has been institutionalized.

Any ongoing social structure with institutionalized power relationships can be referred to as a political institution. This general definition includes many of the institutions of society. The family, the workplace, the school, and even the church or synagogue have structured social inequality in decision making. The most prominent political institution, however, is the state.

The State

The State as the Dominant Political Institution

The **state** is usually distinguished from other political institutions by two characteristics: (1) its jurisdiction for legitimate decision making is broader than that of other institutions, and (2) it controls the use of coercion in society.

Jurisdiction. Whereas the other political institutions of society have rather narrow jurisdictions (over church members or over family members, for example), the state represents the seat of decision making for society as a whole. The kinds of decisions that states may legitimately make vary historically, but most modern states are responsible for reaching and implementing decisions in the following areas (Williams, 1970):

1. Establishing an order of priority among collective goals (environmental protection or cheap energy, inflation or unemployment, guns or butter).
2. Organizing resources and activities to meet collective goals (taxes, clean environment, the draft).
3. Distributing goods and services (facilities, benefits, rights) to individuals and groups, domestic and foreign.
4. Settling conflict between societal units and establishing institutionalized procedures to deal with all recurring or major conflicts of interest (conflict between neighbors or between neighboring states).
5. Defining and maintaining relationships with other societies (treaties, trade negotiations).

Coercion. The state claims a monopoly on the legitimate use of coercion. To the extent that other institutions use coercion (for example, the family or the school), they do so with the approval of the state. And as the state giveth, it also taketh away. Thus the state has withdrawn approval of physical coercion between husband and wife and has sharply restricted the amount of physical punishment that is legitimate for parents to administer to children. Similarly, the state has generally declared physical punishment illegitimate within the school system.

Figure 13.4
Although power is a part of all institutions, the dominant political institution is the state. It is the only institution allowed to maintain armed forces and it controls the use of coercion by all other institutions of society. Thus, police may interfere in coercive relationships in families, churches, or labor unions. The state determines when and where coercion is legitimate.

The **state** is the social structure that successfully claims a monopoly on the legitimate use of coercion and physical force within a territory.

The state uses three primary types of coercion. First, the state uses its police power to claim a monopoly on the legitimate use of physical force. It is empowered to imprison people and even impose the death penalty. This claim to a monopoly on legitimate physical coercion has been strengthened in recent years by the declining legitimacy of coercion in other institutions, such as the home and the school. Second, the state uses taxation, a form of legitimated confiscation. Finally, the state is the only unit in society that can legally maintain an armed force and that is empowered to deal with foreign powers.

A variety of social structures can be devised to fulfill these functions of the state. Here we will review the two basic political forms: democracy and authoritarian systems.

Democracy

Democracy is a political system that provides regular, constitutional opportunities for a change in leadership according to the will of the majority.

There are several forms of **democracy**, many of them rather different from that of the United States. All democracies, however, share two characteristics: there are constitutional procedures for changing leaders and these leadership changes reflect the will of the majority.

In a democracy, there exist two basic groups: the group in power and one or more legal opposition groups that are trying to get into power. The rules of the game call for sportsmanship on both sides. The losers have to accept their loss and wait until the next constitutional opportunity to try again, and the winners have to refrain from eliminating or punishing the losers. Finally, there has to be public participation in choosing among the competing groups.

Although there are a variety of democratic governments, three general conditions must be met before democracy can flourish. There must be competing interest groups, an absence of fundamental cleavages, and a high level of economic development.

Competing Interest Groups.   Democracy is a mechanism for arbitrating conflict between competing groups. It can flourish only in a society in which there are many competing groups, each less than a majority (Williams, 1970:271). The fracturing of the population into competing groups has two vital consequences for democracy. First, it means that no single group can win a majority of the votes without negotiating and compromising with other groups in order to build a coalition. Second, it means that since each group is, by itself, a minority group, effective safeguards for minority political groups are in the interest of everybody. Both of these characteristics help support the rules of good sportsmanship that are essential to a democracy.

Absence of Fundamental Cleavages.   Although competing interest groups are vital for sustaining democracy, it is equally vital that these interest groups have basically compatible values. When groups emerge that are not merely competitive but bitterly opposed to the existence of each other, then they are not likely to be able to abide by the rules of the game. For example, a party dedicated to the overthrow of the government or the elimination of some minority group would be neither a gracious winner nor a gracious loser. Class conflict, racial or ethnic conflict, and religion are but a few of the dimensions that have historically been sources of major cleavages. In U.S. history, the Civil War was the result of such a cleavage, and the secession of the South demonstrated that the issues were too vital for it to maintain the pretense of being a gracious loser. The existence of major cleavages between blacks and whites in Rhodesia/Zimbabwe or between Catholics and Protestants in Northern Ireland are additional examples of cleavages that make democracy difficult to maintain.

Economic Development.   No observer could fail to notice that contemporary democracy is found almost exclusively in the wealthier nations of the world. In fact, economic development is one of the best predictors of stable democratic government (Hannan & Carroll, 1981). Why this is so is a matter of some debate. In part, it may be simply because it is easier to be a gracious loser if you are not on the edge of subsistence. When there appears to be plenty to go around, it may be easier to believe that it does not matter much one way or another who wins this round (Lipset, 1978:96). The impact of economic development on democracy, however, is probably more complex than this. Economic development is part of the entire transformation of society caused by industrialization: greater education, urbanization, greater social and geographic mobility. Many believe that these changes have made democracy possible in the modern world (Jackman, 1974; Lipset, 1959; Rubinson & Quinlan, 1977; Tyree et al., 1979).

The political institutions of a society do not exist independent of its other social structures. Without the support of these three factors—competing groups, absence of fundamental cleavages, and high levels of economic development—it would be difficult for any society to maintain a democratic form of government. Democracy cannot be exported like Coca-Cola; it is integrally related to a society's other institutions.

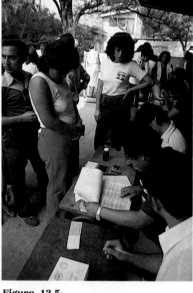

Figure 13.5
Democracy is a delicate institution which will not thrive unless three conditions are met: 1) competing interest groups, 2) the absence of fundamental cleavages, and 3) a high level of economic development. Where one or more of these conditions is absent, democracy is likely to be unstable and ineffective. Despite holding of elections, democracy is unlikely in El Salvador.

Authoritarian Systems

Most societies have lacked the conditions for democracy. As a result, most people in most times have lived under **authoritarian systems**. Authoritarian governments go by a lot of other names: dictatorships, military juntas, despotisms, monarchies, theocracies, and so on. What they have in common is that the leadership was not selected by the people and legally cannot be changed by them.

Authoritarian structures vary in the extent to which they attempt to control people's lives, the extent to which terror and coercion are used to maintain power, and the purposes for which control is exercised. Some authoritarian governments, such as monarchies and theocracies, govern through traditional authority; others have no legitimate authority and rest their power almost exclusively on coercion.

Authoritarian systems are political systems in which the leadership is not responsible to the people and in which there is no legal method of changing leadership short of forceful overthrow.

Legitimacy of the State

A political structure has been institutionalized when the distribution of power is affirmed by norms and values attached to a network of statuses. If consensus on these norms and values exists, the state can exercise

Figure 13.6
For most of history, people throughout the world have lived under authoritarian political, regimes: the people have not chosen their leader and they have lacked the legal right to change leaders. Authoritarianism, however, ranges from extremely oppressive and punitive regimes to those which rule from the general consensus of their people. As the cheerful faces of these Chinese soldiers indicate, many authoritarian regimes have generated great patriotic fervor among the masses and rule with little explicit coercion.

power through authority. If consensus does not exist, the state must rely on coercion. This is an extremely unstable condition that requires the state to spend a considerable proportion of its resources overcoming resistance and securing obedience. This requirement reduces the state's ability to meet its other functions and such states are unlikely to survive long.

American Political Structures

It is a simple task to give a straight forward description of the formal structure of American political institutions. A description of the actual patterns of authority and influence, however, is a different matter and it should not surprise you that viewpoints about the American political process are, well, political. The following section outlines the essential formal elements of the American political structure, explains the values that underlie it, and explores several opinions on how it works in practice.

Liberal Democracy

The legal structure of the American government, as embodied in the U.S. Constitution and the Bill of Rights, is described in every high school civics

Figure 13.7
In the U.S., all political parties which do not advocate the overthrow of the government are legal. This includes the American Nazi Party, whose leader, Frank Collins, is pictured here describing a planned march through the heavily Jewish suburb of Skokie, Illinois. Extremist and minority parties like this are not very influential in American politics. Because of our winner-take-all rules, and because of a heterogeneous society, only a political party with a broad, centrist appeal is likely to have much power.

book. This formal structure is important, but it should not be overemphasized. It was created to embody and support values on which the American people were able to reach consensus; 200 years later, it still rests on consensus. If values change, then the formal structure can be amended.

One of the central values shaping Americans' attitudes toward the state is a distrust of government. This distrust is the hallmark of the form of democracy practiced in the United States—**liberal democracy**. In this form of democracy, the state is regarded as a necessary evil and the structure of government is designed to limit and restrict the ability of the state or of the majority to interfere with individual freedom.

The U.S. Constitution is largely a reflection of these values. Thus the first 10 amendments (the Bill of Rights) specify individual rights that the state cannot abridge. For example, they guarantee freedom of speech and freedom of the press. The creation of an independent judiciary, which can strike down laws passed by Congress and supported by a popular majority, is another reflection of the basic values underlying liberal democracy.

It is important to recognize that the Constitution has authority only insofar as it continues to be supported by the majority. As noted in the discussion of Japanese Americans interned during World War II, (chapter 9) our rights rest ultimately not on law but on the consensus of the people. When that consensus changes, the law may be changed or simply bypassed.

The Two-Party System

Many of the practices governing American politics are not included in the Constitution. The most important of these extra-legal practices is the **political party**—an association specifically organized to win elections and secure access to the power of the state.

Liberal democracy is a democratic form of government characterized by distrust of government power. Many of the formal elements of liberal democracy are designed to restrain the government or a popular majority from interfering with the rights of individuals.

A **political party** is an association specifically organized to win elections and secure power over the personnel and policies of the state.

In a stable democratic system, political parties have two vitally important characteristics: (1) they use nonviolent means and are both gracious winners and gracious losers, and (2) they are voluntary associations with open recruitment—membership is by self-designation. If you want to call yourself a Democrat, the Democratic Central Committee cannot stop you. In the United States, we have a relatively stable two-party system, each party representing a loose coalition of competing interests. Because of this last characteristic, the differences between parties are not great and there are differences of opinion among members of the same party as well as between members of different parties.

These characteristics are not mandated by the Constitution, which indeed does not mention parties at all. Rather, the character of American political parties can be seen as an outgrowth of our stratification system, our basic values, and our formal system of government (see Figure 13.8).

Formal Structure and the Winner-Take-All Rule. An important characteristic virtually unique to the American brand of democracy is the winner-take-all rule. In most European democracies, legislative seats are apportioned according to the popular vote. Thus a party getting 10 percent of the vote gets 10 percent of the seats. In the United States, a group that got only 10 percent of the vote would come out with nothing. Thus, in order to gain any representation at all in our system, the small group must ally itself with others in a coalition that may ultimately appeal to at least 50 percent of the voters. Similarly, the federal system of government requires that a group with a particular agenda to push, whether of isolationism or of a war on poverty, control many branches of government in order to implement its program. It is not enough simply to elect a president; the group must also control Congress. This need to affect elections in local units across the nation as well as attaining a national majority requires that political parties have broad national appeal.

Heterogeneity and Social Mobility. In a homogeneous nation, broad national appeal might be attained with a very specific, even extreme, program of action. In a heterogeneous society, however, majority backing can be gained only by a program that combines and balances the interests of many smaller groups—farmers, labor, blacks, big-cities, conservationists, heavy-industry, and so on. The strength and stability of American political parties is thus partly attributable to the diversity of the American population and the many crosscutting interest groups that affect the population. It is also attributable to relatively weak class boundaries and an ideology that stresses mobility rather than class identification. These aspects of the stratification structure prevent the emergence of strong class-based parties (Jackman, 1972; Tyree et al., 1979).

Each political party, then, represents a loose coalition of competing interest groups rather than a single interest with a unified agenda. This has two consequences:

1. It helps maintain the requirement of being a gracious loser. When you agree with only 60 percent of your own party's platform and probably agree with 30 percent of the other party's platform, it is likely that you can tolerate one party's victory almost as easily as the other's. The lack

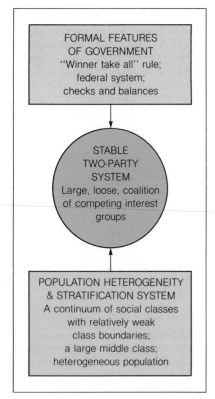

Figure 13.8 Determinants of a Stable Two-Party System
Our form of democracy is not simply a result of a sound constitution; it is also the product of our stratification system and our population structure. Nations that lack these features may not be able to maintain democracy even if they adopt a democratic constitution.

FORMAL FEATURES
OF GOVERNMENT
"Winner take all" rule;
federal system;
checks and balances

STABLE
TWO-PARTY
SYSTEM
Large, loose, coalition
of competing interest
groups

POPULATION HETEROGENEITY
& STRATIFICATION SYSTEM
A continuum of social classes
with relatively weak
class boundaries;
a large middle class;
heterogeneous population

of single-issue parties takes much of the heat out of politics and contributes enormously to the stability of the system.

2. It makes it unlikely that government will enact any extreme or radical programs. There are philosophical differences between the parties (see Table 13.1), but both are necessarily centrist. Each needs to capture 51 percent of the vote across the country to win a presidential election. Because of the diversity of the population, this majority can occur only with a centrist (some would say wishy-washy) platform. This aspect contributes also to the stability of the two-party system.

Thus the remarkable stability of America's two-party system is a function both of the formal structure of government and of the stratification system. The formal structure might not provide stability, however, if the stratification system changed drastically.

Who Governs? Models of American Democracy

This broad picture of the American political structure is generally supported by observers from all theoretical and political backgrounds. The consensus breaks down, however, when we begin to discuss how decisions are actually made. Is there an elite group pulling the strings? Are we adrift without a rudder? This section outlines three viewpoints on how decisions are made: pluralist, power-elite, and conflict/dialectic.

The Pluralist Model.   The central idea of the pluralist model is that there is a continual process of coalition and competition among many organized groups, none of which is consistently a winner. There is no

Table 13.1   Perceptions of Party Differences, 1982
Although both of the major political parties in the United States are centrist parties, there are ideological differences between them. Generally, Republicans are seen as stronger on defense and fiscal responsibility and Democrats as stronger on helping the poor and working class.

"From this list, name the three or four issues you feel the Democrats and the Republicans would do the best job on."

	DEMOCRATS	REPUBLICANS
Helping the poor and disadvantaged	41%	3%
Reducing unemployment and stimulating new jobs	22	7
Protecting social security	30	5
Protecting the environment	14	3
Keeping world peace	12	7
Reducing taxes	6	14
Reducing government regulation and interference	4	20
Balancing the federal budget	4	24
Reducing government spending	5	24
Strengthening America's national defense	7	31

SOURCE: Opinion Outlook, a *National Journal* publication, February 12, 1982

Figure 13.9
The pluralist model of American politics stresses the importance of Congress in making decisions. Congress is seen as an area where competing interest groups vie for votes and power. According to this model of the American political process, no side consistently wins and there is a shifting balance of power.

A **veto group** is an interest group or coalition of interest groups that can block action by other groups but that is less effective in pushing its own programs.

elite in this model, rather the key concept is **veto group**—an interest group or coalition of interest groups that can block action by other groups but is less effective in pushing its own programs. For example, farmers stand almost alone in trying to raise the price supports for agriculture (and thus the cost of food) and have been relatively unsuccessful in recent years in this endeavor. However, they can join together with longshoremen, the maritime industry, and the railroads to prevent an embargo on the export of U.S. grain.

Another vital part of the pluralist model is the existence of shifting allegiances. According to pluralist theorists, different coalitions of interest groups arise for each decision. Thus agriculture and labor will work together to oppose the embargo but against each other on commodity supports. This pattern of shifting allegiances keeps any interest group from consistently being on the winning side and keeps political alliances fluid and temporary rather than allowing them to harden into permanent and unified cliques (Dahl, 1961, 1971). As a result of these processes, pluralists see the decision-making process as relatively inefficient but also relatively free of conflict, a process in which competition between interest groups keeps any single group from gaining significant advantage.

The **power elite** is the people who occupy the top positions in three bureaucracies—the military, industry, and the executive branch of government—and who act together to run the United States in their own interests.

The Power-Elite Model.   Theorists associated with the power-elite model wave aside the competition among organized interest groups as the middle levels of power. Unlike the pluralists, power-elite theorists contend that there is a higher-level of decision making where an elite makes all the major decisions—in its own interests. In his classic work, *The Power Elite*, C. Wright Mills (1956) defined the **power elite** as the people who occupy the top positions in three bureaucracies: the military, industry, and the executive branch of government. From these "command posts of power" and through a complex set of overlapping cliques, these people share decisions having at least national consequences (Mills, 1956:18). The

Figure 13.10
The power elite model of American politics argues that the real power to make decisions affecting U.S. policies rests with individuals who occupy the top spots in three bureaucracies: major corporations, the military, and the federal bureaucracy. According to this model, major decisions are made by elites in rooms such as this rather than in the rough and tumble competition in Congress.

power-elite argument is based on three factors: elite control of vast bureaucracies, similar interests among elites, and interchangeability of elites.

BUREAUCRATIC CONTROL.   Mills argues that the power to influence American life, in fact to structure the conditions that determine which issues will be raised, is most clearly found in the modern bureaucracy. Bureaucracies such as those of the Department of Health and Human Services, the military, or major corporations represent organizations of thousands or hundreds of thousands of employees, all controlled by a rigid hierarchy of authority. (For example, the Department of Health and Human Services employed more than 162,000 people in 1980.) The people who occupy the command posts in these bureaucracies do not have absolute power, but their power is far less constrained than is the power of the legislature. Thus, Mills argues, these men (and, less often, women) have vast power. This point cannot be denied.

SIMILARITY.   The suggestion that the individuals occupying the top positions represent a unified elite is supported by evidence of a strong similarity in background among the top members of these three bureaucracies. They have gone to the same colleges and prep schools, summered at the same resorts, skied at the same lodges, and joined the same clubs. The role of their social ties is described in Domhoff's study of a prestigious men's social club, the Bohemian Grove. President Reagan belongs to this club, as do Vice-President Bush and several members of the Reagan cabinet.

> The Bohemian Grove, as well as other watering holes and clubs, are relevant to the problem of class cohesiveness in two ways. First, the very fact that rich men from all over the country gather in such close circumstances as the Bohemian Grove is evidence of the existence of a socially cohesive upper class. It demonstrates that many of these men do know each other, that they have face-to-

face communications, and that they are a social network. In this sense we are looking at [clubs] as a *result* of social processes that lead to class cohesion. But such institutions also can be viewed as facilitators of social ties. Once formed, these groups became another avenue by which the cohesiveness of the upper class is maintained. [Domhoff, 1974:88]

THE REVOLVING DOOR.   In addition to similarity of personnel, there is substantial evidence of direct interchangeability of personnel—the so-called revolving door between business and industry and the military. For example, Reagan cabinet members Caspar Weinberger and George Shultz were pulled into elite positions in the executive branch of government from elite positions in business (president and vice-president, respectively, of the huge multinational corporation Bechtel). Similarly, Alexander Haig went from general to secretary of state (not as big a jump as Eisenhower made, but Eisenhower fought a more popular war).

Significant empirical evidence shows that there is such an elite and that it is highly overrepresented in top positions in the executive branch (Kerbo & Della Fave, 1979). Similarity, interchangeability, and power, however, are not sufficient to demonstrate that an elite group controls decision making in the United States and wields it for its own benefit. Evidence on the latter point is lacking. On the side of the power-elite model, it can be demonstrated that government policy has not seriously threatened established elites. Successive government programs such as social security and inheritance and income taxes have failed to produce any substantial redistribution of privilege or wealth (see figures on income and wealth distribution in chapter 8). The lack of change, of course, can be attributed as easily to the stalemate of the pluralist model as to the defensive actions of the elite. Even if the elite is not as united or powerful as Mills and others suggest, however, it may still be more powerful than any other coalition likely to be assembled against it (Domhoff, 1970:299).

The Conflict/Dialectic Model.   A Marxist vision of class conflict is at the root of the conflict/dialectic model. The major power in society is held by the dominant class by virtue of its control of the means of production. The subordinate class, however, has its own resources for power: class consciousness and the possibility of class action. The power of the subordinate class can be likened to that of a sleeping rattlesnake; the snake is not hurting you now, but you want to be certain not to awaken it. Thus the conflict/dialectic model sees underlying tensions between the elite (dominant class) and the nonelite that are largely missing from the power-elite model.

A further element of this model is its emphasis on the dialectic as the process of social change. As noted in earlier chapters, the dialectic suggests that social change will emerge as a result of contradictions and conflicts within and between social institutions. Marxists believe that

social institutions, economic systems, and political institutions contain inherent contradictions. These produce conflicts and strains that eventually lead to the transformation of those institutions and systems. *Contradictions* are thus engines of social change and their analysis is central also to understanding the dynamics of political power. [Whitt, 1979:84]

In terms of the American political structure, the dialectic suggests that the elite has to be constantly on its toes to ward off the potential consciousness and power of the subordinate class in a climate of shifting economic and political conditions. Change rather than stability is the key to the conflict model. Whereas the power-elite model sees the elite striving to maintain privilege, the conflict model envisions a more rough-and-tumble battle in which both sides strive to structure change for their benefit. This conflict is seen to occur within as well as between classes. Unlike the power-elite model, the conflict model does not require a unified elite. Rather, various elements of the elite may be in conflict on particular issues. Thus the model alerts us to contradictions and strains within the elite that may ultimately weaken it and lead to change.

CONCEPT SUMMARY

Comparison of Three Models of American Political Decision Making

	PLURALIST	POWER-ELITE	CONFLICT/DIALECTIC
Basic units of analysis	Interest groups	Institutional elites	Social institutions, social classes
Basis of group power (resources)	Many: economic, organizational, governmental, social, personal	Institutional position, common social background and interests	Class position, class consciousness and class organization
Distribution of power	Dispersed among competing diverse groups	Concentrated in relatively homogeneous elite	Held by dominant class, potentially available to lower class
Limits of power	Limited by shifting and crosscutting loyalties	No identifiable limits to elite dominations	Limited by class conflict and contradiction among social institutions

A Speculative Case Study: Who Gets Wyoming?

The different implications of the models can be illustrated by speculation on how each would envision the political decision to strip-mine in Wyoming. If the large and virtually untouched deposits of coal in Wyoming can be mined, the United States won't face an energy shortage for a long time. However, the process will be dirty, destructive of the environment, and disruptive of the current use of the land as well as of the economic and social life of the small communities currently in the area. The land containing the coal deposits is controlled largely by the U.S. Bureau of Land Management. How will the decision be reached about what to do?

The pluralist model would envision competition among various interest groups: cattlemen and ranchers (the so-called Sagebrush Rebellion), the environmentalists, and coal companies. Each group will seek allies among peripherally affected groups, such as federal agencies, the Wyoming government, Indian reservations, and the railroads, and will put together a broad coalition to block the other groups or, less probably, to get its own way. Ultimately, no side will win a clear victory, and some compromise will be reached.

The power-elite model would suggest that while all this is going on, the heads of the energy company and the Interior Department will be sharing lunch at their club and deciding how to run their program. The elites will act together. Often they work together even without planning to do so; they simply have similar interests and values. At other times, however, they actively conspire to manipulate the situation for their own advantage. This latter process is illustrated by a memo from the chairman of Standard Oil of California during a recent California election. The memo, which was not intended for public consumption, suggests a strategy for defeating an environmentalist group:

> In short, the campaign ... must not be spearheaded *publicly* by business and industry. *It should be publicly launched by responsible conservationists, by academicians, labor spokesmen, leaders of the Democratic Party,* and joined at the appropriate time in the appropriate fashion by business, industry, and the Republican Party leadership. ... The involvement of the principal oil companies and the principal utilities ... is not a *public* involvement. Rather, in a nonpublicized sense, it is a means of directing the campaign under the aegis of a public citizens committee as outlined. In the doing, total control of the public campaign is maintained. [Cited in Whitt, 1979:93]

The essence of the power-elite model, as evidenced in this memo, is the assumed cohesiveness of business, industry, and the utilities and their intent to work together to manipulate the public and control decision making.

The conflict/dialectic model would assume that the elite is divided, not unitary—that the bureaucrats in the Bureau of Land Management would like to retain control of the land as much as the energy companies would like to gain it. Furthermore, this model would see a historical contradiction (dialectic) emerging. The century-long rape of fossil fuels has exhausted the easily accessible (and most profitable) sources of conventional energy. As the costs of conventional fuels go up, more and more people are turning to alternative technologies such as solar and wind power. Although energy companies are trying to gain monopoly control over patents for solar and other alternative technologies, these new forms of production fall outside the current relations of production. Nobody owns the wind or the sun. Thus the very success of the current system may contain the seeds of its own destruction.

Individual Participation in American Government

Democracy is a political system that explicitly includes a large proportion of adults as political actors. Yet it is easy to overlook the role of individual citizens while concentrating on leaders and organized interests. This section describes the American political structure and process from the viewpoint of the individual citizen.

Who Participates?

The average citizen is not politically oriented. A significant proportion of the voting-age population (approximately one-third in 1982) does not even register to vote; of those people who do register, many do not vote. In

FOCUS ON ANOTHER CULTURE

The Soviet Union—
Totalitarianism or Institutionalized Pluralism?

Almost all communist societies include the word *democratic* in their name. East Germany is formally the German Democratic Republic, and Cambodia is now Democratic Kampuchea. Few communist societies, however, meet the definition of democracy given here; instead we would call them authoritarian states. How authoritarian are they?

Following World War II, most Americans agreed that the Soviet system was not merely authoritarian but totalitarian. *Totalitarianism* is a new kind of authoritarianism, one in which the state tries to "pulverize all existing associations in society in order to remake that society and subsequently, even man

himself, according to certain 'ideal' conceptions" (Brzezinski, 1956:752). The word *totalitarian* was developed specifically to apply to Nazi Germany, but it also seems to apply to Stalin's Russia (1925–1953). The characteristics of a totalitarian government are as follows (Brzezinski & Huntington, 1964:202–209):

1. An official ideology covers almost all aspects of existence, and all citizens are expected to adhere to it. This ideology rejects the current state of society and desires to remold society and individuals into a new image.
2. There is a single political party led by a single individual. The goals

of the party are passionately supported by a hard core of party ideologues, though not by the masses.
3. The leaders use a system of police terror to supervise the party. The system also is directed against enemies of the regime and certain arbitrarily chosen classes of the population.
4. The party exercises nearly complete control over all aspects of daily life by controlling the major bureaucracies, the mass media, and all other major institutions: economy, church, school, and family.

During the decades of Stalin's rule, it is likely that this model described the Soviet political system. With Stalin's death in 1953, however, the system seems to have mellowed considerably. There is less stress on the ideology of changing society, there is less use of police terror, power is less concentrated in a single individual, and the party no longer strives to enforce rigid adherence to a party line. Certainly, dissidents are imprisoned, punished, deported, and exiled, but there appears to be much greater tolerance that there was before 1953.

As is the case with the United States, it is easier to describe the formal structure of the Soviet government than it is to assess the processes by which decisions are made. Increasingly, however, students of that government are coming to describe Soviet political processes in much the same terms that are used to describe the

Figure 13.11

The Soviet Union is an authoritarian political structure, but it is not totalitarian. Recently, students of Soviet politics have argued that disagreement and competition are tolerated in the Soviet system. A major distinction between the Soviet system and our own, however, is that in the Soviet Union only bureaucrats are allowed to voice dissent and to compete for economic and political favors.

American political process. A major school of thought suggests that decision making in the Soviet Union represents institutionalized pluralism. Bureaucratic actors (representing the command posts of power) compete against each other for a share of the national budget. The school system, the military, and industry compete with each other for priority. Much of the most intense conflict, however, takes place within policy areas rather than between them. People whose careers hinge on particular policy decisions compete with one another over scarce dollars and authority. Thus the navy competes with the space-program, people in the fields of scientific and technical education compete with those who teach foreign languages, and people who want heavy industry in the heartland compete with those who want to develop energy resources in Siberia. Through this system of institutionalized pluralism, dissent over policy reaches to the highest levels of the Soviet system. According to this viewpoint, the elite acts as a broker, mediating the demands of conflicting groups.

No one would be likely to argue that decision making in communist societies is as open as it is in the United States. The Soviet Union is an authoritarian nation in which the people have no power to change the leadership or the system. Nevertheless, there are institutionalized mechanisms by which vested interests compete. To the extent that individuals are plugged into one of these bureaucracies, they can participate in decision making.

The Soviet system [is] a highly participatory one for the individual as well as for the institution. The distinctive feature of individual participation in the Soviet Union is that people must work through official channels.

They cannot picket, hand out leaflets, speak on the street corner, or the like; they cannot form interest groups around issues; they cannot organize political factions or parties. . . . Legitimate political process must take place within an institutional process. [Hough & Fainsod, 1979:547]

Questions to Consider

1. How different is the political power of the average Soviet citizen from that of the average U.S. citizen?
2. Does the Soviet system seem closer to the pluralist, the power-elite, or the conflict/dialectic model? Explain.

SOURCE: Hough and Fainsod. 1979. How the Soviet Union Is Governed. Cambridge: Harvard University Press.

recent presidential elections, 40 to 50 percent of the voting-age population has not bothered to go to the polls. Electoral participation declines markedly as one gets closer to the local level and often only 20 to 25 percent vote in local elections.

Voting is in many ways the easiest and most superficial means of participating in politics. If we include letter-writing, returning congressional questionnaires, and making campaign contributions as elements of political activity, we will have to conclude that less than 20 percent of U.S. citizens take an active part in politics. And, of course, only a very small proportion take part to the extent of running for or occupying elective office.

The studies demonstrating low levels of political participation and involvement pose a crucial question about the structure of power in American democracy. Who participates? If they are not a random sample of citizens, then some groups probably have more influence than others. Studies show that voters differ from nonvoters on social class, race, and age.

Social Class.   One of the firmest findings in social science is that political participation (indeed, participation of any sort) is strongly related to social class. Whether we define *participation* as voting or letter-writing, people with more education, more income, and more prestigious jobs are more likely to be politically active. They know more about the issues, have

Figure 13.12
When the United States was founded 200 years ago, it was widely hailed as the first modern democracy. In 1789, however, only white men of property were allowed to vote. Since that time, the electoral franchise has been more widely distributed: black men were given the right to vote in 1863, women in 1919, and Native Americans in 1924. Despite universal suffrage, however, only a bare majority of citizens exercise the right to vote.

stronger opinions on a wider variety of issues, and are much more likely to try to influence the nature of political decisions. This conclusion is supported by data on voting patterns from the 1982 election (see Table 13.2). The higher the level of education, the greater the likelihood of voting; those who have graduated from college are nearly twice as likely to vote as those who have not completed high school.

Table 13.2 Participation in the 1982 Election
Political participation is greater among establishment types—people who are older, better educated, and non-Hispanic.

	PERCENT REGISTERED	PERCENT ACTUALLY VOTING
TOTAL	64%	48%
EDUCATION		
8 years or less	52	36
9–11 years	53	38
12 years	63	47
13–15 years (college)	70	53
16 or more years (college graduate)	79	66
RACE/ETHNICITY		
White	66	50
Black	59	43
Hispanic*	35	25
AGE		
18–24	42	25
25–34	57	40
35–44	68	52
45–64	76	62
65+	75	60

SOURCE: U.S. Bureau of the Census, *Statistical Abstract of the United States, 1984,* table 441.

*Underestimates participation among eligible voters; 32 percent of Hispanics ineligible to register because not citizens.

Figure 13.13
In the 1984 presidential election, despite a major effort on the part of the Democrats to lure lower socioeconomic groups to the polls, voting was disproportionately drawn from the well educated and better off—those with a stake in preserving the status quo.

Race.   Political participation is also strongly related to race. Because of the civil rights movement of the 1960s, this differential is much smaller than it was 30 years ago. Today, the differences between black and white political participation are due almost entirely to social-class differences (Guterbock & London, 1983). In fact, after social class has been taken into consideration, it seems likely that being black increases political participation. Blacks are more apt than whites to want changes made in the system, and they turn to political participation as a means to effect these changes (Guterbock & London, 1983:440). Low Hispanic participation is traceable partly to low socioeconomic status, but much of the apparent low participation of Hispanics is an artifact of the measurement procedure: 32 percent of the voting-age population of Hispanics are aliens (legal as well as illegal) and are not eligible to register or to vote.

It should be stressed that lower voting participation by underprivileged groups is not a characteristic of all democratic systems. Rather, the low participation of minorities and of the working class in the United States can be attributed to the absence of a political party that directly represents their interests (Zipp et al., 1982). In European political systems with pro-worker parties, this class differential in political participation is largely absent. In the United States, however, there is no exclusive political vehicle for the working class or for minorities. Again, this is a function of the stable two-party system and the winner-take-all rule.

Age.   Another significant determinant of political participation is age. There is a steady increase in political interest, knowledge, opinion, and participation with age. One-third of all voters in the 1980 election were 55 or older. Even in the turbulent years of the Vietnam War, when young antiwar demonstrators were so visible, young adults were significantly less likely to vote than were the middle aged. In that period, young adults engaged in other forms of political participation that did, in fact, influence political decisions. In most time periods, however, the low participation of younger people at the polls is a fair measure of their overall participation.

The data on voting patterns demonstrate that establishment people are more likely than others to try to influence political decisions. These people are middle aged, middle to upper class, well educated, and with vested economic interests. They are the people who have the highest stake in preserving the status quo. Thus differential patterns of participation give added weight to conservative positions and reduce the voice of the dissatisfied.

Differentials in Office Holding.   By law, almost all native-born Americans over the age of 35 are eligible to hold any office. In practice, elected officials tend to be white men from the professional classes. Thus, for the most part, the political activities of other groups (women, minorities, non-elites) have been directed at choosing the white elite males to represent them. This practice has been changing, however; blacks, Hispanics, and women (though not nonelites) are increasingly holding elected office, especially at local levels. Still, only about 4 percent of all state legislators are black, and only 12 percent are female. The proportions in Congress are much smaller (U.S. Bureau of the Census, 1984).

Political Alienation

An important determinant of whether citizens participate in political decision making is their judgment of the usefulness of the exercise. Citizens who believe that they can influence outcomes through their participation are apt to be active. Those who are **politically alienated**, who cynically believe that voting is a useless exercise that has no influence on decision making, are not going to be active. Alienated voters are likely to think that their vote doesn't count, that no one cares what they think, and that the system is run for the benefit of the few. Opinion poll results show that alienation has increased substantially among voters since the mid-1960s (see Table 13.3), and it has contributed to the overall decline in voter participation.

In addition to being alienated from the political process, many citizens are simply ignorant about it. In 1978, only half of the adult population knew that each state had two senators (Erikson et al., 1980:19). It is difficult to know whether alienation leads to ignorance or vice versa, but in general the people who are most ignorant of government are those most turned off by it.

Political Affiliation

In spite of the fact that both of the major political parties in the United States are necessarily centrist, there are philosophical distinctions between them. As suggested by Table 13.1 earlier in the chapter, most Americans see the Democratic party as more socially responsible and the Republican party as more fiscally responsible and tougher on defense.

Because of these characteristics, the Republicans tend to attract people with higher incomes, who tend to be fiscally conservative. The Democrats tend to attract the highly educated, who tend to be more liberal on social issues, as well as voters of lower socioeconomic status (Kourvetaris &

Political alienation is a cynical belief that voting is a useless exercise and that individual citizens have no influence on decision making.

Table 13.3 Political Alienation in the United States, 1966–1982
Political events of the last 15 years have left an increasing number of Americans feeling alienated. A majority now feel helpless to affect the course of government.

	PERCENT WHO AGREE THAT:	
	What You Think Doesn't Count Very Much Anymore	The People Running the Country Don't Really Care What Happens to You
1966	37%	26%
1971	44	41
1974	60	63
1976	63	64
1978	52	50
1980	59	48
1982	58	50

SOURCE: Harris Survey. Cited in *Opinion Outlook*, a *National Journal* publication, July 15, 1982.

Figure 13.14
Voting is the easiest way for citizens to participate in the political process, but it may not always be the most effective. Political demonstrations and protests are an effective means for concerned interest groups to gather national attention and to place issues on the national agenda.

Dobratz, 1982). There is a particularly sharp pattern by race; nonwhites are overwhelmingly associated with the Democratic party. In addition to these class-based affiliations, there is also a long-standing association between religion and political affiliation: Catholics and Jews tend to be Democrats more often than Protestants do. These class and religious differentials have decreased in the last 30 years; however, as Table 13.4 shows, they are still substantial.

There is some evidence that American voters have become more issue-oriented in the last 20 years (Nie et al., 1979). Prior to 1960, political affiliation, like religion, was inherited; whether you were a Republican or a Democrat depended more on the affiliation of your parents than on your own characteristics (Berelson et al., 1954). Under these circumstances, voting was easy. Some states still allow people to vote a straight ticket by providing a lever that will automatically select all of the Republican or all of the Democratic candidates. In this way, the voter doesn't even have to know who is running. The switch to issue-oriented voting has made voting more difficult. Some would argue that issue voting is a more responsible form of political participation; however, the increased difficulty has contributed to lower participation on the part of the traditional but uninvolved voter.

One sign of the switch to issue voting is the sharp increase in the proportion of voters who call themselves independents. Independents are not themselves a political party. They are disproportionately young and well-educated voters who have declared an intent to vote on the basis of

Table 13.4   Political Affiliation, 1980

Although American parties do not regard themselves as speaking for any particular social class, the better off tend to be Republicans and the poor and nonwhite tend to be Democrats. The growing proportion who identify themselves as independent tend to be young, well educated, and white.

"In politics, as of today, do you consider yourself a Republican, a Democrat, or an Independent?"

	REPUBLICAN	DEMOCRAT	INDEPENDENT
NATIONAL	26%	43%	31%
Race:			
White	28	38	34
Nonwhite	7	80	13
Education:			
College	31	34	35
High school	24	45	31
Grade School	22	55	23
Income:			
Over $25,000	33	34	33
$20,000–$24,999	27	41	32
$15,000–19,999	22	42	36
Under $15,000	23	49	28
Religion:			
Protestant	30	42	28
Catholic	20	48	28
Jewish	12	54	34

SOURCE: Gallup Opinion Index, December 1980, no. 183, p. 63.

issues rather than party loyalty. When the 31 percent of the voters who call themselves independents go to the polls, however, they usually have to choose between a Republican and a Democratic candidate.

Consequences of Differential Participation

Elite theorists see popular elections as little more than games designed to delude the masses. Since real decisions aren't made in Congress, much less by the governor or the mayor, level of participation is irrelevant. These theorists point out that opinion polls show a drop in political alienation immediately after elections (Ginsberg & Weissberg, 1978), and they interpret elections as a ritualized form of participation that serves to confirm the legitimacy of the system.

Pluralists, as one would expect, put much more emphasis on the importance of elections. Nevertheless, they acknowledge that the balancing of interest groups, blocs, and veto groups effectively operates to keep much from being accomplished by representatives, even those who are responsive to their constituents.

One thing on which many agree is that lack of participation, even apathy, is functional for the stability of the American political system (Greer & Orleans, 1964). The large body of citizens who don't care very much one way or the other reduces the amount of political conflict in society. In addition, many studies have shown that nonvoters are less supportive of democratic values; they are less supportive of civil rights, more authoritarian, and less tolerant of nonconformity (McClosky, 1964; Nunn et al., 1978). They are certainly more ignorant of the issues and of the system. This evidence suggests that nonparticipation may serve a useful purpose in contributing to the continued tolerance of diverse opinions that is a requirement of democracy. It does mean, though, that the government is unrepresentative of the whole and, in particular, that it underrepresents the poor and the poorly educated.

The Political Consequences of Scarcity

American politics has been largely free of conflict between the haves and the have-nots. Although there are class-related differences between the political parties, there are also enough crosscutting loyalties to keep politics from being a direct expression of class conflict. Why is class conflict largely absent from American politics? If the working class outnumbers the upper class (and it does), why don't its members vote to change the system?

For the most part, Americans have not been interested in absolute equality. As noted in chapter 8, they are interested in equality of opportunity rather than equalization of wealth (Robinson & Bell, 1978). The desire of lower-class members—successive waves of immigrants, blacks, and Hispanics—has been "deal me in" rather than "soak the rich."

This attitude has been traced to the astounding economic expansion characteristic of the first 200 years of the United States. Although our abundance is accompanied by significant disparities in income, our standard of living is luxurious by almost any comparison. As a 19th century socialist noted with chagrin in describing the failure of the United States to sustain a socialist movement: "On the reefs of roast beef and apple pie, socialistic

Figure 13.15
A moderate degree of economic development appears to be essential to maintain democracy. It reduces conflicts over scarce resources and makes it possible to take care of the poor without great sacrifices by the rich. When resources become scarce, as they did in the late 1970s with gasoline shortages, then competition over scarce resources—and between social classes—becomes more direct.

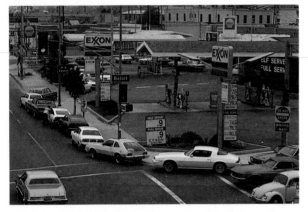

utopias of every sort are sent to their doom" (Sombart, 1906/1974:87).

Perhaps more important than the richness of the American economy is its growth. If one is not rich, it is possible that one's children will do better. The future was rather accurately foreseen to offer the promise of further prosperity. Thus, instead of seeing themselves as the have-nots, America's lower-class members have tended to see themselves as the going-to-haves.

Many scholars have argued that affluence and growth have worked to produce a peculiarly nonpolitical approach to inequality. For the most part, Americans have believed that it is easier to improve economic position by education and hard work than by joining a political party that will change the way wealth is distributed. If these theories are correct, then an end to growth could seriously alter the way the political process works in the United States. These consequences are most likely in two areas: the distribution of scarce resources and the redistribution of income.

THE DISTRIBUTION OF SCARCE RESOURCES

In capitalist societies, a common means of distributing scarce resources (for example, gasoline) has been on a market basis. The resources go to those who can afford to pay the most for them. This allocation process seems nonpolitical in the sense that it represents a decision not to interfere directly. Reliance on economic forces, however, contains a hidden political decision; wealth will determine access to the scarce resources. Earlier generations of economists referred to this phenomenon as the invisible hand of the market. The procedure causes few problems when a resource is plentiful or cheap. When gasoline becomes dear enough that there is not enough to go around, when water becomes scarce enough that we can irrigate or flush toilets but not both, then the invisible hand has to come out into the open. When this happens, conflict seems likely to erupt. Do we ration? Do we assign priority to some groups? Do we make the poor do without?

PROGRAMS OF REDISTRIBUTION

Over the past decades, the growth of American productivity has made it possible to meet demands for new programs and new benefits without having to redistribute income significantly. That is, new programs have been funded out of surplus growth, and it has been possible to give to the poor without taking from the rich. Without this surplus, any further giving to the poor will require taking from the rich. When the pie is growing, each of us is able to increase our share without taking away from the others. If the pie stops growing, we can increase our share only by taking some away from other groups. Thus, in a static economy, rich and poor will be pitted against one another far more directly than they are in an expanding economy. It seems reasonable, then, to expect politics to become more concerned with class issues.

THE SPECTRE OF SCARCITY

The spectre of scarcity first arose for most Americans with the 1973 oil embargo. This event startled millions of Americans into considering that growth and affluence might not be permanent conditions of the American economy; natural-resource shortages, overpopulation, and the limits to growth became real. This shock was followed by stagflation, a decade-long period of high inflation accompanied by slow economic growth. The result was that many Americans perceived that their standard of living was declining. And it was. In the last decade, our houses have become smaller, and they are hotter in the summer and colder in the winter; our cars are smaller, and we have to drive them more slowly. No one knows whether these recent reversals are temporary or the beginning of a no-growth society. A substantial portion of the population, however, believes that they are permanent. In 1979, nearly two-thirds of the population agreed with the statement "Americans should get used to the fact that our wealth is limited and that most of us are not likely to become better off than we are now" (Yankelovich et al., 1979).

Regardless of whether the future holds feast or famine, it is clear that growth and affluence have reduced political conflict in America. If growth ceases, it is likely that our political process will be more strongly class-linked, more bitter, and more likely to lead to fundamental cleavages (Blumberg, 1980; Gappert, 1979; Ophuls, 1977), Could this possibly be a good thing? Marxists believe that an increase in the political consciousness of the working class will lead to a better deal for the majority of the population. Others believe that scarcity will make the upper class more defensive and reduce the likelihood of redistribution programs (Lipset, 1978).

SUMMARY

1. Power may be exercised through coercion or through authority. Authority may be traditional, charismatic, or rational-legal. Influence is less effective than power since it does not allow one to compel another's obedience.

2. Any ongoing social structure with institutionalized power relationships can be referred to as a political institution. This definition includes the family, the school, and the church, but the most prominent political institution is the state.

3. The state is distinguished from other political institutions because it claims a monopoly on the legitimate use of coercion and it has power over a broader array of issues.

4. Democracy comes in many forms. The American form, liberal democracy, is supported by values, norms, and statutes that limit the authority of the government and protect the individual from both government interference and the tyranny of the majority.

5. Democracy is not just a matter of having the right values; it also requires a supportive institutional environment. Such an environment is characterized by competing interest groups, the absence of fundamental cleavages, and economic development.

6. The stable two-party system is a product of our stratification system and of the formal structure of government. It results in the creation of two centrist parties, each representing a coalition of interest groups.

7. There are three major models describing the American political process: the pluralist model, the power-elite model, and the conflict/dialectic model. None of the three suggests that the average voter has much power to influence events.

8. The Soviet system is authoritarian rather than democratic. Nevertheless, there are some similarities between political process in the United States and the Soviet Union. In large, complex societies, individuals can most effectively influence decisions if they are part of a bureaucratic structure.

9. Political participation is rather low in America; fewer than half of the people of voting age vote in most national elections, and fewer yet take an active role in politics. Political participation is greater among those with high social status and among middle-aged and older people—establishment types who are more likely to support the status quo.

10. Abundance has reduced political conflict in America. If the pie stops growing, it seems likely that conflicts over inequality will become more central in our political processes.

SUGGESTED READINGS

Dye, Thomas R. (1983). Who's Running America? (3rd ed.). Englewood Cliffs, N.J.: Prentice-Hall. A study of the elite power structure in America, focusing on the strength of interlocking corporations and on decision making that has national and international consequences.

Ebenstein, William. (1980). Today's Isms. Englewood Cliffs, N.J.: Prentice-Hall. A classic that offers a straightforward, understandable discussion of the major political and economic forms. It is useful for understanding socialism, capitalism, and communism—both their theoretical underpinnings and their work in practice.

Lipset, Seymour Martin. Political Man: The Social Bases of Politics. (1963). Garden City, N.Y.: Anchor/Doubleday. Concerned with the sociology of politics, a comprehensive examination of the relationships between politics and democracy, with particular emphasis on American society. Special attention is given to class-based political participation in America and the implications this has for policy and governance.

Mills, C. Wright. The Power Elite. (1956). New York: Oxford University Press. One of the most important discussions of the relationships among three areas of power in America: government, business, and the military. Mills, a conflict theorist, argues that a small but elite group of individuals make the decisions that control American society.

Ophuls, William. Ecology and the Politics of Scarcity. (1977). San Francisco: W. H. Freeman. Is democracy in America safe? This readable book is a consciousness-raising experience, drawing attention to democracy as a political form of governance that coexists with affluence. A central thesis is that democracy is threatened by scarcity. A help in understanding the implications of increased scarcity for the democratic way of decision making.

Williams, Robin W., Jr. (1970). American Society (3rd ed.). New York: Knopf. An examination of the basic values of American culture, with an emphasis on how these values are embedded in our political, economic, and family institutions.

CHAPTER 14

ECONOMIC INSTITUTIONS

PROLOGUE

Have You Ever . . . taken one of those tests that asks questions such as "Would you rather read to a sick person or do the laundry?" If you took the SAT or the ACT tests while you were in high school, then you know about those kinds of questions. The application forms for both of the tests include interest inventories that can be used to guide you into an appropriate major. The tests indicate whether you would rather work with people or things, whether you prefer to work alone or with others, and what kinds of rewards motivate you.

If you stop to think about it, the existence of such tests is a tribute to a remarkable change in the attitude toward work. The tests imply that work need not be a burden; they suggest that you should be able to find work that you like. Some people do find enjoyable and satisfying careers, others are happy just to have a job.

For all of us, however, whether homemaker, professor, or mechanic, our occupation is a central determinant of our social identity. Occupations are also central to our economic institutions. This chapter describes economic institutions in terms of social structures such as corporations and the networks of roles, statuses, and norms that make them up. It is useful to remember, however, that each morning this complex system of interacting parts is set off by 100 million alarm clocks. Economic institutions are people working.

One of Karl Marx's most influential ideas was that economic institutions are the foundation of society. In its extreme form this idea leads to the argument that all other institutional arrangements in society (marriage, religion, law) arise out of economic relationships. Many would take exception to this total economic determinism (Marx himself acknowledged exceptions), but no thoughtful observer of society could fail to be struck by the tremendous importance of economic institutions.

Economic institutions are social structures concerned with the production and distribution of goods and services. Such issues as scarcity or abundance, guns or butter, craftwork or assembly lines are all part of the production side of economic institutions. Issues of distribution include what proportion goes to the worker versus the manager, who is responsible for supporting nonworkers, and how much of society's production is distributed on the basis of need rather than effort or ability. The distribution aspect of economic institutions intimately touches the family, stratification systems, education, and government.

Sociology is not concerned with the intricate workings of economic systems. Such issues as the Federal Reserve System, the causes of inflation, and the national debt are all left to the discipline of economics. Some understanding of such issues is required, of course. For example, do high interest rates lead to an increase or decrease in income inequality? However, sociologists focus on the enduring pattern of norms, roles, and statuses that make up the economic system (Turner, 1972).

In this chapter, we will look at the economic system from two points of view. At the macroeconomic level, we will examine the social structures of economic institutions and their relationships to other social institutions. Then we will turn to an examination of the microeconomic level, looking at the economic system from the point of view of the individual. In the case of economic institutions, this means a concern with jobs and the organization of work.

> **Economic institutions** are social structures concerned with the production and distribution of goods and services.

Types of Economic Institutions

All societies must deal with the problems of producing and distributing goods. At a minimum, each must produce food, clothing, and shelter and must institutionalize some set of rules to distribute them. In a historical and cross-cultural view, we distinguish three major types of economic systems: preindustrial, industrial, and postindustrial. They differ from one another in the typical organization of work as well as in the kind and amount of goods produced.

Preindustrial Economic Structures

In a simple society, most goods are produced by the clan or family unit. There may be limited barter or trade, but most of the goods consumed by a family are also produced by it. The family also serves as the distribution system. Family ties obligate the more productive to share with the less productive; thus children, the elderly, and the sick are provided for by ties of family responsibility.

Preindustrial economic structures were characteristic of Europe until 500 years ago and are still typical of many societies. Although the economies vary in complexity, their dominant characteristics are:

1. Production units are small, and settlements are small and widely dispersed.
2. The major sources of energy are human and animal power, occasionally supplemented by primitive waterwheels.
3. The vast majority of the labor force is engaged in **primary production**, extracting raw materials from the environment. Prominent among primary production activities are farming, herding, fishing, foresting, hunting, and mining. As late as 1900, 36 percent of the U.S. labor force was engaged in primary production.

Primary production is extracting raw materials from the environment.

In large part because of limited energy resources, preindustrial economies do not produce much more than they need. Some have produced enough surplus to support giant cities such as Rome, Cairo, and Tenochtitlán, as well as artistic and scholarly elites, but this standard of living for the few required great inequality. It also required that the vast majority of the population continue to give constant attention to primary production.

For the average person, a preindustrial economy means a close integration of work with all other aspects of life. Work takes place at or near home in family or neighborhood units. Some observers who deplore modern industrial work organization (assembly lines, time clocks, and so on) have romanticized preindustrial work organization as a situation in which people set their own pace, organize their own work, and have the satisfaction of seeing the results of their own labor. In fact, the average person in preindustrial societies probably works very hard; and if the impetus to go to work is the needs of the stock or the amount of work to be done, there is little individual choice about working. Getting to organize one's work is probably limited to deciding which end of the field to weed first, and the products of one's labor are undoubtedly too few to give rise to a great deal of satisfaction. Nevertheless, a preindustrial style of work organization does offer flexibility and variety. Its content and tempo change with the seasons; the hectic pace of the harvest is followed by the relative relaxation of harness mending and stock tending in the winter. All too often, it is also followed by malnutrition in the early spring, as last season's small surplus dwindles (Wrigley, 1969).

Figure 14.1
Primary production—food, ore, and timber—is important in industrial as well as preindustrial societies. The key difference is that mechanization allows a much greater surplus to be produced by many fewer people. This greater productivity of the primary sector sets the stage for the explosion of wealth and technology that characterizes industrial and postindustrial society.

Industrial Economic Structures

Industrialization means a change in both the organization and the content of production. Its major characteristics are:

1. Reliance on new sources of energy (gasoline, electricity, coal, steam) rather than on muscle power.
2. Large and bureaucratically organized work units.
3. A shift to **secondary production**, the processing of raw materials.

Secondary production is the processing of raw materials.

For example, ore, cotton, and wood are processed by the steel, textile, and lumber industries; other secondary industries will turn these materials into automobiles, clothing, and furniture. Obviously, some part of the labor force must still be involved in producing ore, cotton, and timber, but the proportion involved in primary production drops steadily as greater use of nonmuscle energy decreases the labor requirements for primary production.

The shift from primary to secondary production is characterized by growing surpluses. The surpluses of the primary sector make possible the expansion of secondary production, and secondary production provides yet more goods. Even with substantial inequalities in distribution, this abundance generally leads to better education, better health, and a higher standard of living for the entire population.

The transformation of the economic structure, however, does more than increase the standard of living; it also transforms the entire social fabric. As Figure 14.2 suggests, stratification systems, the family, and political institutions may all be altered; change rather than tradition becomes the natural condition (Bollen, 1983; Jackman, 1973; Rubinson & Quinlan, 1977). Some of these changes are attributable simply to greater abundance; others are due to changes in the organization of work itself.

Many of the transformations that have accompanied industrialization are universally valued: long life, democracy, reduction of intolerance, more education. Other changes, however, are not so desirable: population growth, the assault on the environment, and the growth of cities. (Many of these problematic aspects of industrialization are covered in Unit 5, which deals with change.) In spite of its drawbacks, industrialization has been eagerly sought by most societies. As a means of increasing productivity and the standard of living, its advantages have been unquestioned.

Postindustrial Economic Structures

Tertiary production is the production of services.

Postindustrial development rests on a third stage of productivity, **tertiary production**. This stage is the production of services. Service industries include government, medical care, education, fast food, repairs, and entertainment. The tertiary sector of the economy has grown tremendously in the United States, gradually replacing the blue-collar workers of primary and secondary industries with either the white-collar workers of the professional service industries or the pink-collar workers of restaurants and salons. Figure 14.3 shows the transformation of the labor force that has accompanied the shift to a postindustrial economy in the United States. The proportion engaged in primary industry is growing smaller,

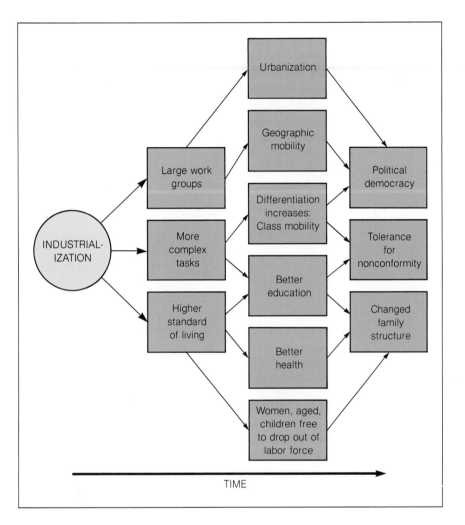

and a full 50 percent of the labor force is now employed in the tertiary sector.

The transformation is both a cause and a consequence of greater surpluses. The productivity of industrial economies frees more and more workers for such non-essential tasks as teaching, research, and health care. The advances in knowledge and technology that result from these people's work cause even further increases in productivity, which frees even more people from involvement in primary or secondary production.

Like the industrial revolution before it, the shift to a postindustrial economy is associated with changes in the organization of society. Within the tertiary sector, few employees work with machines; instead they work with people and with paper. This means that the ability to manipulate people and language has become more important than strength, endurance, and dexterity. Furthermore, within the major service sectors (government, education, and health) public service has replaced profit as the major goal. Thus service industries tend to produce and demand a different kind of worker than was needed before.

Figure 14.3 Changing Labor Force in the United States
Since 1900, the labor force in the United States has changed drastically. The proportion of workers engaged in primary production has declined sharply while the proportion engaged in service work has expanded greatly.

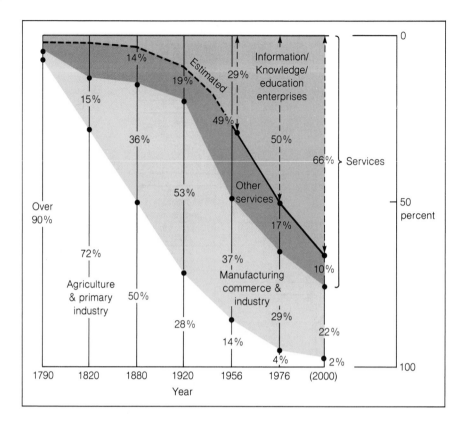

Figure 14.4
Nearly half of the U.S. labor force is employed in tertiary production. Those who work in government, education, and health care often spend a great deal of their time in committees such as this where the ability to influence others, make a good impression, and speak effectively are vital to their career success. Thus, postindustrial work environments demand a much different kind of employee than is demanded by industrial organization.

A classic postindustrial personality is the **other-directed individual** described by David Riesman. This person is sensitive and attentive to others, guided not by firm principles and values but by the signals picked up from the social environment (Riesman, 1963). For example, school administrators will move back to the basics in the 1980s with the same ease that they went along with the liberal curriculum of the 1960s and 1970s. This flexibility of purpose means high adaptability in a period of rapid social change, and it is eminently suitable to people whose jobs require manipulating people rather than the physical environment.

Another important characteristic of postindustrial society is that it represents the first time that a substantial portion of a society's energy has been devoted to studying and managing itself (Etzioni, 1968). This characteristic creates enormous potential for deliberate social change. With fewer organizational and economic resources, previous generations eliminated illiteracy, smallpox, and 90 percent of infant deaths. If the vast resources of the postindustrial society are committed to new social projects—say the elimination of segregation, cancer, blindness, or poverty—they have enormous potential for good. Of course, these resources may be turned to less admirable goals, but a postindustrial society is in a unique position in regard to its ability to produce deliberate social change.

The transitions from preindustrial to industrial to postindustrial economic structures have occurred within a few centuries. These revolutions in production have transformed social institutions and the daily lives of individuals who work in them. From monarchy to democracy, from country to city, from illiteracy to literacy, the transforming effects of economic growth and change are felt in all aspects of social life.

Modern Economic Systems

In the modern world, there are basically two types of economic systems: capitalism and socialism. Because economic systems must adapt to different political and natural environments, however, there are few instances of pure capitalism or pure socialism. Most modern economic systems represent some variation on the two and often combine elements of both.

Capitalism

The economic system in which most wealth (land, capital, and labor) is in private hands and is used to create more wealth for its owners is **capitalism** (Dushkin, 1974). Since an individual's gain is greatest when the most product has been squeezed out of the least expenditure of resources, this system is effective at using individual self-seeking as an incentive to increase productivity and the material standard of living for the society.

In theory, the capitalist economy is self-regulating. It automatically adjusts changing supplies and demands to maximize the use of resources. The theory assumes that many small producers are trying to maximize their own gain by producing what the public wants at prices it can afford. If they fail in this effort, the capital and labor they had tied up will move to more productive enterprises. This system is said to ensure that capital and labor will be put to their highest and best use. More prosaically, it ensures that they are put to their most profitable use. If an industry is wasteful, it will fold in favor of a less wasteful one. If an industry produces too much, causing a glut on the market and a drop in prices, it may go out of business. If public tastes change, the market will shift resources to the new area of demand. In this way, a balance between supply and demand is created (Williams, 1970).

Even when capitalism works to produce a balance between supply and demand, it is still an incomplete system. It maximizes production at the expense of distribution. The capitalist system is created to be a fruitful exchange between owners of capital and labor. Those who have neither are in a vulnerable position. With nothing to exchange, they are outside the market—the major device for distributing goods and services. Whereas the family can be expected to continue caring for members who cannot sell their labor (children, the elderly, the disabled), what happens when whole families, indeed whole communities, have no one who is willing to buy their labor? In theory, it is assumed that labor, like capital, will move to a new area of demand. An unemployed steelworker in Youngstown, Ohio, however, cannot easily transform himself into a computer repairman or a frogman for an off-shore oil rig (Thurow, 1980). Another problem with pure capitalism is that it does not provide for public goods: streets, watersheds, sewers, defense. These goods must be provided even if they offer profit to no one. Thus capitalist systems must have some means of distribution other than the market.

The **other-directed individual** is sensitive and attentive to others, guided not by firm principles and values but by the signals picked up from the social environment.

Capitalism is the economic system in which most wealth is in private hands and is used to create more wealth for its owners.

Socialism

If capitalism is an economic system that maximizes production at the expense of distribution, socialism is a system that stresses distribution at the expense of production. As an ideal, **socialism** is an economic structure in which productive tools are owned and managed by the group as a whole or by their representative, the state.

In theory, socialism has several major advantages over capitalism. First, societal resources can be used for the benefit of society as a whole rather than for a few. This advantage is most apparent in regard to common goods such as the environment. A related advantage is that of central planning. Because resources are controlled by the group, they can be deployed to help reach group goals. This may mean diverting them from profitable industries (say those making bicycles, televisions, or washers) to industries that are seen as more likely to benefit society in the long run: education, agriculture, or steel. The major advantage claimed for socialism, however, is that it produces equitable (though not necessarily equal) distribution.

The creed of pure socialism is from each according to ability, to each according to need. An explicit goal of socialism is to eliminate unequal reward as the major incentive to labor. Cuban revolutionary Che Guevera, argued that "one of the fundamental objectives of Marxism is to remove

Socialism is an economic structure in which productive tools (land, labor, and capital) are owned and managed by the group as a whole or by their agent, the state.

Figure 14.5

Marx predicted that bringing the working classes together in mines and factories would increase the likelihood that they would share their grievances and realize that their numbers gave them a source of strength. Miners, such as those in this picture, have been among the most radical groups in industrial society. Not only were their working conditions terrible, but geographical isolation encouraged them to feel a class apart.

interest, the factor of individual interest and gain from men's psychological motivations" (cited in Hollander, 1982). Workers are expected to be motivated by loyalty to their community and their comrades. Unfortunately, the childless woman is not likely to be motivated to do her best when the incompetent next to her takes home a larger paycheck simply because she has several children and thus a greater need. Nor is the farmer as likely to make the extra effort to save the harvest from rain or drought if his rewards are unrelated to either effort or productivity. Because of this factor, production is usually lower in socialist economies than in capitalist economies. To combat low productivity, socialist economies provide incentives for individual productivity (Hollander, 1982). For example, China currently allows agricultural communes that exceed their quotas to sell the surplus for profit (van der Tak, 1983).

The Political Economy

The form that an economic system takes depends significantly on the institutional structure of society. The economic system is particularly dependent on the political system, so much so that earlier generations referred to them as a single institution—the political economy. Recognition of this close relationship is essential for understanding the major forms of socialism that exist in the world today.

Several varieties of socialist thought flowered in the 19th century. Writers who based their idealism on humanist or Christian principles (including John Humphrey Noyes of Oneida) laid the foundations for Fabian or Christian socialism. This democratic socialism became an important political force in Western Europe. Simultaneously, Marx's version of socialism, as interpreted by Lenin, became the basis of communism.

Marx envisioned a society that was both socialist and democratic. He believed that a democratic coalition of workers would form a temporary dictatorship of the proletariat, which would last only as long as it took to dismantle bourgeois institutions. This vision of the future was based on the existence of a united, urban working class that was conscious of its own best interest.

Marx's theory posed a dilemma for Russian intellectuals in the early 20th century. They wanted a revolution but lacked an urban working class. Thus Marxism had to be substantially reinterpreted before it could be used to guide the Russian Revolution. The reinterpretation was provided by Lenin, who argued that the revolution need not come from the working class; rather, the lower classes could be led by the intellectuals. Until the masses became urban, united, and conscious, the intellectuals would have to guide them. Lenin argued that Russia's circumstances required a dictatorship of the Communist party over the proletariat (Ebenstein, 1973:33).

Communism is socialism grafted onto an authoritarian political system. It is a socialist economy guided by a political elite and enforced by a military elite. The goals of socialism (equality, efficiency) are still there, but the political form is authoritarian rather than democratic. In evaluating the merits of socialism versus capitalism, it is important to keep in mind the political structure in which the economy exists.

Figure 14.6
Socialism was an active political and economic movement in Europe even before Karl Marx issued his Manifesto in 1848. In Russia, however, there was no industrial working class to support the revolution and Lenin had to reinterpret Marx to suit an essentially feudal economy. Because Russia lacked most of the necessary conditions of democracy, the Russian Revolution established socialism in an authoritarian political system, a combination we call communism.

A **dual economy** consists of an industrial core made up of giant organizations and a periphery made up of small, competitive firms.

Mixed Economies

Most Western societies in the late 20th century represent a mixture of both capitalist and socialist economic structures within a more-or-less democratic framework. In many nations, services such as the mail and the railroads and key industries such as steel and energy have been socialized. These moves to socialism are rarely the result of pure idealism. Rather, public ownership is often seen as the only way to ensure continuation of vital services that are not profitable enough to attract private enterprise. Other services—for example, health care—have been socialized because societies have judged it unethical for these services to be available only to those who can afford to pay for them. Education is a socialized service, but it went public so long ago that few recognize the public schools as one of the first socialized industries.

In the case of many socialized services, general availability and progressive tax rates have gone far toward meeting the maxim from each according to ability, to each according to need. There are still inequalities in education and health care, but many fewer than there would be if these services were available on a strictly cash basis. The United States has done the least among major Western powers toward creating a mixed economy, but undoubtedly the trend, at least in human services, is toward increased socialism.

The U.S. Economic System

The U.S. economic system can be viewed as a **dual economy**. Its two parts are the large industries of the industrial core and the small, competitive organizations that form the periphery. These two segments of the contemporary economic system differ significantly in a variety of characteristics, including size, relationship to government, recruitment, rewards, and job characteristics.

The Industrial Core: Corporate Capitalism

The corporation system has allowed the pooling of vast amounts of capital, much as the factory system allowed the pooling of a large labor force. Thus, in place of the small, independent producers assumed by capitalist theory, the modern economy is peopled with industrial giants. This growth in size and interdependence of economic units has meant a significant change in the way capitalism operates.

Size of Units.   There are more than 250,000 businesses in the United States, but most of the nation's capital and labor are tied up in a few giants that form the industrial core. The top 20 U.S. companies (see Table 14.1) have over $477 billion worth of assets. The largest of these companies, General Motors, employs nearly two-thirds of a million people; it has 1.3 million stockholders (Dolbeare & Edelman, 1981). These giants loom large on both the national and the international scene: 13 of them are also among the top 20 companies in the world. They exceed many nations of the world in wealth and population.

Table 14.1 The 20 Largest Industrial Corporations in the United States, 1983

The largest corporations in the United States have more assets than many nations. Their financial health is of vital concern to local and national leaders, and their influence often stretches far past the borders of the United States.

RANK 1983	1982	COMPANY	SALES $Millions
1	1	Exxon (New York)	88,561,134
2	2	General Motors (Detroit)	74,581,600
3	3	Mobil (New York)	54,607,000
4	5	Ford Motor (Dearborn, Mich.)	44,454,600
5	6	International Business Machines (Armonk, N.Y.)	40,180,000
6	4	Texaco (Harrison, N.Y.)	40,068,000
7	8	E.I. du pont de Nemours (Wilmington, Del.)	35,378,000
8	10	Standard Oil (Ind.) (Chicago)	27,635,000
9	7	Standard Oil of California (San Francisco)	27,342,000
10	11	General Electric (Fairfield, Conn.)	26,797,000
11	9	Gulf Oil (Pittsburgh)	26,581,000
12	12	Atlantic Richfield (Los Angeles)	25,147,036
13	13	Shell Oil (Houston)	19,678,000
14	15	Occidental Petroleum (Los Angeles)	19,115,700
15	14	U.S. Steel (Pittsburgh)	16,869,000
16	17	Phillips Petroleum (Bartlesville, Okla.)	15,249,000
17	18	Sun (Radnor, Pa.)	14,730,000
18	20	United Technologies (Hartford)	14,669,265
19	19	Tenneco (Houston)	14,353,000
20	16	ITT (New York)	14,155,408

Because dollar totals are in millions, the sales for Exxon, for example, should be read as 88 billion dollars.

SOURCE: Reprinted from the 1984 FORTUNE Directory; © 1984 Time Inc. All rights reserved.

Interdependence.   Economic units are not only increasingly large, they are also increasingly interdependent. One symptom of this interdependence is **interlocking directorates**. Figure 14.7 provides an example of the institutional affiliations of the directors who sit on the board of General Motors (Mintz & Schwartz, 1981). This network links General Motors directly to 29 other companies. Moreover, the boards of directors of these companies also have interlocks. For example, the board of Procter & Gamble is connected to 23 other boards besides that of General Motors. Through such complex ties and through equally complex networks of financing and credit, the independence assumed by classic theory has been eroded. The banks and insurance companies that hold increasing proportions of U.S. stocks put the stability of the network ahead of the profitability of an individual unit (Kerbo & Della Fave, 1983).

The effect of institutional interdependence has been the creation of giant interlocking economic structures that cannot be allowed to fail—by either their partners, the communities they support, or their governments.

An **interlocking directorate** exists when common membership on a board of directors ties many companies together.

Figure 14.7   The Interlocking Directorate of General Motors

The people who sit on the board of directors at General Motors sit on 29 other boards. The numbers next to firm names represent the total number of corporations to which the organization is intertied. Thus, the people who sit on the board of directors at American Express are also linked to the boards of 25 other corporations. As a result of this tight network of financial ties, stability of the network becomes more important than the profitability of any particular unit.
SOURCE: Beth Mintz and Michael Schwartz, "Interlocking Directorate and Interest Groups," *American Sociological Review*, Vol. 46, 1981, pg. 857.

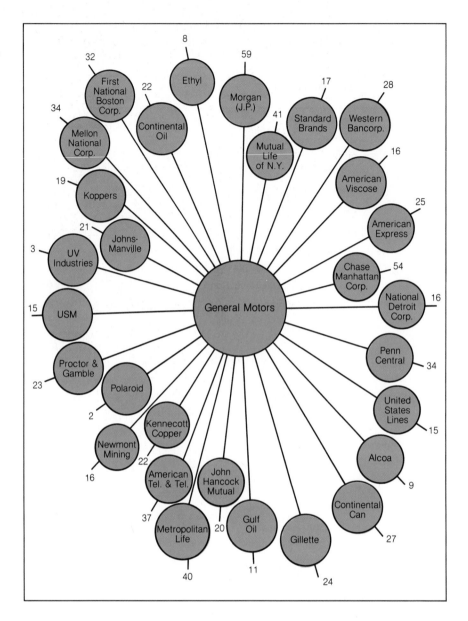

If one of these giants fell, the consequences would echo through the national and international economy. For this reason, the U.S. government now considers stepping in to help struggling giants such as Lockheed and Chrysler.

Capitalism in the United States is a very different economic system than it was in the 18th century. Monopoly has reduced the spur to efficiency and greater productivity. Large size and interdependence have made failure impossible to contemplate, putting a premium on stability rather than profit. The very large capital investment required by many modern industries means that capital cannot easily leave an unprofitable industry and flee to one that is more profitable. Neither capital nor labor is as flexible as theory demands and both may find themselves bogged down in such depressed industries as steel. As a consequence of these changes, the market is no longer an efficient regulator of supply and demand. Increasingly, this regulation is being provided by the federal government.

Corporate Capitalism and Government: Are They Too Close?
Economic theorists of the right and the left agree that the conditions of modern capitalism require government intervention. The government can spur lagging demand by reducing interest rates; it can slow down an overheated economy by reducing the money supply and tightening credit. Through tariffs and international trade agreements, wheat sales and wheat embargoes, it can further affect economic conditions. As a result of these factors, the interdependence between government and the economy has grown increasingly strong. Some people believe it has grown too much.

On the one hand, many liberals believe that there is an unbridgeable gap between the goals of government and industry; whereas industry exists to make private profits for the few, government is supposed to serve the many. These critics view close ties between government and industry with alarm; they fear that government is being used to support the economic goals of the corporate elite. This is, in fact, one of the primary arguments of the power-elite thesis reviewed in chapter 13.

A frequent target of liberal critics is the so-called military-industrial complex. In his final presidential address, Dwight Eisenhower warned that the similarity of interests between major defense industries and the military was creating a military-industrial complex. He suggested that national defense spending was responding more to self-interest on the part of corporate America than to national interest. In more reent years, critics have wondered whether the space program and various missiles and bombers haven't done more for Boeing, Lockheed, and other contractors than they have for the United States.

There can be no doubt that many industries rely heavily on military spending and that they encourage government spending out of their own self-interest. A critical analysis of the last couple decades, however, suggests that if an alliance exists between the military and industry, it is remarkably ineffective (Dye, 1983). In the years following the Vietnam War, for example, defense spending has declined as a share of the national budget. Even under President Reagan, defense spending remains a far smaller part of the federal budget than it was in the 1960s (U.S. Bureau of the Census 1984:342). Thus, although the tie certainly exists between the military and defense contractors, their alliance does not appear to represent a growing threat to government independence.

Another area in which government and economic ties are often alleged to be too close is that of federal regulatory commissions. In this case, as in that of the military-industrial complex, there is a high level of interchangeability of personnel between industry and government. A recent report found that "about half those appointed to regulatory commissions come from regulated companies or the law firms that work for them. On leaving office, about half went to work for such companies" (Patterson et al., 1983). Private law firms hire away the best antitrust lawyers of the Federal Trade Commission, and the possibility of lucrative work in the private sector is a powerful incentive to distinguish oneself in a temporary government career (J. Q. Wilson, 1980).

Figure 14.8
Although the economic philosophy of the United States is basically capitalistic, an increasing number of Americans work in nonprofit organizations—hospitals, schools, government agencies. These organizations often put service before profit and many are committed to providing service regardless of ability to pay. Most other industrialized nations have moved much farther in this direction than the United States, but in recent decades we have moved away from strict capitalism and toward a mixed economy.

What does this interchangeability mean? Many critics have alleged that private industry has captured regulatory agencies, that agencies that should be protecting the public are instead protecting the profitability of private enterprise. Increasingly, however, political analysts are inclined to offer a less critical view. They suggest that the two goals are not contradictory and that protecting private enterprise may be a service to the public (Behrman, 1980). For example, many would agree that it is in our best interest to have a healthy airlines industry, one that will allow us, say, to fly twice daily, nonstop, to Chicago.

Whereas liberals worry that economic interests have too much influence on government, conservatives worry that government has too much influence on business. The latter charge is directed especially at government regulations that restrict trade and manufacturing practices of U.S. industry. Government regulation has grown tremendously, and there are undoubtedly some foolish and unnecessary regulations. Nevertheless, regulation has for the most part grown up to meet real societal needs rather than being an extension of red tape by officious bureaucrats. For example, the Environmental Protection Agency was a response to public alarm related to having to cancel recess in Los Angeles schools because breathing outdoors was dangerous to children's health (Thurow, 1980). The Occupational Safety and Health Act of 1970 was passed as a result of a demand from labor for safer working conditions (Donnelly, 1982).

To a significant extent, government regulations support rather than restrict business. For example, regulation of the transportation and communications industry involves setting aside certain markets for specific companies, establishing minimum charges, and otherwise eliminating the costs of damaging competition (Thurow, 1980). Where government regulation is damaging, however, is in the peripheral economy; there small businesses and the self-employed find little compensation for the extra paperwork and regulation.

Regardless of the value judgment one places on it, there is clearly a strong tie between the industrial core and the federal government. Government affects business, and business affects government. The same tie also exists at the state and local levels, although at these levels the tie is frequently less equal. Major corporations dwarf many cities in their assets and power, and local governments are often in a subservient position with regard to these businesses, having to bargain tax packages, zoning exceptions, and environmental quality in order to gain or retain jobs.

The Multinationals.   The link between government and large economic actors is of particular concern when the economic actors become international actors. The large international companies (mostly American in origin)—the **multinationals** such as International Telephone and Telegraph, IBM, and General Motors—are so large that they dwarf many national governments in size. Their ability to bring capital, jobs, and prosperity from one nation to another makes them political actors. Unlike the government, however, they are motivated by a search for profit rather than by the national interest.

There is a great deal of debate about the possible effects, good and ill, of such international economic enterprises. A few observers hope that ties

Multinationals are large corporations that operate internationally.

result looks quite different than does the unemployment rate. Table 14.2 compares the various definitions for two time periods. Despite the generous definition of *actively looking*, there were close to a million discouraged workers in 1981. This figure may be even higher now, and it is likely that many of the people designating themselves as retired at 55 and 60 and many of the women who call themselves homemakers have simply given up.

Some critics charge that a new definition should be created to reflect the full range of pressure in the job market; the Labor Department wants to maintain a definition consistent with its earlier series of reports. The data on discouraged and involuntary part-time workers are, however, routinely gathered by the Labor Department to be used by labor-market analysts—and by presidential candidates.

Table 14.2   Changing Components of Unemployment, 1970 and 1981

The usual unemployment rate does not fully measure the amount of pressure in the job market. Inclusion of involuntary part-time and discouraged workers sharply increases our estimate of people who cannot find work.

	1970	1981
Total labor force	82,772,000	106,770,000
Unemployed	4,113,000	8,273,000
Unemployment rate	5.0%	7.7%
Hidden unemployment and underemployment:		
Involuntary part-time workers	2,446,000	4,767,000
Discouraged workers	437,000	808,000
Total unemployment and underemployment rate*	8.4%	12.9%

SOURCE: U.S. Bureau of the Census, 1982, tables B–14 and B–15.

*Discouraged workers were added to the count of the labor force as well as to the count of unemployed and underemployed workers.

Questions to Consider

If you were trying to assess a president's record on unemployment, what kind of measure would you like to see? What would tell you that the president had done a bad or good job on employment?

respect of their family; they may find themselves expected to help with low-status household jobs formerly done by their wives and children. Studies of unemployment in the Depression showed that men whose self-esteem was severely damaged by their role loss were tense, hard to live with, and emotionally explosive (Liker & Elder, 1983). It is little wonder, then, that unemployment tends to be associated with high levels of divorce, unhappiness, abuse, and violence (Hicks & Platte, 1970). The detailed description of Tally's Corner in chapter 2 is a vivid example of what can happen when unemployment persists in a community.

The Structure of Work: Occupations

Aside from the simplest consequences of working (income and filling up 40 hours of your time), what one does at work is probably as important as whether one works. Here some of the important differences between the professions and white- and blue-collar work are described.

Professions.   Occupations that demand specialized skills and creative freedom are **professions**. Their distinctive characteristics include (1) the production of an unstandardized product, (2) a high degree of personality involvement, (3) a wide knowledge of a specialized technique, (4) a sense of obligation to one's art, (5) a sense of group identity, and (6) a significant service to society (Gross, 1958). This definition was originally created for the so-called learned professions (law, medicine, college teaching), but it

Professions are occupations that demand specialized skills and creative freedom.

applies equally well to skilled craft workers whose work is a matter of art rather than of following patterns. Perhaps the most important thing separating the professions from other highly skilled jobs is the high involvement of the individual with the job. Illustrative of this involvement are the results of a survey that asked people from all walks of life what they would do with the extra time if the day were stretched to 26 hours. Professionals said they would spend it at work. Those in other occupations, even the highly skilled, were apt to say they would spend it in leisure activity or in work unconnected with their paid employment (Wilensky, 1966).

In the social science literature, *profession* and *professional* have technical meanings. Outside social science, however, one frequently sees *professional* used as a synonym for "highly trained." Thus there are professional muffler installers and professional car-rental agents, neither of whom are likely to demonstrate much interest in coming to work on weekends because they like their work so much.

The professions are both growing in number and changing in character. In the past, all professions were characterized by a high degree of autonomy. Doctors and lawyers were usually self-employed; college professors, though working for bureaucratic structures, enjoyed a great deal of self-governance in the United States (Loether, 1982). Increasingly, however, people in the professions work for others within organizational structures that constrain many of the most characteristic aspects of professionalism.

Blue-Collar/White-Collar.   Fifty years ago, the color of your collar was a pretty good indication of the status of your job. People who worked with their hands wore blue (or sometimes flannel) collars; managers and others who worked in clean offices wore white collars. Those days are past. The labor force is far more diversified, and some of the old guidelines no longer work. The bagger at the Safeway and the milk deliverer both wear white shirts and ties; the librarian wears blue jeans and sandals. Yet the librarian is a white-collar worker and the milk deliverer is not.

Traditional white-collar workers are managers, professionals, typists, salespeople—those who work in clean offices, wear their own clothes, and are expected to be able to think independently. White-collar workers use their head instead of their hands. Blue-collar workers are people in primary and secondary industry who work with their hands; they farm, dig ditches, build houses, and weld joints. Although some blue-collar workers earn more than some white-collar workers, their jobs are characterized by less security; layoffs are common during economic slumps and bad weather. On the average, blue-collar workers are characterized by lower incomes, lower status, lower security, closer supervision, and more routine. The strength of one's back is more important than one's smile, pronunciation, or intelligence.

Fifty years ago, this simple, two-part division of the labor force included most workers. These days it leaves out a growing category of low-skilled, low-status service workers. Some have called these people the pink-collar workers, but they as often appear in company-supplied brown polyester suits or turquoise jackets. They fry hamburgers, stock K-Mart shelves, and collect money at the "U-Serv" gas station. An important characteristic of the jobs these workers hold is that they have a short or nonexistent career ladder and they pay the minimum wage or close to it.

Figure 14.12

A growing sector of employment is the minimum-wage service sector. Fast foods, child care, and self-service gas stations are but some of the industries that require low-skill, low-paid employees. Unlike traditional blue-collar work, these industries are nonunionized and do not pay a wage on which an individual could support a family.

Blue-Collar Woes. The coming of a postindustrial economy means a permanent reduction in the number of blue-collar jobs in primary or secondary industry. Further changes in production, such as the rapidly expanding use of robots in heavy industry and the automation of supermarket checking, will mean even less need for traditional blue-collar workers. The result is that the shift to a postindustrial society means more unemployment or worse employment for the traditional working class.

This reduction is being made more abruptly and more painfully than we once anticipated. Increased concern about pollution and natural resources and a national economic recession have hurried a predicted decline in employment in secondary industry—the sector in which most blue-collar workers are employed. Some of these jobs will come back with prosperity, but changes in the U.S. industrial structure are likely to mean that significant unemployment will persist, especially for the less skilled blue-collar workers.

New jobs are developing, but they are very different from the jobs that are disappearing. Table 14.3 shows some of the projected changes in the occupational structure. As you can see, the new labor market is not totally concentrated in jobs involving high levels of education and high status. Some workers—for example, computer and data-processing mechanics—are simply a new generation of repair people with perhaps two years of vocational training. These new jobs should continue to provide opportunities for stable and relatively highly paid manual work. The other class of growing jobs, however, represents major downward mobility. Certainly, unemployed steelworkers could easily develop the skills to sell hamburgers or doughnuts—but they could not support a family on the wages usually paid in the lower-status service sector. The symbolism of shifting from a blue to a pink collar, from overalls to a cute polyester uniform, rightly signals a loss of status, income, and power.

Table 14.3   The Shifting Job Market: Projected Changes between 1978 and 1990*

	PERCENT DECLINE IN EMPLOYMENT
Some jobs are going . . .	
Shoemaking-machine operators	−13%
Farm laborers	17
Railroad-car repairers	10
Secondary-school teachers	12
Housekeepers, private households	15
Timber-cutting and logging workers	11
	PERCENT GROWTH IN EMPLOYMENT
Some jobs are growing . . .	
Data-processing-machine operators	+147%
Paralegal personnel	132
Computer-systems analysts	108
Office-machine operators	81
Tax preparers	64
Fast-food restaurant workers	69
Childcare attendants	56

SOURCE: Carey, Max L. 1981: 42–55.

*These projections assume moderate growth in GNP and a decline in inflation.

It is likely that the high unemployment rates of the early 1980s are at least partly a result of the dislocation caused by shifting modes of production. Even after the economic recession is over, however, some of the jobs that have been lost will not come back. What do we do with the people who used to hold those jobs? Some of them can be retrained for new jobs that have benefits similar to those of the relatively well-paid jobs that they have lost. Retraining programs are not a complete answer, however, for there is expected to be a severe shortage of really good jobs for manual workers. The growing occupations require either years of advanced education and specialized knowledge or almost no skill, and the latter offer very little reward. Thus the transformation of the labor market is likely to mean problems for the traditional working class.

The Meaning of Work

For most people, work is essential as the means to earn a livelihood. As noted in chapter 8, one's work is often the most important determinant of one's position in the stratification structure and, consequently, of one's health, happiness, and life-style.

Work is more than this, however. It is also the major means that most of us use to structure our lives. It determines what time we get up, what we do all day, who we do it with, and how much time we have left for leisure. Over a lifetime, our work will be our longest and most enduring task. Thus the nature of our work and our attitude toward it can have a tremendous impact on whether we view our lives as fulfilling or painful. For most of us—whether we work at home, at school, or in the labor force—our work is a major determinant of self-esteem and identity (O'Toole, 1973:4). If we are good at it, if it gives us a chance to demonstrate competence, and if it is meaningful and socially valued, then it can be a major contributor to life satisfaction.

The Protestant Ethic

What is meaningful work? According to the **Protestant ethic**, what you do is less important than that you work hard. This work ethic, whose religious associations are discussed in chapter 15, is no longer the property of any particular creed or faith. It is a general cultural belief that work is good and idleness is wicked.

This attitude toward work is neither human nature nor a cultural universal. In many cultures, work is seen as an unhappy curse, and this idea finds some expression in our own culture. In Genesis, a life of toil is one of the burdens placed on Adam when he is expelled from the garden (Genesis 3:19), and many people's idea of heaven is of a place where they are free of work.

This mixed cultural heritage leads many Americans to have an ambivalent attitude toward work. We place a great deal of emphasis on working as opposed to idleness, but we want work that is fulfilling. Surveys show that three-quarters of U.S. workers would want to continue working even if they inherited enough money that they didn't need the income (see Table 14.4). Of course, many, or even most, of those who would continue to work would prefer another job, perhaps trying their hand at a novel, starting their own business, or piloting charter boats. As a rule, however, Americans express a clear preference for work over idleness, and many feel anxious and at loose ends when they have no work to do.

The current work ethic differs sharply from the old Protestant ethic, though. Few people now (if ever) are satisfied with the idea that all work is moral and hence meaningful. Instead, people want work that allows them to use their talents, that challenges their minds and their skills, and that brings social and economic rewards.

Alienation

Many jobs do not have these characteristics. To paraphrase Marx, some individuals do not fulfill themselves in work, but rather deny themselves; some individuals find misery rather than well-being at work, and some find their mental and physical energies exhausted by work. When these things occur, we speak of **alienation**. Because work is such a central part of our lives, individuals who are alienated from their work become alienated from themselves and from society (Gruenberg, 1980).

The factory system of the mid 19th century prompted Marx to predict widespread worker alienation. The assembly line, the monotony, the high levels of supervision and task specialization almost completely eliminated people's ability to make a personal investment in their work. Marx anticipated that continued mechanization of production would totally alienate the working class.

Many changes have occurred in the organization of work since Marx wrote about alienation, and many of them are in the direction he predicted. Increased mechanization has reduced the skill level needed for many jobs to the point where it is difficult to take pride in craft or in a job well done (Wallace & Kalleberg, 1982). Typesetting and even typing have been transformed by technology into low-skill jobs. In the days before word processors, photocopying, and self-correcting typewriters, a typist had to be

The **Protestant ethic** is a belief that work is good and idleness is wicked. Its name comes from its importance to the early Puritans.

Table 14.4 Americans' Attitudes toward work
Americans retain a strong commitment to work. Indeed, as women increase their commitment, it can be said that the work ethic is growing.

"If you inherited enough money that you didn't need the income, would you keep working anyway?"

	PERCENT RESPONDING YES
Women	
1957	58%
1976	77
Men	
1957	85
1976	84

SOURCE: Institute for Social Research, cited in Yankelovich, 1981:95.

Alienation occurs when conformity to role expectations estranges the individual from personal creativity and judgment.

Figure 14.13
Automation has eliminated many jobs altogether. Many of those that are left have been reduced to such low levels of skill and monotony that they cannot provide a feeling of accomplishment or worker satisfaction. Women and men with jobs such as this quality control specialist are apt to find their work alienating and unsatisfactory. Their major compensations are their wages and relatively short work week.

good; one mistake and the whole thing might have to be redone. A good typist could therefore take pride in the work. With the new technologies, almost anyone can turn out decent-looking copy. Thus, although few of us work on assembly lines, much of the work that we do has been reduced to such simple tasks that it is hard to take pride in our work. Also, at all levels, high and low, work is increasingly bound by the regulations of the large bureaucracies in which we work, so there is little scope for personal judgment.

Working with machines is not the only way to become alienated from work. People can become alienated by having to sell their personality as well as their muscle. This is especially obvious in sales, where personality is an important instrument for getting the job done. Just as an auto worker brings a tool kit to work, the salesperson brings a cheerful, outgoing personality—leaving behind the real self (Mills, 1951).

Of course, the shifting nature of work has not all been in the direction of increasing alienation; there are some compensating features. One is that the labor force works with increasingly complex and expensive machines. There can be pleasure and pride in working with technological miracles, and although less skill is required, people may take more pride in working with word processors than with typewriters, in working with computerized automobile diagnostic machines than with the car itself. The major compensation, however, is pay and leisure. The unprecedented productivity of our economy has made it possible to produce a large surplus with relatively little labor input, which has made it possible to increase wages and decrease hours of work. These increased benefits may not make the work itself less alienating, but a good wage certainly improves the likelihood that individuals will consider their work—and themselves—worthwhile.

Work Satisfaction

A concern with the alienation of labor has prompted a rich literature on work satisfaction or the lack of it. This literature suggests that a great many people are satisfied with their work. Recent surveys demonstrate that 80 percent of U.S. workers report being either very satisfied or satisfied with their jobs; only 20 percent report being dissatisfied or very dissatisfied (National Opinion Research Center, 1978). Although a report of satisfaction with one's job may represent an acceptance of one's lot rather than a real enthusiasm for the work, it is remarkable that 51 percent of U.S. workers choose to say that they are very satisfied and only 4 percent choose to report that they are very dissatisfied.

Studies of job satisfaction concentrate on two kinds of rewards that are available from work. **Intrinsic rewards** arise from the process of work; you experience them when you enjoy the people you work with and feel pride in your creativity and accomplishments. **Extrinsic rewards** are more tangible benefits, such as income and security; if you hate your job but love your paycheck, you are experiencing extrinsic rewards.

Ideally, work would be most satisfying if it provided high levels of both intrinsic and extrinsic rewards. A review of dozens of studies shows that the most satisfying jobs are those that provide (1) autonomy and freedom from close supervision, (2) good pay and benefits, (3) job security, (4) opportunity for promotions, (5) use of valued skills and abilities, (6) variety, (7) interesting work, and (8) occupational prestige (Mortimer, 1979). There is, however, a great deal of variability in the extent to which these attributes are attached to jobs. Some jobs score high on all of them and some score low on nearly all of them.

Generally, the most satisfied workers are those in the learned professions, people such as lawyers, doctors, and professors. These people have considerable freedom to plan their own work, to express their talents and creativity, and to work with others; furthermore, their extrinsic rewards

Intrinsic rewards are rewards that arise from the process of work; they include the enjoyment of creativity, accomplishment, and working with others.

Extrinsic rewards are tangible benefits such as income and security.

Figure 14.14
Individuals who are free to use their creativity in their job typically enjoy their work more. If they receive a good income, that is an additional reward. The intrinsic rewards that come with using one's talents and working with others are not equally available to all workers. Instead, white-collar and professional workers tend to receive both more intrinsic and more extrinsic rewards from their work.

are substantial. The least satisfied workers are those who work on automobile assembly lines. Although their extrinsic rewards are good, their work is almost completely without intrinsic reward; they have no control over the pace or content of the work and are generally unable to interact with coworkers. A survey of automotive assembly-line workers showed that only 8 percent would choose the same occupation again, whereas 93 percent of urban university professors would choose the same occupation (Kohn, 1972). In between these extremes, professionals and skilled workers generally demonstrate the greatest satisfaction; semiskilled, unskilled, and clerical workers indicate lower levels of satisfaction.

The criteria for a satisfying job vary by occupation. Professionals and skilled workers tend to take extrinsic rewards for granted; for them, job satisfaction depends on the amount of intrinsic rewards they receive. Unskilled, semi-skilled, and clerical workers, however, receive few intrinsic rewards. Whether these workers find their jobs satisfying is thus likely to depend entirely on their wages; for them a good job is a job that pays well (Gruenberg, 1980). This does not mean that these workers would not like an opportunity to use their talents and their minds; it simply means that, lacking any such opportunity, they base their job satisfaction on its extrinsic rewards.

Managing the Worker

Social science has been concerned with work satisfaction and work alienation because they represent a central part of the socially structured environment. Unlike some concerns of social science, the same topics have also been of concern to business and industry. The practical interest in alienation by the business community has led to a unique marriage of theory and practice.

Managers are interested in the application of social science findings about alienation for a variety of reasons (Gardell, 1975). Most important is the economic motive; it has generally been assumed that satisfied workers will show greater productivity and lower turnover rates than unsatisfied workers, thus contributing to greater profitability. Next in importance is the humanistic motive, in which meaningful jobs that are neither physically nor mentally degrading are seen as desirable for their own sake. Finally, there is the ideological reason; many believe that a highly authoritarian workplace is incompatible with a democratic political structure.

Figure 14.14

The scientific management school suggested that productivity would increase if work tasks were broken down to the smallest possible units so that each worker would repeat the same task all day. Thus, a seamstress might sew inseams or insert zippers all day. More recent schools of thought suggest that workers will be more productive, more careful, and less often absent from work if they are allowed to invest some talent and creativity in their tasks. The Industrial Democracy school suggests that a democratic workplace is a necessary step toward a fully democratic society.

The involvement of social science in industrial management began in the 1930s with the *human relations school* of industrial sociology. This group, founded by Elton Mayo, stressed treating workers as human beings with social and emotional needs. As obvious as this type of treatment seems now, it contradicted the earlier scientific management school, which viewed workers simply as pieces of equipment. The earlier school tried to increase productivity by breaking down each task as much as possible so the worker, like a machine, could stand in one spot and do the same thing all day. This strategy was supposed to reduce training, increase speed, and reduce mistakes. Instead, in many instances, it led to deadly boredom, daydreaming, absenteeism, and absentminded mistakes.

The human relations school grew out of a series of pioneering experiments at Western Electric's Hawthorne plant in Cicero, Illinois, in the late 1920s. The company was interested in a management program that would help it increase productivity, so it gave a team of social scientists relatively free rein to experiment with working conditions. For the studies, one group of workers was separated from the others to become the experimental group. Various experimental conditions were applied to this group, and its productivity was then compared to that of the other workers, the control group. The experiments involved relatively minor adjustments in working conditions: brightening the workplace, changing from piece rates to hourly wages, changing break periods, introducing soft lights or music. The problem was that no matter what condition was introduced, productivity went up. It went up when the lights were brightened, and it went up even more when they were dimmed.

Finally, Mayo and his coworkers concluded that productivity was going up in response to the experiment itself rather than in response to the experimental conditions. That is, the experimental group of workers had been selected for important scientific work and set apart from the other workers, interactions within the group became more intense and there was always a management crowd fussing over the group. (This is one of the first observations of the guinea-pig effect, noted in chapter 2, and it is sometimes called the Hawthorne effect as a result of this early association.)

The human relations school has generally advised business that the most effective way to increase productivity is to increase informal work-group solidarity and interaction and to provide evidence that management considers workers and their ideas worthwhile. Thus management efforts may take the form of company-sponsored recreation such as softball and bowling leagues, suggestion boxes, employee lunchrooms, and company newsletters to promote a we-feeling at all levels. Essentially, management tries to increase some of the intrinsic rewards people might get from work without making substantive changes in either extrinsic rewards or the organization of work. This approach has been subjected to serious criticism on the ground that it manipulates workers, which leads to even greater exploitation than before (Perrow, 1979).

The *industrial democracy school* can be regarded as an outgrowth of the human relations school, but along more radical lines. It advocates democratic decision making within the organization and reduced authoritarianism in the work environment. Democracy is suggested to be to the advantage of the employer as well as the employee. A management consultant to Polaroid lists the following advantages of greater worker participation (Lytle, 1975):

1. Employees more committed to high production and high quality, lower costs, and other corporate goals.
2. Increased opportunity for employees to gain satisfaction, growth, and enjoyment from their work, which helps fulfill the corporate goal of providing a work life for all employees in which they can . . .

—Exercise their talents fully.
—Express their opinions.
—Make their work a fully rewarding, important part of their lives.
—Share in the progress of the company as far as their capabilities permit.

3. Reduced absenteeism and turnover.
4. Open flows of ideas from employees about better methods, processes, equipment, procedures, and so on.
5. More effective handling of plant discipline problems through increased self-discipline of employees.
6. More openness to change on the part of employees.
7. Increased opportunity for supervisors to manage rather than having to provide detailed direction.

This description of industrial democracy suggests that both workers and management will benefit. As with most such schemes, however, it seems to have a flaw. Recent studies have found that although democracy produces more satisfied workers, satisfied workers don't produce significantly more than do dissatisfied workers (Greenberg, 1980; Hall, 1983; Perrow, 1979). Thus one of the major

incentives for employers is reduced. Are the other benefits of industrial democracy worth the possible costs?

Within the United States, few firms have been willing to commit themselves to a full-scale experiment in industrial democracy. Attempts to introduce democracy have been limited largely to flextime, in which individuals are given some flexibility in arranging their 40 hours of work a week. This flexibility is usually rather limited (for example, forgoing lunch and leaving work an hour early) and is an option open most often in clerical and other white-collar occupations. A recent Chrysler labor settlement, which placed a worker representative on the management team in exchange for wage concessions, is, however, a modest step toward real industrial democracy.

The major interest in industrial democracy has occurred in Sweden, where the government has encouraged experiments in nationalized firms. Since profit is not the only goal of socialized industries, these industries can afford to tolerate possible decreases in productivity in exchange for long-run benefits, either social or economic. Private enterprise, however, does not have tax dollars to fall back on if a transformation in management causes temporary loss of income; nor can it generally afford humanitarian or ideological benefits unless they also produce economic benefits.

Teams of social scientists have carefully monitored the Swedish experiments in industrial democracy. One of the pioneering studies of these experiments was done in a branch plant of a tobacco manufacturing company in Avrika. In this experiment, the employees were to work with management to implement a democratic scheme that the employees desired. The stated goals of the worker-management team at the Avrika factory included job rotation, worker participation in decisions about hiring and firing, and, more generally, a decision-making process that provided for sufficient agreement, solidarity, and stability in the work group (Agersvold, 1975). The experiment resulted in a 15 to 20 percent increase in productivity for the Avrika plant and work satisfaction significantly higher in that plant than in the plants that served as the control group. The greater productivity may have been caused by the guinea-pig effect, but the improved morale and attitude are real enough. Thus the experimenters concluded that industrial democracy provides benefits for both the employer and the employee as well as a work environment that is compatible with and supportive of basic democratic institutions.

Think about where you work. How democratic is the decision making? Would you be more satisfied with your job if you had more opportunity to influence the pace and organization of your work? Would you work harder or be more productive under such a system? Would the same thing be true of all your coworkers?

SUMMARY

1. The economic institution has a profound effect on other institutional structures, particularly government, stratification systems, education, and the family. Changes from preindustrial to industrial to postindustrial economies have thus had profound effects on social organization.

2. Approximately half of the U.S. labor force is involved in tertiary production. This change in employment has meant a devaluation of physical strength and dexterity in favor of skill in manipulating ideas and people.

3. Capitalism is an economic system that maximizes productivity but tends to neglect aspects of distribution; socialism emphasizes distribution and neglects aspects of production. Most contemporary economies include elements of both.

4. Economic and political institutions are especially interdependent, and the actual operation of an economic system depends on the political structure in which it operates. Communism is a socialist economy in an authoritarian political system; Christian or democratic socialism is socialism in a political democracy.

5. The U.S. has a dual economy containing two distinct parts: the industrial core and the competitive sector at the periphery. These are paralleled by a segmented labor market.

6. The industrial core of the U.S. economy has grown far beyond the scope embraced by traditional capitalist theory. Instead of containing independent producers who balance supply and demand, the economy is peopled with giant corporations that are tightly bound together in networks of finance and management. This economy is no longer self-regulating.

7. In the United States, one's work has a tremendous psychological importance, being a major determinant of self-identity and self-esteem as well as of one's position in the stratification system.

8. U.S. workers value jobs that give them both intrinsic and extrinsic rewards. These rewards are more common for white-collar and professional jobs, however, and people who have these jobs are more likely to enjoy their work and find satisfaction in it.

9. Worker satisfaction is significantly increased when work environments are made more democratic and less authoritarian. Although this move toward industrial democracy does not increase worker productivity, it may reduce costs of supervision and create a work environment more supportive of the basic values of democracy.

SUGGESTED READINGS

Ebenstein, William. (1980). Today's Isms. Englewood Cliffs, N.J.: Prentice-Hall. A classic that offers a straightforward, understandable discussion of the major political and economic forms. It is useful for understanding socialism, capitalism, and communism—their theoretical underpinnings and how they work in practice.

Kimzey, Bruce. (1983). Reaganomics. St. Paul, Minn.: West Publishing. A short but excellent review of Reagan's economic policies written by an economist for noneconomists. Helps one understand how capitalism works in the United States and how current economic policies are based on past capitalist ideology.

O'Toole, James (Ed.). (1974). Work in America. Cambridge, Mass.: MIT Press. A collection of readings assembled by a special task force for the secretary of the Department of Health, Education, and Welfare.

Rubin, Lillian. (1976). Worlds of Pain. New York: Basic Books. What does it mean to be working class in the United States today? What kinds of jobs are available for this segment of society? Are jobs secure? Do current economic conditions affect the working class adversely in terms of quality of life? These important questions are answered by Rubin in her detailed study of 50 working-class families.

Terkel, Studs. (1975). Working. New York: Avon. The personal accounts of U.S. workers, describing the diversity of jobs in our society, how people feel about the occupations they have chosen, and the work involved in their jobs. An enjoyable book, especially for those contemplating an occupation and wanting to know how people in that occupation feel about it.

Thurow, Lester C. (1980). The Zero-Sum Society. New York: Basic Books. Another book about the effect of slow economic growth on U.S. political and economic institutions. A wide-ranging book that gives special attention to the close relationship between economics and politics.

CHAPTER 15
RELIGION

PROLOGUE

Have You Ever . . . *seriously considered the possibility that God has a position on the Equal Rights Amendment? Phyllis Schlafly is certain that God is against the Amendment: "I'm a Christian and all good Christians believe that women are special and that God made men to take care of women, to protect them and go to war for them, to help them with their jackets and make sure nobody else messes with them" (cited in Bollier, 1982:222). Some pro-ERA people also believe that God is on their side. Luckily, this text does not have to concern itself with which side is right. Its concern is the relationship between religious belief and social institutions.*

Whether they search for the answer in the Bible, the Talmud, the Koran, the Bhagavad Gita, or the stars, people have made religion an important part of their culture. The important rituals of life—birth, death, marriage—are tied to religion. In fact, whether you believe in God or not, you are likely to be prayed over at commencement, at your funeral, and at several points in between. More generally, you live in a society whose values and institutions have been shaped by religious belief and heritage.

The pope goes to Poland, and everyone wonders whether it might lead to invasion or mob violence. In our nation, people are being fined and sent to jail for operating church schools that do not meet state standards for teacher certification. Commencements and legislative sessions are opened by prayer.

Religion is an important part of social life. It is intertwined with politics and culture, and it is intimately concerned with integration and conflict. At the microsociological level, sociologists examine the consequences of religious belief and involvement for individuals. How does being religious

407

affect the integration, activities, and attitudes of ordinary people? On a macrosociological level, sociologists examine how society affects religion and how religion affects society. Of particular concern is the contribution of religion to social order and social change.

The Scientific Study of Religion

What Is Religion?

The first step in studying religion is to agree on what it is. How can we define religion so that our definition includes the contemplative meditation of the Buddhist monk, the speaking in tongues of a modern Holy Roller, the worship of nature in Native American cultures, and the formal ceremonies of the Catholic church? Sociologists define **religion** as the system of shared beliefs and practices by which people invoke supernatural forces as explanations of earthly struggles (Stark & Bainbridge, 1979:121). This definition includes belief systems that attribute personality and will to nature and belief systems that encompass one or more gods. It does not, however, include belief systems whose explanations of earthly events omit any reference to the supernatural, such as Marxism and science.

Religion is the system of shared beliefs and practices by which people invoke supernatural forces as explanations of earthly struggles.

The Sociological Perspective

Sociologists who study religion treat it as a set of values. As with monogamy or democracy, the concern is not whether the values are true or false. The scientific study of religion does not ask whether God exists, whether salvation is really possible, or which is the true religion. Rather, it examines the ways in which culture, society, and class relationships affect religion and the ways in which religion affects individuals and social structure.

Figure 15.1
This Trappist monk, a member of a Roman Catholic religious order in France, spends much of his day in meditation, silence, and fasting. The monastic life demands an austere and self-disciplined religious devotion that is very different from the religious practices of most Christians.

Why Religion? Some Theoretical Answers

Religion is a fundamental feature of all societies. Whether primitive or advanced, each society has forms of religious activity and expressions of religious behavior. Why? The answer appears to lie in the fact that every individual and every society must struggle to find explanations for events and experiences that go beyond personal experience. The poor man looks around him and wonders, "Why me?" The woman whose child dies in its sleep wonders, "Why mine?" The community struck by flood or tornado wonders, "Why us?" Beyond these personal dilemmas, people wonder why the sun comes up every morning, why there is a rainbow in the sky, and what happens after death. These appear to be questions that all individuals and societies struggle with. The answers vary enormously from culture to culture, but each culture provides answers that help individuals understand their place in the universe. In the words of Weber, religion deals with "the fundamental problem of meaning."

Religion helps us interpret and cope with events that are beyond our control and understanding; tornadoes, droughts, and plagues become meaningful when they are attributed to the workings of some greater force. Beliefs and rituals develop as a way to control or appease this greater force, and eventually they become patterned responses to the unknown. Rain dances may not bring rain, and prayers may not lead to good harvests; but both provide a familiar and comforting context in which people can confront otherwise mysterious and inexplicable events. Regardless of whether they are right or wrong, religious beliefs and rituals help people cope with the extraordinary events they experience.

Within this general sociological approach to religion, there are two distinct theoretical perspectives. One school, associated with Durkheim, sees religion as a thinly disguised worship of society, serving to create and maintain social solidarity. The second school, associated with Weber, views religion as an intellectual force that may challenge society as well as support it.

Durkheim: Religion as the Worship of Society

Durkheim's structural-functionalist analysis began with the assumption that if religion is universal, then it must meet basic needs of society; it must serve important functions. Durkheim identified three universal aspects of all religions, which he called the elementary forms of religion. Having established the universal form of religion, he then discussed universals in the functions or consequences of religion.

The Elementary Forms of Religion. Durkheim (1915) compared religions from all over the world and concluded that all share three elements: (1) a distinction between the sacred and the profane, (2) a set of beliefs, and (3) a set of rituals.

THE SACRED AND THE PROFANE. A central component of all religions is the division of human experience into the sacred and the profane. The **profane** represents all that is routine and taken for granted in the everyday

> The **profane** represents all that is routine and taken for granted in the everyday world, things that are accepted because they are familiar and common.

The **sacred** consists of things outside the sphere of everyday life that are approached with an attitude of awe and reverence.

world, things that are known and familiar and that we can control, understand, and manipulate. The **sacred,** by contrast, consists of the events and things that we hold in awe and reverence—what we can neither understand nor control.

In the cultures of premodern societies, a large proportion of the world is viewed as sacred. Many events are beyond control and manipulation. As advances in human knowledge increase a society's ability to explain and even control what was previously mysterious, fewer and fewer events require supernatural explanations; less is held sacred. When an event can be explained without reference to supernatural forces, then it is no longer sacred. This process of transferring things or ideas from the sacred to the profane is called **secularization.** Science and technology have been major contributors to secularization. They have given us explanations for lightning, rainbows, and death that rely on physical rather than supernatural forces. Thus they have come to be viewed as enemies of religion (Hargrove, 1979:27).

Secularization is the process of transferring things or ideas from the sacred realm to the profane realm. The transfer occurs when an event can be explained without recourse to supernatural forces.

BELIEFS, MYTHS, AND CREEDS.   A second common dimension to all religions is a set of beliefs about the supernatural. Religious beliefs center around uncertainties associated with birth, death, creation, success, failure, and crisis. They become part of the world view constructed by society as a rationale for the human condition and the recurrent problems experienced. As beliefs become organized into an interrelated set of assumptions about the supernatural, they form the basis for official religious doctrines, which find expression in the rituals of the church.

RITUALS.   Religion is a practice as well as a belief system. It brings people together to express through ritual the things that they hold sacred. In contemporary Christianity, rituals are used to mark such events as births, deaths, weddings, the resurrection, and Christ's birth. In an earlier era,

Figure 15.2

Most religions hold marriage to be a sacred event. In The Unification Church, new recruits are required to spend the first few years celibate, giving their time and energy to the church. After their commitment to the church has been established, however, they are allowed to marry. In this photograph in 1982 the Reverend Sun Myung Moon officiates at the mass wedding ceremony of 2200 couples in Madison Square Garden.

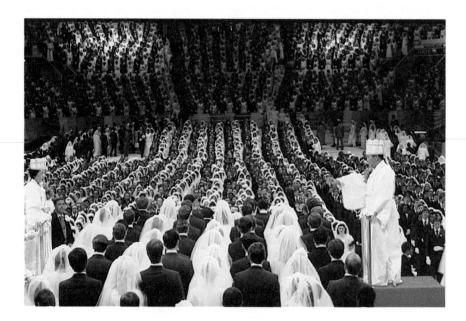

when the world was more rural and more uncertain, planting and harvest were occasions for important rituals in the Christian church; they are still important ritual occasions in many religions.

The Functions of Religion. Durkheim argued that religion serves functions for individuals who believe in it and for society as a whole. For individuals, the beliefs and rituals of religion offer support, consolation, and reconciliation in times of need. On ordinary occasions, many people find satisfaction and a feeling of belongingness in religious participation.

On a societal level, Durkheim argued, the major function of religion is that it gives tradition a moral imperative. Most of the central values and norms of any culture are taught and reinforced in its religion. These values and norms cease to be merely the usual way of doing things and become the only moral way of doing them. They become sacred. When a tradition is sacred, it is continually affirmed through ritual and practice and is largely immune from change.

Within the functionalist perspective, the worship of God is seen as a barely disguised worship of society (Durkheim, in O'Dea, 1966:12). Religion is seen as a means of lending supernatural authority to traditional practices, a way of giving usual practice the unchallengeable standing of supernaturally established laws.

Weber: Religion as an Independent Force

Durkheim looked at the forms of religion and asked about the kinds of functions they performed. Weber was concerned with the process by which religious answers were developed and how their content affected society.

For most people, religion is a matter of following tradition; people worship as their parents did before them. To Weber, however, the essence of religion is the search for knowledge about the unknown. In this sense, religion is similar to science; it is a way of coming to understand the world around us. And as with science, the answers provided may be uncomfortable; they may challenge the status quo as well as support it.

Where do the answers to questions of ultimate meaning come from? Often they come from someone who has **charisma**—extraordinary personal qualities that are thought to be supernatural in origin (Weber, 1910/ 1970e:295). Charisma has been attributed to such historical figures as Christ, Muhammad, and, more recently, John Humphrey Noyes (Oneida community), Joseph Smith (Mormonism), and Jim Jones (People's Temple). The answers provided by such individuals often disagree with traditional answers. Thus Weber sees religious inquiry as a potential source of instability and change in society.

In viewing religion as a process, Weber gave it a much more active role than did Durkheim. This is most apparent in Weber's analysis of the Protestant Reformation.

The Protestant Ethic and the Spirit of Capitalism. In a classic analysis of the influence of religious ideals on other social institutions, Weber (1904–1905/1958) argued that the Protestant Reformation paved the way

Charisma is extraordinary personal qualities that are thought to be supernatural in origin.

Figure 15.3
The hard work, sacrifice, and frugal living that were so much a part of our ideal American culture in 1930 are symbolized in Grant Wood's painting, American Gothic. Weber argued that these values, nurtured by Protestantism, became the foundation of capitalism as a form of economic activity. To Weber, religion was an important source of social change.

for bourgeois capitalism. He suggested that three aspects of Protestantism were essential in creating a new morality: predestination, the concept of a calling, and rationalism.

Predestination is the theological argument that we cannot earn our way to salvation; we are predestined for either salvation or damnation (see Isaiah 42:25 for one of the supporting Scriptures). Our salvation is God's decision, not our own work. No priests or popes can intercede on our behalf; each of us stands alone before God. The result, argued Weber, was an awful isolation, in which individuals searched for signs of grace that would tell them whether they were among the saved or the damned.

An additional element of Protestantism was Martin Luther's concept of calling. Luther argued that God calls each of us to some earthly duty and that our best service to God is through hard work at our allotted task. This emphasis on earthly work contrasted sharply with the 15th century Catholic teaching that the best service to God was withdrawal into a monastery.

A final element of early Protestantism was an emphasis on rationalism as a means to salvation. Rationalism led to adult baptism (the decision to be baptized had to represent a serious desire on the part of the individual rather than something imposed by parents), the translation of the Bible from Latin into the common language so that individuals might interpret the Scriptures on their own, and the elimination of music and ritual from church services. These three elements were most fully developed among the Puritans. For them, religion was an intellectual exercise; God was to be worshipped with work, not with song.

The combination of the three elements produced what Weber called the Protestant ethic, a belief that work, rationalism, and plain living are moral virtues, whereas idleness and indulgence are sinful. What happens to a person who follows this ethic? Someone who works hard and makes business decisions on rational rather than emotional criteria (Scrooge, for example, bases Crachet's wages on business considerations, not on what Crachet needs to support his crippled son, Tiny Tim) will grow rich. But what can the money be spent on? It cannot be spent on wine or fine clothing, for that would be wicked indulgence. Therefore, it is reinvested in the business—in more land, more machines, more wagons. This close relationship between religion and wealth was acknowledged by the founder of the Methodist church, John Wesley:

> Religion must necessarily produce both industry and frugality, and these cannot but produce riches. But as riches increase, so will pride, anger, and the love of the world in all its branches. . . . Is there no way to prevent this—this continual decay of pure religion? We ought not to prevent people from being diligent and frugal; we must exhort all Christians to gain all they can, and to save all they can; that is, in effect to grow rich. [Cited in Niebuhr, 1929/1957:70]

In the Protestant ethic, wealth was an unintended consequence of behavior that was directed by religious motives. The shift from the Protestant ethic to the spirit of capitalism required only that wealth become the end itself rather than a means to an end.

This brief sketch of Weber's thesis illustrates the thrust of his approach to religion: that religious ideas can be the source of change. Weber viewed religion as an ongoing process of inquiry, a dynamic aspect of society.

Modern Conflict Theory: Beyond Marx

Like Durkheim, Marx saw religion as a supporter of tradition. This support ranges from relatively mild injunctions that the poor and oppressed should endure rather than revolt (blessed be the poor, blessed be the meek, and so on) and that everyone should pay taxes (give unto Caesar) all the way to the extreme endorsement of inequality implied by a belief in the divine right of kings.

Marx differed from Durkheim by interpreting the support for tradition in a negative light. Marx, an atheist, saw religion as a delusion deliberately fostered by the elite—a sort of shell game designed to keep the eyes of the downtrodden on the hereafter so they would not notice their earthly oppression. This position is hardly value-free; and much more obviously than either Weber's or Durkheim's, it does make a statement about the truth or falsity of religious doctrine.

Modern conflict theory goes beyond Marx's interpretation of religion as the opiate of the masses. The major contribution of Marxism to the analysis of religion is the idea of the dialectic—that contradictions build up between existing institutions and that these contradictions lead to change. Sometimes contradictions between other institutions erupt into religious expression. On other occasions, the basic tension is between society and religion. This tension is addressed in the next section of the chapter.

Tension between Religion and Society

A society's religions are part of its culture, its traditional ways of doing things. The Muslim religion is an integral part of Middle Eastern culture, just as Judeo-Christianity is an important part of Western culture. Despite this overlap between culture and religion, there is a universal tension between them.

Each religion is confronted with two contradictory yet complementary tendencies: the tendency to compromise with the world and the tendency to reject the world (Troeltsch, 1931). When a religion denounces adultery, homosexuality, and fornication, does the church categorically exclude adulterers, homosexuals, and fornicators, or does it adjust its expectations to take common human frailties into account? If a rich man is as likely to enter the kingdom of heaven as a camel to go through the eye of the needle, must the church require that all members forsake their worldly belongings?

How religions resolve these dilemmas is central to their eventual form and structure. Scholars distinguish two ideal types of religious organizations: The *church* represents the successful compromisers, and the *sect* represents the virtuous outsiders.

Churches are religious organizations that have become institutionalized, that have endured for generations, that are supported by society's norms and values, and that have become an active part of society. Their societal activity does not necessarily mean that they have compromised essential values. They still retain the ability to protest injustice and immorality. From the abolition movement of the 1850s to the antiwar move-

Churches are religious organizations that are institutions of society, supporting and supported by its other institutions. They tend to be large and bureaucratically organized, with professional clergy and formal rituals of participation.

Sects are religious groups that reject the social environment in which they exist. They are generally small, low in ritual, and demanding of high levels of personal participation.

ment of the 1960s, churchmen and women have been in the forefront of social protest. Nevertheless, churches are generally committed to working with society. They may wish to improve it, but they have no wish to abandon it.

Sects are religious organizations that reject the social environment in which they exist (Johnson, 1957). Religions that reject sexual relations (Shakerism), automobiles (Amish) or monogamy (19th Century Mormonism) are examples of sects that differ so much from society's norms that their relationships with the larger society are often hostile. They reject major elements of the larger culture and are in turn rejected by it.

The chief distinguishing features of churches and sects are summarized in Table 15.1. Many religious groups fall somewhere between these polar opposites; the distinction is meant to guide our analysis rather than to serve as boxes into which current religions can be sorted. The following sections will elaborate on major differences in religious organization, differences that stem from the balance between compromise and rejection of society's institutions.

Churchlike Religions

Within the rough category of religions that exhibit a low degree of tension with society and a high degree of integration with society's institutions are two major types: the ecclesia and the denomination.

An **ecclesia** is a churchlike religious group that automatically includes every member of a society.

Ecclesia. The most institutionalized of all religious structures is an **ecclesia**—a religious body that automatically includes every member of a society. People do not join ecclesiae; membership comes with citizenship (Becker, in Yinger 1957:149). The Roman Catholic church in Europe was an ecclesia during the Middle Ages. Ecclesiae represent the highest degree of religious institutionalization. There is little tension between the religion

Figure 15.4
Religion in the United States is predominantly Christian with 87 percent of the population being either Protestant or Catholic. Even so, there is a wide range of religious practice and diversity in our society. The Holy Ghost People, for example, include the unusual practice of handling live poisonous snakes as part of their religious rituals. The practice is a demonstration of their faith that God will protect them and they will not be harmed.

Table 15.1 Distinctions between Churches and Sects

These characteristics of churches and sects anchor two ends of a continuum along which we can place the religious organizations of society. Catholicism and Lutheranism are obviously churches, whereas the Unification Church (Moonies) is clearly a sect. Many organizations such as southern Baptist and Mormon fall somewhere in between.

	CHURCHES	SECTS
Degree of tension with Society	Low	High
Attitude toward other institutions and religions	Tolerant	Intolerant; rejecting
Type of authority	Traditional	Charismatic
Organization	Bureaucratic	Informal
Membership	Establishment	Disinherited

and society—the religion is society. The fate of the church and the fate of the nation are wrapped up in each other, and the church is vitally involved in supporting the dominant institutions of society.

Denomination, or Mainline, Churches. Religious groups that have accommodated to society and to other religions are **denominations** (Robertson, 1970). Most of the largest religious groups in the United States fit this definition: Catholic, Lutheran, Methodist, and Episcopalian. Their clergy meet together in ecumenical councils, they pray together at commencements, and they generally adopt a live-and-let-live policy toward one another. Denominations have adjusted to the existing social structure of society. They support and are supported by the other institutional structures. This endorsement of the broad and basic fabric of the social order assures members that the ways of both their religion and their society are moral and just.

Denominations are churchlike religious groups that are large and bureaucratically organized and that adopt a tolerant attitude toward other religions.

Structure and Function of Churchlike Religions. Ecclesiae and denominations tend to be formal bureaucratic structures with hierarchical positions, specialization, and official creeds specifying their religious beliefs. Leadership is provided by a professional staff of ministers, rabbis, or priests, who have received formal training at specialized schools. These leaders are usually arranged in a hierarchy from the local to the district to the state and even the international level. Religious services almost always prescribe formal and detailed ritual, repeated in much the same way from generation to generation. Congregations often function more as audiences than as active participants. They are expected to stand up, sit down, and sing on cue, but the service is guided by ritual rather than by the emotional interaction of participants.

Generally, people are born into churchlike religions rather than being converted to them. People who change churches, who become Methodists instead of Lutherans, Catholics instead of Presbyterians, usually do so for practical reasons. They marry somebody of the other faith, the other church is nearer, or their friends go to the other church. Although churches do not actively recruit new members, they have confirmation classes for adults and children to educate newcomers to the doctrines of their adopted faith. As a result, individual commitment is based more on tradition or intellectual commitment than on the emotional experience of conversion.

Denominations tend to be large in size and to have well-established facilities, financial security, and a predominantly middle-class membership. As part of their accommodation to the larger society, they generally support a liberal interpretation of the Scriptures. Jewish, Catholic, and Protestant denominations usually allow the Scriptures to be interpreted in ways that are relevant to modern culture. Because of these characteristics, denominations are frequently referred to as *mainline*, a term denoting their centrality in society.

Sectlike Religions

For the religions that have greater tension with society, we can distinguish three levels of tension. First are cults, with the greatest tension, then sects, and finally established sects. The latter begin to approach institutionalization.

Cults.   A religious group that is independent of the religious traditions of society is a **cult** (Stark & Bainbridge, 1979). Most often, cults are new religions, but established religions may also be called cults when they are

A **cult** is a religious group that is independent of the religious traditions of the society in which it develops. It usually rejects and is rejected by society.

Figure 15.5
Stoned rastafarians . . . very stoned. The Ras Tafari cult movement originated in 1930 among lower class men in Jamaica as a semi-religious, semi-political movement. In addition to being violently anti-white, rastas regard Emperor Haile Selassie of Ethiopia as God, and advocate the return of blacks to Africa. In recent years, the movement's hostility has quieted and members are largely unemployed Jamaicans residing in crowded, blighted areas. Street meetings twice weekly and Sunday services typically include speech making, singing, and, for some, getting stoned.

transported to a different society. Scientology is an example of the former, and Hinduism in the United States is an example of the latter.

Cult movements typically come into existence during times of societal stress. Some survive, but many do not. Because of their dependence on charismatic leaders who claim exclusive insight into the truth, cult movements experience a high state of tension with the sociocultural environment, and other religions resist their claims to truth. To the extent that they are able to reduce this tension as time passes, they move along the continuum, securing increased size, financial security, and acceptance. What begins as a cult may eventually become a sect or even a church.

Sects. As already defined, sects are religious groups that consider themselves the one true religion and that reject the institutions of the larger society. They typically seek to preserve their spiritual purity by remaining apart from the world and by exercising close control over their members (Robertson, 1970).

The primary distinction between a cult and a sect is that a cult is independent of society's cultural heritage, whereas a sect is an offshoot of society's religious traditions. Sects often view themselves as restoring true faith, which has been mislaid by religious institutions too eager to compromise with society. They see themselves as preservers of religious tradition rather than innovators. Like the Reformation churches of Calvin and Luther, they believe they are cleansing the church of its secular associations. However offbeat in comparison to mainline churches, if a religious group in the United States uses the Bible as its source of inspiration and guidance, then it is probably a sect rather than a cult.

Established Sects. A religious group that straddles the gap between church and sect is an **established sect.** It still believes that it is the one true church, but it is less antagonistic to other faiths than are sects. It remains aloof from the world except for the purpose of spreading its message (Robertson, 1970).

An **established sect** is a religious group that has adapted to the ways of society in order to spread its message and gather converts but that still holds itself aloof.

Established sects have reduced some of the tensions that sects experience with the rest of society. Whereas sects often seek withdrawal from the world, established sects are active participants. A sect that sets out to change the world must also participate in the world. In order to acquire power and produce change, it is forced to accommodate itself to some of the values of society. Resources are required for producing religious materials, promoting the word, providing facilities for meetings and worship, and so on. Increased membership size is essential if enough political strength is to be developed to influence voting behavior and subsequent legislative decisions. These demands ultimately mean that the sect itself must undergo some changes if it is to be successful in producing social change. When it makes these changes, it is likely to become an established sect.

The distinction between sects and established sects is based primarily on whether members withdraw from the world or attempt to influence it. The Amish and the Hutterites have been happy to be left alone; and although they have endured for centuries, they remain sects. The Mormons in contrast, have increased their accommodation to the larger so-

CONCEPT SUMMARY

A Fivefold Division of Religions

This fivefold division of religions helps us define the sociologically relevant categories of religious bodies. It is not always easy to categorize a religion. For example, some Baptist groups have the characteristics of established sects whereas others are clearly denominations.

CONCEPT	TENSION WITH SOCIETY'S INSTITUTIONS	DISTINGUISHING FEATURES	U.S. EXAMPLE
CHURCHLIKE			
Ecclesiae	Low	Come with citizenship	None
Denominations		Tolerant of and supported by other social institutions	Methodists, Lutherans, Catholics
SECTLIKE			
Established Sects		Reject truth claims of other churches; in the world in order to spread the word	Mormons, Jehovah's Witnesses
Sects		Reject worldly institutions; withdraw from the world	Amish, Oneida, Hutterites
Cults	High	Religion alien to society's traditions	Moonies, Scientologists

ciety. They have abandoned plural marriage (see chapter 4) and have left the seclusion of a virtual ecclesia in Utah in order to seek converts. They still retain sectlike characteristics, however, including the lack of a paid clergy and an emphasis on conversion.

Structure and Function of Sectlike Religions.   The hundreds of cults and sects in the United States exhibit varying degrees of tension with society, but all are opposed to some basic societal institutions. Not surprisingly, these groups tend to be particularly attractive to people who are left out of or estranged from society's basic institutions—the poor, the underprivileged, the handicapped, and the alienated. For this reason, sects have been called "the church of the disinherited" (Niebuhr, 1929/1957). Sects provide a sense of identity and belonging for the disinherited and a sense that society's institutions rather than the people themselves are at fault.

Sect membership is often the result of conversion or emotional experience. Members do not merely follow their parents into the church; they are reborn or born again. Religious services are more informal than for churches; and even in such established sects as the Mormon or Christian Scientist, church members may be called upon to give testimony of religious experience.

Leadership remains largely unspecialized, and there is little, if any, professional training for the calling. Lay ministers assume part-time responsibility for administering religious rituals, conducting services, and teaching the gospel. The religious doctrines emphasize other worldly rewards, and the Scriptures are viewed as of divine origin subject to literal interpretation.

Sects and cults share many of the characteristics of primary groups: small size, informality, and loyalty. They are relatively closely knit groups that emphasize conformity and maintain significant control over their members. Members may be required to observe specific norms related to patterns of dress (Amish, Oneida), speech (Quaker), use of modern innovations (Amish), and so on. These requirements are symbolic reminders to community members of their religious identity. They function to foster cohesion and reinforce group identity.

Many, if not all, of the denominations in the world today were at one time sects. As they made the transition from sect to church, they became increasingly secularized; this secularization reflected accommodation to and compromise with the institutional structures of society. Not all sects, of course, adjust and become assimilated in this way. Some remain established sects, antagonistic to many institutions in the general society; others suffer eventual extinction.

Case Studies of Sectlike Religions

Two examples of sectlike religions, the Old Order Amish and the People's Temple, demonstrate the diversity and vitality of religious belief in the United States.

Old Order Amish. A sect that developed from the Protestant reform movement in Switzerland in 1520 and that migrated to Lancaster County, Pennsylvania, in 1727 is the Old Order Amish. This sect believes in the Scriptures as the literal word of God, in adult rather than infant baptism, and in strict separation from the ways of the world (Hostetler, 1963).

The Amish pride themselves on being a "peculiar" people who follow the Bible rather than the ways of the world. As a result, they differ sharply from the other residents of Pennsylvania in dress and behavior. The Amish use Bible verses to support a clothing style that is modest, shows a distinction between the sexes, and does not appeal to vanity. All women dress alike in dark-colored skirts, blouses, and matching aprons (no prints, only home-dyed solids); unmarried girls differ slightly in that they wear white aprons. All women wear homemade bonnets (following a biblical injunction that women who pray with their heads uncovered are dishonored), and none wear jewelry. Men too must all dress alike, in jackets that have no lapels, no outside pockets, and no buttons. Even zippers are forbidden except in utilitarian work clothes. These distinctive dress patterns serve a vital function; they provide a constant reminder to members of the group that they are outside the ways of the world. Neither the Amish nor their neighbors are likely to forget that they are a peculiar people.

The Amish reject almost all modern conveniences. They are not allowed to have rugs, electricity, telephones, or any modern appliances except sewing machines. Most importantly, they are not allowed to use automobiles. Instead, both farm equipment and pleasure vehicles are horse-drawn. The Amish are forbidden to dance, to go to movies, to live in cities or towns, to serve in the military, to go to court, to join any association other than the church, to go to public school, and to attend even Amish schools past the 8th grade.

Both boys and girls attend Amish schools for 8 years. They learn reading, writing, and arithmetic from teachers who have had the same 8th grade education. The purpose of education is to allow the Amish to read the Bible and to manage farm accounts. Any further learning is considered not only unnecessary (for the Bible is the source of all knowledge) but

Figure 15.6
These Old Order Amish pride themselves on being a "peculiar" people. They have managed to successfully withdraw from the ways of the modern world which surrounds them by adopting a life-style based on self-sufficiency. They reject modern conveniences, make almost all of their goods by hand, and are excellent farmers. This photograph of a large family saying grace before their meal shows the typical dress worn by members of the Amish community.

actually wrong, as it will expose youth to the ways of the world and make them unhappy with Amish society. All adults, however, are expected to be able to read and study the Bible. The Amish have no established clergy; the leadership positions in the church are established by lot. Thus every man in the community is expected to be familiar with the Bible and with church doctrine.

The Amish have managed to escape from secularization almost completely for more than 400 years. They have withdrawn physically—in the 18th century moving all the way from Germany to Pennsylvania—to escape the influence of the world. They seek neither converts nor worldly influence; they wish only to be left alone.

Whether the Amish can continue to ward off the world is questionable. The world is intruding on their way of life and making it more difficult. For example, hard-surface roads cripple buggy horses within 12 to 18 months. This kind of intrusion, as well as the increasing price of land, is changing the Amish way of life more or less by accident. More direct challenges are offered by the draft, taxes, and education. For example, the Amish refuse to pay social security taxes, believing that such a plan indicates distrust of God's care. After much legal skirmishing, Congress exempted the Amish from the taxes and the benefits of social security. More troubling is education. In Pennsylvania, officials have long since worked out an accommodation to allow the Amish to have their own schools without state certified teachers and to have their children stop at the 8th grade. Population pressure (the Amish often have eight children), however, is pushing the Amish way of life into others states, which are unwilling to make this accommodation. For example, the governments of Iowa and Nebraska have levied heavy fines on Amish families who refuse to send their children to public schools.

As a result of these changes, the Amish are finding it increasingly difficult to remain aloof from the world. Amish young people inevitably see some of the pleasures available in American society and many are reluctant to turn their back completely on dancing, driving, and other amusements. As a result, many Amish communities now allow their young people a year in the larger world, hoping that they will get their curiosity out of their system and be willing to return to the Amish way of life.

People's Temple. In 1978, the world was fascinated and appalled by the grisly tale of mass suicide and murder in Jonestown, Guyana. Altogether, 912 people died in Jonestown after drinking cyanide-laced Kool-aid on the direction of their "Bishop" and "Father," Jim Jones.

The early career and beliefs of Jones (1931–1978) are unclear. He himself said in later years that he used a religion in which he did not believe to spread the gospel of communism and social justice. At the time he began preaching, however, he appeared to be a Christian crusader. After traveling the circuit of poor black and white neighborhoods in Indianapolis, Jones—who had no formal theological training—raised $55,000 to start the People's Temple. Jones's temple, affiliated with the Disciples of Christ, appealed particularly to the poor and black. Jones preached racial integration, opened soup kitchens, distributed clothes to the needy, found jobs for ex-addicts and ex-convicts, and started nursing homes. In recognition of his social services to the community, he was named director of the Indianapolis Human Rights Commission.

Jones justified his activism by reference to the New Testament. Christ, he said, would not recognize his church if he found it to consist only of praying and singing on Sunday mornings. Christ, he said, demanded action. A favorite text was Matthew 25:35–40: "For I was hungered and ye gave me meat, I was thirsty and ye gave me drink; I was a stranger and ye took me in; Naked and ye clothed me; I was in prison and ye came to me. . . . Verily I say unto you, Inasmuch as ye have done it unto one of the least of these, ye have done it unto me." Thus the so-called Jonestown cult was really a sect, nourished and supported by Christian tradition. (The term *cult* tends to be applied to any religious group, of which society disapproves, regardless of its theology. In this case, societal disapproval came late in the day; until a few months before the People's Temple moved to Guyana, Jim Jones and his temple were considered pillars of the community.)

Many sects begin as antithetical to society's institutions but gradually reduce this tension. The People's Temple followed the opposite course. Over the years, Jones became increasingly estranged from the secular world. He believed that civil authorities (FBI, CIA, and so on) were plotting against the People's Temple. He also became convinced that the end of

Figure 15.7

The People's Temple was a Christian-based sect founded by the Reverend Jim Jones. Its message rested more on the desirability of curing earthly problems through socialism than on eternal life and it was disproportionately attractive to the poor, the black, and the alienated. Jones became increasingly isolated from Christianity and from American society, first moving his people to the jungles of Guyana and finally demanding mass death as the only escape.

the world was near. Like many other sect leaders, he interpreted the Book of Revelations to mean that the end of the world would come through a nuclear war between the United States and the Soviet Union. As a result of his beliefs, he first moved his temple to Ukiah, California (one of the locations in the United States supposed to be least damageable by a nuclear attack), and then to the jungles of Guyana.

Jones was a charismatic leader. His followers believed him to be speaking directly with God; indeed, they came to believe he was the Messiah. The faith of his followers rested partly on standard brainwashing procedures; Jones kept temple members tired and busy, cut off from their nontemple friends, and frightened. As a result, their critical faculties were suspended. In addition, however, his followers had a Christian heritage, and they believed that Christ would come again. Why not this man? Why not this place and time? Jones used the Christian heritage of his followers to manipulate them, but in fact he abandoned Christianity and the Bible's God, who he disparagingly called the sky God, very early in his career. "What's your sky God ever done? . . . He never gave you a bed and He never provided a *home*. But *I, Your socialist worker God*, have given you *all* these things" (cited in Reiterman, 1982:148-149).

The members of his congregation hungered for salvation and a heavenly reward. They also sought respite from the hardship of Jonestown. Thus, when they were ordered to drink the poison in November 1978, more than 900 did so. Some were coerced, and some (such as the 200 children who died) did so unknowingly; others, however, drank the poison willingly. Jones himself died of a gunshot wound to the head, presumably fired by someone who subsequently drank the poison. Despite a number of rumors on the subject, there is no evidence that Jones intended not to die with his people. The temple's property was willed to the Communist party of the Soviet Union.

The Jonestown "cult" was, up until its last year, similar to many other sects. It was a religion of the disinherited, and it was led by a charismatic leader. Its congregation formed a strong primary group that bound its members so tightly that they could not conceive of any disloyalty; their whole existence became one with temple membership. Although initially based on Christian tradition, however, the doctrine and rituals of the group became increasingly cultlike during the last year.

The amount of coercion and intimidation at Jonestown clearly distinguishes it from other sectlike religions in the United States. Yet violence does not in itself make a religion a cult. The witch hunts and inquisitions of the Middle Ages, the Holy Wars of Islam, self-immolation by Buddhist monks in Saigon, and numerous other kinds of martyrdoms remind us that violence is often part of ecclesiae and denominations as well as of cults and sects.

Summary

The concepts of church and sect and denomination and cult are designed to help us recognize what various religions have in common. They are useful yardsticks for measuring the essential characteristics of religions. As the descriptions of the Amish and the People's Temple aptly illustrate, however, two sects may share sociologically relevant characteristics (smallness, rejection of society) and still be very different in religious content.

Religion in the United States

The vast majority of Americans consider themselves to be religious. In a recent Gallup Poll, 94 percent of U.S. adults interviewed claimed a belief in God, and virtually all said that they believed in the power of prayer (Gallup Report, 1982). In fact, more than half of the U.S. population prays every day (Greeley, 1979:122).

The U.S. Religious Heritage

Out from the Wilderness. The United States was not always a religious nation. Although some persecuted groups sought religious freedom in North America, most early settlers came for nonreligious reasons. They came as servants, as convicts, and as adventurers and seekers of fortune. In 1800, only 7 percent of the U.S. population belonged to a church. In 1779, a traveling preacher told of meeting a man in the backwoods of Delaware and asking him, "Do you know Jesus Christ?" "Can't say as I

Figure 15.8

Most people in America consider them-
selves to be religious and on any given
Sunday approximately forty percent of
the adult population attends church ser-
vices. As this picture depicts, those who
attend most frequently and regularly are
somewhat older and disproportionately
female.

do," replied the man. "He must not live in these parts." Even as late as the
mid-19th century, it was generally held that Sunday stopped at the Missouri River (Phares, 1964:1).

The lack of religiosity in this period was not simply ignorance. Many of
the prominent citizens who were instrumental in designing our government were Deists, not Christians. Washington, Jefferson, Franklin, and
others believed that there was a supreme being, but they did not believe
that there was a personal God who concerned himself with the workings
of this world; nor did they accept the Bible as the word of God. Whether
believers or nonbelievers, however, the political and economic elite of the
early colonies came from Protestant cultural backgrounds and supported
values that arose from this heritage.

Pluralism: Catholic, Protestant, or Jew.   The growth and development
of different religious groups in the United States parallels the historical
patterns of immigration and ethnicity outlined in chapter 9. It was not
until the massive immigration of Irish Catholics in the mid 19th century
that Catholicism was firmly established in the United States. Catholicism
in this country is a religion of immigrant groups; it is the religion of
Hispanics, Poles, Italians, and Irish. Judaism too is a religion of immigrants.
To be Jewish in the United States is as much an ethnic label as a religious
affiliation.

The three major religions in the United States thus differ not only in
theology but also in the timing and origin of their immigration to the
United States. To be Catholic, Protestant, or Jew means more than a particular creed; it signals something about ethnicity and status in our society.

Contemporary Religious Affiliation.   When asked what religion they
belong to, only 7 percent of the people in the United States say that they

belong to no church. The vast majority are able to identify themselves not only as religious but as affiliated with some particular religious organization. Most (59 percent) call themselves Protestants, but 29 percent are Catholics and 2 percent are Jews (see Table 15.2). Within the category of Protestants and among the 4 percent of the population who belong to other religious faiths, there is a great deal of variability. The 1982 *Yearbook of American and Canadian Churches* lists more than 200 religious organizations, and researchers have identified more than 500 cult movements and more than 400 sects currently in existence in the United States (Stark & Bainbridge, 1981).

Despite their differences, the three major religions in the United States embrace a common Judeo-Christian heritage. They accept the Old Testament, and they worship the same God. They rely on a similar moral tradition (the Ten Commandments, for example), which reinforces common values. This common religious heritage supplies an overarching sense of unity and character to U.S. society—providing a framework for the expression of our most crucial values concerning family, politics, economics, and education.

U.S. Civil Religion

In addition to their common religious heritage, Americans also share what has been called a civil religion (Bellah, 1974:29; 1975). The rituals of **civil religion** include giving the pledge of allegiance and singing the national anthem; they also include folding and displaying the flag in ways that protect it from desecration. This civil religion provides the same function as religion in general: It is a source of unity and integration.

The sacred beliefs of civil religion are found in the Constitution, the Declaration of Independence, and the inaugural addresses of presidents. They include a sacred and almost worshipful attitude toward liberty, justice, and freedom. Through civil religion, the American way of life becomes not merely the usual way of doing things but also the only moral way of doing them—a way of life, an economic and political system, that is blessed by God.

Correlates of Religiosity and Commitment

Although almost everybody expresses a belief in God, some people are consistently more likely than others to emphasize the role of religion in their lives. These patterns of religious commitment, or **religiosity,** are summarized in Table 15.3. The data come from a national probability sample of 10,000 adults interviewed in 1980.

Two-thirds of the adults in this country are members of churches or synagogues, and 40 percent are found in church on a weekly basis. A clear majority (55 percent) define religion as very important to their lives. On both measures of religiosity (church attendance and importance of religion), people who live in the Midwest and the South report greater religiosity than people who live in the West or the East.

The most striking differences in religiosity, however, are found by age and gender. Older people and women report greater attachment to religion

Table 15.2 Religious Affiliation in the United States, 1981

Although nearly 90 percent of Americans call themselves Protestant, Catholic, or Jewish, there are more than 200 religious organizations in the United States and as many as 1,000 cults and sects.

Catholic		28%
Protestant		59
Baptist	19%	
Methodist	10	
Lutheran	6	
Presbyterian	4	
Episcopalian	2	
Mormon	1	
Other Protestant	13	
Nonspecific Protestant	4	
Jewish		2
Other		4
None		7

SOURCE: The Gallup Report, No. 201–202, June–July 1982.

Civil religion is the set of institutionalized rituals, beliefs, and symbols sacred to the American nation, including reverence for the flag and belief in capitalism and democracy.

Religiosity is a measure of the extent to which a person's attitudes, beliefs, and behaviors are influenced by religion.

Table 15.3   Religious Participation and Attitudes, 1980

There are some pronounced patterns in U.S. religiosity. Men are less religious than women, young people are less religious than their elders, Westerners are less religious than people in other regions, Jews are less religious than people of other religions. The well educated go to church, but they are not otherwise as religious as the less well educated.

	PERCENT OF ADULTS WHO	
	Attend Church or Synagogue Weekly	Say Religion Is Very Important
National	40%	55%
Region:		
Midwest	45	54
South	42	66
East	40	49
West	29	51
Age:		
Below 30	31	43
30–49	40	55
50 and older	47	65
Gender:		
Male	36	48
Female	44	62
Education:		
Grade school	43	69
High school	39	55
College	40	50
Religion:		
Protestant	39	61
Catholic	53	56
Jewish	25	31

SOURCE: The Gallup Report, 1982.

than do younger people and men. These differences are highly reliable and have been reported in national studies over several decades (Greeley, 1979:120). Young adults, particularly those under the age of 30, are approximately three times more likely to indicate no religious preference than are those over 50; they are less likely to be members of a congregation, they have lower weekly attendance than adults in other age groups, and they are less likely to view religion as very important to their lives.

On these items, Jews appear to be far less religious than Catholics or Protestants. To a significant extent this is because *Jew* is an ethnic label that people retain even after they give up Judaism as a religion.

A question that has consistently interested students of religious affiliation is the relationship between socioeconomic status and religiosity. To many people, it has seemed logical that religion should appeal disproportionately to the poor, who may stand in greater need of hope and help in dealing with this world. Empirical research, however, demonstrates that the relationship between religion and social class is more complex. As the data in Table 15.3 indicate, people with a college education are as likely to attend church as are people with a grade school education. They are, however, significantly less likely to say that religion is important to

Figure 15.9
The majority of Americans are religious in the sense that they believe in God, belong to a church, and think religion is important to their lives. They practice their religion in a more passive way, however, than do the persons pictured above who actively attempt to spread the word through street proselytizing. A characteristic of sects is the tendency to recruit new members through missionary work and proselytizing.

them. Higher-status people also belong to somewhat different religious organizations. They are more often members of churchlike religions, whereas lower-class individuals are more often members of sects and cults.

Why does religion appeal to some groups more than others? After examining several competing explanations, Roof and Hoge (1980) concluded that religious involvement for adults is strongly associated with community attachment and conventional values. People who are attached to and involved in their communities—who belong to voluntary associations and civic groups and are integrated into their neighborhoods—tend to extend that involvement to religious participation. Liberal attitudes toward sexual morality, gender roles, civil liberties, and drug use, however, tend to be inconsistent with church involvement. These factors help explain why well-educated people participate in church despite their lack of enthusiasm for it and why young people are less likely to participate or believe.

Consequences of Religiosity and Religious Affiliation

Because religion teaches and reinforces values, it has consequences for attitudes and behaviors. These consequences are most obvious in areas of life that are strongly tied to moral values, but they are also apparent in other areas.

FOCUS ON MEASUREMENT

How Religious Are You, and How Can You Tell?

How do you tell whether a person is religious or not? One way is to ask—but what is the question? Is it enough just to go to church regularly? What if you go to church just to please your mother or to impress your business contacts? An alternative strategy would be to ask whether you pray or abide by the Ten Commandments.

The two measures of religiosity used by the Gallup Poll (in Table 15.3) are relatively superficial measures of religious commitment and belief. Sociologists usually assume that there are at least three dimensions of religiosity: belief, ritual, and experience (Glock & Stark, 1965). Repeated tests show that the dimensions are not necessarily highly related; people may be high on ritual and low on belief (we call these people hypocrites) or high on belief and low on experience. The following questions from the Glock and Stark Scale should tell you something about how religious you are.

Belief

1. Do you believe in a personal God, a supreme being who concerns Himself with the workings of the world?
2. Do you believe that Jesus Christ is the Divine Son of God?
3. Do you believe miracles actually happened just as the Bible says they did?
4. Do you believe the devil actually exists?

Ritual

5. How often do you attend Sunday worship services?
6. How often, if at all, are table prayers or grace said before or after meals in your home?

Experience

7. Have you ever had a feeling that you were somehow in the presence of God?
8. Since you have been an adult, have you ever had a sense of being saved in Christ?
9. Have you ever had a feeling of being punished by God for something you have done?

These questions have the major defect of measuring religiosity only for Christians. Even among Christians, however, the three dimensions do not exhaust the ways in which we could measure religiosity. None of the questions asks about general behavior— whether you drink or cheat on your spouse or steal—and none taps the intellectual roots of religiosity, such as whether you know and understand your church's position on baptism, the creation, and Holy Communion. Nevertheless, these nine questions provide a reliable mechanism for ranking Christians on religiosity. There would be general agreement that an individual who could answer yes to all nine is more religious than one who could answer yes to only four.

Questions to Consider

1. Do some of these questions seem unfair to you? Do they make you look more or less religious than you think you are?
2. What if you are Jewish? or Hindu? Can you think of any way to measure religiosity that would be equally applicable to all religions?

Two decades ago, to be Catholic or Jewish or Protestant meant major differences in the propensity to divorce, the use of contraceptives, and family size. Today these differences have almost disappeared (Jones & Westoff, 1978). There is still a sharp difference between Catholics and non-Catholics on approval of abortion, but increasingly it is religious fervor rather than religious affiliation that is important. Policy issues related to religious fundamentalism are discussed more fully in the Issues in Social Policy section of this chapter.

Religious involvement and participation have far-reaching personal consequences. Survey data from a 1982 Gallup Poll (see Table 15.4) suggest that religion provides personal satisfaction and integration. On all three Gallup measures, people who have high religious involvement are signif-

Table 15.4 Religiosity and Social Values

Religious participation has consequences for many aspects of people's lives. People who are most involved in their church report significantly greater personal happiness; they are also significantly less liberal on such social issues as marijuana use and public spending.

MEASURE OF RELIGION	PERCENT VERY HAPPY	PERCENT FAVORING DEATH PENALTY	PERCENT FAVORING MORE MONEY ON SOCIAL PROGRAMS	PERCENT FAVORING LOWER MARIJUANA PENALTIES
AFFILIATION				
Mainline Protestant	40%	59%	38%	10%
Evangelical Protestant*	59	57	49	9
Catholic	42	56	56	13
None	31	51	58	36
RELIGIOUS INVOLVEMENT				
Very high	69	49	47	4
Fairly high	59	53	44	5
Fairly low	30	55	56	22
Very low	32	55	53	26
CHURCH ATTENDANCE				
Within last week	55	53	45	7
7 days to 6 months ago	43	57	47	14
Not in last 6 months	30	58	53	21

SOURCE: The Gallup Report, Nos. 201–202, June–July, 1982.

*Evangelical Protestants are Protestants who say that they consider themselves born-again Christians and Protestants who believe that the Bible is the literal word of God. This group includes 18 percent of all Protestants.

icantly happier with their personal lives than are people who are not religiously involved. They are also more conservative on social issues. They oppose the reduction of marijuana penalties, and they oppose further spending on government social programs. Those who have no religious affiliation and those who practice their religion the least are the most liberal but the least happy. Although there is little difference by religion in approval of the death penalty, there is some evidence that more religious people are apt to practice Christian forbearance. The most religious and those who most recently attended church are least apt to favor a mandatory death penalty.

Current Religious Trends in the United States

Religion is a dynamic social structure. It simultaneously influences and is influenced by its environment. Changes in technology, knowledge, and social setting challenge the church to find new ways to make life meaningful. Similarly, the church tries to direct and sometimes resist social change.

There are competing religious trends in the United States. On the one hand, there is a widespread belief that religion is no longer as important as it used to be. Premarital sex, extramarital sex, and just plain sex are everywhere more visible, bad language is common, homosexuals have come out of the closet, one-third of all pregnancies end in abortion, and nobody wants to be a priest anymore. Contrasted with this widespread impression that religion is in decline is the resurgence of fundamentalism and the growth of evangelical Protestantism. Bob Dylan and Jimmie Carter have been born again, and the moral majority and other conservative Christian movements are out to remake the United States into a Christian nation. This section will review three major religious issues in the United States: (1) changing religious commitment, (2) the decline of the mainline denominational churches and the rise of fundamentalism, and (3) electronic churches.

Has Religion Declined in the United States?

Descriptions of colonial times suggest that our religious history is far from one ongoing fall from grace. However, if we compare 1980 with 1950, we do find signs of decline. As the data in Table 15.5 demonstrate, these signs are relatively minor. In the last 25 years, there has been only a modest decrease in the proportion of people belonging to and attending a church or synagogue. The vast majority (93 percent) express some religious preference, and 87 percent want their children to receive religious instruction.

Despite these continuities in outward religious observance, some important changes have occurred in the way people feel about religion. The proportion who say religion is very important to their own lives has dropped substantially, and there has been a sharp decrease in the proportion believing that the Bible is the actual word of God.

In sum, people still say that they have a religion, they still go to church, and they still want their children to have a religious education. For many, however, these issues have less meaning than they used to.

Growing Fundamentalism

One of the most striking changes in religion today is the vitality and growth of the fundamentalist churches compared to that of mainline denominations. In the 1950s, the mainline denominations grew in both numbers and financial security (Roof & Hadaway, 1979). At the time, it was hypothesized that there were two primary reasons (Stark & Glock, 1968):

1. The people who were pushed into upward social mobility by the transformation of industry and education sought to cement their new status by joining establishment churches.
2. Many were finding the demythologized beliefs of the mainline denominations more compatible with modern life.

Beginning in the 1960s, this trend reversed its direction, and the reversal continues unabated to the present time. The liberal mainline denominations are losing membership, and the conservative and fundamentalist religions are experiencing a resurgence of growth.

Fundamentalism is a grass-roots conservative movement that began at the turn of the century in an attempt to purify the churches and restore the original teachings—the fundamentals—of a particular version of

---

Table 15.5 Changing Religious Commitment, 1947 to 1981

Over the last 25 years there has been little decline in outward religious observance. There has, however, been a substantial drop in the proportion who say that religion is very important to their lives, and there has been a sharp decrease in the proportion who think that the Bible is the actual word of God.

	1947–1952	1978–1981
Belong to a church or synagogue	76%	69%
Attended church last week	46	40
Have no religion	6	7
Want their children to have religious instruction	98	87
Religion is very important to their own lives	75	55
Believe Bible is actual word of God, to be taken literally word for word*	65	37

SOURCE: Gallup Report, 1982.

*The first measure on this variable was taken in 1963.

Fundamentalism is a movement to restore original religious principles to both religious practice and society.

Figure 15.10
Religious rituals are often used to mark the transition from one major status to another; birth, marriage, and death. This picture depicts a jazz funeral in New Orleans for musician Fats Houston. Like an Irish wake, jazz funerals are unusual in that they celebrate life rather than death. Because events such as birth and death are among the least understood, they continue to be held sacred and celebrated through religious ritual.

Christianity. It was a countermovement to liberal trends that seemed to be casting aside the differences between Christianity and the secular and sinful world (Hargrove, 1979:284).

Fundamentalists can be found in all religions; there are fundamentalist Catholics, Baptists, Presbyterians, and Lutherans. Their common aim is to bring the church back to its tension with society. The split between the fundamentalists and the modernists is one of the most significant religious cleavages in the United States. On many social and political issues, it is much more important than whether one is Catholic or Protestant. For example, consider the issue of creationism in the schools. Fundamentalists generally favor a requirement that the Genesis story be taught in the schools along with, or even instead of, evolutionary theory. They believe that the two theories are incompatible, and they wish to make certain that students are exposed to Christian theory. Leaders of established churches are generally not in favor of creationism in the schools. They have interpreted the Genesis story as a parable rather than as literal truth, and they see no contradiction between scientific evolution and religion. A Catholic authority, for example, notes: "We're more concerned with God as the creator of the world than with how he created. . . . So long as whatever is taught in the schools allows room for that interpretation, there's no problem" (Rev. Thomas Gallagher, Secretary for Education, U.S. Catholic Conference, cited in Bollier, 1982:196).

Figure 15.11

All religions tend to develop symbols for those things which are held sacred. These symbols serve the purpose of constantly reminding persons of their religious vows and obligations. Statues, altars, crucifixes, and special clothing are only a few of the many religious symbols used. This 84 year old Hindu priest in Sri Lanka is responsible for guarding the leaves of this 2600 year old sacred fig tree.

The Lure of Fundamentalism.   Research comparing mainline and fundamentalist churches indicates that an important reason for the growth of fundamentalist churches is that they do a better job of meeting the functions of religion for individuals. They provide, for example, a greater sense of community for their members. They create a strong sense of group identity by requiring new members to make public declarations of their beliefs and by providing a rigorous program of education and greater opportunities for members to be active in carrying out responsibilities and duties related to church functions. For example, at a recent national convention of Jehovah's Witnesses, the 10,000 delegates spent several evenings canvassing the convention city together. They did not just talk about fund-raising and church budgets; they were out working together. These organizational features of the fundamentalist church result in greater meaning and a sense of belonging for individual members and strengthen the social bonds of membership.

Electronic Religion

Increasingly, people find it possible to enjoy religious participation without leaving their homes. There are several religious television networks, 95 nationally syndicated religious television programs, and perhaps 1,500 religious radio broadcasters. The television shows alone are estimated to reach an audience of 25 million people (Bollier, 1982).

People who subscribe to electronic religion are similar to those who attend churches; they are older, mostly female, Protestant, and disproportionately from the southern and midwestern regions of the country. They also tend to be low in education and socioeconomic status.

There is much controversy over electronic churches and their impact on religious behavior. The most successful of the television evangelists—Jerry Falwell, Oral Roberts, Pat Robertson—bring in annual revenues of $50 million each through solicitations of and sales to their listeners. Mainline religions oppose the blatant use of God's name in these fund-raising efforts. Others have worried that religious broadcasts sandwiched between *Gilligan's Island* and *Love Boat* reruns on Sunday mornings will trivialize religion and detract from attendance at local churches. Recent evidence, however, indicates that these fears may be unfounded; as many as one-third of those watching religious programs on television increase their involvement in local church activities, and only about 7 percent are negatively affected (Gallup Report, 1981). This suggests that electronic churches may stimulate rather than diminish involvement in local congregational activities. Also on the positive side, electronic churches make religion available to many people who otherwise would be shut off from participation: the elderly, the physically handicapped, and other isolated individuals.

The Moral Majority—Can Church and State Really Be Separated?

The Bill of Rights of the U.S. Constitution gives Americans the right to freedom of religious expression, and the Constitution mandates a separation of church and state. Yet, if the sociological perspective has any merit, it should be impossible to have one institution that is independent of the others. Institutions are interdependent, not independent.

For this reason, it has proved difficult to keep church and state separate. To the extent that the values and practices of one institution challenge those of another, there will be tension between them. This tension is likely to cause changes in both.

THE MORAL MAJORITY

Moral Majority, Inc., is an organization founded in 1979 by the Reverend Jerry Falwell, a television evangelist on

Figure 15.12

The separation of church and state is basic to the Constitution of the United States. This separation, however, is more ideal than real since both are major institutions of society. The Moral Majority, a political organization led by evangelist Jerry Falwell, attempts to insert right wing Christian morality into the political process. On his fifty state tour in 1981, Falwell mixed Christian values with patriotic and religious song, the flag, and the Bible at rallies held on the steps of state capitals across the nation.

the *Old-Time Gospel Hour*, which appears on several hundred television stations across the country. The Moral Majority, Inc., is a formal organization with membership cards, dues, and so on, but more generally we can say that the **moral majority** is a political movement, designed to legislate evangelical Christian morality. It is a political rather than a religious organization; it seeks to affect public legislation. Specifically, it wants to remake public education, government, law, and the family into Christian organizations. Following is a brief review of the social issues that the moral majority sees as legitimate religious concerns.

The Separation of Church and State

The moral majority believes that Christians have an obligation to be politically active. It believes that a Christian has a right and a duty to try to reform the state through the political process. That is, rather than going after individual souls and reforming individuals, it believes that it has an obligation to create a Christian state:

> The idea that religion and politics don't mix was invented by the Devil to keep Christians from running their own country. [Falwell, cited in Bollier, 1982:54]

> Not voting is a sin against God. . . . Perverts, radicals, leftists, Communists, liberals, and humanists have taken over the country because Christians didn't want to dirty their hands in politics [Robinson, cited in Bollier, 1982:70]

Public Education

One issue that the moral majority believes is a legitimate concern of Christian citizens is public education. It believes that the schools should be actively supporting Christianity. It argues that failure to support Christian doctrine in the schools undermines what children learn at home and in church. Among the aspects of public education that it criticizes most is values clarification. It believes that children should not be taught to question and evaluate their own beliefs—that to do so may undermine their faith:

When a student reads in a math book that there are no absolutes, suddenly every value he's been taught is destroyed. And the next thing you know the student turns to crime and drugs. [Gabler, cited in Bollier, 1982:132]

If we are to stem the tide of lawlessness, drug addiction, and sexual perversion which adversely affects academic performance, we must start with putting God back into our school system. [McAteer, cited in Bollier, 1982:208]

Putting God back in the schools usually means school prayer, the elimination of sex education, textbooks stating that the United States is a divinely guided nation that is always on the side of righteousness, and a curriculum that concentrates on the basics rather than on independent thinking.

WHO ARE THE MORAL MAJORITY?

Studies suggest that support for the moral majority comes from three groups—those who watch televised religion, those who desire to preserve the status quo, and those who support the Christian right wing (Johnson & Tamney, 1982).

Many of the leaders of the moral majority are, like Jerry Falwell, television evangelists. They ask their "partners in faith" to help them in various political causes—defeating homosexual legislators, putting prayer in the schools, or defeating Medicaid funding for abortion. The television medium has been very effective for reaching portions of the population not normally among the politically active.

Studies show that the people who support the moral majority tend to be from groups who have lost status in recent decades. They are the lower-middle-class and working-class whites who have seen their jobs threatened by blacks; they are the women and men whose values and jobs are threatened by women's liberation; most of all they are the people whose major accomplishment in life is respectability and who have found that respectability no longer counts. Like the people who supported Prohibition in the 1930s, they tend to be groups who want to return to an earlier era—one in which they had more prestige and respect.

Finally, the moral majority is drawn heavily from the people who favor the Christian right wing. These people believe that the United States is God's chosen instrument to fight communism and that it is a Christian obligation to support capitalism and democracy.

It should be emphasized that not all fundamentalists are members of the moral majority or the Christian right wing. As David Riesman said 20 years ago: Not all "fundamentalists in religion are right wingers in politics. Many reject politics as one of things of this world that is alien to the devout and otherworldly; many others find in the Gospels the basis for often courageous Christian social action for peace or racial integration" (1963:123).

A Gallup poll in December 1981 suggests that the moral majority has relatively little support from the general public. Even among those who categorized themselves as conservative in their religious beliefs, there were as many who did not favor the moral majority as there were who did. For the rest of the public, opinion ran two to one against the moral majority (Gallup Report, 1982).

THE ISSUE

Whether you agree or disagree with the moral majority, it raises an important issue. Church and state are not independent institutions. If the state changes, if its educational system changes, then the church is bound to be affected. If the educational system gives girls and boys equal opportunities or if the state gives men and women equal political power, what happens to the church that is still saying that women must be subordinate to men? One of the things that happens is that people quit paying attention to religious teachings because the teachings contradict what they have learned elsewhere. If religion wants to be more than a passive object of such external changes, then it has to fight back. The moral majority is simply one of the latest contenders in this battle. Just as labor, environmentalists, farmers, and the handicapped have organized in order to protect their interests, the moral majority represents the political arm of a particular form of Christian fundamentalism.

SUMMARY

1. The scientific study of religion concerns itself with the consequences of religious affiliation for individuals and with the interrelationships between religion and other social institutions. It is not concerned with evaluating the truth of particular religious beliefs.

2. There are two distinct viewpoints about the role of religion in society. One, associated with Durkheim, suggests that religion provides support for the traditional practices of a society and is a force for continuity and stability. The other, associated with Weber, suggests that religion provides new ideas and challenges the institutions of society.

3. All religions are confronted with a dilemma: the tendency to reject the secular world and the tendency to compromise with it. The way religion resolves this question determines its form and character. Those who make adaptations to the world are called churches, whereas those who reject the world are called sects.

4. The primary distinction between a cult and a sect is that a cult is outside a society's traditional religious heritage whereas a sect often sees itself as restoring the true faith of a society. Both tend to be primary groups characterized by small size, intense we-feeling, and informal leadership. Both tend to be churches of the disinherited.

5. The vast majority of Americans consider themselves religious, and this has not changed very much in the last 25 years. Nevertheless, religion tends to have less influence on people's daily lives than it did 25 years ago.

6. American civil religion is an important source of unity for the American people. This religion is not associated with any particular set of religious beliefs. It is composed of a set of beliefs (that God guides the country), symbols (the flag), and rituals (pledge of allegiance) that many Americans of all faiths hold sacred.

7. Religion in the United States shows two contradictory tendencies. The mainline denominations have become increasingly secularized; they place less emphasis on the supernatural and on rejecting the secular world. There has also been a growth of fundamentalism, an ecumenical movement that stresses a return to religious principles as a basis for everyday living and for society.

8. The church is not independent of other institutions. As government, law, economics, and education change, religion is affected. Fundamentalist groups try to halt this one-way flow of communication, hoping to create a political movement through which religion will affect law, education, and government.

SUGGESTED READINGS

Hadden, Jeffrey K., & Swann, Charles E. (1981). Prime Time Preachers: The Rising Power of Tele-Evangelism. Reading, Mass.: Addison-Wesley. A study of the men and women who preach on television and their effect on religion in the United States.

Kephart, William M. (1983). Extraordinary Groups: The Sociology of Unconventional Lifestyles (2d ed.). New York: St. Martin's Press. A book that covers the Amish as well as many other religious sects: the Hutterites, the Shakers, and the Oneidans, for example.

Pope, Liston. (1942). Millhands and Preachers. New Haven, Conn.: Yale University Press. A classic study of the confrontation between economic and religious forces in a textile mill strike in the South in 1929. An illuminating narrative of the very real tension between religion and society.

Weber, Max. (1904/1958). The Protestant Ethic and the Spirit of Capitalism. New York: Scribner. An influential essay by Max Weber that is also enjoyable reading for anyone who has a knowledge of U.S. history and a familiarity with Protestantism.

Wilson, John. (1978). Religion in American Society: The Effective Presence. Englewood Cliffs, N.J.: Prentice-Hall. A textbook that thoroughly reviews theory and research in the sociology of religion.

CHAPTER 16

SECONDARY INSTITUTIONS: SPORT, SCIENCE, AND MEDICINE

PROLOGUE

Have You Ever . . . considered the parallels between sport and religion? Sports events usually occur on Saturday or Sunday afternoon rather than Saturday or Sunday morning, but the functions are very similar. Both promote social integration and affirm basic values.

College football is a prime example. From Seattle to Chapel Hill, from Notre Dame to Stanford, football is a chief avenue of community integration. Traffic disappears while everyone is either at the game or tuned in to it. People stop in checkout lines to cheer a new score. And people who have other loyalties are well advised to keep them to themselves.

Like the vast cathedrals of the Middle Ages, our stadiums stand as extravagant monuments to the ideals of our society. Used only once a week for only a few months a year, they are symbolic of the things we hold dear—achievement and competition.

The institutions of society are the chief embodiments of our culture. Although each meets a unique need, each in a different way reflects society's central values. This chapter will introduce some less central, but nevertheless important, institutions—sport, science, and medicine. Like the economy, the family, and government, they not only reflect our society's central values but also help individuals and society cope with recurrent problems.

Institutional Development

An **institution** is a social structure built around a relatively distinct and socially important set of values that endures over generations (Williams, 1970). The chief examples of institutions are the five basic ones covered in previous chapters—economy, family, government, education, and re-

437

An **institution** is a social structure built around a relatively distinct and socially important set of values that endures over generations.

ligion. Each has a relatively distinct set of norms and positions that are of central importance to society.

Institutional arrangements are evolutionary rather than constant, however. They change in response to changes in technology, environment, and culture. Just as roles that used to be attached to family statuses (for example, teaching the young) have become attached to statuses in educational and religious institutions, so new institutions emerge to meet new needs.

In preindustrial societies, there is often only one well-developed institution: the family. Many or all religious, economic, political, and educational roles are attached to family statuses. At this stage of institutional development, family statuses (husband/father, wife/mother, grandparent, brother-in-law) include political, educational, religious, and economic obligations. As societies become more complex, specialization occurs and unique social structures develop to fill distinctive needs.

The process continues. Within the 20th century, science, medicine, sport, the military, and law have clearly emerged as institutions. Each of these areas has a distinct grid of statuses linked by compelling norms. For example, the legal institution has a network that includes such statuses as judge, police officer, correctional officer; a body of interrelated norms that constitute the law; and a set of sanctioning systems that compel each of us, whether citizen, lawyer, or enforcer, to take the norms into account (Turner, 1972).

These new institutions can be regarded as secondary, in the sense that they are not found in all societies or even in all industrial societies. Although they are relevant to survival in the modern world, they are irrelevant to many kinds of human societies. They are thus secondary both in the timing of their development and in their importance for understanding human societies.

The chief characteristic of institutions is their stability. Their major function is to produce continuity in social organization from one generation to the next. Yet institutions are also responsive. Old ones adapt, evolve, and change; new ones emerge to meet new needs. Although the basic five should remain as a foundation, undoubtedly new institutional patterns will be added in the generations to come—and they will reflect new technologies, new environments, new social needs.

Leisure and the Institutionalization of Sport

The Sociology of Leisure

If you think about the way you spend your average day, you will find that most of your activities are structured by the five basic institutions covered in chapters 11 to 15. Between going to school, going to work, doing your shopping, paying your bills, doing your housework, taking care of your family obligations, and maybe going to church (plus washing, sleeping, and eating), most of your days and nights are filled up. These obligatory acts structure your life with things that you should or must do. Luckily, however, you usually have a little time left over in which you can do what you want. This residual category is called **leisure**—all the voluntary activities that people undertake after they have finished their required work.

Trends in Leisure Time.   Any comparison of contemporary work schedules with those of the previous century demonstrates that Americans now spend less time at work. Over the last 50 years there has been a sustained decrease in the average workweek, an increase in vacation and holiday time, and a decrease in the number of years spent in the labor force (Wilson, 1980). Does this mean that we have more leisure time? Not necessarily. During the same period, other obligations have increased. We have bigger houses and yards, and we expect them—and ourselves—to be cleaner and better cared for than before. Thus, in spite of washing machines, vacuum cleaners, and power mowers, we spend more time on maintenance than we used to. One study, in fact, calculated that despite spending less time at work, the average American had lost 2 hours of leisure time a day between 1930 and 1965 (Robinson & Converse, 1972:79).

In 1975, a national study asked a sample of adults to keep time diaries in which they would record how they spent their days. The results show that the average adult has 4 hours of free time each weekday, 6 hours on Saturday, and nearly 8 hours on Sunday. What do people do with their

Leisure is all the voluntary activities that people undertake after they have finished their required tasks.

Figure 16.1
For many Americans, leisure means relaxing from work by watching television, going to the movies, or listening to music. A larger proportion of people, however, use their leisure time to engage in physical recreation and sport. Jogging is one form of recreation that has been taken up by persons from varied backgrounds; young and old, female and male. As this picture suggests, leisure is not equivalent to rest—it is simply voluntary activity.

34 hours a week of spare time? How do their leisure activities relate to their other social roles? Are they alienating or fulfilling? These are the questions addressed by the sociology of leisure.

Leisure Activities.   People undertake an immense variety of voluntary activities to fill their free time. Some garden, some play guitars, some go to movies, some play flag football, and many watch television. Studies of leisure habits in the United States agree that television has replaced many of the leisure activities that people engaged in 30 or 40 years ago.

Television has not eliminated all competing activities, however; increasing proportions of people fill their free time with indoor and outdoor recreation. Since 1970, the number of adult softball teams has increased from 29,000 to 102,000. In addition to these organized types of recreation, in 1983, 20 percent of Americans went camping, 31 percent went fishing, 22 percent bicycled just for enjoyment, and 19 percent jogged (U.S. Bureau of the Census, 1984). The types of recreation that people engage in vary by gender, race, class, and age. Most Americans, however, are involved in some form of recreation.

Although some of the activities engaged in for recreation are forms of play that have no rules, most of them have performance standards. There are conventions that tell us how to run, quilt, and play bridge or the guitar. For the most part, however, these pursuits are not governed by any distinct normative complexes; no set of appropriate behaviors governs the entire set of activities. One area of recreation, however, that is governed by such norms is sport.

Sport as an Institution

Competitive physical activities that base winning and losing on a set of structured rules are **sports.** In addition to the specific rules that govern each sport, the entire field of sport is governed by a common set of norms and values that can be summarized by the words "be a good sport." These words mean that you should be a cheerful loser and a gracious winner, play fair, and give your best effort. According to the norms of sport, not trying to win is almost as damning as cheating. If you're behind 44 to 12 and it is impossible for you to win, you still have to try. If you give up— if you just sit on the ball for three downs, if you do a somersault instead of your usual floor routine, if you quit the game—this is taken as a demonstration of lack of character.

Sport is competitive physical activity that bases winning and losing on a set of structured rules.

Sport is indeed a distinctive social structure with norms and values that set it apart from other institutions. It is also an increasingly important institution. Keeping Americans supplied with rackets, balls, sweat clothes, and season tickets is a major industry. In addition to being a big business, sport involves a large proportion of the population either as active participants or as observers.

Among participants and nonparticipants alike, sport is a major spectator activity. It is an interest that includes all classes, races, and ages. The sports page is the first section, sometimes the only section, of the newspaper that many people read, and no reasonable public figure would schedule a speech that would preempt a major ball game.

Perhaps nothing is as common to U.S. society as the idea that sport is a good thing. Sport is often said to be good for society and for the individual athlete. It builds good citizens and strong character. This belief in the goodness of sports is so pervasive that a former California State School Superintendent, Max Rafferty, once said, "Critics of collegiate football are kooks, crumbums, and commies" (cited in Edwards, 1973). Sport embodies and reinforces the values and perspectives of U.S. society; to some, criticism of sport is criticism of the United States. The following sections will evaluate some of the claims made for sport and review some of the more critical analyses.

The Functions of Sport

Sport may contribute to the maintenance of society in a variety of ways. Most importantly, it serves as a mechanism to reinforce important societal norms and values, including competition, teamwork, and obedience:

1. *Competition.* Sport teaches young people the importance of giving their best and trying to be winners. It thus reinforces expected values in educational and economic arenas. These values would be out of place in a society where status was completely ascribed; competition is part and parcel of a relatively open class system.

2. *Teamwork.* Team sports teach young people the advantages of putting the group above the individual, the virtues of loyalty, and the merits of cooperation. These values are consistent with society's expectations in the workplace and the community. The team is the ultimate metaphor for the idea that each person's work, no matter how menial, is vital to group success.

3. *Obedience.* In much sport activity there is a rigid hierarchy of authority. Neither the position one plays nor its duties are open to individual or group decision making. Sport is thus an important reinforcer of the need for an authority structure and the importance of obedience in reaching collective goals. Learning these values in sport may contribute to tolerance of inequality and authoritarian relationships in economic and political life.

Figure 16.2
Sport is distinguished from other forms of physical recreation in that the activities are competitive and guided by a set of agreed upon rules. Participation in team sports such as softball supports the values of competition and achievement, but it also encourages teamwork and the subordination of individual goals for a team win.

Basically, all sport has a conservative influence (Edwards, 1973). This is especially true of team sports such as football and baseball, which teach obedience, discipline, cooperation, and competition within the rules. Although sport is often linked to the American way of life, it has been useful in the political structures of many other countries too. As the tremendous success of East German, Romanian, and Soviet athletes demonstrates, sport is hardly unique to democracy or freedom. Rather, in all societies, sport is a way to impose discipline on young people.

In many ways, sport serves some of the same functions as religion. It teaches values that are important for society, and it reinforces them with ceremonial rituals. Consider the following maxims as illustrations of values taught through sport (Snyder, 1971):

— There is no I in TEAM.
— Who passed you the ball when you scored?
— The way you live is the way you play.

Figure 16.3

Organized sports are some of the clearest examples of how social structure patterns behavior. A division of labor, a clear hierarchy of authority, and conformity to assigned roles are all important to team success. A functional view of sport argues that these conditions apply in most other spheres of life and that participation in sport reinforces norms and values underlying other institutions.

— A quitter never wins; a winner never quits.

— To explain triumph, start with the first syllable.

The ideals of sport are basically the same as those that underlie other U.S. institutions. In fact, it can be argued that the learning of social values takes place as much in gymnasiums and on Little League playing fields as it does in church, synagogue, or classroom.

Thus sport teaches and reinforces society's values. It contributes to the maintenance of society by legitimizing the values that underlie most of the other major institutions.

In addition, sport may serve to channel hostility and aggression. At a general level, it provides a legitimate channel for the aggressive behavior of young people who may have more energy and aggression than they can express in acceptable ways. For lower-class youths, it may serve the additional function of providing a nondestructive means of gaining status recognition from peers as well as an opportunity for upward mobility.

There is, however, some evidence that sport participation encourages aggressive behaviors and ideologies (Stevenson, 1975).

Sport and the Athlete: Does Sport Build Character?   The general belief that sport is good for athletes as well as society is nicely summed up by former President Gerald Ford, who played football at the University of Michigan: "Outside of a national character and an educated society, there are few things more important to a country's growth and well-being than competitive athletics. If it is a cliché to say that athletics builds character as well as muscle, then I subscribe to the cliché" (cited in Coakley, 1982). To a large extent, the claim that sport builds character is an untestable hypothesis. To test it, we would have to set up an experiment (see chapter 2) in which young people were randomly divided into two groups. The experimental group would be required to engage in sport, and the control

Figure 16.4

In a close analogy to military battles, national teams compete in the Olympics to demonstrate the superiority of their nation's economic and political system. The conflict perspective of sport would see this U. S. victory over the Soviets at the Winter Olympics in 1980 as promoting false consciousness and exploiting athletes.

group would have to refrain from it. Over the years, we could test the two groups to see which group had the best character—assuming we were able to reach some consensus about how to measure character.

Because sport is voluntary, however, participation in athletics is far from random, and such an experiment is impossible. Some people choose to participate, and others do not. It is entirely likely that people who possess the traits supposedly built by sport (discipline, industriousness, competitiveness) had these traits before they engaged in sport. It is also likely that athletes who do not possess these traits soon drop out; thus, by the time athletes reach high school, they are a highly select group. For these reasons, it is hard to assess empirically whether sport does build character.

Some observers believe that it is unrealistic to think that sport might build character. Critics charge that the vast emphasis on winning at all costs encourages cheating, excessive violence and aggression, and the exploitation of athletes. Fuel for this argument comes from several recent autobiographies by former professional ball players as well as from recent scandals about steroid use among amateur athletes. Occasionally, the evidence is provided unintentionally by those claiming that sport builds character. For example, the coach of the 1954 Little League championship team had this to say about his philosophy of winning:

> You have to be ruthless, because the other guys are ruthless . . . and you have to have kids on your team who are tough, fighters, rough-and-ready kids who aren't going to take any bullshit [cited in Coakley, 1982:56]

One of his young players commented:

> He used to try to break kids; he would scream and yell at us and put the pressure on, to see which of us would break down and cry. If you broke down and cried in practice, he figured you'd break down and cry in a game. I don't think it hurt me a bit because that's what life is all about anyway, pressure and competition. Yeah, I'd like my son to go through what I went through. . . . It would be good for him. [cited in Coakley, 1982:189]

This is character-building of a special type. It emphasizes mental and physical toughness and the ability to take punishment. It says nothing about integrity, honesty, or empathy.

Despite the difficulties of measuring the effects of sport on character, there have been several attempts to do so. One review of this literature concluded that the best that could be said was that there is no evidence that athletic participation actually damages character (Ogilvie & Tutko, 1971).

A Conflict Perspective on Sport

Conflict theorists analyze social institutions by looking for the ways in which institutionalized norms are used to rationalize and support patterns of inequality. They also look for contradictions between institutions that might pave the way to social change. A conflict perspective on sport deals with such potentially embarrassing questions as: "Is sport really good for

you, or is it good only for the people who sell sporting goods and sporting events?" This perspective seldom appears on *Wide World of Sports* or on the sports pages of newspapers, but it offers a valuable balance to the prevalent functionalist view that sport contributes to societal and individual welfare.

Basically, conflict theorists suggest that sport contributes to sexism and to militarism, that it exploits athletes, and that it serves as a mechanism to support current inequalities in the class structure. Let us briefly examine each of these claims.

Does Sport Contribute to Sexism?   There is no worse thing to say to a group of athletes than "You played like a bunch of girls out there." More than any other life activity, sport segregates women and men. It also presents a dramatic arena for demonstrating male superiority (see Table 16.1). Critics of sexism in sport do not deny that male athletes can run faster, hit harder, throw longer, and jump higher. What they object to is that sport takes these relatively unimportant differences between women and men and magnifies them into seemingly major differences in worth and ability. These differences are then used to support attributions of differential status to women and men in industry, home, church, and government.

Women and girls are increasingly active in athletics. In high schools, girls' participation rates increased eightfold between 1970 and 1978 (Siedman, 1979). This increase is due in large part to Title IX legislation, which makes gender discrimination in any part of educational institutions illegal. Passed in 1972, but not enforced until 1976, this legislation mandates that female athletes get the same budgets, the same training facilities, and the same kinds of exhibition schedules as do male athletes. The full consequences of the legislation were just beginning to be felt when the Reagan

Table 16.1   The Olympic Story
The increasing encouragement of women's athletics has resulted in rapid progress for women's achievements. In many sports, women's advances are greater than men's; and in several sports, the best women in 1980 are better than the best men were 50 years ago. The gender gap will not disappear, but it is getting smaller.

	GOLD-MEDAL WINNER'S TIME	
	Men's	Women's
Track, 800-Meter Run		
1928 games	1 min 51.8 sec	2 min 16.8 sec
1948 games	1 min 49.2 sec	*
1980 games	1 min 45.4 sec	1 min 53.5 sec
Swimming, 400-Meter Freestyle		
1924 games	5 min 4.2 sec	6 min 02.2 sec
1948 games	4 min 41.0 sec	5 min 17.8 sec
1980 games	3 min 51.3 sec	4 min 08.8 sec
Running High-Jump		
1928 games	6'4"	5'3"
1948 games	6'6"	5'6"
1980 games	7'9"	6'5"

SOURCE: The World Almanac and Book of Facts, 1984, edition, copyright © Newspaper Enterprise Association, Inc., 1983, New York, NY 10166.

*The women's 800-meter race was not included in the 1948 games.

administration announced in 1984 that it would no longer punish gender discrimination in athletics by withholding federal dollars from educational programs. This change in federal policy may bring a reversal of women's gains in athletics.

Sport poses a real dilemma for gender equality. Whereas radical critics suggest that sport is bad because it overemphasizes the physical differences between men and women, other critics demand that women be allowed to participate fully in sport and to exercise their physical and competitive abilities. No one has yet suggested a reasonable structure in which equality and competition can be achieved (Theberge, 1981).

Does Sport Encourage Militarism?   The Duke of Wellington is alleged to have said, "The Battle of Waterloo was won on the playing fields of Eton." Many observers since that time have noted the similarities between sport and the military: the emphasis on obedience, teamwork, loyalty, and authority—even the haircuts and the uniform. And, in fact, there appears to be a strong tie in many people's minds between patriotism and sport. The parade of colors, the singing of the national anthem, and many other patriotic rites are part of most sports events. Similarly, any expression of political dissent (for example, a black power salute) at a sports event is considered not merely inappropriate but somehow in violation of the ideals of sport itself.

Does Sport Exploit Athletes?   There is no denying that many athletes benefit through participation in sport. Some are highly paid; others gain esteem from their performance. The conflict perspective stresses, however, that for every winner, there are countless losers. College athletes are a particularly poignant case in point; they are five times more likely than other students to leave school without a degree (Coakley, 1982). Is this exploitation?

Careful studies show that at both the high school and college level, athletes enter school with poorer academic backgrounds than the average student. The big-money sports—football and men's basketball—are especially likely to recruit players who have inadaquate academic backgrounds (Hauser & Lueptow, 1978; Purdy et al., 1982). Many would not have gone to college at all without their athletic scholarships. There is little convincing evidence that college athletic participation hinders the academic progress of good students; it may instead give opportunities to those who would not otherwise have them.

On another dimension, however, there is substantial evidence that sport exploits athletes. In high school and college, as well as at professional levels, athletes are either encouraged or allowed to ruin their long-term health in pursuit of short-term gains. Athletes receive tapings, cortisone shots, and other treatments that encourage them to play despite injury, possibly creating chronic injuries that will last long after the end of their careers in competitive athletics. Thus, although athletes may be strong and muscular, they are also often racked with the pain of knee injuries, elbow injuries, and torn ligaments. This element of sport suggests that long-term gains go to owners, coaches, and advertisers rather than to the athletes themselves.

Figure 16.5
The economic inequalities in athletics are most evident in professional big money sports where a few athletes are disproportionately rewarded. Carl Lewis, for example, winner of four gold medals in the 1984 Olympics, annually receives a small fortune in endorsements; this enables him to practice without worrying about money and also allows him to support an affluent life-style. Most athletes are not so fortunate. These inequalities, conflict theorists point out, are the forces which lead to corruption, cheating, and payoffs in some college and professional sports.

Does Sport Contribute to Class Inequality?   Functionalists regard the work of sport in teaching young people the values of obedience and authority as a contribution to the maintenance of society. Conflict theorists see it as a form of manipulation that will serve to perpetuate the class structure.

Karl Marx suggested in 1848 that religion was the opiate of the masses. Contemporary critics see sport serving the same purpose. It provides entertainment for the lower classes and keeps them from focusing on their class injuries. The Romans offered their people bread and circuses to keep them happy; we get bowl games and ball games and the Olympics. In addition to keeping the lower classes occupied, radical critics suggest, sport builds an altogether false sense of community. For example, the whole city may celebrate when its team wins the pennant, or the entire school may be united by a crucial game. The conflict perspective suggests that this feeling of unity is false consciousness and that the oppressed classes would be better off focusing on their own problems.

A Summary of Sport and Society

Sport is an institution in American life. As it gains attention as a social structure, it also gains criticism. The comparison of the structural-functional and conflict perspectives is a useful approach in ensuring that we

CONCEPT SUMMARY

A Comparison of Structural-Functional and Conflict Theories of Sport

	STRUCTURAL-FUNCTIONAL THEORY	CONFLICT THEORY
ASSUMPTIONS ABOUT THE SOCIAL ORDER	Social order based on consensus, common values, and interrelated subsystems.	Social order based on coercion, exploitation, and subtle manipulation of individuals.
MAJOR CONCERNS IN THE STUDY OF SOCIETY	How do social systems continue to operate smoothly? How are parts interrelated?	How is power distributed and used in society? How do societies change, and what can be done to promote change?
MAJOR CONCERNS IN THE SOCIOLOGY OF SPORT	How does sport contribute to the maintenance of society? How does it support other institutions?	How does sport create personal alienation? How is it used to control thoughts and behaviors of people and maintain economic and political systems serving the interests of those in power?
MAJOR CONCLUSIONS ABOUT THE SPORT-SOCIETY RELATIONSHIP	Sport is a valuable secondary institution benefiting society as well as individual athletes. It is basically a source of inspiration on the personal and societal level.	Sport is a distorted form of physical exercise shaped by the needs of an autocratic and production-conscious society. Sport lacks creative and expressive elements of play; it is an opiate.

SOURCE: Adapted from Coakley, Jay J.: Sport in society, ed. 2, St. Louis, 1982, The C.V. Mosby Co.

see both sides of a social structure that we are accustomed to viewing positively. Both perspectives agree that sport reinforces traditional American values, but each points out different consequences of these values.

Science: An Institutionalized Way of Knowing?

Sociology of Knowledge

Science was defined in chapter 2 as a process of inquiry, a way of knowing based on systematic empirical observation. It is hardly the only way of knowing, however. Knowledge—the acceptance of statements as truth— can come from an authoritative source, say the church or someone you admire, from a supernatural experience, or from personal interpretation of your own experience (Montague, 1925).

In our culture, we rely extensively on scientific rules of evidence to determine what is or is not true. For example, a scientific study tells us that Special K is less nutritious than Lucky Charms ("Which cereal," 1981). Although this conclusion contradicts our personal interpretation of the evidence, we accept it as fact because we accept laboratory experiments as a valid means of authorizing knowledge. Similarly, we accept the fact that the moon rotates around the earth but the sun does not, despite our own observations that both move across the sky.

In most areas of life, modern societies give preference to science as a way of knowing. The Bible speaks of creation in 7 days, but science provides evidence of evolution. Faced with conflicting knowledges of this sort most people in the United States have revised their religious knowledge to make it consistent with scientifically authorized knowledge; they define the creation story as an allegory, for example. A sizable minority, however, have solved the dilemma of conflicting knowledge by revising scientific knowledge to fit their religious knowledge. Politics and economics can also be the source of conflicting knowledge. In Stalinist Russia, the opinions of "the Great Teacher, Stalin" were taken as authorized knowledge on matters in the natural world as well as the political world.

The **sociology of knowledge** is concerned with the development and change of criteria for authorizing knowledge. It asks, for example, why rationalism—the expectation that events are logical—emerged in the modern era as the primary criterion for accepting knowledge. (As any *Star Trek* watcher knows, Spock's total reliance on logic can lead to absurdity; intuition and emotion are also important ways of knowing.) Those who study the authorization of knowledge examine how the cultural values of society determine whether new knowledge gets accepted or rejected and how this affects society.

Marxist sociologists trace the acceptance of new knowledge to economic relationships. They argue that the knowledge that society accepts is that which helps provide a rationale for the dominant relationships of production (Habermas, 1970). Thus, in the pre-Civil War South, slaveholders were eager to accept knowledge that justified slavery. They used the Bible, theories of evolution, and early anthropology as sources of knowledge that blacks were inferior. Cases such as this, where one generation's or culture's knowledge is another generation's nonsense, make the relativity of knowledge obvious. Although non-Marxists look at factors beyond the rationalization of the relationships of production, all students of knowledge conclude that what a society accepts or rejects as knowledge and the standards by which it chooses are related to dominant values and social structures (Merton, 1957).

As contemporary society's most respected process of gaining and validating knowledge, science has become an institution. It has acquired a fairly unique set of norms relating to an important arena of life that has endured over generations. Analysis of this institution rests heavily on the contributions of one man, Robert Merton, whose work is the springboard for the sociological analysis of science.

Figure 16.6

Knowledge can come from many sources. For these Jews, the Talmud is an important source of knowledge. In modern society, truth claims based on tradition, religion, and authority have tended to give way to science as a way of knowing. Over the past century, science has emerged as an institution, complete with a set of norms and rules related to generating, accepting, and validating new knowledge.

The **sociology of knowledge** is concerned with the development and change of criteria for authorizing knowledge.

Ideal Norms of Science

"The institutional goal of science is the extension of certified knowledge" (Merton, 1973:270). In his classic work, "Science and democratic social structure" (1942/1957), Merton identified four norms of science that are essential to achieve this goal: *communalism, universalism, disinterestedness,* and *organized skepticism.* (The acronym CUDOS, which is used in the sociology of science literature, may help you remember these norms.) Merton argued that the norms are moral imperatives in science. When scientists violate them, they are not merely odd or mistaken—they are immoral. Merton suggested that the norms apply to science in all societies and all time periods. Thus, although such technical norms as sampling,

Figure 16.7
Science is guided by a set of ideal norms intended to guide the search for new knowledge: the norms of communalism, universalism, disinterest, and organized skepticism. Albert Einstein, achieved fame though not fortune for his work in physics and mathematics. Such fame and fortune is not supposed to be a goal for the individual; truth not glory is the ultimate object of science.

measurement strategies, and rules of evidence may change over time, the moral imperatives of science are constant.

The **norm of communalism** specifies that scientists must freely share new knowledge with others.

Communalism. The **norm of communalism** specifies that scientists must freely share new knowledge with others. Because the development of knowledge often proceeds by the piecing together of many small bits of evidence, it will proceed faster if all investigators share their little bits. This norm requires that a scientist's new discoveries be made public honestly and completely and that other scientists have access to the person's data and techniques.

The **norm of universalism** specifies that new knowledge claims be judged on technical merit only, not on the characteristics of the individual scientist.

Universalism. The **norm of universalism** specifies that new knowledge claims be judged on technical merit only, not on the characteristics of the individual scientist. According to this norm, new knowledge will not be judged on the basis of the race, gender, social class, or prestige of the individual scientist. According to the ideal norms of science, the social origins of knowledge are irrelevant to its validity (Mulkay, 1979).

The **norm of disinterest** requires that the scientist place the search for truth above personal gain.

Disinterestedness. The **norm of disinterest** requires that the search for truth be placed above personal gain. Thus scientists are expected to evaluate evidence fairly, with no preference for support of their own pet theories. Furthermore, they are expected to pursue research topics regardless of whether the topics are currently popular or unpopular, regardless of the likelihood of acquiring recognition or reward, and regardless of political or religious barriers. The goal is truth, not glory.

The **norm of organized skepticism** requires that all new knowledge claims be critically examined to see if they meet technical standards.

Organized Skepticism. The **norm of organized skepticism** requires that all new knowledge claims be critically examined to see if they meet technical standards. In practice, this norm means that little is ever regarded as proven in science and that new claims to knowledge are accepted only after careful scrutiny.

An Additional Norm: Emotional Neutrality. Since Merton's initial description of the norms of science in 1942, an additional norm has been added to the list. The **norm of emotional neutrality** specifies that a scientist may not allow personal preferences to affect the outcomes of research. Thus a social scientist investigating the effects of child abuse on human development is expected to be open to the possibility that abuse may have positive effects. Similarly, the physicist who has made a career out of watching atoms go clockwise is expected to be open to evidence that demonstrates the opposite.

> The **norm of emotional neutrality** requires that the scientist's personal preferences not affect the outcomes of research.

Real Science: Conformity, Nonconformity, and Sanctions

Merton is one of the chief architects of contemporary structural-functional theory. It is not surprising, therefore, that the picture he draws of science as an institution fits a functionalist perspective. In Merton's picture, the norms of science are integrated with and support the norms and values of society. As Merton describes science, it is a perfect illustration of the functional theory of stratification: The rewards an individual receives are based solely on contributions to knowledge that are critically and fairly evaluated. Thus inequality in prestige and reward are both justifiable and necessary, reflecting real differences in the contributions that scientists make to society.

Not all observers of the scientific institution have been so positive about it. Indeed, science as an institution has been criticized on a number of grounds. There are two major strands of criticism. The first accepts the ideals of science as desirable but suggests that the norms may be incompletely institutionalized and that many violations occur. The second suggests that the ideals themselves may be faulty and that science serves capitalist society. The latter criticism attacks the belief that science is an impartial certifier of knowledge, apart from the culture in which it exists.

Living Up to Scientific Norms. The moral imperatives of science identified by Merton are ideal norms. All institutions have such norms. Parents are supposed to put their children's interests above their own, nuns and priests are supposed to lack sexual interest, and scientists are supposed to lack self-interest. The fact that the human beings who occupy these statuses may not be able to live up to the ideal norms does not negate the importance of the norms in channeling behavior. As ideals, they serve to guide and inspire. They are thus important even if no one lives up to all of them.

FRAUD. In his initial work, Merton argued that the norms of science led to the "virtual absence of fraud" in science (1942/1957:559). Nevertheless, occasional cases of outright fraud have been uncovered. A recent example is the case of Richard Spector, a graduate student researcher at Cornell University (Broad & Wade, 1983). Spector claimed to have experimental evidence that confirmed a particularly elegant and attractive theory of cancer; many expected him to win a Nobel Prize. Other scholars quickly began to incorporate his findings into their own work. The only problem was that they could not replicate the first step in his process, breaking down an enzyme. Because Spector's findings were so attractive, however, fellow scientists chose to believe that Spector had a knack with this notoriously tricky process rather than that he was in error. In fact, it was neither error nor knack; it was fraud. Spector was a convicted forger who had falsified his educational credentials to gain admission to the school and was merely practicing another type of fraud, this time on the scientific community. He was eventually found out and banished from his laboratory.

Replication is the repetition of empirical studies again and again to make sure that different observers get the same results.

THE ROLE OF REPLICATION.   The primary mechanism for uncovering error and fraud is **replication**—the repetition of empirical studies again and again to make sure that different observers get the same results. The more eminent the scholar and the more important the knowledge claim, the more likely it is that research results will be reexamined. Eventually, as in Spector's case, replication tends to replace faulty knowledge with more accurate knowledge. The process of replication occurs in a sequence that looks something like this list of hypothetical articles:

"The effect of spring on the sex lives of sponges" (1972)
"New evidence on the effect of spring on the sex lives of sponges" (1974)
"The effect of spring on the sex lives of sponges: A critique" (1975)
"Reply" (1975)
"A reconsideration of the effect of spring on the sex lives of sponges" (1979)

Eventually, the process results in the identification of a core of knowledge in the area of inquiry. If three scientists find the same effect in three different laboratories, using several different techniques, then we can feel confident that they are on the right track. If nobody can confirm the original findings, they eventually will be consigned to the dustbin. In the short run, faulty or even fraudulent knowledge may be accepted; in the long run, the process of replication eliminates such knowledge.

Science: Is It Culture-Free?   The ideal norms of science suggest that scientific knowledge exists independently of its social origins. Is this possible? Critics say no. Some suggest that science is a way of knowing that is uniquely compatible with capitalism; others link it to Christianity, to industrial society, or to democracy (Sklair, 1972).

It seems safe to conclude that no social process is culture-free. First, the level of material culture determines the tools and techniques with which science can be pursued. Second, culture may determine which subjects are open to scientific (as opposed to political or religious) knowledge. In the 17th century, Galileo was condemned by the Catholic church for advancing a theory of the universe that challenged religious knowledge. In our own society, some liberals are opposed to research on genetic differences among human races. They argue that evidence of any such differences may be used to promote or perpetuate racial injustice. Similarly, many people are opposed to research that can be used to create destructive weapons or new life. Cultural restrictions on research topics are imposed not only behind the Iron Curtain. Many are imposed simply by the cultural blinders that all members of a culture share and that define some matters as naturally out of the realm of science. For example, in criticizing a research grant to investigate the causes of love, Senator William Proxmire has said, "200 million Americans want to leave some things a mystery and right at the top of those things they don't want to know is why a man falls in love with a woman and vice versa" (cited in Skolnick, 1983).

CULTURAL BIAS.   Most of us are more eager to accept good news than bad. We are more apt to believe someone who tells us our dog is smart than someone who tells us our dog is stupid. Not only are we more apt to believe statements that are personally gratifying, we are more apt to believe statements that fit into our previous experience. New evidence that requires us to reorganize our opinions and beliefs is uncomfortable; we don't like it. Thus we have a tendency to reject knowledge that is awkward for us and to accept evidence that confirms what we already know.

It appears that the same process occurs in science. Kuhn (1962) has described how science deals with inconvenient facts that do not fit into current ways of thinking. When new evidence contradicts an accepted theory, quite often it is just ignored instead of being taken as an indicator that the theory is wrong. Occasionally, enough evidence accumulates that the old theory is overthrown and a new one is put in its place. The tendency of science is plain: to accept what fits with current thinking and to reject what does not.

A clear example from social science is the recent controversy about Margaret Mead's work on Samoa (Mead, 1928). Her anthropological work appeared to offer scientific evidence that sexual activity among young people was normal and that it helped promote a healthy attitude toward sexuality. The people she studied in 1923 were not afflicted by rape, frigidity, or any of the hangups common to Western sex lives of the 1920s. Her writings provided convenient justification for what might be called the first sexual revolution, and her book was embraced by scholars and the public. Over a 50-year period, millions of undergraduates were assigned to read *Coming of Age in Samoa* as an example of scientifically valid knowledge. A recent work by an anthropologist who spent 40 years in Samoa, however, argues that Mead's training for scientific field work in anthropology was wholly inadequate (though not by the standards of 1923), her evidence inconsistent, and her conclusion just plain wrong (Freeman, 1983). Yet her conclusion was accepted without question because it was convenient.

In sum, the focuses and techniques of scientific knowledge are undoubtedly influenced by culture. To the extent that scientific knowledge is channeled by these cultural influences, it will differ from culture to culture and perhaps from class to class. Although science offers a set of guidelines that should lead to universal agreement on the evidence, there are many processes at work that bias the questions that are asked, the evidence that is permissible, and the attention that will be given to findings. Science is a system for answering questions. As long as different cultures and classes ask different questions and as long as some answers benefit one group more than another, science will not be culture-free.

The Organization of Science

As a group, scientists have no unique organizational home. Some appear in the military, some in government, some in business, some in hospitals, and some in universities. This dispersion of scientists among so many institutions is one reason that science is called a secondary institution. Because science lacks a unique organizational base, some have argued that it can best be understood as a profession.

Figure 16.8
Science as profession includes people working in very different areas of inquiry: physics, biology, and sociology to name only a few. As this chemist's technique for purifying DNA from a solution of ethidium bromide demonstrates, each discipline has somewhat unique techniques. What they share in common, what makes them all sciences, is their agreement on a set of criteria for certifying knowledge. All rely on empirical data, critically evaluated by peers, and carefully replicated.

Science as a Profession.   Science possesses many of the characteristics of a profession. Scientists are highly trained, their work is self-directed and creative, they see themselves as performing a service to society, and they have a sense of identity with other scientists. The norms and sanctions of science are informal; they are imposed by colleagues and by the profession, not by the employing organization.

A characteristic of scientists, as of all professionals, is that their first loyalty is usually to their profession rather than to their employing organization. Although their paycheck comes from a specific industry or university, it is their professional identification that gives them a sense of identity and self-esteem. The division of loyalties between profession and employer creates tension for the bureaucracies in which scientists work as well as for the scientists themselves.

On the surface, science and bureaucracy are like oil and water; they do not mix. Bureaucracies are based on control—control of communication, authority, work standards, and work assignments. Science is based on freedom—freedom of inquiry, freedom from authority, and freedom of communication. Although current research suggests that the dilemma is more apparent than real (Ritzer, 1977), scientists often claim that they need to be treated differently than other employees. For example, they claim that creativity cannot be scheduled from 9 to 5, so they demand (and frequently get) the freedom to come and go as they please and to work at home, at midnight, or perhaps not at all. These successful claims may be one of the reasons that scientists are among the most satisfied with their jobs.

Some scientists, referred to disparagingly as locals, develop a loyalty to their employing university or business. They are interested in and seek to promote the welfare of their own organization. The norms of science, however, clearly favor the cosmopolitan, the scientist who is interested in larger issues, not in the success or failure of a particular organization (Gouldner, 1957). This lack of identification with the employing bureaucracy may lead to a phenomenon known as whistle-blowing—going public with some information that will serve the greater good at the expense of the employing organization. Thus an engineer may leak the news that a new train is unsafe (Perrucci et al., 1980). Any public-spirited employee can blow the whistle (Karen Silkwood is a good example), but whistle-blowing is more likely among those whose professions give them clear guidelines about the importance of putting truth before other goals. As a result, scientists are often regarded warily by the bureaucracies that employ them.

The Changing Organization of Science.   It is estimated that 95 percent of all scientists ever born are alive right now. The number of scientists now being trained in graduate schools far exceeds the total number of practicing scientists 50 years ago. Increasingly, the PhDs being turned out by U.S. graduate schools will go into government work, college teaching, or administration rather than into direct research. Nevertheless, the number of people trained in scientific research is growing at an astounding rate.

Along with the growth in the number of scientists has come a tremendous growth in the resources available to science and the bureaucracy administering them. It used to be that major scientific contributions could be made by a lone individual working in a simply equipped laboratory. Increasingly, major contributions require teams of specialists working with expensive equipment and vast financial resources. Since World War II, we have made the organizational shift from little science to big science (Price, 1963).

One of the most important aspects of the shift to big science is the increasing expense of scientific research. Physicists, chemists, and engineers need expensive equipment; sociologists use national sample surveys that, like the Zelnik and Kantner research described in chapter 2, cost half a million dollars or more. The increasing cost of research means that scientists have less independence in choosing projects; they have to work

Figure 16.9

In recent years the organization of science has shifted away from individuals working independently to teams of researchers working collectively on major projects requiring expensive equipment and facilities. The costs of high technology and sophisticated research equipment, such as that being used in this computer factory, are largely borne by either the federal government or large corporations with their own research and development departments.

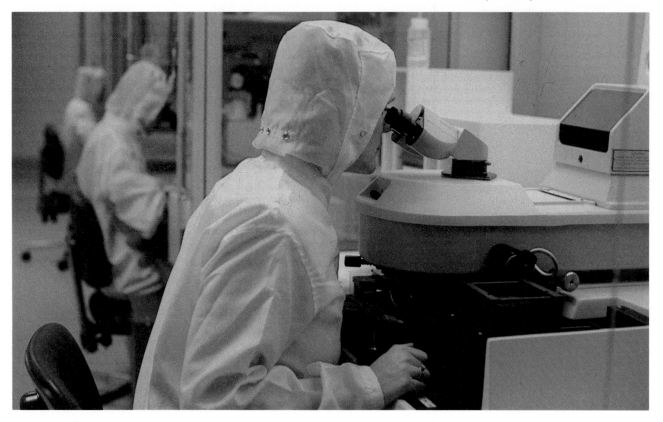

where the money is. Although some money is available from private foundations, most research money comes from business or the federal government. A full one-third of all research money spent in the United States goes for defense and space-related projects (U.S. Bureau of the Census, 1984). In sociology, two areas that are currently well funded are aging and adolescent pregnancy; divorce and mental health are two areas that the Reagan administration has explicitly said it does not want to know about. Thus the shift to big science reduces the likelihood that science will be a culturally free, questing enterprise.

Science remains a matter of individual creativity rather than the application of routine techniques to routine questions. Nevertheless, the shift to big science has changed the organization of science. It is possible that the changes may lead to even greater acceleration of scientific productivity. As more individuals work together in better-equipped laboratories and with greater financial support, science may become more creative and more productive. However, this change in the organization of science explicitly leaves out the person who lacks proper credentials (usually the PhD) or who does not have a position at a well-funded private laboratory or research-oriented university. Increasingly, science is becoming an activity of credentialed specialists at specific institutions rather than an activity in which any person of creative bent can engage.

Health and the Institution of Medicine

The Sociology of Health

In every society, people are concerned about their health. They take steps to ensure continued good health and establish procedures for avoiding ailments and injuries. These efforts may take the form of avoiding black cats, making burnt offerings, or taking vitamins. Needless to say, some efforts are more effective than others.

In all societies, there are normative responses to health and sickness. In preindustrial societies, these norms are seldom attached to unique statuses. Rather, the roles of healer and preventor of sickness are attached to statuses within the family or religious institutions. In many societies, illness and injury are associated with being cursed; thus religious ceremonies are seen as appropriate responses.

Advances in technology and medical science have led to a redefinition of the causes of illness. We now define illness as the result of biological or physical factors instead of supernatural causes. This redefinition has transformed the treatment of illness. When people think illness has a supernatural cause, they often consider it illegitimate to interfere. When illness is redefined as something merely physical, however, then human efforts become acceptable. The redefinition of illness occurred at approximately the same time that science developed the skills to effect cures. As people gained control of illness, medicine ceased to be sacred and became profane (see chapter 15).

Parallel to the transformation of illness has come the development of medicine as a unique social institution. This new institution has a distinct

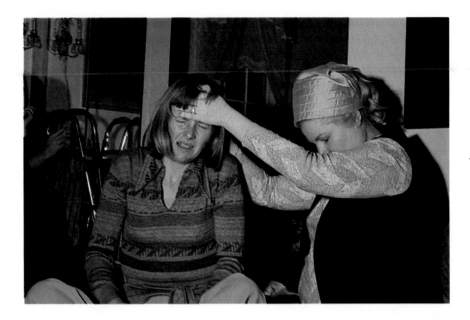

Figure 16.10
In the modern world, the treatment of sickness and poor health rests primarily on medical science and technology. There are a few religions that reject modern medicine totally, but most religions have accepted medical advances and combined them with religious practices. In fact, many hospitals are sponsored by churches and those that are not frequently have chapels for patients and others to use. In the premodern world, however, the treatment of illness is often the responsibility of faith healers, shamans, or witch doctors.

set of statuses and norms and a complex of values that set it apart from the other institutions of society. Although many hospitals are church-related and all have chapels, healing is now seen as the primary obligation of physicians rather than priests. There are, however, still religions in the modern world that reject medical intervention into God's intentions for the sick (Christian Science, for example). Many others believe in the use of prayer, consecrated oils, or ritual as important auxiliary means to regaining health.

The medical institution is a complex one. All of us hold some status in this institution, although for most it is only the status of patient. All are governed in daily life by norms about health and illness. The following sections treat the norms for health and illness, the health professions, and the U.S. health-care delivery system.

Norms within the Institution of Medicine

Some of the norms that govern the institution of medicine are specialties; they apply to only some statuses within the institution. For example, the Hippocratic oath applies only to physicians. There are also universal norms defining how all of us ought to behave with regard to health and illness. Among the most important are the norms that define illness and our responses to it.

The Sick Role. Talcott Parsons's (1951) concept of the **sick role** is one of the most important concepts in medical sociology. Parsons's major insight was that the designation *sick* brings with it a set of rights and obligations. Parsons claimed that being sick is a social role in that illness entitles us to the role only when the illness has been socially recognized.

According to Parsons, the following are the rights, duties, and obligations associated with the sick role:

The **sick role** is the rights and obligations that accompany the social label *sick*.

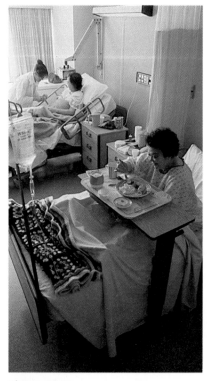

Figure 16.11

Being sick is a social role that carries certain rights as well as obligations. These hospital patients can expect to be excused from their usual role obligations and to be treated for their illness. At the same time, they are obligated to try to get well by following instructions and co-operating with the medical staff.

1. *Sick people are exempt from normal social roles.* They can stay home from school and work, shirk committee meetings, and not clean their houses—all without incurring censure from others. It is acceptable that the sick not fulfill normal obligations.

2. *Sick people are not responsible for their condition.* No one will suggest that they deserve it, that God is punishing them, or that it is their fault that they are sick. Their illness is regarded as an unfortunate accident. Not only are they not responsible for the illness, it is not thought that they could get well just by wanting to. In short, being sick is a physical matter, not a moral one.

3. *Sick people should try to get well.* Although it is not their fault that they are sick, it is their obligation to follow instructions and to wish to be well.

4. *Sick people should seek technically competent help and cooperate with physicians.* Not only should they abstain from behaviors that will extend the sickness, they should also actively seek to get better.

Being exempt from usual duties is the right of the sick; trying to get better and seeking help are the obligations. If you do not carry out the obligations of the role, you soon find that the rights are withdrawn. If others believe that you are not trying to get better or that you are sick through your own fault, then you will not be allowed to stay in the sick role. For example, if a coworker who is allergic to horses nevertheless goes to the racetrack, no one is going to find the resulting asthma a good reason for missing work. The asthma will be just as real as if it had another, more excusable cause, but the sick role will not be granted because the illness is seen as self-inflicted. People who have diseases caused by obesity or cigarette smoking may be denied the sick role.

Thus the social reality of illness depends in large part on the extent to which other people know about and accept the legitimacy of the illness. This raises the challenging question: What is illness? Certainly, we would all agree that a broken leg constitutes an illness. But what about being too depressed to hold a job? Is this a legitimate illness? Although there are some biological and chemical clues to distinguish normal from abnormal conditions, calling a behavior an illness is basically a process of social labeling. In some times and places, a condition may be defined as an illness; in others it may be a crime; in yet others it may be the normal condition. The following sections briefly describe how illness is defined.

Health is the state of mind and body that permits a person to occupy the usual social roles.

Illness and Deviance.   One definition of **health** is that it is the state of mind and body that permits a person to occupy the usual social roles. A person who cannot fulfill the usual obligations is referred to as sick. By this definition, pneumonia and the flu are illnesses; the sufferer is confined to bed and cannot fulfill normal roles. The same can be said about massive depression or anxiety, which also may confine a person to bed.

The extreme of the social definition of health and illness is to define anybody who does not fill normal social roles as sick. Thus many people regard all deviants as mentally ill. Whether deviants are sick or just bad is an issue still being thrashed out; the issue itself is the culmination of a long process in which more and more deviant behaviors are coming to be regarded as illnesses. For example, many now consider alcoholism to be a disease. This means that alcoholics are considered eligible to assume the sick role. Their behavior is judged to be beyond their control. It is no longer their fault that they are alcoholics; rather it is a chemical dependency. When a form of deviance becomes accepted as illness, then social reaction changes. It is no longer appropriate to put people in jail for being public drunks; instead they are put in hospitals. Physicians and counselors, rather than judges and sheriffs, treat them. Other forms of deviance, such as laziness, murder, and rape, also may be regarded as forms of mental illness that are better treated by physicians than sheriffs. Presently, we have reached no firm decision on these issues. The public seems to believe that although there are some murderers, rapists, and so on who are mentally ill and should be treated by physicians, there are others who are just bad and should be put in jail.

Regardless of where the lines eventually are drawn on these particular issues, the trend is clear. More and more deviant behaviors are coming to be defined as illnesses—conditions that should be diagnosed and treated by health-care professionals.

The Social Structuring of Illness. If illness is said to occur whenever we cannot perform our usual social roles, then whether we are ill depends very much on our social roles. For example, the irresponsibility that may be regarded as eccentricity in the idle rich may be defined as mental illness in the person who has to hold a routine job. Similarly, anxiety or depression may have a greater impact on the housewife, who spends a lot of time in unstructured activity, than it does on the person with a highly structured job. Thus the same condition is defined as an illness for one person but not for another, depending on social roles. To a significant extent, then, illness is relative rather than absolute; it depends on the social situation.

The Profession of Medicine

Only 10 percent of the medical work force is physicians. Yet this status is central to understanding the medical institution. Physicians are responsible for both defining ill health and treating it. Their definitions set the stage for the other actors. They define what is appropriate for those with the status patient as well as for all the other participants in medical practice. They play a crucial role in setting hospital standards and in directing the behavior of the nurses, technicians, and auxiliary personnel who provide direct care.

The concept *profession* describes a special kind of occupation and no occupation fits this concept better than that of physician. Consider the six characteristics of a professional: (1) specialized knowledge, (2) a sense of obligation to one's field, (3) service to society, (4) a strong feeling of identity with others in one's field, (5) high personal involvement in one's work, and (6) an unstandardized product.

The professionalization of physicians has paralleled the institutionalization of medicine. Until 100 or 150 years ago, physicians neither possessed much specialized knowledge nor had a strong identity with others in the field. Almost anyone could claim the title of doctor; training and proce-

China Rejects Modern Medicine

When modern medicines and medical technology were exported to less developed countries, the Western medical institution was shipped along with the sulpha drugs and contraceptives. Thus physician training, hospitals, and the norms and statuses surrounding the delivery of health care were transferred intact from Boston and London to Bangkok and Zaire.

The Western medical institution is not a culture-free product of science and technology; it is the product of an affluent society. This makes it difficult to export it to less developed nations. For example, when the Rockefeller Foundation helped bring modern medicine to Thailand, it demanded that only fully trained physicians from the hospital in Bangkok be allowed to practice medicine. As that hospital could turn out only 50 doctors a year, however, all of whom preferred urban rather than rural practice, the elimination of intermediate medical personnel such as midwives and independent nurses worked a hardship on the Thai people—denying them any medical care unless they could have the best (Goldstein & Donaldson, 1979).

China is one of the few nations that has accepted Western medical knowledge but rejected the institution of medicine. Its alternative structure of medicine is a rational adaptation of medical knowledge and technology to a low-income, rural population in a socialist society.

The Chinese mode of health care is based on seven principles:

1. Emphasis on the rural population, the bulk of the people.
2. Demystification of medicine; health-care workers are like all others working for the state, no better and no worse.
3. Emphasis on preventive medicine rather than treatment.
4. Heavy reliance on part-time workers.
5. Health as everybody's responsibility—a community responsibility.
6. Emphasis on medical resources directed at the poor.
7. Heavy emphasis on prevention of disease through provision of adequate food, housing, and sanitation.

Many of these principles stand in sharp contrast to those of Western medicine, but they provide a realistic model for maintaining a healthy population at a low cost and with low investment. Since 1960, China has halved its mortality rate, and its life expectancy has risen from 57 to 68. This is a remarkable achievement for a society whose per capita GNP is less than 3 percent of that in the United States.

The Chinese system is organized from the grass roots upwards. The population is divided into production teams, brigades, and

Figure 16.12

Modern medical technology, such as this computerized life support system for premature babies, has greatly enhanced our ability to extend and save lives. It is, however, extraordinarily expensive. In China, a largely rural society with a population in excess of 1 billion, expensive western-style medicine has been rejected in favor of prevention, community organization for health care delivery, and improved sanitation, housing, and food. China's medical practices have effectively reduced the death rate at a relatively low cost.

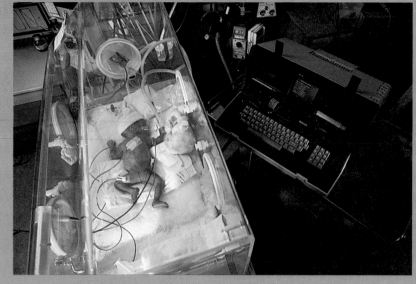

communes. The production team is the smallest unit, and it consists of 100 to 200 people. Each team elects three individuals who will have part-time responsibility for health care: the barefoot doctor, the health aide, and the midwife. In exchange for their responsibilities, they are released from some of their usual work. Periodically, the positions are rotated. The barefoot doctor, who is given a 3-month training course, is charged with basic health education and illness prevention, treatment of minor illnesses, vaccinations, and contraception. Since the barefoot doctor is responsible for only 100 to 200 people, he or she is expected to know them intimately and to be able to provide suggestions that will lead to a healthier life. The health aide's primary responsibility is sanitation—making sure that water and food supplies are clean. It is only at the commune level, 40,000 to 60,000 people, that physicians

with Western-style training are available. Even these physicians, however, have much shorter training periods than do U.S. physicians. Referrals are made to them by the brigade health workers. This system of health-care delivery almost completely eliminates the profession of medicine as it appears in the West.

The Chinese system has some costs, however. The emphasis on prevention at the local level means significant loss of privacy. It is somebody's job to check frequently and remind you that you smoke too much, drink too much, or don't keep your house clean enough; it is also somebody's business to make sure you change to a healthier life-style. In addition to loss of privacy, there is also some loss in quality of care. A difficult birth is more likely to result in either infant or maternal mortality when the attendant is a midwife rather than an obstetrician;

it is likely to take longer before a stomach pain can be diagnosed as cancer rather than gas. Nonetheless, China's system has allowed the rapid dispersal of medical knowledge and technology at relatively low cost. It has made possible major strides in life expectancy despite extreme poverty. It has also eliminated, to a significant extent, the inequality in health care inherent in the capitalist model of professional medicine.

Questions to Consider

Would there be any advantages to having a system like China's in a relatively rich country such as the United States, or is it useful only for poor countries that cannot afford the Western-style health system? How would you like to have one of your neighbors in charge of helping you live a healthy life-style?

dures were highly variable and mostly bad. About the only professional characteristic of these early practitioners was that the product was highly unstandardized.

In the United States, the professionalization of medicine began in 1848 with the establishment of the American Medical Association (AMA) and was virtually completed in 1910, when strict standards were set up for medical training. At the same time, AMA-supervised state examinations began to be required before one could assume the title of physician and begin to practice medicine.

Understanding Physicians' Income and Prestige.   The medical profession provides a controversial case study of stratification theories. Why are physicians predominantly male and nurses predominantly female? Why are physicians among the highest-paid and the highest-status professionals in the United States.

A structural-functional explanation of the status of physicians would directly follow the Davis and Moore theory outlined in chapter 8: Physicians have scarce talent and ability and must undergo long periods of training; consequently, high rewards must be offered to motivate the few who can do this work to devote themselves to it.

The conflict perspective would contend that the high income and prestige accorded physicians has more to do with physicians' use of power in their self-interest than with what is best for society. Its theorists argue

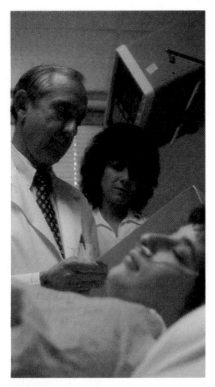

Figure 16.13
Physicians are among the highest-paid and most prestigious professionals in the United States. Theirs is also a profession with considerable power, both in terms of other medical personnel and patients. This picture of the interactions among a physician, nurse, and patient leaves little doubt about the relative status of these actors in the institution of medicine.

that the relatively small size of medical schools has more to do with a desire to keep supply low than it does with quality training. They also question whether the talents necessary to become a physician are as rare as is alleged or whether 10 years of training are really required to diagnose measles or deliver babies. A variety of people's health movements—for example, women's health cooperatives and community food cooperatives—have grown up in opposition to the medical profession; they argue that the layperson can prevent many illnesses and treat many minor problems once the techniques are removed from the monopolistic control of capitalist physicians (Illich, 1976).

Critics of the medical profession point out that the definition of *profession* that we use is an ideal norm created by the medical profession as part of its drive to justify high power and privilege (Freidson, 1970). These critics suggest that a more realistic way to evaluate a profession is in terms of its power relationships with other occupations and its clients. Freidson lists three major elements of professions:

1. *Monopoly*. The ability to monopolize control and performance of a set of tasks.
2. *Autonomy*. Being sole definer, controller, and evaluator of professional activities.
3. *Clinical mentality*. Emphasis on responsibility to one's colleagues and clients, not to the community as a whole.

Although medicine is one of the clearest examples of these characteristics of a profession, you might ask yourself whether the same criticisms can be applied to other professions. Just as it does not take 8 years of postgraduate education to recognize a cold, it probably does not require 16 years of education to teach kindergarten or a PhD to teach introductory sociology. Professionals—physicians, scientists, lawyers, and professors—are self-conscious groups of workers who seek to maintain and enhance their prestige and income. Because they can lay claim to specialized knowledge, they are in a unique position to define and defend their job demands.

ISSUES IN SOCIAL POLICY

The U.S. Health-Care Delivery System

A major focus of medical sociology has been the evaluation of the health-care delivery system. Reflecting sociology's concern with the distribution of power and privilege in society, medical sociologists have been especially concerned with patterns of inequality in health care. Three general problems with the U.S. system of health-care delivery have been noted: (1) unequal distribution of services—too many doctors in New York City and too few in rural areas, (2) too many specialists and not enough general practitioners, and (3) inadequate access to medical care by the poor. Increasingly, research in these areas has led to social policy attempting to solve the problems.

OVERSPECIALIZATION.

A middle-class family may have a pediatrician for the children, a gynecologist for the wife, and perhaps an internist for the husband, who has high blood pressure. Who do they call for hemorrhoids or the flu? The increased specialization of medicine leaves them with no one who will take responsibility for their whole self—including not only routine ailments but the interaction between mind, body, and social roles.

Since 1950, the number of general practitioners in the United States has declined from 112,000 to 55,000 (Cockerham, 1982) while the number of specialists has mushroomed. In part, specialization is an adaptation to the growing body of medical knowledge; it allows a physician to learn one aspect of medicine well as opposed to learning a little about a lot of areas. However, it contributes to one of the other major problems of U.S. medicine: overurbanization. A physician who only delivers babies or only does coronary bypass operations must work in a populous area to have a reasonable demand for the service. Thus specialization and overurbanization go hand-in-hand, leaving out not only the routine ailments and the whole self but also rural and small-town areas.

INABILITY TO AFFORD CARE

In the United States, the prevailing mode of health-care delivery has been on a fee-for-service basis. It is regarded as a service, like dry-cleaning, that you purchase for a price. Many people criticize the concept of capitalist health-

Figure 16.14
Advances in medical technology have contributed to major increases in life expectancy and significantly better health in our society. Further improvements, however, cannot rest on medical technology alone. Longer life and better health require decent housing, good nutrition, and social integration. Advances in medical technology alone will not eliminate the health deficit for youngsters growing up in environments like this.

care delivery. They point out that this system necessarily provides less and lower-quality health care to the poor.

Several sociological studies have documented the unequal access to medical care of the poor, the rural, and the elderly (Aday & Anderson, 1975; Davis, 1975). These are precisely the people who are omitted from most private health-insurance plans. Medicaid and Medicare were instituted in 1965 to redress this inequality. Current proposals for national health insurance are being promoted in order to remove remaining inequalities.

BEYOND HEALTH CARE

In evaluating proposals to equalize health care, one point must be clarified. Access to health care can be divided up more or less equally among the population: health cannot. Health is not a fixed quantity, like income or years of school, that can be divided up among a population (Fuchs, 1974). Nor is health merely the product of medical care. To an important extent, it is a product of individual life-style and social class. It depends on habits of eating, drinking, sleeping, driving, smoking, and working. In addition, health and long life may require adequate housing, a fulfilling occupation, and freedom from fear and discrimination.

For the most part, social policy is directed at ensuring that if you get lung cancer or cirrhosis of the liver, you will have access to medical care regardless of your geographic location or social class. It is clear, however, that this policy alone cannot improve health standards. A social policy designed to produce better health requires not only equal access to health care but also more equality in all life chances. It also requires that individuals make a choice to be healthy—that they get enough exercise and eat right, that they reduce or eliminate smoking and drinking. How far should social policy go? Is a healthy America important enough that life-style decisions—such as smoking and seat-belt use—should be part of social policy?

SUMMARY

1. Institutions evolve to meet the changing needs of society. In addition to the five basic institutions, recent and emerging institutions meet important but less central needs of society. Among these new institutions are sport, science, and medicine.

2. Sport is one area of leisure activity that is becoming institutionalized. It has a set of positions whose actions are governed by a relatively distinct normative complex. Although sport is not as crucial to society as is the economy or the family, it is an important activity involving billions of dollars and millions of participants.

3. The norms of sport emphasize teamwork, obedience, and competition. Because these same norms underlie many of our other institutions, sport serves to teach and reinforce societal values much as religion and education do.

4. Many people have asserted that sport builds character, yet critics charge that sport encourages sexism, militarism, and class inequality. The evidence is mixed, but it is clear that sport is seldom an agent of change; instead it reinforces traditional values.

5. Knowledge is relative. One generation's or culture's knowledge may be another's nonsense. Science is only one way of certifying knowledge, and, like other ways, it is related to the dominant values of its social environment.

6. There are five ideal norms of science—communalism, universalism, disinterest, organized skepticism, and emotional neutrality. Merton argued that if these norms were followed, there would be an efficient and accurate production of certified knowledge. Critics charge that there are

many norm violations and that science is affected by fraud and cultural bias.

7. Big science means teams of specialists working with expensive techniques. It also means that scientific research is being increasingly channeled by research priorities of government funding agencies and business rather than by intellectual curiosity.

8. The cause of illness and the cure of disease have only recently been transferred from religion to the new institution of medicine. This new institution has a distinctive grid of statuses guided by a distinctive normative complex.

9. In many ways, being sick is a social role with specific rights and obligations. Whether a person is regarded as sick, immoral, or normal depends on processes of social labeling and varies sharply by culture and social status.

10. The U.S. system of health-care delivery results in overspecialization, overurbanization, and a neglect of lower-income groups. However, equality in health cannot be achieved simply by equalizing access to health care. Health is a matter of life-style and life chances and can be understood only within the larger social context.

SUGGESTED READINGS

Brannigan, Augustine. (1981). The Social Basis of Scientific Discoveries. New York: Cambridge University Press. A review of some of the most memorable discoveries in modern science, with documentation of the social conditions that fostered their acceptance.

Broad, William, & Wade, Nicholas. (1983). Betrayers of the Truth. New York: Simon & Schuster. An attempt to demonstrate that there are few sanctions to support the norms of science and that the norms remain unrealized ideals. Includes fascinating accounts of fraud and carelessness in science.

Coakley, Jay J. (1982). Sport in Society: Issues and Controversies. St. Louis, Mo.: C. V. Mosby. A review of the major issues in the sociology of sport (sexism, racism, exploitation) in a manner that is thorough and fair but spiced with enough criticism to make it interesting.

Cockerham, William C. (1981). Medical Sociology (2d ed.). Englewood Cliffs, N.J.: Prentice-Hall. A textbook that offers a thorough description of the sociology of health and the development of modern medical institutions.

Edwards, Harry. (1973). Sociology of Sport. Homewood, Ill.: Dorsey Press. A biting critique of the U.S. sport institution, with emphasis on the special relationship between sport and race in the United States.

Gould, Stephen Jay. (1981). The Mismeasurement of Man. New York: W. W. Norton. An entertaining description of the appalling ways in which "science" has been used to support theories of racial inequality. Includes a critique of intelligence tests from the 19th century to the present that provides a serious challenge to our belief that we might ever have a culture-free science.

Starr, Paul. (1983). The Social Transformation of American Medicine. New York: Bantam Books. Describes how disorganization and quackery in the 19th century gave way to a highly controlled profession. An important but controversial book that critics charge unfairly blames physicians for working in a capitalist economy.

UNIT FIVE

Change

CHAPTER 17
POPULATION

468

PROLOGUE

Have You Ever . . . considered having a child? If you've given it any thought at all, you've probably come up with a long list of pros and cons. For most people, the list of cons is a long one: Children are expensive, they tie you down, they interfere with school or work, and they give you a frightening level of responsibility. Yet, every year, about 70 out of every 1,000 women in the United States have a baby. Of course, some bumble into it by accident and some do it unthinkingly as part of the normal adult role, but others look over the long list of pros and cons, gulp, and take the plunge. The amazing thing about fertility is that in spite of the diversity of motives on the individual level, the result on the societal level is very similar year after year.

Whether you have children and how many you have are likely to depend on your other goals. If you are committed to a career or to getting a graduate degree, the likelihood is that, male or female, you will postpone having children or even decide not to have any. Your decision will have ramifications far beyond your own life. If you and many others of your generation look at the list of disadvantages and decide that childrearing isn't for you, you may skip elementary education as a career and try social services for the elderly or health care instead. If domesticity appeals to you, however, the problems with the social security system will soon be over and property taxes will probably rise to build new schools. Having a child is one of the most intimate and private of experiences, yet perhaps nothing else we do has so much public impact.

This chapter explores the interrelationships between social structures and population. In doing so, it takes a historical and cross-cultural perspective to illustrate how social structures and population problems can be better understood when their interrelationships are acknowledged.

The Demographic Transition

The Current Situation

In 1984, the world population was 4.8 billion, give or take a couple hundred million. It is growing—rapidly. By the time current college students reach retirement age, the world population is likely to be 9 billion. This tremendous growth is totally alien to most human experience. Most societies before the industrial revolution grew either slowly or not at all (see Figure 17.1).

The world today has twice as many people in it as it did as recently as 1950. In part because of this growth, millions are poor, underfed, and undereducated. In part because of this growth, 15 to 20 percent of the world's species of plant and animal life will disappear by the end of this century. In part because of this growth, the world economic system is in danger of bankruptcy. Perhaps no other issue is so vitally connected to so many of our era's crises. This section will describe the current world population and then the process by which it was reached.

Although population is concerned with such intimate human experiences as birth and death, the big picture of population growth and change can be understood only if we use statistical summaries of human experience. Three measures are especially important: the crude birthrate, the crude deathrate, and the natural growth rate.

$$\textbf{Crude birthrate (CBR)} = \frac{\text{Number of births in year}}{\text{Total Population}} \times 1{,}000$$

$$\textbf{Crude Deathrate (CDR)} = \frac{\text{Number of deaths in year}}{\text{Total population}} \times 1{,}000$$

$$\textbf{Natural growth rate} = \frac{\text{CBR} - \text{CDR}}{10}$$

Table 17.1 shows these rates in 1984. For the world as a whole, the crude birthrate in 1984 was 28 births per 1,000 population; the crude deathrate was a much lower 11 per 1,000. Because the number of births exceeded the number of deaths by 17 per 1,000, the natural growth rate of the world's population was 1.7 percent. If your savings were growing at the rate of 1.7 percent per year, you would undoubtedly think that the growth rate was very low. A growth rate of 1.7 percent will double the principal in 41 years, however, and if this population growth rate continues, in 2025 the world population will be 9.6 billion.

The frightening prospect of welcoming another 4.8 billion people in our lifetime is complicated by the fact that the growth is uneven. As Table 17.1 shows, growth rates are startlingly different across the areas of the world. Africa is the world's fastest-growing continent. At a growth rate of 2.9 percent per year, it will double its population size in only 24 years. In Europe, by contrast, births barely exceed deaths and population is barely growing.

These differentials in growth are of tremedous importance. Almost all the additions to world population in the next several decades will take

The **crude birthrate (CBR)** is the number of births divided by the total population and then multiplied by 1,000.

The **crude deathrate (CDR)** is the number of deaths divided by the total population and then multiplied by 1,000.

The **natural growth rate** is the percentage growth rate implied by the excess of births over deaths. It is measured as the crude birthrate minus the crude deathrate and then divided by 10.

Figure 17.1   The Growth of World Population

Until the last 100 years or so, world population grew very slowly or not at all. The population bomb is as much a child of the 20th century as is the atom bomb.
SOURCE: van der Tak et al., 1979.

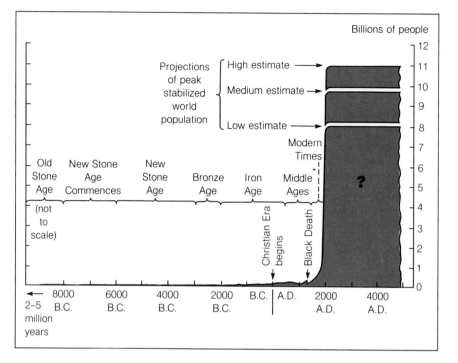

place in the less developed nations. As a result, the world is likely to be proportionately poorer in 2025 than it is now. How did we get into this fix?

Population in Preindustrial Times

Fertility is the incidence of childbearing.

Mortality is the incidence of death.

For most of human history, **fertility** (childbearing) was barely able to keep up with **mortality** (death) and the population grew little or not at all. Historical demographers estimate that in the long period before popula-

Table 17.1   The World Population Picture, 1984

In 1984, the world population was 4.8 billion and growing at the rate of 1.7 percent per year. Growth was uneven, however; the less developed areas of the world were growing much more rapidly than the more developed areas. As a result, most of the additions to the world's population were in poor nations.

AREA	CRUDE BIRTHRATE	CRUDE DEATHRATE	NATURAL GROWTH RATE	TOTAL POPULATION (in Millions)
World	**28**	**11**	**1.7%**	**4,762**
Africa	45	16	2.9	531
Asia	29	11	1.8	2,782
Latin America	31	8	2.3	397
Soviet Union	20	10	1.0	274
North America	15	8	0.7	262
Europe	13	11	0.2	491

SOURCE: Population Reference Bureau, 1984 World Population Data Sheet.

tion growth exploded, both the birth- and deathrates hovered around 50 per 1,000. (Birthrates are still 45 in Africa.) This means that each year, out of every 1,000 people, 50 died and 50 were born. What do birth- and deathrates of 50 per 1,000 mean for individuals and social structures?

Fertility. A birthrate of 50 babies per 1,000 population means that out of 1,000 people, 50 women spent the year pregnant and gave birth. This does not sound like a big burden, except that most of those 1,000 people cannot give birth. In terms of an individual woman's experience, we can break the birthrate down this way:

1. Begin with 1,000 people.	1,000	people
2. Not all of these people can have children. Take away all of the males, say 50 percent.	−500	
	500	females
3. Only women between the ages of 15 and 45 can bear children. Take away the roughly 60 percent who are younger or older.	−300	
	200	women 15 to 45
4. Only women in marriage or other sexual unions will bear children. Take away a minimum of 15 percent.	− 30	
	170	sexually active women between 15 and 45
5. At least 10 percent of women between 15 and 45 are involuntarily sterile. Take away 10 percent.	− 17	
	153	potential mothers

In a typical preindustrial population of 1,000, then, we have 153 potential mothers, of whom 50 bear a child each year. Assuming that the 153 women take turns, this means that each woman bears a child every 3 years: 1 year pregnant, 1 year nursing, 1 year off, and then do it again . . . and again. Thus a birthrate of 50 per 1,000 means a lifetime of childbearing for the average woman—potentially 10 children to bear between the ages of 15 and 45. In the United States, the 1790 census showed an average of 8 children per woman, with a crude birthrate of 55 per 1,000.

A lifetime of childbearing has a powerful effect on the role of women; it virtually precludes any participation in social structures outside the family. The woman will undoubtedly work, at home and in the fields, but she will be tied close to home and excluded from participation in political, community, or economic affairs beyond the household.

Mortality. During the long millenia in which there was little population growth, the number of deaths approximately equaled the number of births. The human meaning of a crude deathrate of 50 is best understood by equating it to an average life expectancy of 25 to 30 years. A life expectancy of 30 does not mean that a 35-year-old is considered old; instead it means that a high proportion of the population dies in infancy.

Life expectancy is the average number of years that a group of infants can expect to live.

Life expectancy is the average number of years lived by a group of infants. A simple example will show how high childhood mortality can bring down this average. Let's take a hypothetical group of 10 infants: 3 die in infancy and therefore live 0 years; 2 die at the age of 10; the other 5 live to 70. The total number of years lived by these 10 infants is 370:

$$3 \times 0 \text{ years } = 0$$
$$2 \times 10 \text{ years } = 20$$
$$5 \times 70 \text{ years } = \underline{350}$$
$$\text{Total} 370$$

The average number of years lived by this group of 10 infants—their life expectancy—is 37 (370 divided by 10). Thus high mortality rates in infancy and early childhood produce a low life expectancy despite the fact that many of those who escape the perils of childhood manage to live to an old age.

A crude deathrate of 50 means that death is a frequent visitor to most households. The stepmothers and stepfathers who appeared in fairy tales were a page out of real life; loss of spouses was common, and remarriage was speedy. One set of church records for 16th century England shows that the average husband remarried within 3 months of his wife's death (Wrigley, 1969).

In preindustrial societies, the deathrate was high and probably fluctuated from year to year with weather and disease; the birthrate was high and nearly constant. In some years, births outnumbered deaths, but overall they nearly balanced each other, and the population didn't change much.

The Transition in the West

Demography is the study of population—its size, growth, and composition.

The **demographic transition** is the change from high birth- and deathrates to low birth- and deathrates associated with modernization. During the transition, birthrates are higher than deathrates and population growth is much more rapid.

The industrial revolution set in motion a whole series of events that revolutionized population in the West. First, mortality dropped; then, after a period of rapid population growth, fertility declines followed. Because studies of population are called **demography,** this process is called the **demographic transition.**

Decline in Mortality.   General malnutrition was a major factor supporting high levels of mortality. Though few died of outright starvation, poor nutrition increased the susceptibility of the population to disease. Improvements in nutrition were the first major cause of the decline in mortality. New crop varieties from America (corn and potatoes especially), new agricultural methods and equipment, and increased communication all helped improve nutrition. Productivity increased, and greater trade reduced the consequences of localized crop failure. The second major cause of the decline in mortality was a general increase in the standard of living: better shelter and clothing . . . and soap. Changes in hygiene were vital in reducing communicable diseases, especially those affecting young children, such as typhoid fever and diarrhea (Razzell, 1974). Because of these factors, the deathrate gradually declined between 1600 and 1850. Despite its decline, though, the life expectancy for women in the United States was only 40 years at the time of the Civil War.

The Calamitous Century

In the 5th decade of the 14th century, one-third of the world died. An international epidemic of the bubonic plague struck first in China, then followed the caravan routes to the Mediterranean and traveled by ship to Western Europe. In 1351, a ghost ship with a cargo of wool and a dead crew ran aground in Norway, and the disease spread to Scandinavia and Russia. In its first assault, perhaps one-third of the population of Europe and Asia died. The plague came back again and again throughout the century until the population of Europe was reduced to half of what it had been before.

The immediate effect of the plague on social relationships was disastrous. Among those who caught the plague, death was both certain and quick. Stories were recorded of people who caught the plague in their sleep and died before they awoke. The deathrate was enormous; people died faster than they could be buried. Bodies piled up in the streets, and shallow mass graves were filled as fast as they could be dug.

The disaster was too large to comprehend in ordinary terms, and many believed that it meant the end of the world. This belief, plus the very realistic expectation of sudden death, meant that normal social relationships stopped. Crops went unharvested and fields unplowed; cathedrals being built were abandoned, never to be completed; livestock went untended and died almost as fast as their masters.

Overwhelming fear did not encourage human kindness. Each person was afraid to go near another, and the usual social ties were torn. Parents abandoned children, and wives left husbands.

In yet a darker spirit, people looked for a scapegoat to blame for their misfortune. The answer in the 14th century, as it was in the 20th, was the Jews. Despite a papal statement that it was unreasonable to think that the Jews were poisoning the wells they too used, a flame of anti-semitism swept Europe: 6,000 Jews were burned to death in Maintz (Germany) on August 24, 1349; in Worms, York, Antwerp, and Brussels, entire Jewish communities were exterminated. The survivors moved eastward to Poland and Russia, and by 1350 there were few Jews left in Germany or the Low Countries.

In the long run, the 50 percent reduction in population had significant economic impact and may have hastened the end of feudalism. The 14th century was a preindustrial agricultural society. Without mechanical aids, the productivity of the soil was directly proportional to the amount of labor put into it. The plague cut the amount of labor by half. The immediate consequence was an enormous fall in productivity. In the long run, the very foundations of feudalism were shaken. Labor's bargaining power rose sharply, and wages for craftsmen and laborers doubled. Tenant farmers no longer had to stay with exploitive masters

but could choose among manors competing for their services. Rents tumbled, and many tenant farms went empty; fields returned to the wild. Attempts were made to arrest this rapid change in economic relationships by legally restricting wage increases to 35 percent and by binding tenants to their land. In the face of severe competition for labor, however, these laws were ineffective and labor gained significant advantage.

A change in the supply and demand of labor did not revolutionize society. The people of the Middle Ages, both landlords and tenants, were still bound to one another by ties of custom. Nevertheless, the loss of half the population and the subsequent economic response deeply affected medieval society.

Questions to Consider

1. How would our social structure be affected by the death of half our population—say by nuclear war? How would your opportunities and obligations change?
2. Would the effect of sudden massive mortality from nuclear war be different from the effect of a more gradual disaster caused by infectious disease? Explain.

SOURCES: Tuchman (1978), McNeil (1976), and Hatcher (1977).

Figure 17.2

In the West, mortality declined largely because of an increasing standard of living. In the Third World, however, mortality reductions have been due to the introduction of western technology such as vaccination and only secondarily to improved diet and living conditions. The sudden drop of the death rate in the Third World is a major cause of the current population explosion.

In the late 19th century, public-health engineering led to further reductions in communicable disease by providing clean drinking water and adequate sewage. Medical science did not have an appreciable effect on life expectancy until the 20th century, but its contributions have sparked a remarkable and continuing increase in life expectancy. In the first 78 years of this century, the life expectancy of U.S. women increased 50 percent, from 49 to 77 years. Thus, although mortality began a steady decline in about 1600, the fastest decreases have occurred in the 20th century. This decline reflects the almost total elimination of deaths from infectious disease and the steady progress in eliminating deaths caused by poor nutrition and an inadequate standard of living (McKeown & Record, 1962; McKeown et al., 1975).

Decline in Fertility. The industrial revolution also affected fertility, though much later and less directly. The reduction in fertility was not a response to the drop in mortality or even a direct response to industrialization itself. Rather, it appears to have been a response to changed values and aspirations triggered by the whole transformation of life (Coale, 1973).

Industrialization meant increasing urbanization, greater education, the real possibility of getting ahead in an expanding economy, and, most importantly, a break with tradition—an awareness of the possibility of doing things differently than they had been done by previous generations. The idea of controlling family size in order to satisfy individual goals spread even to areas that had not experienced industrialization, and by the end of the 19th century, the idea of family limitation had gained widespread currency (van de Walle & Knodel, 1980). In England and Wales, the average number of children per family fell from 6.2 to 2.8 between 1860 and 1910, the space of just two generations (Wrigley, 1969).

This decline in fertility took place without benefit of modern contraceptives. Toward the end of the decline, diaphragms and condoms were important, but much of the fertility decline in Europe was achieved through the ancient method of withdrawal—coitus interruptus.

As Figure 17.3 shows, the demographic transition in the West will come nearly full circle by the end of the 20th century. Throughout Europe and North America, birth- and deathrates are again about even, and there is little population growth. In the non-West, the transition is taking a very

Figure 17.3 The Demographic Transition in the West

Because mortality declined while fertility remained high, Europe experienced substantial population growth during its demographic transition. Because the decline in mortality was slow and because many of the excess people moved to North America or Australia, this growth did not cause dramatic problems for Europe.

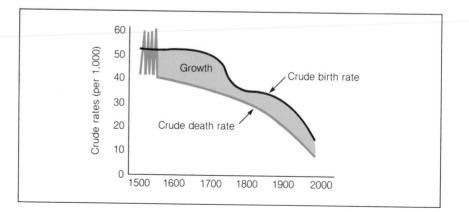

different course; in many of its nations, the transition from high birth-
and deathrates to low ones has just begun.

The Transition in the Non-West

In the non-West, birth- and deathrates remained at roughly preindustrial
levels until World War II. After that, modern medicine and public-health
engineering caused deathrates to tumble. Unlike the mortality decline in
the West, this change was not caused by changes in social structure or
standard of living; nor was it gradual. It was sudden change brought in
from outside. As Figure 17.4 demonstrates, the result has been massive
and sudden population growth.

Many people have looked at the demographic transition that occurred
in the West for clues as to how to effect a transition of fertility in the non-
West. What caused the fertility decline in the West? Not better contraceptives, not urbanization and new technology, but a transformation of the
entire social structure—including the class structure, the role of the family
and women, and religious and secular values. The following sections will
explore contemporary relationships between social structure and population and then return to the question of what this tells us about solutions
to the world population problem.

Fertility, Mortality, and Social Structure

The Effects of Social Structure

Social Structure and Fertility. In Kenya, the average woman has six
or seven children; in East Germany, the average woman has only one or
two. These differences are not the result of biological differences; they are
the product of values, roles, and statuses in very different societies. The
average woman in Kenya wants seven or eight children, and the average
woman in East Germany wants only one or two.

The level of fertility in a society is strongly related to the roles of women.
Generally, fertility is higher where women marry at younger ages, where
they have less access to education, and where their roles outside the

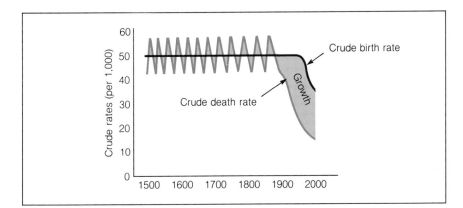

Figure 17.4 The Demographic Transition in the Non-West

In the non-West, mortality rates fell suddenly while fertility continued at very high levels. The result was dramatic growth. Fertility rates have begun to decline but are still far higher than mortality rates.

Figure 17.5
The level of fertility in any society is closely related to the roles women play. These women attending an open market near Nairobi (Kenya) are either choosing their family's groceries or marketing their farm's produce, tasks for which the women are largely responsible. Neither activity is hampered by having many children. As long as women's roles remain restricted to household activities, there is little incentive to have small families.

The **dependency ratio** is the ratio of dependents per productive worker, usually calculated as the number of people under 15 and over 65 divided by the population 15 to 65.

household are limited. Fertility also reflects the development of society's institutions. When the family is the source of security, income, social interaction, and even salvation, fertility is high.

Social Structure and Mortality.   The single most important social factor to affect mortality is standard of living—access to good nutrition, safe drinking water, protective housing, and decent medical care. Differences in standard of living account almost entirely for the fact that the average American can expect to live 25 years longer than the average Nigerian and that the average white in the United States can expect to live 4 years longer than the average black.

More subtly, social structure affects mortality through its structuring of social roles and life-style. Overeating and underexercising are causes of mortality as surely as are undereating and overworking. Race, religion, and gender all affect exposure to dangerous life-styles. In 1980 in the United States, 19,000 young men died at the ages of 20 to 24, compared to 6,600 young women. Most died in automobiles, and the difference in number is a product of the different norms that structure the lives—and deaths—of men and women. Another example is the low cancer rate in Utah, apparently attributable to the fact that the Mormon religion forbids the use of alcohol and tobacco and emphasizes a family oriented life-style (Clark, 1979).

The Effects of Fertility and Mortality on Social Structure

Fertility Effects.   Fertility has powerful effects on the roles of women. The greater the number of children a woman has and the older she is at the time of the last birth, the less likely she is to have any involvement in social structures outside the family. When the average woman bears only two children, the second of whom is in school by the time the woman is 30, fertility places much less restriction on her social involvement.

AGE STRUCTURE.   In addition to affecting women's roles, fertility has a major impact on the age structure of the population: The higher the fertility, the younger the population. This is graphically shown in the population pyramid in Figure 17.6. When fertility is low, the number of young people is about the same as the number of adults; when fertility is high, there are many more children than adults and the age structure takes on a pyramidal shape.

One measure of a society's age structure is the **dependency ratio**—the ratio of the number of people under 15 and over 65 per person aged 15 to 65. This ratio is a rough measure of the number of dependents per productive adult. On a worldwide basis, it varies from 0.94 in Africa to 0.54 in the West. This means that in Africa there is nearly one dependent for every producer and in the West there is one dependent for every two producers (see Figure 17.7). On an individual level, this is the difference between a family where one parent supports one child and a family where two parents support one child. Obviously, the two-parent family is better off. Not only is it better off now, but it is more likely to be able to set aside some savings for the future, with the result that in the long run it will be even better off.

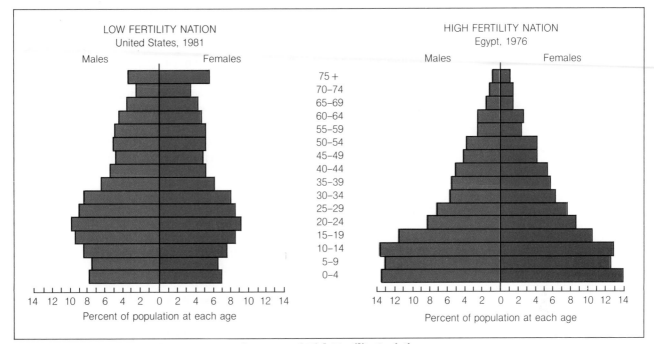

Figure 17.6 A Comparison of Age Structures in Low- and High-Fertility Societies
When fertility is high, the number of children tends to be much larger than the number of parents. When this pattern is repeated for generations, the result is a pyramidal age struc- ture. When fertility is low, however, each generation has a similar size, and a boxier age structure results.
SOURCE: van der Tak et al., 1979.

Mortality Effects. Like fertility, mortality has particularly strong effects on the family. A popular myth about the preindustrial family is that it was a multiple-generation household, what we call an extended family. A little reflection will demonstrate how unlikely it is that many children lived with their grandparents when life expectancy was only 25 to 30 years and when fertility was seven to eight children per woman. Reconstructions tell us that only a small percentage of all families could have been three- generational. Even if the grandparents survived, they could live with only one of their surviving children, leaving the other households without a grandparent. And quite often, if the children lived with their grandparents, it was because their parents were dead. In short, the three-generation household was impossible for many and affordable by few (Wrigley, 1969). The household of a high-mortality society was probably as fractured, as full of stepmothers, half-sisters, and stepbrothers, as is the current house- hold of the high-divorce society.

Population and Social Structure: Three Examples

Kenya: The Highest Fertility in the World

Kenya is an example of a society where traditional social structures en- courage high fertility. It is also an example of a society where high fertility may ensure continuing traditionalism—and poverty.

Figure 17.7 Age Composition and Development
In the less developed nations of the world, high fertility means that children are a large proportion of the population. This means that much of current produc- tion has to go to feed new mouths.
SOURCE: Population Reference Bureau, 1984 World Population Data Sheet.

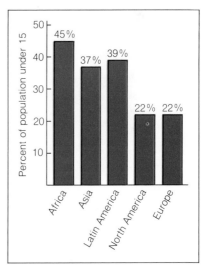

The Effects of Social Roles on Fertility.   Almost alone among the nations of the world, Kenya still has a crude birthrate of 52 per 1,000 population. Mortality, however, is down to 12 per 1,000. This means that the population of Kenya is growing at 4 percent per year. If that rate continues, the population will double in just 18 years. An aggressive family planning program is unlikely to reduce this growth: The average woman in Kenya has 7.1 children; she would like 7.3 (Kent & Larson, 1982).

The high value placed on fertility in Kenyan society is a reflection of several **pronatalist** (profertility) pressures. Among the pressures are tribal loyalties, women's roles, and the need for economic security (Mott & Mott, 1980).

TRIBAL LOYALTIES.   Kenya is a diverse nation in which there is jealous competition among tribal groups. Because the size of each tribe's population is an important factor in political power, large families are seen as politically advantageous. This is a common pronatalist pressure in any diverse society. Among French Canadians, it is called the revenge of the cradle.

WOMEN'S NEED FOR CHILDREN.   Regardless of the needs of their tribe or nation, most women give first consideration to how another child will affect them and their family. For the 80 percent of Kenyan women who are responsible for family farms, children are an asset. A substantial minority of Kenyan men work away from the family farm; even when they are there,

Pronatalism refers to social forces that encourage childbearing.

Figure 17.8
In Kenya, the family continues to be the center of economic and social relationships. Women and men find that having many children enhances their prestige, helps with their work, and provides them with economic security for their later years. Because there are few costs associated with having children, the average woman in Kenya desires—and has—seven children.

their role is largely supervisory. Women bear the chief responsibility for planting, ploughing, and harvesting and have full responsibility for cooking, drawing water, and finding firewood. As a result, three-quarters of Kenyan women list "help with work" as a reason for having children. In addition to helping with the work, children are an important, perhaps the only, source of esteem and power open to women. This is especially true of the 30 percent of Kenyan women who live in polygamous unions. The number of children, especially the number of sons, is an important determinant of a woman's position relative to that of other wives.

ECONOMIC SECURITY.   Children add to their parents' economic security in a number of ways. They are the only form of old-age insurance available. When they grow up and marry, they may also add to the family's economic and political security by their marriages. The greater the number of children, the greater the number of in-laws. A family that can bind itself to many other families has greater political power and more security.

In short, a family's income, status, and long-term security are all enhanced by its having many children. There are comparatively few rewards for having a small family. Children are virtually cost-free—no expensive medical treatment is available, what schooling there is has no direct cost to the parents, and there are no designer jeans or $75 tennis shoes. With a cost-benefit ratio of this sort, it is not surprising that Kenyans desire many children.

The Effect of Population Growth on Society.   Although high fertility may appear to be in the best interests of individual women, it has clearly negative consequences for the society. At current rates of fertility and mortality, Kenya's population is doubling every 18 years. As a result, development goals are shooting at a moving target. In order to double the proportion of children getting an elementary school education (from 45 to 92 percent), the government had to raise the dollars spent on education fourfold because the total number of children needing schooling doubled. Simply to maintain that level over the next 18 years, the Kenyan government would have to again double the dollars spent on education. Unfortunately, there are other demands on the budget—for defense, for highways, for development, for agriculture. All these areas face the same problem of escalating demand.

Thus a decision that is rational on the individual level turns out to be irrational on the societal level. Occasionally, people in the West make remarks of the sort: "Are they stupid? Can't they figure out they would be better off if they had fewer children?" Unfortunately for the argument, nations don't have children; women do. High fertility continues to be a rational choice for Kenyan women—and for Kenyan men.

Kenya was the first sub-Saharan African nation to establish an official family planning program, but the program has had very limited success. Only 17 percent of married women want no more children, and only 17 percent of this small group is using contraceptives (Mott & Mott, 1980). Like most family planning programs, Kenya's is voluntary. It tries to make services available conveniently and inexpensively to women who want them. When women plan families of seven or more, however, they require little help from family planning programs. Unless pronatalist forces are reduced, the most active of family planning programs is unlikely to have an impact on Kenya's fertility. The pronatalism built into Kenya's basic social institutions cannot be quickly eliminated just because official policy is **antinatalist.**

Antinatalism refers to social forces that discourage childbearing.

The Soviet Bloc: Official Pronatalism

At least officially, the nations of the Soviet bloc have the opposite problem: They think fertility is too low. Accordingly, these nations have official policies that attempt to encourage large families.

Concerns about Low Fertility.   In the western part of the Soviet Bloc, population growth has virtually ceased; in Hungary, the population is actually diminishing. In the eastern part of the Soviet bloc and in the Soviet Union itself, however, population continues to grow. Official concern appears to be stimulated by three factors: (1) fear of labor shortages, (2) uneven growth among ethnic groups, and (3) a changing age structure (Feshbach, 1982).

LABOR SHORTAGES.   Agriculture and industry are much more labor-intensive in the Soviet Union than in the West. Demands for increased productivity have thus placed heavy labor demands on the Soviet population: 88 percent of both women and men between 18 and 60 work full time, compared to about 70 percent in the United States. Whereas the labor force grew by nearly 2 percent each year during the 1970s, it will grow by 0.5 percent each year in the 1980s. This declining labor force growth will make it difficult to increase productivity.

A special concern is the lack of young men for military service. The Soviet military is staffed largely by draftees, and few young men escape the 2 years of required military service following their 18th birthday. The drop in the birthrate means a drop in the number of young men. In 1980, 2.5 million males turned 18; in 1990, only 2.1 million will. If the Soviet army is not to become smaller, the Russians will have to draft more civilians. This would mean a reduction in the civilian labor force and a subsequent decline in productivity. The Soviet government believes that higher fertility is a more attractive alternative.

ETHNIC DIFFERENTIALS.   An important concern for Soviet planners is the wide differences in growth rates among the 125 ethnic groups in the Soviet Union. The country traditionally has been dominated by Western or Slavic republics, and, in fact, these are the only Russians who speak Russian. In the Slavic republics, fertility has fallen to very low levels. Almost all the growth in the Soviet population comes from the high fertility of Asian and Middle Eastern minority groups. As a result, the Soviet army and economy are becoming increasingly dependent on these non-Slavic, non-Russian minorities. If this continues, far-reaching changes will be required. An army in which an increasing proportion of recruits do not speak the same language as the officers is in trouble.

CHANGING AGE STRUCTURE. The Soviet bloc faces the same problems as do all societies with declining fertility: An increasing proportion of the population consists of the dependent elderly. In 1980, 10 percent of the population was over 65; in 2000, the figure will be 19 percent. As with the other population problems, the aging of the population is aggravated by ethnic differentials. Already, 22 percent of the population in Slavic republics is over 65. The aging of the population is particularly problematic for the Soviet bloc because it has long-standing difficulties in providing human services.

For these reasons, as well as concerns in some nations about an actual decline in their population's size and, presumably, its power, planners in the Soviet bloc have concluded that low fertility poses a population problem.

Determinants of Fertility. Most adult women in the Soviet bloc work full time. This in itself is a disincentive to have children, especially when daycare services are not easily available and when there are relatively few labor-saving devices. In addition to full-time work, many women in Eastern Europe spend 2 hours a day standing in line to get groceries and other basic items. The housing shortage is severe, and most young families live in a one-bedroom apartment or with their parents (David, 1982). There are no neighborhood laundromats, much less private washers and dryers. If you have a baby in Eastern Europe, it will sleep in your room and you will have to wash its diapers in the bathroom sink. Considering these circumstances, it is amazing that women have even one or two children. Of course, women in Kenya or in preindustrial Europe have had many children under worse conditions. The women of Eastern Europe, however, have alternatives. They have opportunities for status and achievement outside the family, opportunities that are largely incompatible with large families. In these circumstances, many women have chosen to have very small families.

Although informal pressures from the social structure discourage fertility, official policy is pronatalist. Incentives to encourage fertility usually include paid maternity leave, cash bonuses for extra children, longer vacations for mothers, and graduated family allowances. Czechoslovakia provides the most generous incentives. New mothers are eligible for 6 months of paid maternity leave, and many benefits (family allowances, housing subsidies, and even a lower age at retirement) are graded according to the number of children. Low-interest loans are available to newly married couples for buying and furnishing homes; and with each additional child, an increasing proportion of the loan is written off. Few of the other Soviet bloc nations can afford such generous incentives, and in most cases, incentives are not large enough to surmount the lack of a washing machine or daycare facilities.

Throughout most of the Soviet bloc, fertility rates did edge upward during the 1970s. To a significant extent, this increase occurred because of a severe restriction on abortions. Since World War II, Eastern Europe has relied heavily on abortion as a method of birth control. In the Soviet Union itself, for example, there were twice as many abortions as live births in 1970. When abortion was suddenly restricted, fertility rose sharply (in

Figure 17.9
The Soviet Union is officially pronatalist. Because of declining birth rates, the generation now being born is somewhat smaller than the current generation. This means that there will be fewer people to staff Soviet institutions, in particular, the army, but also the labor force. Thus, the Soviet Union is one of a handful of nations that is encouraging fertility and offers incentives for large families.

Romania births doubled in a 1-year period). Although contraceptives are still not generally available in Eastern Europe (withdrawal remains the most commonly used method of birth control), couples seem to have adjusted to the new policy and are avoiding childbearing anyway.

The new rewards for large families have encouraged a small response. Couples who were going to have two children sometime in the future have sped up their schedule. There is no evidence, however, that the benefits have encouraged people to have more children than they otherwise would. Thus the long-term prospects are for a continuing decline in fertility rather than an increase.

China: Official Antinatalism That Works

In 1982, China conducted its first modern census. The results confirmed what experts had estimated—a population of slightly over 1 billion people—one-quarter of the world's population. Currently, China has an aggressive antinatalist policy, one that is apparently working successfully. Both social structure and official incentives have been transformed to discourage fertility.

Effects of Population on Social Structure.   Traditionally, Marxists have asserted that there is no such thing as a population problem; there is simply a distribution problem. Thus, when the Communists first came to power in China, in 1949, they claimed that China had no population problem:

> It is a very good thing that China has a big population. Even if China's population multiplies many times, she is fully capable of finding a solution; the solution is production. The absurd argument of Western bourgeois economists . . . that increases in food cannot keep pace with increases in population was not only thoroughly refuted by Marxists long ago, but has also been completely exploded by the realities in the Soviet Union. . . . Of all things in the world, people are the most precious. Under the leadership of the Communist party, as long as there are people, every kind of miracle can be performed. [Mao Zedong (Mao Tsetung), September 1949, cited in Aird, 1972]

Not until 1970 was this naive approach to population finally abandoned. The shift to a more pragmatic stance was dictated in part by periodic food shortages and fear of famine. In addition, China has extremely ambitious plans for economic development and agricultural improvement. These plans require high levels of investment and, consequently, a lower proportion of income going for immediate consumption. Lower fertility will free women for societal work rather than family work, it will make possible more education and training by dividing the education dollars among fewer students, and it will require that less money be spent on housing, highways, and health services. In the long run, however, lower fertility will mean an older population, which will bring a new set of problems.

Structuring a Low-Fertility Society.   China has been aided in its effort to reduce fertility by the vast transformation of its society that accompanied the Communist revolution. The structure of government, education, labor, and religion were all overturned by the new regime. In contemporary China, a woman's esteem, security, and income depend not on her children but on the state and community. Her self-interest lies in economic production and Communist party work rather than in many children. In fact, under the current structure of rewards, a large family is a cause of both short- and long-term disadvantage.

China has established a maximum of two children per family and strongly urges couples to stop at one. Incentives for a one-child family include supplementary food and housing, free health care, preferential treatment in choice of schooling and jobs, larger farm allotments in rural areas, and higher pensions. Couples who sign a one-child pledge begin to receive these benefits immediately; the benefits must be paid back if a second child is born. Contraceptives and abortion are widely available, and sterilization is encouraged.

In many nations, family size is considered personal business. In China, fertility is everybody's business ("In China," 1980). The most striking example is the practice of making one woman in each work group responsible for the fertility of the others. This responsibility includes making sure that they have contraceptives, chatting frequently about the importance of the one-child family, and carefully noting missed periods or weight gain. Because large families cause problems for communities, the woman who has a second pregnancy will be under intense community pressure to get an abortion or at least to stop at two. If she gets pregnant a third time and does not agree to an abortion, she and her husband may lose their jobs and their home and be shunned by their families, left out of community affairs, and denied basic privileges.

Officially, China's birthrate has dropped from 33 to 22 per 1,000 between 1971 and 1984, and its growth rate has dropped from 1.8 to 1.3 percent. (Applied to a base of 1 billion, this is still enormous growth.) Observers believe that these low rates and, in fact, the whole antinatalist policy may

Figure 17.10
This billboard shows a newly married Chinese couple being admonished to have only one child. In China, fertility is everybody's business and the government, employers, and neighbors engage in a concentrated program to provide formal and informal sanctions against large families. China's population is now over 1 billion people, however, and even with very small families, their future population problems will be substantial.

be more effective in the urban areas around Beijing (Peiking) than in rural areas, but all agree that China has made remarkable strides in providing both informal and formal supports for low fertility (Tien, 1983).

It is interesting to speculate on the consequences if the one-child family becomes widespread. With one child per family there would be no aunts, no uncles, no cousins, no brothers or sisters, no nieces or nephews. If China succeeds in creating a social structure that discourages fertility, low fertility will in turn have new effects on the social structure.

The Population Problem: Dilemmas and Approaches

The Population/Poverty Problem

There are nearly 5 billion people in the world. Only one-quarter of them live in what is called the developed world. The other three-quarters live in less developed nations, where the gross national product (GNP) per capita is one-tenth that of the developed world. Perhaps 500 million are seriously undernourished (Brown, 1981), and each year there are outbreaks of famine and starvation in Africa and Asia; a billion more are poorly nourished, poorly educated, and poorly sheltered. These are the same nations with high population growth. How is population growth related to poverty? Does high fertility cause poverty, or does poverty cause high fertility?

The Effects of Poverty on Population Growth.   For most of human existence, the normal pattern has been for women to devote most of their adult lives to bearing and rearing children. In the West, this pattern was disrupted by the transformation of society triggered by the industrial revolution. Changes included institutional development outside the family, formal education, a rise in the standard of living and in mobility, and a shift in values. This disruption of traditional practice has yet to occur in the less developed world. The high fertility of women in less developed nations is not caused by their poverty, but the lack of economic growth helps maintain fertility at traditionally high levels.

The Effects of Population Growth on Poverty.   In some of the poorest nations of the world, the population grows as fast as the economy. Despite relatively steady economic growth, increases in productivity are eaten up by high fertility, and there is nothing left over to invest in equipment or training. Were fertility to decline, more money would be freed for investment, which would set off a spiral of growing productivity and greater investment.

The Nature of the Problem

High fertility and poverty thus form a vicious circle in the less developed world; high fertility discourages economic growth, and lack of economic growth discourages fertility reduction. This complex connection between

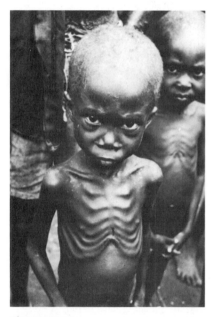

Figure 17.11
Perhaps half a billion people in the world are seriously malnourished and some, such as this starving child, face permanent physical and intellectual damage or even death. Few such cases are directly related to overpopulation. Instead, they are due to war, drought, and poverty—and an economic system in which rich countries have storehouses of grain and poor nations starve. When the world population reaches 9 billion in 40 to 50 years, however, there may actually be too little food to go around even with equal distribution.

fertility and poverty is of grave concern, first for humanitarian reasons and then for pragmatic and political reasons.

High population growth causes intense environmental pressure: Forests are stripped by governments seeking export dollars and by villagers seeking firewood. The overwhelming need to find wood for today's cooking fire prevents concern for tomorrow's needs, and new trees and shrubs are stripped before they get a chance to grow. The results are soil erosion and the beginning or extension of deserts. One estimate suggests that as a consequence of pollution and lack of habitat, 15 to 20 percent of the world's plant and animal species will become extinct by the year 2000 (Barney, 1981).

Self-interest on the part of the developed world raises other concerns about the poverty/population problem. Nations with severe problems may be politically unstable, and there is concern among Western policy makers that misery loves communism, or at least revolution. Thus they fear that political instability may result if the problems of poverty are not resolved. Is it coincidence that El Salvador has the highest growth rate in Latin America, or has rapid growth helped destabilize that nation?

Approaches to the Problem

As a result of these diverse pressures, the population/poverty problem is of concern to world leaders in both more and less developed nations. There are three primary approaches to the problem: family planning, development, and redistribution.

Family Planning Approach.   Advocates of family planning argue that the major cause of poverty in the less developed world is high fertility. They suggest that the best path to prosperity is to reduce fertility through family planning; reduced fertility will in turn make development possible. To this end, they support increased financial aid and technical assistance for family planning programs in less developed countries.

Development Approach.   Others refer instead to a poverty problem and prefer to attack it from the other end: first development, then lowered fertility. They suggest that development is the best contraceptive. Most advocates of this approach recommend aid in the form of trade agreements and loans that will help the struggling economies of poor nations. At the 1984 World Population Conference in Mexico City, President Reagan caused the United States to support a version of the development approach. He believes that private enterprise and enterprising individuals will allow the less developed countries to pull themselves up by their bootstraps.

Redistribution Approach.   Even without the acceptance of Marx's belief that all instances of poverty are simply distribution problems, it must be acknowledged that current poverty could be reduced by a more even distribution of goods, both within and between nations. A redistribution of goods is one possible point of entry into the vicious circle between poverty and population. Whether it takes the form of land reform within nations or major transfers between nations, however, this alternative is

Figure 17.12
Although children impose burdens on parents, they also bring joy and entertainment. Moreover, children are one of the few sources of joy and reward equally available to rich and poor. As this photograph indicates, women and men with few economic rewards may still find pleasure in their children. Thus, poverty and children are not incompatible and poor people find it rational to have children.

often unpopular. It is unpopular with the elites in less developed countries and with the citizens and leaders of the world's rich nations.

Recent experience suggests that neither family planning nor development is sufficient by itself. Development is slow and extremely expensive; changed social structures might not affect fertility patterns for two generations, by which time the population may already have doubled or tripled. Providing contraceptives and encouraging small families, however, is likely to be relatively ineffective within impoverished and traditional societies. The most successful programs—China's, for example—have used all three strategies: strong family planning programs, high investment in economic development, and special attention to land reform and other programs that assure that the benefits from development go to the poorest of the poor.

The Good News: Declining Fertility

Despite the massive difficulties involved in altering such a major social role as motherhood and such a central social institution as the family, the world fertility rate has been declining since 1970. The decline is uneven, but it is visible in almost all corners of the world (see Table 17.2).

Declining fertility rates are most evident among nations and groups that have made the greatest steps toward economic development. Even in very traditional nations such as Kenya and Nepal, there have been fertility declines among women who are urban, educated, and working outside the home. When the elite and urban women in a society accept birth control, it becomes increasingly acceptable at all levels, even in the absence of development.

The Bad News: Momentum

Regardless of current decreases in average family size, the world population will double within the next 40 to 50 years. The reason for this gloomy prediction lies in the current age structure. The next generation of mothers

Table 17.2   Changes in Average Family Size
In the last 15 years there has been a 24 percent decrease in the average number of children being born per woman. This decrease has been noticeable in all parts of the world except Africa. Because mortality has fallen too, however, and because of the momentum of the age structure, population is still growing rapidly.

	AVERAGE NUMBER OF CHILDREN PER WOMAN		PERCENT CHANGE
	1968–1972	1984	
World	4.7	3.8	−24%
Africa	6.4	6.4	0
Asia	5.4	4.0	−35
Latin America	5.5	4.2	−31
Europe and North America	2.8	1.8	−36

SOURCE: Data for early years from Freyka, 1973, T. 4–1; 1984 data from Population Reference Bureau, 1984 World Population Data Sheet.

is already born—and there are a lot of them. As the pyramidal shape of the age structure in Figure 17.4 demonstrated, high-fertility nations have a population of children (future parents) that is much larger than the current generation of parents. This force for population growth is called **momentum,** and it is roughly measured by the ratio of girls aged 0 to 4 to the number of women aged 25 to 29. In Kenya, the ratio is 3:1. This means that the next generation will have three times as many mothers as does this generation. The ratio for the United States is about 1:1.

Momentum has tremendous implications for the future of population. Consider Kenya's problem. If fertility per woman remains unchanged, Kenya will have three times as many babies in 25 years as it does now. In order to keep the number of babies in 2010 the same as the number in 1985, the vast new generation of mothers would have to reduce its fertility by two-thirds, a decrease in family size from 7.1 to 2.4. This is an enormous change to expect so rapidly; it is also unlikely. Even if it occurred, though, it would not eliminate population growth; it would simply maintain the number of births at today's very high rate.

ZERO POPULATION GROWTH. In describing demographic goals, demographers distinguish two different ends: zero population growth and replacement. **Zero population growth (ZPG)** means that the number of births is the same as the number of deaths; no growth occurs. This goal is almost impossible when the age structure is pyramidal. When the population bearing children is much larger than the elderly population, it is likely that there will be many more births than deaths.

REPLACEMENT-LEVEL FERTILITY. A more modest reproductive goal is **replacement-level fertility.** This requires that each woman have approximately two children, one to replace herself and one to replace her husband. When this occurs, the next generation will be the same size as the current generation of parents. In the short run, replacing the large generation of current parents will mean relatively rapid population growth. In the long run, however, say four generations, the generation dying will be the same size as the one having children, and replacement-level fertility will create zero population growth. Neither replacement nor ZPG is on the immediate horizon, however, and we must plan for a future that will contain 9 billion people—twice the number currently in the world.

Population in the United States

The dilemma of population growth and change is not as stark in the United States as it is in the less developed world. Nevertheless, patterns of fertility, mortality, and migration continue to influence our social relationships. This section briefly describes current demographic patterns in the United States and sketches some of their consequences for the social structure.

Fertility

In the United States, fertility patterns have had a lot of ups and downs this century, but the long-term trend is toward the two-child family (Ryder,

Momentum is a force for population growth that occurs when the number of people in future reproductive generations is larger than the number in the current generation.

Zero population growth (ZPG) means that the number of births is the same as the number of deaths, so the population does not grow.

Replacement-level fertility requires that each woman bear approximately two children so that she replaces her and her partner; this results in the next generation being the same size as the current generation of parents.

Figure 17.13

Although large families in the United States are a rarity today, fertility has not gone out of style. The average family in the U.S. plans to have two children, with luck one boy and one girl. The children will be born sometime in the mother's twenties and she will have approximately 50 years of active life after her last child enters school.

1979). Across all segments of the population, there is increasing convergence on the two-child family, and old differentials between Protestant and Catholic, black and white, and middle and working class are disappearing. Some women will have their children as teenagers and some will postpone them until they are 30, but increasingly they will stop at two. Also, an increasing proportion will stop at one or have none at all (Huber, 1980; Ryder, 1979).

The long-term decline in fertility is due to the rising costs of having children, the increasing alternatives for women outside the home, and the spread of contraceptive knowledge and acceptance. Almost all marital fertility is now planned. An increasing proportion of couples cap their successful contraceptive career with sterilization (48 percent of all white couples aged 35 to 44).

In addition to a decline in large families, current trends also show a sharp increase in the number of childless women. In 1965, only 12 percent of the women who had ever been married were still childless at ages 25 to 29. In 17 years, this proportion more than doubled; and by 1982, fully 28 percent of the ever-married women in the peak childbearing years were still childless (U.S. Bureau of the Census, 1983:68). Many women who are childless at 30 may yet have children, but the increase in the proportion of women who are postponing or entirely forgoing childbearing is one of the sharpest changes since the baby boom.

Unmarried women are a different story. Lower marriage rates have increased the number of unmarried women at the same time that changes in sexual behavior have increased their risk of pregnancy. As a result, an increasing proportion of U.S. babies are born to unmarried women, many of whom are still teenagers: 18 percent of the next generation will start life in a fatherless home. This a major change in fertility patterns and family structure.

The Future of Fertility.   Over the last 200 years, U.S. fertility has fallen from an average of 8 children per woman to an average of 1.8. Is there any reason to think that the decline might continue? Some scholars believe that we have become an antinatalist society and that fertility will continue to decrease until the population actually shrinks (Huber, 1980; Ryder, 1979). Is this likely?

The question of what will happen to fertility in the future raises the question: Why do people have babies? Research suggests that most people are well aware of the disadvantages of childbearing: Large majorities agree that children are expensive, tie you down, impose burdensome demands, and eat up most of your free time (Blake & del Pinal, 1981). Nevertheless, most people say they want children. The major advantages that people expect, the ones that outweigh the costs and demands, are stimulation, fun, love, and companionship.

Increasingly, however, women are finding that stimulation and companionship are available outside the family. As women's economic opportunities develop outside the family, childlessness is expected to increase and family size to continue its decline. Many women and men will no doubt continue to find children a satisfying investment of their time, energy, and money, but as the number of alternative investments increase and as the costs of children rise, it seems likely that fertility will decline further.

Mortality

In the United States, mortality declined spectacularly in the earlier part of this century, and the decline continues. Within the decade of the 1970s, another 2 years were added to life expectancy (see Table 17.3).

The spectacular gains in life expectancy during this century are attributable largely to the conquering of infectious disease. At the turn of the century, the top three causes of death were pneumonia-influenza-bronchitis, tuberculosis, and diarrhea. (Diarrhea is a major killer of infants in high-mortality societies.) By 1980, the top three causes of death were diseases of the elderly: heart disease, cancer, and stroke. The most recent advances in life expectancy are due to better diagnosis and treatment of these degenerative diseases. In addition, increases in overall life expectancy have been made possible by bringing the advantages of modern medicine to some of the more disadvantaged segments of the population.

Race and class still have an effect on mortality, but the gap is closing. At the time of World War II, white females could expect to live 12 years longer than non-white females; by 1980, the gap had shrunk to 6 years. If further progress is made in equalizing racial and class life chances, the average life expectancy of Americans will continue to rise.

These changes in mortality have made death almost a stranger to U.S. families. The average age at death is now in the 70s, and people who survive to 65 can expect to live to 85. Parents can feel relatively secure that their infants will survive; and newlyweds, if they don't divorce, can safely plan on a golden wedding anniversary.

Table 17.3   Trends in U.S. Life Expectancy, 1850–1980

Life expectancy has climbed spectacularly during this century. The gains have been greater for women than men, with the result that women now outlive men by 7 to 8 years. The gap between white and nonwhite life expectancy, has been reduced, but life expectancy for non-whites is still 6 to 7 years below whites.

	WHITE		NONWHITE	
	Male	Female	Male	Female
1850*	38	40	—	—
1878–1882	42	44	—	—
1900	47	49	32	33
1910	49	52	34	38
1920	54	56	46	45
1930	60	64	47	49
1940	62	67	52	55
1950	66	72	59	63
1960	67	74	61	66
1970	68	76	61	69
1980	71	78	64	72

SOURCE: Data for 1970 and before are taken from Omram, 1977; 1978 data are from the U.S. Bureau of the Census, 1983.
*Note: Data prior to 1900 are estimates based on the total population of Massachusetts.

Figure 17.14

A newborn in the United States today can look forward to a lifetime of 70 to 80 years. At 60, the average woman still has 25 years ahead of her. These changes in life expectancy have created a society in which being old is no longer a novelty and no longer a condition of physical and economic dependence. Because increases in life expectancy have favored women over men, however, the older population is disproportionately female.

Figure 17.15

In a free society it is considered illegitimate for a government to tell people where they may move within its boundaries. The government is considered to have the right, and even duty, however, to control the movement of people across its boundaries. Here, U. S. officials are recording the movement of Cuban refugees in 1980. These refugees were permitted to enter the United States only after special legislation was passed in Congress where annual limits are set on the number of refugees accepted.

Migration

Population size and composition are jointly determined by three variables: fertility, mortality, and migration. In the discussion of world population growth and development, no attention was given to the third demographic variable—migration. In most nations, migration has much less effect on population growth than do fertility and mortality. The United States however, is one of several nations in which migration has a major impact.

A significant portion of U.S. population growth is attributable to **immigration**—the permanent entrance of people into a country. At the present time, approximately one-third of U.S. population growth comes from immigration instead of natural increase. Continued low fertility, however, will mean that the United States will soon cease to grow from natural increase. By 2020 or 2030, it will have reached zero population growth, where births and deaths are approximately equal. When that occurs, immigration will account for all population growth in the country (Population Reference Bureau, 1982:21).

Estimates suggest that during the 1980s the United States can expect to add between 800,000 and 1 million people annually through immigration. About half will be illegal immigrants from Mexico and Latin America. If current trends continue, fully 10 percent of the U.S. population will be Hispanic by the year 2000 (see Figure 17.16). By the year 2080, some 40 percent of all schoolchildren will be descended from post-1980 immigrants, and a full 80 percent of all California schoolchildren will be descended from newcomers to the United States—few of whom will be of white, European stock (Davis et al., 1983).

These changes in composition will offer grave challenges to U.S. institutions. Unlike earlier immigrant groups, Hispanic migrants have not abandoned their language and culture. Moreover, they are geographically concentrated, which gives them significant political power. Already Anglos

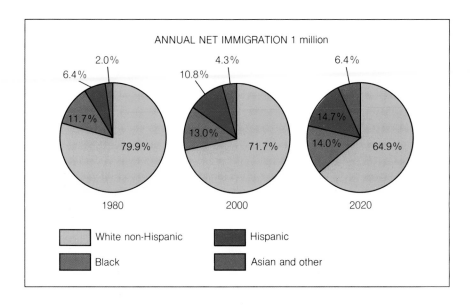

ANNUAL NET IMMIGRATION 1 million

2.0%
6.4%
11.7%
79.9%
1980

4.3%
10.8%
13.0%
71.7%
2000

6.4%
14.7%
14.0%
64.9%
2020

White non-Hispanic
Black
Hispanic
Asian and other

Figure 17.16 Changing Composition of U.S. Population
If annual migration remains at 1 million and if fertility remains low, the racial and ethnic composition of the U.S. population will change substantially in the decades ahead. The most noticeable effect will be a sharp rise in the proportion who are Hispanic and a corresponding decrease in the proportion who are Anglo.
SOURCE: Davis et al., 1983: 39.

are a minority in California, and Hispanics are likely to wield strong political clout throughout the Southwest as their numbers increase. This makes it more likely that bilingualism and Hispanic culture will survive and perhaps even gain legal protection. In short, it appears likely that U.S. institutions will have to adapt to this wave of immigrants as much as the immigrants have to adapt to U.S. institutions.

ISSUES IN SOCIAL POLICY

The New Immigrants—Aliens or Amigos?

Unlike fertility, mortality, and internal migration, immigration is seen as something that can be governmentally regulated in a free society. Beginning with the Chinese Exclusion Act of 1882, much of U.S. immigration policy has been frankly racist and ethnically biased. Since 1965, however, immigration policies have ceased to give preference to people from northern and western Europe; as a result, our population composition is changing.

CURRENT POLICY

U.S. immigration policies are changed relatively frequently. The last version (passed by Congress in 1979) contained the following limitations and provisions:

Legal Migration

— Numerically limited migration: 270,000 migrants are accepted per year, with a maximum of 20,000 from any one country. Among applicants from a single country, preference is given to relatives of U.S. citizens or permanent resident aliens and to persons "of exceptional ability" in the professions or workers in occupations with labor shortages.
— Unlimited legal migration: Spouses, minor children, and parents of U.S. citizens, former U.S. citizens, and employees or retired employees of the U.S. government.

Refugees

— Congress sets the number of refugees to be admitted on an annual basis. The suggested maximum in the 1980 legislation is 50,000. The number can be raised in exceptional circumstances, and in most recent years the number has been far larger as we have accommodated Vietnamese, Laotian, Cuban, and Haitian refugees.

Illegal immigrants

— Estimates vary widely, but it is generally accepted that between 350,000 and 500,000 enter the U.S. each year (some estimates run as high as 1 million per year), 90 percent of whom are from Mexico or other countries in Latin America.

As a result of the policies and practices indicated here, an estimated 1 million immigrants entered the United States in 1981. They accounted for 30 to 33 percent of the growth in the U.S. population in 1980 and 1981. If immigration stays this high, however, and fertility continues to decline, immigration will soon account for 100 percent of U.S. population growth.

POLICY CONSIDERATIONS

U.S. immigration policy attempts to balance several goals. On the one hand, many people believe that it is important for the United States to be an open country that offers freedom and refuge. On the other hand, there is concern

Figure 17.17
Migration from Mexico (about half of it illegal) now accounts for nearly one-quarter of the population growth in the U.S. Although many people believe that immigration should be controlled, the task is extraordinarily difficult and expensive. This is because the U.S.-Mexico border is the only place in the world where a very rich nation exists side-by-side with a poor one. One solution is a stepped up border patrol, another is to support economic development in Mexico.

about the impact of large-scale immigration on the U.S. economy and culture.

The level of immigration is widely recognized as an issue that should be regulated by the federal government. The policy question is: What should be done? Many lobbying groups have been formed to encourage sharp reductions in immigration. These groups enjoy substantial public support. A 1980 Roper Poll showed that 80 percent of the public favored reducing legal immigration and 91 percent favored eliminating illegal immigration (Murphy & Cancellier, 1982).

On the other side are groups that oppose sharp restrictions on legal immigration and strong attacks on illegal immigration. Their arguments rest largely on an ideological commitment to welcoming the poor and huddled masses. Both ideologically and politically, walling our nation and its prosperity off from the rest of the world would be an untenable position. It would hurt our self-image and our position in the world.

Research documents that illegal immigrants rarely threaten the employment opportunities of Anglo or black workers (Mindiola, 1979). Illegals are willing to do unpleasant jobs at lower wages than are Anglo or black workers, thus contributing substantially to agricultural profit in the Southwest and in northern areas that use migrant labor. They do, however, compete with legal and native Hispanics. There is substantial evidence that the availability of illegal (cheap) labor reduces the income of legal and native-born Hispanics (Gerking & Mutti, 1980; Jones & Rice, 1980; Majka, 1981). Despite documented negative economic consequences to Hispanic citizens, however, most are gravely concerned about any policies designed to punish illegal aliens (Flores, 1983). They fear that any U.S. government program directed against Hispanics will affect them much more negatively than will additional labor competition.

The major line of controversy is with the question of illegal immigration—not so much with whether it should be stopped or at least reduced but with whether the consequences of doing so will be acceptable. Many people believe that they will not be. Rounding up illegal immigrants often means harassing legal immigrants and U.S. citizens of Hispanic ancestry, who may be called upon to produce proof of their citizenship or face deportation. To members of the Hispanic community, these demands seem equivalent to having to wear a Star of David to identify themselves to a police state. Keeping out illegal immigrants may mean establishing a completely closed and well-patrolled Mexico-U.S. border, the so-called tortilla curtain. There is the further question of how we can do any of this without offending Mexico, a country whose friendship is vital to our national security and on whom we are increasingly dependent for oil.

Given these constraints and diverse opinions, the issue emerges as: What reasonable laws should be enforced in a reasonable way by a reasonable people? (Briggs, 1975). The decision will have to be political. It will reflect the need for friendship with Mexico, internal political and economic pressures, budgetary constraints (keeping a half million eager and nearby people out of the country each year will not be cheap), and pressure from organized groups on each side.

As a result of these counterpressures, any decision is difficult to make. In recent years, the Simpson-Mazzoli proposal to sharply restrict illegal immigration has been considered in each session of Congress. During 1984, both the House and the Senate passed a version of this bill, but were unable to reconcile their differences and enact it into law. Passing the bill will not solve the problem of illegal aliens, however, for both the constitutionality and the effectiveness of its provisions are in doubt. In the long run, however, it seems likely that doing something about immigration will continue to be a major item on the national agenda.

SUMMARY

1. For most of human history, fertility was about equal to mortality and the population grew slowly or not at all. Childbearing was a lifelong task for most women, and death was a frequent visitor to most households, claiming one-quarter to one-third of all infants in the first year of life.

2. The demographic transition in the West began with a decline in mortality. Major causes of the decreased mortality, in order of occurrence, were increased nutrition, an improved standard of living and hygiene, improved public sanitation, and modern medicine.

3. The decline of fertility in the West is attributable to the entire transformation of the social fabric that occurred as a result of industrialization, especially the changing roles of women and the family and a break with traditional values.

4. Social structure, fertility, and mortality are interdependent; changes in one affect the others. Among the most important consequences of high fertility are restricted roles for women and a high dependency ratio.

5. The level of fertility in a society has much to do with the balance of costs and rewards associated with childbearing. In traditional societies, such as that of Kenya, most social structures (the economy, religion, and the family, for example) support high fertility. In many modern societies, such as those of the Soviet Union, China, and the United States, social structure imposes many costs on parents (deliberately in the case of China).

6. There is a close relationship between poverty and population growth. Poverty helps maintain traditionally high fertility, and high population growth makes economic growth difficult. Three alternatives, each with its own political costs, are family planning, development, and redistribution. A combination, as in China, appears to be most effective.

7. The age structure of the less developed nations provides momentum for high fertility. Because of the large number of future parents already born, it is unlikely that either zero population growth or replacement-level fertility will be achieved any time soon, and world population will probably reach 9 billion within 45 to 50 years.

8. Natural increase is very small in the United States; the birthrate is not much higher than the deathrate. The long-term pattern for births in the United States is downward, and it is anticipated that there will be fewer larger families and an increase in childlessness. A major change in fertility and family structure is the growing proportion of children born to unmarried women.

9. Currently, 30 to 33 percent of U.S. population growth is due to immigration; this proportion is likely to become larger as fertility declines. Because many of the new Americans are Asian or Hispanic, the composition of the U.S. population is likely to change significantly if immigration continues at current levels.

SUGGESTED READINGS

Barney, Gerald O. (1980). The Global 2000 Report to the President of the U.S. New York: Pergamon Press. The report of a commission ordered by President Carter to investigate the long-term consequences of population growth. The conclusions are alarming and disconcerting.

Birdsall, Nancy. (1981). "Population growth and poverty in the developing world." Population Bulletin 35(5):1–45. A short pamphlet summarizing the major issues and latest data on the population and poverty debate.

McNeill, William H. (1976). Plagues and Peoples. Garden City, N.Y.: Anchor Press. An entertaining trip through history. Relates the effects of mortality on history from the time of Alexander the Great through World War II.

Population Reference Bureau. (1982). "U.S. population: Where we are; where we're going." Population Bulletin 37(2):1–50. A pamphlet summarizing recent trends in fertility, mortality, and migration, with some projections about the future of the U.S. population.

Wrigley, E. A. (1969). Population and History. New York: McGraw-Hill. A detailed description of the demographic transition in Europe along with some lessons for today's developing world.

Wrong, Dennis. (1977). Population and Society (4th ed.). New York: Random House. An excellent short textbook on demography that will provide a thorough overview of the field.

CHAPTER 18

URBAN LIFE

PROLOGUE

Have You Ever . . . gone into a cafe in a small town and felt like a conspicuous stranger? Anyone who has traveled through the United States by car must have had the experience of going into a place where it appears that everybody knows everybody else and everybody is looking at you and wondering where you came from.

This is the kind of experience we expect to have as strangers in a small town. However, the same kind of experience is almost as common in big cities. Restaurants, bars, and other public establishments have their own clientele. These regulars know the social structure of the establishment, and strangers who don't know the rules may be almost as conspicuous there as in small towns. For example, strangers may sit in the booth informally reserved for certain regulars; they may play country and western music on the jukebox when the usual fare is rock; they may be much older or younger than the usual clientele or over- or underdressed or of the wrong sexual persuasion. In short, cities are not collections of anonymous individuals; they consist of small, well-defined social worlds.

There are many significant differences between living in big cities and living in small towns or rural areas, but there are also a great many similarities. This chapter contrasts social life in rural and urban places and describes the human consequences of urbanization.

If all human experience were condensed into a single day, the beginning of large-scale urban life would not begin until a few minutes before midnight. In fact, the world's population is still more rural than urban. Nevertheless, for most people in the contemporary United States, to speak of social life is to speak of urban life. Over 75 percent of this generation's college students were born and raised in metropolitan areas. Similarly, at least 75 percent of the mothers, lawyers, and junkies in the United States are urbanites. Thus, throughout this book, we have been examining largely urban experience. This chapter takes a self-conscious look at the settings of contemporary social activity. Among the questions it considers are the consequences of urban living for human social behavior, the uniqueness of urban problems, and the changing nature of urban living.

Urban Growth and Change

Urban growth and change is largely a story of the last century. It has been estimated that as late as 1850 only 2 percent of the world's population lived in cities of 100,000 or more (Davis, 1973). Today, nearly a quarter of the world's population and over half of the U.S. population lives in cities larger than 100,000. Paralleling this increasing urbanization of the world is an evolution in the character of the city. The modern city is very different from the city that developed in the 2nd century—or even the 19th.

The Preindustrial City

The preindustrial economy is dominated by primary production. Whether it is farming, herding, mining, or forestry, economic activity is essentially rural activity. The cities that emerge under these conditions are largely trading and administrative centers. The ancient cities Rome, Byzantium, and Tenochtitlán grew up to administer empires and control trade. Many early cities were founded on trade routes—natural breaking points where caravans crossed or where land portage changed to sea. With few excep-

Figure 18.1
Carcassonne in France is one of the finest examples of a medieval walled city in Europe. Originally constructed on a double-walled Roman city in 400 A. D., the city was rebuilt in the 600s and enlarged in the 1100s and 1200s. It was restored in the 1800s and stands today as a monument of the crowded fortress-like preindustrial trade centers of the past.

tions, they would hardly be classified as villages in the modern scale of things. Nevertheless, archaeologists estimate that the Aztec capital, Tenochtitlán, may have had 100,000 inhabitants at its height; imperial Rome may have had as many as 300,000. The size of these giants can be put in perspective by our remembering that the Los Angeles Coliseum seats 100,000 and that imperial Rome was smaller than Omaha or Wichita.

The preindustrial city was not only a much smaller affair than the modern city, it was very differently organized. Of primary importance in understanding it is the fact that most people got from place to place by walking. The result was a great concentration of social life into crowded, teeming squares. Because transportation was difficult, people lived and worked in the same building. In the preindustrial city there was no central business district whose only occupants were men in three-piece togas. Instead, children, cooking odors, and laundry pervaded all parts of the city. Segregation was not between business and family but between kinds of businesses. People who needed to see one another in the course of business lived together in one quarter of the city. Thus craftsmen occupied one quarter, traders another, and officials yet another.

Then, as now, the city was a major force in the development of art, culture, and technology. It was also a crowded, filthy, and dangerous place. Until the last century, cities had higher deathrates than rural areas. Human and animal waste turned streets and canals into open sewers. Disease was spread through contaminated water, dirt, and flies. The dense housing conditions fostered the rapid spread of epidemics such as bubonic plague and smallpox. Children and infants were especially vulnerable to the dirt and disease of cities, and the birthrate in cities could not keep up with the deathrate. The only way cities could maintain their populations was by constantly drawing new recruits from the countryside.

This description probably fit most of the world's cities until at least 1800. In 1790, Philadelphia, with a population of 44,000, was the largest U.S. city. Like New York and Boston, it was a trading and commercial center, a port where primary goods from the interior were exchanged for goods from overseas. Like Damascus or Cairo, these early U.S. cities lacked sewers and safe drinking supplies. And far from offering bright lights, the absence of streetlights made the cities close down at nightfall.

The Industrial City

With the advent of the industrial revolution, production moved from the countryside to the urban factory, and industrial cities were born. These cities were mill towns, steel towns, shipbuilding towns, and, later, automobile-building towns; they were home to slaughterers, packagers, millers, processors, and fabricators. They were the product of new technologies, new forms of transportation, and vastly increased agricultural productivity that freed most workers from the land.

Fired by a tremendous growth in technology, the new industrial cities grew rapidly during the 19th century. In the United States, the urban population grew from 2 to 22 million in the half century between 1840 and 1890. In 1860, New York was the first U.S. city to reach 1 million. The industrial base that provided the impetus for city growth also gave the

Figure 18.2
Hong Kong, one of the most densely populated countries of the world, illustrates the vertical city growth that occurs when available land mass is limited. The former British colony is an island of affluence on the south coast of China that has attracted millions of migrants. Many poor families live in crowded, dilapitated waterfront housing where several families share a single room and people sleep on crowded rooftops. Over the past three decades, however, over a million squatters have moved from hillside shacks to high rise housing units that dominate the landscape.

industrial city its character: tremendous density, a central business district, and a concentric zone pattern of land use.

Density. Two factors are critical in explaining the character of the industrial city as it developed in the 19th century. First, the city was built around dirty, noisy manufacturing plants. Second, most people still walked to work—and everywhere else, for that matter. The result of these two factors was dense crowding of working-class housing around manufacturing plants. Even in 1910, the average New Yorker commuted only 2 blocks to work. Thus the industrial city saw much more crowding than either the preindustrial or late-industrial city. Entire families shared a single room; and in major cities such as New York and London, dozens of people crowded into a single cellar or attic. The crowded conditions, accompanied by a lack of sewage treatment and clean water, fostered tuberculosis, epidemic diseases, and generally high mortality. A glimpse of these conditions is provided by a letter that appeared in the London Times in 1849:

> Sur,—May we beg and beseach your proteckshion and power. We are Sur, as it may be, livin in a Wilderness, so far as the rest of London knows anything of us, or as the rich and great people care about. We live in muck and filth. We aint got no priviz, no dust bins, no drains, no water-splies, and no drain or suer in the hole place. The Suer Company, in Greek St., Soho Square, all great, rich powerfool men take no notice whasomdever of our complaints. The Stenche of a Gulley-hole is disguistin. We all of us suffer, and numbers are ill, and if the Cholera comes Lord help us.
>
> Some gentelmans comed yesterday.... They was much surprised to see the sellar in No. 12, Carrier St., in our lane, where a child was dying from fever, and would not believe that Sixty persons sleep in it every night. This here seller you

couldent swing a cat in, and the rent is five shillings a week; but theare are great many sich deare sellers....

Praeye Sir com and see us, for we are livin like piggs, and it aint faire we should be so ill treted. [Cited in Thomlinson, 1976]

Central Business District (CBD). The lack of transportation and communication facilities also contributed to another characteristic of the industrial city, the central business district (CBD). The CBD is a dense concentration of retail trade, banking and finance, and government offices, all clustered close together so messengers could run between offices and business men could walk to meet one another. By 1880, most major cities had electric streetcars or railway systems to take traffic into and out of the city. Because most transit routes offered service only into and out of the CBD rather than providing crosstown routes, the earliest improvements over walking enhanced rather than decreased the importance of the CBD as the hub of the city.

Concentric Zone Pattern. Spatial analysis of early industrial cities suggests that they often approximated a series of rings, or concentric zones (see Figure 18.3). Zone 1, the CBD, was characterized by dense building where land values were so high that only the most profitable commercial operations could afford to locate there. Residential use and large commercial operations were pushed to the periphery of the city. Meanwhile, high land values encouraged vertical growth, and eventually skyscrapers came to dominate the landscape of the CBD.

Zones 2 and 3 included the manufacturing plants and the families who worked in them. The working class was still largely dependent on walking to work; thus most workers lived close to the plants. Noise, smoke, and pollution reduced the attractiveness of Zone 3 for residential use, thereby bringing housing prices into the reach of the working class. For the most part, Zone 3 housing consisted of tenements, apartment blocks, and row houses.

In the industrial city, everyone who could afford to live away from the noise and smoke and smell did so. The upper class could best afford a relatively long commute; consequently, it occupied the periphery of the city, Zone 5. The middle class occupied the intermediate area, Zone 4. Again, because of transportation problems—the middle class did not have access to automobiles until 1920—all areas of the industrial city were densely packed. Even middle-class families more often lived in duplex and row houses than in single-family homes; as drives through older neighborhoods still indicate, single-family homes occupied small lots, with the houses almost touching each other.

Sectoral Pattern. Although no city ever formed a perfect concentric zone pattern, this model helps us understand the processes that affected the growth of industrial cities. A common variant of the pattern is the sectoral model, which takes into account the radial patterns of urban transportation and illustrates the tendency of use patterns to follow arterials rather than rings. As Figure 18.4 demonstrates, the sectoral model retains some aspects of concentric zones but adds to them a recognition that vectors of activities may radiate outward from the city center. This

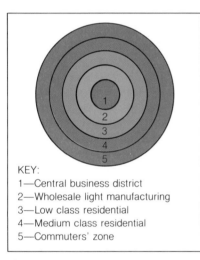

KEY:
1—Central business district
2—Wholesale light manufacturing
3—Low class residential
4—Medium class residential
5—Commuters' zone

Figure 18.3 Concentric Zone Model of Urban Spatial Patterns
The early industrial city developed a characteristic circular pattern. Because transportation was limited, business activity and working-class housing were densely concentrated toward the center. Only the more affluent could afford to live on the edges, away from the bustle.
SOURCE: Harris & Ullman, 1945.

pattern explicitly reflects the limited transportation routes available before the automobile.

The Late-Industrial City

The industrial city was a product of a manufacturing economy plus a relatively immobile labor force. Beginning about 1950, these conditions changed and a new type of city began to grow. Among the factors prominent in shaping the character of the late-industrial city are the greater ease of communication and transportation, the greater mobility of the labor force, the consolidation of production units, and the great expansion in single-family living. These closely related changes have led to a much diminished role for the central business districts; a dispersion of retail, manufacturing, and residential areas; and a much lower urban density.

Consolidation of Production Units. As pointed out in chapter 14, small firms employing dozens of workers have been replaced with large firms employing thousands. As plants spread over acres of land, they moved from the center of the city, where land was expensive, to less expensive locations on the periphery. Where manufacturing industries and jobs went, so went working-class housing and the retail stores to serve the working class. Eventually, manufacturing jobs, retail stores, and working-class housing were spread across all parts of the city.

Easier Communication and Transportation. The development of the telephone, good highways, and inexpensive trucking has reduced the importance of being close to other businesses. More recently, telecommunications has further reduced this need, in some instances making it possible for people to work from home by remote terminals. The central business district of the industrial city was held together by the need for physical proximity. Once this need was eliminated, high land values and commuting costs led more and more businesses to locate on the periphery, where land was cheaper and housing more desirable.

The Growth in Single-Family Homes. With the very notable exception of the Great Depression, real incomes have risen sharply in this century. One of the first things families did with their greater income was to invest in single-family homes, perhaps the closest thing to a universal American Dream.

The major growth in single-family living occurred immediately after World War II and was subsidized largely by the federal government. First, the government created an income tax deduction for the interest on home mortgage payments, providing an attractive tax shelter for the middle class. This tax incentive meant that prudent families bought the most expensive house they could and, when it was paid for, moved up and started paying on another. Second, the government guaranteed millions of suburban home loans through the Federal Housing Administration (FHA) and Veterans Administration (VA). Finally, the government subsidized quick, convenient expressways and freeways, which made possible longer distances between work and home.

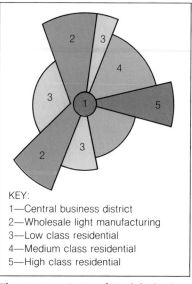

KEY:
1—Central business district
2—Wholesale light manufacturing
3—Low class residential
4—Medium class residential
5—High class residential

Figure 18.4 Sectoral Model of Urban Spatial Patterns
The sectoral pattern is a common variant of the concentric zone pattern. It reflects the tendency of commercial and residential zones to follow transportation routes that radiate out from the city center.
SOURCE: Harris & Ullman, 1945.

All of these developments moved housing away from the central business district and farther and farther into suburbia. Little villages 20 miles from the city center, where upper-class people used to have their summer homes, suddenly became part of the city itself.

The Automobile.   All of these changes were made possible by the increased individual mobility provided by the automobile. Without the automobile, plants could not have amassed a daily work force of thousands, workers and businesses could not have moved to the city periphery, and space-gobbling single-family homes would not have been possible. In this sense, the automobile has been the chief architect of U.S. cities since 1950. It has given them a freedom of form that older cities did not have.

Multiple Nuclei.   The new cities are much larger in geographical area than the industrial cities were. The average city in 1940 was probably less than 15 miles across; now many metropolitan areas are 50 to 75 miles across. Spatial analysis of new cities suggests that they are no longer divided into concentric zones or sectors and are far less dominated by the central business district. The vertical growth so apparent before World War II has been partially replaced by horizontal growth in the form of urban sprawl. The general configuration of modern cities appears to conform to a multiple nuclei pattern (see Figure 18.5). No longer are people bound by subway and railway lines that go only back and forth to downtown. Instead, retail trade is dominated by huge, climate controlled, pedestrian safe suburban malls. A great proportion of the retail and service labor force has also moved out to these suburban centers, and many of the people who live in the suburbs also work in them. The cities that have grown up in the last few decades have adapted rather easily to this new spatial pattern. Their central business districts are relatively small, housing primarily government offices, banking and commercial firms, and some professional offices. They have never been retail trade centers. In the cities that grew up before 1950, however, the development of the periphery has caused real problems, as the once-vital central business district is increasingly abandoned by business and shoppers, leaving behind empty buildings, unprofitable businesses, and a declining tax base.

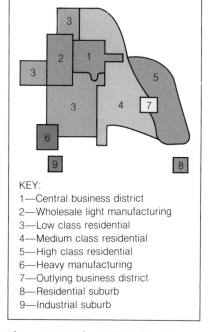

KEY:
1—Central business district
2—Wholesale light manufacturing
3—Low class residential
4—Medium class residential
5—High class residential
6—Heavy manufacturing
7—Outlying business district
8—Residential suburb
9—Industrial suburb

Figure 18.5   The Multiple Nuclei Model of Urban Spatial Patterns
The automobile has given the late-industrial city a freedom of form that its predecessors did not have. Commercial and residential areas are spread throughout the city and the suburbs. The city center has declined in importance, and many smaller centers have developed.
SOURCE: Harris & Ullman, 1945.

Rural is the U.S. Census Bureau term for places with fewer than 2,500 people.

Urban is the U.S. Census Bureau term for places with 2,500 people or more.

U.S. Cities: Terms and Definitions

Rural and *urban* are relative terms, anchoring a continuum that runs from isolated farmhouses to extremely large and dense masses of individuals. What might be considered urban in one century or nation might be rural in another. In the United States, the Bureau of the Census uses two basic distinctions, one between rural and urban and the other between metropolitan and nonmetropolitan. The rural-urban distinction is simple. **Rural** refers to all settlements of fewer than 2,500 people; **urban** refers to all settlements of 2,500 and more. Thus quite small villages and towns are considered urban by the Census Bureau definition. The simple rural-urban dichotomy has the disadvantage of ignoring the degree to which a small settlement might be within the social and economic orbit of a larger city. In order to make this distinction, the Census Bureau uses the terms *metropolitan* and *nonmetropolitan*. A **metropolitan county** either has a city of 50,000 or more in it or is significantly linked, economically and socially, with a county that does have such a city. A **nonmetropolitan county** has no major city in it and is not closely tied to a county that does have such a city. The metropolitan-nonmetropolitan distinction is based on county units under the assumption that all county residents, even those who live on isolated farms, will be affected by a large city within the county in terms of economic, educational, and social opportunities. Thus the character of the county is either metropolitan or nonmetropolitan. Within a metropolitan county, the Census bureau distinguishes between those who live within the urban area, or central city, and those who live in the balance of the county.

The rural-urban and nonmetropolitan-metropolitan distinctions overlap but are not equivalent. A town of 1,500 outside Cleveland may be rural but still metropolitan; a county seat of 30,000 may be urban but nonmetropolitan. In 1980, 75 percent of the U.S. population was metropolitan (see Table 18.1).

Third World Cities

Whereas the West has been predominantly urbanized since at least 1950, the less developed areas of the world—roughly Africa, Asia, and Latin America—are still predominantly rural. This is changing within our lifetime, however, on a scale that is difficult to grasp (see Figure 18.7).

The growth of large cities and an urban way of life has occurred everywhere very recently; in the Third World it is happening almost overnight.

A **metropolitan county** either has a city of 50,000 or more in it or is significantly linked, socially and economically, to a county that does have such a city.

A **nonmetropolitan county** has no major city in it and is not closely linked to a county that does have such a city.

Table 18.1   Distribution of the U.S. Population, 1980
Although two-thirds of the U.S. population is both urban and metropolitan, one-quarter lives in nonmetropolitan counties, which are not linked to a major city and are not substantially urban in character.

METROPOLITAN POPULATION		75%
Urban	64%	
Rural	11	
NONMETRPOLITAN POPULATION		25%
Urban	9%	
Rural	16	

SOURCE: U.S. Bureau of the Census, 1984, table 24.

Figure 18.6
*Third world urbanization is characterized by dense population growth unparalleled elsewhere in the world. It is fueled by high urban fertility as well as migration from countryside. This **favelas** (urban slum) in Rio de Janerio is occupied by low-income families living in shacks on steep hillsides. Inadequate sanitation, roads, housing, and schools plague the city, an important center of Brazilian trade, finance, and transportation.*

Figure 18.7 Urbanization Trends in the Developed and Less Developed World, 1950, 1975, 2000

Although the world is still more rural than urban, this is changing within our lifetimes. Urbanization is growing particularly quickly in the less developed world. Between 1950 and 2000, there will be an eightfold increase in the urban population of the world.

SOURCE: Beier, George. 1976. "Can third world cities cope?" Population Bulletin 31 (December): 2.

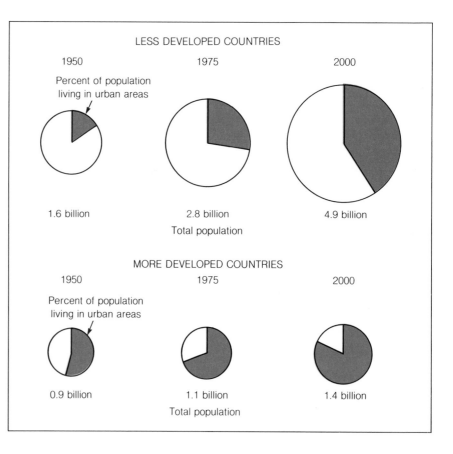

Mexico City, Sao Paulo, Bogota, Seoul, Kinshasa, Karachi, Calcutta—these and other Third World cities are growing at 5 to 8 percent per year. This means that their populations will double in approximately a decade. The roads, the schools, and the sewers that used to be enough no longer are; neighborhoods triple their populations and change their character from year to year. These problems are similar to the problems that plagued Western societies at the onset of the industrial revolution (see Chapter 1), but they are on a much larger scale. Despite the obvious drawbacks, cities continue to attract new migrants. No matter how poor they are, the urban poor are better off than the rural poor. Most importantly, opportunity is in the city. In rural areas, the only means to wealth is land, and that means is static; its quantity never changes, and its ownership is seldom transferred. Thus the possibility for self-improvement lies almost entirely in urban areas.

Third World urbanization differs from that of the developed world not only in pace but also in causal factors. Few of the large and growing Third World cities are industrial centers; rather, like earlier preindustrial cities, they are trade and administrative centers. This means that they have relatively few working-class jobs to offer. The new migrants therefore become part of a shadow labor force of the self-employed—artisans, peddlers, bicycle renters, laundrywomen, and beggars.

Mexico City—32 Million?

Mexico City is the most dramatic example of Third World urbanization. At 16 million, it is currently the third largest city in the world (after New York and Tokyo); by the year 2000, it is projected to be the largest city in the world, with a population of 32 million people. Mexico City is currently growing at about 4.5 percent each year—750,000 new inhabitants each year, 14,000 each week. Nearly two-thirds of this growth is due to natural increase, the excess of births over deaths. Only one-third is attributable to migration from the countryside.

Tremendous size, rapid growth, and lack of job opportunity have resulted in multiple problems. Among the worst are dangerously high air pollution, severe overload on water and sewer systems, abject poverty, and a serious housing shortage.

Mexico is among the richest of the less developed countries. Nevertheless, the poverty is appalling by our standards. At least 4 million (25 percent) of Mexico City's inhabitants live in squatter housing on the outside of the city. They lack water, sewers, public transportation, electricity, and employment. They live in tar-paper, scrap-lumber, or cardboard shacks. Because they lack legal title to their land, it does not pay them to invest either money or effort in improving their housing. And because of the relative impermanence of the housing, the government does not provide public services (Beier, 1976).

In the mid 1960s, anthropologist Oscar Lewis drew a dramatic picture of life in these neighborhoods with a simple research technique: He went into a tenement and calculated the value of every possession owned by the people living there, from ashtrays to underwear. The tenement he studied was not the poorest of the poor, for the building was a permanent adobe structure with electrical service and a central water spigot. Nevertheless, 83 people lived in 14 one-room, dirt-floor apartments. On the average, these families owned $338 worth of

material possessions; they had 23 beds for their 83 members. Almost all their goods had been purchased secondhand and would be pawned or sold off in times of economic emergency (Lewis, 1969).

Like many other less developed countries faced with rapid urban growth, Mexico is trying to encourage decentralization. Growth in rural areas and smaller cities is being encouraged by the provision of electric power, transportation links, and low-interest loans for capital investment outside Mexico City. This strategy is unlikely to be very effective. In the first place, capital-intensive industries are not the ones likely to employ the unskilled urban poor or the rural migrants. In addition, part of Mexico's problem is overall population growth. With a 4 percent annual growth rate, the countryside too is overcrowded. The best long-range strategy to slow the growth of Mexico City is to reduce fertility as fast as possible and to improve conditions in the countryside as a means of reducing migration flow. In the meantime, reforms that will help the city accommodate its vast new population, including legalizing the tenure of squatters and redirecting urban investment into poor neighborhoods, are desperately needed.

Questions to Consider

What would happen if your community doubled its population in 10 years? Are there any acceptable ways in which you could forbid people to move to your community?

Urbanism

Urbanization is the process of population concentration.

Urbanism is a distinctively urban mode of life that is developed in the cities but not confined there.

Urbanization is the process of population concentration. Those who study it are concerned with the extent of urban growth and the forces that encourage the development of urban living. Although this is an important area of study, sociologists have been more often concerned with **urbanism**—a distinctively urban mode of life that is developed in the city though not confined there (Wirth, 1938). Sociologists have been concerned with the extent to which social relations and the norms that govern them differ between rural and urban settlements.

Theoretical Views

The Western world as a whole has an antiurban bias; urbanism as a way of life has generally been negatively viewed. Big cities are seen as haunts of iniquity and vice, corruptors of youth and health, and destroyers of family and community ties. Cities are despised as artificial creations that compare poorly to creations of nature. City dwellers are characterized as sophisticated but artificial; rural people are characterized as possessing homegrown goodness and warmth.

This general antiurban bias (which has been around at least since the time of ancient Rome), coupled with the very real problems of the industrial city, had a great deal of influence on early sociologists. For the most part, Durkheim, Weber, and others believed that the quality of human social life was significantly worse in the cities. Only recently has evidence emerged that rural life is not as idyllic and city life is not as bleak as was supposed.

Gemeinschaft communities are dominated by personal and diffuse ties among individuals. They are more often characteristic of rural society.

Gesellschaft communities are characterized by instrumental and impersonal relationships. They are more common in urban environments.

Early Writers.   In the late 19th and early 20th centuries, the rapid urbanization of human social life stirred intense interest. It also drew a lot of bad press. Ferdinand Tönnies (1855–1930) offered one of the earliest sociological descriptions of the differences between urban and rural society. He gave the name **gemeinschaft** to the rural communities dominated by primary group ties. He called urban society, which is dominated by the impersonal and instrumental ties characteristic of secondary groups, **gesellschaft**. Durkheim saw the essence of urbanization as a shift from social cohesion built on similarity (mechanical solidarity) to a cohesion built on a complex division of labor and high interdependence (organic solidarity). Weber spoke of a shift from tradition to rationalism as a guide to social activities.

These early writers were not blind to the drawbacks of rural society. They recognized that rural society was static and confining, that tradition bound individuals to a station in life and to ways of thinking that left little room for innovation or individualism. Their preference for rural life was based on the security it provided—the security of knowing exactly what was expected of you, what your place in the social order was and what your neighbor's place was. Although there was no changing the rules of the game, there was also no anxiety about what the rules were. Many of the early social observers believed that this certainty was vital to individual

happiness and social cohesion. In addition, the long-lasting personal relationships characteristic of rural society were thought to be essential to
informal social control. Many were concerned that when people did not
have to worry about what the neighbors would think, deviance would
become commonplace and the social order would be threatened.

Wirth: Urban Determinism.   The classic statement of the negative consequences of urban life for the individual and for social order was made
by Louis Wirth in 1938. In his influential work "Urbanism as a Way of Life",
Wirth suggested that the greater size, heterogeneity, and density of urban
living necessarily led to a breakdown of the normative and moral fabric
of everyday life.

Greater size means that many members of the community will be strangers
to us. Greater density means that we will be forced into close and frequent
contact with these strangers. Wirth postulated that individuals would try
to protect themselves from this crowd by developing a cool personal style
that would allow them to ignore some people (including people who were
physically close, such as in a crowded elevator) and to interact with others,

Figure 18.8
*Because urbanites may rub shoulders
with dozens and even hundreds of
strangers everyday, they develop an impersonal attitude. This dirty bus full of silent passengers symbolizes the apathy
and indifference with which urbanites regard their environment and each other.*

such as sales clerks, in an impersonal style so that their personality would not be engaged. The Kitty Genovese incident, described in chapter 2, is rightly cited as the kind of thing that is more apt to happen among strangers than among lifelong neighbors. Wirth did not suggest that urbanites had no friends or primary ties, but he did think that the city bred a personal style that was cold and calculating (Fischer, 1976).

The heterogeneity of the city is also hypothesized to lead to an awareness of alternative normative frameworks or subcultures. Wirth suggested that this awareness would lead to normative confusion for the individual and lack of integration for the community. Faced with a welter of differing norms, Wirth thought, the dweller in a heterogeneous city was apt to conclude that anything goes. Such an attitude, coupled with the lack of informal social control brought on by size, would lead to greater crime and deviance and a greater emphasis on formal controls.

In sum, Wirth argued that city living brought negative consequences for individuals and society. That is, he believed that if a well-integrated, warm, and conforming person from the farm moved to the city, that person would change and become calculating, indifferent, and nonconforming.

CONCEPT SUMMARY

Differences between Rural and Urban Society According to Wirth and Classical Theorists

	RURAL SOCIETY	URBAN SOCIETY
SOCIAL ORGANIZATION	Small social units Simple social organization Kin-based informal organizations Strong extended kinship system	Large social units Complex social organizations Bureaucratic organizations Weak, unstable nuclear family
CULTURE	Sacred and traditional Homogeneity and mechanical solidarity	Secular and rational Heterogeneity and organic solidarity
SOCIAL RELATIONSHIPS	Personal, emotionally based primary ties Total	Impersonal secondary ties Segmental
CONSEQUENCES FOR INDIVIDUALS AND SOCIETY	Society well organized Psychology security Little alienation	Social disorganization Psychological stress High alienation

SOURCE: Urban Problems in Sociological Perspective, by Thomas R. Shannon. Copyright 1983 by Random House, Inc. Reprinted by permission of the publisher.

The Compositional Model. Later theorists have provided a more benign view of the city. Compositional theorists suggest that individuals experience the city as a mosaic of small worlds that are manageable and knowable. Thus the person who lives in New York City does not have to cope with 18 million people and 500 square miles of city; rather the individual's private world is made up of family, a small neighborhood, and an immediate work group. Compositional theorists argue that the primary group lives on in cities and that the quality of interpersonal ties is not affected even though the number of impersonal contacts is much greater than in rural areas.

The compositional model does recognize that deviance, loneliness, and other problems are greater in cities than in rural areas. It suggests, how-

Figure 18.9
Compositional theorists suggest that the urban environment is a mosaic of small private worlds where individuals develop primary ties and relationships with others. These young people, for example, reside in a restricted environment bounded by their neighborhood and friendship groups. Although they live in a large metropolitan area, on a day-to-day basis their interactions are confined to a smaller and more manageable world.

ever, that deviants, singles, people without children, the lonely, and the alienated are attracted to the cities rather than created by them. Those with families and those willing to conform are attracted to the suburbs.

The Subcultural View. In Wirth's view, the city has essentially negative effects; in the compositional view, urban environment has few direct consequences. The subcultural view straddles the two positions and provides a more moderate picture of the city. The essential idea of the subcultural view is that of critical mass. Subcultural theorists suggest that special subcultures—intellectuals, radicals, gays—cannot develop until there are

Figure 18.10
The subcultural view of the city suggests that a relatively large heterogeneous population provides sufficient diversity for subcultures to develop and thrive. Because of the development of a critical mass, urban environments provide the opportunity for people who share a similar but minority interest to participate in activities not available in smaller places. This includes the seedier side of city life like the pornographic district pictured here, as well as the enriching opportunities for music, art, and professional sports.

a relatively large number of people sharing some relatively uncommon set of norms or values. For example, one homosexual in a small community will be under constant pressure to conform to general standards; only when there are many others will it be possible to sustain a gay community with its own set of norms and values. Similarly, a symphony orchestra, a football team, and a synagogue all await the development of a critical mass of people who share the same interest. Once they identify one another, they will have group support for their identities and standards. In this way, the greater diversity and size of the city leads to development of subcultures with different, perhaps even deviant, norms and values. Wirth might interpret these subcultures as evidence of a lack of moral integration of the community, but they can also be seen as private worlds within which individuals find cohesion and primary group support.

Empirical Consequences of Urban Living

One theory suggests that urban living has negative consequences, another that it has few consequences, and still another that it leads to the development of subcultures. This section reviews the evidence about the effects of urban living on personal integration, life satisfaction, deviance, and community integration.

Personal Integration: Family and Friends.   The effects of urban living on personal integration are rather small. Surveys asking about primary ties show that urban people have as many intimate ties as rural people. There is a slight tendency for urban people to name fewer kin and more friends than rural people, but the kin omitted from the urban lists are not parents, children, and siblings but more distant relatives. Thus urban living may narrow the kin group and expand the number of nonkin who are listed as intimates (Fischer, 1981). Over all, however, urban residents have the same number of intimate ties as do rural people and they see their intimates as often. Thus there is no evidence that urban people are disproportionately lonely, alienated, or estranged from family and friends.

There is evidence, however, that urban people develop a hard shell (protective or otherwise) against nonintimates. Research on the bystander effect and on helping behavior has consistently demonstrated that people in big cities are less apt to help a stranger in trouble than are people in rural areas. One research project looked at community size differentials in bystanders' response to a tearful child asking for help in finding his mother. The results show a substantially lower willingness to help in bigger cities than in small ones (Korte, 1980; Milgram, 1970). In big cities, many people ignored the child altogether or said something to the effect, "Go away, I can't be bothered." Thus it does appear to be true that urban living creates an indifference to others.

Personal Integration: The Neighborhood.   Because the existence of neighborhoods provides a crucial test of contradictory theories, it has generated a great deal of research over the last half century. If neighborhoods continue to exist in big cities, then Wirth's argument is challenged; however, the validity of both the compositional and the subcultural theories depends on the continued existence of neighborhoods.

Sociologically speaking, a **neighborhood** is something more than just a collection of streets; it has a common sense of identity and some basis of shared ties. The shared ties may be to a common social institution, such as a school or park, or it may be to such social characteristics as ethnicity, race, or life-style. Strong neighborhoods allow the establishment and enforcement of agreements about public behavior—for example, standards for the maintenance of homes, the behavior of children, or the acceptable level of noise. Unlike contemporary zoning ordinances, which often spell out the same kinds of things, strong neighborhoods ensure conformity through informal channels of neighbors and peers (Schoenberg, 1979). Thus, in a strong neighborhood, a truant child is likely to have someone recognize him and report him to his parents.

For most city dwellers, however, the neighborhood is a very weak group. Even in suburbia, where relatively long distances and inconvenience result in more reliance on neighbors, frequent moves retard the formation of strong neighborhoods. Another factor making strong neighborhoods less likely is the sharp decline in the number of women who are housewives, with the time, interest, and need to develop close ties with their neighbors. The survival of the neighborhood as a primary group is most often documented when ethnic or other subcultures are spatially segregated. Thus the Italians of Boston's West End (Gans, 1962), the Hispanics in a southwestern barrio, or the Poles in Chicago may form neighborhoods whose common identity and long interaction lead residents to recognize mutual rights and obligations.

Most city dwellers, whether central city or suburban, find that city living has freed them from the necessity of liking the people they live next to and has given them the opportunity to select intimates on a basis other than physical proximity; this freedom is something that people in rural areas do not have. There is growing consensus among urban researchers that physical proximity (neighborhood) is no longer a primary basis of intimacy. Rather, people form intimate networks on the basis of kin, friendship, and work groups; and they keep in touch by telephone rather than relying solely on face-to-face communication. When in trouble, they call on their parents or their children for help (Wellman, 1979). In short, urban people do have intimates, but they are unlikely to live in the same neighborhood with them.

Neighborhoods are more than anonymous collections of people, however. Neighbors are not strangers, and there are instances in which being nearby is more important than being emotionally close. Many surveys demonstrate that in times of emergency—we're locked out of our house, we need a teaspoon of vanilla, or we want someone to accept a United Parcel package—we still rely on our neighbors (Dono et al., 1979). Although we generally do not ask large favors of our neighbors and don't want them to rely heavily on us, most of us expect our neighbors to be good people who are willing to help in a pinch. This has much to do with the fact that neighborhoods are often segregated by social class, race and ethnicity, and stage in the family life cycle. Thus we know that our neighbors will be people pretty much like us.

Life Satisfaction. On most measures of life satisfaction, urban people score lower then rural people; and the larger the city, the more dissatisfied

A **neighborhood** is a geographically bounded set of streets that has a common sense of identity and some basis of shared ties.

Figure 18.11
Neighborhood block parties, such as this one on Charles Street in New York City, function to integrate neighborhoods and strengthen the ties between residents. Neighborhoods that share ethnic or subcultural characteristics are more apt to experience events such as this thereby reducing the need for more formal types of social control.

they are (see Table 18.2). Urbanites are more afraid to be out after dark in their neighborhoods and are less satisfied with their lives, homes, and communities.

Survey after survey demonstrates that many city dwellers would prefer to live in small towns or rural areas. Few people from these smaller places want to live in central cities, however. A Gallup Poll from 1980 found that one out of three urban residents wanted to move out of the city. The chief reasons were a high crime rate (mentioned by 49 percent of those wanting to leave central districts of large cities) and a general preference for sub-urban living—that is, a desire to exchange dense apartment living for home ownership and less crowding ("Who would leave," 1981). Having to rub shoulders with undesirable groups is another frequently mentioned reason for wanting to leave central cities.

Despite these complaints, few would deny that large cities offer many more public amenities than do small towns or rural areas. The availability of libraries, museums, zoos, parks, concerts, and galleries increases with city size. So does the quality of medical services and police and fire protection. Thus there are many positive aspects of city living that give a great deal of satisfaction and that encourage people to want to live at least close to a big city (Christensen, 1979).

Some subgroups in the population prefer to live in big cities rather than small ones. These groups are racial or subcultural minorities, who find that the development of a critical mass of similar others provides them with greater power and a stronger sense of community than they would have if they constituted only a handful in a smaller community. For example, blacks have been shown to have greater political power, better education, and more black-oriented institutions (banks, beauty shops, formal organizations) in large than small cities (Karnig, 1979). For black

Table 18.2 Quality of Life by City Size, 1981
Although there are many advantages to living in big cities, there are also personal costs. People who live in big cities are less satisfied with their communities and their personal lives; they are also much more fearful of their environment than are rural people.

Generally speaking, how happy would you say you are? Very happy, fairly happy, or not too happy?

CITY SIZE	PERCENT VERY HAPPY
1,000,000 +	35%
500,000–999,999	38
50,000–499,999	50
2,500–49,999	51
Rural	47

Is there any area right around here—that is, within a mile—where you would be afraid to walk alone at night?

CITY SIZE	PERCENT AFRAID
1,000,000 +	55%
500,000–999,999	49
50,000–499,999	52
2,500–49,999	43
Rural	33

SOURCE: Gallup Report, April 1981, no. 187; June 1981, no. 189.

Americans, then, big-city living allows an escape from some of the consequences of being a minority group.

Crime and Deviance. Urban residents quite rightly believe that crime rates are higher in the city than in the countryside. Their anxiety about being out on the streets at night seems justified. Table 18.3 presents the number of reported crime incidents per 100,000 population in the United States in 1982 according to the size of the place where the incident occurred. The data show that crime rates decrease as city size decreases; this is especially true of the kind of crime that people fear most—violence against the person.

Crowding. A persistent criticism of urban living is that crowded living conditions foster mental illness, irritability, and deviance. Studies of animal behavior show that crowding does increase a variety of deviant behaviors, including homosexuality, poor mothering, and aggression. Many people expect urban crowding of human beings to have the same effect.

Research, however, demonstrates that urban people are not significantly more crowded than rural people. Certainly, there are larger crowds on the sidewalks and in the stores; but in their own homes, urban people often have more rooms and more room per person than do rural people. That is, unlike laboratory animals, they have a relatively uncrowded place to which they can retreat (Fischer, 1976). In addition, humans have a variety of adaptive mechanisms for structuring spatial use in such a way that there is relatively little interaction. Once such mechanism is television, which allows several people to use the same room simultaneously (Gillis, 1979). Outside the household, high-density living can actually encourage neighborliness if the physical environment provides front porches, benches, and other facilities for group interaction (Fox et al., 1980). In short, there is no evidence that high urban densities lead to human pathologies (Booth, 1976).

Other Rural-Urban Differences. According to stereotype, rural people, especially farmers, are hicks, rednecks, and rubes. They use bad grammar and think that if it was good enough for grandpa, it is good enough for me, that a woman's place is in the home, and that children should be

Table 18.3 United States Crime Rates by City Size, 1982
There is a basis in fact for the greater fearfulness of urban residents. The crime level is higher in big cities, especially for the violent personal crimes that people fear most.

CITY SIZE	NUMBER OF CRIMES REPORTED PER 100,000 POPULATION	
	VIOLENT CRIMES	PROPERTY CRIMES
250,000 +	1,354	7,851
100,000–249,999	779	7,576
50,000– 99,999	561	6,019
25,000– 49,999	431	5,553
10,000– 24,999	320	4,546
2,500– 9,999	284	4,211
Rural	184	2,041

SOURCE: U.S. Bureau of the Census, 1983, table 288.

seen and not heard. In contrast is the stereotype of the sophisticated city dweller, who is aware of current events, innovative, and upbeat.

Although they are exaggerated, there is some truth to these stereotypes: As size of place declines, people become more conservative in their moral and political beliefs. Table 18.4 points out that people in rural areas are more likely than city dwellers to oppose drinking, labor unions, marijuana, and handgun control. And regardless of where they currently live, people who were raised in rural and small-town environments tend to be much less tolerant of such deviant life-styles as homosexuality or cohabitation (Stephan & McMullin, 1982).

There are many issues, however (churchgoing, attitude toward abortion, and desired family size, for example), on which there is little division between town and country. Thus, although differences continue to exist between rural and urban ways of thinking, they should not be exaggerated. In fact, many of the traditional differences between rural and urban society are diminishing. All but the remotest cabins have access to national culture via television, radio, movies, and news magazines. The automobile and a good freeway system have also increased the access of rural people to urban amenities.

The city continues to be the major source of innovation and change: New dress styles, music, educational philosophies, and technologies originate in the city and spread to the countryside. Thus the rural-urban difference is constantly created anew and seems unlikely ever to be totally eliminated (Fischer, 1979). Because the speed of cultural diffusion is now much more rapid than before, however, rural-urban differences are far less profound than they were in the past.

Suburbanism

Spatially, suburbia is halfway between the countryside and the central city; culturally, it shares some of the characteristics of both. There are working-class suburbs and middle-class suburbs, Jewish suburbs and Polish suburbs. What they all share is the predominance of single-family detached homes on individual lots—a low density housing pattern that provides room for dogs, children, and barbeques. This is the life-style to

Table 18.4   Rural-Urban Differences in Attitudes
There is some truth in the stereotype that rural and small-town residents are more conservative than people who live in big cities. On most issues, however, the differences are not dramatic; rural people are very much a part of mainstream American culture.

CITY SIZE	NEVER USE LIQUOR	OPPOSE LABOR UNIONS	APPROVE LEGALIZING MARIJUANA	FAVOR HANDGUN CONTROL	FAVOR BAN ON ABORTION
1,000,000 +	24%	28%	32%	61%	41%
500,000–999,999	18	29	27	44	36
50,000–499,999	28	31	28	43	44
2,500–49,999	34	43	20	31	47
Rural	37	42	18	31	39

SOURCE: Gallup Reports, June 1980; March 1981; July 1981; August 1981.

which the majority of Americans aspire; and, in general, suburbanites are happier with their lives and communities than are people living in central cities.

There are, however, several drawbacks to suburban living, both for the individual and for society. A chief drawback for the individual is the relatively greater inconveneince of shopping and services that results from the low-density land use. The supermarket is likely to be 5 miles away rather than just around the corner, children in elementary school are likely to be bused to school, and employees typically commute longer distances to their work sites. This inconvenience factor is particularly important for teenagers, the elderly, and the carless, who are virtually isolated by the lack of public transportation and the distances required. These groups of the population often express greater dissatisfaction in suburbia than in the city.

Although suburbs differ from one another, there tend to be a number of similarities within each suburb. In part, this is because houses of similar size and price are put up within each development. Thus a development of three-bedroom houses in the $80,000 to $90,000 range attracts a different group of people than does a development of five-bedroom houses in the $125,000 to $150,000 range. Within each suburb, new homeowners are roughly similar in income, education, and occupational prestige. They probably all have children and are between the ages of 30 and 60. For most suburbanites, their home is their major investment, and a concern about property values gives them a keen interest in the identity and lifestyle of their neighbors.

In addition to this initial similarity, the low population density of the suburbs serves to enhance conformity. The population is too small to produce a critical mass for subcultural development; and unless interests (such as gardening, bridge, or children) are widely shared, suburbanites are unlikely to find anybody to join with them. Thus they tend to restrict their activities and interests to those that are widely shared and to forgo the development of more esoteric interests. Some people find this conformity stifling, but in general the suburbs attract people who are willing to play the game by the rules.

An important consequence of suburban development is the increased segregation of blacks from whites. Although blacks make up nearly 30 percent of central cities, they make up only a small portion of the suburbs. The combination of large-scale immigration of white families to the suburbs and large-scale immigration of rural blacks to central cities has created an increase in housing segregation since World War II.

Figure 18.12
This housing development in San Jose, California is characteristic of contemporary suburban housing. Each family has its own house, its own yard, and two cars. House structures, incomes, life-styles, and values tend to be very similar within each development. Because of this, suburbs emphasize conformity. Nevertheless, this affluent life-style is the one most Americans aspire to.

Moving In, Moving Out, Moving On

Many of the unique characteristics of the central cities, suburbs, and small towns arise out of the kinds of people they attract. In the last 30 years, there have been three dramatic trends in population distribution: (1) the decline of metropolitan areas and the increased growth of nonmetropolitan areas, (2) the growth of suburbs, and (3) the move to the Sunbelt (see Figure 18.13). Because groups are not equally likely to move, these redis-

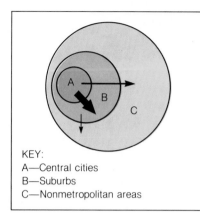

KEY:
A—Central cities
B—Suburbs
C—Nonmetropolitan areas

Figure 18.13 Residential Flows during the 1970s

During the 1970s, there were three primary trends in residential mobility. The width of arrows indicates approximate relative size of net migration flow. The largest group of movers went from the central cities to the suburbs, but there were also important streams from the central cities and the suburbs to nonmetropolitan areas.

SOURCE: Urban Problems in Sociological Perspective, by Thomas R. Shannon. Copyright 1983 by Random House, Inc. Reprinted by permission of the publisher.

tributional trends have had substantial impact on the size and composition of urban and rural areas.

Metropolitan Decline and Nonmetropolitan Resurgence

For 180 years, U.S. censuses showed a steadily increasing degree of urbanization. Beginning in 1970, however, the process was reversed; for the first time, nonmetropolitan areas grew faster than metropolitan ones. The biggest losers were the largest central cities. Between 1970 and 1980, Baltimore lost 19 percent of its population, Buffalo 25 percent, Pittsburgh 21 percent, and Washington, D.C. 25 percent ("U.S. Census update," 1980). The people did not move just to bedroom communities elsewhere in the metropolitan area; many left the region altogether.

A significant and increasing proportion of people in the United States say they would prefer to live in rural areas; even suburbanites would prefer lower density and more space ("Who would leave," 1981). A small, but increasing, number act on this preference, and there is noticeable growth in nonmetropolitan areas. This trend is fostered by a variety of social, economic, and technological changes. First, nonmetropolitan areas are no longer as remote as they were. Good highways, the extension of electricity to rural areas, the telephone, and television make it possible for people to experience rural living without losing touch. There is also an increase in the number of people whose incomes are not tied to a particular location (for example, the retired).

Few of the people moving from metropolitan to rural areas are returning to the land or adopting a rural life-style. Rather, they have above-average educations and incomes and are taking urban culture into the countryside (Kasarda, 1980). When they get there, they demand many of the services that were available in the city and thus contribute to rising taxes in rural areas. The result of the growth of nonmetropolitan areas may, therefore, be an extension of urban culture rather than a move toward a more conservative rural culture. Although the whole phenomenon causes some resentment among long-time rural residents, it is usually offset by their satisfaction at having new jobs and greater income (Price & Clay, 1980).

Shift to the Suburbs

The availability of affordable suburban housing after World War II led to a massive exit of the middle class from the central cities. Business left at about the same time. Retail business followed the middle class to the suburbs, and manufacturing plants fled because of high land values in the central city. Between 1947 and 1972, the 33 largest metropolitan areas lost nearly 1 million working-class jobs; more than half of all retail sales are now in suburban malls (Kasarda, 1980).

Into the gap left by the vanishing middle class moved the rural poor from the South and Appalachia, who were drawn to northern industrial cities by high wages (see Figure 18.14). The result has been the creation of class and racial barriers between the suburb and the central city. The compositional differences of central cities and suburbs account for much of the urban-suburban difference in satisfaction, crime, and life-style.

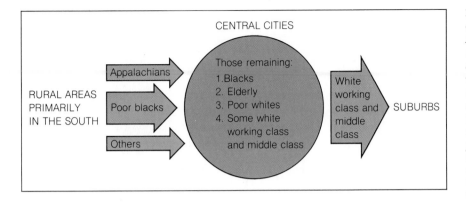

Figure 18.14 Changing Composition of the Cities
Population shifts during the 1950s and 1960s resulted in dramatic changes in the composition of U.S. central cities. The white working and middle classes left for the suburbs and were replaced by poor migrants from Appalachia and the South, including many blacks. The size of the arrows indicates the relative size of the population movements.
SOURCE: Urban Problems in Sociological Perspective, by Thomas R. Shannon. Copyright 1983 by Random House, Inc. Reprinted by permission of the publisher.

The growth of the suburbs has altered their character. As larger numbers of people have settled in limited land areas, suburban lots have become smaller and neighborhoods of townhouses and duplexes have started appearing in suburbia. These low-maintenance homes offer the advantages of home ownership to those who earlier found the three-bedroom ranch too much trouble. As a result, childless couples, singles, and retired couples are now more common in suburbia. Suburbia has become more crowded and less dominated by the station wagon set.

Move to the Sunbelt

The move to the Sunbelt is a simple extension of the trends just noted. People are leaving northern industrial cities and going to suburbs and nonmetropolitan areas in the South and Southwest. Some are following jobs, and some are simply looking for a better climate and open spaces. During the last decade, both traditional manufacturing jobs and new industries were lured to the Sunbelt by lower taxes, lower land costs, lower wages, and less unionization (Kasarda, 1980).

Urban Problems

The changes in the distribution of population and industry have created problems for U.S. cities. Among the most important are poverty, fiscal crisis, and racial segregation.

Poverty

A drive through most large cities reveals slums, ghettos, and other obtrusive signs of real poverty. News coverage of the rundown areas of Watts, Detroit, Miami, and Newark reveals massive and oppressive poverty. Poverty, however, is not a uniquely urban problem. In fact, it has been and continues to be a disproportionately rural problem.

Like the rest of the population, however, the poor have become increasingly urbanized over the last several decades. When the poor live in cities, they tend to be found disproportionately in the urban core rather than

Figure 18.15

The post-World War II boom in suburban housing led most of those who could afford good housing to leave the city. As a result, central city housing has increasingly deteriorated. As illustrated in this picture of the South Bronx in New York City, many areas have fallen into serious decay. Lacking lawns, parks, and other recreational facilities, children in central cities make do with what's available; abandoned cars, fire escapes, and rubble.

in the suburbs. Aged housing, noise, and pollution have reduced the desirability of the central city to the point where the poor can afford to live there. In addition, living there is convenient for the poor, many of whom depend on public transportation or on walking.

Whether in Appalachia or on the South Side of Chicago, poor people tend to live in neighborhoods with other poor people. In the city, however, their neighborhoods are much larger and denser. This density gives poverty a visibility in the city that it does not have in the country, where isolated shacks and mobile homes far from the road are easily overlooked. No one who drives through Chicago can ignore poverty.

An important aspect of urban poverty is that it is disproportionately black poverty. Whereas the rural poor are 25 percent black, the central city poor are 46 percent black. This too contributes to the greater visibility of poverty in the cities; the poor population is set off not only by income but by color. Visibility has increased special programs for the urban poor; thus, in terms of education and health programs, the urban poor are much better off than the rural poor.

The greater density and visibility of the urban poor also increases the likelihood that poor people will recognize themselves as a group and act as a group. In fact, the greater potential for revolt among the urban poor was one of the keystones of Marx's ideas about revolution. In the United States there has been no sustained revolutionary or even reformist movement coming from the urban lower class, but all the black radical movements have originated in big cities. The urban riots of the past few decades certainly suggest that the density of urban poverty has and will continue to have important consequences. (These riots and social movements are examined in greater detail in chapter 19.)

Urban Fiscal Woes

The movement of middle-class property and retail business to outside the city limits has seriously damaged the tax base of large cities. In many northern cities, in fact, the absolute value of land and buildings in the central city has decreased in recent years. This declining tax base leaves cities three choices: (1) increase taxes, (2) decrease services, or (3) go broke. A large number of cities are doing all three. Raising taxes is disastrous because it drives even more businesses and residents out of the city. Reducing services is impossible because the changing composition of the city (more elderly, more poor) means that more services are required.

Racial Segregation and Racial Steering

A substantial amount of racial segregation results inadvertently from the operation of economic factors. Whites more often than blacks can afford to gratify their housing preference, which for almost all means suburbia. Overt discrimination does, however, play an important role in maintaining segregation. Blacks who want to and can afford to move out of black neighborhoods are discouraged from doing so. This discouragement has a variety of forms, some overt and some subtle. The most overt form of housing segregation—the refusal to sell or rent to a family because of its race or ethnicity—has been outlawed by open housing legislation. Intent to discriminate is difficult to prove, however, and many find a plausible excuse for turning away unwanted customers without providing obvious grounds for discrimination.

Housing segregation is achieved more subtly through **racial steering**— realtors encouraging black families to buy or rent in black neighborhoods and white families to buy or rent in white neighborhoods. This discrim-

Racial steering occurs when realtors encourage black families to buy or rent in black neighborhoods and encourage white families to buy or rent in white neighborhoods.

Figure 18.16
Changes in population composition have compounded the problems of America's biggest cities. A shrinking tax base has meant less money for the support of public facilities at the same time that public demands have grown. Thus, central city governments find it increasingly difficult to meet the tab for public education, sanitation, and fire and police protection. These problems increase the likelihood that those who can afford to leave the city will do so.

ination on the part of realtors results in the maintenance of racially segregated neighborhoods.

The way racial steering works was neatly captured in an experiment by Pearce (1979), who sent a total of 20 black and white couples out to 50 real estate offices in Detroit. The 20 couples were all provided with nearly equal backgrounds (education, occupation, income, age, and number of children) and demands (three-bedroom house in the suburbs, near an elementary school). In order to avoid suspicion, the standard biographies for blacks and whites differed slightly, and the white couples had slightly lower incomes. One white couple and one black couple were sent, some weeks apart, to each real estate agent.

Pearce's study demonstrates substantial differences in treatment. In the first place, black couples were significantly less likely to be shown any houses at all. Of the realtors who showed houses, 97 percent showed them to white couples; only 35 percent showed them to similar black couples.

There were also substantial differences in the houses that black and white couples were shown. Although the black couples had somewhat higher incomes than the white couples did, 47 percent of the black couples, compared to only 22 percent of the white couples, were shown houses that cost less than $25,000. Black couples, however, were more likely than white to be shown really expensive homes (perhaps to discourage them).

Solutions

Because the middle class and business have largely abandoned the central city, multiple problems have arisen there. They include a poorer and blacker population and an urban government hovering on the brink of bankruptcy. One solution often suggested to the problems of racial segregation and urban fiscal crisis is the extension of local government to the suburbs. In effect, this extension would replace city government with county government. If it were done, integrated school districts could be created to draw from central cities and suburbs, and suburban populations and industry could be taxed to support the city.

Supporters of this plan argue that suburbanites are currently parasites. They ride the city's buses, go to its theaters and nightclubs, drive to work on its streets, shop in its stores. Therefore, they should have to help support it. Detractors argue that government is too big already and that the current system helps maintain some community control over decisions about the level and variety of taxes and services. Prior to 1960, most cities had the right to annex surrounding communities almost at will, and the communities did not object. Increasingly, however, suburbs and fringe communities are successfully resisting annexation, preferring to maintain their autonomy and their lower taxes.

ISSUES IN SOCIAL POLICY

Decaying Central Cities

A major problem for most U.S. cities is an aging housing stock. Entire neighborhoods slide gradually into disrepair and finally are abandoned. Owners are replaced by renters; and as the more affluent leave the city for the suburbs, landlords must decrease their rents to attract renters. Declining rental income and higher taxes mean a decline in maintenance and upkeep. As buildings deteriorate, so do rents, and the cycle continues until the buildings are uninhabitable and eventually abandoned. This cycle is hardly inevitable. Some of the most elegant neighborhoods in U.S. cities are 50 or even 150 years old. Why do some decline and others not?

Good housing means a higher tax base. It also means less need for public housing and the attraction of a stable working- and middle-class population. Thus every housing policy for 30 years has emphasized the need for maintaining quality housing in central cities. The reality, however, is a steady decline; parts of our central cities are so derelict that they look like Beirut after the bombings. This condition persists in spite of social policy and, to a significant extent, because of it. Three factors that have contributed to the decay of urban housing are redlining, home loan programs, and urban renewal.

REDLINING

The housing market rests on two commodities: loans and insurance. Both are controlled by the biggest commercial firms in the United States. Before a family can obtain a mortgage loan, it must have insurance; the same thing is true for remodeling loans. A substantial body of research demonstrates that both home insurance and mortgage loans are more difficult to obtain in some parts of the city than in others. The process whereby these financial investments are systematically denied to one area of the city and diverted to other, more favored areas is called **redlining**. Typically, the areas discriminated against are heavily minority and low-income, and the favored areas are suburban. Insurance companies, for example, charge rates for central city areas that are much higher than is justified by the increased risk of fire or vandalism; they may also terminate policies in redlined areas or simply define such areas as outside their territory (Squires et al., 1979). The same process occurs in home mortgages (U.S. Department of Housing and Urban Development, 1977).

These discriminatory practices are part of a systematic process of disinvestment in low-income and minority—that is, central city—neighborhoods. Rather than being a natural cycle of aging, urban decay is the result of deliberate action. The lack of investment in a neighborhood means no construction jobs, no repairs, and deteriorating housing. Ultimately, it leads to simple abandonment, a critical and rapidly growing problem in U.S. cities. Gaping windows and sagging doors provide targets for vandalism and havens for junkies, criminals, and rats; they also contribute to further decline.

FEDERAL LOAN PROGRAMS

Nearly half of all mortgage loans for home purchases are guaranteed by the federal government through either the VA or FHA. The federal guarantees remove the risk for local savings and loan associations and encourage them to offer loans to people whose ability to buy is marginal, especially working-class and lower middle-class people. These federal programs give preference to new housing and thus have been used almost exclusively to encourage suburban development rather than the purchase and up-

Figure 18.17

The Pruitt-Igoe Project, a low-income housing project in St. Louis, was a classic example of a failed attempt at urban renewal. When it was built in 1954, it was hailed as a modern, spacious, and much-improved form of public housing. However, the project soon became a center for vandalism and crime. By 1970, only 16 of 43 buildings were occupied. It is shown here being demolished in 1972.

keep of established central city neighborhoods. Because loan guarantees are unavailable for older homes, renting becomes the rule and the long decline begins. The lack of federal loan guarantees works in parallel with redlining practices to almost exclude central city home ownership.

URBAN RENEWAL

The chief objective of urban renewal was to replace unsafe, rundown tenement housing with higher-quality housing. This renewal was expected to beautify downtowns and provide a better standard of living for the poor. All evaluations of urban development suggest that the first objective was pursued at the expense of the second. Urban renewal was a dismal failure; it significantly decreased the quality of urban housing and contributed to racial segregation, higher crime rates, and alienation. This is an amazing record for a policy designed to make things better.

Essentially, urban renewal bulldozed square miles of low-rise tenement buildings and replaced them with modern high-rise apartment buildings. The space saved was often used for freeways or public buildings. Despite the fact that the apartments were superior to the destroyed housing, the change had substantial negative consequences. First, unlike the destroyed units, the new housing was public housing. Thus the working poor were displaced, and a dense aggregation of the poorest of the poor was created. Second, dense high-rises are poor places in which to raise children. Children who are playing 20 stories below their parents are effectively beyond parental supervision. Finally, by eliminating the front porch as a neighborhood meeting ground, the physical basis for neighborhood cohesion and integration was eliminated at the same time that increased density vastly increased the possibilities of neighbors annoying one another. Furthermore, all the new projects were located in heavily minority areas, thus contributing to the continuity of segregation.

In short, urban renewal eliminated needed housing for the working poor and herded the very poor into dense congregations where parental supervision and neighboring were physically discouraged. Not surprisingly, therefore, the new projects became scenes of vandalism, violent crime, and desperation—places where even the poorest of the poor feared to live. Many of these projects were abandoned within 15 to 20 years of their construction.

Urban renewal could have been a success. Hindsight suggests at least two strategies that would make public housing contribute to social policy objectives.

First, small, low-rise units of no more than 15 to 20 families should be built. Each project should include public space where neighbors can interact, benches where parents can sit and watch their children, and windows that look out over play areas, streets, and alleys. It should also be small enough to encourage neighborhood cohesion and informal control and to provide *defensible space*—an area that inhibits crime (Newman, 1973). Such a space is small enough and central enough to be (1) defined by the community as its space, a space for which residents are responsible; and (2) within sight of many or most units so that strangers will be noted and, if necessary, challenged. Defensible space is more likely to occur when 20 rather than 500 families are using the playground and when all apartments provide oversight of

Figure 18.18
Georgetown, a wealthy neighborhood in Northwest Washington, D. C., is an example of regentrification. Although many of the row houses in this section of the city are between 100 and 200 years old, they have been refurbished over the past two decades and are now largely occupied by upper class and upper-middle class residents.

public spaces. Thus small projects would contribute to lower crime rates, better cohesion, and lower levels of delinquency (Roncek et al., 1981).

Second, the low-rise housing projects should be scattered throughout the city and suburbs to help achieve racial integration and prevent the development of subcultures of poverty. Of course, the reason that this hasn't been done is that working- and middle-class homeowners worry that their property values will be reduced by the presence of public housing. City and county governments have the legal power to put public housing anywhere they wish; they haven't wished to risk their jobs, however, by annoying established citizens. Thus housing projects have served to concentrate rather than disperse poverty and minority groups.

REGENTRIFICATION

A word should be said about the much-heralded return of the middle and upper middle classes to the central city. Magazine spreads frequently show an old brick rooming house or factory turned into an elegant home. This process of vastly upgrading decaying neighborhoods, called *regentrification* (bringing back the gentry), is supported by federal loan programs that provide favorable loan rates to families attempting such projects. In spite of the financial aid, however, the number of middle-class families drawn back to decayed neighborhoods is a mere trickle compared to the continuing stream of middle-class families to the suburbs. The major impact of regentrification programs has been to further reduce the amount of housing available to the poor and near

poor by turning rooming houses for five families into elegant single-family homes.

THE RESULT: DEFEATED NEIGHBORHOODS

The end result of these processes—redlining, disinvestment, and urban renewal—is the creation of the *defeated neighborhood*—a neighborhood that has disintegrated in both physical and social structure so that it can no longer act on its own behalf or protect itself. It is

> subject to insufficient or quixotic enforcement of building standards, zoning rules, police protection, and wide disparities in the delivery of all available community services. Above all it is a community which citywide, regional, and federal agencies treat as an object without much fear of retaliation from a local constituency. . . . It is a community so heavily stigmatized and outcast that its residents retreat from most forms of public participation out of shame, mutual fear, and an absence of faith in each other's collective concern. [Suttles, 1972:239]

In short, others feel free to put freeways through defeated neighborhoods, close their schools, and renew their housing—all of which would lead to an uproar in defended neighborhoods. In extreme cases, the police may decide to ignore certain crimes, such as prostitution or vagrancy, within some rundown neighborhoods, thus tacitly handing the neighborhood over to criminal control. This last stage completes the process of urban decay.

SUMMARY
▬▬

1. The development of cities during the industrial revolution was influenced by two factors: The cities were built around manufacturing plants, and most people still relied on walking to get around. These factors gave the industrial city its three distinctive features: high density, a central business district, and a concentric, or sectoral, spatial pattern.

2. The chief architect of the late-industrial city is the automobile. As a result, this city is characterized by multiple nuclei and low density.

3. Urbanization is exploding in the less developed world; many of its large cities will double in size in a decade. This urban growth is the result not of industrialization but of high urban fertility and the high density and poverty that drive peasants toward the city.

4. Wirth's urban determinism theory suggests that the size, density, and heterogeneity of the city inevitably lead to nonconformity and indifference to others.

5. Compositional theory suggests that urbanites experience the city as a mosaic of small, manageable worlds. Although they see many strangers, their degrees of warmth and conformity are not affected by living in the city.

6. Subcultural theory suggests that the size of the city provides for the development of a critical mass of individuals with uncommon interests. Thus subcultures are more apt to grow up in the city, lending an appearance of diversity.

7. Urbanites are less satisfied with their lives and communities than are people who live in small towns and rural areas. Although there is little difference in number of intimate ties, city dwellers tend to rely more on close family and friends and less on distant kin and neighbors.

8. Rural-urban differences are declining, but rural people continue to be more traditional on social and political issues. Because new ideas usually originate in the cities, this difference is unlikely to be completely eliminated.

9. There have been three major U.S. population shifts in recent decades: the move from metropolitan to nonmetropolitan counties, the move to suburbia, and the move to the Sunbelt.

10. In part because of the middle-class move to suburbia, the biggest U.S. cities are faced with problems of poverty, impoverished urban governments, and segregation.

11. The urban housing stock in the United States is decaying. The three factors primarily responsible are urban renewal, federal loan programs that have sponsored suburban growth at the expense of urban maintenance, and the practice of redlining.

SUGGESTED READINGS

Banfield, Edward C. (1974). The Unheavenly City Revisited. Boston: Little, Brown. A critical and controversial look at cities and U.S. urban policies.

Berry, Brian J. C. (1981). Comparative Urbanization: Divergent Paths in the Twentieth Century. New York: St. Martin's Press. A historical and cross-cultural description that concentrates on the human consequences of urbanization. The thesis is that the consequences of living in cities are anything but uniform and differ substantially among world regions.

Fischer, Claude S. (1984). The Urban Experience (2d ed.). San Diego: Harcourt Brace Jovanovich. A readable book that covers theoretical views of the city as well as contemporary research about urban problems and the quality of life in the city.

Riis, Jacob A. (1971). How the Other Half Lives. New York: Dover Publications. (Original work published 1901). A liberally illustrated essay on conditions in U.S. urban slums at the turn of the century. Riis's early photographs provide ample documentation of the poverty and filth of the industrial city.

Shannon, Thomas R. (1983). Urban Problems in Sociological Perspective. New York: Random House. A laundry list of urban problems—poverty, housing, taxation, transportation—that also provides an integrated sociological perspective.

CHAPTER 19

COLLECTIVE BEHAVIOR

PROLOGUE

Have You Ever . . . *been swept up into the excitement of a crowd? At a ball game or a concert, have you shouted, clapped, stomped, and cheered with hundreds or thousands of others? Being part of a crowd is exciting and exhilarating. It provides a remarkable sense of group feeling.*

Concerts and football games are intended to give us that good feeling of exhilaration in a safe and harmless way. They make us feel good without threatening the usual way society does business. Some crowds and demonstrations, however, do threaten the status quo. Crowds generate a tremendous sense of solidarity and power, a belief that so many people dedicated to a cause must be able to change the world—to eliminate poverty, injustice, and war, for example. A homosexual who attended one of the first gay rights conferences in Los Angeles spoke of this excitement: "Can you imagine what it was like? . . . You looked up and all of a sudden the room became vast—well, you know, was there anyone in Los Angeles who wasn't gay? We'd never seen so many people" (cited in Altman, 1983:119).

This chapter is about the episodes and movements that occur when people are drawn outside the daily routine of social institutions to form crowds, mobs, and movements.

— In November, 1984, hundreds died in mob violence in India after a Sikh bodyguard killed President Indira Gandhi. The assassination was the result of long-smouldering conflict between the Hindu-led government and the Sikh minority. In the days following the assassination, mobs of Hindus avenged their leader's death by rampaging through Sikh neighborhoods killing, looting, and burning.

— In January 1983, a race riot erupted briefly in Miami. A young black man was killed by a Hispanic police officer under ambiguous circumstances. Stories spread rapidly through the Overtown section of Miami, and soon more than 200 people were looting, burning cars, and vandalizing. The eruption of violence was blamed on the recession and cutbacks in federal programs, on alienation from the legal system, and on the continued exclusion of blacks from social, economic, and political institutions. The disturbance lasted 3 days and brought with it tens of millions of dollars of property damage, 26 arrests, and two deaths. ("Racial outburst," 1983:23).

— In March 1983, a million people marched down Fifth Avenue in New York in protest over nuclear weapons. This was one of the largest protests ever recorded.

What place do such incidents have in the study of patterned interaction? Despite the fact that riots, demonstrations, and social movements occur with some frequency, they are not part of the conventional social structures that guide people through their daily lives, providing ready-made patterns for loving, worshipping, and competing. Still, they are hardly random events. Rather they are intimately connected with the social structures in which they take place. This chapter examines the relationships between social structures and noninstitutionalized group behaviors.

The sociology of collective behavior covers two related but distinct topics: collective actions and social movements. **Collective actions** are episodic crowd actions that are prompted by nonroutine events; they include riots and mobs. **Social movements** are deliberate, organized attempts to change social institutions—society's patterned norms and values—from the outside; they include the gay rights, antinuclear, and feminist movements.

All collective behavior is a challenge to the status quo; that is, it challenges the usual way a society does business. These challenges are likely to arise in times of rapid social change and are often attempts to control and direct that change. When collective behavior occurs, it directs attention to sources of strain and tension in society, places where change is causing a dislocation in ordinary social relationships.

In this chapter, we will examine the social structure of collective behavior; the circumstances under which people step outside the usual conventions; the processes through which some disorganized protests, riots, and outbreaks become organized; politicized social movements; and, finally, the responses of institutions and people who wish to maintain the status quo.

Collective actions are episodic crowd actions that occur in irregular ways and that are triggered by nonroutine events.

Social movements are deliberate, organized attempts to change social institutions from the outside.

Crowds and Mobs: Nonroutine Collective Action

Types of Crowds

A **crowd** is a relatively large number of people drawn to a common location by some nonroutine event. This definition excludes concert audiences, football spectators, and church congregations, all groups that are drawn together as part of a routine activity. A crowd is not a group in the sociological sense; nor is it routine. The nonroutine attraction that draws

A **crowd** is a relatively large number of people drawn to a common location by some nonroutine event.

people into joint action may be war, catastrophe, economic crisis, or outside aggression; it may be simply a traffic accident. Whenever the traditional and anticipated way of doing things is disrupted, crowds are likely to form (G. Marx & Wood, 1975).

The behavior of the crowd depends on many things, including the cause of its formation, the response from authorities, and the organization, resources, and ideology possessed by the crowd. Table 19.1 summarizes six of the more common types of crowds.

Theories of Crowd Behavior

Some crowds are quiet, some are noisy but safe, and some are explosive and dangerous. What accounts for the ways crowds behave? In ongoing groups, there are norms, roles, and sanctions that set goals and structure conformity. In the absence of social structure, how is conformity to crowd behavior, whether quiet, noisy, or destructive, secured? Three general explanations have been offered to account for the seeming unanimity and conformity of crowd behavior: contagion theory, convergence theory, and emergent-norm theory.

Contagion Theory. According to **contagion theory** the crowd situation leads to the development of unanimous and intense feelings and behaviors that are at odds with the usual predispositions of the individual participants (Turner, 1964). This theory attempts to explain only one kind of crowd behavior: the escalating response. It suggests that crowds are moved to extreme and irrational behaviors—lynchings, prison riots, mass suicide, religious frenzy—through a vicious circle of exchange. One person yells an obscenity, another throws a rock, and a third shoots a gun. Finally, the crowd is fired up to an emotional level that its members would not have reached if they had coolly considered the matter on their own. Many contagion theorists believe that this circular stimulation heightens and reinforces antisocial behavior, stripping away the effects of socialization so that crowd responses become irrational and instinctual (Blumer, 1934; LeBon, 1896).

Convergence Theory. Whereas contagion theory argues that the crowd situation leads to escalating extremism among otherwise conforming in-

> **Contagion theory** suggests that the crowd situation leads to the development of unanimous and intense feeling and behavior that are at odds with the usual dispositions of the individual participants.

Table 19.1 Types of Crowds

TYPE OF CROWD	TYPICAL TRIGGERING EVENT FOR CROWD BEHAVIOR
Rampage or riot	Response to smoldering discontent, triggered by minor incident or pretext (example: modern race riot)
Looting	Temporary incapacity of law enforcement (example: looting following hurricane)
Mob	Inflammatory incident; perceived injustice (example: lynch mob)
Demonstration	Grievance of middle or working class (example: protest of school closing)
Panic	Fear (example: fighting over last lifeboat)
Spectator	Interesting, nonroutine event (example: a sidewalk preacher)

SOURCE: The first four of these crowd types are identified by Banfield, 1974.

Convergence theory contends that the cause or pretext for crowd action selectively draws persons who share a common set of predispositions.

dividuals, **convergence theory** attempts to explain quiet as well as rowdy crowds. It contends that the cause, or triggering event, for crowd action selectively draws people who share a common set of predispositions. For example, street riots draw unattached, alienated, and angry young men. The convergence of many like-minded people provides the critical mass for their predispositions to be put into action. Similarly, crowds triggered by a sad event (such as the crowds who mourned John Lennon's death) draw people who share another set of predispositions. According to convergence theory, there is no process within crowds; nothing new develops. Rather the crowd represents a convergence of like-minded individuals. Thus the lynch mob is not a group of well-meaning citizens whipped up into a frenzy by circular stimulation; it is instead a collection of racist killers.

The major criticism of convergence theory is that it ignores the heterogeneity of most crowds. Crowds generally contain many different kinds of people; they are drawn by different motives, and they exhibit different levels of involvement. Some are spectators and some are leaders; some are eager participants and some are confused passersby. Convergence theory does not explain the processes whereby such a heterogeneous group arrives at apparently unanimous acts; nor does it explain how peaceful demonstrations occasionally turn into violent scenes of looting and destruction.

Emergent-norm theory suggests that a crowd is governed by norms that are developed and validated by group processes within the crowd.

Emergent-Norm Theory.   These dilemmas are addressed by **emergent-norm theory**, which suggests that each crowd is governed by norms developed and validated by group processes within the crowd (Turner & Killian, 1972). The theory, which has its roots in small-group research (see chapter 6), sees the crowd situation as roughly similar to the situation that occurs when a group of strangers are put into a laboratory and given

Figure 19.1

Looting is a form of collective action that takes place when some unusual event has broken down the barriers which normally ensure conformity. This may be when a demonstration or other protest gets out of hand or it may be when an event such as a blackout reduces the ability of civil authorities to maintain order. Looting is a short-lived, disorganized activity; it may draw in people from all social classes and walks of life. Contagion, emergent norm, or convergence theory may all be used to explain looting.

an ambiguous task to perform. A variety of roles emerge—leader, follower, suggestion maker—and, through interpersonal exchange processes, some consensus is reached in terms of goals and strategies. As with the subject in Asch's experiment who didn't want to disagree publicly about which line was longest (see chapter 6), many crowd members will conform without actually being convinced.

Crowds are both larger and less structured than the small-group laboratory, but observation shows that social processes at work in them produce their definitive character. Occasionally, these processes may resemble contagion. An essential aspect of the emergent-norm perspective, however, is that the unruly crowd, far from representing a stripping away of normative inhibitions, actually develops new norms and internally validates them. That is, the crowd develops a shared conviction that looting, lynching, or whatever is appropriate behavior in the situation. Usually, this conviction is rationalized by reference to generally shared values and symbols. Emergent-norm theory is broader than either contagion theory or convergence theory. It is applicable to both quiet and unruly crowds, and it points to the process by which strangers come to act as a group.

The normative content of crowd behavior is most apparent when we look at crowd behavior cross-culturally or over time. Even violent crowds tend to differ systematically from culture to culture and region to region. Like other cultural responses, crowd behavior is patterned. Whether mob violence is directed at Jews, women, blacks, Catholics, or other groups depends on cultural norms. Prior to 1943, race riots in the United States almost always consisted of whites rampaging through black neighborhoods, looting, burning, and killing. After World War II, race riots changed direction; blacks rampaged, and whites were often the targets.

The form of crowd behavior also changes over time. The witch-hunt and the lynch mob have almost disappeared as forms of collective action; the demonstration and the sit-in, however, have gained in popularity. The fact that certain crowd behaviors remain characteristic of specific times and places suggests that each society has a repertoire of crowd behaviors from which to choose (Tilly, 1979). This repertoire represents patterned responses to recurrent situations rather than any spontaneous or instinctive aspect of human nature.

CONCEPT SUMMARY

A Comparison of Theories about Crowd Behavior

	CONTAGION THEORY	CONVERGENCE THEORY	EMERGENT-NORM THEORY
BASIC ASSUMPTIONS	Through circular stimulation and reinforcement, irrational and extreme acts develop	Crowds are characterized by like-minded people drawn together by common interest	New norms emerge during crowd interaction and validate group actions
EVALUATION	Explains only the escalating response	Ignores the heterogeneity of most crowds; assumes that crowds cause no change in individual behavior	Explains quiet crowds as well as the escalating response

Three Case Studies of Nonroutine Collective Action

Theory is useful to the extent that it provides an understanding of past events and helps predict future ones. One way to evaluate the theories and typologies of collective action is to test them against concrete experience. Three very different types of crowds—the spectator crowd, the riot, and the mob—will now be analyzed using these perspectives.

The 1983 Rape Spectator Crowd.   In March 1983, a woman was repeatedly raped in a New Bedford, Massachusetts, tavern while the bartender and at least 15 male customers watched. None came to her aid or called the police; some cheered.("Tavern rape," 1983).

The 21-year-old mother of two had entered the bar to buy cigarettes, but stayed for a drink when she met a woman she knew there. After her friend left, a man seized her, stripped off her clothing, and raped her on the barroom floor. Two other men then forced her to perform oral sex. In spite of her cries for help, no one interfered as several men lifted her onto the pool table and raped her repeatedly. Many members of the audience cheered and clapped. One man reportedly hollered, "Knock it off—this is getting out of hand," but to no avail. Others later reported that they were too frightened to call for help. Finally, the woman escaped. Four men between the ages of 22 and 26 were convicted of aggravated rape ("Gang rape," 1984:38).

This is an example of a spectator crowd. A collection of people are turned into an interactive crowd by their observance of a nonroutine event. If contagion theory is correct, we would expect the members of the crowd to be characterized by substantial unanimity and intensity in their atti-

Figure 19.2

In 1930, these two black men were lynched by a mob in Marion, Indiana "by parties unknown." Between 1890 and 1930, there were over 1000 lynchings in the United States. Most of these were in the South, where 90 percent of those lynched were black. Although lynching is often attributed to contagion that drives people to act differently than their better natures, it is possible to see the common racial pattern of lynchings as evidence of shared values: racism. The same argument can be used to describe the witch hunts of the middle ages.

tudes and by everybody getting carried away and acting in ways that violated their usual values and afterwards left them ashamed and repelled. If convergence theory is correct, we would also expect to find substantial unanimity and intensity in the crowd. In this case however, we would expect these men to share general beliefs that justified the rape to them (for example, that women who go into bars alone deserve what they get) and to regret only that they were caught. Because there is no evidence that news of the incidence caused such people to flock to the scene, convergence theory would have to assume that this bar's usual patrons were men of this character. If emergent-norm theory is correct, we would expect diversity among the spectators—some eager and amused, some embarrassed, and some appalled. We would also expect to find a great deal of discussion and questioning among the spectators, who would be trying to find some definition of the situation that would justify or normalize their passive participation.

Because no insightful social scientist was at the scene and because a great deal of contradictory evidence was presented during the subsequent legal proceedings, no conclusive answer about the validity of the three theories is possible. Both contagion theory and convergence theory have some plausibility. This antisocial crowd behavior is exactly the type that contagion theory purports to explain. It is also feasible, however, that the men who hung out in this notoriously tough bar represented a convergence of violently inclined sexists who needed little stimulation, circular or otherwise, to put their predispositions into practice. Emergent-norm theory provides a compelling explanation of the process by which the men defined it as appropriate to put this possibly shared, but deviant, feeling into operation at this time and this place and why some who disagreed nevertheless did not intervene. The inaction of the anxious witnesses can be explained by the usual motives by which people seek to conform to the group's norm rather than strike out on their own against the group.

The 1967 Newark Race Riot.   Racial tension in Newark, New Jersey, smoldered with increasing intensity throughout the early 1960s. Between 1960 and 1966, the city went from 65 percent white to 35 percent white; tax revenues sagged, schools were on double shifts, and poverty and discontent were rampant. In the summer of 1967, two issues heightened the tension. The first was the city's choice of secretary to the board of education. The black community's preference was for a black accountant with a master's degree; the mayor's candidate was a white man who had never attended college. Because over 70 percent of the students in the public school system were black and because of their candidate's higher educational achievement, the black community believed that the appointment of the white would be a major injustice. The second and related issue was an attempt by the city planning commission to clear 150 square blocks of black housing in the central ward for urban renewal. The black community was opposed to the plan, seeing it as a political move designed to break up black neighborhoods and dilute black voting power.

Tension escalated throughout the summer, exacerbated by intense media coverage of race riots in other cities. On July 12, the triggering event occurred. A black cab driver was taken to jail for tailgating and harassing patrol cars. Residents of the high-rise housing project overlooking the police station saw the man being dragged into the station, and soon the story had spread that he had been beaten and was near death. Residents of the high-rise formed a crowd outside the police station. Black leaders tried to channel the crowd into a peaceful march to city hall, but the march disintegrated when children began throwing rocks at the demonstrators and some demonstrators started throwing rocks back. Soon the rocks were aimed at police and at storefronts. A little looting and vandalism took place that night, but things were quiet by morning.

During the next 24 hours, inflammatory rumors circulated throughout the central ward, and a demonstration was scheduled for that evening. Again, rocks and other missiles thrown by isolated individuals caused both the police and the crowd to become violent and disorderly. The ensuing riot ebbed and flowed for several days. As it became clear that police had merely cordoned off the neighborhood rather than entering it, many residents were drawn into general looting. The next few days saw escalating responses as the police and the national guard tried to enter the central ward to restore order. Neither the police nor the national guard were trained to face such a situation, and their actions served to escalate rather than suppress the civil disobedience. For example, at 3:30 p.m. on July 14, three carloads of police officers opened fire on a group of looters. bullets sprayed into nearby apartments, and one bullet struck a 3-year old girl. She survived, but she lost an eye and her hearing. In similar incidents, the national guard and police opened fire on looters and spectators alike, frightening and angering the black community. When the police and national guard were withdrawn on July 17, the riot was over (National Advisory Commission on Civil Disorders, 1968).

This seems like a classic case of contagion on the part of both the rioters and the armed authorities. As rumor followed rumor and as rock throwing escalated into shooting and violence, both sides progressed far past their usual predispositions. The guardsmen were young and generally inexperienced; they had received no training for riot work. A firecracker was mistaken for a sniper's bullet, a volley of rifle fire was directed at the source of the noise, and the conflict thus escalated past what either side considered reasonable. Contagion certainly existed, but contagion theory is inadequate to describe fully the course of the riot. Frenzy and irrationality can explain neither the shifts in tempo and mood during the 5-day riot nor the fact that most of the action took place during evenings and weekends, when people were finished with their regular jobs. Such scheduling hardly indicates frenzy.

Emergent-norm theory, however, helps explain how the black community first defined the riot as a protest and then redefined it as a white attack; it also helps explain why the police and national guard defined themselves as being in an us-against-them confrontation with a dangerous and hostile enemy. These definitions of the situation emerged during the course of the riot and helped guide the responses of participants.

The Fourteenth Century Mob: Witch-Hunts.   Between 1300 and 1650, Europe was obsessed with hunting witches. During these centuries, an estimated 200,000 to 500,000 "witches," 85 percent of them women, were killed. Observers reported that "Germany was almost entirely occupied in building bonfires. . . . Switzerland had to wipe out whole villages in order to keep (witches) down. Travellers in Lorraine may see thousands and thousands of stakes" (Trevor-Roper, cited in Ben-Yehuda, 1980). The victims were burned, drowned, beheaded, or strangled. Burning with green wood was recommended for the grossly impenitent, and torture was explicitly advocated by the Roman Catholic church to extract confessions. At first, the victims were old and single women; but at the height of the witch-hunting craze, women of all ages, married or unmarried, were suspect.

Witch-hunting is a bizarre chapter in European history. (It is a much smaller, but still bizarre, chapter in North American history; fewer than a dozen "witches" are thought to have been put to death in North America.) Why did it occur when it did, and why did it subsequently die out? Why was the most virulent form of witch-hunting confined largely to France, Germany, and Switzerland? Why were women the chief victims? Whatever else it was, witch-hunting was hardly a random pattern of mob violence. It was a classic situation of a normatively shared target and a normatively shared strategy.

Late medieval society was rocked by the rumblings of massive change. Urbanization, world exploration and the discovery of extraordinary and

Figure 19.3
The demonstration or protest is one form of collective action. It occurs when large numbers of people are drawn together to protest some injustice. This may be a draft law, new taxes, school closings, or, in this case, the downing of a Korean jetliner in 1983 by the Soviets. The distinctive feature of this form of collective action is that it is not part of any larger movement designed to bring about social change; it is a relatively spontaneous and short-lived demonstration of public sentiment.

alien cultures, the collapse of the rural feudal order, and the beginnings of science and humanism were exciting events that were breaking down the old order and fostering a belief in the possibilities of almost limitless change and variety. Shadowing all of these events was the Black Death—the plague that killed one-third of Europe (chapter 17). The church itself was splintered by the Reformation.

How were these strange and apparently uncontrollable events to be explained? The answer was found in the activities of a negative supernatural power—the devil and his agents. Rather than blaming the church or other social institutions, people blamed the societal crisis on imaginary demons. Such demons were always part of the Christian religion (Exodus 22:10: "Thou shalt not suffer a witch to live"), but a minor part. In the late medieval period, this developed into the belief that Satan and his handmaidens were actively trying to gain control of the earth.

The witch-hunt served at least two functions. It provided a seeming explanation of the chaos of the late medieval period, and it suggested a way in which people could do something about it. It is an example of blatant scapegoating, where the frustrations of a changing and troubled society are taken out on a vulnerable subordinate group (Ben-Yehuda, 1980).

Summary

Collective action is, by definition, nonroutine and irregular. As the examples just given demonstrate, however, it is also related to the institutional patterns of society. The norms, frustrations, and values of society help determine when and where outbreaks of collective action will occur.

Rumor and the Mass Media

Rumor

Rumor is unauthenticated information spread by word of mouth.

One of the most important processes of crowd behavior is the dissemination of information and the collective definition that arises from it. The chief instrument of such collective information is **rumor**—unauthenticated information spread by word of mouth. Rumor thrives on ambiguous situations where it is impossible or difficult to get authorized news but where people are keenly interested in knowing what is going on (Shibutani, 1966).

In crowds, the flow of information generally begins by everyone asking a neighbor, "What's going on?" Occasionally, somebody really does know what is going on and the response may spread more or less accurately through the crowd. More often, one person, the so-called keynoter, will offer an explanation that is readily acceptable—usually because it lines up with previous conditions and beliefs. The keynoter's suggestion or speculation may then set the tone for further discussion and ultimate consensus. In other crowds, rumoring may be more equivalent to verbal milling about, where a variety of unconfirmed speculations are tossed around. Until there is some consensus, however, the crowd is unlikely to act; verbal milling about will be accompanied by physical milling about.

Only after consensus has been reached on the meaning of the situation will there be collective action.

Rumors and those who spread them often have a negative image. False rumors can cause unnecessary trouble, and even true rumors can lead to trouble. For example, as a ship is sinking, the rumor that there are not enough lifeboats for all the passengers may lead to unnecessary panic and loss of life; a rumor of bank insolvency can cause massive withdrawals that will destroy an otherwise healthy bank. Studies of the major race riots of the late 1960s found that the spread of false rumors (in Newark, these rumors included the story that the police had beaten the taxi driver and a story that a sniper was firing at the national guard) was a major factor in the explosion of violence (National Advisory Commission on Civil Disorders, 1968).

The Rumor Process. A great deal of research has focused on how the content of a rumor changes as the rumor passes through a population. Three general processes have been noted: sharpening, leveling, and assimilation. Sharpening and leveling are parallel processes; some details are sharpened in succeeding versions, and others are leveled. Basically, the story becomes shorter and less detailed. Empirical studies show that two or three points are usually sharpened and that details are dropped quickly. Assimilation is a process of distortion in which the story is altered to make it fit better with the beliefs of the teller. Details are filled in (that is, made up) so the story hangs together better or fits more comfortably with preconceived notions and stereotypes. For example, whites describing a poorly seen struggle between a black man and a white man are likely to describe the black man as the assailant; blacks are likely to describe the white man as the assailant. The assimilation process is often an unconscious attempt to make the story more coherent rather than a deliberate attempt to mislead.

The Mass Media

The old-fashioned rumor has not been replaced by the mass media, but the media do provide a faster (and not always more accurate) rumoring process that can be vital in creating and sustaining collective behavior. Mobs, demonstrations, riots, and movements owe a great deal to the media's dissemination of information.

Publics. A mass media audience, or **public**, differs from a crowd in two ways: (1) the public is dispersed whereas the crowd is physically concentrated, and (2) division of opinion is expected from the public, whereas at least the appearance of consensus is expected from the crowd. Nevertheless, the public can be a vital force in collective action. Crowd processes can occur even among people not in close physical proximity. Rumors can fly, keynoters can note, and consensus can be formed in living rooms and offices all across the city and nation as well as in a compact group.

In such dispersed settings it is less likely that contagion will catch hold, but it is possible to inform and capture the public interest very swiftly. For example, it is estimated that 95 percent of the people in the United

A **public** is a dispersed group of people interested in and divided about an issue.

States knew of President Kennedy's assassination within 2 hours of its occurrence. Had there been any action required, a huge population could have been quickly mobilized. Similarly, an inflammatory incident can now spark demonstrations all across the country, not just in the community where it occurred. Norms about appropriate response can emerge in a dispersed public as well as in a crowd.

The Mass Media and Collective Action. The mass media contribute to nonroutine collective action in three ways: (1) by publicizing the triggering event, (2) by demonstrating collective action techniques, and (3) by providing rationales for collective action.

PUBLICIZING EVENTS. Obviously, the media provide an important means of quickly spreading the news. If a policeman shoots a minority youth, if a plane crashes in the Potomac, or if someone holds the Washington Monument hostage, then it will be on radio and television within minutes and in the newspapers within hours. The media reach the isolated as well as the integrated, the passive as well as the active. Thus the mass media publicize triggering events faster and more thoroughly than rumor can.

DEMONSTRATING TECHNIQUES. As Tilly (1979) has noted, each culture has a repertoire of possible collective actions. One of the ways this repertoire is now learned is by watching the evening news. Publicity surrounding one sit-in, riot, or crowd may stimulate a rash of similar events in other communities.

PROVIDING RATIONALES. Nonroutine collective actions are typically spontaneous reactions to nonroutine events. Although norms may emerge to justify the actions, they are not well thought out. Many would not stand

Figure 19.4
The mass media have partially replaced rumor as a source of information about collective action. When a shooting incident takes place in one block, news may spread by rumor throughout the neighborhood. As soon as the media picks up the news, however, newsbreaks on television and radio will spread news of the incident throughout the city and soon throughout the nation. In this way, the news media increase the impact of collective action. They also spread knowledge of inflammatory incidents and of possible strategies of collective action.

up under careful consideration at a later time. The media's attempt to explain events to the public may provide better-developed rationales. In the late 1960s, for example, both black and white leaders were widely publicized as saying that the root causes of civil disorder were poverty, discrimination, and injustice. These well-intentioned statements designed to raise the public's consciousness about poverty and racism may also have made rioting appear normal, reasonable, and even expected under the circumstances.

Social Movements

Defining Social Movements

Crowds, mobs, and riots are nonroutine collective actions. Although the same collective acts (for example, witch-hunts or riots) may recur frequently, they are not the result of ongoing organizations pursuing specific ends; therefore, they are not social movements—organized attempts to change social structure or ideology that are carried on outside legitimate channels or that use these channels in innovative ways (Ash, 1972). The antinuclear movement, the environmental movement, and the civil rights movement are ongoing efforts that have stepped outside the usual legislative process in their attempts to challenge the status quo. What makes such movements arise? Why do people step outside their usual social roles and attempt to change the world?

Theories of Social Movements

Smelser's Theory. In 1962, Neil Smelser presented a list of six conditions that he argued were necessary for the emergence of a social movement. He suggested that, taken together, the presence of all six conditions is sufficient to create a social movement. The conditions are

1. *A conducive social structure.* According to Smelser, a social structure must meet two conditions before a social movement develops. The structure must be complex and differentiated enough to produce sustained divergence of interests, and it must be less than completely authoritarian. In a completely authoritarian society, divergent opinions would not be tolerated. Revolution might be possible in such a society, but not reform. The more authoritarian the regime, the more limited the forms of social movement.

2. *Structural strain.* For a social movement to develop, there must be a strain in the structure of society. Classical Marxist scholars insist that this source of strain is in the relations of production. Another source of strain, however, is rapid change in any aspect of society—for example, natural disaster, mass immigration, or loss of status. Whenever there are conflicts, deprivations, ambiguities, and discrepancies in the social order, a social movement is possible (G. Marx & Wood, 1975).

3. *General belief about the source of strain.* A set of beliefs that defines the stressful situation as unjust and that identifies the cause of the problem must develop. There are strains in all societies; certainly, inequality and

poverty seem to be universal. Only when poverty comes to be defined as illegitimate and as caused by, say, capitalism or drinking or overpopulation or racism will it become the focus of a social movement. Poverty, discrimination, and disaster by themselves are not sufficient to create a social movement. Many people date the current feminist movement in the United States to the publication of Betty Friedan's book *The Feminine Mystique* and the ecology movement to Rachel Carson's *Silent Spring*. These books served as consciousness-raisers that led to redefining some familiar conditions as unjust.

4. *Precipitating factor.* A social movement needs a triggering event. Such an event may give substance and urgency to an already defined problem, or it may serve as the catalyst for defining a situation as problematic. In the early civil rights movement, one such catalyst was the ejection of a middle-aged black cleaning woman from a Montgomery, Alabama, bus. Rosa Parks was on her way home from work and was just too tired to go to the back of the bus the way she had done every other day. She was ejected from the bus, a group of church leaders met to discuss the event, and the civil rights movement was launched.

5. *Mobilization.* A social movement requires that a group not only hold common beliefs but also act on them. Thus a social movement does not arise until people commit their time and goods to see that action takes place. Demonstrations must be held, lobbyists hired, committees formed, letters written, and newsletters sent out. All these activities require the mobilization of time and money. Without these resources, a set of beliefs will go nowhere, regardless of the rightness of the cause of the strength of the sentiment.

6. *Ineffective opposition.* All social movements are designed to challenge the status quo; they are deliberate attempts to change the social structure. Thus they always generate opposition. The character of this opposition— its strength, timing, and consistency—will affect whether a social move-

Figure 19.5

Mass demonstrations such as this June, 1982 protest at Indian Pt., New York serve to gain publicity for social movements and to re-invigorate rank-and-file members. The real work of most social movements, however, goes on in committee meetings, at fundraisers, and other methodical tasks designed to mobilize resources and influence public opinion.

ment forms and whether it is successful. Opposition to a social movement can come either from the elite or from a countermovement (examples of the latter include the anti-ERA and antiabortion movements). Opposition can interrupt the development of a social movement during any of the previous five steps. For example, the opposition can quash publicity about possible triggering events or forbid gatherings and other forms of mobilization. Simply specifying the organizations to which donations are tax-deductible is a mild method by which government elites attempt to control social movements. In some cases of overreactive or inconsistent opposition, the opposition can spur rather than retard mobilization. For example, the violent response of British military authorities to Gandhi's nonviolent tactics was a key to mobilizing support for India's independence.

Smelser's theory of social movements provides a useful description of the process through which such movements develop. It does not, however, describe the conditions under which people will define a condition of strain to be illegitimate or the conditions that will lead to mobilization. These issues are addressed by relative-deprivation theory and mobilization theory. **Relative-deprivation theory** stresses the role of social disorganization and discontent in encouraging social movements. **Mobilization theory** stresses the competing interests of organized groups as the crucial factor in movement formation.

Relative-deprivation theory stresses the role of social disorganization and discontent in encouraging social movements. Also known as breakdown theory.

Mobilization theory suggests that social movements arise when competition develops among organized groups. Also known as solidarity theory.

Relative-Deprivation Theory.   Poverty and injustice are universal phenomena. Why is it that they so seldom lead to social movements? According to relative-deprivation theorists, deprivation leads to social movements only when it is defined as illegitmate. This definition can be reached by comparing one's own condition to that of some other reference group or to expectations based on past experience. It refers to deprivation relative to other groups or other times rather than to absolute deprivation; hence the label *relative-deprivation theory.*

Figure 19.6 diagrams three conditions for which relative-deprivation theory would predict the development of a social movement. In Condition A, disaster or taxation suddenly reduces the absolute level of living. If there is no parallel drop in what people rightfully expect, then they will feel that their deprivation is illegitimate. In Condition B, both expectations and real standard of living are improving, but expectations continue to rise even after the standard of living has leveled off. Consequently, people

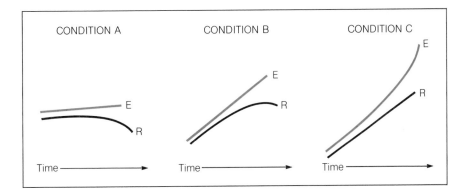

Figure 19.6 The Gap between Expectations and Reality
Relative-deprivation theory suggests that whenever there is a gap between expectations (E) and real standard of living (R), relative deprivation is created. It may occur when conditions are stable or improving as well as when the real standard of living is declining.

feel deprived relative to what they had anticipated. Finally, in Condition C, expectations rise faster than the standard of living, again creating a gap between reality and expectations. Relative-deprivation theory has the merit of providing a plausible explanation of the fact that many social movements occur in times when objective conditions either are improving (Condition C) or are at least a major improvement over the past (Condition B).

Because people may feel relatively deprived whether conditions are declining, stable, or even improving, the key to social movements is expectations. According to deprivation theorists, unmet expectations are most likely to emerge when rapid social change disorganizes and disrupts traditional solidarities (Gurr, 1970; Piven & Cloward, 1977). Discontent occurs when rapid change breaks down traditional social structures that have defined the inequality as natural. For example, unequal wages for women and men came to be seen as unjust when paid employment ceased to be a temporary, premarital activity for women and became a major female role. Because relative-deprivation theory relies ultimately on the disorganizing effects of social change, it is often referred to as *breakdown theory.*

CRITICISMS OF RELATIVE-DEPRIVATION THEORY.   There are two major criticisms of relative-deprivation theory. First, the theory is basically an individualistic and psychological explanation. It asserts that individuals become discontented and thus available for mobilization into a social movement. This assertion implies that members of social movements will be not only homogeneous but also malcontents. These implications are not borne out in empirical studies of social-movement membership, however. This individualistic theory also does not explain how individuals come together to work collectively on common goals. Second, the theory fails to specify the conditions under which relative deprivation will lead to social movements. It does not, for example, specify why some, but not all, white ethnic groups mobilized in response to perceived deprivation relative to nonwhite minority groups (chapter 9). Empirical studies suggest that relative deprivation by itself is not a good predictor of the development of social movements (Gurney & Tierney, 1982).

Mobilization Theory.   According to mobilization theory, the key to the formation of a social movement is the existence of organized groups. This theory argues that relative deprivation and other strains are universal and thus relatively unimportant as predictors of social movements (Oberschall, 1973). Solidarity, rather than disorganization, is the key to the formation of social movements.

In mobilization theory, the organized group is argued to be the precondition of a social movement. The most effective social movements emerge from groups that share two characteristics: relative homogeneity and many overlapping ties (Tilly, 1978:63). An implication of this theory is that a black civil rights group that admitted whites would be less effective than one consisting only of blacks; similarly, a women's rights organization with male members would have a reduced capacity for action. Groups will be stronger if, in addition to homogeneity, their members share a strong network of ties—if they belong to the same clubs and organizations, if they work together, if they live in the same neighborhood.

In addition to a group of people ready to act, a social movement also needs resources. Mobilization is "the process by which a unit gains significantly in the control of assets it previously did not control" (Etzioni, 1968:388). These assets may be weapons, technologies, goods, money, or loyalties and obligations. The resources available to a social movement depend on two factors: the amount of resources controlled by group members and the proportion of their resources that the members are willing to commit to the movement. Thus mobilization can proceed by increasing the size of the membership, increasing the proportion of assets that members are willing to give to the group, or by recruiting richer members.

In mobilization theory, the coincidence of an organized group with the mobilization of many resources will lead to a social movement. The theory assumes that strains and stresses that provide the issues for social movements are permanent and recurring (Oberschall, 1973) and that group solidarity, not disorganization and discontent, is the crucial factor.

Mobilization theory is often referred to as *solidarity theory* because it suggests that the building blocks of social movements are organized groups, not alienated, discontented individuals. Empirical analysis indicates that this is a generally valid picture of how a number of social movements, especially reform movements, operate. Movement members are integrated members of the community, often belonging to many community organizations and groups. Studies of social-movement organizations (SMOs) show that effective organizations often take advantage of this characteristic through **bloc mobilization**—a process by which the SMO recruits other organizations to support its cause rather than recruiting single individuals. One of the more effective civil rights organizations, the National Association for the Advancement of Colored People (NAACP), built its organization by working through black churches. The Communist party, in contrast, tried to recruit individual disaffected and alienated blacks and was singularly ineffective.

People who are not integrated into the community respond to strain either through apathy and withdrawal or, if they happen to be young, male, and lower class, through rioting. Social movements, however, are essentially group rather than individual phenomena.

An Integration. Relative-deprivation theory focuses on the role of strain and discontent in rousing individuals to participate in social movements. Mobilization theory focuses on group solidarity in providing an organization for a social movement. (See Figure 19.8 for a comparison of the two theories.) In a study of the Boston antibusing movement, Useem (1980, 1981) provides an integration of these two theories.

Useem found that people who supported or participated in the antibusing movement did feel relatively deprived. Much more than the nonsupporters, supporters tended to believe that blacks had been making faster economic and social progress than whites and that blacks were being given unfair advantages. In short, they felt deprived relative to blacks. Useem also found, however, that participants in and supporters of the

Figure 19.7
Social movements tend to attract people who are already participating in their communities—people who vote, who belong to voluntary associations, who are relatively well educated and well off. The sustained and methodical attempt to reform and change social structure is seldom attractive to the angry and the alienated. For that reason, many social movements grow through bloc mobilization: they recruit people who already belong to related social movements. The many bumper stickers on this automobile reflect the tendency for many social movements to share the same membership.

Bloc mobilization is the process whereby social-movement organizations recruit other organizations to support their cause rather than trying to recruit single individuals.

**Figure 19.8 A Comparison of
Deprivation/Breakdown Models with
Mobilization/Solidarity Models**
SOURCE: Adapted from Useem, 1980.

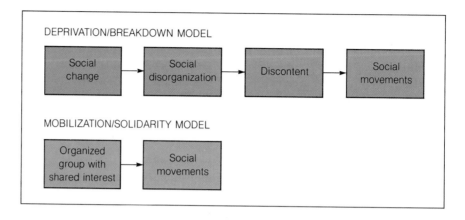

antibusing movement were more integrated into the community than
nonsupporters were. Supporters had greater attachment to and integration with their neighborhoods and were more active in secondary organizations.

Useem suggests that group solidarity and relative deprivation are both
essential ingredients in creating a social movement. Relative deprivation
without solidarity is likely to lead to apathy or withdrawal; solidarity
without a grievance leads to expressive voluntary organizations rather than
to social movements. Useem suggests that only when relative deprivation
is defined as a group phenomenon (our group is deprived relative to their
group) is it likely to result in a social movement. Thus solidarity of both
the challenging and the challenged group contributes to the likelihood
that relative deprivation will be defined in political terms.

Countermovements

A **countermovement** seeks to resist
or reverse the change advocated by a
social movement; it is a defender of
the status quo.

A major and growing category of social movements is the **countermovement,** which seeks to reverse or resist change advocated by a social movement (Lo, 1982; Mottl, 1980). Countermovements are almost always right-
wing in orientation. They seek to maintain traditional structures of status,
power, and values.

Mobilization theory is particularly appropriate for understanding countermovements. Because they defend the status quo, they are often closely
tied to vested-interest groups (Lo, 1982; Mottl, 1980), and bloc mobilization
is a chief means of recruiting members and resources. For example, the
Boston antibusing movement made heavy use of existing PTAs, and the
antiabortion movement has relied strongly on the preexisting organization
and networks of the Catholic church.

Social-Movement Organizations

It is essential to distinguish social-movement organizations from social
movements. A social movement is generally a loose coalition with a general
goal. Within a broad social movement, it is likely that several competing
SMOs will exist. The existence of these competing groups may be func-

Figure 19.9
When a social movement seems potentially successful and large enough to challenge established groups, a countermovement may develop. A countermovement attempts to preserve the status quo by rallying opposition to the social movement and perhaps rolling back reforms or changes instituted by the social movement. The anti-abortion movement did not emerge as a powerful countermovement until after the pro-abortion movement had achieved substantial success in 1973.

tional for the social movement, providing avenues of participation for people with a variety of styles and goals.

Within the feminist movement, for example, there are basically two types of SMOs. The first type is the formal organization, which is made up largely of middle-class and professional women and which seeks to effect legislative reforms in affirmative action, economic opportunity, and other specific areas. An example is the National Organization for Women (NOW). At the other end of the continuum are hundreds of consciousness-raising groups and support groups. Some of them seek to overthrow the entire patriarchal social structure; others seek merely to help individual women restructure their own values and roles. This wide disparity in SMOs makes it likely that anybody who is vaguely committed to the feminist movement can find an organization to work in. A similar diversity of organizations exists in the civil rights movement and the environmentalist movement.

Revolutionary Social-Movement Organizations. The form taken by SMOs depends on a movement's goals. Movements that seek total transformation, either of society or of individuals, usually exhibit two characteristics: (1) isolation of members from conventional social contacts by the withdrawal of members from the usual networks of family, friends, and coworkers, and (2) charismatic leadership and the reduction of most members to discipleship status (Bromley & Schupe, 1980). These characteristics are most obvious in the case of religious movements, such as the Unification Church (the Moonies) and the People's Temple, but they also occur in dedicated revolutionary groups. They help foster an undiluted radical dedication, encourage high commitment of resources to the organization, and maintain the secrecy of the organization.

Reform Social-Movement Organizations. Movements seeking only partial reforms tend to have very different social structures. They allow and even encourage their members to participate in other groups, and their leaders have much more limited authority over followers. As befits groups that want only to tinker with the status quo, not destroy it, SMOs representing reform movements are usually run very similarly to establishment organizations and require only a partial commitment from their members.

A Case Study: The Gay Rights Movement

In recent Western thought, homosexuality has been considered a sin or a sickness. As a result, it has often been furtive and concealed. There is now an active social movement to change this situation. Like many social movements, it is diverse and fragmented, replete with competing SMOs and even a countermovement.

History of the Gay Rights Movement. Homosexual acts are illegal in most states. Homosexuals are barred from service in the military and are dishonorably discharged if discovered, they are often barred from teaching in public schools, and they may be denied custody of their children and, in some cases, even visiting rights. Until a few years ago, they were barred from employment in the federal civil service and from immigration to the United States. In addition, they suffer social ostracism. They are often shunned by their family and coworkers, forced out of their jobs, and subjected to taunts and jeers.

As a result, most homosexuals have concealed their sexual preference. As long as they did so, there could be no social movement. For a movement to exist, there must be a group of people who acknowledge to themselves and to one another that they are members of the same group and share a common interest.

The beginning of the gay rights movement came when sufficient numbers of prominent individuals were willing to step forward and define themselves as homosexuals. This development began in Germany at the end of the 19th century. It was abruptly halted by Hitler, however, who included homosexuals among the undesirables of the world and who sent known homosexuals to concentration camps. In the United States, the gay rights movement began in the 1920s, when the Society for Human Rights was established to "protect the rights of people who by reasons of mental and physical abnormalities are abused and hindered in the legal pursuit of the happiness which is guaranteed by the Declaration of Independence" (cited in Altman, 1983:133). The organizers were quickly driven back into the closet by a police raid, and it was not until after World War II that the two founding SMOs of the gay rights movement—the Mattachine Society for male homosexuals and the Daughters of Bilitis for female homosexuals—were founded.

The early gay rights movement, as indicated in the preceding quote, seemed to accept society's view of its members as handicapped and abnormal. During the 1960s and 1970s, this view changed radically. Gay activists began to demand not just tolerance, not just the absence of persecution, but acceptance. They wanted homosexuality to be recognized as a simple variation of sexual orientation—not viewed as sin or sickness.

The Current Movement.　The gay rights movement is not unified. There are splits within it by gender, class, race, and political ideology. Broadly, however, the movement seeks to do four things (Altman, 1983:122):

1. *To define a gay community and a gay identity.* The movement seeks to help gay individuals realize that they are not alone. As C. Wright Mills might have put it, they want homosexuals to recognize that their problems are not merely personal troubles but are shared by others.
2. *To establish the legitimacy of a gay identity.* The movement seeks to reduce the shame, to overcome the internalized self-hatred and doubts of people who have been socialized to believe that they were wicked and sick.
3. *To achieve civil rights for homosexuals.* The movement seeks to decriminalize homosexual acts and to establish antidiscrimination laws to protect homosexuals.
4. *To challenge the general ascription of sex roles in society.* The movement seeks to give people the right to choose roles rather than being forced to act out a role thrust on them by reason of their gender.

Conflict within the Movement.　There are several major schisms within the gay rights movement. The most important is that between men and women. Homosexual men (gays) and women (lesbians) have some goals in common—in particular, civil rights goals. However, lesbians face a situation of double jeopardy. They may be discriminated against on the basis of gender as well as sexual preference. Lesbian women often believe that they will make more progress working with straight women than with gay men; they believe that improvements in the status of women (especially in economic terms) will be more beneficial than will general improvements for homosexuals. Furthermore, gay men can be as patriarchal as straight men, and lesbian women have even less interest than straight women in

Figure 19.10
Public demonstrations by the Gay Rights Movement are designed to bring homosexuality out of the closet, to make it seem a less deviant and dangerous practice. By publicly acknowledging their sexual preference, men such as the ones in this parade, force society to acknowledge that there are relatively large numbers of people—many of them apparently normal and decent people—who are homosexuals. Thus, the public demonstration is a particularly important weapon in the social movement for homosexual rights.

being in male-dominated organizations. As a result, there is relatively little cooperation among male and female homosexual groups.

A second schism is of class and politics. On the one side are the middle-class professionals who wear gender-appropriate suits and insist that homosexuals are respectable, decent people—good parents, good credit risks, good neighbors. On the other side are people who insist that gay rights means the freedom to wear lavender and leather and who wish to dismantle the entire system of sex roles and status politics. These are, respectively, the people who want to tinker with the system—to extend the basic rights package just a little further—and the people who think that the whole system is a sham and want to overthrow it.

Successes, Failures, and Prospects.   When a social movement mobilizes sufficiently that its goals begin to look at least possible, a countermovement often arises. In this case, there are several, most of them from the Christian rightwing. The moral majority campaigns vigorously against homosexuality, and many local legislative battles have been fought to reduce the rights of homosexuals—to make it illegal for them to teach in the public schools, for example.

Despite this, the gay rights movement has seen some notable successes. The American Psychological Association voted in 1974 to declare that homosexuality is not a sickness, Wisconsin has passed laws making discrimination on the basis of sexual orientation illegal, acknowledged homosexuals have been elected to public office—not just in California but in Massachusetts and Minnesota—and in offices and families around the country it is becoming possible to be an open homosexual without losing the respect of others. There are still many homes, offices, and neighborhoods, however, where the position of an acknowledged homosexual would be awkward at best. In terms of general community acceptance, the goals of the movement have been only partially reached. The military remains adamantly opposed to homosexuality, and in many states homosexual acts are still a crime.

Recently, the male homosexual community has been galvanized by the spectre of AIDS (acquired immune deficiency syndrome), an apparently incurable blood disease now suffered by an estimated 2,500 people. Although the disease is not confined to homosexuals, 71 percent of the AIDS sufferers are male homosexuals. Many gays see the slow response of government funding for AIDS research as another form of discrimination. This new feeling of injustice as well as fear and anxiety have provided an impetus for organization. AIDS hotlines and information meetings have provided a trigger for homosexual networks that cut across class, race, and political cleavages. By increasing the solidarity of the group, these new networks may increase the effectiveness of the gay rights movement.

The Mass Media and Social Movements

A social movement is a deliberate attempt to create change. To do so, it must reach the public and create the appearance that the public's opinion is on its side. The relationship between the media and social movements is one of mutual need. The movements need publicity, and the media

A Dirty, Filthy Book

The practice of birth control became a trend in 18th century France. Without the aid of any organized social movement, it spread from the urban bourgeoisie to the rural and poorer classes. It was in England and the United States that birth control became an organized social movement. A number of liberal reformers seized on excessive population as the chief cause of poverty and other social problems. These reformers suggested that the use of birth control by the poor would reduce welfare costs and, by decreasing the numbers of the poor, increase the demand for their labor and cause wages to rise.

In this period, a U.S. physician, Charles Knowlton, produced a book entitled *The Fruits of Philosophy: The Private Companion of Young Married People*. In it, he discussed coitus interruptus (withdrawal), but he favored postcoital douching; he stated that he was "quite confident that a liberal use of pretty cold water would be a never-failing preventative" (Himes, 1936:227). (In fact, of course, douching is almost totally ineffective as a contraceptive.)

The advocates of birth control created their first SMO in 1860, with the formation of the Malthusian League. The movement did not take off, however, until 1877, when the British government prosecuted Annie Besant and Charles Bradlaugh for distributing Knowlton's book in England. The charge was distributing obscene material, and the resulting publicity

was exactly what the new movement needed. The trial was widely reported in the only mass media of the day, the newspapers, which included the prosecutor's accusation that "this is a dirty, filthy book, and the test of it is that no human being would allow that book on his table, no decently educated English husband would allow even his wife to have it" (cited in Chandrasekhar, 1981:1). The methods and morals of birth control were given detailed discussion in the popular press, and sales of Knowlton's book went from only 1,000 a year to more than 200,000. In a ground swell of free publicity, Malthusian Leagues were formed in almost every Western nation. Among the reasons produced for using birth control were that it would reduce both the misery and numbers of the poor, make early marriage possible and thus eliminate prostitution, and even lead to world peace. The birth control movement was an idealistic social movement that hoped to improve society by reforming individuals. (In succeeding generations, the Women's Christian Temperance Union—WCTU— sought to achieve the same goals by getting everyone to give up alcohol.)

The first birth control clinic in the United States was opened by Margaret Sanger in 1916. Throughout New York City, she distributed 5,000 leaflets in Yiddish, Italian, and English. They began: "Mothers! Can you afford to have a large family? Do you want any more children? If not, why do you have

them? DO NOT KILL, DO NOT TAKE LIFE, BUT PREVENT." After her clinic had been open 10 days, the police closed it and arrested her on a charge of "maintaining a public nuisance." She was held overnight and released on bail; she immediately reopened the clinic and was rearrested and sentenced to 30 days in jail. After several more convictions, she established the first permanent clinic, in 1923.

The birth control movement challenged many cherished values. It was opposed by physicians on the ground that the practice was injurious to health, by moralists on the ground that it encouraged pleasure-seeking without concern for the consequences, by traditionalists on the ground that it altered women's natural functions, by nationalists on the ground that there would be too few soldiers, and by legal authorities on the ground that it was obscene. The birth control movement was ultimately successful and is now a part of the institutional structure rather than an attacker of it. In fact, the government itself is now the chief provider of contraceptives to the poor.

Questions to Consider

What social movements of our own day can you think of that probably would never have gotten off the ground if not for media attention? Which social movements receive generally positive publicity, and which are given a negative slant?

Figure 19.11

There is a mutual dependency between social movements and the mass media. The media need material; the movement needs free publicity. In this relationship, however, the media has the advantage and movement organizations may call press conferences that no press attend. Often the media focus on a particular movement leader who may be particularly photogenic or articulate. Cesar Chavez has become the media symbol of the Farm Workers Union and the Mexican-American community. Probably few Americans could name a single other figure in this movement.

need material. Sometimes both needs can be met satisfactorily. In this mutual exchange, however, most of the power belongs to the media. The media can affect a social movement's success by giving or withholding publicity and by slanting the story positively or negatively. What the media choose to cover "not only affects the success of the movement, but also shapes its leadership and its meaning to the general public and to its own adherents—in short, what the movement actually is" (Molotch, 1979:81).

One result of the interdependence between social movements and the media is the development of media stars (Gitlin, 1980). The media make the news interesting by personalizing social movements, focusing their coverage on movement leaders who make good copy. The celebrity status of some leaders may be detrimental to the solidarity and success of the movement. Among the consequences of personalized publicity are inflamed rhetoric, greater conflict within the organization, and disproportionate attention to publicity rather than to other movement goals. Of course, if the alternative is no publicity at all, then the elevation of some leaders to star status may be a price the movement has to pay. Without free publicity, the cost to a social movement of spreading its message is greatly increased.

Factors Associated with Movement Success

Empirical analysis of social movements in the United States and around the world suggests that a number of factors are important to the success of a movement or countermovement (G. Marx, 1971):

1. The demands of the movement are seen to be consistent with the broader values of society. For example, the movement seeks to increase freedom or reduce injustice.
2. The movement has the support of influential third parties or can demonstrate that its demands will benefit other groups as well. For example, the abolitionist movement gained the support of the early feminist movement because women believed that extending suffrage to blacks would help women gain suffrage.
3. The movement's demands are concrete and focused. A protest against a specific urban renewal project is more likely to succeed than is a general protest against poor housing.
4. The movement is able to exert pressure directly on the responsible party without harming uninvolved third parties. For example, a fruit boycott that hurts truckers as well as fruit growers will generate more opposition and less support.
5. The movement adopts techniques with which the authorities have had little experience. The nonviolent sit-in had tremendous impact when it was first employed during the early civil rights movement; in 1980, however, hundreds of protestors sitting in at the Seabrook Nuclear Plant were hauled away with little publicity and little effect. The police now know how to deal with the tactic, and the media no longer find it newsworthy.

6. Neutral third parties who have an interest in restoring harmony are present.

7. The movement's demands are negotiable rather than absolute.

8. The movement's demands involve a request for acceptance of social diversity, equal treatment, or inclusion, rather than a fundamental redistribution of income and power.

9. The movement seeks to veto proposed policies rather than implement new ones.

10. The movement is large enough to organize itself for conflict but not so large as to be perceived as a serious threat to the dominant group.

Controlling Collective Behavior

Psychologist Kurt Lewin once said that there is nothing as practical as a good theory. If our theories of collective behavior are any good, we should find that the police and the FBI as well as the radical underground have found them useful guides.

The police are concerned with collective action and social movements. The goal of keeping the public peace and protecting lives and property requires that the police prevent rampages and mob actions; they are likewise obliged to prevent demonstrations from getting out of hand and turning into more violent crowd forms. Less obviously, authorities have been concerned with monitoring and obstructing social movements. Their techniques for controlling collective behavior are based on a sociological understanding of the processes of collective action.

CONTROLLING NONROUTINE COLLECTIVE ACTION

In 1947, a sociologist wrote a riot manual for the Chicago police that is still being used. It describes five techniques for interrupting the development of collective violence (cited in Turner & Killian, 1972:165):

1. Remove or isolate the individuals involved in the precipitating incident before the crowd has begun to achieve substantial unity.
2. Interrupt communication during the milling about process by dividing the crowd into smaller units.
3. Remove crowd leaders if it can be done without force.
4. Distract the attention of the crowd from its focal point by creating diversions at other places.
5. Prevent the spread and reinforcement of the crowd by isolating it.

These 1947 guidelines and more recent police procedures are based essentially on contagion theory. In the words of a 1977 police manual, the "primary aim is to relieve emotional contagion caused by circular stimulation" (Radelet & Reed, 1980:236). Recent police manuals also show some profit from emergent-norm theory. For example, they suggest thinning the crowd of those who are not really committed to crowd action but who are afraid to rock the boat. Similarly, recent manuals recognize the importance of rumor and recommend setting up police press offices to get the police version of the action to the press quickly.

CONTROLLING SOCIAL MOVEMENTS

A social movement, by definition, challenges the status quo. When this threat is perceived as a serious challenge to basic institutions, the authorities are likely to try to damage the movement. In the United States, social movements on the left have traditionally been viewed as more threatening than those on the right; thus most of the official energy devoted to damaging social movements has been directed at liberal and left-wing movements rather than at conservative and right-wing movements. As society itself has become more liberal, however, certain right-wing groups, such as the Ku Klux Klan, have

Figure 19.12
Collective behavior is usually a strike against the status quo, either it interrupts the usual way society does business or it is a deliberate attempt to change social structure. For this reason, the power of the state and other established institutions are often directed at halting collective behavior. If done inconsistently or inappropriately, however, such opposition can create support for the movement and increase its chance of success. Here police officers are nonviolently carrying off demonstrators at a rally at the United Nations in 1982. In this case the police response was carefully orchestrated to create no new publicity and no support for the "poor protesters."

come to be viewed as threatening and have therefore also become official targets.

What does theory suggest about the best ways to sabotage a social movement? Relative-deprivation theory suggests only that one should eliminate racial injustice, poverty, social change, and other stresses in society. This is hardly helpful. As far as practical utility is concerned, mobilization theory provides a much clearer set of guidelines: Limit mobilization and reduce solidarity. Some practical applications of these principles by the FBI have included planting informers and rumors of informers in SMOs and discrediting leaders. (G. Marx, 1979).

Planting Informers and Rumors of Informers in SMOs

Fear of informers causes a movement to develop a more secretive and antidemocratic structure, deters many people from participating, and requires that an increasing proportion of resources be used for defense. It is estimated that in 1976, nearly 2,000 of the Ku Klux Klan's total membership of 10,000 were paid FBI informants. One of these men testified before a House Select Committee that he was instructed to sleep with as many of the wives of members as possible. The tactic was ostensibly to get information, but it had the important latent function of causing distraction and tension within the

movement. Another FBI directive suggested that the aim of agents' tactics should be to "enhance the paranoia endemic in these circles and . . . to get the point across that there is an FBI agent behind every mail box" (Wise, cited in G. Marx, 1979).

Discrediting Leaders

The tactic of discrediting leaders has been tried with varying degrees of success. In 1966, the FBI circulated stories about Martin Luther King's sexual exploits. In another case, the FBI circulated a leaflet showing the pictures of four New Left leaders under a "Pick the Fag" headline. In the early 1970s, the FBI planted forged documents on a long-time leader of the Communist party; the documents suggested that he was an FBI informer. As a result, he was kicked out of the party and the party was forced to go more deeply underground.

Understanding collective behavior is one of the most practical outcomes of sociological analysis. Whether you intend to join a SWAT team, the radical underground, or the Sierra Club, knowledge of the strategies and tactics that successfully challenge the existing social structure can be of important practical value.

SUMMARY

1. The study of collective behavior is the study of occasions when groups of people step outside the usual conventions of the social structure. The occasions include sporadic and episodic events such as riots and mobs (collective actions) as well as sustained attempts to deliberately change the social structure (social movements).

2. There are three theories explaining crowd behavior: contagion theory, convergence theory, and emergent-norm theory.

3. Although sporadic, episodic, and often outside the law, crowd behavior is not random. Each society has a repertoire of collective actions from which to choose. In contemporary society, the mass media are an important source of information about this repertoire.

4. Rumor is an essential ingredient in the development and validation of crowd norms. In rumoring, stories are leveled, sharpened, and assimilated. Through a process of verbal milling about, a consensus develops on what is going on and which actions are appropriate.

5. Smelser's theory of social movements suggests that six conditions must exist before a social movement occurs: (1) a conducive social structure, (2) a source of structural strain, (3) a belief that the strain is unjust, (4) a

precipitating event, (5) a mobilization of resources, and (6) an ineffective opposition.

6. Relative-deprivation theory is also known as breakdown theory because it relies heavily on the disorganization of society; mobilization theory is also known as solidarity theory because it relies on the previous solidarity of organized groups. An integration of the two suggests that social movements occur when deprivation and solidarity coincide—when our group is deprived relative to your group.

7. Within a social movement, there may be many social-movement organizations, each differing substantially from the others in style and political philosophy. SMOs favoring the radical restructuring of society tend to demand total commitment from their members, whereas SMOs wanting to adjust rather than replace the status quo demand much less of their members' time, loyalty or money.

8. The success of a movement depends not only on its mobilization and solidarity but also on its aims. Movements with gradualist approaches and with demands that do not damage the status of others and that may bring benefits to others are more likely to succeed.

9. Relative-deprivation theory is relatively useless for dealing with anything practical in regard to social movements. Mobilization theory, however, suggests a number of practical ways in which a social movement can be countered through creating cracks in its solidarity and hindering its mobilization.

SUGGESTED READINGS

Ash, Roberta. (1972). Social Movements in America. Chicago: Markham Publishing. A general introduction to the study of social movements, followed by detailed histories of the most prominent social movements in the United States. The material on the temperance movement is particularly interesting.

Gitlin, Todd. (1980). The Whole World Is Watching. Berkeley: University of California Press. Focus on the relationship between the mass media and the New Left of the 1970s, with special emphasis on how the media changed the movement.

Rose, Jerry D. (1979). Outbreaks. New York: Free Press. Concentration on episodes of collective action, including panic and disaster-related group acts.

Rosnow, Ralph L., & Fine, Gary Alan. (1976). Rumor and Gossip. New York: Elsevier. A review of the classic works and of the more recent history of gossip and rumor as they affect collective action.

Tilly, Charles. (1978). From Mobilization to Revolution. Reading, Mass.: Addison-Wesley. An advanced treatment of mobilization theory, with the ideas about social movements integrated into the sociological theories of Marx, Durkheim, and Weber. The examples are largely historical rather than contemporary.

Turner, Ralph, and Killian, Lewis. (1972). Collective Behavior (2d ed.). Englewood Cliffs, N.J.: Free Press. The classic text on collective behavior. Although it does not cover more recent developments, especially mobilization theory, it gives hundreds of fascinating accounts of collective behavior.

CHAPTER 20

SOCIAL CHANGE

PROLOGUE

Have You Ever . . . considered what the world will be like for your children? In 25 years, there will be another 3 billion or so people in the world—assuming that it has not been blown up by then. As if that weren't bad enough, you have to worry about whether social security will go broke. You may anticipate that in some ways your life will be better than your parents' life, but you probably also have some real anxieties. The last few decades have brought us such wonders as the neutron bomb (it can kill all the living things in a wide radius without destroying buildings) and the test-tube baby, pornographic video games for the home computer, microwave ovens, and the almost worldwide elimination of smallpox. We still have churches, schools, and families, but even these traditional institutions are different than they were 25 years ago.

Many of the changes that have occurred may have reached you personally. Perhaps the changes in the family mean that your parents have been divorced and that you have stepparents and half-sisters. It is likely that one of your siblings or cousins has had an illegitimate child or an abortion. Changes in economic and educational opportunities also directly affect you. Many of the ways society is changing have been pointed out in earlier chapters. This chapter summarizes some of the major trends in U.S. society and the forces that create change.

The Importance of Social Change

If the last 50,000 years of human existence were compressed into lifetimes of 62 years each, there would be 800 of them. People emerged from caves sometime during the 650th lifetime, printing began only 6 lifetimes ago, the electric motor has been used in only the last 2 lifetimes, and most of the material goods we use today were developed in the present lifetime (Toffler, 1970).

Another way of looking at change is that almost as much change has occurred since you were born as took place in the entire history of humankind prior to your birth. Moreover, there is good reason to believe that change will continue to be rapid and far-reaching in your generation. New ideas, inventions, and ways of doing things will make it necessary for you to learn how to respond differently.

If the past is any indication, accepting change and adapting to it will not be easy. Most of us tend to resist change. Although we are curious, we are also uneasy about the untried, untested, and unfamiliar. (Will microwaves give us cancer? Does cohabitation mean the end of the family as we know it?) Some resist change not because it is disquieting but because it is potentially damaging to self-interest. The central business districts of major cities, for example, resist the development of suburban malls; the television and motion picture industries resist the marketing of video recorders to home viewers; the clergy of major denominations adamantly oppose electronic churches.

Despite the fact that we sometimes drag our heels about accepting change, most of us have become committed to the idea that change will occur. We no longer expect things to be the same for our children as for ourselves; we expect next year's models to be different from this year's (Vago, 1980). Some of these changes will represent progress: longer life, better health, more justice, and a higher standard of living. (The Japanese are even working on a pill that will allow you to eat all the pizza you want without gaining a pound.) Other changes may be less universally beneficial.

Social change is significant alterations over time in material or nonmaterial culture.

The concept of social change has to be very broad to incorporate all these events. Therefore, **social change** is defined here as significant alterations over time in patterns of material or nonmaterial culture. This definition allows the inclusion of everything from norms, values, and statuses to technology and physical artifacts. Underlying an awareness of these alterations are specific concerns about what is changing, how fast, in which direction, and how much? These concerns point to some of the major analytic dimensions of social change.

Dimensions of Change

Duration.   Changes may be permanent or very temporary alterations in society. Much of the change that takes place between one generation and the next or between one year and the next is of the short-term variety called fad or fashion.

Fads are widely dispersed patterns of behavior that develop rapidly and end almost as rapidly.

Fads are widely dispersed patterns of behavior that develop rapidly and end almost as rapidly. They are often of minor significance, but because they represent something new, they gain attention and temporary value. (Some examples are pet rocks, Rubik cubes, and Cabbage Patch dolls.) Through strategic advertising in the mass media, we have the means to popularize a fad very quickly. This same machinery ensures that fads are short-lived—here today, gone tomorrow. Once a fad spreads, its value diminishes; what was new becomes old and uninteresting.

Fashions are longer-lasting cultural patterns, usually of dress and adornment; they tend to last for a year or two before they are replaced. They typically begin and are supported by established status groups in society. New styles symbolically distinguish innovators from the masses; when the styles are imitated by lower-status groups, they lose their symbolic value and are abandoned (Turner & Killian, 1972). In short, by the time some version of a fashion is being sold at K-Mart, Vogue has moved on to something else. This characteristic leads to the observation that fashion operates only in open class societies, where there is competition for elite status (Simmel, 1957). When status is fixed at birth, there is no need to reassert it again and again.

In recent years, there have been some reversals in who sets fashion. Lower-status subcultures and countercultures have been major contributors to new fashion. Blue jeans, for example, long a staple of working-class attire, have become expensive designer jeans; the transformation of tennis shoes and sweat clothes into fancy jogging attire is equally dramatic. The fashion for men's earrings and for women to have their ears double- or triple-pierced did not originate with higher-status groups, and it remains to be seen if these fashions will spread upwards. If punk-rock hairstyles can spread to the elite salons and punk clothes appear in the J. C. Penney catalog, however, it appears safe to say that fashion origination is no longer a unique province of the well-off.

Direction. The direction of change may be toward development and progress or toward decay and decline. Three major models of change are presented in Figure 20.1. The optimistic model sees change as equivalent to progress, with each alteration leading to a better world (A). The pessimistic model sees change as a form of growth and decay (B). It views societies as organisms that are born, grow, and die. People who adopt this model are often on the lookout for signs showing that we have passed the crest and are on a path toward decay and decline. More complex patterns of change allow for alternating periods of growth, stability, and decline (C). Though Rome did indeed rise and fall, the next civilization built upon the ruins.

Magnitude and Impact. Some changes, such as fads, may affect only limited segments of the population, and then only briefly. Major transitions, however, such as industrialization, permanently and significantly alter culture. These transitions disrupt the existing social order and produce ripple effects that extend to all major facets of society. For example, the development of the automobile led to new uses for rubber and gasoline, which led to increased economic ties to Latin America and the Middle East. And by giving us new mobility, the automobile also gave us suburbia and changed the nature of courtship.

The most radical and far-reaching kind of change is **revolution,** a sharp break with the past and a change in the basic patterns of life. Revolutions may be intentional and violent (for example, political revolutions); they may be gradual (for example, the industrial revolution); they may even be only partial, in that they replace some aspects of society (say economics or government) but keep others intact (for example, the American Revolution).

Fashions are cultural patterns, usually of dress and adornment, adopted by a segment of the population for a relatively brief period of time and then abandoned.

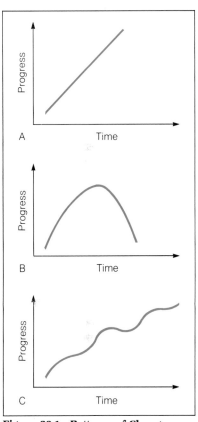

Figure 20.1 Patterns of Change
Evolutionists tend to see change as leading to progress (A), but other observers believe that change is not necessarily the same as improvement. Some believe societies undergo processes of growth and decay (B); others believe that progress is sporadic (C).

Revolution is the most radical form of social change; one that makes a sharp break with the past and results in significant changes in basic social structure.

Rate. Change may be fast, slow, continuous, orderly, or uneven. Not surprisingly, rapid and fitful change has more disruptive consequences than does slow, steady change. An excellent example of the disruptive effect of rapid change is the price of gasoline. The price has not grown any more than that of other commodities over the last 30 years; however, it was effected almost entirely in a single year, whereas the price of eggs and housing increased more slowly. When the price of gasoline more than doubled within 3 or 4 months, it caused serious dislocations. Sales of gas-guzzling cars plummeted, Detroit was in disarray, local small-car dealers were besieged with customers, and people canceled their vacations and decided that they couldn't afford to visit their friends. In contrast, slow and even change may go unnoticed until one day people realize that the world has changed.

Mechanisms of Social Change

The world is a dynamic and interdependent system of elements. Because of this interdependence, changes snowball. We can never change just one thing; a change in one element leads to changes in others. A convenient way of summarizing the set of dynamic elements is the POET model (see Figure 20.2)—the set of interrelationships of population (P), social organization (O), the physical environment (E), and technology (T). Any of these elements may be the source of change. When there is change in one, however, it is likely to reverberate throughout the system. The following sections briefly address the roles of each of these elements in causing change.

Population

Alterations in the composition, distribution, and size of population are important sources of social change. Earlier chapters have noted how differential migration creates de facto school segregation, how changing mortality affects social structure, and how the changing age structure of a population creates problems for school systems, the job market, and retirement. The potentially disruptive changes caused by shifts in the age structure are especially evident in the United States. The baby boom followed by the birth dearth produced significant dislocations in the ability to deliver social services to specific age groups. The post-World War II baby boom generation was such a large increase in size over the previous generation that hospital delivery rooms and then schools were vastly overcrowded; there were too few teachers and now there may be too few jobs. The sharp fall in birthrates in the 1970s created the opposite problems: empty classrooms, school closings, and teachers unable to find school employment. On the positive side, however, the crime rate is going down too.

In the developed world, population growth tends to be slow. The adjustments required are relatively minor ones involving changes in age structure, ethnic composition, and internal settlement. In the less devel-

Figure 20.2 The POET Model
The POET model summarizes the interdependence of the elements of life. A change in one element leads to changes in others.

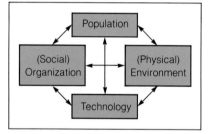

oped world, population change is explosive. For every two persons in an underdeveloped country right now, there will be three by the year 2000. The amount of agricultural land will diminish. Thus the tremendous growth in population will force negative changes in the level of nutrition, in the distribution of wealth and food, in the deathrate—or maybe in all three. The potential for population growth to effect social change is obvious. As we saw in the case of the Black Death (chapter 17), population decline can also cause significant social change.

Social Organization

Social change often originates from within the social organization of society. Changes in political, economic, or even religious organization can provide the spark for changes in technology and population. Marx argued that changes in economic organization were the major impetus to social change. Weber responded that changes in values and ideologies could lead the way to economic change. Although Weber's analysis emphasized the role of religious ideologies, it is ironic that Marxism itself has become one of the most powerful ideologies inspiring economic and social change today.

In a sense, the previous 19 chapters of this book have been an examination of the social causes of social change. Changes in the economy affect the family; changes in the family affect education; changes in education affect government; changes in government affect race relations. These changes in social institutions affect not only other social institutions but also population, technology, and the physical environment. The declining economic significance of the family, for example, leads to reduced fertility, an older age structure, and, eventually, less pressure on the physical environment.

The Physical Environment: A Fragile Ecosystem

Culture represents an adaptation to the physical as well as the social environment. Changes in the physical environment or in our relationship to it can be a vital spur to social change. Some of these changes occur naturally. Currents shift, and volcanoes erupt. More importantly, the environment is altered by our own actions. We dam the rivers and level the mountains; we plough the plains and plant a single strain of artificially developed grain across a whole continent; we drain underground water, oil, and gas reserves to maintain our standard of living; we pollute the air, denude the forests, and extinguish hundreds of species of animal life.

So far, we have been able to change the physical environment to suit our convenience. It is increasingly obvious, however, that there are limitations to the physical environment and that these limitations will eventually cause us to change some of our cultural practices. Most obviously, we are being pressured to reduce our birthrates, but we are also being pressured into using less fuel for cars and homes, living in townhouses rather than detached single-family dwellings, controlling pollution emission even at major costs in productivity, and changing our methods of agriculture to preserve rather than exploit our farmland.

Figure 20.3
This boy huddles with his sister in a Cambodian refugee camp inside Thailand. During the last decade, the entire population of Southeast Asia has sharply altered: death rates have risen and refugee streams have spread across Southeast Asia, the Philippines, the United States, and elsewhere. To understand social change of this magnitude requires placing population change in a larger context and understanding its interdependence with social organization, the environment, and technology.

Figure 20.4

During the explosion of industrialization, many people believed that we had conquered nature. As a result, we created artificial environments such as this one in New York, assuming that we could do with nature as we wished. Increasingly, however, problems of pollution, population growth, and exhaustion of natural resources remind us that the natural and social worlds are interdependent.

Figure 20.5

This fully automated production plant in Missouri uses robots to weld frames on Chrysler LeBarons. In the last decade, computer technology has significantly altered the production of goods and correspondingly our conceptions of work. Tedious mechanical jobs can now be done by automated equipment, thus freeing people for more creative work. There may be an awkward period of cultural lag, however, before new jobs are found for those displaced.

Technology, Science, and Knowledge

The ideas and tools that are used by society to solve problems are called technology. The vast majority of technological advances are of relatively recent origin (Freeman, 1974). The greater a society's commitment to science and the more advanced its technology, the greater the rapidity of its changes in material culture. Technology itself grows exponentially. Each new development is potentially a basis for further development.

For most of the history of human existence, however, the rates of technological growth were relatively slow and there were few changes from one generation to the next. In terms of material and nonmaterial culture, it was expected and desired that the future would be like the present. The advent of science and the industrial revolution changed all this. We accept change as normal and expect the creation of new products and the continual refinement of existing ones. We wonder whether we should buy a calculator or a microwave this year or wait until next year, when it will be better—or cheaper. Change is now a normal and expected part of our view of the world.

The numerous instances of social change sparked by technological breakthroughs have led many scholars to argue that technology is the basis for all major transformations of society (Boulding, 1964). Certainly, examples supporting this argument abound. The silicon chip, electricity, and the automobile all provide evidence of societal changes that occurred because of particular technological breakthroughs. The silicon chip, for example, has revolutionized our information-oriented society, enabling small businesses, homeowners, and students to store and retrieve information easily and rapidly on microcomputers. The same advance has led to illegal entry into the classified information of banks, the military, and government.

It is important to recognize, however, that "a new device merely opens a door; it does not compel us to enter" (White, 1966:28). Thus a technological device may exist for decades, even centuries, before society develops a practical use for it. The Greeks, for example, developed a toy steam engine in 100 AD. Until social and economic institutions were ready for mass factory production, however, it remained a toy. Often social change creates a demand for technological development. For example, the major declines in fertility (see chapter 17) took place prior to breakthroughs in birth control technology.

Thus technology is hardly the only factor contributing to social change. The acceptance of technology, the varied applications to which it is put, and the impact it has on society depend to a large extent on the broader sociocultural patterns that exist.

Sources of New Knowledge and Technology. New knowledge and new technology come through one of four processes: discovery, invention, acculturation, or diffusion.

DISCOVERY. The independent uncovering of a new piece of knowledge, called **discovery,** often refers to physical matters—fire, electricity, or the laws of genetics, for example. Discovery is a change in our understanding of events or processes, not the development of new events or processes.

> **Discovery** is the independent uncovering of a new piece of knowledge.

INVENTION. When existing knowledge is combined in novel ways to enhance its usefulness, we speak of **invention**. Many decades after Mendel discovered the elementary laws of heredity, scientists have invented ways to apply that knowledge to cloning, gene splitting, and controlling hereditary traits through artificial insemination, gene transplants, and test-tube babies. Sperm banks, a social invention of modern society, are a novel way in which discoveries in genetics are combined for such purposes as artificial insemination to preserve the genes of geniuses.

> **Invention** occurs when existing information is combined in novel ways that enhance its usefulness.

ACCULTURATION. Change that comes about because of contact and exchange between two cultures is called **acculturation**. It involves accepting parts of the material or nonmaterial cultures of the other society and is almost always the result of prolonged contact: war and conquest, colonization, missionary work, migration, slavery, or similar situations.

Acculturation seldom occurs equally in both cultures. Where one culture is technologically more advanced than the other, the typical pattern is for the less advanced culture to adopt the ways of the dominant (more advanced) one. Status enhancement serves as a stimulant to change in the direction of the dominant culture. The Focus on Another Culture section of this chapter offers an example of this process.

> **Acculturation** occurs when continuous contact causes the subordinate group to take on the material or nonmaterial culture of the dominant group.

DIFFUSION. A special case of acculturation is **diffusion**—the transmission of a relatively small piece of material or nonmaterial culture (such as Kentucky Fried Chicken to Japan or bowler hats to Peru). Diffusion is more limited than acculturation and may occur without contact.

The spread of cultural innovations through diffusion depends on several conditions. Merely coming into contact with another culture does not ensure that cultural elements will be borrowed and transmitted. For diffusion to take place, the innovation itself must be perceived as having some advantage to the receiving society. It must also be compatible with the existing values, practices, and past experiences of the receiving society.

> **Diffusion,** is a process by which an aspect of material or nonmaterial culture is spread from one culture to another.

The Acculturation of the Manus

Anthropologists have contributed significantly to our understanding of social change through diffusion and acculturation. Of the many studies reported, Margaret Mead's detailed analysis of social change among the Manus, a New Guinea tribe situated in the Admiralty Islands, is one of the best known. Mead first visited the Manus in 1928, at a time when the Territory of New Guinea was just coming under the influence of Western civilization. In 1928, the Manus were a Stone Age people living in what seemed to the Western world a strange and savage society. When Mead returned in 1953, the islanders had made the transition to the 20th century, accomplishing "a kind of change that is unprecedented in history" (Mead, 1970:38). Her book *New Lives for Old* (1956) is an account of the incredible changes that occurred in the space of just 25 years.

1928. The Manus were an isolated people in 1928. Their world consisted of 11 villages, where approximately 2,000 nearly naked natives lived in thatched-roof houses built on poles over shallow salt lagoons. Technology was limited to that required to sustain a simple fishing economy. Limited bartering brought the Manus into biweekly contact with the "land people," with whom they traded fish for vegetables and fruit, lime for betel nut and pepper leaves, and salt water for fresh water. Some long-distance trading with villages from other islands also occurred.

In 1928, the Manus had no writing, no schools, no formal political structure. It was a society in which children's play was confined to waterways between houses and in which the clothing of both men and women consisted of bark cloth G-strings and grass aprons. The children did not wear clothes. Women's heads were shaved and their earlobes weighted down with shells. Men wore their hair in great knots or combed up to look like halos. Ceremonial costumes, constructed mainly from beads and dogs' teeth, had monetary value and were worn on special occasions. The ghosts of the recently dead were central elements of religious belief and ritual.

World War II. Extensive contact with Western civilization came abruptly when World War II extended itself to the Territory of New Guinea. The Manus were exposed first to the Japanese and later to more than a million U.S. troops stationed on the island. Discrepancies about the treatment of the Manus by the Japanese abound, but their first experience with civilization was apparently extremely uncivil. Some Manus were killed, some were tortured, and many were driven out of their homes, to hide in the swamps, as Japanese warplanes machine-gunned their houses.

The arrival of U.S. troops brought escape and relief from Japanese oppression. It also brought more than a million people to the Admiralty Islands. The U.S. soldiers cleared land for airstrips, built barracks, and knocked down mountains with the most highly developed machine technology the world had ever seen. Because they were there temporarily, they showed little interest in long-term colonization or domination. They did, however, use the hardworking Manus extensively as construction workers. In a short period of time, the Manus became exposed to U.S. technology and culture. Under these conditions, the U.S. servicemen and the Manus developed a friendly and sympathetic relationship. The process of acculturation had begun.

1953. When Mead returned to the Admiralty Islands in 1953, she found the Manus culture dramatically changed. She was greeted by a man in neatly ironed clothing, shoes, and a tie, who was an elected official of the community. She was handed a letter written by the local school teacher, who had been just a baby in 1928. She stepped ashore on the site of the new Peri village, which consisted of 67 U.S.-style houses built on the land. The houses were arranged in rows, and dominating the village center were a church, a village square, and a dock. The Manus also had a workshop for building canoes, a children's playground, a cemetery, and latrines.

Acculturation. The new Manus culture skipped thousands of years of change ordinarily thought to be essential stages in development and modernization. Mead attributed the rapid change to many factors. Clearly, the Manus saw in the Euro-American culture elements of advantage to them, elements that fit into some of their existing culture and could be modeled. In addition, their old culture was seriously disrupted by events surrounding the outbreak of World War II. The war had led to social upheaval and the development of cargo cults—religious movements that looked forward to a new era of peace and prosperity ushered in by the arrival of huge cargo shipments of Western goods. Under the influence of Paliau, a leader who emerged during the cargo-cult outbreaks, the whole society moved at once. All three generations (including the elderly) became involved in planning and carrying out the acquisition of U.S. social forms. In this goal, the Manus have proved remarkably successful. Within 12 years after establishing the first school, they were contributing teachers, clerks, interpreters, and nurses to the Territory of New Guinea, and their students were being sent to the new University of Paua and New Guinea—all this from a society that in 1928 had no written language.

Questions to Consider

What negative consequences of rapid social change would you expect to uncover among the Manus?

Perspectives on Social Change

We have not yet considered directly why social change occurs. There are three major perspectives on the subject: evolutionary, structural-functional, and conflict.

Figure 20.6
The hats of these Peruvian women are a particularly striking example of diffusion. The bowler derbies worn by visiting Englishmen earlier in this century have become a standard part of female attire in the Andes.

Evolutionary Theory

The use of technology and specific social practices to help people adapt to changes in their social or physical environment is **cultural evolution**. In the evolutionary perspective, change is gradual, in only one direction (toward better adaptation and more complexity), and lasting in its consequences. It is seen as building on what went before, producing progress as opposed to mere difference.

Cultural evolution is the use of specific social arrangements and technology as mechanisms for adapting to environmental and social change.

Social thinkers from all eras have had a strong tendency to assume that their society was a step in the right direction (Nisbet, 1969). In this sense, the idea of social evolution predates Darwin's work on evolution of biological forms. Combined with Mendel's studies of genetics, however, Darwin's work provided scientific support for a theory of evolution based on the notion of natural selection. This idea became very popular at the end of the 19th century and influenced the work of scholars in many areas, including sociology.

Early evolutionary theories in sociology were often based on the assumption that there were a fixed number of specific stages that each society must pass through as it progressed and developed over time (for example, from savagery through barbarism to civilization). For the most part, these theories were unilinear theories of social change; they assumed that all societies evolve in the same way, from less civilized to more civilized through the same necessary stages. Auguste Comte, for example, described three stages that each society must pass through: theological, metaphysical, and positive. The positive stage was characterized by industrialization and science. Western civilization, Comte believed had reached the positive stage and was on the verge of being able to control the physical environment. Sociology, which Comte called the highest of all sciences, was envisioned as the means to control the social environment.

Figure 20.7

Charles Darwin (1809–1882) was a naturalist whose theory of evolution through natual selection created a storm of controversy in the biological sciences. Although the ideas of social evolution predate Darwin, evolutionary theory in the social sciences has not been as popular as in the biological sciences. Skeptics have been unwilling to label all social change as adaptation or to see it as the outcome of neutral forces.

Spencer, another early social evolutionist, saw society as developing from relatively simple patterns of social organization to higher levels of complexity, organization, and specialization. Change was a natural evolutionary process, and Spencer believed that the state should not interfere with nature by legislating and regulating society. The early U.S. sociologist William Sumner advocated the same philosophy; states could not change folkways, since improvement and progress came from natural evolution, not legislation.

Evolutionary theory has often been criticized for associating Westernization with progress (Etzioni-Havely, 1981). This assumption of Western superiority has kept evolutionary theory from being widely embraced. Recently, however, the ideas of social evolution have been rehabilitated in a more objective form. Lenski and Lenski (1978) offer a theory of sociocultural evolution in which change is merely cumulative; new elements of a culture are gradually adapted into the existing cultural base and elaborated on. There is a continuity with past cultural elements as new sociocultural elements are incorporated into the customs and institutions of society. When the new elements are introduced, sometimes as alternatives to present ones, the old elements are no longer useful and become extinct. This theory makes no assumptions about progress or adaptation; it merely describes how innovations accumulate to produce change.

In sociology and anthropology, the ideas of unilinear evolution have given way to multilinear theories, which recognize that evolution can occur in different ways. There are no fixed stages; instead there are alternative routes to the same destination (Stewart, 1953). Because societies differ to begin with, the cultural patterns of change evolve differently. Contemporary evolutionary theories generally see societies as moving from small, homogeneous social structures and cultural patterns to larger, more heterogeneous, and more complex ones. Because the meaning of advancement, progress, and development is relative, the goals of Western society are no longer hailed as the ultimate ones. Contemporary evolutionists recognize that the association of Westernization with progress represents value judgments and ethnocentrism rather than evolution.

Structural-Functional Theory

Structural functionalism emphasizes the relationship between the various parts of society and the need for integration in the maintenance of society. As long as the parts of society are mutually compatible and fulfill functions for one another, the social system will remain relatively stable and enduring. This emphasis on the maintenance of society suggests a static image, which some argue diminishes the ability of structural functionalism to explain social change. Talcott Parsons, the most influential and best-known functional theorist, contends, however, that there is really "no difference between processes which serve to maintain a system and those which serve to change it" (Parsons, 1966:21). Social systems are never perfectly integrated; there are always strains and tensions between the various parts. Institutions exist to manage and control these strains.

Functionalists argue that the parts of society are in **dynamic equilibrium**, constantly adjusting to preserve the stability of the system as a whole. The easiest way to understand this concept is to think of the thermostat that turns the heater and the air conditioner off and on in order to achieve a constant result in the face of changing conditions. Society is viewed as constantly changing and adjusting—with the intent of preserving the system in the face of changes in its parts or its environment. In this view, functional change helps institutions adapt.

As indicated throughout the book, a significant amount of sociological theory is based on functional theory, or the idea of equilibrium. Interrelated parts function together to maintain the stability of a social system. The mechanisms that preserve or reestablish equilibrium after internal or external disturbances have allowed functionalists to incorporate social change into their explanations. They do not, however, explain major revolutions such as the Bolshevik revolution in Russia or Mao's cultural revolution. In both of these cases, significant internal strains produced rapid social change, disrupting the equilibrium of society and altering many of the basic social structures.

Evolutionary Functionalism.
As one might suspect, evolutionary and functional theory overlap in many places. In contemporary functionalism,

Figure 20.8
Industrialization and modernization proceed slowly in the third world—as they did in the West. The availability of female employment outside the home, for example, does not automatically alter old attitudes toward the family. Women may still find much pressure to have children and may still bear almost the entire responsibility for their care. The pace of social change may be faster in the third world because of diffusion, but social institutions encourage continuity in social relationships.

Dynamic equilibrium is the constant adjustment of the various parts of a social system to preserve the stability of the system as a whole. In functional theory, dynamic equilibrium is functional change.

evolutionary theory is most evident in the work of Talcott Parsons, who assumes that social change consists of three general processes: (1) societies become more highly differentiated, with a more complex division of labor; (2) this greater differentiation leads to more integration and interdependence; and (3) the society becomes more adaptive and flexible (Turner, 1982). Parsons's belief that progress consists of greater differentiation leads him to conclude that socialism is regressive evolution. He argues that both the increasing connections between political and economic institutions and the declines in religion as an institution have simplified society, reducing its level of differentiation. This simplification, he argues, will in turn reduce the level of societal integration and ultimately the ability of the society to adapt to changing circumstances and to maintain itself (Gorin, 1980).

One of the earliest and most respected theories of social change, put forth by William F. Ogburn, also involves a synthesis of social evolution and functional theory. Material culture (technology), Ogburn argued, advances in a smooth and cumulative fashion, with ever-increasing complexity. Because of the continuity in the development of inventions and discoveries, new aspects of material culture develop out of the old. Nonmaterial culture, however, adjusts to these changes in a less continuous fashion. Technical innovations throw the norms, values, attitudes, and beliefs of the population into disequilibrium, and there is a period of **cultural lag**—a period in which nonmaterial culture adapts to changes in material culture.

Cultural lag is the period of adjustment of the nonmaterial culture to the new material culture.

Automation is an example of one technological innovation to which we are having difficulty adapting. As industry turns to robots and automation, the factory of the future may become void of human energy. General Motors currently has a factory under construction that will build locomotive motor frames completely by automation. "Where it now takes 68 skilled machine operators 16 days to build huge locomotive frames, the new factory will turn them out in 1 day—with no human workers" ("The factory of the future," 1982:69). This displacement of workers will lead to unemployment, retraining, and replanning. The young people who assumed that they would stay in their community and work at the same plant that their parents did are having to make new plans. Similarly, the introduction of personal computers has brought revolutionary changes in communications. The full impact of this revolution in terms of individual adjustments and organizational developments has scarcely begun to be realized.

On a more value-laden level, consider birth control technology. As a result of safe, inexpensive, virtually foolproof contraceptives, a major reason for avoiding premarital sexual contacts has been eliminated. Many people are therefore increasing their sexual activity. Values, however, are changing more slowly; they are lagging behind changes in technology and changes in behavior. (This statement does not assume that increased sexual behavior represents progress; it is merely an example of older values being challenged by technology.) The period of time it take people to adjust to innovations and restore equilibrium is what Ogburn meant by cultural lag.

Conflict Theory

The most influential and significant figure in the development of conflict theory is Karl Marx. His theory of dialectic materialism is a theory of social change. It asserts that change takes place as a result of competition and conflict between opposing forces (the dialectic) and that the fundamental basis of this conflict is economic (or material) interest. In Marx's theory, changes in the modes of production (technology and resources) are the driving forces behind social change. As the modes of production change, corresponding changes develop in the social relations of those tied to production. For example, industrialization results in massive shifts in the labor force, creating a marginal population of the unemployed, whose skills are no longer required. Others are exploited for their labor in factories owned and operated by a ruling class. The increasing complexity of labor caused by industrialization divides society into opposite camps, the powerful elites and the exploited workers. The struggle between these two classes, Marx maintained, will inevitably result in the emergence of political structures to represent class interests. For Marx, the only solution to this conflict was revolution—the violent overthrow of the ruling elites—and the reorganization of the forces of production.

Marx's approach to social change was somewhat restricted by his insistence that modes of production are the only basis of change. Modern conflict theory takes a broader view, applying the dialectic and the emphasis on conflict as a basis of change to ideological and status conflicts as well as to material ones. Dahrendorf (1959), for example, suggests that conflict is based on the legitimacy of authority rather than on class struggle. Within any social group or organization, there are positions and roles

Figure 20.9

The conflict approach assumes that social change stems from class struggle and changes in economic relationships. This picture of the 1917 Bolshevik Revolution in Russia portrays the successful attempt by Lenin and others to overthrow the existing class relationships in Russia and to transform major institutions. Initially, chaos, confusion, and destruction swept the countryside, but eventually a new social order was established.

that cause some people to be dominated by others. Dominant groups will seek to maintain the status quo; subordinate groups will challenge the legitimacy of authority and seek social change. As subordinate groups organize, develop leadership, and become more aware of their common interests, conditions of conflict will become more apparent and intense. From Dahrendorf's perspective, most conflicts are resolved through compromise rather than revolution. Dahrendorf has consistently maintained that social conflict rests in the social structure and that these conflicts, not individual psychological or social psychological characteristics such as aggression, explain social change.

Conflict Functionalism. One modern conflict theorist, Lewis Coser, notes that conflict has both negative and positive effects in society. Conflict frequently leads to the resolution of disagreements and restores unity. In this sense, it leads to adjustment and adaptation, enabling different groups to work out their differences and live side-by-side. Coser also believes that conflict strengthens the in-group cohesion of members by providing them with a common opposition. Coser's position is a combination of conflict theory and functionalism (Turner, 1982), stressing adaptation and positive functions on the one hand and the presence of conflict and change in society on the other.

Social Change in the United States

One approach to analyzing social change in the contemporary United States is to summarize the changes examined in the previous 19 chapters. Such a list would include increases in illegitimacy and educational attainment, decreases in religious commitment and political party affiliation, and increases in assault and decreases in mortality. Instead of reviewing these changes, however, this section will use the work of contemporary scholars to summarize four of the most important trends. Following John Naisbitt's (1982) analysis of social change, we can refer to these trends as megatrends, because they transcend any single institution and are felt in many areas of social life. The trends are a shift to postindustrial society and greater flexibility, more diversity, and scarcity.

Industrial Society to Postindustrial Society

One of the profoundest changes in modern history is the rise of tertiary industry and the relative decline of secondary and primary industry. What is tertiary industry? It includes service work such as waitressing and cooking, but for the most part it involves information-processing. It is a matter of clerks and teachers, typists and technicians. Among the consequences of this change are that we work with our minds instead of our hands; education is the best capital we can have and brains the best raw material. This change favors the individual who is adaptable, has excellent communication skills, and learns quickly.

Although the people who lack these skills will be at a serious disadvantage, the high-information society opens up a wide range of opportunities. If we accept that the people who control the nation's financial capital do not have a monopoly on brains, then we can see how this social change provides opportunities for mobility. In the high-technology–low-capital investment economy, the person with a better idea can more easily get ahead. The computer field is perhaps the best example. The young men who started Apple Computer on a shoestring are now millionaires.

Technological Alienation to Freedom through Technology

The capacity of technology to alienate the worker was the starting point of Marx's analysis. As the size of the task got smaller and smaller, as the machine did more of the work and the worker was left with less creativity, technology threatened to reduce the individual worker to a robotlike creature who would simply respond to the demands of a machine. Naisbitt (1982) argues that technology has now come full circle, liberating us and giving us greater flexibility. The computer, for example, makes it possible for a large company to design individual benefit plans for its 40,000 employees, each of whom can choose a different combination of vacations, flextime, holidays, and insurance.

Figure 20.10
The latest innovations in technology are providing individuals with greater personal freedom and life-style choices. Biogenetic engineering, for example, now enables infertile couples to become parents through the use of fertility drugs, ovum transplants, or donor sperm.

The computer and associated telecommunications systems may further liberate us from the need to congregate by the thousands in huge factories and offices. Increasingly, we are able to tune in from home and send our memos, reports, and charts via telephones connected to computers. Teachers can communicate with faraway students through electronic blackboards; and even in the traditional classrooms, computers allow teachers to devise individualized exams for each of their students.

The latest innovations in technology appear, therefore, to be giving us greater freedom. A simple example of this freedom is electronic religion. Say you like to sing, but you are not fond of sermons—or you like some sermons better than others. If you attend church, you are bound to stay through the entire service. If you participate in electronic religion, however, you can turn the channel until you find a sermon you do like or you can turn down the sound until the sermon is over. If you want, you can dial a prayer. From work to worship, technology is giving us more freedom.

Conventionality to Diversity

One of the most obvious trends in our society is an increased opportunity to choose among a wide range of options. Society now tolerates greater diversity than it used to. If you want to cohabit, have children without marriage, have marriage without children, or join a religious sect, you are relatively free to do so. There has always been diversity in the United States, but often individuals had little choice. They were different because of their class, race, or region. Now people are freer to choose a life-style that suits them. If one compares 1985 with 1945 or even 1965, the increase in options is startling. In everything from automobiles to fashions to family forms, there is more opportunity for individual choice.

Abundance to Scarcity

Scholars vary in the degree of urgency they assign to problems of population growth, resource depletion, and environmental pollution. Some believe crisis is imminent and unavoidable; others believe that urgent action is required to avoid disaster. After spending a year hearing expert testimony and putting together complex projections of resource use, President Carter's Global 2000 Commission concluded:

> The world in 2000 will be more crowded, more polluted, less stable ecologically, and more vulnerable to disruption than the world we live in now. Serious stresses involving population, resources, and environment are clearly visible ahead. Despite greater material output, the world's people will be poorer in many ways than they are today. [Barney, 1981:1]

The commission report includes a long list of the problems that will face the world in general and the United States in particular in the very near future: acid rain, loss of cropland to erosion and salinization, regional water shortages, depletion of animal and plant species because of pollution and loss of habitat, and possible shortages of natural resources. The report concludes with the hope that these problems can be dealt with if they are addressed immediately.

Regardless of the steps we ultimately take to bring our life-styles and population into harmony with our physical environment, it is clear that a major trend in the United States is an increasing awareness of the limits of growth. We have wasted natural resources and taken their abundance for granted; we are now increasingly aware of the need to conserve them. Evidence of this trend includes legislation regarding fuel conservation in automobiles and insulation in homes. Some cities (Boulder, Colorado, is the leader) have attempted to conserve open space and retard urban sprawl by legislating a green belt around the city. New city growth

Figure 20.11
Increasing scarcity over the past decade has contributed to major social changes throughout the world. In most western countries, individuals now drive smaller more fuel efficient automobiles, turn down thermostats, car pool, and weatherproof their homes. Among the latest adaptations is Japan's hotel capsules, subcompact rooms at modest prices. The New Rubia Hotel in Osaka, open since June of 1981, requires about one-third the space needed for an equivalent economy hotel and boasts a nearly 100 percent occupancy rate.

will have to be in apartment or townhouse building instead of in space-consuming single-family homes. Environmental groups are becoming increasingly vocal and some, such as the Greenpeace movement to save the whales, are actively radical. Although it is not certain who will win these competitions over resource use, we will not take our resources for granted in the future.

Summary

If 10 scholars were asked to summarize the four most important trends in U.S. society, the result would probably be 10 different lists. Each scholar would emphasize some changes instead of others. We present these 4 trends not as the only important ones in contemporary life but as 4 that cross many institutions. These trends are evident in schools, churches, families, and workplaces. They underlie such varied changes as increased cohabitation, growth of political Independents, the resurgence of non-metropolitan living, and increased education.

Social Change in the World: A Macrosociological View

Change occurs not only within societies but also in the relations among them. In the world today there is consensus that one change is both necessary and desirable: an increase in the standard of living for the world's poorer nations and a decrease in their population growth—in short, economic development.

The analysis of social change at the macro level is highly complex and almost always political. Two perspectives at the center of it are modernization theory and world system theory. The former rests on evolutionary and functional theory; the latter is a conflict perspective of world social change. Both theories organize observations about the differences between more and less developed countries.

The divisions among the world's nations are glaringly obvious: Developed countries are more politically stable and their people are healthier, more educated, and, most importantly, richer. In the long run, wealth leads to better health, better education, and more political stability. There is consensus in the world that, on these dimensions, developed countries are not just different but better. Every nation wants to be as rich as the developed nations. Less developed countries therefore want massive social change, and they want it quickly. Modernization theory and world system theory offer two very different perspectives to explain these sets of observations.

Modernization Theory

Modernization is the advancement of a society's social, political, and economic development through stages of increasing differentiation and complexity (Moore, 1979; Parsons, 1951). It is an evolutionary process in which traditional societies adopt scientific methods and technology, gradually mature into a period of industrialization, and eventually arrive at a level of high consumption with a high standard of living (Rostow, 1960). It is assumed to be a comprehensive process resulting in simultaneous changes in several areas: industrialization, urbanization, family form, education, sex roles, and bureaucratization.

Modernization theory, a functionalist theory of development based on Western experience, assumes that developing nations can follow the Western path to wealth through industrialization.

Modernization theory uses Western experience as a model for developing nations. It assumes that the process used in the West can be initiated in three ways: through industrialization, through acculturation, and through induced change (Chodak, 1973). In Europe, in the 18th and 19th centuries, it was the forces of industrialization that gave birth to modernization. Industrialization, however, is not always a crucial factor in modernizing underdeveloped or developing countries. As we learned from Mead's account of rapid social change in the Admiralty Islands, modernization also can occur through acculturation and diffusion. In addition, it can be deliberately created through the imposition of modern systems of education and health care. The development of industry may follow the acquisition of Western norms and values.

As a theory of macro social change, modernization was advanced throughout the 1950s and 1960s as a means to explain how developing nations could increase their standard of living. Many believed that foreign aid, educational and technological advice, the Peace Corps, and the reform of economic and legal structures would allow underdeveloped nations to move rapidly into development, taking their place alongside the nations that had already made this transition. The period of the 1970s, however, largely discredited this notion. The Third World countries (Latin America, most of Asia, and Africa) did not catch up with the rich nations; in fact, the gap was increasingly widened.

Figure 20.12

Attempts at modernization in third world countries have been only modestly successful. Dependence on one or two trade goods has dislocated rural and urban economies and intensified class differences between elites and non-elites. Displaced peasants move to shanty towns on the periphery of the city, but without a diversified economy there are few job opportunities.

This failure is the result of flaws in modernization theory, which does not fully consider the differences between 17th century Yorkshire and 20th century Uganda. England, for example, did not go through these stages of development on its own resources alone. It moved into industrialization with the aid of surpluses acquired from societies that it systematically exploited for raw materials. When improving conditions caused an overpopulation problem in 19th century Europe, industrializing nations were not burdened with the care of large numbers of people. Instead, the excess population was shipped to North America or Australia. In short, England and the other industrialized Western nations reached their present state of development under conditions that no longer prevail. Underdeveloped and developing nations today exist in an international context that was not present during the earliest periods of industrialization. Realistically, they do not have the opportunity to follow the Western path to modernization.

Moreover, the already industrialized nations have developed economic and political structures that impede the opportunities of underdeveloped and developing nations to compete on the international market. These formidable obstacles have given rise to an alternative view of macro social change—world system theory.

World System Theory

The entire world may be viewed as a single economic system in which there is a division of labor among nations. For example, some nations produce raw materials and some fabricate the raw materials into finished products. **World system theory** looks at this economic system through a distinctly Marxist eye: Some countries are the bourgeoisie of the world capitalist system, and others are the proletariat. The division of labor between them is justified by a prevailing rationale (capitalism) and kept in place by an exploitive ruling class (rich countries) that seeks to maximize its benefit at the expense of the working class (poor countries).

World system theory distinguishes two classes of nations: core societies and peripheral societies. **Core societies** are rich, powerful nations that are economically diversified and relatively free of outside control. **Peripheral societies** are poor and weak, with highly specialized economies over which they have relatively little control (Chirot, 1977). For example, in 1980, coffee and cocoa made up 70 percent of Cameroon's exports, coffee made up 97 percent of Uganda's exports, and jute made up 76 percent of Bangladesh's exports. The economies of these and many other developing nations are extremely fragile, resting on world demand for one or two products. In addition, they are usually highly dependent on one or two buyers: 60 percent of Cameroon's coffee went to France and the Netherlands, and 25 percent of Egypt's exports went to Italy (Europa Yearbook, 1983). As a result, the economies of peripheral nations are vulnerable and largely beyond their own control.

The outcome of this exchange relationship is more far-reaching, however, than mere inequality in national wealth. According to world system theory, this economic colonialism has three negative effects on the peripheral nations: (1) it tends to produce a small, local elite whose economic interests are tied to foreign investors in core countries; (2) the emphasis on production of raw materials for foreign trade retards economic diversification; and (3) the lack of diversification increases income inequality within the peripheral nation (Stack & Zimmerman, 1982). The classic examples of this kind of economy are the large coffee plantations of Brazil and Uganda. Land owners with foreign ties control the major capital and

World system theory, a Marxist analysis of the relationship between developing and developed countries, suggests that the economic dominance of core societies will prevent the progress of peripheral societies.

Core societies are rich and powerful nations that are economically diversified and relatively free of outside control.

Peripheral societies are poor and weak, with highly specialized economies over which they have little control.

Figure 20.13
For centuries pastoral nomads provided the only social and economic activity on the Sahara desert. In the late 20th century, however, the nations of the middle East discovered a natural resource which they have sold at great profit to more developed countries. Ironically, the world's total amount of crude oil may well be used up by rich industrialized countries before these less-developed countries have adjusted to industrialization.

often invest it overseas rather than in their own nation. Lack of alternative industry prevents the development of a middle class and keeps the population divided between a large mass of peasants and a small elite.

A major insight provided by world system theory is that individual economies cannot be understood in isolation. One cannot fully explain a particular society's level of industrialization by looking only within that country; rather, one must look at the country's relationships with other countries (Wallerstein, 1974). This idea takes us back to chapter 1, which discussed Mills' idea of the distinction between personal troubles and public issues. Whether we are looking at individuals or at nations, the lesson seems to be that they must be viewed in the context of their relations with others. Nations can also be viewed as the intersection of biography and history.

Summary

Regardless of whether one accepts the Marxist implications of world system theory, its reminder that a larger view is necessary to understand change is useful. The 20th century, with its exploding technology and population, unprecedented richness and unparalleled poverty, and vastly different political ideologies, requires global attention to social change. Societies no longer exist independently of one another but are locked into international relationships. The forces of change occurring in one part of the world cannot be ignored by other nations.

Predicting the Future

Prediction is one of the objectives of science. In his science fiction book, *Foundation Trilogy*, Isaac Asimov (1953) fantasizes about a society in which scholars have enough knowledge about social behavior to be able to predict life hundreds and thousands of years into the future. His hero, Hari Seldon, successfully predicts political and economic crises and even the ends of empires on the basis of mathematical equations which model human social relations. Most sociologists would express their goal more humbly as an interest in having "some rough estimate of what is going to happen next" (Lemert, 1981:299).

From the beginning, sociology has had its share of prophets. Comte, Spencer, Durkheim, and Marx all made attempts to use information from their study of society to assess change at some future period. We still continue to make predictions about the future of marriage, religion, and democracy.

Predicting the future is a difficult and complex task—one that many sociologists shy away from. Perhaps the strongest objection to it is lack of accuracy. For every success there is a disastrous failure (Lipset, 1979). One of the most well known failures concerns the prediction of the future of the U.S. population. Between 1880 and 1930, U.S. fertility declined sharply. It reached a low point during the early years of the Depression, when the average family had fewer than two children. Scholars in that period looked backward to a continuous downward path; they saw no reason that it should not continue. As a result, they predicted that the U.S. population would quit growing and even shrink. This prediction caused serious concern, and several major studies of fertility intentions were designed in the late 1930s. These studies were shelved during World War II but begun again afterwards. By the time the studies were complete, the researchers were embarrassed to find that they were looking not at the death of fertility but at its resurgence (Dorn, 1950).

Since that time, sociologists have become much more careful in their statements of the future. They no longer make *predictions*—statements about what future trends will be; instead they make *projections* of the form "if

present trends continue, then the future will look like . . ." Thus, for example, we say that blacks and whites would reach occupational equality in 50 years if they had the same pattern of occupational mobility (Daymont, 1980).

Despite past failures and difficulties in gauging the complex dynamics of social change, there are good reasons for sociologists to make forecasts. With the rapid changes in population, natural-resource depletion, and technology, it becomes increasingly important that we ascertain future alternative states as best we can. Projections are needed for planning, setting priorities, and directing social change (rather than reacting to it).

The problems and potentials of forecasting are demonstrated in the Global 2000 study. In 1980, an executive group from several U.S. agencies tried to project the condition of the world in the year 2000. To make this projection, they assembled long-term trends in population, resource use, economic activity, and environmental damage. Then they projected these trends into the future, assuming that the future will indeed be an extension of present trends. The result was a grim picture of what life will be like in the year 2000 if trends continue unchanged. Because trends are unlikely to continue unchanged, however, the projections are undoubtedly going to be somewhat inaccurate. Their merit is in warning us. If we do not want the world to look like the projection, then we had better do something about it—quickly. These projections serve much the same function as a gas gauge; they warn us that trouble is ahead unless we take steps now.

Sociologists have become increasingly active in projecting social change. Many federal programs now require environmental impact statements to assess the long-term consequences of policy alternatives. These statements must include effects on the social as well as the physical environment. The reliance on sociologists for aid in assessing and projecting change has moved sociology in the direction of being an applied science—something that Comte, sociology's founding father, advocated in the 19th century.

SUMMARY

1. Accelerating social change is significantly altering our patterns of culture and social structure. Although many people are uneasy about change, most people in modern society accept change as normal and desirable.

2. Sociologists analyze social change by considering its duration, direction, magnitude, and rate.

3. Because the world is an interdependent system, a change in one element causes other changes in the system. The POET model summarizes the four major elements in this system: population, organization, environment, and technology.

4. There are three dominant perspectives on social change. Evolutionary theory explains social change as a gradual development in which the future builds on the past. Structural-functional theory views social change as a process of adjustment to external conditions. Conflict theory emphasizes that social change results from competition over scarce resources.

5. Four major changes occurring in the United States today are the shifts from an industrial to a postindustrial society, from technological alienation to freedom through technology, from conventionality to diversity, and from abundance to conservation. These four shifts can be regarded as megatrends because they affect social structures in many institutions.

6. Modernization theory, a functionalist perspective of social change, rests on the assumption that less developed countries can move toward industrialization by adopting the technologies, science, and forms of social organization that were used by the developed countries.

7. World system theory, a conflict perspective, views the world as a single economic system where the already industrialized countries control world resources and wealth at the expense of the less developed countries. The processes of economic exchange favor the developed countries in such a way that the gap between rich and poor nations is increasing.

8. The future is difficult to predict; yet there is a great need to understand the implications of today's behavior and to plan for the future. This necessity has moved sociology toward becoming an applied science, particularly in the areas of population projections and environmental impact assessments.

SUGGESTED READINGS

Barney, Gerald O. (1980). The Global 2000 Report to the President of the U.S.: Entering the 21st Century: Vol. 1: The Summary Report. New York: Pergamon Press. Required reading for anybody concerned about the future, though it is unlikely to cheer one up.

Bell, Daniel. (1973). The Coming of Post-Industrial Society: A Venture in Social Forecasting. New York: Basic Books. The classic book on the postindustrial society. Not light reading, but not technically difficult either.

Chirot, Daniel. (1977). Social Change in the Twentieth Century. New York: Harcourt Brace Jovanovich. A powerful book that presents world-system theory in a compelling fashion.

Moore, W. E. (1979). World Modernization: The Limits of Convergence. New York: Elsevier. A contemporary look at modernization theory, including a discussion of the factors that prevent developing nations from raising their standard of living.

Naisbitt, John. (1982). Megatrends: Ten New Directions Transforming Our Lives. New York: Warner Books. A book written for a popular audience by a consultant whose job is advising business and industry about the probable future. Interesting reading.

Glossary

Absolute poverty is the inability to provide the requirements of life.

Abuse is deliberate action that is intended to harm another emotionally or physically and that is contrary to social norms.

Accommodation is a process of intergroup interaction in which two groups live side-by-side as parallel cultures.

Acculturation occurs when continuous contact causes the subordinate group to take on the material or nonmaterial culture of the dominant group.

An **achieved status** is one that is optional and that a person can obtain in a lifetime.

Achievement motivation is the continual drive to match oneself against standards of excellence.

Ageism is the belief that chronological age determines the presence or absence of socially relevant characteristics and that age therefore provides a legitimate reason for unequal treatment.

An **aggregate** is people who are temporarily clustered together in the same location (e.g., busloads of people, those attending a movie, and shoppers in a mall).

Alienation occurs when conformity to role expectations estranges the individual from personal creativity and judgment.

The **American dream** is the ideology that Americans use to rationalize their class positions. It suggests that there is equality of opportunity in the United States, and everyone gets the class position they deserve.

Anglo-conformity is the process of acculturation in which new immigrant groups adopt English language and English customs.

Anomic deviance occurs among individuals who accept society's goals but are blocked from achieving them through the usual means.

Anomie is a situation in which the norms of society are unclear or no longer applicable to current conditions; the individual has few guides as to what is expected.

Anticipatory socialization is role-learning designed to prepare the individual for future roles.

Antinatalism refers to social forces that discourage childbearing.

Art of impression management is the attempt to control others' conduct and influence their definition of the situation and their impression of the actor.

An **ascribed status** is one that is fixed by birth and inheritance and is unalterable in a person's lifetime.

Assimilation is the integration of the minority group into the institutions of the majority group and the end of its identity as a distinct group.

Authoritarian systems are political systems in which the leadership is not responsible to the people and in which there is no legal method of changing leadership short of forceful overthrow.

Authoritarianism is the tendency to be submissive to those in authority coupled with an aggressive and negative attitude toward those lower in status.

Authority is power supported by norms and values that legitimate its use.

Behaviorism assumes that individual acts are conditioned by events external to the individual. We learn to repeat behavior that brings rewards and avoid behaviors that give us pain.

Bloc mobilization is the process whereby social-movement organizations recruit other organizations to support their cause rather than trying to recruit single individuals.

The **bourgeoisie** is the class that owns the means of production.

Bureaucracy is a complex organization characterized by rational operation of a hierarchical authority structure and explicit procedures and rules.

Capitalism is the economic system in which most wealth is in private hands and is used to create more wealth for its owners.

577

Caste systems use ascribed statuses as the basis for unequal resource distribution.

A **category** is a collection of people who share a common characteristic (for example, the elderly, females, managers, and students).

Charisma is extraordinary personal qualities that are thought to be supernatural in origin.

Charismatic authority occurs when an individual is granted the right to make decisions for others because of perceived extraordinary personal characteristics.

Churches are religious organizations that are institutions of society, supporting and supported by its other institutions. They tend to be large and bureaucratically organized, with professional clergy and formal rituals of participation.

Civil religion is the set of institutionalized rituals, beliefs, and symbols sacred to the American nation, including reverence for the flag and belief in capitalism and democracy.

Class refers to a person's relationship to the means of production (proletariat or bourgeoisie).

Class consciousness occurs when people are aware of their relationship to the means of production and recognize their true class interests.

Class systems use achieved status as the basis of unequal resource distribution.

Coercion is the exercise of power through force or the threat of force.

Cohabitation occurs when couples live together without legal marriage.

Cohesion refers to the forces that attract members to the group.

Collective actions are episodic crowd actions that occur in irregular ways and that are triggered by nonroutine events.

Competition is a struggle for scarce resources that is regulated by shared rules.

Complex organizations are large in size and characterized by complex interrelationships among their parts.

Conflict is a deliberate attempt to destroy or neutralize one's rivals in order to attain valued ends.

Conflict theory addresses the points of stress and conflict in social structures and the ways they contribute to social change.

Contagion theory suggests that the crowd situation leads to the development of unanimous and intense feeling and behavior that are at odds with the usual dispositions of the individual participants.

Control variables are background factors whose effects must be eliminated in order to understand the relationship between study variables.

Convergence theory contends that the cause or pretext for crowd action selectively draws persons who share a common set of predispositions.

Cooperation is when people work together to achieve shared goals.

Core societies are rich and powerful nations that are economically diversified and relatively free of outside control. This is a central idea of world system theory.

Correlation is a statistical association between two variables showing that they have a patterned relationship.

Countercultures are groups that have acquired a set of unique values, interests, beliefs, and life-styles that are in conflict with the dominant characteristics of the larger culture.

A **countermovement** seeks to resist or reverse the change advocated by a social movement; it is a defender of the status quo.

Credentialism is the practice of using educational degrees as job requirements to ward off any encroachment of the lower class on upper-class jobs.

Crimes are deviant acts that are subject to criminal or civil penalties.

The **cross-sectional design** uses a sample (or cross section) of the population drawn from a single point in time. It is a form of survey research.

A **crowd** is a relatively large number of people drawn to a common location by some nonroutine event.

The **crude birthrate (CBR)** is the number of births divided by the total population and then multiplied by 1,000.

The **crude deathrate (CDR)** is the number of deaths divided by the total population and then multiplied by 1,000.

A **cult** is a religious group that is independent of the religious traditions of the society in which it develops. It usually rejects and is rejected by society.

Cultural evolution is the use of specific social arrangements and technology as a mechanism for adapting to environmental and social change.

Cultural lag is the period of adjustment of the nonmaterial culture to the new material culture.

Cultural relativity refers to evaluating the traits of a culture on the basis of how a trait fits into the overall cultural patterns.

Cultural universals are behavioral patterns and institutions that are found in all human cultures; among them are inequality, marriage, body adornment, and religious ritual.

Culture is the total way of life shared by members of a society. It includes material products as well as patterned, repetitive ways of thinking, feeling, and acting.

Cuture of poverty is a set of values that emphasizes living for the moment rather than thrift, investment in the future, and hard work.

De facto segregation is not legally mandated separatism; it is separatism that evolves over time because of economic and social circumstances.

A **defeated neighborhood** is a neighborhood that has disintegrated in both physical and social structure so that it can no longer act on its own behalf or protect itself.

Defensible space is an environment that inhibits crime; it is small enough and visible enough to be considered a neighborhood responsibility.

De jure segregation is legally required separation in housing.

Deduction is the process of moving from theory to observations by devising tests of hypotheses drawn from existing theory.

Defensive pluralism is an assertion of group identity motivated by competition with other organized groups that are making claims for special treatment.

Definition of the situation suggests that "if men define situations as real, they are real in their consequences."

Democracy is a political system that provides regular, constitutional opportunities for a change in leadership according to the will of the majority.

The **demographic transition** is the change from high birth- and deathrates to low birth- and deathrates associated with modernization. During the transition, birthrates are higher than deathrates and population growth occurs.

Demography is the study of population—its size, growth, and composition.

Denominations are churchlike religious groups that are large and bureaucratically organized and that adopt a tolerant attitude toward other religions.

The **dependency ratio** is the ratio of dependents per productive worker, usually calculated at the number of people under 15 and over 65 divided by the population 15 to 65.

The **dependent variable** is the effect in cause-and-effect relationships. It is dependent on the actions of the independent variable.

Developmental theory assumes that there are a series of stages of cognitive and moral development that correspond to physiological maturation.

Deviance involves acts of nonconformity that violate significant norms and are negatively viewed by society.

Dialectic philosophy views change as a product of conflict and contradictions among the parts of society.

Differential association theory assumes that deviance is learned through the same mechanisms as conformity—essentially through interaction with intimates.

Differentials are differences in the incidence of a phenomenon across subcategories of the population.

Diffusion is a process by which an aspect of material or nonmaterial culture is spread from one culture to another.

Discovery is the independent uncovering of a new piece of knowledge.

Disengagement theory is the functionalist theory of aging that argues the elderly voluntarily disengage themselves from active social participation.

Division of labor is the interdependence of individuals with specialized tasks and abilities.

The **divorce rate** is calculated as the number of divorces each year per 1,000 married women.

Dominant roles are established when individuals assign priorities to their roles and choose to act in terms of normative demands of the most important role.

Double or triple jeopardy means having low status on two or three different dimensions of stratification.

A **double standard** exists when premarital or extramarital sexual activity is acceptable for men but not for women.

Dramaturgy is a version of role theory that views social situations as scenes, complete with stages, actors, scripts, props, and audiences.

A **dual economy** consists of an industrial core made up of giant organizations and a periphery made up of small, competitive firms.

Dynamic equilibrium is the constant adjustment of the various parts of a social system to preserve the stability of the system as a whole. In functional theory, dynamic equilibrium is functional change.

Dysfunctions are consequences of social structures that have negative effects on the stability of society.

An **ecclesia** is a churchlike religious group that automatically includes every member of a society.

Economic determinism suggests that economic relationships are the basis for all other social relationships.

Economic institutions are social structures concerned with the production and distribution of goods and services.

Egalitarianism emphasizes that spouses jointly share in decision making, control of family resources, and childrearing.

Emergent-norm theory suggests that a crowd is governed by norms that are developed and validated by group processes within the crowd.

Environmental deprivation syndrome is a condition of neglect, isolation, and absence of mothering.

An **established sect** is a religious group that has adapted to the ways of society in order to spread its message and gather converts but that still holds itself aloof.

An **ethnic group** is a category of people who are distinct because of cultural characteristics handed down from generation to generation.

Ethnocentrism is the tendency to view the norms and values of one's culture as absolute and to use them as a standard against which to judge the practices of other cultures.

Exchange is the mutual giving and receiving of material or nonmaterial benefits.

An **experiment** is a method in which independent variables are manipulated in order to test theories of cause and effect.

Expressive describes activites or roles that provide integration and emotional support to group members.

An **extended family** exists when the wife-husband pair and their children live with other kin and share economic and childrearing responsibilities with them.

Extrinsic rewards are tangible benefits such as income and security.

Fads are widely dispersed patterns of behavior that develop rapidly and end almost as rapidly.

False consciousness occurs when people are fooled by differences in income and prestige and fail to recognize their true class interests (that is, their relationship to the means of production).

A **family** is a relatively permanent group of persons linked together in social roles by ties of blood, marriage, or adoption who live together and cooperate economically and in the rearing of children.

Fashions are cultural patterns, usually of dress and adornment, adopted by a segment of the population for a relatively brief period of time and then abandoned.

Fertility is the incidence of childbearing.

Folkways are norms that are the customary, normal, habitual ways in which a group does things.

Formal social controls are administrative sanctions such as fines, expulsion, and imprisonment.

Functions are consequences of social structures that have positive effects on the stability of society.

Fundamentalism is a movement to restore original religious principles to both religious practice and society.

Gemeinschaft communities are dominated by personal and diffuse ties among individuals. They are more often characteristic of rural society.

Gender is biological sex, male or female.

Generalized other is Mead's term for our awareness of social norms; it is the composite expectations of all the other role-players with whom we interact.

Gesellschaft communities are characterized by instrumental and impersonal relationships. They are more common in urban environments.

Group is a collection of people who interact together on the basis of a shared social structure.

Groupthink is a process of decision making in which we-feeling and unanimity rate higher than critical evaluation and rationality.

The **guinea-pig effect** occurs when participants in an experiment act differently than they would outside the laboratory because of their knowledge that they are participating in an experiment.

Health is the state of mind and body that permits a person to occupy the usual social roles.

Homogamy is similarity in characteristics between individuals.

The **hidden curriculum** is the unofficial program of studies in the schools, the three Rs of which are rules, regulations, and routines.

The **human relations school** stresses treating workers as human beings with social and emotional needs.

Hypotheses are statements about the expected relationships between two or more variables.

Ideology is a set of norms and values that rationalize the existing social structure.

Incidence is the frequency with which an attitude or behavior occurs.

The **independent variable** is the variable that does the causing in cause-and-effect relationships.

The **indirect inheritance model** argues that parents' status and income structure children's surroundings and aspirations so that children end up in the same social class as their parents.

Induction is the process of moving from observations to theory.

The **industrial democracy school** advocates democratic decision making within the organization and reduced authoritarianism in the work environment.

Informal social control is self-restraint exercised because of fear of what others will think.

Institutionalized racism is an indirect form of discrimination, one in which unjustifiable preconditions and prerequisites exclude a disproportionate number of minority group members.

An **institution** is a social structure built around a relatively distinct and socially important set of values that endures over generations. They are relatively stable clusters of interconnected statuses and roles centered around the basic needs of society.

Instrumental describes activities or roles within a group that are task oriented.

Integration describes biracial interaction in which the minority group is accepted on a completely equal basis.

An **interlocking directorate** exists when common membership on a board of directors ties many companies together.

Internalization occurs when we accept the norms and values of our group as the appropriate way to behave—when conformity becomes part of our self-concept.

Intragenerational mobility is the change in social class within one person's career.

Intergenerational mobility is the change in social class form one generation to the next.

Intrinsic rewards are rewards that arise from the process of work; they include the enjoyment of creativity, accomplishment, and working with others.

A **kin group** is a status network composed of people related by common ancestry.

Labeling theory is concerned with the processes by which some groups are able to attach the label *deviant* to the behavior of other groups or individuals.

Latent functions are consequences of social structures that are neither intended nor recognized.

Laws are norms that are officially enforced and sanctioned, generally by the authority of government.

Leisure is all the voluntary activities that people undertake after they have finished their required tasks.

Liberal democracy is a democratic form of government characterized by distrust of government power. Many of the formal elements of liberal democracy are designed to restrain the government or a popular majority from interfering with the rights of individuals.

The **life course** is the structure of expectations and relationships through which one passes sequentially.

The **lifetime divorce probability** is the probability that a marriage will ever end in divorce.

The **longitudinal design** follows a sample over a period of time, during which some portion of the sample experiences the independent variable. It is a form of survey research.

Looking-glass self is Cooley's term for a self-concept that is based on how we think we appear to others.

Macrosociology studies human social behavior by identifying the basic patterns of society and their interrelationships.

A **majority group** is a group that is culturally, economically, and politically dominant.

Manifest functions are consequences of social structures that are intended and recognized.

Marriage is a socially recognized and institutionalized mating arrangement between males and females.

Matriarchal authority is normatively approved female dominance.

Matrilocal residence occurs when the rules of residence require newly married couples to take up residence with the wife's kin.

The **melting pot** goes beyond assimilation to include a physical and cultural blending of groups.

A **metropolitan county** either has a city of 50,000 or more in it or is significantly linked, socially and economically, to a county that does have such a city.

Microsociology analyzes interactions among individuals.

Mid-life crisis is an awareness that goals not yet reached are probably forever beyond one's reach.

A **minority group** is a group that is culturally, economically, and politically subordinate.

Mobilization theory suggests that social movements arise when competition develops among organized groups. Also known as solidarity theory.

Modernization theory, a functionalist theory of development based on Western experience, assumes that developing nations can follow the Western path to wealth through industrialization.

Modernization theory of aging argues that modernization reduces the power of the elderly by reducing the value of their traditional resources: land, labor, and experience.

Momentum is a force for population growth that occurs when the number of people in future reproductive generations is larger than the number in the current generation.

Monogamy is marriage in which there is only one wife and one husband.

Moral entrepreneurs are people who are in a position to create and enforce new definitions of morality.

The **moral majority** is a political movement designed to legislate evangelical Christian morality.

Mores are norms for which fairly strong ideas of right or wrong have developed; they carry a moral connotation.

Mortality is the incidence of death.

Multinationals are large corporations that operate internationally.

Mutable self is a self-concept based more on personality characteristics than on institutional statuses and roles; it is highly flexible and adaptable.

The **natural growth rate** is the percentage growth rate implied by the excess of births over deaths. It is measured as the crude birthrate minus the crude deathrate and then divided by 10.

A **neighborhood** is a geographically bounded set of streets that has a common sense of identity and some basis of shared ties.

Neolocal residence occurs when the rules of residence require that a newly married couple take up residence away from their relatives.

A **nonmetropolitan county** has no major city in it and is not closely linked to a county that does have such a city.

The **norm of communalism** specifies that scientists must freely share new knowledge with others.

The **norm of disinterest** requires that the scientist place the search for truth above personal gain.

The **norm of emotional neutrality** requires that the scientist's personal preferences not affect the outcomes of research.

The **norm of organized skepticism** requires that all new knowledge claims be critically examined to see if they meet technical standards.

The **norm of reciprocity** specifies that people should return favors and should seek to maintain a balance of obligation in their social relationships.

The **norm of universalism** specifies that new knowledge claims be judged on technical merit only, not on the characteristics of the individual scientist.

Norms are shared expectations of how people are supposed to behave.

A **nuclear family** consists of a husband, wife, and their dependent children.

Operational definitions describe the exact procedures by which a variable is to be measured.

The **other-directed individual** is sensitive and attentive to others, guided not by firm principles and values but by the signals picked up from the social environment.

Overeducation occurs when the level of education attained exceeds what is necessary for an occupation.

Participant observation is a method that uses interviewing, observation, and participation in order to examine the context of human interaction and their meanings for the individuals involved.

Party is a person's ability to influence communal action in Weber's analysis of class systems.

Patriarchal authority is normatively approved male dominance.

Patrilocal residence occurs when the rules of residence require a newly married couple to take up residence with the husband's kin.

Patterned social regularities are social phenomena that occur over and over in the same way.

Peripheral societies are poor and weak, with highly specialized economies over which they have little control. They are a central component of world system theory.

Personality is the unique attributes and abilities of the individual.

Political alienation is a cynical belief that voting is a useless exercise and that individual citizens have no influence on decision making.

Political institutions are institutions concerned with the social structure of power.

A **political party** is an association specifically organized to win elections and secure power over the personnel and policies of the state.

Polyandry is a form of marriage in which one woman may be married to two or more men at a time.

Polygamy is any form of marriage in which a person may have more than one spouse at a time (polygyny or polyandry).

Polygyny is a form of marriage in which a man may be married to two or more women at a time.

Positivism is the belief that the scientific method can be applied directly to the study of social behavior.

Power is the ability to get others to do something against their wishes, the ability to overcome resistance.

The **power elite** is the people who occupy the top positions in three bureaucracies—the military, industry, and the executive branch of government—and who act together to run the United States in their own interests.

Predictions are statements about what the future will be like that represent the predictor's best guess about probable trends.

Prejudice is irrationally based negative attitudes toward categories of people.

Primary deviance is an individual's first instance of a nonconforming act. If the act is labeled deviant and the person accepts the label, then the person may become a real or secondary deviant.

Primary groups are groups characterized by intimate, face-to-face association and cooperation.

Primary production is extracting raw materials from the environment.

Primary socialization is personality development and role learning that occurs during early childhood.

Primary ties are people for whom we have feelings of love, loyalty, and caring.

The **profane** represents all that is routine and taken for granted in the everyday world, things that are accepted because they are familiar and common.

Professions are occupations that demand specialized skills and creative freedom.

Projections are extrapolations of current trends into the future.

The **proletariant** is the class that does not own the means of production and must sell its labor to the bourgeoisie in exchange for a wage.

Pronatalism refers to social forces that encourage childbearing.

Propinquity is spatial nearness.

The **Protestant ethic** is a belief that work is good and idleness is wicked. Its name comes from its importance to the early Puritans.

A **public** is a dispersed group of people interested in and divided about an issue.

A **race** is a category of people who are socially defined as distinct because of genetically transmitted physical characteristics.

Racial steering occurs when realtors encourage black families to buy or rent in black neighborhoods and encourage white families to buy or rent in white neighborhoods.

Racism is a belief that inherited physical characteristics determine the presence or absence of socially relevant abilities and characteristics and that such differences provide a legitimate basis for unequal treatment.

Rational-legal authority occurs when an individual is granted the right to make decisions for others because of submission to a set of rationally established rules.

Redlining is the process by which financial investments (mortgages, loans, and home insurance) are systematically denied to one area of the city and diverted to other, more favored areas.

Regentrification is the process whereby middle-classs or upper-middle-class families take over a decaying neighborhood and vastly upgrade the quality of housing.

Relative-deprivation theory stresses the role of social disorganization and discontent in encouraging social movements. Also known as breakdown theory.

Relative poverty is poverty relative to the average standard of living in a society.

Religion is the system of shared beliefs and practices by which people invoke supernatural forces as explanations of earthly struggles.

Religiosity is a measure of the extent to which a person's attitudes, beliefs, and behaviors are influenced by religion.

Replacement-level fertility requires that each woman bear approximately two children so that she replaces her and her partner; this results in the next generation being the same size as the current generation of parents.

Replication is the repetition of empirical studies again and again to make sure that different observers get the same results.

Resocialization occurs when we abandon our self-concept and way of life for one that is radically different.

Revolution is the most radical form of social change; one that makes a sharp break with the past and results in significant changes in basic social structure.

Risky shift is a process of decision making during which group members converge on a decision that is more adventurous than their initial individual choices.

Rites of passage are formal rituals that mark the end of one status and the beginning of another.

Romantic love is a combination of such physical symptoms as breathlessness and a pounding heart with a sexual yearning for the other and a disregard of practical and economic consequences.

Roles are the rights and obligations of persons performing special functions for a group.

Role conflict occurs when the role expectations of two or more statuses held by an individual are incompatible or inconsistent.

Role identity is our evaluation of our performance in a specific social role.

Role segmentation occurs when roles are compartmentalized and used in some situations but not others.

Role strain results whenever there are tensions or contradictions built into the role expectations of a particular status.

Role theory suggests that the social roles we acquire shape both our behavior and personality.

Role transition is the process of shedding old roles and adopting new roles over the life course.

Rumor is unathenticated information spread by word of mouth.

Rural is the U. S. Census Bureau term for places with fewer than 2,500 people.

The **sacred** consists of things outside the sphere of everyday life that are approached with an attitude of awe and reverence.

A **sample** is a systematic selection of a group of individuals from a larger pool using random procedures.

Sanctions are rewards for conformity and punishments for nonconformity.

Scapegoating is the practice of placing the blame for one's own frustrations on another group.

Science is a way of knowing based on systematic, critical and empirical investigation.

Secondary deviance occurs when a person accepts the label of deviant and elects to play that role in society by repeatedly engaging in deviant acts.

Secondary groups are groups that are formal, large in size, and impersonal.

Secondary production is the processing of raw materials.

Secondary ties are people known in the context of specific instrumental relationships.

Sects are religious groups that reject the social environment in which they exist. They are generally small, low in ritual, and demanding of high levels of personal participation.

Secularization is the process of transferring things or ideas from the sacred realm to the profane realm. The transfer occurs when an event can be explained without recourse to supernatural forces.

The **segmented labor market** has systematically different patterns of hiring, advancement, and benefits in the industrial core than in the periphery.

Segregation is the practice of physically separating minority and majority group members.

Self consists of two parts, one (the I) responding to individual needs and the other (the me) responding to social demands.

Self-concept is the individual's evaluation of his or her personality and social roles in comparison to others'.

A **self-fulfilling prophecy** occurs when, by acting on a belief that a situation exists, it becomes real.

The **semicaste structure** is a hierarchical ordering of classes within castelike boundaries based on ascribed characteristics such as race or ethnicity.

Sex roles are the rights and obligations assigned to males and females in a particular society.

Sexism is a belief that women and men have biologically different capacities and that these differences form a legitimate basis for the subordination of women.

Sexual harassment consists of unwelcome sexual advances, requests for sexual favors, and other unwelcome verbal or physical conduct of a sexual nature.

The **sick role** is the rights and obligations that accompany the social label sick.

Significant others are those occupying roles that deal intimately with us.

Social change is significant alterations over time in material or nonmaterial culture.

Social control is the forces and processes that encourage conformity, including internalization, informal social control, and formal social control.

Social control theory assumes that deviance is a natural condition which may be controlled by strong bonds that tie the individual to society.

Social-desirability bias is the tendency of respondents to make themselves sound better and more desirable than they really are.

Social distance is the degree of intimacy in relationships between two groups.

Socialism is an economic structure in which productive tools (land, labor, and capital) are owned and managed by the group as whole or by their agent, the state.

Social mobility is a change in occupation or social-class position between generations or over the career of an individual.

Social movements are deliberate, organized attempts to change social institutions from the outside.

A **social network** is the total set of linkages a person has with others through participation in social groups.

Social processes are mechanisms of interaction. They are concerned with change, development, and the dynamic aspects of social relationships.

Social structure is a network of interconnected statuses and corresponding roles that structure interaction.

Societies are groups of interacting individuals who share the same territory and are bound together by economic and political ties.

Socialization is the process of learning the roles, statuses, and values necessary for participation in social institutions.

Sociobiology focuses on the biological and evolutionary bases of social behavior.

Socioeconomic status (SES) is a measure of social class that is based on indicators of income, occupation, and education.

Sociological imagination is the ability to place personal troubles in the context of social structures and see them as public issues.

Sociology is the systematic study of human social interaction.

The **sociology of knowledge** is concerned with the development and change of criteria for authorizing knowledge.

Specialty norms pertain to only certain groups or subgroups.

Sport is competitive physical activity that bases winning and losing on a set of structured rules.

The **state** is the social structure that successfully claims a monopoly on the legitimate use of coercion and physical force within a territory.

Status is the collection of roles associated with a specialized position in the group.

Status is social honor, expressed in life-style in Weber's analysis of class systems.

Status network is the total set of interacting statuses within a group, organization, or social system.

Stratification is an institutionalized pattern of inequality in which social categories are ranked on the basis of their access to scarce resources.

Street-level justice is the decisions the police make in the initial stages of an investigation.

Structural functionalism addresses the question of social organization and how it is maintained.

Subcultures are groups that share in the overall culture of society but that have their own distinctive values, norms, and life-styles.

Survey research is a method that involves asking a relatively large number of people the same set of standardized questions.

Symbolic interactionism addresses the subjective meanings of human acts and the processes through which people come to develop and communicate shared meanings. It emphasizes interaction, negotiation, and role-taking as mechanisms for learning social roles and self-identity.

Systems model of education (input/output model) focuses on how the output from schools depends on both the diversity of input (children) and life in the schools.

Tame shift is a process of decision making during which group members converge on a decision that is more conservative than their initial individual choices.

Tertiary production is the production of services.

Theory is an interrelated set of assumptions that provides an explanation of why correlations exist.

Total institutions are facilities in which all aspects of life are strictly controlled for the purpose of radical resocialization.

Tracking occurs when evaluations relatively early in a child's career determine the educational programs the child will be encouraged to follow.

Traditional authority occurs when an individual is given the right to make decisions for others because of the sanctity of time-honored routines.

Trends are changes in a variable over time.

The **triple-melting pot** is the intermarriage and cultural blending of whites within the three major religions: Catholic, Protestant, and Jewish.

The **underclass** is the group that is unemployed and unemployable, not an integrated part of the nation but a miserable and useless substratum.

Universal norms are norms that are binding on all members of society.

Urban is the U. S. Census Bureau term for places with 2,500 people or more.

Urbanism is a distinctively urban mode of life that is developed in the cities but not confined there.

Urbanization is the process of population concentration.

Value-free sociology concerns itself with establishing what is, not what ought to be.

Values are shared standards of desirability.

Variables are measured characteristics that vary from one individual or group to the next.

Verstehen sociology emphasizes the subjective meanings of human actions.

A **veto group** is an interest group or coalition of interest groups that can block action by other groups but that is less effective in pushing its own programs.

Victimless crimes are illegal acts for which there is no complainant.

Voluntary associations are nonprofit organizations designed to allow individuals an opportunity to pursue their shared interests collectively.

Weak ties are people known personally but not intimately.

White-collar crime is crime committed by people of respectability and high status in the course of their profession.

Withdrawal is a mechanism for resolving role conflict in which individuals choose not to meet the expectations of either role.

World system theory, a Marxist analysis of the relationship between developing and developed countries, suggests that the economic dominance of core societies will prevent the progress of peripheral societies.

Zero population growth (ZPG) means that the number of births is the same as the number of deaths, so the population does not grow.

References

ABC News/Washington Post Poll. (1983, October 15–October 28).

Adams, Bert N. (1971). The American Family: A Sociological Interpretation. Chicago: Markham Publishing.

Adams, Bert N. (1979). "Mate selection in the United States: A theoretical summarization." In W. R. Burr, Reuben Hill, F. Ivan Nye, & Ira L. Reiss (Eds.), Contemporary Theories about the Family (Vol. 1, pp. 259–267). New York: Free Press.

Aday, Lu Ann, & Anderson, Ronald. (1975). Development of Indices of Access to Medical Care. Ann Arbor, Mich.: Health Administration Press.

Agersvold, Mogens. (1975). "Swedish experiments in industrial democracy." In L. Davis, B. Cherns, and associates (Eds.), The Quality of Working Life (Vol. 2, pp. 46–65). New York: Free Press.

Aird, John S. (1972). Population Policy and Demographic Prospects in the People's Republic of China. U.S. Department of Health, Education and Welfare. Washington, D.C.: U.S. Government Printing Office.

Alexander, Karl, Cook, Martha, & McDill, Edward L. (1978). "Curriculum tracking and educational satisfaction: Some further evidence." American Sociological Review, 43(1):47–66.

Alfred, Randall. (1976). "The church of Satan." In Charles Y. Glock, & Robert N. Bellah (Eds.), The New Religious Consciousness (pp. 180–202). Berkeley: University of California Press.

Allen, Walter R. (1980). "Preludes to attainment: Race, sex, and student achievement orientations." The Sociological Quarterly, 21(Winter):65–79.

Altman, Dennis. (1983). The Homosexualization of America. Boston: Beacon Press. (Original work published 1982).

Amir, Menachem. (1971). Patterns of Forcible Rape. Chicago: University of Chicago Press.

Angell, Robert. (1936). The Family Encounters the Depression. New York: Scribner's.

Aries, Philippe. (1962). Centuries of Childhood: A Social History of Family Life. New York: Knopf.

Asch, Solomon E. (1955). "Opinions and social pressure." Scientific American, 193(November):31–35.

Ash, Roberta. (1972). Social Movements in America. Chicago: Markham Publishing.

Asimov, Isaac. (1953). Foundation Trilogy. New York: Doubleday.

Astin, Alexander. (1977). Four Critical Years. San Francisco: Jossey-Bass.

Atchley, Robert C. (1982). "Retirement as a social institution." American Review of Sociology, 8:263–287.

Babbie, Earl R. (1983). The Practice of Social Research (3rd ed.). Belmont, Calif.: Wadsworth.

Baldwin, Frances. (1926). "Sumptuary legislation and personal regulation in England." Johns Hopkins University Studies in Historical and Political Science, 44(1):1–282.

Balkan, Sheila, Berger, Ronald J., & Schmidt, Janet. (1980). Crime and Deviance in America: A Critical Approach. Belmont, Calif.: Wadsworth.

Banfield, Edward C. (1974). The Unheavenly City Revisited. Boston: Little, Brown.

Barfield, Richard E., & Morgan, James N. (1979). "Trends in planned early retirement." In Jon Hendricks & C. Davis Hendricks (Eds.), Dimensions of Aging: Readings. Cambridge, Mass.: Winthrop Publishers.

Barnet, Richard J., & Muller, Ronald E. (1974). Global Research: The Power of Multinational Corporations. New York: Simon & Schuster.

Barney, Gerald O. (1981). The Global 2000 Report to the President of the U.S.: Entering the 21st Century: Vol. 1. The Summary Report. New York: Pergamon Press.

Barone, Michael, & Ujifusa, Grant. (1981). The Almanac of American Politics, 1982. Washington, D.C.: Barone and Company.

Becker, Howard S. (1963). Outsiders: Studies in the Sociology of Deviance. New York: Free Press.

Beckwith, Carol. (1983). "Niger's Wodaabe: 'People of the taboo.'" National Geographic, 164(October):482–509.

Behrman, Bradley. (1980). "Civil aeronautics board." In J. Wilson (Ed.), The Politics of Regulation (pp. 75–120). New York: Basic Books.

Beier, George J. (1976). "Can Third World cities cope?" Population Bulletin, 31(December):1–34.

Bell, Wendell, & Robinson, Robert V. (1978). "An index of evaluated equality: Measuring conceptions of social justice in England and the United States." In Richard F. Tomasson (Ed.), Comparative Studies in Sociology (Vol. 1, pp. 235–270). Greenwich, Conn.: JAI Press.

Bellah, Robert N. (1974). "Civil religion in America." In Russel B. Richey & Donald G. Jones (Eds.), American Civil Religion. New York: Harper & Row.

Bellah, Robert. (1975). The Broken Covenant: American Civil Religion in Time of Trial. New York: Seabury Press.

Bem, Sandra L. (1976). "Probing the promise of androgyny." In A. G. Kaplan & J. P. Bean (Eds.), Beyond Sex-Role Stereotypes (pp. 48–62). Boston: Little, Brown.

Bendix, Reinhard. (1968). "Max Weber." In David J. Sills (Ed.), International Encyclopedia of the Social Sciences (Vol. 16, pp. 493–502). New York: Macmillan and Free Press.

Bennis, Warren. (1979). "Response to Shariff: Beyond bureaucracy baiting." Social Science Quarterly, 60(1):20–24.

Ben-Yehuda, Nachman. (1980). "The European witch craze of the 14th to 17th centuries: A sociologist's perspective." American Journal of Sociology 86(July):1–31.

Berelson, B. R., Lazarsfeld, Paul, & McPhee, W. N. (1954). Voting. Chicago: University of Chicago Press.

Berger, Peter L. (1963). Invitation to Sociology: A Humanistic Perspective. Garden City, N.Y.: Doubleday.

Berger, Peter L., Berger, Brigitte, & Kellner, Hansfried. (1972). The Homeless Mind. New York: Vintage Books.

Bianchi, Suzanne. (1980). "Racial differences in per capita income, 1960–1976: The impact of household size, headship, and labor force participation." Demography 17(May):129–146.

Black, Donald. (1976). The Behavior of Law. New York: Academic Press.

Blake, Judith. (1979). "Is zero preferred? American attitudes toward childlessness in the 1970's." Journal of Marriage and the Family, 41(May):245–257.

Blake, Judith. (1981). "Family size and the quality of children." Demography, 18(4):421–442.

Blake, Judith, & del Pinal, Jorge. (1981). "The childlessness option: Recent American views of nonparenthood." In Gerry E. Hendershot & Paul J. Placek (Eds.), Predicting Fertility:

Demographic Studies of Birth Expectations (pp. 235–261). Lexington, Mass.: Lexington Books.

Blau, Peter M. (1964). Exchange and Power in Social Life. New York: Wiley.

Blau, Peter M. & Duncan, Otis Dudley. (1967). The American Occupational Structure. New York: Wiley.

Blau, Peter M., & Meyer, Marshall W. (1971). Bureaucracy in Modern Society (2d ed.). New York: Random House.

Blumberg, Abraham S. (1970). Criminal Justice. Chicago: Quadrangle Books.

Blumberg, Paul. (1980). Inequality in an Age of Decline. New York: Oxford University Press.

Blumenbach, Johan. (1975). "On the Natural Variety of Mankind." Cited in M. Banton & J. Harwood, The Race Concept. Newton Abbot, U.K.: David and Charles. (Original work published in 1775).

Blumer, H. (1934). "Collective behavior." In A. M. Lee (Ed.), New Outlines of the Principles of Sociology (pp. 165–220). New York: Barnes & Noble.

Blumstein, Phillip, & Schwartz, Pepper. (1983). American Couples. New York: William Morrow.

Bohland, James R. (1982). "Indian residential segregation in the urban Southwest: 1970 and 1980," Social Science Quarterly 63(December):749–761.

Bollen, Kenneth. (1983). "World system position, dependency, and democracy: The cross-national evidence." American Sociological Review, 48(August):468–479.

Bollier, David. (1982). Liberty and Justice for Some. New York: Frederick Ungar Publishing.

Boocock, Sarane S. (1975). "The social context of childhood." Proceedings of the American Philosophical Society, 119(6):419–429.

Boocock, Sarane. (1976). Students, Schools, and Educational Policy. Aspen, Colo.: Aspen Institute for Humanistic Studies.

Booth, Alan. (1976). Urban Crowding and Its Consequences. New York: Praeger.

Booth, Alan, Johnson, David R., White, Lynn K., & Edwards, John. (1984). "Women, outside employment, and marital instability." American Journal of Sociology, forthcoming.

Booth, Alan, & White, Lynn. (1980). "Thinking about divorce." Journal of Marriage and the Family, 42(August):605–616.

Bose, Christine E., & Rossi, Peter H. (1983). "Gender and jobs:Prestige standings of occupations as affected by gender." American Sociological Review, 48(June):316–330.

Boulding, Kenneth Ewart. (1964). The Meaning of the Twentieth Century: The Great Transition. New York: Harper & Row.

Bouvier, Leon F. (1980). "America's baby boom generation: The fateful bulge." Population Bulletin, 35(1):1–45.

Bowen, Howard R. (1977). Investment in Learning. San Francisco: Jossey-Bass.

Bowers, William J., & Pierce, Glenn. (1983). "What is the effect of executions: Deterrence or brutalization?" Unpublished paper cited in Ernest van den Haag & Jon P. Conrad, The Death Penalty: A Debate. New York: Plenum Press.

Bowlby, J. (1969). Attachment and Loss. New York: Basic Books.

Bowles, Samuel. (1972). "Unequal education and the reproduction of the social division of labor." In Martin Conroy (Ed.), Schooling in a Corporate Society, New York: David McKay.

Bowles, Samuel, & Gintis, Herbert. (1976). Schooling in Capitalist America: Educational Reform and the Contradictions of Economic Life. New York: Basic Books.

Braithwaite, John. (1981). "The myth of social class and criminality reconsidered." American Sociological Review, 46(February):36–58.

Brake, Mike. (1980). The Sociology of Youth Culture and Youth Subcultures. London: Routledge & Kegan Paul.

Briggs, Vernon. (1975). "Illegal aliens: The need for a more restrictive border policy." Social Science Quarterly, 56(December):485–491.

Brinkerhoff, Merlin B., & Kunz, Phillip R. (Eds.). (1972). Complex Organizations and Their Environments. Dubuque, Iowa: Wm. C. Brown.

Broad, William, & Wade, Nicholas. (1983). Betrayers of the Truth. New York: Simon & Schuster.

Bromley, David G., & Schupe, Anson D., Jr. (1980). "Financing the new religions: A resource mobilization approach." Journal for the Scientific Study of Religion, 19(3):227–239.

Bronfenbrenner, U. (1970). Two Worlds of Childhood: U.S. and U.S.S.R. New York: Russell Sage Foundation.

Brookover, Wilbur, Beady, Charles, Flood, Patricia, Schweitzer, John, & Wisenbaker, Joe. (1979). School Social Systems and Student Achievement: Schools Can Make a Difference. New York: Praeger.

Brossi, Kathleen B. (1979). A Cross-City Comparison of Felony Case Processing. Washington, D.C.: U.S. Government Printing Office.

Brown, Judith K. (1970). "A note on the division of labor by sex." The American Anthropologist, 72(5):1073–1078.

Brown, Lester R. (1981). "World food resources and population: The narrowing margin." Population Bulletin, 36(September):1–43.

Brown, R. (1974). "Further comment on the risky-shift." American Psychologist, 29(June):468–470.

Brzezinski, Zbigniew. (1956). "Totalitarianism and rationality." American Political Science Review, 50(September): 751–763.

Brzezinski, Zbigniew, & Huntington, Samuel P. (1964). Political Power USA/USSR. New York: Viking Press.

Bullock, Charles S., III, & Rodgers, Harrel R., Jr. (1976). "Institutional racism: Prerequisites, freezing, and mapping." Phylon, 37(3):212–223.

Bumpass, Larry. (1984). "Children and marital disruption: A replication and update." Demography, 21(February):71–82.

Bumpass, Larry, & Rindfuss, R. (1979). "Children's experience of marital disruption." American Journal of Sociology, 85(January):49–65.

Burgess, Robert L., & Akers, Ronald L. (1966). "A differential association-reinforcement theory of criminal behavior." Social Problems, 14(Fall):128–147.

Burke, Peter J. (1980). "The self: Measurement requirements from the interactionist perspective." Social Psychological Quarterly, 43(1):18–29.

Burris, Val. (1983). "The social and political consequences of overeducation." American Sociological Review, 48(August):454–467.

Bybee, Rodger W. (1979). "Violence toward youth: A new perspective." Journal of Social Issues, 35(Spring):1–14.

Campbell, Ernest Q. (1969). "Adolescent socialization." In David A. Goslin (Ed.), Handbook of Socialization Theory and Research (pp. 821–860). New York: Russell Sage Foundation.

Cantor, Marjorie. (1976). "Effect of ethnicity on life styles of the inner-city elderly." In Jon Hendricks & C. Davis Hendricks (Eds.), Dimensions of Aging: Readings (pp. 278–293). Cambridge, Mass.: Winthrop Publishers.

Caplow, Theodore, & Chadwick, Bruce. (1979). "Inequality and life style in Middletown, 1920–1978." Social Science Quarterly, 60(December):367–386.

Carey, Max L. (1981). "On occupational employment growth through 1990." Monthly Labor Review 104(August):42–55.

Carneiro, Robert L. (1968). "Herbert Spencer." In David J. Sills (Ed.), International Encyclopedia of the Social Sciences (Vol. 15, pp. 121–127). New York: Macmillan and Free Press.

Catalano, R., & Dooley, D. (1977). "Economic predictors of depressed mood and stressful life events in a metropolitan community." Journal of Health and Social Behavior, 18(September):292–307.

Chandrasekhar, S. (1981). A Dirty, Filthy Book. Berkeley: University of California Press.

Chappell, Neena L., & Havens, Betty. (1980). "Old and female: Testing the double-jeopardy hypothesis." Sociological Quarterly, 21(Spring):157–171.

Cherlin, Andrew. (1981). Marriage, Divorce, Remarriage. Cambridge, Mass.: Harvard University Press.

Chirot, Daniel. (1977). Social Change in the Twentieth Century. New York: Harcourt Brace Jovanovich.

Chodak, Symon. (1973). Societal Development: Five Approaches with Conclusions from Comparative Analysis. New York: Oxford University Press.

Christensen, James A. (1979). "Urbanism and community sentiment: Extending Wirth's model." Social Science Quarterly, 60(December):387–400.

Clark, Leon. (1979). Mortality American Style: A Tale of Two States. Washington D.C.: Population Reference Bureau.

Clausen, John A. (1972). "The life course of individuals." In Matilda White Riley, Marilyn E. Johnson, & Anne Foner (Eds.), Aging and Society: Vol. 3. A Sociology of Age Stratification (pp. 457–514). New York: Russell Sage Foundation.

Clear, Todd R., Hewitt, John D., & Regoli, Robert M. (1978). "Discretion and the determinate sentence: Its distribution, control, and effect on time served." Crime and Delinquency, 24(October):428–445.

Coakley, Jay J. (1982). Sport in Society (2d ed.). St. Louis: C. V. Mosby.

Coale, Ansley. (1973). Cited in M. Teitelbaum. (1975). "Relevance of demographic transition theory to developing countries." Science, 188(May 2):420–425.

Cockerham, William G. (1982). Medical Sociology (2d ed.). Englewood Cliffs, N. J.: Prentice-Hall.

Cohn, Richard M. (1978). "The effect of employment status change on self attitudes." Social Psychology, 41(June):81–93.

Cohn, Richard M. (1982). "Economic development and status change of the aged." American Journal of Sociology, 87(5):1150–1161.

Coleman, James S. (1961). The Adolescent Society. New York: Free Press.

Coleman, James S., Campbell, Ernest Q., Hobson, Carol J., McPortland, James, Mood, Alexander M., Weinfeld, Frederic D., & Link, Robert L. (1966). Equality of Educational Opportunity. U.S. Department of Health, Education, and Welfare, Office of Education. Washington, D.C.: U.S. Government Printing Office.

Collins, Randall. (1979). The Credential Society. New York: Academic Press.

Comstock, George S. (1977). "Types of portrayal and aggressive behavior." Journal of Communication, 27(Summer):189–198.

Conklin, Mary E., & Daley, Ann Ricks. (1981). "Does consistency of parental encouragement matter for secondary school students?" Sociology of Education, 54(October):254–262.

Conrad, John P. (1983). "Deterrence, the death penalty and the data." In Ernest van den Haag & John P. Conrad (Eds.),

The Death Penalty: A Debate. New York: Plenum Publishing.

Conrad, Peter, & Schneider, Joseph W. (1980). Deviance and Medicalization: From Badness to Sickness. St. Louis: C. V. Mosby.

Cooley, Charles Horton. (1902). Human Nature and the Social Order. New York: Scribner's.

Cooley, Charles Horton. (1967). "Primary Groups." In A. Paul Hare, Edgar F. Borgotta, & Robert F. Bales (Eds.), Small Groups: Studies in Social Interaction (rev. ed., pp. 15–20). New York: Knopf. (Original work published 1909).

Coser, Lewis A. (1956). The Functions of Social Conflict. Glencoe, Ill.: Free Press.

Cowgill, Donald O. (1974). "Aging and modernization: A revision of the theory." In Jon Hendricks & C. Davis Hendricks (Eds.), Dimensions of Aging: Readings (pp. 54–68). Cambridge, Mass.: Winthrop Publishers.

Crain, Robert L., Mahard, Rita E., & Narot, Ruth E. (1982). Making Desegregation Work: How Schools Create Social Climates. Cambridge, Mass.: Ballinger Publishing.

Crèvecoeur, J. Hector. (1974). "What is an American?" In Richard J. Meister (Ed.), Race and Ethnicity in Modern America (pp. 3–8). Lexington, Mass.: D. C. Heath. (Original work published 1782).

"Crime in the suites: On the rise." (1979, December 3). Newsweek, pp. 67–68.

Crull, Sue R., & Bruton, Brent T. (1979). "Bogardus social distance in the 1970s." Sociology and Social Research, 63(4):771–783.

Dahl, Robert. (1961). Who Governs? New Haven, Conn.: Yale University Press.

Dahl, Robert. (1971). Polarchy. New Haven, Conn.: Yale University Press.

Dahrendorf, Ralf. (1959). Class and Class Conflict in Industrial Society. Stanford, Calif.: Stanford University Press.

Dale, Roger. (1977). "Implications of the rediscovery of the hidden curriculum of the sociology of teaching." In Denis Gleeson (Ed.), Identity and Structure: Issues in the Sociology of Education (pp. 44–54). Driffield, England: Nafferton Books.

Daniels, Roger, & Kitano, Harry H. L. (1970). American Racism: Exploration of the Nature of Prejudice. Englewood Cliffs, N. J.: Free Press.

David, Henry. (1982). "Eastern Europe: Pronatalist policies and private behavior." Population Bulletin 36(6):1–45.

Davis, Cary. (1982, September–October). "The future racial composition of the U.S." Intercom, pp. 8–10.

Davis, Cary, Haub, Carl, & Willette, JoAnne. (1983). "U.S. Hispanics: Changing the face of America." Population Bulletin, 33(June):1–43.

Davis, Karen. (1975). "Equal treatment and unequal benefits: The medicare program." Milbank Memorial Fund Quarterly, 53:449–488.

Davis, Kingsley. (1940). "Extreme social isolation of a child." American Journal of Sociology, 45(May):554–564.

Davis, Kingsley. (1947). "Final note on a case of extreme isolation." American Journal of Sociology, 52(March):432–437.

Davis, Kingsley. (1961). "Prostitution." In Robert K. Merton & Robert A. Nisbet (Eds.), Contemporary Social Problems (pp. 262–288). New York: Harcourt, Brace & World.

Davis, Kingsley. (1973). "Introduction." In Kingsley Davis (Ed.), Cities (pp. 9–18). San Francisco: W. H. Freeman.

Davis, Kingsley, & Moore, Wilbert E. (1945). "Some principles of stratification." American Sociological Review, 10(April):242–249.

Daymont, Thomas N. (1980). "Racial equity or racial equality." Demography, 17(4):379–393.

DeLamater, J., & McCorquodale, P. (1979). Premarital Sexuality: Attitudes, Relationships, Behavior. Madison, Wisconsin: University of Wisconsin Press.

DeWitt, J. L. (1943). Japanese in the United States, Final Report: Japanese Evacuation from the West Coast, p. 34. Cited in Paul E. Horton & Gerald R. Leslie. (1955). Social Problems, p. 287. New York: Appleton-Century-Crofts.

Dibble, Ursula, & Straus, Murray. (1980). "Some social structure determinants of inconsistency between attitudes and behavior: The case of family violence." Journal of Marriage and the Family, 42(February):71–82.

Dobyns, Henry F. (1966). "Estimating aboriginal American population: An appraisal of techniques with a new hemispheric estimate." Current Anthropology, 71(October):415.

Dolbeare, Kenneth M., & Edelman, Murray J. (1981). American Politics: Policies, Power, and Change (4th ed.). Lexington, Mass.: D. C. Heath.

Domhoff, G. William. (1970). The Higher Circles. New York: Random House.

Domhoff, G. William. (1974). The Bohemian Grove and Other Retreats. New York: Harper & Row.

Donnelly, Patrick G. (1982). "The origins of the Occupational Safety and Health Act of 1970." Social Problems, 30(October):13–25.

Dono, John E., et al. (1979). "Primary groups in old age: Structure and function." Research on Aging, 1(December):403–433.

Dore, Ronald P. (1973). British Factory, Japanese Factory. Berkeley: University of California Press.

Dorn, Harold F. (1950). "Pitfalls in population forecasts and projections." Journal of the American Statistical Association, 45(September):311–333.

Douglas, Jack D., & Waksler, Frances C. (1982). The Sociology of Deviance: An Introduction. Boston: Little, Brown.

Duberman, Lucille. (1975). The Reconstituted Family: A Study of Remarried Couples and Their Children. Chicago: Nelson Hall Publishers.

Duncan, Otis Dudley, Featherman, David L., & Duncan, Beverly. (1972). Socioeconomic Background and Achievement. New York: Seminar Books.

DuNouy, Pierre. (1936). Biological Time. London: Methuen.

Durkheim, Emile. (1915). The Elementary Forms of the Religious Life. London: George Allen & Unwin.

Durkheim, Emile. (1964). The Division of Labor in Society (George Simpson, Trans.). New York: Macmillan and Free Press. (Original work published 1893).

Durkheim, Emile. (1966). Suicide (J. Spaulding and George Simpson, Trans.). New York: Free Press. (Original work published 1897).

Dushkin Publishing Group. (1974). Encyclopedia of Sociology. Guilford, Conn.: Dushkin Publishing Group.

Dye, Thomas R. (1983). Who's Running America (3rd ed.)? Englewood Cliffs, N. J.: Prentice-Hall.

Ebenstein, William. (1973). Today's Isms. Englewood Cliffs, N.J.: Prentice-Hall.

Eblen, Jack E. (1974). "New estimates of the vital rates of the United States black population during the 19th century." Demography, 11(2):301–320.

Edwards, Harry. (1973). Sociology of Sport. Homewood, Ill.: Dorsey Press.

Eisenhower, M., (1969). Commission Statement on Violence in Television Entertainment Programs. National Commission on the Causes and Prevention of Violence. Washington D.C.: U.S. Government Printing Office.

Eitzen, D. Stanley. (1975). "Athletics in the status of male adolescents: A replication of Coleman's The Adolescent Society." Adolescent, 10(Summer):267–276.

Elder, G. H., Jr. (1969). "Appearance and education in marriage mobility." American Sociological Review, 34(August):519–533.

Elder, G. H., Jr. (1974). Children of the Great Depression. Chicago: University of Chicago Press.

Elliott, Delbert S., & Ageton, Suzanne S. (1980). "Reconciling race and class differences in self-reported official estimates of delinquency." American Sociological Review, 45(February):95–110.

Emerson, Richard M. (1962). "Power-dependence relations." American Sociological Review, 27(February)31–41.

Engels, Friedrich. (1965). "Socialism: Utopian and scientific." In Arthur P. Mendel (Ed.), The Essential Works of Marxism (pp. 45–82). New York: Bantam Books. (Original work published 1880).

Engels, Friedrich. (1972). The Origins of the Family, Private Property, and the State (Eleanor Burke Leacock, Trans.). New York: International Publishers. (Original work published 1884).

Erikson, Robert S., Luttbes, Norman S., & Tedin, Kent L. (1980). American Public Opinion: Its Origins, Content and Impact (2d ed.). New York: Wiley.

Eron, L. D. (1980). "Prescription for reduction of aggression." American Psychologist, 35(March):244–252.

Etzioni, Amitai. (1968). The Active Society. New York: Free Press.

Etzioni-Havely, Eva. (1981). Social Change: The Advent and Maturation of Modern Society. London: Routledge & Kegan Paul.

The Europa Yearbook. (1983). A World Survey (Vols. 1 and 2). London: Europa Publications.

"The factory of the future." (1982, September 6). Newsweek, p. 69.

Farley, Reynolds. (1977). "Residential segregation in urbanized areas of the U.S. in 1970: An analysis of social class and racial differences." Demography, 14(November):497–518.

Farley, Reynolds. (1982). "The white flight controversy: Policy implications." In Alan C. Kerckhoff & Ronald G. Corwin (Eds.), Research in Sociology of Education and Socialization. Greenwich, Conn.: JAI Press.

Feagin, Joe R. (1972). "Poverty: We still believe that God helps those who help themselves." Psychology Today 6(November):101.

Feldman, Harold. (1971). "The effects of children on the family." In A. Michel (Ed.), Family Issues of Employed Women in Europe and America (pp. 104–125). Leiden: E. Brill.

Feshbach, Murray. (1982). "The Soviet Union: Population trends and dilemmas." Population Bulletin, 37(3):1–45.

Festinger, Leon, Schachter, Stanley, & Back, Kurt. (1950). Social Pressure in Informal Groups. New York: Harper & Row.

Figley, Charles R. (1973). "Child density and the marital relationship." Journal of Marriage and the Family, 35(May):272–282.

"Final research regulations approved: Most social science research exempt." (1981, March 1). Footnotes, pp. 1, 9.

Fischer, Claude S. (1976). The Urban Experience. New York: Harcourt Brace Jovanovich.

Fischer, Claude S. (1979). "Urban-to-rural diffusion of opinion in contemporary America." American Journal of Sociology, 84(July):151–159.

Fischer, Claude S. (1981). "The public and private worlds of city life." American Sociological Review, 46(June):306–317.

Fischer, Claude S. (1982). To Dwell among Friends: Personal Networks in Town and City. Chicago: University of Chicago Press.

Fischer, D. H. (1979). Growing Old in America. New York: Human Sciences Press.

Fitzpatrick, Joseph P. (1978). "Puerto Rican on the mainland." In Kananur V. Chandras (Ed.), Racial Discrimination against Neither-White-Nor-Black American Minorities (pp. 68–79). San Francisco: R & E Research Associates.

Flores, Estevan. (1983). "The impact of undocumented migration on the United States labor market." Houston Journal of International Law, 5(Spring):287–321.

Form, William. (1982). "Self-employed manual workers: Petty bourgeois or working class?" Social Forces, 60(June):1050–1070.

"The Fortune Directory of the largest U.S. industrial corporations." (1984, April). Fortune.

Fox, B. J., Fox, J., & Marans, R. W. (1980). "Residential density and neighbor interaction." The Sociological Quarterly, 21(Summer):349–359.

Frazier, Charles E., Bock, E. Wilbur, & Henretta, John C. (1983). "The role of probation officers in determining gender differences in sentencing severity." The Sociological Quarterly, 24(Spring):305–318.

Freeman, David M. (1974). Technology and Society: Issues in Assessment, Conflict, and Choice. Chicago: Rand-McNally.

Freeman, Derek. (1983). Margaret Mead and Samoa: The Making and Unmaking of an Anthropological Myth. Cambridge, Mass.: Harvard University Press.

Freeman, Richard B. (1976). The Declining Economic Value of Higher Education and the American Social System. Aspen, Colo.: Aspen Institute for Humanistic Studies.

Freidson, Eliot. (1970). Profession of Medicine. New York: Dodd, Mead.

Freyka, Tomas. (1973). The Future of Population Growth: Alternative Paths to Equilibrium. New York: Wiley.

Friedsam, H. J. (1965). "Competition." In Julius Gould & William L. Kolb (Eds.), A Dictionary of the Social Sciences (pp. 118–119). New York: Free Press.

Fuchs, Victor. (1974). Who Shall Live? New York: Basic Books.

Gagnon, J. H. (1977). Human Sexualities. Glenview, Ill.: Scott, Foresman.

Gagnon, J. H., Roberts, E., & Greenblat, C. (1978). "Stability and change in rates of marital intercourse." Paper presented at the annual meetings of the International Academy of Sex Research, Toronto, Canada (August).

Galliher, John. (1971). "Explanations of police behavior." The Sociological Quarterly, 12(Summer):308–318.

Galliher, John F., & Cross, John Ray. (1982). "Symbolic severity in the land of easy virtue: Nevada's high marihuana penalty." Social Problems, 29(4):380–386.

Gallman, R. (1969). "Trends in the size of distribution of wealth in the nineteenth century: Some speculations." In

Lee Soltow (Ed.), Six Papers on the Size Distribution of Wealth and Income. (pp. 1–24). New York: Columbia University Press.

The Gallup Opinion Index. (1978, November). Report No. 160.

The Gallup Opinion Index. (1979, July). Report No. 168.

The Gallup Opinion Index. (1980, June). Report No. 178.

The Gallup Opinion Index. (1980, December). Report No. 183.

The Gallup Opinion Index. (1981, January). Report No. 184.

The Gallup Report. (1981, March). No. 186.

The Gallup Report. (1981, April). No. 187.

The Gallup Report. (1981, June). No. 189.

The Gallup Report. (1981, July). No. 190.

The Gallup Report. (1981, August). No. 191.

The Gallup Report. (1982, June–July). No. 201–202.

The Gallup Report. (1982, November). No. 206.

The Gallup Report. (1983, March). No. 210:4–6.

The Gallup Report. (1983, May). No. 212.

The Gallup Report. (1983, June). No. 213.

The Gallup Report. (1984, January/February). No. 220–221.

Gans, Herbert J. (1969). "Culture and class in the study of poverty: An approach to anti-poverty research." In Daniel P. Moynihan (Ed.), On Understanding Poverty (pp. 201–228). New York: Basic Books.

Gans, Herbert J. (1973). More Equality. New York: Random House, Pantheon Books.

Gans, Herbert J. (1962). The Urban Villagers. New York: Free Press.

Gappert, Gary. 1979. Post–Affluent America. New York: New Viewpoints.

Gardell, Bertil. (1975). "Compatibility-incompatibility between organization and individual values: A Swedish point of view." In Louis E. Davis, Albert B. Cherns, & Associates (Eds.), The Quality of Working Life (Vol. 1, pp. 317–326). New York: Free Press.

Gardner, David. (1983). A Nation at Risk: The Imperative for Educational Reform. Report of the National Commission on Excellence in Education. Washington, D.C.: U.S. Government Printing Office.

Gardner, Howard. (1983). Frames of Mind: The Theory of Multiple Intelligences. New York: Basic Books.

Gardner, L. I. (1972). "Deprivation dwarfism," Scientific American, 227(July):76–82.

Gardner, R. Allen, & Gardner, Beatrice T. (1969). "Teaching sign language to a chimpanzee." Science, 165(August):664–672.

Garrison, Howard H. (1979). "Gender differences in the career aspirations of recent cohorts of high school seniors." Social Problems, 27(December):170–185.

Gaston, Jerry. (1980). "Sociology of science and technology." In Paul T. Durbin (Ed.), A Guide to the Culture of Science, Technology, and Medicine (pp. 465–526). New York: Free Press.

Gecas, Victor. (1981). "Contexts of socialization." In Morris Rosenberg & Ralph H. Turner (Eds.), Social Psychology: Sociological Perspectives (pp. 165–199). New York: Basic Books.

Gecas, Victor, & Schwalbe, Michale. (1983). "Beyond the looking-glass self: Social structure and efficacy-based self-esteem." Social Psychological Quarterly, 46(2):77–88.

Gelernter, Carey Quan. (1981, August 30). "Japanese Canadians." Seattle Times.

Gelles, Richard J. (1980). "Violence in the family: A review of research in the seventies." Journal of Marriage and the Family, 42(November):873–885.

Gerking, Shelby, & Mutti, John H. (1980). "Costs and benefits of illegal immigration: Key issues for government policy." Social Science Quarterly, 61(June):71–85.

Gerth, H. H., & Mills, C. Wright (Eds. and Trans.). (1970). From Max Weber: Essays in Sociology. New York: Oxford University Press. (Original work published 1946).

Gerzon, Mark. (1982). A Choice of Heroes: The Changing Faces of American Manhood. Boston: Houghton Mifflin.

Gilbert, L., Hansen, G., & Davis, B. (1981). "Perceptions of parental responsibilities: Differences between mothers and fathers." Family Relations, 31(April):261–269.

Gillis, A. R. (1979). "Coping with crowding: Television, patterns of activity, and adaptation to high density environments." The Sociological Quarterly, 20(Spring):267–277.

Ginsberg, Benjamin, & Weissberg, Robert. (1978). "Elections and the mobilization of popular support." American Journal of Political Science, 22(February):31–55.

Girdner, Audrie, & Loftis, Anne. (1969). The Great Betrayal. London: Macmillan.

Gitlin, Todd. (1980). The Whole World Is Watching. Berkeley: University of California Press.

Glenn, Norval D. (1975). "Psychological well-being in the postparental stage: Some evidence from national surveys." Journal of Marriage and the Family, 37(February):105–110.

Glick, Paul C., & Norton, Arthur J. (1977). "Marrying, divorcing, and living together today." Population Bulletin, 32(5):1–40.

Glick, Paul C., & Spanier, Graham B. (1980). "Married and unmarried cohabitation in the United States." Journal of Marriage and the Family, 42(February):19–30.

Glock, Charles Y., & Stark, Rodney. (1965). Religion and Society in Tension. Skokie, Ill.: Rand-McNally.

Goffman, Erving. (1959). The Presentation of Self in Everyday Life. New York: Doubleday.

Goffman, Erving. (1961). Asylums: Essays on the Social Situation of Mental Patients and Other Inmates. Garden City, N.Y.: Doubleday Anchor Books.

Goffman, Erving. (1963). Stigmas: Notes on the Management of Spoiled Identity. Englewood Cliffs, N.J.: Prentice-Hall.

Goldberg, S., & Lewis, M. (1969). "Play behavior in the year-old infant: Early sex differences." Child Development, 40(March):21–30.

Goldblatt, Philip B., Moore, Mary, & Stunkard, Albert. (1965). "Social factors in obesity." Journal of the American Medical Association, 192(June):97–102.

Goldstein, M. S., & Donaldson, P. J. (1979). "Exporting professionalism: A case study of medical education." Journal of Health and Social Behavior, 20(December):322–337.

Goode, William. (1959). "The theoretical importance of love." American Sociological Review, 24(February):37–48.

Gordon, Henry A., & Kammeyer, Kenneth C. W. (1980). "The gainful employment of women with small children." Journal of Marriage and the Family, 42(May):327–336.

Gorin, Zeev. (1980). "Socialism and dependency in Parson's theory of evolution." The Sociological Quarterly, 21(Spring):243–258.

Gortmaker, Steven L. (1979). "Poverty and infant mortality in the United States." American Sociological Review, 44(April):280–297.

Gouldner, Alvin. (1957). "Cosmopolitans and locals: Toward an analysis of latent social roles." Administrative Science Quarterly, 2(December):281–306.

Gouldner, Alvin. (1960). "The norm of reciprocity." American Sociological Review, 25(February):161–178.

Gove, Walter S. (1972). "The relationship between sex roles, mental illness, and marital status." Social Forces, 51(1):34–44.

Granovetter, Mark. (1973). "The strength of weak ties." American Journal of Sociology, 78(May):1360–1380.

Granovetter, Mark. (1974). Getting a Job: A Study of Contacts and Careers. Cambridge, Mass.: Harvard University Press.

Greeley, Andrew M. (1979). "Ethnic variations in religious commitment." In Robert Wuthnow (Ed.), The Religious Dimension: New Directions in Quantitative Research (pp. 113–134). New York: Academic Press.

Greenberg, Edward S. (1980). "Participation in industrial decision making and work satisfaction: The case of producer cooperatives." Social Science Quarterly, 60(March):551–569.

Greenblat, Cathy Stein. (1983). "The salience of sexuality in the early years of marriage." Journal of Marriage and the Family, 45(May):289–300.

Greenfield, Kent R. (1918). "Sumptuary law in Nurnberg." Johns Hopkins University Studies in Historical and Political Science, 36(2):1–139.

Greer, Scott, & Orleans, Peter. (1964). "Political Sociology." In R. E. L. Faris (Ed.), Handbook of Modern Sociology (pp. 808–851). Chicago: Rand-McNally.

Gross, Edward. (1958). Work and Society. New York: Thomas Y. Crowell.

Gruenberg, Barry. (1980). "The happy worker: An analysis of educational and occupational differences in determinants of job satisfaction." American Journal of Sociology, 86(September):247–271.

Gurney, Joan N., & Tierney, Kathleen J. (1982). "Relative deprivation and social movements: A critical look at twenty years of theory and research." The Sociological Quarterly, 23(Winter):33–47.

Gurr, Ted R. (1970). Why Men Rebel. Princeton, N.J.: Princeton University Press.

Guterbock, Thomas M., & London, Bruce. (1983). "Race, political orientation and participation: An empirical test of four competing theories." American Sociological Review, 48(August):439–453.

Habermas, J. (1970). Toward a Rational Society: Student Protest, Science, and Politics (translated by J. Shapiro). Boston: Beacon Press.

Hall, Edward T. (1976). Beyond Culture. Garden City, N.Y.: Doubleday Anchor Press.

Hall, Richard H. (1983). "Theoretical trends in the sociology of occupations." The Sociological Quarterly, 24(Winter):5–24.

Hanks, Michael. (1981). "Youth, voluntary associations and political socialization." Social Forces, 60(September):211–223.

Hannan, Michael T., & Carroll, Glenn R. (1981). "Dynamics of formal political structure." American Sociological Review, 46(February):19–35.

Hare, Nathan, & Swift, David. (1976). "Black Education." In David Swift (Ed.), American Education: A Sociological View (pp. 303–332). Boston: Houghton Mifflin.

Hargrove, Barbara. (1979). The Sociology of Religion: Classical and Contemporary Approaches. Arlington Heights, Ill.: AHM Publishing.

Harlow, H. F., & Harlow, M. K. (1966). "Learning to love." Scientific American, pp. 244–272.

Harrington, Michael. (1962). The Other America: Poverty in the United States. New York: Macmillan.

Harris, Chauncey D., & Ullman, Edward L. (1945). "The nature of cities." The Annals of the American Association of Political and Social Science, 242(November):7–17.

Harris, Louis, & Associates. (1975). The Myth and Reality of Aging in America. Washington, D.C.: National Council on Aging.

Hartman, Heidi. (1981). "The family as the locus of gender, class and political struggles: The example of housework." Signs, 6(3):366–394.

Hartnagel, Timothy F. (1982). "Modernization, female social roles, and female crime: A cross-national investigation." The Sociological Quarterly, 23(Autumn):477–490.

Harwood, Edwin. (1983). "Alienation: American attitudes toward immigration." Public Opinion, 6(June–July):45–51.

Hatcher, John. (1977). Plague, Population and the English Economy 1348–1530. London: Macmillan Press.

Hauser, W. J., & Lueptow, Lloyd. (1978). "Participation in athletics and academic achievement: A replication and extension." The Sociological Quarterly, 19(Spring):304–309.

Hedges, Janice N., & Barnett, Jeanne K. (1972). "Working women and the division of household tasks." Monthly Labor Review, 95(4):9–14.

Hendricks, Jon, & Hendricks, C. Davis. (1981). Aging in Mass Society: Myths and Realities (2d ed.). Cambridge, Mass.: Winthrop Publishers.

Heyl, Barbara. (1979). The Madam as Entrepreneur: Career Management in House Prostitution. New Brunswick, N.J.: Transaction Books.

Heyns, Barbara. (1978). Summer Learning and the Effects of Schooling. New York: Academic Press.

Hickok, Kathleen. (1981). "The spinster in Victorian England: Changing attitudes in popular poetry." Journal of Popular Culture, 15(3):118–131.

Hicks, Mary W., & Platte, Marilyn. (1970). "Marital happiness and stability: A decade review of the research of the sixties." Journal of Marriage and the Family, 32:553–574.

Himes, Norman E. (1936). The Medical History of Contraception. Baltimore: Johns Hopkins University Press.

Hindelang, Michael J. (1981). "Variations in sex-race-age specific incidence rates of offending." American Sociological Review, 46(August):461–474.

Hindelang, Michael J., Hirschi, Travis, & Weis, Joseph. (1981). Measuring Delinquency. Beverly Hills, Calif.: Sage Publications.

Hirschi, Travis. (1969). Causes of Delinquency. Berkeley and Los Angeles: University of California Press.

Hochschild, Jennifer. (1981). What Is Fair? American Beliefs about Distributive Justice. Cambridge, Mass.: Harvard University Press.

Hodge, Robert W., Siegel, Paul, & Rossi, Peter. (1964). "Occupational prestige in the United States, 1925–63." American Journal of Sociology, 70(November):286–302.

Hodge, Robert W., Treiman, Donald J., & Rossi, Peter. (1966). "A comparative study of occupational prestige." In Reinhard Bendix and Seymour Martin Lipset (Eds.), Class, Status, and Power (2d ed., pp. 309–321). New York: Free Press.

Hoelter, Jon W. (1982). "Race difference in selective credulity and self esteem." The Sociological Quarterly, 23(4):527–538.

Hoffman, L. W., & Nye, Ivan (Eds.). (1974). Working Mothers. San Francisco: Jossey-Bass.

Hollander, Paul. (1982). "Research on Marxist societies: The relationship between theory and practice." American Review of Sociology, 8:319–351.

Homans, George. (1950). The Human Group. New York: Harcourt, Brace & World.

Hoover, Sue Epstein. (1983). "Why do women live longer than men?" Science, 83(4):30–31.

Hopkins, J. Roy. (1983). Adolescence: The Transitional Years. New York: Academic Press.

Hopper, Grace M., & Mandell, Steven L. (1984). Understanding Computers. St. Paul, Minn.: West Publishing.

Horowitz, Ruth. (1983). Honor and the American Dream: Culture and Identity in a Chicano Community. New Brunswick, N.J.: Rutgers University Press.

Hostetler, John. 1963. Amish Society. Baltimore: Johns Hopkins University Press.

Hough, Jerry F., & Fainsod, Merle. (1979). How the Soviet Union Is Governed. Cambridge, Mass.: Harvard University Press.

Houston, Jeanne Wakatsuke, & Houston, James D. (1973). Farewell to Manzanar. Boston: Houghton Mifflin.

Howard, Susan. (1980). Title VII Sexual Harassment Guidelines and Educational Employment. Washington, D.C.: Project on the Status and Education of Women, Association of American Colleges.

Howery, Carla. (1983). "Sociologists shaping public policy: Two profiles." Footnotes, 11(August):12.

Hoyt, Danny, & Babchuk, Nicholas. (1983). "Adult kinship networks: The selective formation of intimate ties." Social Forces, 62(September):84–101.

Huber, Bettina. (1983). "Sociological practitioners: Their characteristics and role in the profession." Footnotes, 11(May):1, 6–7.

Huber, Joan. (1980). "Will U.S. fertility decline toward zero?" The Sociological Quarterly, 61(Autumn):481–492.

Huber, Joan, & Form, William H. (1973). Income and Ideology: An Analysis of the American Political Formula. New York: Free Press.

Hughes, Helen M. (1968). "Robert E. Park." In David J. Sills (Ed.), International Encyclopedia of the Social Sciences (Vol. 11, pp. 416–419). New York: Macmillan and Free Press.

Humpreys, Laud. (1970). Tearoom Trade: Impersonal Sex in Public Places. Chicago: Aldine Publishing.

Hunt, Morton. (1974). Sexual Behavior in the 1970's. Chicago: Playboy Press.

Illich, Ivan. (1976). Medical Nemesis. New York: Pantheon Books.

"In China, family planning is everybody's business." (1980, June). Intercom, p. 7.

"Institutions and values outlook." (1982, July 15). Opinion Outlook, pp. 3–4.

Istvan, Joseph, & Griffit, William. (1980). "Effects of sexual experience on dating desirability and marriage desirability: An experimental study." Journal of Marriage and the Family, 42(May):377–385.

Jackman, Mary. (1972). "Social mobility and attitude toward the political system." Social Forces, 50(June):462–472.

Jackman, Robert W. (1973). "On the relation of economic development to democratic performance." American Journal of Political Science, 17(August):611–621.

Jackman, Robert. (1974). "Political democracy and social equality." American Sociological Review, 39(February):29–45.

Jackson, Philip W. (1972). "The student's world." In Melvin L. Silberman, Jerome S. Allender, & Jay M. Yanoff (Eds.), The Psychology of Open Teaching and Learning: An Inquiry Approach. Boston: Little, Brown.

Janis, I. L. (1971). "Group Think." Psychology Today, 5(November):43–46, 74–76.

Jencks, Christopher, Crouse, James, & Mueser, Peter. (1983). "The Wisconsin model of status attainment: A national replication with improved measures of ability and aspiration." Sociology of Education, 56(1):3–19.

Jencks, Christopher, Smith, M., Acland, H., Bane, J.J., Cohen, D., Gintis, H., Heyns, B., & Michelson, S. (1972). Inequality: A Reassessment of the Effect of Family and Schooling in America. New York: Basic Books.

Johnson, Benton. (1957). "A critical appraisal of the church-sect typology." American Sociological Review, 22(1):88–92.

Johnson, Richard E. (1980). "Social class and delinquent behavior: A new test." Criminology, 18(1):86–93.

Johnson, Stephen D., & Tamney, Joseph B. (1982). "The Christian right and the 1980 Presidential election." Journal for the Scientific Study of Religion, 21(2):123–131.

Jones, Elise, & Westofff, Charles. (1979). "The end of 'Catholic' fertility." Demography, 16(2):209–218.

Jones, James H. (1981). Bad Blood: The Tuskegee Syphilis Experiment. New York: Free Press.

Jones, Lamar, & Rice, G. Randolph. (1980). "Agricultural labor in the Southwest: The postbracero years." Social Science Quarterly, 61(June):86–94.

Jones, W. H., Chernovitz, M. E., & Hansson, R. O. (1978). "The enigma of androgyny: Differential implications for males and females?" Journal of Consulting and Clinical Psychology, 46(April):298–313.

Kanter, Rosabeth Moss. (1977). Men and Women of the Corporation. New York: Basic Books.

Kanter, Rosabeth Moss. (1981). "Women and the structure of organizations: Explorations in theory and behavior." In Oscar Grusky & George H. Miller (Eds.), The Sociology of Organizations (2d ed., pp. 395–424). New York: Free Press.

Karnig, Albert A. (1979). "Black economic, political and cultural development: Does city size make a difference?" Social Forces, 79(June):1194–1211.

Kasarda, John D. (1980). "The implications of contemporary redistribution trends for national urban policy." Social Science Quarterly, 61(December):373–400.

Katz, Michael B. (1975). Class, Bureaucracy and Schools: The Illusions of Educational Change in America (expanded ed.). New York: Praeger.

Kazdin, Alan. (1978). History of Behavior Modification. Baltimore: University Park Press.

Kennedy, Robert E. (1976). "Behavior modification in prisons." In W. Edward Craighead, Alan E. Kazdin, & Michael J. Mahoney (Eds.), Behavior Modification: Principles, Issues, and Applications (pp. 321–340). Boston: Houghton Mifflin.

Kent, Mary M. & Larson, Ann. (1982). "Family size preference: Evidence from the World Fertility Surveys." Reports on the World Fertility Survey, No. 4 (April). Washington, D.C.: Population Reference Bureau.

Kephart, William M. (1983). Extraordinary Groups: The Sociology of Unconventional Life-Styles (2d ed.). New York: St. Martin's Press.

Kerbo, Harold R., & Della Fave, L. Richard. (1979). "The empirical side of the power elite debate: An assessment and critique of recent research." The Sociological Quarterly, 20(Winter):5–22.

Kerbo, Harold R., & Della Fave, L. Richard. (1983). "Corporate linkage and control of the corporate economy: New evidence and a reinterpretation." The Sociological Quarterly, 24(Spring):201–218.

Kerckhoff, Alan C., & Davis, Keith E. (1962). "Value consensus and need complementarity in mate selection." American Sociological Review, 27(June):295–303.

Kessler, Ronald C. (1982). "A disaggregation of the relationship between socioeconomic status and psychological distress." American Sociological Review, 47(December):752–764.

Kifner, John. (1973). "At Wounded Knee, two worlds collide." In David R. Colburn & George E. Pozzetta (Eds.), America and the New Ethnicity (pp. 79–90). Port Washington, N.Y.: Kennikat Press.

Kinsey, A. C. (1948). Sexual Behavior in the Human Male. Philadelphia: W. B. Saunders.

Kinsey, A. C. (1953). Sexual Behavior in the Human Female. Philadelphia: W. B. Saunders.

Kleck, Gary. (1981). "Racial discrimination in criminal sentencing: A critical evaluation of the evidence with additional evidence on the death penalty." American Sociological Review, 46(December):783–805.

Kleck, Gary. (1982). "On the use of self-report data to determine the class distribution of criminal and delinquent behavior." American Sociological Review, 47(June):427–433.

Kluegel, James R. (1978). "Causes and costs of racial exclusion." American Sociological Review, 43(June):285–301.

Knoke, David. (1981). "Commitment and detachment in voluntary associations." American Sociological Review, 46(2):141–158.

Kogama, Joy. (1981). Obason. Toronto: Lester and Orpen Dennys.

Kohlberg, Lawrence. (1980). The Development of Socio-moral Knowledge. New York: Cambridge University Press.

Kohn, Melvin L. (1969). Class and Conformity: A Study in Values. Homewood, Ill. Dorsey Press.

Kohn, Melvin L., & Schooler, C. (1978). "The reciprocal effects of the substantive complexity of work and intellectual flexibility: A longitudinal assessment." American Journal of Sociology, 84(1):25–52.

Kohn, Robert L. (1972). "The meaning of work: Interpretation and proposals for measurement." In A. Campbell & P. Converse (Eds.), The Human Meaning of Social Change. New York: Basic Books.

Konig, René. (1968). "Auguste Comte." International Encyclopedia of the Social Sciences (Vol. 3, pp. 201–206). New York: Macmillan and Free Press.

Korte, C. (1980). "Urban-nonurban differences in social behavior: Social psychological models of urban impact." Journal of Social Issues, 36(1):29–51.

Kourvetaris, George A., & Dobratz, Betty A. (1982). "Political power and conventional political participation." American Review of Sociology, 8:289–317.

Krohn, Marvin D., Akers, Ronald L., Radosevich, Marcia J., & Lanza-Kaduce, Lonn. (1980). "Social status and deviance." Criminology, 18:303–318.

Krohn, Marvin D., & Massey, James L. (1980). "Social control and delinquent behavior: An examination of the social bond." The Sociological Quarterly, 21(Autumn):529–543.

Kuhn, D., Langer, J., Kohlberg, L., & Haan, N. (1977). "The development of formal operations in logical and moral judgment." Genetic Psychology Monographs, 95(February):97–188.

Kuhn, Thomas. (1962). The Structure of Scientific Revolutions. Chicago: University of Chicago Press.

Kummer, Hans. (1971). Primate Societies: Group Techniques of Ecological Adaptation. Chicago: Aldine Atherton.

Larson, Reed. (1978). "Thirty years of research on the subjective well-being of older Americans." Journal of Gerontology, 33(January):109–125.

Lebergott, Stanley. (1975). Wealth and Want. Princeton, N.J.: Princeton University Press.

LeBon, Gustav. (1896). The Crowd: A Study of the Popular Mind. London: Ernest Benn.

Lee, Gary R. (1977). "Age at marriage and marital satisfaction: A multivariate analysis with implications for marital stability." Journal of Marriage and the Family, 39(August):493–504.

Lee, Gary R., & Stone, Loren Hemphill. (1980). "Mate-selection systems and criteria: Variation according to family structure." Journal of Marriage and the Family, 42(May):319–326.

Lemert, Edwin. (1981). "Issues in the study of deviance." The Sociological Quarterly, 22(Spring):285–305.

Lenski, Gerhard. (1966). Power and Privilege: A Theory of Social Stratification. New York: McGraw-Hill.

Lenski, Gerhard, & Lenski, Jean. (1978). Human Societies: An Introduction to Macrosociology (3rd ed.). New York: McGraw-Hill.

Levin, R., & Levin, A. (1975, October). "Sexual pleasure: The surprising preferences of 100,000 women." Redbook, pp. 38, 40, 42, 44, 190, 192.

Levinger, George, & Moles, Oliver C. (1978). "In conclusion: Threads in the fabric." Journal of Social Issues, 32(1):193–207.

Lewis, Oscar. (1969). "The culture of poverty." In Daniel P. Moynihan (Ed.), On Understanding Poverty (pp. 187–200). New York: Basic Books.

Lewis, Robert A. & Spanier, Graham. (1979). "Theorizing about the quality and stability of marriage." In Wesley R. Burr, Reuben Hill, Nye, F. Ivan, & Reiss, Ira L. (Eds.), Contemporary Theories about the Family (Vol. 1, pp. 268–294). New York: Free Press.

Leyburn, James. (1968). "William Graham Sumner." In David J. Sills (Ed.), International Encyclopedia of the Social Sciences (Vol. 16, pp. 1–7). New York: Macmillan and Free Press.

Liebow, Elliot. (1967). Tally's Corner. Boston: Little, Brown.

Liker, Jeffrey K., & Elder, Glenn. (1983). "Economic hardship and marital relations in the 1930's." American Sociological Review, 48(June):343–359.

Lin, Nam, Ensel, Walter M., & Vaughn, John C. (1981). "Social resources and strength of ties: Structural factors in occupational status attainment." American Sociological Review, 46(August):393–405.

Lincoln, James R., Olson, Jon, & Hanada, Mitsuyo. (1978). "Cultural effects on organizational structure: The case of Japanese firms in the United States." American Sociological Review, 43(December):829–847.

Linton, Ralph. (1936). The study of Man: An Introduction. Englewood Cliffs, N.J.: Prentice-Hall.

Lipset, Seymour Martin. (1959). "Some social requisites for democracy: Economic development and political legitimacy." American Political Science Review, 53(March):69–105.

Lipset, Seymour Martin. (1978). "Growth, affluence, and the limits of futurology." In Richard Snyder (Ed.), From Abundance to Scarcity: Implications for American Tradition (pp. 65–108). Columbus: Ohio University Press.

Lipset, Seymour Martin (Ed.). (1979). The Third Century: America as a Post-Industrial Society. Stanford, Calif.: Hoover Institution Press, Stanford University.

Litwak, Eugene. (1961). "Voluntary association and neighborhood cohesion." American Sociological Review, 26(April):266–271.

Lo, Clarence Y. H. (1982). "Countermovements and conservative movements in the contemporary U.S." Annual Review of Sociology, 8:107–134.

Locksley, Anne. (1980). "On the effects of wive's employment on marital adjustment and companionship." Journal of Marriage and the Family, 42(May):337–346.

Loether, Herman J. (1982). "Organizational context and the professional role." In Phyllis L. Steward & Muriel G. Cantor (Eds.), Varieties of Work (pp. 137–152). Beverly Hills, Calif.: Sage Publications.

Long, Theodore, & Hadden, Jeffrey. (1983). "Religious conversion and the concept of socialization: Integrating the brainwashing and drift models." Journal for the Scientific Study of Religion, 22(March):1–14.

Lynch, J. J. (1979). The Broken Heart: The Medical Consequences of Loneliness. New York: Basic Books.

Lytle, William O., Jr. (1975). "A smart camel may refuse the last straw: A case study of obstacles to job and organizational design in a new manufacturing operation." In Louis E. Davis, Albert B. Cherns, and associates (Eds.), The Quality of Working Life (Vol. 2, pp. 110–137). New York: Free Press.

Majka, Linda C. (1981). "Labor militancy among farm workers and the strategy of protest, 1900–1979." Social Problems, 28(June):533–547.

Mannheim, Karl. (1929). Ideology and Utopia: An Introduction to the Sociology of Knowledge. New York: Harcourt, Brace.

Marsh, Robert M. & Mannari, Hiroshi. (1976). Modernization and the Japanese Factory. Princeton, N.J.: Princeton University Press.

Martindale, Don. (1968). "Verstehen." In David J. Sills (Ed.), International Encyclopedia of the Social Sciences (Vol. 16, pp. 308–313). New York: Macmillan and Free Press.

Marx, Gary T. (Ed.). (1971). Racial Conflict. Boston: Little, Brown.

Marx, Gary T. (1979). "External efforts to damage or facilitate social movements: Some patterns, explanations, outcomes and complications." In M. Zald & J. McCarthy (Eds.), The Dynamics of Social Movements (pp. 94–125). Cambridge, Mass.: Winthrop Publishers.

Marx, Gary T., & Wood, James L. (1975). "Strands of theory and research in collective behavior." Annual Review of Sociology, 1:368–428.

Marx, Karl, & Engels, Friedrich. (1964). On Religion. New York: Schocken Books. (Original essays published 1841–1895)

Marx, Karl, & Engels, Friedrich. (1965). "The communist manifesto." In Arthur Mendel (Ed.), Essential Works of Marxism (pp. 13–44). New York: Bantam Books. (Original work published 1848).

Masatsugu, Mitsuyuki. (1982). The Modern Samurai Society: Duty and Dependence in Contemporary Japan. New York: American Management Association.

Massey, Douglas S. (1979). "Residential segregation of Spanish Americans in U.S. urbanized areas." Demography, 16(4):553–563.

Massey, Douglas S. (1981). "Social class and ethnic segregation: A reconsideration of methods and conclusions." American Sociological Review, 46(October):641–650.

McClosky, Herbert. (1964). "Consensus and ideology in American politics." American Political Science Review, 58(June):361–382.

McKeown, T. & Record, R. G. (1962). "Reasons for the decline of mortality in England and Wales during the nineteenth century." Population Studies, 16(March):94–122.

McKeown, T., Record, R. G., & Turner, R. D. (1975). "An interpretation of the decline of mortality in England and Wales during the twentieth century." Population Studies, 29(November):390–421.

McNeil, William H. (1976). Peoples and Plagues. Garden City, N.Y.: Anchor Press.

McPherson, J. Miller, & Smith-Lovin, Lynn. (1982). "Women and weak ties: Differences by sex in the size of voluntary organizations." American Journal of Sociology, 87(January):883–904.

Mead, George Herbert. (1934). Mind, Self, and Society: From the Standpoint of a Social Behaviorist (Charles W. Morris, Ed.). Chicago: University of Chicago Press.

Mead, Margaret. (1928). Coming of Age in Samoa. New York: William Morrow.

Mead, Margaret. (1935). Sex and Temperament in Three Primitive Societies. New York: William Morrow.

Mead, Margaret. (1956). New Lives for Old: Cultural Transformation—Manus, 1928–1953. New York: William Morrow.

Mead, Margaret. (1970). Culture and Commitment: A Study of the Generation Gap. New York: Doubleday.

Medley, Morris. (1976). "Satisfaction with life among persons sixty-five years and older." Journal of Gerontology, 32(July):448–455.

Merton, Robert. (1949). "Discrimination and the American creed." In Robert MacIver (Ed.), Discrimination and National Welfare (pp. 99–126). New York: Harper & Bros., 1949.

Merton, Robert. (1957). "Science and democratic social structure." In Social Theory and Social Structure (1957, 2d. ed.). New York: Free Press. (Original work appeared in 1942)

Merton, Robert. (1957). Social Theory and Social Structure (2d ed.). New York: Free Press.

Merton, Robert. (1973). The Sociology of Science: Theoretical and Empirical Investigations (N. W. Storer, Ed.). Chicago: University of Chicago Press.

Messenger, John C. (1969). Inis Beag: Isle of Ireland. New York: Holt, Rinehart and Winston.

Meyer, Marshall W. (1979). "Debureaucratization?" Social Science Quarterly, 60(1):25–34.

Milgram, Stanley. (1970). "The experience of living in cities." Science, 167(March):1461–1468.

Miller, Brent. (1976). "A multivariate developmental model of marital satisfaction." Journal of Marriage and the Family, 38(November):643–657.

Mills, C. Wright. (1951). White Collar. New York: Oxford University Press.

Mills, C. Wright. (1956). The Power Elite. New York: Oxford University Press.

Mills, C. Wright. (1959). The Sociological Imagination. London: Oxford University Press.

Mindiola, Tatcho, Jr. (1979). "Age and income discrimination against Mexican Americans and Blacks in Texas, 1960 and 1970." Social Problems, 27(December):196–208.

Mintz, Beth, & Schwartz, Michael. (1981). "Interlocking directorates and interest group formation." American Sociological Review, 46(December):851–869.

Molotch, Harvy. (1979). "Media and movements." In M. Zald & J. McCarthy (Eds.), The Dynamics of Social Movements (pp. 71–93). Cambridge, Mass: Winthrop Publishers.

Monk-Turner, Elizabeth. (1983). "Sex, educational differentiation, and occupational status: Analyzing occupational differences for community and four-year college entrants." The Sociological Quarterly, 24(3):393–404.

Montague, William Pepperell. (1925). The Ways of Knowing or the Methods of Philosophy. New York: Macmillan.

Moore, Wilbert E. (1967). "Economic and professional institutions." In Neil J. Smelser (Ed.), Sociology: An Introduction. New York: Wiley.

Moore, Wilbert E. (1979). World Modernization: The Limits of Convergence. New York: Elsevier Scientific Publishing.

Mortimer, Jeyland T. (1979). Changing Attitudes toward Work. Scarsdale, N.Y.: Work in America Institute.

Mortimer, Jeyland T., & Simmons, R. G. (1978). "Adult socialization." Annual Review of Sociology, 4:421–454.

Mott, Frank, & Mott, Susan. (1980). "Kenya's record population growth: A dilemma of development." Population Bulletin, 35(3):1–45.

Mottl, Tahi L. (1980). "The analysis of countermovements." Social Problems, 27(June):620–635.

Mulkay, Michael. (1979). Science and the Sociology of Knowledge. London: George Allen & Unwin.

Mulvihill, Donald J., Tumin, Melvin M., & Curtis, Lynn A. (1969). Crimes of Violence (Vol. 11). Washington D.C.: U.S. Government Printing Office.

Murdock, George Peter. (1949). Social Structure. New York: Free Press.

Murdock, George Peter. (1957). "World ethnographic sample." American Anthropologist, 59(August):664–697.

Murphy, Elaine M. (1984). Food and Population: A Global Concern. Washington, D.C.: Population Reference Bureau.

Murphy, Elaine M., & Cancellier, Patricia. (1982). Immigration Questions and Answers. Washington, D.C.: Population Reference Bureau.

Murstein, Bernard I., Cerreto, M., & MacDonald, M. G. (1977). "A theory and investigation of the effect of exchange-orientation on marriage and friendship." Journal of Marriage and the Family, 39(August):543–548.

Myrdal, Gunnar. (1962). Challenge to Affluence. New York: Random House.

Nagel, John. (1978). "Mexico's population policy turnabout." Population Bulletin, 33(5):1–45.

Naisbitt, John. (1982). Megatrends: Ten New Directions Transforming Our Lives. New York: Warner Books.

National Advisory Commission on Civil Disorders. (1968). Report of the National Advisory Commission on Civil Disorders. New York: Bantam Books.

National Opinion Research Center. (1978). General Social Surveys, 1972–1978: Cumulative Codebook. New Haven, Conn.: Roper Public Opinion Research Center of Yale University.

Neugarten, Bernice. (1968). "The awareness of middle age." In Bernice Neugarten (Ed.), Middle Age and Aging (pp.93–98). Chicago: University of Chicago Press.

Newman, Oscar. (1973). Defensible Space: Crime Prevention through Urban Design. New York: Collier Books.

Nie, Norman H., Verba, Sidney, & Petrocik, John. (1979). The Changing American Voter. Cambridge, Mass.: Harvard University Press.

Niebuhr, H. Richard. (1957). The Social Sources of Denominationalism. New York: Henry Holt. (Original work published in 1929)

Nilsen, Linda B. (1981). "Reconsidering ideological lines: Beliefs about poverty in America." The Sociological Quarterly, 22(4):531–548.

Nisbet, Robert H. (1969). Social Change and History: Aspects of the Western Theory of Development. New York: Oxford University Press.

Norman, Jane, & Harris, Myron. (1981). The Private Life of the American Teenager. New York: Rawson, Wade Publications.

Noyes, John Humphrey. (1961). History of American Socialism. New York: Hillary House. (Original work published 1869)

Nunn, Clyde, Crockett, Harry, & Williams, J. Allen, Jr. (1978). Tolerance for Nonconformity: A National Survey of Americans' Changing Commitment to Civil Liberties. San Francisco: Jossey-Bass.

Nye, F. Ivan (1958). Family Relationships and Delinquent Behavior. New York: Wiley.

Oberschall, A. (1973). Social Conflict and Social Movements. Englewood Cliffs, N.J.: Prentice-Hall.

O'Brien, Robert M., Strichor, David, & Decker, David L. (1980). "An empirical assessment of the validity of UCR and NCS crime rates." The Sociological Quarterly, 21(Summer):391–401.

O'Dea, Thomas F. (1966). The Sociology of Religion. Englewood Cliffs, N.J.: Prentice-Hall.

Ogilvie, Bruce, & Tutko, Thomas A. (1971). "Sport: If you want to build character, try something else." Psychology Today, 5(5):61–63.

Oliver, Melvin L., & Glick, Mark A. (1982). "An analysis of the new orthodoxy on black mobility." Social Problems, 29(June):511–523.

Omran, Abdul. (1977). "Epidemiological transition in the U.S." Population Bulletin, 32(2):1–45.

Ophuls, William. (1977). Ecology and the Politics of Scarcity. San Francisco: W. H. Freeman.

Ortega, Suzanne T., Crutchfield, Robert D., & Rushing, William. (1983). "Race differences in elderly personal well being." Research on Aging, 5(March):101–118.

O'Toole, James (Ed.). (1973). Work in America: Report of a Special Task Force to the Secretary of HEW. Cambridge, Mass.: MIT Press.

Palazzolo, Charles S. (1981). Small Groups. New York: Van Nostrand.

Palmore, Erdman B. (1983). "Cross-cultural research: State of the art." Research on Aging, 5(March):45–57.

Parelius, Ann Parker, & Parelius, Robert J. (1978). The Sociology of Education. Englewood Cliffs, N.J.: Prentice-Hall.

Parenti, Michael. (1967). "Ethnic politics and the persistence of ethnic identification." In Meister (Ed.) Race and Ethnicity in Modern America (1974, pp. 124–136). Lexington: Heath.

Parsons, Talcott. (1942). "Age and sex in the social structure of the United States." American Sociological Review, 7(October):604–616.

Parsons, Talcott. (1951). The Social System. Glencoe, Ill.: Free Press.

Parsons, Talcott. (1964). "The school class as a social system: Some of its functions in American society." In Talcott Parsons (Ed.), Social Structure and Personality (pp. 129–154). New York: Free Press.

Parsons, Talcott. (1966). Societies: Evolutionary and Comparative Perspectives. Englewood Cliffs, N.J.: Prentice-Hall.

Parsons, Talcott, & Bales, Robert F. (1955). Family Socialization and Interaction Process. New York: Free Press.

Patterson, Francine (1978). "Conversations with a gorilla." National Geographic 154(October):438–465.

Patterson, Thomas, Clifford, J. G., & Hagan, Kenneth. (1983). American Foreign Policy. Lexington, Mass.: D. C. Heath.

Pearce, Diana. (1979). "Gatekeepers and homeseekers: Institutional forces in racial steering." Social Problems, 26(3):325–342.

Pearlin, Leonard I. (1982). "Discontinuities in the study of aging." In Tamara K. Hareven & Kathleen J. Adams (Eds.), Aging and Life Course Transitions: An Interdisciplinary Perspective (pp.55–74). New York: Guilford Press.

Pebley, Anne R., & Westoff, Charles F. (1982). "Women's sex preferences in the United States: 1970 to 1975." Demography, 19(2):177–190.

Perrow, Charles. (1979). Complex Organizations: A Critical Essay (2d ed.). Glenview, Ill.: Scott, Foresman.

Perrucci, Robert, Anderson, Robert, Schendel, Don, & Trachtman, Leon. (1980). "Whistle blowing: Professionals' resistance to organizational authority." Social Problems, 28(December):149–164.

Petersen, David M. & Friday, Paul C. (1975). "Early release from incarceration: Race as a factor in the use of 'shock probation.' " Journal of Criminal Law and Criminology, 66(March):79–87.

Peterson, William. (1978). "Chinese Americans and Japanese Americans." In Thomas Sowell (Ed.), American Ethnic Groups (pp. 65–106). Washington, D.C.: Urban Institute.

Pettigrew, Thomas F. (1982). "Prejudice." In Thomas F. Pettigrew, George M. Fredrickson, Dale T. Knobel, Nathan Glazer, & Reed Ueda (Eds.), Prejudice: Dimensions of Ethnicity (pp. 1–29). Cambridge, Mass.: Harvard University Press.

Phares, Ross. (1964). Bible in Pocket, Gun in Hand. Lincoln: University of Nebraska Press.

Phillips, David P. (1983). "The impact of mass media violence on U.S. homicides." American Sociological Review, 48(August):560–568.

Piaget, Jean. (1929). The Child's Conception of the World. New York: Harcourt, Brace.

Piaget, Jean. (1932). The Moral Judgment of the Child. New York: Free Press.

Pinney, Roy. (1968). Vanishing Tribes. New York: Thomas Y. Crowell.

Pitts, Jesse R. (1964). "The structural-functional approach." In Harold T. Christensen (Ed.), Handbook of Marriage and the Family (pp. 51–124). Chicago: Rand-McNally.

Piven, Frances Fox. (1981). "Deviant behavior and the remaking of the world." Social Problems, 28(5):489–508.

Piven, Frances Fox, & Cloward, Richard. (1977). Poor People's Movements: Why They Succeed, How They Fail. New York: Pantheon.

Pollock, Philip H., III. (1982). "Organizations and alienation: The mediation hypothesis revisited." The Sociological Quarterly, 23(Spring):143–155.

Pope, Hallowell, & Mueller, Charles W. (1976). "The intergenerational transmission of marital instability: Comparisons by race and sex." Journal of Social Issues, 32(Winter):49–66.

Pleck, Joseph. (1981). The Myth of Masculinity. Cambridge, Mass.: Massachusetts Institute of Technology Press.

Population Reference Bureau. (1982). "U.S. population: Where we are, where we're going." Population Reference Bureau, 37(June):1–50.

Population Reference Bureau. (1984). World Population Data Sheet 1983. Washington D.C.: Author.

Premack, Ann James, and Premack, David. (1972, October). "Teaching language to an ape." Scientific American, pp. 92–99.

Price, Derek J. (1963). Little Science, Big Science. New York: Columbia University Press.

Price, M. L., & Clay, D. C. (1980). "Structural disturbances in rural communities: Some repercussions of the migration turnaround in Michigan." Rural Sociology, 45(4):591–607.

Projector, D. S., & Weiss, G. S. (1966). Survey of Financial Characteristics of Consumers. Washington, D.C.: Board of Governors of the Federal Reserve Board.

Provence, Sally, & Lipton, Rose. (1962). Infants in Institutions: A Comparison of Their Development with Family-Reared Infants during the First Year of Life. New York: International Universities Press.

Purdy, Dean A., Eitzen, D. Stanley, & Hufnagel, Rich (1982). "Are athletes also students? The educational attainment of college athletes." Social Problems, 29(April):439–448.

Quinney, Richard. (1980). Class, State and Crime (2d ed.). New York: Longman.

"A racial outburst in Miami." (1983, January 10). Newsweek, p. 23.

Radbill, S. (1974). "A history of child abuse and infanticide." In Ray E. Helfer & C. Henry Kempe (Eds.), The Battered Child (2d ed., pp. 3–17). Chicago: University of Chicago Press.

Radelet, Louis A., and Reed, Hoyt Coe. (1980). The Police and the Community (2d ed.). Encino, Calif.: Glencoe Press.

Rawlings, Stephen. (1978, December). "Perspectives on American husbands and wives." Current Population Reports, Special Studies Series P–23 No. 77. U.S. Department of Commerce, Bureau of the Census. Washington, D.C.: U.S. Government Printing Office.

Razzell, P. (1974). "An interpretation of the modern rise of population in Europe: A critique." Population Studies, 28(March):5–15.

Reckless, Walter C. (1973). The Crime Problem (5th ed.). New York: Appleton-Century-Crofts.

Reiss, Albert J., with Duncan, O. D., Hatt, Paul K., & North, C. C. (1961). Occupations and Social Status. Glencoe, Ill.: Free Press.

Reiss, Ira L. (1980). Family Systems in America (3rd ed.). New York: Holt, Rinehart and Winston.

Reiterman, Tim. (1982). Raven: The Untold Story of the Rev. Jim Jones and His People. New York: Dutton.

"Revised code of ethics." (1982). Footnotes, 10(March):9–10.

Rheingold, Harriet L., & Cook, Kaye V. (1975). "The content of boy's and girl's rooms as an index of parents' behavior." Child Development, 46(June):459–463.

Riesman, David. (1963). "The intellectuals and the discontented classes: Some further reflections." In Daniel Bell (Ed.), the Radical Right (pp. 137–159). Garden City, N.Y.: Doubleday.

Riesman, David, in collaboration with Denney, Reul, & Glaser, Nathan. (1950). The Lonely Crowd. New Haven, Conn.: Yale University Press.

Riley, Matilda White & Foner, Anne. (1968). Aging and Society, Vol. 1. New York: Russell Sage Foundation.

Risman, Barbara J., Hill, Charles T., Rubin, Zick, & Peplau, Letitia Anne. (1981). "Living together in college: Implications for courtship." Journal of Marriage and the Family, 43(February):77–83.

Ritzer, George. (1977). Working: Conflict and Change (2d ed.). Englewood Cliffs, N.J.: Prentice-Hall.

Robbins, Thomas, Anthony, Dick, & Curtis, Thomas. (1975). "Youth culture religious movements: Evaluating the integrative hypothesis." Sociological Quarterly 16:48–64.

Robertson, Roland. (1970). The Sociological Interpretation of Religion. Oxford: Basil Blackwell.

Robinson, I. E., & Jedlicka, D. (1982). "Change in sexual attitudes and behavior of college students from 1956 to 1980: A research note." Journal of Marriage and the Family, 44(February):237–240.

Robinson, J., & Converse, P. (1972). "Social change reflected in the use of leisure time." In Angus Campbell & Philip E. Converse (Eds.), The Human Meaning of Social Change (pp. 17–86). New York: Russell Sage Foundation.

Robinson, James Lee, Jr. (1980). "Physical distance and racial attitudes: A further examination of the contact hypothesis." Phylon, 41(4):325–332.

Robinson, Robert V., & Bell, Wendell. (1978). "Equality, success, and social justice in England and the United States." American Sociological Review, 43(April):125–143.

Roche, Thomas, & Smith, David L. (1978). "Frequency of citations as criteria for the ranking of departments, journals, and individuals." Sociological Inquiry, 48(1):49–57.

Rogan, Arleen. (1978). "The threat of sociobiology." Quest, 4(Summer):85–93.

Rogers, Everett M. (1960). Social Change in Rural Society: A Textbook in Rural Sociology. New York: Appleton-Century-Crofts.

Roncek, D. W., Bell, R., & Francik, J. M. A. (1981). "Housing projects and crime: Testing a proximity hypothesis." Social Problems, 29(December):151–166.

Roof, Wade Clark, & Hadaway, Christopher K. (1979). "Denominational switching in the seventies: Going beyond Stark and Glock." Journal of the Scientific Study of Religion, 18(4):363–379.

Roof, Wade Clark, & Hoge, Dean R. (1980). "Church involvement in America: Social factors affecting membership and participation." Review of Religious Research, 21(4):405–426.

Rose, Peter. (1981). They and We: Racial and Ethnic Relations in the United States (3rd ed.). New York: Random House.

Rosenthal, A. M. (1964). Thirty–Eight Witnesses. New York: McGraw-Hill.

Rosenthal, Robert, & Jacobson, Lenore. (1968). Pygmalion in the Classroom. New York: Holt, Rinehart and Winston.

Ross, H. L., & Sawhill, I. V. (1975). Time of Transition: The Growth of Families Headed by Women. Washington, D.C.: Urban Institute.

Rostow, W. W. (1960). The Stages of Economic Growth: A Non-Communist Manifesto. Cambridge, Eng.: Cambridge University Press.

Roszak, Theodore. (1969). The Making of a Counterculture. Garden City, N.Y.: Doubleday.

Rothschild-Whitt, Joyce. (1979). "The collectivistic organization: An alternative to rational bureaucratic models." American Sociological Review, 44(4):509–527.

Rubel, Maxmilien. (1968). "Karl Marx." International Encyclopedia of the Social Sciences (Vol. 10, pp. 34–40). New York: Macmillan and Free Press.

Rubin, Lillian Breslow. (1976). Worlds of Pain. New York: Basic Books.

Rubinson, Richard, & Quinlan, D. (1977). "Democracy and social inequality." American Sociological Review, 42(August):611–623.

Rumbaugh, Duane M., Gill, Timothy V., & von Glasersfeld, E. C. (1973). "Reading and sentence completion by a chimpanzee (Pan)." Science, 182(November):731–733.

Rutter, Michael. (1974). The Qualities of Mothering: Maternal Deprivation Reassessed. New York: Aronson.

Ryder, Norman. (1979). "The future of American fertility." Social Problems, 26(February):359–370.

Rytina, Joan Huber, Form, William H., & Pease, John. (1970). "Income and stratification ideology: Beliefs about the American opportunity structure." American Journal of Sociology, 75(4):703–716.

San Miguel, Guadalupe, Jr. (1982). "Mexican American organizations and the changing nature of school desegregation in Texas, 1945–1980." Social Science Quarterly 63(December):701–715.

Schachter, Stanley. (1964). "The Interaction of cognitive and physiological determinants of emotional state." In L. Berkowitz (Ed.), Advances in Experimental Social Psychology (Vol. 1, pp. 49–80). New York: Academic Press.

Schaffer, Kay T. (1981). Sex Roles and Human Behavior. Cambridge, Mass.: Winthrop Publishers.

Schoenberg, S. (1979). "Criteria for the evaluation of neighborhood vitality in working class and low income areas in core cities." Social Problems, 27(October):69–78.

Schur, Edwin M. (1979). Interpreting Deviance: A Sociological Introduction. New York: Harper & Row.

Schwartz, Shalom H., & Gottlieb, Avi. (1980). "Bystander anonymity and reaction to emergencies." Journal of Personality and Social Psychology, 39(3):418–440.

Schwitzgebel, Ralph, and Kolb, David. (1974). Changing Human Behavior. New York: McGraw-Hill.

Sclar, E. D., & Hoffman, V. J. (1978). Planning Mental Health Service for a Declining Economy. Final Report to NHS. Waltham, Mass: Brandeis University.

Seaman, Barbara. (1972). Free and Female. New York: Fawcett.

Sellin, Thorsten. (1980). The Penalty of Death. Beverly Hills, Calif.: Sage Publications.

Sennett, Richard. (1978). The Fall of Public Man. New York: Vintage Books.

Sewell, William H., Haller, Archibald O., & Portes, Alejandro. (1969). "The educational and early occupational attainment process." American Sociological Review, 34(February):82–92.

Sewell, William H., & Hauser, R. M. (1975). Occupation and Earnings: Achievement in the Early Career. New York: Academic Press.

Shankman, Arnold. (1982). Ambivalent Friends. Westport, Conn.: Greenwood Press.

Shannon, Thomas R. (1983). Urban Problems in Sociological Perspective. New York: Random House.

Shariff, Zahid. (1979). "The persistence of bureaucracy." Social Science Quarterly, 60(June):3–19.

Sherif, Muzafer. (1936). The Psychology of Social Norms. New York: Harper & Row.

Shibutani, Tamotsu. (1966). Improvised News: A Sociological Study of Rumor. Indianapolis: Bobbs-Merrill.

Simmel, Georg. (1955). Conflict (Kurt H. Wolf, Trans.) Glencoe, Ill.: Free Press.

Simmel, Georg. (1957). "Fashion." American Journal of Sociology, 62(May):541–558.

Sjoberg, Gideon. (1960). The Preindustrial City. New York: Free Press.

Skinner, B. F. (1948). Walden Two. New York: Macmillan.

Skinner, B. F. (1971). Beyond Freedom and Dignity. New York: Knopf.

Skjei, Eric, & Rabkin, Richard. (1981). The Male Ordeal: Role Crisis in a Changing World. New York: G. P. Putnam's Sons.

Siedman, C. (1979, December 30). "Women athletes gained recognition and respect." The New York Times, p. 87.

Sklair, Leslie. (1972). "The political sociology of science: A critique of current orthodoxies." The Sociological Review Monograph, 18:43–60.

Skolnick, Arlene. (1983). The Intimate Environment: Exploring Marriage and the Family. Boston: Little, Brown.

Sloan, Irving. (1981). Youth and the Law. Dobbs Ferry, N.Y.: Oceana Publishers.

Smelser, Neil J. (1962). Theory of Collective Behavior. New York: Free Press.

Smith, A. Wade. (1981). "Racial tolerance as a function of group position." American Sociological Review, 46(October):558–572.

Smith, Douglas A., & Visher, Christy A. (1981). "Street-level justice: Situational determinants of police arrest decisions." Social Problems, 29(2):167–177.

Snow, David A., & Phillips, Cynthia L. (1982). "The changing self-orientations of college students: From institution to impulse." Social Science Quarterly, 63(September):462–476.

Snyder, Eldon E. (1971). "Athletic dressing room slogans as folklore: A means of socialization." Paper presented at the 1971 annual meeting of the American Sociological Association. Cited in Edwards, Harry. (1973). Sociology of Sport. Homewood, Ill.: Dorsey Press.

Soldo, Beth. (1981). "The living arrangements of the elderly in the near future." In Sara B. Kiesler, James N. Morgan, & Valerie Kincade Oppenheimer (Eds.), Aging, Social Change (pp. 491–512). New York: Academic Press.

Sombart, Werner. (1974). "Why is there no socialism in the U.S.?" Excerpted in John Laslett & S. M. Lipset (Eds.), Failure of a Dream: Essays in the History of American Socialism (pp. 593–608). Garden City, N.Y.: Doubleday Anchor Books. (Original work published 1906).

Sone, Monica. (1953). Nisei Daughter. Boston: Boston, Little, Brown.

Sorenson, A., Taueber, K. E., & Hollingsworth, L. J., Jr. (1975). "Indexes of racial residential segregation for 109 cities in the U.S.: 1940–1970." Sociological Focus, 8(April):125–142.

Sowell, Thomas. (1981). Ethnic America: A History. New York: Basic Books.

Spanier, Graham B. (1983). "Married and unmarried cohabitation in the United States: 1980." Journal of Marriage and the Family, 42(May):277–288.

Spence, J., Helmreich, R., & Stapp, J. (1975). "Ratings of self and peers on sex-role attributes and their relation to self-esteem and conceptions of masculinity and femininity." Journal of Personality and Social Psychology, 32(July):29–39.

Spitz, René. (1945). "Hospitalism: An inquiry into the genesis of psychiatric conditions in early childhood." In Anna Freud, Heinz Hartman, & Ernst Kris (Eds.), The Psychoanalytic Study of the Child (Vol. 1, pp. 53–74). New York: International Universities Press.

Squires, Gregory D., Dewolfe, Ruthanne, & Dewolfe, Alan. (1979). "Urban decline or disinvestment: Uneven development, redlining, and the role of the insurance company." Social Problems, 27(October): 79–95.

Stack, Steven, and Zimmerman, Delore. (1982). "The effect of world economy on income inequality: A reassessment." The Sociological Quarterly, 23(Summer):345–358.

Stark, Rodney, & Bainbridge, William Sims. (1979). "Of churches, sects and cults: Preliminary concepts for a theory of religious movements." Journal for the Scientific Study of Religion, 18(2):117–133.

Stark, Rodney & Bainbridge, William Sims. (1981). "American-born sects: Initial Findings." Journal for the Scientific Study of Religion, 20(2):130–149.

Stark, Rodney, & Glock, Charles Y. (1968). American Piety: The Nature of Religious Commitment. Berkeley: University of California Press.

Stearn, Peter N. (1976). "The evolution of traditional culture toward aging." In Jon Hendricks & C. Davis Hendricks (Eds.), Dimensions of Aging: Readings (pp. 38–53). Cambridge, Mass.: Winthrop Publishers.

Steffenmeier, Darrell J. (1980). "Sex differences in patterns of adult crime: A review and assessment." Social Forces, 58(June):1080–1108.

Steffenmeier, Darrell J., & Cobb, Michael J. (1981). "Sex differences in urban arrest patterns, 1934–79." Social Problems, 29(1):37–50.

Stephan, Edward G., & McMullin, Douglas R. (1982). "Tolerance of sexual nonconformity: City size as a situational and early learning determinant." American Sociological Review, 47(June):411–415.

Stephens, W. N. (1963). The Family in Cross-Cultural Perspective. New York: Holt, Rinehart and Winston.

Stevenson, C. L. (1975). "Socialization effects of participation in sport: A critical review of the research." Research Quarterly, 46:286–301.

Stewart, Julian. (1953). "Evolution and progress." In A. L. Kroeber (Ed.), Anthropology Today (pp. 313–326). Chicago: University of Chicago Press.

Stolte, John F. (1983). "The legitimation of structural inequality." American Sociological Review, 48(June):331–342.

Stryker, Sheldon. (1981). "Symbolic interactionism: Themes and variations." In Morris Rosenberg & Ralph H. Turner (Eds.), Social Psychology: Sociological Perspectives (pp. 3–29). New York: Basic Books.

Suomi, S. J., Harlow, H. H., & McKinney, W. T. (1972). "Monkey psychiatrists." American Journal of Psychiatry, 128(February):927–932.

Sutherland, Edwin H. (1961). White Collar Crime. New York: Holt, Rinehart and Winston.

Suttles, G. D. (1972). The Social Construction of Communities. Chicago: University of Chicago Press.

Swigert, Victoria Lynn, & Farrell, Ronald A. (1976). Murder, Inequality, and the Law. Lexington, Mass.: D. C. Heath.

Sykes, Gresham M. (1974). The Society of Captives: A Study of a Maximum Security Prison. Princeton, N.J.: Princeton University Press.

Tamir, Lois M. (1982). Men in Their Forties: The Transition to Middle Age. New York: Springer Publishing.

Tannenbaum, Frank. (1979). "The survival of the fittest." In George Modelski (Ed.), Transnational Corporations and the World Order (pp. 180–186). San Francisco: W. H. Freeman. (Original work published 1968).

"The tavern rape: Cheers and no help." (1983, March 31). Newsweek, p. 25

Theberge, Nancy. (1981). "A critique of critiques: Radical and feminist writings on sport." Social Forces, 60 (December):341–353.

Thio, Alex. (1983). Deviant Behavior (2d ed.). Boston: Houghton Mifflin.

Thomas, Gail E. (1979). "The influence of ascription, achievement and educational expectations on black-white postsecondary enrollment." The Sociological Quarterly, 20(Spring):209–222.

Thomas, W. I., & Thomas, Dorothy. (1928). The Child in America: Behavior Problems and Programs. New York: Knopf.

Thomlinson, Ralph. (1976). Population Dynamics: Causes and Consequences of World Demographic Change (2d ed.). New York: Random House.

Thompson, Anthony P. (1983). "Extramarital sex: A review of the research literature." The Journal of Sex Research, (February):1–21.

Thornberry, Terrance P. (1973). "Race, socioeconomic status and sentencing in the juvenile justice system." Journal of Criminal Law and Criminology, 64(1):90–98.

Thornberry, Terrance P., & Farnworth, Margaret. (1982). "Social correlates of criminal involvement: Further evidence on the relationship between social status and criminal behavior." American Sociological Review, 47(August):505–518.

Thornton, Arland, Alwin, Duane, & Camburn, Donald. (1983). "Causes and consequences of sex-role attitudes and attitude change." American Sociological Review, 48(April):211–227.

Thurow, Lester C. (1980). The Zero-Sum Society. New York: Basic Books.

Tien, H. Yuan. (1983). "China: Demographic billionaire." Population Bulletin, 38(2):1–42.

Tilly, Charles. (1978). From Mobilization to Revolution. Reading, Mass.: Addison-Wesley.

Tilly, Charles, (1979). "Repertoires of contention in America and Britain, 1750–1830." In M. Zald & J. McCarthy (Eds.), The Dynamics of Social Movements (pp. 126–155). Cambridge, Mass.: Winthrop Publishers.

Tittle, Charles R., Villemez, Wayne, & Smith, Douglas. (1978). "The myth of social class and criminality: An empirical assessment of the empirical evidence." American Sociological Review, 43(October):643–656.

Toch, Hans. (1977). Police, Prisons, and the Problem of Violence. Rockville, Md.: National Institute of Mental Health.

Toffler, Alvin. (1970). Future Shock. New York: Bantam Books.

Tomeh, Aida K. (1973). "Formal voluntary organizations: Participation, correlates and interrelationships." Sociological Inquiry, 43(3–4):89–122.

Troeltsch, Ernst. (1931). The Social Teaching of the Christian Churches. New York: Macmillan.

Trow, Martin. (1973). "The second transformation of American secondary education." In Sam D. Sieber & David E. Wilder (Eds.), The School in Society: Studies in the Sociology of Education (pp. 45–61). New York: Free Press.

Troyer, Ronald J., & Markle, Gerald E. (1982). "Creating deviance rules: A macroscopic model." The Sociological Quarterly, 23(Spring):157–169.

Tuchman, Barbara. (1978). A Distant Mirror: The Calamitous Fourteenth Century. New York: Knopf.

Turner, Jonathan H. (1972). Patterns of Social Organization. New York: McGraw-Hill.

Turner, Jonathan H. (1982). The Structure of Sociological Theory (3rd ed.). Homewood, Ill.: Dorsey Press.

Turner, Ralph H. (1964). "Collective behavior." In R. E. L. Faris (Ed.), Handbook of Modern Sociology (pp. 382–425). Chicago: Rand-McNally.

Turner, Ralph. (1976). "The real self: From institution to impulse." American Journal of Sociology, 81(March):989–1016.

Turner, Ralph. (1978). "The role and the person." American Journal of Sociology, 84(1):1–23.

Turner, Ralph, & Killian, Lewis. (1972). Collective Behavior (2d ed.). Englewood Cliffs, N.J.: Prentice-Hall.

Tyree, Andrea, Semyonov, Moshe, & Hodge, Robert W. (1979). "Gaps and glissandos: Inequality, economic development, and social mobility." American Sociological Review 44(June):410–424.

U.S. Bureau of the Census. (1976). Current Population Reports, Series P–20, No. 297. "Number, timing and duration of marriages and divorces in the United States, June 1975." Washington, D.C.: U.S. Government Printing Office.

U.S. Bureau of the Census. (1977, June). Current Population Reports, Series P–20, No. 312. "Marriage, divorce, widowhood, and remarriage by family characteristics." Washington, D.C.: U.S. Government Printing Office.

U.S. Bureau of the Census. (1982, September). Current Population Reports, P–20, No. 374. "Population profile of the United States, 1981." Washington, D.C.: U.S. Government Printing Office.

U.S. Bureau of the Census. (1982). Current Population Reports, Series P–20, No. 378. "Fertility of American Women: June 1981." Washington, D.C.: U.S. Government Printing Office.

U.S. Bureau of the Census. (1982b). "Labor force statistics derived from the current population survey: A databook," Vol. 1, Bulletin 2096. Department of Labor. Washington, D.C.: U.S. Government Printing Office.

U.S. Bureau of the Census. (1983). Current Population Reports, Series P–20, No. 380. "Marital status and living arrangements, March 1982." Washingon, D.C.: U.S. Government Printing Office.

U.S. Bureau of the Census. (1984). Current Population Reports, Series P–60, No. 144. "Characteristics of the population below poverty: 1982." Washington, D.C.: U.S. Government Printing Office.

U.S. Bureau of the Census. (1975). Historical Statistics of the United States, Colonial times to 1970 (Bicentennial ed., Part 1). Washington, D.C.: U.S. Government Printing Office.

U.S. Bureau of the Census. (1983). Statistical Abstract of the United States 1984. Washington, D.C.: U.S. Government Printing Office.

"U.S. Census update." (1980, August). Intercom, p. 5.

U.S. Department of Housing and Urban Development. (1977). Redlining and Disinvestment as a Discriminatory Practice in Residential Mortgage Loans. Washington, D.C.: U.S. Government Printing Office.

U.S. Department of Justice. (1983). "Uniform Crime Reports for the United States, 1982." Washington, D.C.: U.S. Government Printing Office.

U.S. Education Department. (1982). Condition of Education, 1982 Report. National Center for Education Statistics. Washington, D.C.: United States Government Printing Office.

"U.S. immigration bill dies again." (1983, September/October). Intercom, p. 2.

U.S. National Center for Health Statistics. (1981). Series 23, No. 6. "Socioeconomic differentials and trends in the timing of births." Washington, D.C.: U.S. Government Printing Office.

Unnever, James D., Frazier, Charles E., & Henretta, John C. (1980). "Race differences in criminal sentencing." The Sociological Quarterly, 21(Spring):197–205.

Useem, Bert. (1980). "Solidarity model, breakdown model, and the Boston anti-busing movement." American Sociological Review, 45(June):357–369.

Useem, Bert. (1981). "Models of the Boston anti-busing movement: Polity/mobilization and relative deprivation." The Sociological Quarterly, 22(Spring):275–284.

Useem, Michael. (1979). "The social organization of the American business elite and participation of corporation directors in the governance of American institutions." American Sociological Review, 44(August):553–571.

Vago, Steven. (1980). Social Change. New York: Holt, Rinehard and Winston.

van de Walle, Etienne, & Knodel, John. (1980). "Europe's fertility transition." Population Bulletin, 34(6):1–43.

van den Berghe, Pierre. (1967). Race and Racism. New York: John Wiley.

van den Berghe, Pierre L. (1978). Man in Society. New York: Elsevier North-Holland.

van der Tak, Jean. (1983). "China likely to overshoot year 2000 target." Intercom 11(March/April):3–4.

van der Tak, Jean, Haub, Carl, & Murphy, Elaine. (1979). "Our population predicament: A new look." Population Bulletin, 34(5):1–49.

Vanek, Joann. (1980). "Household work, wage work, and sexual equality." In Sarah Fenstermaker Berk (Ed.), Women and Household Labor (pp. 275–291). Beverly Hills, Calif.: Sage Publications.

Varenne, Herve. (1982). "Jocks and freaks: The symbolic structure of the expression of social interaction among American senior high school students." In George Spinder (Ed.), Doing the Ethnography of Schooling (pp. 210–235). New York: Holt, Rinehart and Winston.

Vedlitz, Arnold, & Johnson, Charles A. (1982). "Community racial segregation, electoral structure, and minority representation." Social Science Quarterly, 63(December):729–736.

Vogel, Ezra F. (1979). Japan as Number One: Lessons for America. Cambridge, Mass.: Harvard University Press.

Volkart, E. H. (1968). "W. I. Thomas." In David J. Sills (Ed.), International Encyclopedia of the Social Sciences (Vol. 16, pp. 1–7). New York: Macmillan and Free Press.

Wallace, Michael, & Kalleberg, Arne L. (1982). "Industrial transformation and the decline of craft: The decomposition of skill in the printing industry, 1931–1978." American Sociological Review, 47(June):307–324.

Wallace, Walter. (1969). Sociological Theory. Chicago: Aldine Publishing.

Wallach, M. A., Kogan, N., & Bem, D. J. (1964). "Diffusion of responsibility and level of risk taking in groups." Journal of Abnormal and Social Psychology, 68(March):263–274.

Wallerstein, Immanuel Maurice. (1974). The Modern World System: Capitalist Agriculture and the Origins of the European World Economy in the Sixteenth Century. New York: Academic Press.

Walster, Elaine, Arenson, V., Abrahams, D., & Rottman, L. (1966). "Importance of physical attractiveness in dating behavior." Journal of Personality and Social Psychology, 4(November):508–516.

Warner, W. Lloyd, Meeker, Marcia, & Eells, Kenneth. (1949). Social Class in America. Chicago: Science Research Associates.

Warren, Earl. (1954). Cited in Nancy H. St. John. (   ). School Desegregation: Outcomes for Children (p. 42). New York: Wiley.

Watson, J. B. (1958). Behaviorism (rev. ed.). Chicago: University of Chicago Press.

Webb, Eugene J., Campbell, Donald T., Schwartz, Richard D., & Sechrest, Lee. (1966). Unobtrusive Measures: Nonreactive Research in the Social Sciences. Chicago: Rand-McNally.

Weber, Max. (1958). The Protestant Ethic and the Spirit of Capitalism (Talcott Parsons, Trans.). New York: Scribner's. (Original work published 1904–1905).

Weber, Max. (1970a). "Bureaucracy." In H. H. Gerth & C. Wright Mills (Trans.), From Max Weber: Essays in Sociology (pp. 196–240). New York: Oxford University Press. (Original work published 1910).

Weber, Max. (1970b). "Class, status, and party." In H. H. Gerth & C. Wright Mills (Trans.), From Max Weber: Essays in Sociology (pp. 180–195). New York: Oxford University Press. (Original work published 1910).

Weber, Max. (1970c). "Religion." In H. H. Gerth & C. Wright Mills (Trans.), From Max Weber: Essays in Sociology (pp. 267–359). New York: Oxford University Press. (Original work published 1922).

Weber, Max. (1970d). "Science as a vocation." In H. H. Gerth & C. Wright Mills (Trans.), From Max Weber: Essays in Sociology (pp. 129–156). New York: Oxford University Press. (Original work published 1918).

Weber, Max. (1970e). "The sociology of charismatic authority." In H. H. Gerth & C. Wright Mills (Trans.), From Max Weber: Essays in Sociology (pp. 245–252). New York: Oxford University Press. (Original work published 1910).

Wechsler, David. (1958). The Measurement and Appraisal of Adult Intelligence (4th ed.). Baltimore: Williams & Wilkins.

Weinberg, Martin S., Swenson, Rochelle Ganz, & Hammersmith, Sue Kiefer. (1983). "Sexual autonomy and the status of women: Models of female sexuality in U.S. sex manuals from 1950 to 1980." Social Problems, 30(February):312–324.

Welch, Charles E., III, & Glick, Paul C. (1981). "The incidence of polygamy in contemporary Africa: A research note." Journal of Marriage and the Family, 43(February):191–194.

Wellman, Barry. (1979). "The community question: The intimate networks of East Yorkers." American Journal of Sociology, 84(March):1201–1231.

"Which cereal for breakfast?" (1981, February). Consumer Reports, pp. 68–80.

White, Lynn, Jr. (1966). Medieval Technology and Social Change. New York: Oxford University Press.

White, Lynn K., Brinkerhoff, David B., & Booth, Alan. (1985). "The effect of marital disruption on children's attachment to their parents." Journal of Family Issues, forthcoming.

Whitt, J. Allen. (1979). "Toward a class-dialectical model of power." American Sociological Review, 44(February):81–99.

Whitworth, John M. (1975). God's Blueprints: A Sociological Study of Three Utopian Sects. Boston: Routledge and K. Paul.

"Who would leave the cities, and why." (1981, July 6). Opinion Outlook, p. 2.

Wiatrowski, Michael D., Griswold, David B., & Roberts, Mary K. (1981). "Social control theory and delinquency." American Sociological Review, 46(October):525–541.

Wilensky, Harold. (1966). "Work as a social problem." In H. Becker (Ed.) Social Problems. New York: Wiley.

Wilkie, Jane Riblett. (1981). "The trend toward delayed parenthood." Journal of Marriage and the Family, 43(August):583–592.

Williams, Kirk, & Drake, Susan. (1980). "Social structure, crime, and criminalization: An empirical examination of the conflict perspective." The Sociological Quarterly, 21(Autumn):563–575.

Williams, Robin M., Jr. (1970). American Society: A Sociological Interpretation (3rd ed.). New York: Knopf.

Williamson, Nancy. (1978). "Boys or girls: Parents' preferences and sex control." Population Bulletin, 33(1):1–50.

Wilson, Edward O. (1975). Sociobiology: The New Synthesis. Cambridge, Mass.: Harvard University Press.

Wilson, Edward O. (1978). On Human Nature. Cambridge, Mass.: Harvard University Press.

Wilson, James Q. (1980). "The politics of regulation." In J. Q. Wilson (Ed.), The Politics of Regulation (pp. 357–394). New York: Basic Books.

Wilson, John. (1980). "Sociology of leisure." Annual Review of Sociology, 6:21–40.

Wilson, William J. 1978. The Declining Significance of Race. Chicago: University of Chicago Press.

Wirth, Louis. (1938). "Urbanism as a way of life." American Journal of Sociology, 44(1):1–24.

Witt, Shirley. (1980). "Pressure points in growing up Indian." Perspectives, 12(Spring):24–31.

Wolf, Wendy, & Fligstein, Neil. (1979). "Sex and authority in the workplace: the causes of sexual inequality." American Sociological Review, 44(April):235–252.

Wolfgang, Marvin E. (1958). Patterns in Criminal Homicide. Philadelphia: University of Pennsylvania Press.

Wolfgang, Marvin E., & Cohen, Bernard. (1970). Crime and Race. New York: Institute of Human Relations Press.

Woodruff, Diana S. (1983). "A review of aging and cognitive processes." Research on Aging, 5(June):139–153.

Woodrum, Eric. (1981). "An assessment of Japanese American assimilation, pluralism, and subordination." American Journal of Sociology, 87(July):157–169.

The World Almanac and Book of Facts, 1984. (1983). New York: Newspaper Enterprise Association.

Wright, Gavin. (1978). The Political Economy of the Cotton South. New York: W. W. Norton.

Wrigley, E. A. (1969). Population in History. New York: McGraw-Hill.

Wrong, Dennis. (1961). "The oversocialized conception of man in modern sociology." American Sociological Review 26(April):183–193.

Wrong, Dennis. (1979). Power. New York: Harper & Row.

Yankelovich, Daniel. (1981a). New Rules. New York: Random House.

Yankelovich, Daniel. (1981b). "New rules in American life: Searching for self-fulfillment in a world turned upside down." Psychology Today, (April):35–91.

Yankelovich, Skelly, & White. (1979). Cited in President's Commission for a National Agenda for the Eighties. (1980). The Quality of American Life in the Eighties. Washington, D.C.: U.S. Government Printing Office.

Yin, Peter. (1982). "Fear of crime as a problem for the elderly." Social Problems, 30(December):240–245.

Yinger, J. Milton. (1957). Religion, Society and the Individual. New York: Macmillan.

Young, Kimball. (1954). Isn't One Wife Enough? New York: Henry Holt.

Zelnik, Melvin, & Kantner, John. (1980). "Sexual activity, contraceptive use, and pregnancy among metropolitan area teenagers: 1971–1979." Family Planning Perspectives, 12(5):230–239.

Zelnik, Melvin, Kantner, John, & Ford, K. (1981). Sex and Pregnancy in Adolescence. Vol. 133 of Sage Library of Social Research. Beverly Hills, Calif.: Sage Publications.

Zipp, John F., Landerman, Richard, & Luebke, Paul. (1982). "Political parties and political participation: A reexamination of the standard socioeconomic model." Social Forces, 60(June):1140–1153.

Zurcher, Louis A. (1977). The Mutable Self: A Self-Concept for Change. Beverly Hills, Calif.: Sage Publications.

Name Index

Subject Index

615

Mulvehill, Photo Researchers; **125** Falk, Monkmeyer Press Photo Service; **127** Costa Manos, Magnum; **129** Freda Leinwand, Monkmeyer Press Photo Service; **131** John Running, Stock, Boston; **132** Ethan Hoffman, Archive Pictures, Inc.; **134** Erika Stone, Peter Arnold, Inc.; **136** Mimi Forsyth, Monkmeyer Press Photo Service; **138** Ken Regan, Camera 5: **142** Fredrik D. Bodin, Stock, Boston; **144** From "Opinions and Social Pressure," Solomon E. Asch, 1955, *Scientific American, 193*, p. 33. Copyright 1955 by Scientific American and William Vandivert; **146** Michael Hayman, Stock, Boston; **147** Fredrik D. Bodin, Stock, Boston; **150** Cary Wolinsky, Stock, Boston; **153** Peter Yates, Art Resource; **154** Peter Southwick, Stock, Boston; **155** Lionel J-M Delevince, Stock, Boston; **157** Steve Eagle, Nancy Palmer Photo Agency; **160** George Bellerose, Stock, Boston; **162** Cathy Chenwy, EKM-Nepenthe; **165** Alex Webb, Magnum; **168** Eric Kroll, Taurus Photos; **170** Jean-Marie Simon, Taurus Photos; **172** Erika Stone, Peter Arnold, Inc.; **173** Jeffrey Sylvester, Freelance Photographers Guild, Inc.; **175** Photo by Authors; **180** J. Berndt, Stock, Boston; **182** Bruce Anspach/EPA Newsphoto; **186** Eric Kroll, Taurus Photos; **188** Bettye Lane, Photo Researchers; **189** Michael O'Brien, Archive Pictures, Inc.; **190** Danny Lyon, Magnum; **192** (top) Billy E. Barnes, Freelance Photographers Guild Inc.; **192** (bottom) Doug Magee, Art Resource; **196** Guy Gillette, Photo Researchers; **197** Stephanie Maze, Woodfin Camp & Associates; **198** Martha Cooper Guthrie, Peter Arnold, Inc.; **199** Cary Wolinsky, Stock, Boston; **203** Wayne Miller, Magnum Photos; **204** Taurus Photos; **205** Paul Shambroom Photo Researchers; **209** (top, left) John Lei, Stock, Boston; **209** (bottom, left) Fredrik D. Bodin, Stock, Boston; **209** (right) Anestis Diakopoulos, Stock, Boston; **214** Kagan, Monkmeyer Press Photo Service; **218** A. Sirdkofsky, Art Resource; **219** Cary Wolinsky, Stock, Boston; **220** Daniel Brody, Art Resource; **222** Burk Uzzle, Woodfin Camp & Associates; **223** Alon Reininger, Woodfin Camp & Associates; **225** (top) Guy Gillette, Photo Researchers; **225** (bottom) Menschenfreund, Taurus Photo; **229** Bob Hammond, Stock, Boston; **230** UPI/Bettmann Archive; **236** John Marmaras, Woodfin Camp & Associates; **237** George Hall, Woodfin Camp & Associates; **239** Brown Brothers; **241** AP Photo; **243** (left) Bill Grimes, Black Star; **243** (right) John Launois, Black Star; **245** Stephanie Maze, Woodfin Camp & Associates; **249** Historical Pictures Service, Chicago; **251** T. Fujihira, Monkmeyer Press Photo Service; **252** UPI/Bettmann Archive; **254** Freelance Photographers Guild; **256** Photo by Authors; **259** © Carol Beckwith from "Nomads of Niger," Abrams 1983; **261** Monkmeyer Press Photo Service; **262** Michal Heron, Woodfin Camp & Associates; **265** Steve Allen, Black Star; **266** Black Star; **271** Frank Siteman, EKM-Nepenthe; **273** Cary Wolinsky, Stock, Boston; **275** Guy Gillette, Photo Researchers; **276** Strickler, Monkmeyer Press Photo Service; **277** Erika Stone, Peter Arnold, Inc.; **278** Victor Friedman, Photo Researchers; **281** Bettye Lane, Photo Researchers; **282** Mimi Forsyth, Monkmeyer Press Photo Service; **285** Mathias T. Oppersdorff, Photo Researchers; **290** The Art Institute of Chicago; **291** Wide World Photos; **292** Paul Fusco, Magnum; **295** © Carol Beckwith from "Nomads of Niger," Abrams 1983; **296** Jerry Irwin; **298** Oneida Community Collection, George Arents Research Library at Syracuse University; **300** Cary Wolinsky, Stock, Boston; **301** Photo by Authors; **302** Robert

V. Eckert Jr., EKM-Nepenthe; **304** Stephen Shames, Black Star; **306** Photo by Authors; **308** Zimmerman, Freelance Photographers Guild; **309** Mike Kagan, Monkmeyer Press Photo Service; **312** Lenore Weber, Taurus Photos; **314** John Lei, Stock, Boston; **315** Cartoon ©1984, reprinted courtesy of Bill Hoest and PARADE; **320** Stephanie FitzGerald, Peter Arnold Inc.; **322** Brown Brothers; **325** Joseph Schuyler, Stock, Boston; **326** David R. Frazier, Photo Researchers; **327** J. Berndt, Stock, Boston; **329** John R. Maher, EKM-Nepenthe; **331** Jean-Claude Lejuene, Stock, Boston; **333** Charles Harbutt, Archive Pictures, Inc.; **334** Brown Brothers; **338** Owen Franken, Stock, Boston; **341** Peter Vandermark, Stock, Boston; **345** David Burnett, Woodfin Camp & Associates; **346** Raimondo Borea, Art Resource; **347** Ellis Herwig, Stock, Boston; **350** Wally McNamee, Woodfin Camp & Associates; **351** Rodgers, Monkmeyer Press Photo Service; **352** Paul Shambroom, Photo Researchers; **353** UPI/Bettmann Archive; **355** Owen Franken, Stock, Boston; **357** Bob Nickelsberg, Woodfin Camp & Associates; **358** Paolo Koch, Photo Researchers; **359** UPI/Bettmann Archive; **362** Paul Conklin, Monkmeyer Press Photo Service; **363** Burt Glinn, Magnum Photos, Inc.; **367** Farrell Grehan, Freelance Photographers Guild; **369** Brown Brothers; **370** Bill Nation, Sygma; **371** Susan Meiselas, Magnum Photos, Inc.; **374** Craig Aurness, Woodfin Camp & Associates; **377** Don Getsug, Photo Researchers; **379** (left) Lynn Lennon, Photo Researchers; **379** (right) Peter Menzel, Stock, Boston; **382** Bohdan Hrynewych, Stock, Boston; **384** Brown Brothers; **386** Photo Researchers; **389** Richard Wood, Taurus Photos; **391** Bob Davis, Woodfin Camp & Associates; **392** Linda Ferrer, Woodfin Camp & Associates; **394** Lionel J-M Delevingne, Stock, Boston; **397** Mike Valeri, Freelance Photographers Guild; **400** T. R. Holland, Stock, Boston; **401** Arthur Glauberman, Photo Researchers; **403** Christopher Morrow, Stock, Boston; **407** UPI/Bettmann Archive; **408** Bill Strode, Woodfin Camp & Associates; **410** UPI/Bettmann Archive; **412** The Art Institute of Chicago; **414** Mike Maple, Woodfin Camp & Associates; **416** Abbas, Magnum Photos, Inc.; **420** Jerry Irwin; **422** Wide World Photos, Inc.; **424** Hank Morgan, Photo Researchers; **427** (left) Freelance Photographers Guild; **427** (right) Bob Ginn, EKM-Nepenthe; **431** Eric Kroll, Taurus Photos; **432** W. H. Hodge, Peter Arnold, Inc.; **433** Ron Cooper, EKM-Nepenthe; **437** Photo by Authors; **439** Mike Button, EKM-Nepenthe; **441** Hugh Rogers, Monkmeyer Press Photo Service; **442** Photo by Authors; **443** Wide World Photos; **447** Bill Ross, Woodfin Camp & Associates; **449** Cary Wolinsky, Stock, Boston; **450** Ernst Haas, Magnum Photos, Inc.; **454** Hank Morgan, Photo Researchers; **455** Robert A. Isaacs, Photo Researchers; **457** Laimute E. Druskis, Art Resource; **458** Joseph Nettis, Photo Researchers; **460** Jim Balog, Black Star; **462** Joseph Nettis, Photo Researchers; **463** Bonnie Freer, Photo Researchers; **466** Yoram Lehmann, Peter Arnold, Inc.; **467** Terry Oing, Freelance Photographers Guild; **468** Martin Bell, Archive Pictures; **474** Jacques Jangoux, Peter Arnold, Inc.; **476** Yoram Lehmann, Peter Arnold, Inc.; **478** Owen Franken, Stock, Boston; **481** John Bryson, Photo Researchers; **483** Lam Cheung, Taurus Photos; **484** Daily Telegraph Magazine, Woodfin Camp & Associates; **486** Owen Franken, Stock, Boston; **488** Cary Wolinsky, Stock, Boston; **490** (top) Bonnie Freer, Photo Researchers; **490** (bottom) Olivier Rebbot, Woodfin Camp & Associates;

492 Olivier Rebbot, Woodfin Camp & Associates; **496** Martin A. Levick, Black Star; **497** Jacques Lang, Photo Researchers; **499** (left) Chuck Fishman, Woodfin Camp & Associates; **499** (right) Brian Brake, Photo Researchers; **503** Georg Gerster, Photo Researchers; **505** Stephanie Maze, Woodfin Camp & Associates; **507** Christina Thomson, Woodfin Camp & Associates; **509** (top) Sepp Seitz, Woodfin Camp & Associates; **509** (bottom) Charles Gatewood, Stock, Boston; **511** Geoffrey Gove, Photo Researchers; **515** Joe Munroe, Photo Researchers; **518** Sepp Seitz, Woodfin Camp & Associates; **519** Barbara Alper, Stock, Boston; **521** Wide World Photos; **522** Don Carl Steffen, Photo Researchers; **525** Christopher Morris, Black Star; **528** Michael Abramson, Black Star; **530** G. D. Hackett; **533** Greg Davis, Black Star; **536** © 1983 Miami Herald, Black Star; **538** Terry Qing, Freelance Photographers Guild; **541** Erik Kroll, Taurus Photos; **543** UPI/Bettmann Archive; **545** Timothy Eagan, Woodfin Camp & Associates; **548** UPI/Bettmann Archive; **550** Ronald Rossi, Freelance Photographers Guild; **553** Ravi Arya, Black Star; **557** AP/Wide World Photos; **558** (top) Wahl's Photographic Service, Inc., Freelance Photographers Guild; **558** (bottom) Tom McHugh, Photo Researchers; **561** EKM-Nepenthe; **562** Brown Brothers; **563** EKM-Nepenthe; **565** Brown Brothers; **567** Douglas Kirkland, Contact Press Images; **568** Kaku Kurita-Gamma; **570** Cornell Capa, Magnum Photos, Inc.; **571** Richard Wood, Taurus Photos.